Bournemouth Heroes

The Patriots of Bournemouth School 1914-1918

![The Patriots of Bournemouth School cartoon]

A cartoon which appeared in *The Bournemouth Graphic* newspaper, 19th November 1915.

The Old Boys who served on the Western Front 1914-1918

Where possible, in this account of the Old Bournemouthians who served on the Western Front, their individual stories are introduced into that stage or those stages of the war in which they served or made a particular contribution. Unfortunately, it is not possible to be sure how many men and stories may have been missed. Certainly there were many who also served, but it is not clear upon which front, so these are omitted from this study, whilst some are included of whom only the barest details are known.

Bournemouth Heroes

The Patriots of Bournemouth School 1914-1918

W D Pyke

Copyright © 2018

Every reasonable effort has been made to trace copyright holders and to obtain their permission for the use of copyright material. The author and publisher apologise for any errors or omissions in this work and would be grateful if notified of any corrections that should be incorporated in future reprints or editions of this book.

All rights reserved. No part of this publication may be reproduced, stored in a retrieval system or transmitted in any form or by any means electronic, mechanical, audio, visual or otherwise, without prior permission of the copyright owner. Nor can it be circulated in any form of binding or cover other than that in which it is published and without similar conditions including this condition being imposed on the subsequent purchaser.

You must not circulate this work in any other form and you must impose this same condition on any acquirer

British Library Cataloguing in Publication Data available.

ISBN: 978-1-9164964-0-8

Published by Croft House in conjunction with WRITERSWORLD, this book is produced entirely in the UK, is available to order from most book shops in the United Kingdom and is globally available via UK-based Internet book retailers.

Cover Design by Jag Lall

Copy edited by Ian Large

WRITERSWORLD
2 Bear Close, Woodstock,
Oxfordshire
OX20 1JX
UK

☎ +44 1993 812500

www.writersworld.co.uk

The text pages of this book are produced via an independent certification process that ensures the trees from which the paper is produced comes from well managed sources that exclude the risk of using illegally logged timber while leaving options to use post-consumer recycled paper as well.

To my lovely, patient wife, Pam

Contents

1: The Build-up to the War 7

2: 1914: The Opening Campaigns and the First in Action 11

3: The Western Front 1915 33

4: 1916 on the Western Front 94

5: The Battle of the Somme 121

6: 1917 on the Western Front 237

7: The Third Battle of Ypres 299

8: 1918 – Difficulties and the Ludendorff Offensive 363

9: The Counter-Attack: The Battle of Amiens and the 100 Days 435

10: The Autumn Advance to Victory 460

11: The Armistice 495

12: Conclusions 500

Appendices: Others Who Served but whose Service Details are Currently Limited ... 501

    Appendix 1: British Soldiers on the Western Front 501

    Appendix 2: Canadian Soldiers on the Western Front 506

Index of Old Bournemouthians on the Western Front 509

A Note on Army Infantry Units

The British Expeditionary Force grew to include several armies, each divided into divisions with brigades (of four infantry battalions until 1918, then of three battalions). The essential infantry unit of the British Army in action was the battalion, a unit of a regiment. Each battalion was divided into companies, which were further divided into platoons and sections, the smallest recognised unit.

Thanks

I am extremely grateful for the assistance I have received from Bournemouth School, from current members of some of the families represented by the Old Bournemouthians described, and from members of the Great War Forum.

Something to Consider:

"Oh the waste, the utter damnable waste of everything out here—men, horses, buildings, cars, everything. Those who talk about war being a salutary discipline are those who remain at home. In a modern war there is little room for picturesque gallantry or picture-book heroism. We are all either animals or machines, with little gained except our emotions dulled and brutalised and nightmare flashes of scenes that cannot be written about because they are unbelievable. I wonder what difference you will find in us when we come home – "

(From *Adventures of a Dispatch Rider*, W.H.L. Watson, 1915. This comment was written in October 1914.)

1: The Build-up to the War

Bournemouth School in 1913-1914

Bournemouth School was only founded in 1901, on the initiative of some enterprising businessmen, supported by Bournemouth Borough and Hampshire County Councils. Its boys, current and past – and staff – were almost all young. The war hit the school hard – with deaths starting in the opening campaigns right through to the last moments. Old Boys of the school experienced the war from all angles: the trenches (in the west and in the east); at sea; and in the air. They experienced the latest technologies: poison gas, flamethrowers, tanks, machine guns, aeroplanes. By December 1918, many awards had been earned by Old Bournemouthians, as former members of the school were, and still are, known.

This book only examines the commitment made to the war by members of the school on the ground of the Western Front, although it must be remembered that members of the school made a huge commitment to other military theatres, the entire naval campaign and the air war.

The argument of the book is that it was not only the great public schools (with their aristocratic or upper middle class pupils) nor the workers (including many, though by no means all, of the Pals battalions) who fought and won the war. Bournemouth School, ably led by Headmaster Dr. Fenwick and mainly educating members of the aspiring working or lower middle class, instilled such attitudes and virtues into its old boys that they fought courageously on the ground of the Western Front.

Officially, a man should only be recruited into the Army if aged eighteen, and was only liable for overseas service if aged nineteen (changed to eighteen and a half in 1918). Several Bournemouth School boys were only seventeen when they died; some served from fourteen or fifteen. As well as those who were killed, many more served and, too often, were severely wounded. Others served, and emerged physically unharmed, though with varying impact on their on-going mental health and life expectancy. As officers were officially allowed to be recruited younger, and 'men' not sent back to England because of youth until 1916, anybody with the sort of education which Bournemouth School offered could volunteer to become an officer, and had a good chance of being accepted.

Although we tend to look at the ages on the gravestones and shudder, even the stones themselves can mislead. Ages were frequently rounded up in the period – a stone might give a boy's age as eighteen, when in reality he was still seventeen. Significantly, for the first three years of the war, the Army tended to accept, record, and perhaps believe, the age given when a volunteer attested in order to join (which could be exaggerated by up to five or six years). We can look with sadness at the death of one aged eighteen in 1918, and not realise that in some cases he might have been in the trenches from much earlier in the war.

Spring 1914

At Bournemouth School the last year of peace passed with stirring football and cricket matches, and exams. There was a thriving Volunteer Cadet Force which had started at the school soon after it had opened. It was given a major boost in 1909 when, following the Haldane Reforms and the Territorial and Reserve Forces Act 1907, it was re-designated as an O.T.C. (Officer Training Corps –

the forerunner of the C.C.F. Combined Cadet Force). Its numbers grew, and its officers became part of the Territorial Force. The Territorial Army (more commonly known as the Territorials) was anxious to build connections with the school, and boys were encouraged to join a special Hampshire regiment cycling section; twelve boys went on camp with the Territorials in 1913.

Unsurprisingly, since the opening campaigns were dominated by existing professional soldiers and sailors, the majority of the Bournemouth School casualties fell in the second half of the war, but even by December 1914 a huge number had volunteered, and 'old boys' had already lost their lives. By 1918 it was almost a landslide of tragedy.

August 1914

Masters and older boys alike were aware of the build-up of tensions across the Channel in the summer of 1914. "With startling suddenness the greatest war of all time has broken in upon the peace of the world, and at our very doors rages the conflict on the issues of which depend not only the Empire's safety but the very existence, perhaps, of our country as a separate nation."[1] By December 1914, the editor of *The Bournemouthian* reported that no fewer than 170 Old Boys had already joined the armed forces – although the oldest Old Boy could only be in his late twenties, and their average age was about 21.

Many of those still in school were swept up with enthusiasm for the war. The new scouting movement, which had begun close to the school on Brownsea Island, was already providing an outlet for junior enthusiasm for Empire and serving King and God through the school scout troop.[2] Once the war got under way, many of these scouts helped out by patrolling the coast to warn of German invasion. The school O.T.C. enthusiastically supplied the much-needed young officers to swell the ranks (and replace those already fallen). An appeal was made to the boys to make weekly contributions from their own pocket money to supply the fighting forces with comforts in the form of clothing. By December, weekly parcels were being sent to the front each week, and these efforts continued throughout the war.

In the first months of the war, recruitment was so popular some units could afford to be precise – even fussy – about the physiques of the men they recruited, so sometimes men had to travel to find a regiment which would accept them. Since the supply of suitable candidates for junior officer was plentiful, unless you were lucky or had contacts it was generally necessary to be recruited as an over-qualified rank-and-file man rather than hold out for officer recruitment and risk missing out on the glory of a war which the public (if not the experts) believed would be over by Christmas. The natural recruitment for Bournemouth would be into the Hampshire Regiment (because before 1974 Bournemouth was in Hampshire) but the Hampshire Regiment initially sent its battalions to India, not to the Western Front. Many boys came from Poole or Wimborne, and their natural regiment was that of Dorset, but at first the Dorset battalions looked as if they might similarly be going to 'miss out' on the war. Of course, many Old Bournemouthians had already left the area and so they volunteered in the parts of the country in which they lived.

---

[1] *The Bournemouthian*, December 1914.

[2] *The Bournemouthian* first seems to include scout notes in December 1916, but from the content of the article it is clear that the scouts had been active for some time before that.

British War Preparations 1914

In 1908, ministers had decided to increase the capacity of both the small Regular Army and the Navy. The Royal Navy began the rapid expansion of its new Dreadnought class battleship fleet, supported by warships ranging from battlecruisers to oceangoing tugs, converted trawlers, or coastal vessels. A Royal Navy Reserve had been created in 1903. In 1908, a Territorial Army was founded to augment the Regular Army and those former Regulars who made up the Army Special Reserve. This Territorial force was expected to act as a home defence force. When the war began, the Minister of the Army, the old war hero Lord Kitchener (with his famous pointing finger poster) called for volunteers – but as he personally despised the 'part-time' Territorials, he called for volunteers to form a new kind of army, the Service Army, for which the new recruits would swear to serve as 'professionals' at home or abroad as required for the duration of the war. This Service Army became commonly known as the 'New Army'.

The first members of the school to see action were those who had already volunteered for the Regular Army or the Territorial Army before the outbreak of the war and had received sufficient military training to be sent to the front. Those in the New Army were called upon to fight later in the war. Since a large number of Old Bournemouthians served in the Hampshire regiment, many ended up spending all or part of the war in India, rather than on the Western Front, since as soon as the war began, the government realised that the professional British army was too small to fight on the continent effectively unless it could be consolidated by recalling its more far-flung units. The Territorials were trained, or semi-trained, troops who could replace the recalled Regulars to protect and control the empire. When Hampshire Territorials were asked if they would volunteer for foreign service, huge numbers volunteered promptly so the Hampshire battalions were selected to replace the Regulars in India, and they started to leave as early as 9th October 1914. First line battalions (for example 1/7th Hampshires) had already done a lot of training before the war; as the volunteers flooded in they formed second, and later third line units. The second line battalions, such as 2/7th followed before the end of the year. As the author of the official Hampshire regiment history put it, "Though they were largely composed of recruits and as yet handicapped by lack of arms and equipment, it showed that any amount of hard work had already been put in to make them fit to go overseas. The invitation was no small compliment, even if they had to make do with sub-standard equipment. Thus the rifles the 2/5th took out were condemned as unfit for use, and only when the battalion was rearmed with 'long' rifles then discarded by the 1/5th could the battalion get any proper musketry

instruction."[3] The artist of *The Bournemouth Graphic* newspaper drew a cartoon imagining these men seeing Bournemouth disappear over the sea as they set sail for India.[4]

The British Plan

British ministers, assuming that Germany would be the enemy, by 1913 had split the Army into a Home Defence Army (mainly Territorials with some Regulars to train additions) and the British Expeditionary Force (B.E.F.) to carry the fight to the enemy.

The trigger of the war was the ultimatum by Austria-Hungary against Serbia, with its time limit of 28th July 1914. The refusal of Serbia (backed by Russia) to give way to Austria-Hungary led to the events which in turn resulted in Germany declaring war on Russia (1st August) and then on France (3rd August), to support Austria-Hungary. The British cabinet confirmed that the B.E.F. would be sent to France according to a contingency plan to land troops in three French ports: Le Havre, Rouen and Boulogne. Even before the ultimatum to Serbia had run out, the British Army was preparing. On 27th July, Reserve officers were ordered to report to their battalions. Two days later, Regular officers and men on leave were recalled and all new leave cancelled. On Sunday 2nd August, all units then training – Regular, Special Reserve or Territorial – were ordered to return to peacetime headquarters.

When Germany invaded Belgium on 4th August, Britain cited the 1839 Treaty of London, which had guaranteed Belgian neutrality, to explain these actions. After an emergency parliamentary debate on the crisis on Bank Holiday Monday, at 11.00am on 4th August, an ultimatum was issued which expired at midnight. Britain then declared war on Germany. Telegrams ordering formal mobilisation had been sent out at 4.40pm so the embarkation process could begin. Within days of the declaration of war, the original B.E.F. had sailed to France. The B.E.F. comprised four infantry divisions and a cavalry division (divided in two in September). At fewer than 100,000 in total, it probably deserved the comment of the Kaiser that Britain had sent only a contemptible little army to support France and Belgium. At home, the second line units – and later the third line battalions – took over home defence until, sooner than expected, they too were called into action abroad. Across the oceans, the dominion governments were swift to begin to mobilise, and before the end of the year the first imperial battalions were arriving in England to help their 'Mother Country'.

---

[3] *The Royal Hampshire Regiment 1914-1918*, C.T. Atkinson, p. 47, published 1952.
[4] *The Bournemouth Graphic*, 9th October 1914.

2: 1914: The Opening Campaigns and the First in Action

Mons and Le Cateau

Eric Bagshaw was one of the first Old Bournemouthians to see action on the Western Front. The B.E.F. advanced into Belgium in conjunction with the French, reaching Mons where they fought the Germans. Forced to retreat, they fought again en route at Le Cateau. Eric was with them. He originally came from South Africa. After school, from 1903-1909, he intended to help his father as a wholesale tanner in Port Elizabeth, South Africa. First, from 1911 to the summer of 1914, he studied science at Leeds University. Eric volunteered on 6th August, asking to join the Royal Engineers. The same day he was promoted to a full corporal and placed in the Motor Cyclist Section of the R.E.; he had cited his school O.T.C. training as prior experience! In the Army, he had the nickname, 'Spuggy'. In 1915, one of his friends, Captain W.H.L. Watson, published a memoir called *Adventures of a Dispatch Rider*. The group of friends had tried to become accepted as intelligence officers, but were turned down by the War Office, and were instead made into dispatch riders. After a few days training in Ireland, on 17th August 1914 they were sent with the B.E.F. to the continent. He – or his parents – described to the headmaster as a 'dispatch rider for General Sir John French', Commander-in-Chief of the British Expeditionary Force. Actually, he held the rank of corporal in the 5th Signalling Company (5th Division) of the Royal Engineers, part of the Motor Cyclist Section.

The dispatch riders enjoyed comparative freedom. "When the Division moves we ride either with the column or go in advance to the halting-place. That morning we rode with the column, which meant riding three-quarters of a mile or so and then waiting for the main-guard to come up, — an extraordinarily tiring method of getting along. The day (August 21) was very hot indeed, and the troops who had not yet got their marching feet suffered terribly, even though the people by the wayside brought out fruit and eggs and drinks. There was murmuring when some officers refused to allow their men to accept these gifts. But a start had to be made some time, for promiscuous drinks do not increase marching efficiency. We, of course, could do pretty well what we liked. A little coffee early in the morning, and then anything we cared to ask for. Most of us in the evening discovered, unpleasantly enough, forgotten pears in unthought-of pockets."[5]

They reached the town of Bavai. "For a long time we were hutted in the Square. Spuggy found a 'friend', and together we obtained a good wash. The people were vociferously enthusiastic. Even the chemist gave us some 'salts' free of charge." Approaching Mons, the dispatch riders' dangers increased: "We knew nothing of what was going on. There was a rumour that Namur had fallen, and I heard certain officers say we had advanced dangerously far. The cavalry was on our left and the Third Division on our right. Beyond the Third Division we had heard of the First Corps, but nothing of the French. We were left, to the best of our knowledge, a tenuous bulwark against the German hosts."[6]

John Turner fought in the Battle of Mons which followed. The British tried to hold up the German advance but were outflanked when the French withdrew on their flanks. John, born 1892, at the

---

[5] *Adventures of a Dispatch Rider*, W.H.L. Watson, William Blackwood and Sons, Edinburgh and London, pp. 21-22. I am indebted to Nick Shelley for pointing me to this book.

[6] ibid, p. 26.

school 1905-1910, was a keen sportsman (football colours 1909; cricket colours 1908, 1909 and 1910). As well as excelling at sport, he did well in his exams. His brothers George and William had also been keen members of the school. He became a prefect and a keen member of the O.T.C. After leaving school he studied law, articled to his father, and he became Honorary Secretary to the Bournemouth and District Law Students Society. He had just passed the Intermediate Law Examination when the war broke out. He had joined the Special Reserve of officers in 1911, soon after leaving school. He became a full lieutenant in the 3rd Battalion of the Dorsetshire Regiment in 1913, its training and depot battalion.

John Turner

Aged 21, John joined the 1st Dorset Battalion on 6th August along with a number of other officers and reservists, and he was placed in 'B' Company. On 14th August, they embarked on the SS *Anthony* for a two-day voyage and on 16th August landed at Le Havre. From there they went by train to Le Cateau and headed north towards the western outskirts of Mons. On Sunday 23rd August, they were ordered to defend the road south from Mons, and at 5pm that afternoon they had their first taste of war as German shells passed overhead, and soon afterwards they saw German infantry advancing towards them. The next day John was in action with the rest of 'B' Company: "B Coy moved at dawn into a railway cutting by a bridge 600 yards W.N.W. of W. of Wasmes. 2 platoons were pushed forward to entrench – about 6am the whole company went into the trenches, having part of A Coy on their right and a part of C Coy on their left. The enemy's infantry advanced supported by heavy artillery fire to within 400 yards but were repulsed. A lull of about an hour followed. The enemy then opened a heavy rifle and artillery fire. It was seen that the enemy had worked round both flanks. About 2pm the Coy was ordered to retire and fell back in the direction of Blaugies [just inside the Belgian frontier]."[7] The fighting had cost the lives of three officers (and a fourth was missing) as well as twelve men killed, forty-nine wounded, and a further sixty-nine missing. John remained with 'B' Company as it covered the continuing retreat from Le Cateau a couple of days later. As they retreated daily that very hot August more men were wounded or disappeared missing.

At one moment, nicknamed the 'mauvais quart d'heure', the battalion looked as if it was doomed. Outnumbered about ten to one, they formed the rearguard. "But 'Do'set sogers' believe in that couplet of the hymn – 'Let courage rise with danger, and strength to strength oppose.' At the critical moment, when all seemed lost, the voice of Colonel Bols [battalion commander] rang out, 'Lads, we are surrounded. There's nothing for it but to cut our way out. Now is the time to sing!' The effect of such words, from so quiet-mannered an officer, was electrifying. 'Sing' the Dorsets did – a tune that the enemy did not at all like. With desperate energy, they shook the Huns from their flanks, and got out and away. However… there was much 'growsing' amongst the Dorsets during the great retreat. In 'Do'set' parlance, they 'didden like drawin back so!'… They showed rare Dorset doggedness in the great retirement…"[8]

---

[7] War Diary of 1st Dorsets, 24th August 1914.

[8] *The Bournemouth Visitors' Directory*, 24th February 1917, reporting from *The Dorsets in the Great War* by Mr Harry Pouncey. Mr Pouncey was first a reporter and later proprietor of the *Southern Times and Dorset County Herald*, though he did serve in the Dorsetshire Regiment during the war.

Eric Bagshaw and the other dispatch riders with the 5th Division also headed back south-westwards as the army retreated. "It seemed a shame that we motor-cyclists should head the retreat of our little column. I could not understand how the men could laugh and joke. It was blasphemous. They ought to be cursing with angry faces,—at the least, to be grave and sorrowful."[9] One particularly sad sight was to see the British cavalry column retreating with the men leading many riderless horses, since the British 2nd Cavalry Brigade had already seen the bitter consequences of charging the German guns, only to find them protected by barbed wire. As they drew near Le Cateau, "Spuggy was sent up to the trenches in the morning. He was under heavy shell fire when his engine seized up. His brigade was retreating, and he was in the rear of it, so, leaving his bicycle, he took to his heels, and with the Germans in sight ran till he caught up a waggon. He clambered on, and so came into St Waast."[10]

As the division retreated, the general was attended by his chief of staff and the captain of the dispatch riders, supported by four telephone operators, a signals clerk, as well as by motorcyclists and cyclists who were to carry the orders to the mobile units. Radios were not yet available. As the column trudged on, Eric and Watson swopped places on a cart and shared the use of the motorbike they had left between them. As maps were in short supply, the dispatch riders were expected to link between the units without the benefit of maps, using only road signs and information they could get from tired troops to whom they spoke.

The Battle of the Marne

In September, the British combined with the French to make the counterattack known as the Battle of the Marne. Eric had another narrow escape. "The morning of September 5th was very hot, but the brigades could easily be found, and the roads to them were good. There was cheerfulness in the air. A rumour went round—it was quite incredible, and we scoffed—that instead of further retreating either beyond or into the fortifications of Paris, there was a possibility of an advance. The Germans, we were told, had at last been outflanked. Joffre's vaunted plan that had inspired us through the dolorous startled days of retirement was, it appeared, a fact, and not one of those bright fancies that the Staff invents for our tactical delectation. Spuggy returned. He had left us at Bouleurs to find a bicycle in Paris. Coming back he had no idea that we had moved. So he rode too far north. He escaped luckily. He was riding along about three hundred yards behind two motor-cyclists. Suddenly he saw them stop abruptly and put up their hands. He fled. A little farther on he came to a village and asked for coffee. He heard that Uhlans [German lancers] had been there a few hours before, and was taken to see a woman who had been shot through the breast. Then he went south through Villeneuve, and following a fortunate instinct, ran into our outposts the other side of Tournan."[11]

The tide had turned. In the battle of the Marne, French General Joffre attacked the Germans with a hastily put together new army, surprising the Germans on their flank and bringing about a partial retreat to the line of the River Aisne. The British advanced and encouraged this fighting retreat before the lines consolidated as the autumn drew on.

---

[9] *Adventures of a Dispatch Rider*, W.H.L. Watson, p. 31.
[10] ibid, p. 36.
[11] ibid, pp. 76-77.

On 8th September, seventy Prussian Guards, who had been taken prisoner, were 'persuaded' to push to Eric's camp the motorbikes of forty of the divisional cyclists who 'danced round them in delight'. The cyclists had actually captured one hundred and fifty, but British shelling had fallen short and reduced their numbers, fortunately without hitting too many of the cyclists, who had made them carry in their kit and equipment as well as to push in the bikes.

When he got his first leave, in November 1914, he made a beeline for Leeds, leaving the front near Ypres at 7am and reaching Leeds (via Boulogne and London) at 9.30pm. There he spent his week, and met the then Vice-Chancellor of the University of Leeds, Michael Sadler, to discuss his experiences. Michael Sadler clearly felt he looked a good deal older. Although Eric no longer expected victory by Christmas, he still was optimistic of a German collapse early in 1915.[12]

John Turner's unit, the 1st Dorset Battalion, was also in the 5th Division, in the 15th Brigade. On 5th September, they had received their first reinforcements, and the next day had turned round and begun to advance until they made cautious contact with German patrols. On 9th September, they crossed the River Marne and came under heavy shell fire. They tried pushing onwards despite heavy gun, rifle and machine gun fire, but were ordered to retire to prepared trenches. Four more officers had been hit – two dying of their wounds, whilst another seven men were killed, thirty-one injured, and four went missing. Later they advanced again as the brigade's advance guard. On 13th September, they crossed the River Aisne at Missy, east of Soissons without further loss, and for the next couple of weeks consolidated their trench defences at Missy, north of the River Aisne, under German shellfire. Watson wrote of this brigade: "There was one brigade there that had a past. It had fought at Mons and Le Cateau, and then plugged away cheerfully through the Retreat and the Advance. What was left of it had fought stiffly on the Aisne. Some hard marching, a train journey, more hard marching, and it was thrown into action at La Bassée. There it fought itself to a standstill. It was attacked and attacked until, shattered, it was driven back one wild night. It was rallied, and turning on the enemy held them. More hard marching—a couple of days' rest, and it staggered into action at Ypres, and somehow—no one knows how—it held its bit of line. A brigade called by the same name, consisting of the same regiments, commanded by the same general, but containing scarce a man of those who had come out in August, marched very proudly away from Ypres and went—not to rest—but to hold another bit of the line. And this brigade was not the Guards Brigade. There were no picked men in the brigade. It contained just four ordinary regiments of the line—the Norfolks, the Bedfords, the Cheshires, and the Dorsets. What the 15th Brigade did, other brigades have done. Now little has been heard of this fighting round La Bassée in October, so I wish I could tell you about it in more detail than I can. To my thinking it was the finest fighting I have seen."[13]

Harold Deans was also on the Marne. Harold had been at King's School, Canterbury and in its O.T.C. before a last school year at Bournemouth, leaving in December 1912 to go to Edinburgh University to study medicine. He had been keen both as a sportsman and in the O.T.C. (becoming a sergeant). At Edinburgh he joined the University O.T.C. In 1913, he had been commissioned on the Unattached List as 2nd lieutenant for service with an O.T.C. in view of his school experiences. (The

---

[12] Details of his university career and first leave were kindly shared by Nick Shelley, who has researched this early group of dispatch riders. Leeds University Archive holds a typescript of the interview, MS 1314/PA/343.

[13] *Adventures of a Dispatch Rider*, W.H.L. Watson, pp.155-156.

account of his career in *The Bournemouthian* of December 1918 was sketchy, confused and inaccurate.)

He had volunteered on 6th August and was commissioned as 2nd lieutenant and was sent to the 2nd King's Own Scottish Borderers Battalion, which had landed at Le Havre on 15th August 1914, part of 13th Brigade of the 5th Division. He landed in France on 25th September and joined the battalion in the field on 15th October. Harold arrived as a replacement junior officer, one of several to make up for losses incurred. Harold's start with the battalion was more auspicious than that of his comrade, 2nd Lieutenant Sandison, who came at the same time – the war diary describes how he "drew his sword, cut his hand, and retired to hospital"![14] On Sunday 18th September, the battalion moved up to Beau Puits and took over trenches from the Duke of Cornwall's Light Infantry. Harold had his first significant taste of fighting. For two days and nights, 14th and 15th October, the 5th Division was subjected to continuous shellfire and night attacks. According to the official history, things reached a dramatic head on the night of 14th October when "according to the war diary of the 2/King's Own Scottish Borderers, about six hundred Germans cheered and about sixty charged, to be mown down almost to a man."[15]

La Bassée

After falling back in the Battle of the Marne, the Germans tried to consolidate on the River Aisne, but the B.E.F. was sent north-west to support the left wing of the French Army. The 1st Dorset Battalion was pulled back out of the line and on 7th October in "great secrecy" marched through the forest to the station at Compiègne to entrain to Abbeville via Amiens. Transported by bus from Abbeville, they took up position on the front line between Béthune and Ypres,[16] and reinforcements from Saint-Omer and Anvers (Antwerp) soon joined them. The British set about establishing a front from Bixschoote, north of Ypres, to La Bassée in France, with the French cavalry filling the gap between two army corps positioned further south, from La Bassée to Armentières.

John and the 1st Dorset Battalion established themselves on the Canal d'Aire bank near a pont fixe north of Cuinchy. By 12th October they had two companies deployed along the canal bank. This was the Battle of La Bassée, fought concurrently with the Battles of Armentières and Messines. These three minor battles are not generally well known but were of considerable significance to the school because they resulted in the deaths of several of its members.

Sir John French, the British Commander-in-Chief, planned to break through from the north and drive the Germans eastwards from Belgium. Sir John wrote, "Early in October a study of the general situation strongly impressed me with the necessity of bringing the greatest possible force to bear in support of the northern flank of the Allies… to effectively outflank the enemy and compel him to

---

[14] War Diary, 2nd King's Own Scottish Borderers, 15th October.

[15] *History of the Great War*, by direction of the Historical Section of the Committee of Imperial Defence, compiled by Brigadier-General J.E. Edmonds, London, 1925.

[16] Ypres was the last uncaptured city of Belgium, and therefore important for the British to defend it from German capture, even though by the end of the war it was a complete ruin. The British tended to use the French spelling of its name – Ypres – which many pronounced as 'Wipers'. Its more correct spelling is the Flemish Iepers, but throughout I have kept to the spelling as more commonly used by British forces 1914-1918.

evacuate his positions... The enemy had been weakened by continual abortive and futile attacks, whilst the fortification of the position had been much improved."[17]

On 12th October, the French lost control of Vermelles, a small town on the edge of the coal basin. John's battalion deployed on either side of a permanent bridge (pont fixe) over the canal and set up a machine gun on the first floor of a nearby factory to try to halt any German advance. That afternoon the Germans appeared, and the machine gun spat out its bullets, driving the Germans back. A follow-up advance in conjunction with the 1st Bedfords unfortunately led to the loss of a company commander, Major Roper. Although the action finished with a sense of success, in that the Dorsets had secured their objectives, they had still lost eleven men killed, fifty wounded, and two missing.

Fierce fighting erupted on both sides of the canal and continued for four days. On 13th October, the "attack... was resumed at 05:30 hours in an early morning mist. The forward platoons of B & C reached the line of a track boarded by willows. The Battalion moved up slowly to allow flanking units to come into line. Lt Col Bols was anxious about his flanks and he could not get into contact with units either side. Nevertheless, at first the Dorsets seemed to do very well."[18] At 7.20a.m. "there appeared to be very little opposition in front."[19] There was a problem though because to their south the village of Cuinchy was still in German hands, and from there the battalion could receive enfilade fire from their flank.

However, by 11.20a.m. they were under shell-fire from La Bassée and enfilade machine gun fire from the south bank and Cuinchy. At midday, 'B' Company started to withdraw. The Germans brought up a field howitzer battery, which concentrated on 'D' Company, which was lying in the open. About midday, John was killed trying to get his men back to the safety of the trenches, which the supporting companies had occupied. Lieut.-Col. Bols later wrote, "Practically the whole of B Coy was destroyed on that awful 13th." Colonel W.C. Smith of the 1st Dorset Battalion wrote to John's parents, "Your son was one of the best types of officer and gentleman that I have ever met and he would undoubtedly have made a name for himself had he been spared." Sir John French wrote in his dispatch, "General... Sir Horace Smith-Dorrien could make but little progress. He particularly mentions the fine fighting of the Dorsets, commanded by Lieutenant Colonel Bols. They suffered no less than 400 casualties, 130 of them being killed, but maintained all day their hold on Pont Fixé."[20] Captain Ransome wrote that he "was one of our most promising young officers and his two previous Company Commanders were loud in his praises. He showed a power of command and common-sense far above the average of his age and service. I had a great regard for him."[21] John was initially buried in an orchard near where he had fallen, but eventually was re-buried nearby at the Guards Cemetery, Windy Corner, Cuinchy.

Harold Dean's unit was in action a few miles to the north of where John was killed. Two days after John was killed, they too tried to attack against a strong German position: "Ordered to attack south on La Bassée... For our battalion to advance by day over the 700 yards or 800 yards of open ground

---

[17] From Sir John French, Fourth Dispatch, published in the *Second Supplement to the London Gazette* of 27th November 1914.
[18] Regimental History of the Dorsetshire Regiment.
[19] War Diary, 1st Dorsets. 13th October 1914.
[20] From Sir John French, British Commander-in-Chief – Fourth dispatch.
[21] *The Bournemouthian*, December 1914.

against it… was not a possible operation of war. Two attacks were started, drawing the fire of 4 or 5 M.G. and a battery. Our own shells fell short and were the direct cause of holding up the two attacks, though the position could never have been taken by us. Our casualties were approximately 12 killed and 44 wounded… the battalion reduced to 13 officers. Ground was gained to about 300 yards… Entrenching."[22]

By October 23rd the battalion was exhausted after fighting continuously for six days. Even resting under bivouac at Richebourg it was still under German shell fire. Harold fell sick and was probably wounded. Even the hospital in Béthune to which he was sent was shelled by German long range guns, leaving men dead and wounded. When he left the battalion he left his kit by the roadside and afterwards the Army charged him for the lost equipment! In February 1915, the battalion was moved north from the La Bassée Sector to the Ypres Salient.

On 22nd November 1914, Harold and William Austin landed together in France as privates in the 1st I.C.S.C. (Indian Cavalry Supply Column), 89th Company. William, born in 1889; at school 1904-1905 (and a corporal in the O.T.C.) and Harold, born 1892; at school 1905-1907, came from Boscombe. They were clearly close and had worked in London and Manchester as civil engineers. They volunteered on 8th August at Bournemouth for 89 Company, Army Service Corps, formed on 15th October 1914 for service on the Western Front. It was given the role of supporting the 1st Indian Cavalry Division and its supply column, as Number 1 Section (MT). Promotion was rapid, perhaps because of their O.T.C. experience at school or because each had completed his apprenticeship in London. On 18th August, at Aldershot, Harold was promoted to corporal. William jumped ahead: he was made a staff sergeant and then, on 23rd November, quarter master sergeant.

Their unit, operating behind the lines, was an Army Service Corps deployment to support the Indian troops, who from the end of 1914 to the end of 1915 formed a large part of the British fighting capacity on the Western Front before being deployed further east against the Turks.

A number of British battalions and units inter-mingled with Indian Army battalions in the Indian brigades. Why were British troops placed in Indian army divisions? "The officers of the Indian Regiments had every confidence in the troops they led; but it would have been a tremendous test to send Indian soldiers unsupported by British troops to face the renowned fighting men of Turkey, organised and directed by Germans, and equipped with all the latest appliances of modern war. As to the value of its [the Indian Army's] work in Europe opinions differed. Some seemed to think little of it. Some declared that during the time when English reinforcements were not yet ready to go into line, the Indian contingent had saved the British Army from being overwhelmed. Both these views were perhaps extreme. The Indian soldier fought under serious disadvantage in the climate and surroundings of Europe, but undoubtedly he fought with great devotion and suffered heavy losses, for which England owes him deep gratitude."[23]

Their immediate task was to repair the radiators of twenty-one lorries. These were meant to have been drained in the expectation of a hard frost, but because they were choked up with red mud they had failed to drain fully and had therefore split on freezing. Then they had to load up the

---

[22] War Diary, 2nd King's Own Scottish Borderers, 18th-19th October 1914.

[23] *The Thirteenth Hussars in the Great War*, the Right Hon. Sir H. Mortimer Durand G.C.M.G., K.C.S.I. K.C.I.E., William Blackwood and Sons, Edinburgh and London, 1921, p. 91.

lorries with one day's supplies for the division, to support 3,000 British and 4,500 Indian troops, with 7,550 horses. The 89th Company had forty-eight light lorries, three workshops, three store lorries, three cars and seven motorcycles. Their work became the onward distribution of supplies to regiments grouped across northern France. Instead of concerns over machine guns and artillery shells, their main concern was loading and unloading, and driving, supply lorries filled with oats, sugar, and other supplies often needed in considerable bulk, though sometimes – as in February 1915 – they were instead transporting hundreds of soldiers in their lorries. From late April they were supporting troops as far east as Watou, west of Poperinghe, inside the Belgian border. Both young men were ambitious to do more, and their commander supported them. In September they applied for commissions, so then they went their separate ways and changed the nature of their service.

William Austin was commissioned into the Royal Garrison Artillery on 17th November 1915, rising to the rank of Captain of 190 Heavy Battery fighting in the eastern Mediterranean. For his valour he was awarded the Military Cross. He survived the war, despite a bout of malaria. Meanwhile, on 4th October 1915, Harold Austin had been detached for what must have been a 'crash course' in officer training at Number 2 Training Camp of the GHQ Cadet School at Blendecques in France and was commissioned 2nd lieutenant in the 1st Duke of Cornwall's Light Infantry Battalion.

Clermont Grantham-Hill had also arrived in France. Born in 1891, he was one of the earliest members of the school, probably from 1901. Later he attended Shrewsbury School and then went on to Cambridge University in which he was a member of the Cambridge University O.T.C. (Sergeant, Royal Army Medical Corps). By 1911 he was a medical student at London University. In November 1912, although a Quaker and still a medical student, he joined the Inns of Court O.T.C., which was part of the Territorial Force. He formally joined the Army in 1912, and was commissioned 2nd lieutenant in the 3rd Hussars on 15th August. Clermont landed in France on 6th November 1914 to join his cavalry regiment, part of the 2nd Cavalry Division. However, the war of movement was already grinding towards a halt. Five days after landing he joined the regiment near Bailleul, south of Poperinghe. As the lines had stabilised, more men were needed to man the line, and so the regiment had just been required to dismount and to man rudimentary trenches. He was one of five subalterns who arrived about this time, and the war diary of his new regiment was somewhat dismissive of them: "The arrival of five very young officers in the last two days gives the Regt. 3 over Establishment, but none of the five can possibly know anything much of Cavalry work all having joined since the Regt left England."[24]

On 15th November, Clermont got his first real taste of the war – not riding into battle as perhaps he might have imagined, but dismounted, relieving the 5th Lancers in support trenches just west of Messines, with their backs to the Belgium village of Wulvergem. In front of their trenches was the front line manned by the French 156th Regiment. Such had been the losses to the B.E.F. infantry that Sir John French had no choice but to use cavalry in an infantry role. The New Army infantry would not be ready for another year at least.

Although they were only in those trenches for a single day, the pattern was repeated on 19th November when they rode forward as far as east of La Clytte, then dismounted and went to trenches just north of the Kemmel–Wytschaete road, relieving the 18/342th French Regiment.

---

[24] War Diary, 3rd Hussars, 11th November 1914.

These trenches were not the advanced trenches of the middle war years and were very inadequate. "The front trenches were mostly mere rifle pits and were not connected nor provided with communications to the rear. They had also to be approached over an area under enfilade fire from hill 75 on the south side of the main road. Eventually by 10.30pm the Regt was all accommodated – still snowing hard – bitterly cold and wet. Sniping incessant throughout the operation and 3 men were wounded in this manner. Horses were sent back to billets."[25]

This pattern of action became the norm. Their commander explained the impossibility of using horses in the traditional role for which they had trained: "Certainly it is hard now to foresee any possibility of Cavalry work and whilst employed holding trenches horses are an absolute encumbrance. Somewhere near 50% of our fighting strength is occupied looking after them and the transport, thus rendering our own firing line terribly thin, and without support."[26] Cavalry units like the 3rd Hussars continued, however, to carry a cachet, and it is no co-incidence that a few days after they were withdrawn from the trenches at the start of December they were inspected, first by the King, Prince of Wales and Generals Allenby and Gough, and two days later by Sir John French.

The First Battle of Ypres

In the north, the British had reached the Belgian city of Ypres. Sir John French was anxious to push the Germans east from the Ypres area. First however, he had to consolidate the positions between Sir Douglas Haig's 1st Corps at Ypres and the other divisions to the south. Haig described the situation in his war diary entry for 16th October: "I see Sir John French on my arrival. He seemed quite satisfied with the general situation and said the Enemy was falling back and that we 'would soon be in a position to round them up'."[27]

Edward R. E. Hickling.

Sir John French's decision to attack coincided with the parallel decision to attack the British I Corps at Ypres by the German commander Falkenhayn. His overall aim by this attack was to push the German line westwards to cut off the British from the sea and force them to retreat in the direction of Boulogne. Falkenhayn launched his attack at Langemarck near Ypres on October 20th, and Edward Hickling was there.

Edward was in the 1st Loyal North Lancashire Battalion, part of I Corps, 2nd Division. Born in 1895 and at school from 1907, by April 1913 he was a school prefect. He was something of an athlete and a keen member of the O.T.C., becoming a sergeant in September 1912. According to *The Bournemouthian*, he "made up his mind when quite a youngster to go into the Army." When Edward left Bournemouth School, he was gazetted to the 3rd Gloucestershire Battalion on October 8th 1913. As with

---

[25] War Diary, 3rd Hussars, 19th November 1914.
[26] War Diary, 3rd Hussars, 25th November 1914.
[27] From Douglas Haig, *War Diaries and Letters 1914-1918*, edited by Gary Sheffield and John Bourne, p. 73.

other regiments, being gazetted to the 3rd Battalion meant being posted into the Training and Reserve unit of his regiment to train through the winter of 1913 and learn the job of a 2nd lieutenant. When war broke out in August, he was promoted to lieutenant and was sent to France in September. Just before he left for the front he was given leave, and in the best of spirits he visited the school.

However, on the front line he did not get a chance to serve with his own battalion, but was instead attached to the 1st Loyal North Lancashire Battalion.

The first phase of the First Battle of Ypres is sometimes known as the Battle of Langemarck, fought 21st-24th October 1914. It involved both 1st and 2nd Divisions of Haig's I Corps, together with the 3rd and 7th Cavalry Divisions of Rawlinson's IV Corps. Sir John French believed that German resistance to Haig and I Corps would be limited.

On 20th October, Edward's battalion led the 1st Division in its advance towards Ypres, past Cassell and through Poperinghe. Their billets were very limited: "71 in one room."[28] Then the next day, they moved into position near Boesinghe Church, just north of Ypres, and to the south and right of the French.

The British had felt let down by the French at Mons, and once again felt the French were unreliable – instead of holding the bridge, they were found "huddled up" further back, so a section had to be sent to hold the bridge for them. Anticipating a German attack, their orders on 22nd October were to hold the trenches on the southern side of the canal if shelling should start. The British had to withstand a series of German attacks, though "Late in the evening the enemy succeeded in penetrating a portion of the line held by the Cameron Highlanders north of Pilckem."[29] In the middle of the night – 2.30a.m. on 23rd October, Edward's battalion assembled quietly and marched to Pilckem. Sir John French wrote, "At 6a.m. on the morning of the 23rd a counter attack to recover the lost trenches was made by the Queen's Regiment, the Northamptons, the Loyal North Lancashires and the King's Royal Rifles, under Major-General Bulfin."

Just after dawn the battalion attacked from the left of the main road near Bixschoote. Edward was in 'B' Company. "'C' on the left of the road and 'A' on their left advanced by sections under Major Burrows. 'D' and 'B' supported."[30] Edward and another officer with about a hundred men formed a guard on the left flank, so they did not advance until about 7.30a.m. "Then we in turn had the order to advance, and went forward over the turnip fields, and then out on to the open ploughed land with not a vestige of cover anywhere, and bullets flying round us like bees. We got to within about 300 yards of the enemy's trenches. I got hit just above the knee and was of course to all intents and purposes 'down and out'. But I yelled to Hickling to take the men on — whether he heard me or not I cannot say — but I saw him afterwards running forwards with his men, and I was told later that he got through all right."[31] "The attack was driven home and about 11a.m. we were about 300 yards just south east of Stenstart. The shell fire and rifle fire was very heavy and we lost rather a lot. At 2p.m. the Germans began to slip out of their trenches. Our left was swung round and with the Rifles (a company) and a few S[outh] Staffords we charged the trenches and surprised them

---

[28] War Diary of the 1st Loyal North Lancashire Battalion, 23rd October 1914.
[29] From Sir John French, British Commander-in-Chief – Fourth dispatch.
[30] From the War Diary of the 1st Loyal North Lancashire Battalion, 23rd October 1914.
[31] From an account by another officer, published in *The Bournemouthian* in December 1914.

with the maxim[32] under Lieutenant Henderson. We captured the trenches and about 150–200 prisoners who surrendered."[33] "We captured a lot of German prisoners and he was detailed to bring a party of them back. He had a guard on them, with fixed bayonets, and of course all the Germans were disarmed, but it appears that the German officer who was with them had a revolver which had not been taken from him, and while poor young Hickling took his eyes off him for a moment, this swine turned round and deliberately shot him. In the space of two or three seconds that German officer had been simply hacked to ribbons by our men's bayonets, but alas that didn't save poor Hickling. It. was altogether a most tragic affair."[34]

Edward, badly wounded in the hip, was taken back behind the lines first to a battalion first aid post, then back first to a dressing station and then on to a casualty clearing station. For the first few stages of this evacuation the stretcher-bearers would certainly have been within firing range, and even the field ambulance that took him back to the casualty clearing station would have been very vulnerable. The casualty clearing station was a few miles west of Ypres at Poperinghe, which had a railway station from which he might have been evacuated further west – perhaps to Boulogne. Although *The Bournemouthian* reported that he died from his wounds on November 2nd, at Boulogne, this was a mistake. The War Office records his death on 26th October, and he was buried in one of the first graves of the British Army in that part of Belgium, in the Poperinghe Communal Cemetery. Edward died at the casualty clearing station in Poperinghe in one of a series of buildings used by the Royal Army Medical Corps until it was destroyed by shell fire in April 1915. The school magazine dramatically summarised his death – but it could equally have been written for both John before him and Jesse whose death followed soon after: "He has fallen, a martyr, in the most righteous war that has ever been waged, and we hope that his sorrowing father and mother—to whom we offer our deepest sympathy—will take comfort from that thought."[35] He was aged just 19. A few days later, by 31st October 1914, the battalion had been reduced to only one officer and thirty five soldiers.[36]

Meanwhile, Francis Lawrance may have been involved in this battle, in his case like the Austin brothers supporting the Indian troops using his mechanical expertise. Francis, born in 1889, was at the school from 1902 to 1905. Probably a member of the O.T.C., later he completed four years' service with the 4th Hampshire Battalion (a Territorial force) in 1909. He served a four year apprenticeship with Wolseley Motors Ltd., which ended in February 1910. When the war broke out he had decided to enlist, and he travelled to Aldershot where he attested on 5th September 1914, and was placed in the Motor Transport Section of the Army Service Corps. The Army spelt his surname Laurance. Within weeks, at really remarkable speed, he was on the Western Front: he travelled overnight to France, 22nd to 23rd September 1914. He served for the whole war, with the Army Service Corps Motor Transport, the 3rd (Lahore) Division, Indian Contingent, normally abbreviated to the Lahore Division to avoid confusion with the British 3rd Division. (Its men were mostly drawn from the Punjab, now eastern Pakistan.)

---

[32] Maxim – the current British machine gun.
[33] From the War Diary of the 1st Loyal North Lancashire Battalion, 23rd October 1914.
[34] From an account by another officer, published in *The Bournemouthian* in December 1914.
[35] *The Bournemouthian*, December 1914.
[36] According to *A History of the Great War*, based on official documents, by direction of the Historical Section of the Committee of Imperial Defence – *Military operations France and Belgium, 1914*, compiled by Brigadier-General J.E. Edmonds, Macmillan and Co. Limited, 1925.

Soldiers of this division went into action on 24th October 1914. The first Indian units – the Indian Cavalry Corps, the 3rd (Lahore) and 7th (Meerut) Divisions – had begun to reach the front line near Ypres only a few days before, after landing at Marseilles on 26th September. Due to the pressing need to strengthen the British battalions already in the line, the 3rd (Lahore) Division was broken up and its battalions and brigades deployed according to need. Consequently, different units fought almost simultaneously on the Messines Ridge south of Ypres, as well as Armentières on the French-Belgian border, and a little further south at La Bassée. In this battle, within days, these formidable soldiers had suffered 1,565 casualties, but they made a vital contribution to the defence of Ypres. Later, from 20th-21st December, the division fought in the battle for the defence of Givenchy, just east of La Bassée.

We do not know how long Francis and his branch of the Army Service Corps was attached to the Lahore Division. The division remained in France for most of 1915, fighting hard, notably in four significant battles: the Battle of Neuve Chapelle, 10th to 23rd March; taking part in the Second Battle of Ypres, between 24th April and 4th May; the Battle of Aubers on 9th May; and the Battle of Festubert from 15th to 25th May. However, as casualties mounted, which could not easily be replaced from half-way across the world; because additional British battalions were slowly becoming available; and because it was felt Indian troops might be better suited in the warmer climes, it was decided to pull the division out of France and send it to Mesopotamia, where it remained fighting valiantly for the duration of the war. But Francis remained on the Western Front, rising in January 1918 to staff sergeant, specialising in mechanics. He survived the conflict and was demobilised on 18th May 1919.

Falkenhayn had also attacked north of I Corps, attacking the Belgian Army which had retreated to form a defence line on the Yser River between Dixmuide and Nieuwpoort. The Belgian Army was small, brave, but already damaged and unlikely to be able to hold off a prolonged German attack. The Belgians made the brave decision to open the sluices that held back the sea at Nieuwpoort. On 27th October, this action meant the Belgians flooded a two-mile wide water barrier between themselves and the Germans along the twenty miles between Dixmuide and Nieuwpoort. This made a German advance north of the British impossible, so Falkenhayn paused to rethink his battle plans.

He turned to his newly created Fourth Army under the Duke of Wurttemberg to attack Ypres itself, supported by a cavalry corps and Bavaria's Sixth Army under Prince Rupprecht. He counted on outnumbering the B.E.F., capturing Ypres, and crashing through the British defence lines. On 31st October, German cavalry drove the British cavalry from the Messines Ridge at the southern end of the salient. Haig's I Corps fought back and held off the German advance. Finally, on 11th November, the Germans used two crack divisions to try to break the British lines just north of the Menin road, leading to terrible fighting around Hooge. At times the situation seemed desperate for the British, but they held on until bad winter weather brought an end to this, the First Battle of Ypres, on 22nd November. So the First Battle of Ypres had failed to achieve the hoped for breakthroughs anticipated either by Sir John French or by Falkenhayn.

As Edward Hickling lay dying in Poperinghe, Bournemouth School teacher Jesse Atkin left England on October 25th for the Western Front. Assistant master Jesse Atkin had been born in 1891, and by 1914 was a strapping giant of a young man – six foot four inches tall. He was a Nottinghamshire lad, educated at University College, Nottingham, gaining his BA degree from London University (which accredited the Nottingham University College). He gained an Elementary School Teacher's Certificate in 1912. Jesse had joined the O.T.C. at the university. When he had completed his degree course and college career he applied and was accepted for the Special Reserve of officers. This coincided with his appointment, aged just 21, to teach at Bournemouth school from January 1913. He was gazetted on 6th May 1913 as 2nd lieutenant in the Sherwood Foresters.

Jesse Atkin

He was appointed as a versatile junior teacher – his special subject knowledge was in English, French and maths, and soon he was teaching English and maths to the younger boys, and Latin to the senior boys. He settled in well as a young teacher. By the end of the summer of 1913 he was scoring well for the staff cricket team. In July 1913, he was also appointed lieutenant in the school O.T.C. He was form tutor for the equivalent of Year 9, and he produced the summer play – excerpts from Julius Caesar, which was well received. Everything changed in August 1914. The school would just have to manage without him, but doubtless the headmaster and boys were more proud that this young teacher was 'doing his bit' than they were disconcerted by any sudden timetabling complications. With the outbreak of war, the Nottinghamshire and Derbyshire Regiment –

Jesse Atkin as assistant master at Bournemouth School.
He is seated middle row, second from the right.

generally known as the Sherwood Foresters – quickly had needed its Reserve officers to support its necessary rapid growth. Initially, Jesse was placed on garrison duty at Plymouth, but soon he was needed abroad.

He arrived in France on 26th October, and was attached to the 3rd Worcestershire Battalion on October 30th – the need was great and the Army did not mind switching junior officers between regiments. Certainly, the Worcestershire Battalion had been taking steady losses on a daily basis for some time: the battalion war diary records that in the fortnight before Jesse arrived, they had lost seven officers killed and a further eleven wounded, as well as fifty-four soldiers killed, two hundred and thirteen wounded, with a further thirty-nine missing.[37]

When Jesse joined the 3rd Worcestershire Battalion, it was part of 74th Brigade, 3rd Division, south of Ypres. This division had not been involved in the First Battle of Ypres, but had held the line south into France. At 7a.m. on 1st November, the battalion was given short notice that it was to be moved out of its billets. By mid-morning they were on buses and were being taken north into Belgium where they arrived at the western edge of Ploegsteert Wood. At Ploegsteert Wood they moved into bivouac positions a little to the south of the Messines Ridge and south of Ypres – just across the frontier from the French town of Armentières. At dusk the next day, 2nd November, Jesse moved with the battalion into trenches dug inside the wood, holding the line and relieving Hampshire Regiment soldiers.

The first night, with only one soldier wounded, was a relatively gentle introduction to the real war for Jesse, but on 3rd November the battalion was shelled by the Germans, and the shelling became more intense as the day went on, with the result that another junior lieutenant was wounded, and six soldiers were killed and sixteen wounded. In contrast, 4th November was a relatively quiet day with less shelling in the middle of the day, and no one was wounded or killed. Perhaps it was during this lull that he found time to write to the headmaster, Dr. Fenwick, from the 'fighting zone' to say that he was "in the best of health and spirits".[38]

By November 1914, the front line had begun to solidify and both sides had been digging trenches for some time. The British viewed such trenches as temporary shelter before pushing the Germans out from their defensive positions. In these, still relatively primitive trenches east of the wood, Jesse and the others had to endure the heavy rain which hammered down on them in the middle of the night of 4th-5th November, followed by a horrid day on the 5th itself when the battalion came under heavy shellfire and "a lot of sniping"[39] killing another three men and wounding six. Heavy shelling continued on 6th November and intensified further for about an hour from 3a.m. on 7th November. Any confusion caused by the guns was made very much worse by the thick fog which engulfed the wood.

Nowhere was safe. That Saturday, 7th November 1914, Haig confided to his diary one of those dismissive entries which show his limited understanding of the conditions for ordinary soldiers. He wrote of the situation a few miles north of Jesse, "The Lincolns, Northumberland Fusiliers and the Bedfords leave their trenches on account of a little shell fire. Several pass Divisional Headquarters while I am there. I order [all] men to be tried by [Court Martial] who have funked in

---

[37] War Diary, 3rd Battalion, Worcestershire Regiment.
[38] *The Bournemouthian*, December 1914.
[39] War Diary, 3rd Worcestershire Battalion, 5th November 1914.

this way, and the [abandoned] trenches to be re-occupied at once."[40]

About 5a.m., the Germans took advantage of the confusion to break through the right hand trenches manned by 'C' Company, rushing to capture a British trench on the eastern side of Ploegsteert Wood. Jesse was with the Reserve ('B' and 'D') Companies in the wood west of the attack. Both companies were launched into a counter-attack to try to recapture the trench. This was a desperate battle – the companies which included Jesse were reinforced by Inniskilling Fusiliers and East Lancashire Regiment companies, and a company of Seaforth Highlanders. Despite their best efforts, the attempts to recover the forward trenches failed, but a lot of men lost their lives.[41]

As Jesse and his men neared the eastern edge of the wood they came under heavy German fire. Jesse turned his head to give instructions to his men, and was shot in the back of the neck. He just had time to say "Goodbye" to the nearest man, who had run over to help him. His body was not recovered because of the thickness of the undergrowth in that part of the wood, as well as the ferocity of the fighting. By the time a patrol went out to look for the bodies it was already dark, and they could not find him. The next day the battalion was relieved and sent back a mile or two to get some rest. A few days later a Somerset Light Infantry patrol reported finding the body of a junior Worcestershire officer near the edge of the wood, and had buried him there. As Jesse was the only junior officer killed in the area at that time, it must have been his body.

Two days after his death, on Monday 9th November, Jesse's younger sister, Bertha, who worked in the local Jacksdale Post Office, received the telegram regretting his death to take to her own family – it must have been a dreadful shock. Jesse's grave has been lost, and today he is commemorated by an entry on Panel 7 of the Ploegstreet Memorial, part of the Royal Berks Extension Cemetery. Sadly, having lost Jesse in 1914, his parents were later to lose their elder son Charles on 30th May 1918. In his obituary, we read how Jesse had "very soon gained the high esteem of masters and boys for the keen and active interests he took in all that concerned the welfare of the School… Mr Atkin's influence was chiefly felt in the deep personal interest he took in the boys, every one of whom regarded him – and with good reason – as a friend."[42]

The battle resumed in its final phase on 11th November with greater British resources committed. Haig's I Corps and its four divisions had additional support from other corps divisions, including the 7th Division.

Dispatch rider Eric Bagshaw and his comrades had also been at La Bassée, and then at the First Battle of Ypres. However, as the war began to become bogged down, so much of the movement and 'fun' of riding his motor cycle between the different units began to fail, and life became much more of a slog to be endured (despite a welcome pre-Christmas week of leave in England). After the Christmas break, Eric and his friends decided to apply for commissions. "There were points in

---

[40] Haig, op cit., p. 79.

[41] War Diary, 3rd Worcestershire Battalion says that between 6th and 7th November, the battalion lost Captain A.S. Nesbitt, Lieutenant J.B. Vandeleur, as well as Second Lieutenants S.A. Goldsmid and Jesse Atkin, whilst Major H.D. Milward and Lieutenant H. Stockley were also wounded. Of the rank and file soldiers, 42 were killed, 121 wounded and a further 39 were found to be missing when the action was called off.

[42] *The Bournemouthian*, December 1914.

being 'an officer and a gentleman'. Dirt and discomfort were all very well when there was plenty of work to do, and we all decided that every officer should have been in the ranks, but despatch-riding had lost its savour. We had become postmen. Thoughts of the days when we had dashed round picking-up brigades, had put battalions on the right road, and generally made ourselves conspicuous, if not useful, discontented us. So we talked it over. Two of us struck upon a corps which combined the advantages of every branch of the service. We drew up a list of each other's qualifications to throw a sop to modesty, sent in our applications, and waited. At the same time we adopted a slight tone of hauteur towards those who were not potential officers. One night after tea 'Ginger' brought in the orders. I had become a gentleman, and, saying good-bye, I walked down into the village and reported myself to the officer commanding the Divisional Cyclists. I was no longer a despatch rider but a very junior subaltern. I had worked with the others for nearly seven months—with Huggie, who liked to be frightened; with George the arch scrounger; with Spuggy, who could sing the rarest songs; with Sadders, who is as brave as any man alive; with N'Soon, the dashing, of the tender skin; with Fat Boy, who loves 'sustaining' food and dislikes frost; with Grimers and Cecil, best of artificers; with Potters and Orr and Moulders and the Flapper. I cannot pay them a more sufficient tribute than the tribute of the Commander-in-Chief:— 'Carrying despatches and messages at all hours of the day and night, in every kind of weather, and often traversing bad roads blocked with transport, they have been conspicuously successful in maintaining an extraordinary degree of efficiency in the service of communications... No amount of difficulty or danger has ever checked the energy and ardour which has distinguished their corps throughout the operations.'"[43]

On 7th February 1915, Eric ('Spuggy') was commissioned 2nd lieutenant in the 1st Divisional Cyclist Company of the Royal Engineers, part of the 1st Divisional Mounted Troops, and served with them for the next year. On 11th March 1916, he was allowed to resign this commission and to return to South Africa. His father, Thomas Bagshaw, had passed away and he was allowed to settle his family affairs in Port Elizabeth because, after enquires with the South African Government in Pretoria and its High Commissioner in London, it was decided that the family company was vitally important to the conduct of the war, and he was the only adult son and was needed to run the company. He did offer to serve in the South West African campaign if his resignation was not allowed, but that was not deemed necessary. This was because, as Eric put it, "My firm, Bagshaw Gibard & Co. are executing important contracts for boots, harness & saddlery for the Union Troops."[44] On 6th July 1916, he arrived back in the United Kingdom from South Africa[45] and began a second career with the Royal Flying Corps (then still part of the Army) to which he was commissioned on 25th August 1917 as an equipment officer. He was again allowed to resign his commission on 4th September 1918 and returned to Port Elizabeth, setting sail the next day.

Meanwhile, Arthur Hame had arrived in the Ypres Salient. Arthur, born 1890, was at school as a day boy and later as a boarder, 1903-1906, and a member of the O.T.C. After leaving school he was a member of the Leicestershire Royal Horse Artillery for about two years up to 1909. He volunteered for the Honourable Artillery Company on 28th August 1914 from his home in Birmingham. He crossed with the 1st Battalion from Southampton to St. Nazaire on the SS

---

[43] *Adventures of a Dispatch Rider*, W.H.L. Watson, pp. 271-272.

[44] From a letter in the Army File of Eric Bagshaw, WO 339/22770.

[45] For this part of his story, in particular, I am indebted to the contributors of the Great War Forum, www.greatwarforum.org. One of the helpful contributors to this forum directed me to Captain Watson's book previously referenced, and explained how 'Spuggy' was the author's nickname for Eric.

Westmeath, landing on 20th September 1914. Arthur was in 'C' Company in which he acted as a stretcher-bearer.

His battalion was not initially pulled into the fight. For the next two months it stayed in western France, training. At the end of October they moved to Abbeville where they joined the 8th Brigade in the 3rd Division on 9th November 1914. It was decided that as the recruits had so far not even fired their rifles, the process of introducing them to the trenches had to be gradual. They started by digging in support areas. On 15th November they suffered their first death when a shrapnel shell burst on the parapet of a trench in which some were working. They finally went into front line trenches on 22nd November at Neuve Eglise. At the end of the month they moved east and got their first sight of Ypres itself.

On 3rd December, Arthur had a very special experience. The official commander-in-chief of the battalion was the King, and he was visiting his troops. "A 'red letter day'. The British Monarch is with his army in the field for the first time for 170 years. His Majesty arrived outside No.3 billet at 1.45p.m., accompanied by General Sir Horace Smith-Dorrien – 2nd Corps Commander, General Haldane – 3rd Division Commander, General Bowes – Brigadier 8th Brigade & many others. The battn was drawn up in line facing the billets & as His Majesty passed each Company he was given the H.A.C. Artillery Fire. His Majesty addressed the CO – 'Colonel Treffery, we meet under rather different auspices to those under which I had the pleasure of inspecting the H.A.C. in London.' He then inspected the straw huts & the CO introduced Captain Ward with whom his Majesty shook hands. His Majesty went in the Sgts' Hut & talked to the Sgts & the men in another hut. H.R.H. the Prince of Wales also went into the huts when the inspection was over. The CO accompanied his Majesty to the road & in reply to his Majesty's enquiries informed him as to the number of casualties & His Majesty expressed his great pleasure that the men looked so well. He then shook hands with the CO & said 'Well Colonel, I am delighted to have had a look at my Battn again & under active conditions & I am very glad your casualties are so slight – I am informed that the H.A.C. is doing extremely well & that your General is very pleased with you. I shall continue to watch your doings with the greatest interest & I wish you all every possible luck.' The CO thanked His Majesty & he again shook hands. He then entered his car & drove off. Immediately after the inspection the Battn marched to the trenches E of Kemmel."[46]

A few days later they switched to the 7th Brigade, Third Division. On 9th December, two companies (Nos. 2 & 3) went into the front line trenches east of Kemmel, with the rest in support, immediately taking casualties from German shelling. Conditions were awful in the wet weather and the diary touchingly describes how some of the men could only stagger around, with much appreciated fresh hot tea being brewed for them. They remained in the trenches over Christmas and do not seem to have enjoyed any truce. Although there were no recorded casualties on Christmas Day, on Boxing Day one sergeant was killed and a corporal wounded by a shot to the head.

Just after Christmas, Leslie Gilbert arrived to join Arthur. Born in 1891, like Arthur, he boarded at the school, 1905-1908. (His older brother Geoffrey boarded 1905-1906.) Working in London as a stockbroker's clerk, he volunteered in Finsbury on 2nd September 1914, also to join the 1st Honourable Artillery Company Battalion. After initial training he was sent to France on 29th December 1914, and joined the battalion in the field on 13th January 1915. (On 14th October 1915,

---

[46] War Diary, 1st Battalion, Honourable Artillery Company, 3rd December 1914.

this battalion was transferred to be General Head Quarter troops, and then was transferred to the 190th Brigade, in the 63rd (Royal Naval) Division on 9th July 1916.)

Christmas 1914

By December there was stalemate on the Western Front. Both sides stared at each other across their trench lines. Christmas 1914 saw the famous truce on a few sections of the line, especially on and near the Messines Ridge south of Ypres and at Ploegsteert.

"Xmas Day 1914. 25 December. St Jans Cappell. Princess Mary's Gifts of an ornamental box containing cigarettes & tobacco, & a pipe & a card of good wishes given out to every man in France. Also a Xmas Card, with a portrait of HM King George V & of the Queen & their good wishes is issued as a surprise to every man. Owing to the kindness of people at home great quantities of warm clothing, tobacco, & eatables are issued to the troops… From hearsay evidence from officers & others – It is reported from the trenches that at various points during Xmas Eve & on Xmas Day the officers & men of the Bavarian Landwehr opposed to us in this portion of the line made overtures of peace for a Xmas holiday. These were generally accepted. At one point a football match was played between the opposing sides. Food & tobacco was exchanged & the opposing sides visited each other's trenches. The Bavarians were reported to be looking well fed & in a good state, but in some cases in want of clothes. They are reported to have been in ignorance of the present state of affairs on the Russian border, to have been told that the Germans had won enormous victories there, & that the war was to be over in a month."[47]

"There are many people in England still who cannot stomach the story of the Christmas truce. 'Out there', we cannot understand why. Good fighting men respect good fighting men. On our front, and on the fronts of other divisions, the Germans had behaved throughout the winter with a passable gentlemanliness. Besides, neither the British nor the German soldier—with the possible exception of the Prussians—has been able to stoke up that virulent hate which devastates so many German and British homes. A certain lance-corporal puts the matter thus: 'We're fightin' for somethink what we've got. Those poor beggars is fightin' cos they've got to. An' old Bill Kayser's fightin' for somethin' what 'e'll never get. But 'e will get somethink, and that's a good 'iding!' We even had a sneaking regard for that 'cunning old bird, Kayser Bill'. Our treatment of prisoners explains the Christmas Truce. The British soldier, except when he is smarting under some dirty trick, suffering under terrible loss, or maddened by fighting or fatigue, treats his prisoners with a tolerant, rather contemptuous kindness. May God in His mercy help any poor German who falls into the hands of a British soldier when the said German has 'done the dirty' or has 'turned nasty'! There is no judge so remorseless, no executioner so ingenious in making the punishment fit the crime."[48]

Two Old Bournemouthians who enjoyed the short spell of the Christmas truce were John Ingram, born in Parkstone in 1891 and at school 1904-1907, and William Hodges from Bournemouth. Both were members of the 1/16th (County of London) Battalion (known as the Queen's Westminster Rifles). After leaving school, John had been articled to become a chartered accountant. He had volunteered to join the London Regiment when war was declared. William Hodges was younger, born in 1896. This 1/16th London Battalion was part of the huge London regiment – an

---

[47] War Diary, 2nd King's Own Scottish Borderers, 25th December 1914.
[48] *Adventures of a Dispatch Rider*, W.H.L. Watson, pp. 237-238.

organisation that was unique in a number of ways. The whole, massive, London Regiment was entirely a Territorial Army force; and each of its battalions was so huge that each battalion was considered a corps in its own right. These battalions were open to the flood of volunteers from the start of the war.

After initial training at Hemel Hempstead, Hertfordshire, the young riflemen were sent with their battalion to France. The battalion landed at Le Havre on 3rd November and, on 12th November, joined 18th Brigade, the 6th Division. Almost immediately they were sent to the front line, despite Kitchener's earlier considerable reservations about using the Territorial Army in this way. But Kitchener's New Army would not be ready for another year, and the line needed strengthening and support immediately. With all the casualties already inflicted on the B.E.F., the Army urgently needed reinforcements and replacements, and although the troops from the professional Indian Army were helping magnificently to bridge the gap, the need was acute.

By the time John and William arrived in the trenches, the trenches of Western Front were already deteriorating into a quagmire. William had a rough time of it – suffering such rheumatism and frostbite in the winter of 1914-1915 that he had to be sent away from the front for a time to recover.

The Army was in a state of flux. It was clear that Sir John French, the Commander-in-Chief, had been under considerable strain; one of his original corps commanders had died of a heart attack in August, and now his heart too was affected. From November 1914 onwards his grip on command began to slip as his heart condition grew worse. There is some debate amongst historians as to how serious this was. He claimed to have had to take to his bed after heart attacks. It has been suggested that his 'heart attacks' might have been used to 'smoke-screen' his own difficulties in controlling subordinates like Sir Douglas Haig, or later exaggerated by others to conceal the semi-political developments, which led to his ousting as Commander-in-Chief at the end of 1915. Other generals were being privately regarded as potential successors – men like General Herbert Plumer (popular with the soldiers, not particularly with the politicians) or Douglas Haig (who enjoyed the King's favour).

Sir John had a long-standing personal dislike of Horace Smith-Dorrien who commanded 2nd Army, which predated the war. He preferred Haig, in charge of 1st Army, who had been his chief of staff in South Africa, but he was also wary of the opinions and designs of Haig. Even before Christmas, Haig had made clear his belief in the tactics which he believed were needed to end the war, as well as his own criticisms of the approach taken by Smith-Dorrien with his army. On 15th December, he had criticised Smith-Dorrien – then commanding II Corps – for allowing a limited attack by 8 Brigade using only two battalions, which had been driven back. Haig wrote, "In my opinion there are only two ways of gaining ground either, (a) a general offensive all along the front, with careful preparation of artillery at special chosen points in order to dominate the Enemy's artillery at specially chosen points, [and] use of trench guns, mortars, hand grenades, etc. to occupy the Enemy's attention everywhere, and press home in force at certain points [where not expected]. The other method (b) is to sap up, as in siege warfare. This is a slow business especially in wet ground. It is sad to see the offensive movement by the British Army 280,000 strong resolve itself into the attack of two battalions!"[49]

---

[49] Haig, *War Diaries and Letters*, op cit., pp. 84-85.

Douglas Haig was being increasingly well regarded after I Corps had defended Ypres in its First Battle, and although his troops were now exhausted, the line still held. He was promoted to full general and recalled briefly to London where a plan was agreed to divide the B.E.F. into two armies. From December 26th, Haig would be General of 1st Army with six divisions – the original 1st to 6th Divisions; a second army under General Smith-Dorrien would consist of seven divisions – 7th, 8th, 27th-29th, and two Indian divisions being brought in from the subcontinent. Sir John French would continue as Commander-in-Chief.

William and John's battalion fell within Haig's 1st Army, as part of the 6th Division. The battalion was sent to the trenches in the Ypres Salient, and then a little further south to Frelinghien, just across the French border. The trenches were miserable: "Dec 10th-12th. Heavy rain. Many sections of trench flooded. Some of the flooded parts dammed & water localised. No chance of draining. Try digging new trenches, some in front, some behind, but water level seems to be everywhere about 18" below surface. Parapets falling in continually & most of our energy required repairing them, so men spend their time standing in 1 to 2 feet of water. Enemy busy bailing. Not much sniping by either side… 16th-18th. Water in trenches rising steadily. Men employed making dams and drains & digging out falls of parapet etc. casualties O.R. 2 wounded. 1 killed. Offs 1 wounded."[50]

On 23rd December, they went back into trenches that the war diary described as "wetter than ever". On Christmas Eve the German snipers were active, killing one man and wounding four more. But on Christmas Day things changed. John and William saw for themselves the famous 'Christmas Truce' of 1914. "No war today. Much conversation with Enemy between trenches. 107 Regt opposite us. Trenches strongly held. Their men of good military age for the most part though a few very young ones. Seemed happy & healthy & well-fed. Some, however, were despondent. Some said that they were just outside Paris having been brought up to the line in closed Railway carriages. They also believed that the Germans were occupying London. Casualties: O.R. missing 3."

A signaller in this battalion, Bob Brookes, kept an unofficial (and illegal) diary, recording how on December 24th, "Towards evening the Germ[an]s became very hilarious, singing and shouting out to us. They said in English that, if we did not fire they would not, and eventually it was arranged that shots should not be exchanged. With this they lit fires outside their trench, and sat round and commenced a concert, coincidentally singing some English songs to the accompaniment of a bugle band. A Germ[an] Officer carrying a lantern came slightly forward and asked to see one of our officers to arrange a truce for tomorrow (Xmas Day). An officer went out (after we had stood at our posts with rifles loaded in case of treachery) and arrangements were made that between 10.00a.m. and 12.00 noon, and from 2.00p.m. to 4.00p.m. tomorrow, intercourse between the Germs[an]s and ourselves should take place. It was a beautiful night and a sharp frost set in, and when we awoke in the morning the ground was covered with a white raiment. It was indeed an ideal Christmas, and the spirit of peace and Goodwill was very striking in comparison with the hatred and death-dealing of the past few months. One appreciated in a new light the meaning of Christianity, for it certainly was marvellous that such a change in the attitude of the opposing armies could be wrought by an event which happened nigh on 2000 years ago."[51] Of course, such relaxation was very unofficial

---

[50] War Diary 10th-12th and 16th-18th December 1914, 1/16th London Battalion (Queen's Westminster Rifles).

[51] *A Signaller's War: Notes Compiled from My Diary 1914-1918*, the personal diary of Bob Brookes, signaller in the Queen's Westminster Rifles, (16th London), pp. 30-31. www.bobbrookes.co.uk/diary_main.htm

and was disliked by the senior staff though at least Haig had sanctioned a more relaxed day (though not a truce) for the troops whilst he went off to Christmas lunch with Sir John French and Horace Smith-Dorrien.

Brookes continued, "During the night two men were reported to be missing and I had to go out early in the morning on my cycle to try to find them. I went to the dressing station in Chappelle d'Armentières a mile or so away, but they had not been there. Later in the day the Bosches told us that two men the night before had walked into their trench in a state which proved that they had 'drunk of the loving cup, not wisely but too well'. We asked that they should be returned to us, but they refused on account of the fact that these men had seen the position of their machine guns. They promised, however, to wire to their Headquarters, and see what could be done in the matter. Later we were informed that it had been decided to intern them in a civilian camp, and not treat them as prisoners of war, so as this seemed fair and the only course open, we left it at that. At 9.0am as I was off duty I received permission to go to Mass at a church which I had discovered whilst hunting for the missing men. This church was terribly shelled, and was within range of rifle fire, as was clearly proved by the condition of the wall facing the trenches; and no effort had been made to clear the wreckage as to attempt this would have been fraught with danger. A Priest, however, had come in from Armentières to minister to the few people who were still living in the district. In this church which would hold about 300, there were some 30 people, and I was the only soldier. It was indeed a unique service, and during a short address which the Priest gave I was about the only one who was not crying, and that because I did not understand much of what was being said. I returned to Headquarters and went on duty from noon to 2.0 pm, during which time I partook of my Christmas fare which consisted of 'Bully' [canned corned beef], 'Spuds', Xmas pudding, and vin rouge, which latter we found in one of the cellars of the farm. In the afternoon I went out and had a chat with 'our friends the enemy'. Many of the Germ[an]s had costumes on which had been taken from the houses nearby, and one facetious fellow had a Blouse, skirt, Top hat, and umbrella, which grotesque figure caused much merriment. Various souvenirs were exchanged which I managed to send home. We also had an opportunity of seeing the famous iron Cross which some of the men wore attached to a Black and White riband. These crosses are very well made and have an edging of silver. The man's name is engraved on one side, and the reason of the award briefly stated on the other. I have also a number of Germ[an] signatures and addresses on a fly leaf of my 'Active Service Pay Book', and it was arranged that at the end of the war we would write one to the other if we come through safely. The Germ[an]s wanted to continue a partial truce until the New Year, for as some of them said, they were heartily sick of the war, and did not want to fight; but as we were leaving the trenches early the next morning, and naturally did not want them to know, we insisted on the truce ending at Midnight, at which time our artillery sent over to them four shells of small calibre to let them know that the truce, at which the whole world would wonder, was ended, and in its place, Death and Bloodshed would once more reign supreme. At 4.30 am next morning we were relieved in the trenches and marched a distance of 3 or 4 miles to Houplines which proved to be our 'home' for the next five months."[52]

By the end of 1914, a considerable number of Old Bournemouthians had volunteered. A few had already been killed on the Western Front; some had gone to sea or embarked on other war

---

[52] *A Signaller's War: Notes Compiled from My Diary 1914-1918*, the personal diary of Bob Brookes, signaller in the Queen's Westminster Rifles, (16th London), a private account of Christmas 1914. www.bobbrookes.co.uk/diary_main.htm

adventures. Most were in training for the new forces which the crisis had called into being. In 1915, the involvement of members of the school in the fighting on the Western Front became much more marked. One who had volunteered was Percy Robertson, but his experience of the trenches was limited to the winter of 1914-1915. Percy suffered considerably with his health.

Percy, born 1893, was one of the earliest members of the school and in 1903 held the record for athletics, so in youth his health did not hold him back. After school he became an assayer. His younger brother Tudor – who probably did not attend Bournemouth School – had already volunteered for the 5th Hampshires from Chandler's Ford on 14th September, and was to be commissioned in 1915. Percy decided to apply for the Regular, rather than the Territorial or Service Army. He joined the King's Royal Rifles Battalion on 18th November 1914 as a rifleman and went to France on 21st December 1914 with the 3rd Battalion, 80th Brigade, the 27th Division. The division concentrated in France in the area between Aire and Arques. The numbers were boosted by bringing into the division battalions of Territorials.

Percy did not survive long on the mud of the trenches. These were conditions that were very testing on the physique, and he seems to have suffered very quickly. On 19th January 1915, he was sent to hospital as his digestion simply could not cope with the conditions and he was in real danger of dehydration. He remained in hospital until he was discharged on 5th February. Even then he was not fit enough to return to the trenches, so was sent to the depot base at Rouen where he stayed until he re-joined his battalion on 12th March 1915. On 16th May 1915, he was again in hospital, this time at Boulogne. He had been admitted suffering from shock. The school magazine the following July recorded, "We are glad that the following Old Boys are recovering satisfactorily: P R M Robertson (who was buried by the explosion of a shell)…"[53] A few days later, on 19th May, he was transferred to Rouen, and then on back to England on 2nd June.

John Aitken was one of those there to help men like Percy. Born in 1892, and at school about 1905, by 1911 he working as a dental mechanic. On 21st December 1914, John landed in France as an orderly with the British Red Cross Society, and remained on the Western Front until February 1915. What happened then, and afterwards, is not clear. He served in a V.A.D. – a Voluntary Aid Detachment which, by 1910 regulations included a pharmacist and other men. (Contrary to popular myth, V.A.D.s were both men and women, in separate sex detachments.) Conditions for enlistment were jointly agreed with the St. John Ambulance Brigade. Men aged between eighteen and thirty-six were only accepted if they could produce good reasons for non-enlistment in combat units. As the Army agreed that John should receive a service medal, he must have satisfied these requirements. However, one puzzle is that he is not listed amongst the Red Cross volunteers recognised by the Red Cross, and V.A.D.s only attended military hospitals as first aiders and nurses in England from early in 1915, and in France from May 1915, but male detachments were sent to France earlier to work as transport officers or hospital orderlies from October 1914. They transported sick and wounded soldiers, for example between ambulance trains and hospitals. All were trained in first aid and some V.A.D.s were trained in nursing, cookery, hygiene and sanitation. Some of these men worked as ambulance drivers, often coming under fire as they transported men away from the front. By the end of the war there had been about 90,000 Red Cross V.A.D.s, male and female.

---

[53] *The Bournemouthian*, July 1915.

3: The Western Front 1915

In January 1915 there was a general lull in the fighting although the Germans continued to make probing attacks south of Ypres to test the resolve of the British troops. John Ingram's battalion had returned to some extremely dangerous trenches on 1st January 1915. "Unfortunately our men had not got used to being so near as 40 to 50 yards to the Germans, and many a man during these days put his head to the loophole instead of using a periscope, which invariably meant death or at least a wound in the head, for the Germans could see and fire at us from holes in the walls of houses in Frelingheim, and we could not see them."[54]

The rain, too, continued to make life miserable: "Jan 8. Parapet falling in. River Lys rising rapidly necessitating evacuation of trenches near it S of river. Barricade just s of road collapsed & stream middle of right centre section rose rapidly necessitating evacuation listening post. Work day & night on repairs. Conditions very bad. Jan 9. Work Day & night on repairs to trenches. Parapets collapsing. River rising, necessitating more trench evacuation. Enemy opposite apparently relieved. Different class of sniping. Apparently m/gun, less accurate & aggressive. Less rain."[55]

On 11th January, a general and the brigade-major decided to inspect the troops in their forward trenches. It was not a good day to be in a shallow trench as German snipers were already very active. As the general reached John, a sniper took a shot at the general, missed, but hit John in the head. Despite the best efforts of the R.A.M.C., John died four days later at a casualty clearing station in Armentières, without regaining consciousness. He was buried two days later, on 17th January 1915. He lies now in the Cité Bonjean Military Cemetery, Armentières.

It is not clear from the records if William Hodges was there the day John was hit. At some point he had had to leave the trenches, suffering from rheumatism and frostbite.[56] As well as muddy cold water in their trench, he had to cope with snow, rain and frost that January. He would not have got much immediate help from the medical teams. "Many suffered from internal chills and exhaustion, but strange to say, there was not a single case of the ordinary domestic cold. Owing to a shortage of doctors at this time, medical officers were forbidden, by order, to come into the trenches... The sick had to struggle back at night, as best they could, to Houplines. The Battalion was beginning to get very weak in numbers, and only the severest cases were kept out of the line; the remainder were given a night's rest at the dressing station and had to return to the trenches before dawn."[57]

Sadly, John Ingram was not the only old boy to die of his wounds at this stage of the war. Frank Moorey was another volunteer member of the London Regiment, in his case the 13th Battalion – the London Kensingtons (or Princess Louise's Kensington Battalion). Like his older brother William (London 10th Battalion, Royal Fusiliers), he had volunteered for service.

Frank (Born 1894; at school 1908-1909) had left school and moved to London to work in the head office of an international bank. He had so much promise: as well as his academic and career achievements, he was well known as an excellent hockey player, and as being very good at rowing,

---

[54] *A Signaller's War: Notes Compiled from My Diary 1914-1918,* Bob Brookes, 9th January 1915.
[55] War Diary 8th-9th January 1915, 1/16th London Battalion (Queen's Westminster Rifles).
[56] *The Bournemouthian*, July 1915, reported his return to the trenches.
[57] *A Signaller's War: Notes Compiled from My Diary 1914-1918*, Bob Brookes.

Frank Leslie Moorey.

football and cricket. His whole life seemed full of opportunities for the future. He volunteered for service on 7th August.

Frank and the battalion had landed at Le Havre on 5th November 1914. Like the Westminsters, the Kensingtons were soon sent into action to fight, alongside John Turner and the Dorsets, at La Bassée in France. He was wounded – shot in the hand and in the arm – a week after John Turner had been killed, on 18th November, helping to repel a German attack. He was taken back behind the lines, and the wound was serious enough for him to require hospitalization within France. Nevertheless he recovered well, and was back in the trenches in time for Christmas 1914, and he was again in the fighting near La Bassée, not far from John Ingram.

In January 1915, within days of John's death, a German shell burst in the dugout where he was, hitting some and almost burying others. Frank was one of those who got out – but like others his mouth, nostrils and ears were filled with clay. This clay was infected, and Frank was already in a weakened state. He was quickly sent back behind the lines – at the time the frostbite he had in both feet might have been a more obvious danger than the virus – and was sent back to England for medical attention. The germs set up an abscess in his throat which deteriorated into septic pneumonia. These were the days before the discovery of antibiotics, and there was relatively little that could be done for him. He arrived in England on 26th January and was transferred to a military hospital in Cambridge. He died on 19th February 1915. *The Bournemouthian* described him as "one who was never known to fail at the call of duty."[58]

Looking back, the editor of the April 1915 *Bournemouthian* magazine commented on John and Frank's deaths, "The whole country is at one in the conviction that the loss of these and other of the best of the nation's manhood will secure a glorious victory for the cause of justice and uprightness, which they typify alike in their lives and in their death. Their sacrifice is not in vain."

1915 was a difficult year for the school, and a dreadful year for the British Army. On 24th January 1915, just after John had been killed and about the time William went ill, Edward Hall arrived in France. He probably joined the 1/16th London Battalion when William was off sick, on 1st February when the war diary reported a draft of three officers and 244 men joining them as they re-entered the same trenches north of Houplines, near German-held Frelinghien. The writer of the war diary commented on these new arrivals: "The men seem a good lot – keen & well set up."[59] (The war diary reported sixty men sick from the battalion in January.) Edward served with them until the autumn, so they would have been together once William returned.

Edward, born in 1889, joined the school in 1905 as a senior boy and by 1908 had become a prefect. After leaving school he trained at the Winchester Teacher Training College and became an elementary school teacher working for the London County Council. He had enlisted for four years

---

[58] *The Bournemouthian*, March 1915.
[59] War Diary 3rd February 1915, 1/16th London Battalion (Queen's Westminster Rifles).

in the 4th Hampshire Battalion in November 1908. He re-joined, volunteering in London, on 3rd September 1914. After a brief few weeks as a rifleman in the 2/16th (County of London) Battalion he was promoted lance corporal on 26th September 1914 and transferred in January 1915 to the 1/16th London Battalion, reverting to the rank of rifleman in the field in February.

The same conditions continued: much sniping by the Germans, and heavy rain making the river rise again and flooding trenches which had only just been painstakingly restored. The sniping intensified when Canadians of the 3rd (Toronto) Battalion joined them for trench experience and proved themselves keen snipers against the Germans, provoking augmented retaliation. These temporary associates impressed as 'hard and sturdy' but their Ross rifles did not. They were recognised to be more accurate for sniping, but frequently jammed so making them less serviceable for rapid fire. Soon these men were replaced with men from the 15th Canadian Battalion, also for trench experience, also well respected.

Edward seems to have spent most of February and March in these trenches without the rotation later normal to such tours of duty. At one point relief was promised, but then postponed, and a number of men from the 1/5th North Staffordshire Battalion came for instruction instead. The battalion seems to have managed with internal rotation of soldiers instead, keeping half the battalion at a time in the line. The unpleasant trench sniping war continued whilst mines were dug out below No Man's Land by specialists, to create listening posts. April saw the 1/7th Worcestershires attached for experience. Finally, on 1st May, the whole battalion were relieved from the trenches for a few days, though even then, in Houplines, they were still subjected to German 5.9 shelling.

The Battle of Neuve Chapelle

That spring, both sides attempted to break through. The British tried at Neuve Chapelle in March 1915 (and later the great Battle of Loos) and the Germans tried again to break through at Ypres. Further south the French launched their own attacks, for which they wanted British army support. Both sides were impatient to force a breakthrough and a quick victory.

These efforts were partly stimulated by internal conflicts within the command structures of both sides. These disagreements tended to be focussed on the events far away east, on the Eastern Front. Falkenhayn was fighting his rival Hindenburg for military leadership, and dared not risk his own position too much by complete opposition to Hindenburg who had saved Prussia from Russian attack in the summer and autumn of 1914. To placate Hindenburg, Falkenhayn sent a few divisions east which he could ill afford to lose from the Western Front.

For Sir John French the east also caused its own complications. The Russians were not finding it easy to hold their line, despite the confident predictions of pre-war pundits that the huge Russian Army would be unstoppable. The Tsar sacked his army commander Grand Duke Nicholas and made himself commander, joining his army at their Mogilev Headquarters and leaving his wife Alexandra to keep an eye on his central government in Petrograd. Sir John was under pressure from the British Government to reinforce the Russians, though the British Government was itself divided. The policy of reinforcing the Russians to win the war is often known as the 'Eastern Policy', and it was particularly championed in London by David Lloyd George, a fiery and determined Liberal minister in charge of the Navy. He had become increasingly critical of the lack of success by the B.E.F. He seemed to believe that the British should support the French (in whom he had greater confidence) to break the Germans in the west. Sir John French had repeatedly pointed out that the B.E.F. was trying to fight with insufficient artillery, which was itself supplied with so few shells that they had to be rationed even in times of battle, so Prime Minister Herbert Asquith gave Lloyd George a new portfolio in 1915 as Minister of Munitions to sort out the problem. The government also embraced a new initiative of diverting precious resources to the eastern campaigns, especially the Gallipoli campaign. This further limited Sir John French's room to manoeuvre and to attack. Sir John was also wary of Haig, as the latter blamed him for not concentrating more resources for the 'big push' on which he placed so much store. Bournemouth School members were amongst those who paid the price for these differences.

So Sir John French needed a victory to take pressure off the Russians, to improve his own standing with the government, and to support the French further south. His chosen target was the capture of the already ruined French town of Neuve Chapelle. This town, immediately north of La Bassée, lay roughly half-way between the Allied bastions of Béthune and Armentières. Its capture would allow the British to move up onto the Aubers Ridge (the French were to attack further south to try to capture the Vimy Ridge nearer to Arras, which would give the Allies a chance to dominate the German positions and to threaten them on the northern flank of the occupied French coalfields). It was believed that the glutinous mud of Flanders further north would make swift advance very difficult; further south the French around Rheims would launch a major attack in Champagne country; further south still the land was deemed too mountainous, or too forested, to make a renewed war of manoeuvre possible. Capture of the Aubers and Vimy Ridges could lead to the recapture of the key French coalfields and the eventual capture of key railway lines, which would hamper German movements on the Western Front and make it difficult for Falkenhayn to use the railways to move reinforcements from the west to help fight the Russians in the east.

Irishman Arthur Wolfe was in the Battle for Neuve Chapelle. He had attended the school until he left to take up a job with the Port of London Authority in about 1910. At the outbreak of the war he had volunteered and was placed in the 1/4th Seaforth Highlanders Battalion, a part of the Territorial Army and was with the battalion when it landed at Le Havre on 7th November 1914, within days of John Ingram and Edward Moorey. Later he had commented on his sadness at hearing of their deaths, especially that of Edward.

On 12th December, Arthur and the 1/4th Seaforth Highlanders Battalion were attached to the Dehra Dun Brigade of the 7th (Meerut) Division on the Western Front, one of the Indian units which had been brought in to reinforce the British on the Western Front. Although Arthur and his comrades were Territorials from the UK, the division was largely made up of Regular Army units from various places around the empire. The historian, Cyril Falls, once described it as "One of the greatest fighting formations Britain ever put into the field" and in its divisional history by C.T. Atkinson in 1926 the author commented, "Few Divisions can have equalled the strong Divisional spirit which inspired the Seventh Division, making it work as a team, working together towards the same end. It has been described as a very happy Division, and therein lies no small part of the explanation of the wonderful record which these pages have sought to outline."[60]

Arthur sent two letters to the Headmaster of Bournemouth School which were printed in the

---

[60] Quoted on the website, The Long, Long Trail – The British Army in the Great War of 1914-1918. www.longlongtrail.co.uk.

school magazine in March 1915.[61] In these letters he described the misery of the trenches in winter: "The trenches when we went in them were muddy but not at all bad, but during the time we occupied them we had rain, snow, hail, or sleet all the time, so that it was not very comfortable or pleasant. During the night a pretty heavy fire was maintained, but at day very little was necessary." He also described being in action four times, but had hated having to shelter in eighteen inches of mud for sixteen hours, whilst he and his friends "suffered intensely from the cold, and came out wet through and through." He described the hazards of movement to the trenches, and how some men had been machine gunned down near him. His main dislike seems to have been the conditions of his billet which was only a few hundred yards behind the front line: "Twice whilst there we made preparations to retire to bomb-proof dug-outs. German shells were flying all round us – the other buildings very close to us were hit, but fortunately we escaped." But despite the effort of marching back three miles and the monotony of look-out duty, he appreciated times when he could make himself feel much better – with a rub down, a good strong dose of rum, plenty of food and twelve hours sleep.

Soon after he wrote his letters, his battalion was chosen to take part in this battle. In planning it seemed the British had many advantages. Neuve Chapelle formed a German salient – a position in which the German lines jutted out between the British lines. The Germans at the start of 1915 only manned single lines of trenches, so they could be broken. (They were to copy the British multiple lines for defence after this battle, as each side tended to learn from each other.) The British planned to cram two sections of Haig's 1st Army (Rawlinson's IV Corps and an Indian Army corps under Sir James Willcocks) into a narrow front attack pincering in to capture Neuve Chapelle from the German VII Corps, and then to push on to capture the Aubers Ridge. In the air, the Royal Flying Corps (R.F.C.) had trained to try to direct artillery shell fire (by using a primitive method of transmitting short Morse code signals, and looking for coloured sheets of cloth spread out by the artillery which were meant to be interpreted by the pilots and observers). The R.F.C. had also taken aerial photographs for the British to study the distribution of the German defences. Despite a chronic shortage of shells, Haig had amassed more artillery than at any previous point so far in the war. Shells were to be fired sparingly in the weeks leading up to the battle so that there should be enough to fight the battle itself.

The battle began at 0730 on 10th March 1915. Three hundred and forty two artillery guns opened up to pound the German positions. It must have been a stirring sight for Arthur who was with the Indian corps attacking from the southern flank of the sector. What might not have been so obvious was that most British shells fired were shrapnel – that is, anti-personnel shells designed to explode in the air to kill an enemy out in the open, mainly because most high explosive shells made pre-war were designed for the Navy, which ended up not needing very many of them! Despite that limitation, most of the barbed wire in front of the Indian corps had been cut open, and the corps was able to attack with success, capturing the German trench line where they found the Germans dead, surrendering, or in retreat. The more northerly British IV Corps had greater difficulties however. At first, because so few casualties were straggling back, there was early excitement that this meant victory. But this turned to horror when they realised that the few returning casualties were because so many had been killed by German machine guns. Even so, IV Corps mostly captured their target trenches as well.

---

[61] *The Bournemouthian*, March 1915.

Arthur was now caught up in an unforeseen shambles caused by their relative success and the primitive state of battlefield communications. The British and Indian troops had occupied the German lines. In front of them was the ruined town, almost empty of defenders as the Germans had fallen back. What the British now wanted, and needed to do, was to advance through the ruined town, mop up any remaining defenders and break through the other side. Ideally this would open up the way for the cavalry to come into action to exploit this breakthrough. However, the artillery had been instructed to shell the ruins to drive out defending Germans. The artillery commanders had no efficient way to communicate with the forward troops, who were desperate to move forward, and so the British artillery shelled the ruins. British troops which were on the forward edge came under 'friendly fire' from their own artillery. Desperate messages were sent back to try to get the artillery commanders to lift their fire and to concentrate on firing further ahead. Such messages had to be sent by runners, at least to the nearest available telephone points since mobile radio was not available. Even when a runner from the 2nd Rifle Brigade did eventually get through with a message, instead of the artillery shifting their targets, the infantry was ordered to remain where they were.

This confusion and delay of over an hour and a half proved fatal. The Germans stopped retreating and instead regrouped beyond the British artillery fire but on the further, eastern edge of the town, ready to destroy a further British advance. The German contingency plan was to regroup with machine guns on the flanks of a potential advance – in effect creating a funnel effect into which advancing British infantry must pass. Even worse, because these were new positions, the British artillery commanders did not know where the Germans were and so were unable to shell them.

Arthur waited with his comrades, pinned down by their own artillery. Eventually, in the late afternoon, Rawlinson ordered the artillery to lift its fire and ordered that the infantry should now advance. By then the light was failing, but it was strong enough for the German machine gunners to wreak havoc on the British and Indian troops as they attempted to move forwards through and beyond the town. Some men of the Indian brigade in which Arthur served encountered a German patrol near the De Biez Wood on their eastern flank and learned that German reinforcements had now been rushed in to defend the Aubers Ridge.

The next day, 11th March 1915, the chaotic battle resumed. The commanders of IV Corps and the Indian division failed to cooperate, sending separate and uncoordinated orders to their units. There was fog, and the British troops fired much ammunition by guesswork into the fog, whilst the artillery similarly guessed at its targets and ended up firing so far ahead of their men that the artillery did very little good in its efforts to support them. All the soldiers could do was to try to advance in the teeth of machine guns and with little clear idea of where the enemy was, only that the British and Indian troops were being shot down by them. At some point Arthur was shot and killed.

Haig was dismissive of the confusion his plans had caused. In his diary, he wrote of the commander of the 8th Division on 11th March that "apparently he had got his brigades much mixed up... His right [wing] is not getting on as he would like." and on March 15th commented, "India Office wired for names of Indian units which had done well in the fighting about Neuve Chapelle... it should be stated that though Indians had done very well the task accomplished by them was not so difficult as that of the British."[62] In ignorance and arrogance, Haig condemned the commander of the 8th

---

[62] Haig's diary, op cit, pp. 109-110.

Division for not pushing on through on the first day, and stated that he was unfit for future command. Sir John French felt compelled to refuse Haig's request for more soldiers for another attempt to break through.

Arthur's body was never recovered, at least in any identifiable condition, so today he has no known grave. His name is recorded on the Le Touret Memorial, on the south side of the main road between Béthune and Armentières, amongst those of over 13,400 British soldiers killed in this sector of the Western Front from October 1914 to September 1915.

Why were so many men's bodies, like that of Arthur, unidentifiable for burial, and so had to be counted as among those "to whom the fortune of war denied the known and honoured burial given to their comrades in death"?[63] Until August 1916, when a man was buried, usually in haste at or near the place where he fell, a cardboard label with his name and details was left with the body while the remaining identification was removed to be used by the Army to inform higher authorities and his family. Later, graves were often disturbed by further fighting, or for re-burial in a more orderly fashion, and the cardboard labels would have rotted. From August 1916, a new system was introduced whereby each man wore two more durable identity discs, of which one would be removed on burial and one left with the body. Even so, before or after, depending on the nature of his death, there might still not be enough left to make an accurate identification. So the graveyards have huge numbers of 'unknown' graves.

The Royal Army Medical Corps and the Royal Army Veterinary Corps

Behind the scenes, and even at the front, were men who risked their lives trying to save the lives of men like these Old Bournemouthians. One of those was Richard Barfoot, who had arrived at the front in November 1914, and was there at Neuve Chapelle.

Richard Barfoot (born 1896, at school 1908-1910) left to take up an apprenticeship in house furnishing. The outbreak of the war found him a private in a Territorial ambulance unit – the 1st Wessex Field Ambulance – normally known as the 24th Field Ambulance in which he served throughout the war. This Field Ambulance served in the 8th Division, formed near Winchester in October 1914. He went, with the unit, to France aboard the SS *Cymric* from Southampton on 5th November 1914, landing at Le Havre the next day. On 16th November they were already in action collecting the sick and wounded from the 25th Brigade area, although soon they were operating in support of the 24th Brigade. On 20th November they found that five days of rain, followed by frost, had produced about thirty frostbite casualties. From December, they had established dressing stations near Neuve Chapelle. The experience of dealing with the casualties of a major battle showed up weaknesses in their organisation – especially as ambulance wagons had been held too far behind the attack lines, and insufficient men had been sent forward as stretcher-bearers. They had many wounded to deal with over the days of the battle, 10th to 13th March 1915.

Richard and his comrades were volunteers. Often, they went into the battle zones armed only with their stretchers and medical kits. Sometimes they went out forward of the front line into No Man's Land to bring in wounded – British or German. Sometimes they carried the wounded over considerable distances – sometimes even miles – using stretchers when they could, but otherwise carrying the men on their backs. Sometimes they were lucky, and no one fired at them; at other

---

[63] Inscription on the Thiepval Monument on the Somme battlefield.

times they risked sniper or shrapnel fire. They could not open fire, as they worked within the Geneva Conventions which only allowed them to fire in self-defence. Some of the men manned advanced dressing stations or the assessment centres further back but even there they were exposed to German shell fire.

When the accumulated casualties dealt with by the ambulance were totalled up on 16th March, they had treated 62 British officers and 1,436 men. In addition they had treated 47 Indian soldiers, as well as three German officers and 147 German soldiers.[64]

From early 1915, many boys who had moved abroad after leaving school, came back to play their part in the war effort. They came from all across the empire from Canada, Australia, New Zealand, South Africa, Ceylon (Sri Lanka), and even further afield. Many served with distinction, though frequently not on the Western Front but some, especially the Canadians, did serve on the Western Front.

Many boys who had settled in Canada between leaving school and the start of the war immediately volunteered to return to fight (Edward's brother Frank was one). Soon these Canadians were gaining an excellent reputation for their fighting qualities, being recognised for their bravery and their capable and aggressive fighting spirit, and were increasingly used as assault troops for that reason. In September 1915, a new Canadian corps was formed. Eventually, by 1917, it contained all four Canadian divisions, and their success (particularly in their first such action at Vimy Ridge, 9th to 12th April 1917) helped mould them into a distinct Canadian Army and to promote the cause of the truly independent Canada which emerged after the war. Initially, however, members of the Canadian Overseas Expeditionary Force did not necessarily remain in the battalions in which they were sent across to Europe, and so some of the Bournemouth boys found themselves switching to regiments which better reflected their old links (such as the Hampshire Regiment) rather than the new life which they had just begun.

One 'Canadian' working, like Edward, with the R.A.M.C. was Gordon Collingwood. He was born in 1892 and at Bournemouth School around 1905. After leaving the school, probably in early 1907, he attended Trent School in Derbyshire until 1908, after which he went to Canada where he was a student at McGill University and a member of the University O.T.C. He attested at Montreal on 18th March 1915, like his brother, naming their sister Dorothy as his next of kin rather than his elderly parents. He immediately left for France – his war service served as a private with the No.3 Canadian General (McGill) Hospital, created by Dr. Herbert Birkett, Dean of McGill's Faculty of Medicine, who received authorisation to create it on 15th March 1915. (Other universities in the empire later copied this example and organised their own hospitals.) Its personnel were recruited from McGill students and from its medical professors.

Gordon and his comrades left Montreal on 6th May 1915 aboard the *Metagama* and arrived at Plymouth on 15th May. They moved to France on 16th June and opened a hospital at Dannes-Camiers on 19th June, north of Le Touquet and south of Boulogne, on the French coast. On 19th August 1915, however, Gordon applied for a temporary commission in the Regular Army. There was some concern about his eyesight and his need for glasses, but the examining ophthalmist was clear that his sight was stable and should be no barrier to him serving in the Army Service Corps (A.S.C.), another branch of the Army which served and supported the fighting troops.

---

[64] Figures from the War Diary of the 24th Field Ambulance, March 16th 1915. The diary separated the number of Indian soldiers from the overall figure of the British treated.

Another Canadian Old Bournemouthian serving, at least for a time, with the R.A.M.C. was Dudley Sherwood. Dudley, born in 1896, attended several schools, being at Bournemouth School for just a few weeks in autumn 1909. In March 1913, he embarked on the SS *Corinthian* to St. Johns via Le Havre, listed as a labourer on the ship's manifest. He attested on 26th September 1914, at Valcartier, joining the No.1 Canadian Expeditionary Hospital, and crossed the Atlantic to England. Unfortunately, it is not clear with which unit he served on the Western Front, but he is extremely likely to have gone to the Western Front in 1915, and was probably at Ypres during the second battle.

During the war, the British Army made extensive use of animals and birds, and men were needed to keep them fit as well. Howard Wright was one who served in that way for most of the war. Howard was born in about 1894 in Bournemouth. (His older brother, Sydney, born in 1888, was also a member of the school, 1904-1905, and served – and was wounded – in Mesopotamia in 1918.) Howard was at the school from 1902-1907. By 1911 he was working as a grocer's assistant. He joined up early and was posted to the 48th Mobile Veterinary Section of the Royal Army Veterinary Corps.

The corps had the duty of caring for the range of animals and birds used by the Army, which in particular meant horses, mules and pigeons. Howard's particular unit, the 48th Mobile Veterinary Section, was attached to the 36th (Ulster) Division. This was a very special division, as it was made up entirely of men of the former Ulster Volunteer Force led by Sir Edward Carson, which had opposed Home Rule for Ireland and which had almost threatened civil war to defend the Protestant position. In the event, they raised thirteen battalions to form parts of the three Irish regiments then based in Ulster – the Royal Inniskilling Fusiliers, the Royal Irish Fusiliers and the Royal Irish Rifles. By July 1915 these battalions were completing their training, in Sussex, and when the division moved to France, Howard went with them, sailing on the SS *City of Chester* from Southampton and landing at Le Havre the next day, on 5th October 1915. By then, Howard was a corporal. Initially, the men of the division were sent to familiarise themselves with trench warfare, attached to units of the 4th Division which then was near Albert on the Somme. Howard's unit, however, went to Flesselles, on the northern edge of Amiens, and began work treating sick or injured horses almost immediately, on 8th October. After a few weeks, including a short spell at Ailly-sur-Somme, west of Amiens, the unit moved north to Doullens, roughly mid-way between Amiens and Arras, where they stayed for most of November until moving to L'Étoile and Bellancourt, on the Somme, north-west of Amiens.

As a mobile veterinary unit they moved round inspecting and caring for the animals (mostly horses) whilst the division they served was deployed in different parts of the battlefield. From February 1916, the division was deployed in various sections of what would soon become the Somme battlefield, and it was to take part in the great battle, attacking the notorious Schwaben Redoubt near Thiepval, an action subsequently commemorated by the construction of the famous Ulster Tower: over the course of 1st-2nd July they had suffered 5,104 casualties, of whom about 2,069 were fatalities. For the vets, however, the great battle made little difference; their tours of bases and making inspections continued behind the fighting lines. When particularly sick horses were discovered, they arranged either for them to be taken to veterinary hospitals, or – if they were 'unserviceable' – to be destroyed, often via a French butcher who would pay them for it.

On 18th April 1917, the unit war diary included a rare mention of an individual soldier: "Recommend Cpl. Wright for a commission."[65] Unfortunately, it does not seem that this recommendation of Howard from the commander of a unit removed from the fighting was accepted. Soon after this, the 36th Division distinguished itself in the Battle of the Messines Ridge (capturing Wytschaete) and later in the Third Battle of Ypres and afterwards in the Battle of Cambrai. The mobile vets were therefore operating on the edge of the Ypres Salient at Poperinghe, with an advanced aid post in Ypres itself – where in August some men fell casualty to the German guns.

At some point towards the end of the war, Howard was transferred, still a private soldier, to the 8th Yorks and Lancaster Battalion, a battalion with which Arthur Stagg and Thomas Searls had served, and been wounded. In November 1917, that battalion moved to Italy, where they remained fighting for the rest of the war. He survived to be demobilised on 15th April 1919.

The Second Battle of Ypres

The most northerly part of the British line was in Belgium, around the city of Ypres, in the salient which was held in conjunction with French and Belgian troops who held the line north to the coast. To the south of the salient was the Messines Ridge, and from there the ground undulates a little through Mesen itself and down again to the Ploegsteert Wood Sector, and then down into France near Armentières.

Falkenhayn recognised that the British Salient at Ypres was a potential weak spot in the Allied line. The Allied line jutted out precariously eastwards from Ypres, but the high ground in the east and immediately to the south had been in German hands since the First Battle of Ypres, the previous October. Falkenhayn intended to break the Allied line at the junction of British troops with French troops. He might even have been aware that, where the two forces adjoined a short way east of the village of Langemarck and at the most exposed part of the salient, the troops were French African colonial troops to the north and British Canadian colonial troops to the south. To break them he intended to use the secret weapon which the German scientists had been carefully preparing in the winter of 1914-1915: Chlorine gas.

In 1914, gas had been experimented with – not deadly, poison gas but rather lachrymatory gas – commonly known as 'tear gas'. Then the idea had been to render defending troops inefficient and distressed since they would not be able to clearly see their opponents, and in their confusion they would become much less effective in their defence. But now the idea was to deliver poison gas, and this was clearly going to take considerable preparation and skilful use. Both sides seem to have ignored the inconvenience that they had signed the Hague Conventions before the war which banned the use of asphyxiating gas.

Chlorine gas mixes with moisture (such as found in eyes or lungs) to form hydrochloric acid. It is lethal if mixed with one part gas to 5,000 parts air. Although chlorine gas was by no means as deadly as gases later used in the war, it was still a terrible weapon to use. Initially, part of its attraction to the Germans might have been the fact that it is exceptionally irritating. That irritation first affects the membranes of an unguarded nose, making the soldier produce much mucous, as well as making him become tearful and to produce a lot of saliva. As the gas was pulled to the lungs by breathing, it would provoke spasms. The body's own defences could mean that the soldier

---

[65] War Diary, 48th Mobile Veterinary Company, 18th April 1917.

would die from lack of oxygen reaching his lungs because of the frothy liquids or the spasms blocking the way. The recipient would almost immediately have a burning pain in his throat and in his eyes and a feeling he was being suffocated. He would experience a bad pain in the chest. As well as coughing and crying, he would probably also start to vomit and feel very weak. If then he fell to the ground he would find a heavier concentration of the gas and so reduce his chances of survival. If a man suffering from chlorine gas survived and was taken back to the casualty clearing station, he would probably have a fight to breathe with these symptoms for about thirty-six hours. Then, typically, he would sleep exhausted, and when he woke would briefly feel considerably better. But after a few hours he would develop bronchitis and sometimes pleurisy, a very high temperature and a shallow heartbeat. He would then either die from gangrene in the lungs or pleurisy or similar, or he would live but be weak and exhausted for a long time, able only to walk slowly, and getting easily out of breath. The wounded varied, but for some, these weaknesses, including panic attacks and headaches, might stay with them for the rest of their lives, whilst others could return more or less to full health.

Falkenhayn seems to have given very little thought that the Allies would soon develop protective respirators, or that they would soon develop their own versions with which to retaliate against the Germans themselves.

This gas was heavier than air, and seemed to onlookers to look like a yellow mist coming towards those unlucky enough to experience it. It could be produced quickly and relatively cheaply by the Germans (and later by the Allies), and could be compressed into cylinders to be transported to the front line, where the plan was to open valves to release it when the wind was in the right direction to blow it against the enemy. Actually, with the Allied line forming a salient, the wind would only ever be favourable from one direction, which the Germans initially thought to be when the wind blew from approximately north-east. The Canadians, including several from Bournemouth School, were to be on the receiving end.

The Governor-General of Canada had offered military help even before the outbreak of the war, and this offer had been accepted by Lord Kitchener on 7th August 1914. Immediately, a Canadian Expeditionary Force began to be assembled at Valcartier, and as swiftly loaded aboard ships for England, sailing on 3rd October. A number of Old Boys were members.

Frank and Reginald Wrenn were amongst the first members of the school to volunteer in Canada. Boscombe boys, the older, Frank, had been born in 1890. After school, Frank, like his father, had become a butcher. He left home to seek new experiences in Canada, but was quick to volunteer on 19th September 1914 at Valcartier in Canada, stating that he had military experience with the 6th Hampshire Battery, Royal Field Artillery. He was placed in 'A' Company of the 9th Canadian Battalion. His younger brother, Reginald, born in 1894, had sailed aboard the *Royal Edward* from Bristol to Halifax, Nova Scotia in 1911, with some other lads as a sixteen-year old to become a farm labourer. He volunteered at Valcartier on the same day as Frank. (Their brother Victor only left school in 1913 and does not seem to have gone to Canada like his brothers. He served as a lance corporal in the M.M.P. (Military Mounted Police Corps) and afterwards in the Hampshire Yeomanry before transferring to a part of the Territorial Force of the Royal Garrison Artillery (R.G.A.) He served for a time in Salonika and by 1918 was with the artillery in France.)

Another was Basil Keogh (born 1893; at school as a boarder 1907-1909). By origin an Irishman from Dublin with his nearest relatives in Dorset, Basil had settled in Canada as a farmer. At the age of 19 he attested at Valcartier three days later, on 22nd September 1914. He was able to state two lots of military experience – with the 5th Canadian Garrison Artillery and previously with the 4th Volunteer Battalion Hampshire. He joined the Canadian Expeditionary Force as a Canadian artilleryman, 2nd Field Battery, became a bombardier, and later a sergeant. His artillery unit was largely composed of men recruited in the Ottawa area. They left Quebec on 29th September 1914 aboard the *Saxonia* and arrived in Devonport on 17th October and moved to Aylesbury. This was a relatively small unit, even though its batteries formed a brigade of only six officers and 213 men originally. The brigade had four artillery batteries, each divided into three sections of two guns. In December 1914, the batteries were reduced to four guns each but returned to six guns each in March 1917. On 4th November 1914, they were reviewed by the King and Queen, and again by the King at Larkhill in February 1915. Four days later, on 8th February, they moved to Avonmouth and embarked for France. It was a stormy crossing to St. Nazaire; they only arrived on 11th February. The 2nd Battery then entrained for northern France, to Meteren near Haasbruck, just south of the Belgian border. Soon they were attached for training at Armentières to several R.F.A. units. They now formed the 1st Brigade, 1st Canadian Divisional Artillery.

At Valcartier, the next day, bank clerk Horace Tollemache (born in London, 1890, the grandson of an MP; at the school 1903-1907) also volunteered. He was the second of four brothers who were all to volunteer to serve on the Western Front before the end. Their widowed mother, the Honourable Mrs Murray Tollemache but more familiarly known as Mardie Tollemache, had remained in Bournemouth. A short, stocky young man, he was nearly 24 in 1914. He and his brother Philip were working as bank clerks in Canada when the war broke out. Despite volunteering in Canada, and being placed in 4th battalion to 12th for the Canadian Overseas Expeditionary Force, he transferred to the British Army – by 1915 he was fighting in the Hampshire Regiment.[66] He was to have a distinguished war record.

Montague Strudwicke from Poole also heard the news that the empire was appealing for volunteers. Born in 1894, he had left the school in 1908 and pursued a career as a draughtsman, working for the Canadian Pacific Railway, for a time from the town of Brooks, Alberta. He crossed and re-crossed the Atlantic in 1913 and 1914 and was in Canada when the war broke out. Montague also went to the recruitment centre and training camp at Valcartier near Quebec, and volunteered on September 25th 1914, also claiming some military experience – not only three years with the Territorials of the 7th Hampshire Battalion, but also two years in the O.T.C. at Bournemouth School! These factors, together with his good health and sturdy physique were sufficient, and he was certified fit for overseas service and assigned to the 13th Canadian Infantry Battalion, the Royal Highlanders, part of the 3rd Canadian Brigade of the 1st Canadian Division.

Philip Tollemache (born 1893 and at school 1904-1910) volunteered on the same day as Montague and two days after his brother Horace. He was initially placed in a Reserve battalion, the 32nd, but was later placed in the 8th Canadian Infantry Battalion, probably after the 32nd Battalion had reached Shorncliffe (where it was treated as a Reserve to supply other battalions sent to fight in Belgium).

The next day Montague's class mate Alexander Sandbrook volunteered there. Alexander had been born in Weymouth in 1894. He was certainly at the school in 1905 when he did well as an under-

---

[66] *The Bournemouthian*, December 1914, recorded him as a member of the Canadian contingent, and his attestation papers have survived.

12 in athletics. He and his father had emigrated to Canada before the outbreak of the war, and for a time he worked there as an electrician. On 26th September 1914, he volunteered and was placed in H Company, the 8th Canadian Infantry Battalion, a battalion also known as the 90th Winnipeg Rifles because all the men from that core unit had volunteered in August and formed the basis of the new, expanded, battalion. This was the unit Philip had eventually joined.

The same day, 26th September, Dudley Sherwood of the R.A.M.C. and William Harrison volunteered there. Perhaps they recognised each other as fellow Old Bournemouthians, though of different years, but we do not know. Bournemouth boy William had already served four and a half years in the Hampshire Carabineers, a volunteer cavalry regiment. After leaving school in 1908 he had continued to live in Southbourne and worked as a grocer's assistant. Like the others, he came over to Europe with the first detachment of Canadians, and in his case specialised as a signaller. It shows the speed of communications even in 1914 that on 2nd October *The Bournemouth Graphic* newspaper printed a photo of him and said he "is now on the way to the front with the 100th Grenadier Guards, of the Canadian contingent."[67] He was actually in the 11th Battalion of the Canadian Contingent, in which he became a corporal. According to an article in the *Bournemouth Visitors' Directory* he got into the "thick of the fighting on the Continent, has had many narrow escapes, and has once been wounded."[68] One thing that made William's story a bit unusual was that his father, also called William, who had been "associated with a boarding house on the West Cliff" according to the same article, had lied about his age in order to be accepted into the Army. The article went on to state that in 1916 he was "fifty years of age, according to his birth certificate, but has an 'official age' five or six years less. He believes he is the oldest Bournemouth resident who has entered the Army since the war, and has now seen upwards of eighteen months' service in the Army Ordnance Corps."

William Harrison

William Harrison and his father

From Valcartier the battalions moved to Quebec. The 13th Battalion embarked on 29th September, and the 8th Battalion embarked two days later on 1st October aboard the SS *Franconia*, reaching Plymouth on 14th October. According to the regimental list of the men of this battalion, which was printed in 1915, most of these "Canadian" soldiers were born in England. Alexander found himself a member of the 1st Canadian Division, the 2nd Canadian Infantry Brigade. Montague's battalion was in the

---

[67] *The Bournemouth Graphic*, 2nd October 1914.
[68] *The Bournemouth Visitors' Directory*, 1st July 1916.

same division, but its 3rd Brigade. The younger William Harrison's unit, the 11th Canadian Battalion, was part of the 4th Canadian Infantry Brigade and sailed from Canada on 3rd October in a fleet of thirty-three liners guarded by the Royal Navy, and arrived in Plymouth Sound on 14th October 1914 where the locals gave them a hearty welcome. The battalions spent the winter of 1914-1915 in intensive training in the south of England. After four months in sodden tents on Salisbury Plain, the 11th Canadian Battalion were inspected by the King and Queen, and then the next day began the movement to later embarkation.

Alexander's 8th Battalion left for France a day before Montague's 13th Battalion, sailing from Bristol on 10th February aboard the SS *Archimedes*, arriving at St. Nazaire after a blustery voyage. By 23rd February they were in the trenches under instruction. Montague's 13th Canadian Infantry Battalion embarked on the SS *Novion* at Avonmouth on 11th February, sailed on 12th, and endured the same gale in the channel, arriving in France at St. Nazaire in France on 14th February 1915. Then, for Montague, it was a two day train journey, and several days marching to Armentières where they were attached to the British 16th Brigade for training purposes. "The system of instruction was to attach a section of the Canadians to a platoon of the English and for everyone then simply to carry on. In this way the newcomers learned trench routine. Almost before they were aware of it, they knew about the posting of sentries, the screening of fires, the establishment of listening posts, the issuing of rum and so forth. In addition they acquired much information about ration parties, wire cutters, loopholes, ammunition, engineering material, bombs, bayonets, trench sanitation and all the scores of things that are of vital import when men gather in opposing ditches to do one another to death."[69]

In the event, William Harrison's 11th Battalion was one of five which remained behind (6th, 9th, 11th, 12th and 17th) to form the base brigade for a Canadian training division. The battalion into which William was transferred is currently unclear, but he fought his way through to the victory of 1918.

Reginald and Frank Wrenn had left Canada with the 1st Canadian Division as part of 'A' Company, 9th Battalion, 101st Infantry. The battalion were disappointed to learn that it was designated the Reserve battalion for the 1st Canadian Division. Almost immediately about five hundred men were drafted into other Canadian battalions. Frank and Reginald were moved into fighting battalions within the Canadian 1st Division, though it is not clear into which battalions.

One Canadian Old Bournemouthian whose distinguished career does not fit neatly into an account of the fighting was Owen Lobley, one of the original Bournemouth School boys. Born in Bournemouth in December 1887, and at the school from 1901 to 1904, he had emigrated to Canada in 1906. Working for the Imperial Bank of Canada in 1914 he was Assistant Accountant in the Winnipeg Branch, and for four years in the 18th Canadian Mounted Rifles of the militia. In August 1914, he volunteered for the Fort Garry Horse, and was given the rank of lieutenant. On 22nd September, at Valcartier Camp, he transferred to the Canadian Army Pay Corps (1st Division) with the promoted rank of captain. He came across to the United Kingdom with the Expeditionary Force.

O. R. LOBLEY
Lieutenant-Colonel. Officer of the Order of the British Empire (Military Division) Mentioned in Despatches.

---

[69] *The 13th Battalion Royal Highlanders of Canada*, R. C. Fetherstonhaugh, 1925, p. 35.

On 6th April 1915, he wrote to the bank in Canada about the experience of the Canadians now in France: "Rumours that have reached you are founded on fact, and the Canadian Division is now in France and has been in the firing line. Needless to say they have acquitted themselves in every respect in a manner worthy of Canada. I have come in contact to a certain extent with some of the Territorial Forces which have come over from England, and while I do not for one minute wish to imply that they are anything but the good old English fighting men, they cannot, in my humble opinion, compare with the Canadians as regards discipline, efficiency or physique. This, of course, is perhaps easily understood when we consider that the Canadians come from probably one of the most healthy countries in the world, totally devoid of crowded cities, unhealthy conditions and all those things which tend toward a deterioration of physique and fighting qualifications. I think we should feel ourselves deeply honoured when we realize that we are the first irregular division to be entrusted with a portion of the line, and when one considers just what this means and the awful possibilities that would ensue were we to be found wanting, it is indeed gratifying to realize what confidence has been placed in us. There is of course one supremely single idea in the minds of everyone here as regards the final outcome of the war, but I am inclined to think that the Johnnies on the spot believe it will take a great deal longer to finish than was originally anticipated."[70]

He was right. Within days the Canadians were proving their mettle in the successful defence against the gas attack of the Second Battle of Ypres. On 14th June 1916, Owen was promoted major, and on 9th May 1918 lieutenant-colonel. This made him the highest promoted member of the school during the years of the conflict. He served as acting field cashier with the 1st Canadian Division in France, later as officer in charge of pay and allowances, and finally as assistant deputy paymaster general when he was promoted to lieutenant-colonel. On 1st January 1918, he was appointed an Officer of the Order of the British Empire (O.B.E.) for "Good Service, Initiative and Devotion to Duty". He had also earlier been mentioned in dispatches for service in the field, which is quite an achievement given his role was crucial but not particularly martial. So as well as being the highest-ranking Old Bournemouthian at the time, he was also one of the most decorated. After the war he returned to Canada and lived in Montreal.

In March, the Canadian battalions had spent a few spells in their own right in the trenches, and suffered their first trickle of casualties (some Canadians fought at Neuve Chapelle, but there is no evidence that Canadian school members were there), but in April they were brought up to the Ypres Salient to join Smith-Dorrien's 2nd Army. The Canadians were deployed by Sir John French to support the British and French forces trying to cover and secure Ypres. This was where Alexander, Montague, and Philip, with their fellow Canadians, were to receive their real baptism of fire.

Smith-Dorrien had promised them a 'lively time' at their welcoming parade, but neither he nor any of them had any idea of what was about to follow: "On the night of Wednesday, April 21st, the 13th Battalion moved up into the line and took over a series of breastwork trenches from the 14th Battalion, Royal Montreal Regiment, the men little dreaming as they accomplished the relief that they were about to write a glorious page in Canadian history. Apart from an unusually severe shelling of Ypres during the afternoon, nothing had indicated that behind the German lines a blow was being prepared such as had never fallen in civilized warfare, and one which its originators

---

[70] Letter from Owen Lobley, quoted in *Letters from the Front* (being a record of the part played by officers of the bank in the Great War) Volume 1, pp. 6-7, edited by C.L. Foster and W.S. Duthie, published for the Canadian Bank of Commerce, 1921 by the Southam Press Ltd of Toronto and Montreal.

hoped would carry them victoriously to Calais and the English Channel."[71] Their battalion war diary simply noted, "Trenches in poor shape. Many unburied dead between the lines. Weather all that could be desired."[72]

The next day, April 22nd, the battle began. After a quiet day, the Germans released poisonous chlorine gas from banks of cylinders against French colonial troops at Langemarck, north-east of Ypres, and some of the gas hit Montague and the 13th Battalion holding the Canadian left flank at St. Julian. The German front line was only 50 to 75 yards away. The gas attack was preceded by an intense bombardment which particularly hit the reserve and support lines, forcing the men to pull back whilst assuring the front trench that they would come forward again if needed. Once released from the cylinders, the gas mix gradually diminished as the gas was buffeted and dispersed by the air, which explains why so many (comparatively) survived the initial attack.

Surprised and terrified, many French troops panicked and retreated, leaving a four mile gap on the Canadian flank. The Canadians held firm and even extended their line by putting men into the French trenches to support the remaining Algerians. "About 5pm... enemy commenced a terrific bombardment and also sent over a great cloud of gas on the frontage held by the Turcos on our immediate left. The Turcos had to retire and this left our left flank open to the enemy. No.5 Company were called up from Reserve, and one Company of the Buffs also reinforced us. Major Buchanan assumed charge of the front line."[73] In desperate fighting the front line Canadians were mostly killed or captured. The remaining 13th Canadians restructured their defences about 300 yards behind the original front line, and were rapidly reinforced by the 2nd East Kent Battalion ('the Buffs'). They counter-attacked and temporarily retook their original front line trench. The Germans tried to trick them by dressing men in French uniforms and shouting "We are French" but the Canadians were not fooled and repelled them. After a further day being shelled and again gassed, the 13th Battalion were ordered to evacuate these trenches, which they managed to do without further loss of men.

Alexander and the 8th Canadian Infantry Battalion suffered "Intermittent bombardment by enemy... 3 officers wounded, 3 men killed and 33 wounded. 4p.m. men seen leaving their trenches... [about four thousand yards to their left]... Report reached Headquarters that French on left of 3rd Can Brigade [Montague's unit] had retreated from their trenches overcome by gas." At 4a.m. on 24th April they saw "the same bluish cloud that had been observed on the 22nd coming from the German trenches over the trenches... The CO sent immediately SOS signals by telephone to the batteries. The report came from one battalion trench to the effect that the Germans were assembling in trenches which were in front of their main trench. A heavy shell and mortar fire was directed onto our trenches for 15 minutes & directly it ceased the Germans advanced but were easily driven back by the artillery fire... and by the rifle fire of such of our men as could still handle their rifles – after the Germans had retired most of our men collapsed from the effects of the gas."[74] They had in fact been in danger of being surrounded, but had held out whilst the supporting battalions prepared defence lines behind them. "Frequent frontal attacks were made... through a high mustard crop which covered an advance and the fold of the ground enabled the enemy to assemble unseen

---

[71] *The 13th Battalion Royal Highlanders of Canada*, R.C. Fetherstonhaugh, 1925, p. 42.
[72] War Diary, 13th Canadian Infantry Battalion, 21st April 1915.
[73] War Diary, 13th Canadian Infantry Battalion, 22nd April 1915.
[74] War Diary, 8th Canadian Infantry Battalion (90th Winnipeg Rifles), 22nd-24th April 1915.

outside their trenches. There were four distinct attacks during daylight & one at night… a part of the attackers reached the wire… When the trenches to our left were vacated a difficult situation arose. Locality C was the only defended part on the ridge to our left – it was 1300* [yards] from the left of the trenches and 500* from Headquarters – a good deal of the ground between these points was dead and covered with growing crops. Between 4 & 5a.m. the Germans occupied the trenches to our left & began working round the left rear of our trenches & into the ground between the trenches & Locality C. Colonel Trafford 5th Batt. very loyally sent every man he could spare. Two of his platoons were sent to the trench North of Headquarters & 20 men into the growing crops, on the slope of the hill down to the… trenches. Locality C was held by a company of the 7th Battalion. No other reserves were available. A vigorous advance by the Germans could not fail to turn our line & after that the lines to the right which were equally denuded of reserves. The trench commanders reported their position critical as so many of their men were down with 'gas' & the Germans were working around their rear. Every man was sent down to reinforce them & they were told they must hold on at all costs… about 3.40p.m. information was received that two regiments were coming up to support us so Major Kirkalay the Adjutant was sent to guide them but unfortunately he was shot through the chest. At dark no reinforcements seemed to be coming and the Germans were working more and more round our flank. Locality C must have been captured during the night as we could get no word from it… The trenches were all attacked at night & all the men in the trenches except the reserves were weak from fumes – in fact some men had already died from fumes." A battalion got through to relieve them and despite the growing light "the CO thought that the men who had had one dose of the gas could not possibly stand another so agreed to try and have the relief carried out before dawn."[75]

Montague and Alexander survived this first use of poison gas in warfare. The school magazine for July 1915 reported that Montague was still suffering from the effects of receiving this poison gas. Reginald Wrenn was also there when the Canadians withstood the first use of poison gas and was amongst those fighting through the night to close the gap the German advance had caused, including the counter-attack that night to try to drive the Germans out of Kitchener's Wood near St. Julien and the two failed attacks the next morning. He had also fought through the next stage of that battle when, on April 24th, the Germans attacked again with another explosive barrage. The Germans again sent in a chlorine gas attack, shrapnel and machine-gun fire, focussed on the Canadian line. Desperately they soaked handkerchiefs to hold in front of their faces to limit the impact of the gas, and managed to hold the line – even when their Ross rifles jammed.

Whilst the 8th Battalion suffered, the men like Montague of the 13th Canadian Battalion were also still under pressure: "Heavily shelled and bombarded. Machine guns very busy. Held the line until 7.50a.m. when the battalion was forced to retire to Reserve Trenches. Held the Reserve Trenches until 2p.m. when we were shelled out and retired to GHQ Trenches. 25th Sunday. Held trenches all day and then marched to Brayling arriving there at 4.00a.m. 26th. Holding old French Reserve Trenches."[76] After several days of fighting, and a retirement at great cost, the Canadians – assisted by several British battalions – covered part of the gap until the French line stabilised. The German advance was slow and too cautious, through anxiety about the effects of their own gas and concern at their lack of potential reinforcements.

---

[75] War Diary, 8th Canadian Infantry Battalion (90th Winnipeg Rifles), 24th April 1915.
[76] War Diary, 13th Canadian Infantry Battalion, 24th-26th April 1915.

Meanwhile, Basil Keogh and the 2nd Canadian Field Battery saw the results of this gas attack for themselves. They had been frustrated since 17th March when they had been ordered to conserve ammunition; only three rounds were to be fired by each gun during a day, except in real emergency. "This due to large shipment of ammunition to Dardanelles and Labour troubles."[77] On 6th April they had moved just inside Ypres Salient, and on 18th April to Poperinghe, then forward to the north of Ypres. The second in command of the brigade was actually a doctor, Major John McCrae. It is still possible to visit the site by the canal, now known as 'Essex Farm' where he worked for the brigade. He described the scenes he, and men like Basil Keogh, witnessed: "As we sat on the road, we began to see the French stragglers: men without arms, wounded men, teams, wagons, civilians, refugees – some by the roads, some across the country, all talking, shouting – the very picture of a debacle. I must say they were the 'tag enders' of a fighting line rather than the line itself. And they streamed on and shouted us scraps of not too inspiring information – while we stood and took our medicine, and picked out gun positions in the fields in case we had to go right in there and then. The men were splendid: not a word: not a shake. And it was a terrific test. Traffic whizzed by: ambulances, transport, ammunition, supplies, despatch riders – and the shells thundered into the town or burst high in the air nearer us, and the refugees streamed. Women, old men, little children, hopeless, tearful, quiet or excited, tired, dodging the traffic – and the wounded in singles or in groups: here and there I could give a momentary help, and the ambulances picked them up as they could. So the cold, moonlight night wore on – no change save that the towers of Ypres showed up against the glare of the city burning – and the shells still sailed in."

On 23rd April: "Yser Canal. At 3.30a.m. went into action point on Yser Canal 2 miles N of Ypres to support counter attack made by Canadians to recover ground lost by French. Troops lost heavily but recovered a good portion of the lost ground."[78] In this fighting the batteries also took casualties – a situation not helped by German air domination. Soon afterwards, it is believed on 2nd May, Macrae wrote his famous poem, *In Flanders Fields*, whilst at this position on the canal bank.

By 5th May, the batteries were experiencing mixed fortunes – Allied aeroplanes were patrolling, which reduced the danger from above but the batteries were now under fire from the north, south, and the north-east. Their ammunition allowance had increased – but the brigade war diary noted that some of it was dated '1905'. Firing was so intense that gun oil was boiling under pressure and breaking springs, putting many of the guns out of action. "Fighting continued all along the line from Steenstraate to Hill 60. 5 attacks made on front 12th Inf. Bde. All repulsed. Nearly all telephone wires cut. At 8p.m. guns were taken out and column moved south reaching Steenwerck at 4a.m. 10th inst. Men and horses very much exhausted."[79]

Clermont Grantham-Hill also saw the effects of this first use of poison gas. For Clermont and the 3rd Hussars, the rotation of half the regiment in and out of the trenches as dismounted cavalry had continued into 1915. As Clermont was a subaltern in 'B' Squadron, he sometimes went with his squadron into the trenches around Ypres, and sometimes his squadron was held back to attend to the horses. Clermont and 'B' Squadron were in the trenches during the Second Battle of Ypres when the Germans launched their later poison gas attacks. They moved forward as dismounted cavalry to assist the French Zoaves for a few hours, when the latter made an attempt to regain

---

[77] War Diary, 1st Canadian Field Artillery Brigade, 17th March 1915.
[78] War Diary, 1st Canadian Field Artillery Brigade, 23rd April 1915.
[79] War Diary, 1st Canadian Field Artillery Brigade, 5th May 1915.

some of the territory they had recently lost. In the early evening of 27th April, things became intense. At the time they were based at Vlamertinge: "At 5p.m. Vlamertinge was heavily shelled. The billets of the three squadrons of the Regiment being in the centre of the shelling they were ordered to move out of the village onto the Poperinghe road. On the way out an officer and two men, and a French interpreter attached to the Regt were wounded. The hospital in the church full of wounded was hastily evacuated. The Regiment halted just outside the village until orders were received to re-join the led horses. On the way out a shell over the Regt stampeded the led horses of the Scots Greys."[80]

They were soon sent forward again into the trenches north-east of Ypres, supporting the infantry who occupied the front lines. "At 5p.m. a wall of green yellow cloud was seen to apparently rise from the ground to the north, and at the same time the enemy commenced an extremely heavy bombardment of the Ypres Salient, especially its northern sector. Very shortly after large numbers of dazed & wounded infantry men suffering horribly from the effects of asphyxiating gas came streaming past the Regiment's trenches. The shelling now was very heavy and can only be described as a continual crash. The gas-dazed infantry were stopped, mainly through the exertions and gallant example of Regimental Sergeant-Major H. Smith, 3rd Hussars, and placed in dug outs behind the Regiment's trenches. Meanwhile the wall of gas though considerably thinned came down on to the Carabiniers, who suffered no serious effects from it, and a very slight and thinned remaining portion of it passed the 3rd with no more evil result than a horrible smell. To this must be added the gas filled German shells which bursting over the regiment emitted an equally horrible smell, and also severely affected the eyes. About 6p.m. a verbal message reported that the front line was broken, and... an unofficial report stated that the gas wall lifted over the front line and came down on the supports, while another Intelligence Summary states that 'The attack on 2nd May was repulsed principally by the supports, who waited until the walls of gas had come up to the support trenches & and then charged through the gas to the front trenches, which they reached before the German assault.' The following published account of a German prisoner is of interest: he stated that the 'smoke-gas detachment' arrived in their front trench, which was evacuated by the troops holding it, who retired to the second line. The detachment wore rubber coats, goggles, & a special head gear & were kept apart from the men in the trenches. They carried cast-iron cylinders on their backs, 1ft 8in to 2ft long with flat bottoms & conical taps. About 45 minutes after their arrival a continuous yellow 'smoke-wall' rose along a length of some 600 yards just in front of the trench, and was blown towards the British trenches."

The original anti-gas measures issued to the Hussars were a failure: "The 3rd Hussars had been issued with respirators during the morning, which have since been re-called as they were made of cotton wool, which it is found impossible to breathe through after becoming well damped. New respirators since issued are made of cotton waste."[81]

Afterwards, Clermont worked in one of three main ways: sometimes with the dismounted squadrons in the trenches; sometimes with the horses at the rear; and sometimes resting and training when the whole unit was given a break – though then the men were frequently set to dig trenches and create redoubts – especially between Ypres and Kemmel, in case of future German breakthrough.

---

[80] War Diary, 3rd Hussars, 27th April 1915.
[81] War Diary, 3rd Hussars, 2nd May 1915.

These Old Boys lost many friends in those days – Canadian casualties have been reckoned at 30%, with more than 2,000 killed. Dudley Sherwood and the 3rd Canadian Field Ambulance saw the horrible impact of these attacks. "Hearing a rush of footsteps outside, we looked out the window, and saw disorderly bodies of Algerian Troops hurrying past, devoid of rifles and without equipment, they were followed by guns – some drawn by only one team of horses – mixed with them were horses without guns, then came engineers' pontoons, and crowds of Refugees each carrying their household goods on their backs, young and old equally burdened. There was a tenseness that held us spellbound until the seriousness of the position suddenly dawned on us, for we were situated within a salient, completely surrounded by the enemy, except for this narrow neck, and if it should have given way, then indeed grave danger, as far as two British and our own Canadian Division were concerned, was not far away... A French officer... reported that great clouds of dense smoke suddenly arose in front of the enemy's trenches which the gentle breeze rolled over and into our trenches, asphyxiating everyone they came in contact with and the line broke in disorder. Trench after trench was evacuated, without a shot being fired. Then the milder gas cases began to stagger in, and soon we had about two hundred patients in our Hospital who brought with them an indescribably acrid odour that clung to their clothes and filled the air with fumes which caused intense smarting of the eyes, running of the nose, dry throat and irritative cough to everyone who came in contact with them. The patients themselves were more or less in a state of stupor, with staggering gait and great exhaustion. Their eyes and nose running and intense irritative cough. Some with marked dyspnoea. Many vomited without warning and soon the wards were indescribable. All had tachycardia, and the severer cases a ghastly ashy colour of the skin. One died shortly after admission. Then the wounded began to pour in. British, French, Algerian, Indian and Canadian – one never-ending stream which lasted day and night for seven days without cessation, in all some five thousand two hundred cases passing through our hands. Wounds here, wounds there, wounds everywhere. Legs, feet, hands missing, bleeding stumps controlled by rough field tourniquets; large portions of abdominal walls shot away; faces horribly mutilated; bones shattered to pieces; holes that you could put your clenched fist into, filled with dirt, mud, bits of equipment and clothing until it all became like a hideous nightmare – as if we were living in the seventh hell of the damned, and the thousand guns seemed to be laughing in fiendish glee at their work as they spurted forth their messengers of hate and destruction."[82]

It was quickly recognised that ammonia neutralised chlorine. After the first attacks, British troops were supplied with masks of cotton pads which could be soaked in urine to acquire the necessary ammonia. Some men soon experimented with using similarly soaked handkerchiefs, socks, or flannel body belts which could also be soaked in a more acceptable solution of bicarbonate of soda and were effective as long as these too were tied to cover their mouths and noses until the gas cloud had passed over them. Very quickly the Army scientists developed increasingly efficient gas masks from the unpleasant and unwieldy "bug-eyed monster with the nipple" to the much more satisfactory box respirators. However, these anti-gas masks always made it harder for the men to fight, to give instructions or pass on information. Scientists on both sides set about improving their defences and at the same time finding new ways of using gas to damage or wipe out their opponents.

When General Smith-Dorien recommended a partial withdrawal after this first gas attack, Sir John French sacked him, and II Army command was transferred to General Sir Hubert Plumer.

---

[82] Extracted from a report in the War Diary, 3rd Canadian Field Ambulance, April 1915.

Despite a series of British counter-attacks up to 25th May, the Germans managed to drive in the British and French lines, making the salient narrower and even more dangerous. Complicating the British position was the fact that after the battle the Germans held most of the limited high ground – the Passchendaele and Messines Ridges – from which their guns could bombard all the British defensive positions. At some point – probably in the summer of 1915 – Montague left the Canadian Corps and joined the Dorsetshire Regiment, rising to the rank of lieutenant. Then, on 6th September 1918, he switched to the Indian Army. After the war, having reached the rank of captain in the Indian Army, he was gazetted to be captain in the Dorsetshire Regiment in 1923.

Hill 60

To the south of Ypres stands a man-made hill, formed mostly from the soil excavated when a railway cutting was dug to carry the line which runs south from Ypres across the ridge. The hill created from these railway spoils was a pleasant place to walk before 1914, because it afforded fine views over the city from its south. War brought it an awful, new significance. This hill was designated by the British war maps as Hill 60. Of all the places in the Ypres Salient, probably even allowing for the Passchendaele Ridge in 1917, Hill 60 was the most deadly. Hill 60 and its neighbour across the railway line, the 'Caterpillar', overlooked the British lines south of Ypres. The Germans had gained control of these positions in December 1914. Attempts to undermine them were begun immediately by the French, and continued by the British from February 1915.

Eric Head was there, in one of the most famous actions of the war. Born in June 1897, Eric was only briefly a member of the school, from February 1912 to November 1913, when he left to train in the Eastern Telegraph Company. This was a company which laid cables to connect the British Empire (and in which a number of Old Bournemouthians served during the war), and serving members were given a lapel badge to wear to indicate their war work. But Eric had left it to volunteer for the Army. He sailed to Le Havre with the 1/9th London Battalion on 4th November 1914, a battalion more commonly known as 'Queen Victoria's Rifles'. On 27th November, the battalion joined the 13th Brigade in the 5th Division in which it remained until February 1916. During his time within the 13th Brigade, Eric's battalion fought at this notorious Hill 60, in the Second Battle of Ypres and also at St. Julien near Ypres. It was on Hill 60 as the battle began that his battalion fought an incredible defensive combat on 20th-21st April, during which several V.C.s were awarded.

After the British exploded five mines under them on 17th April, the 1st Royal West Kent Battalion and the 2nd King's Own Scottish Borderers had attacked, supported by the 2nd Duke of Wellington's, 1/9th London and 2nd King's Own Yorkshire Light Infantry Battalions. At first the British were successful, but on the next two nights, 18th and 19th April, the Germans had counter-attacked in force. On 20th April they increased their attack massively, concentrating heavy artillery shell fire on the hill. That night Eric's battalion took over the British support trenches, in two waves. First 'A' and 'D' Companies moved up through communication trenches congested with the wounded, followed by 'B' and 'C' companies. Immediately they were drawn into action to support the hard-pressed Bedfordshire Battalion then holding the front line.

Soon they were holding, not a continuous trench line, but a series of fragments of trench and hurriedly defended shell holes. German field guns had been brought forward to pound the hill defences. 'B' and 'C' Companies received instructions to pull back, but other groups from the advanced companies – together with groups of men from the East Surreys and Bedfords – were forced to try to hold on, and were supported by grenade throwers from the Northumberland Fusiliers. When the East Surreys too eventually withdrew, two officers had been killed and one had gone missing. Fifteen men had also been killed and a further one hundred and seven been wounded. One surviving officer from Eric's battalion, 2nd Lieutenant Woolley, had for a time been their only officer alive on the hill. He was awarded the Victoria Cross: the first Territorial soldier to be so honoured. We do not know in which company Eric was serving, and whether he was a survivor from the hill or from the support line. This action preceded the main Second Battle of Ypres. It appears from German sources that the Germans fought desperately for Hill 60, partly because they feared the defenders might have left evidence of the secret preparations for using chlorine gas, and they wished this to come as a complete surprise.

Richard Clark was probably in the fighting at the hill a few days later. Richard, born in 1894 and at school from 1909, had left to continue his education at Ardingley College in the summer of 1911, whilst his father continued his Anglican ministry, variously in Boscombe, at Rowde, at Gussage St. Michael, and finally in West Moors. He was known to the Army as Arthur James Richard, though it seems most likely that he preferred to be called Richard rather than Arthur, and that is how he signed his name. His early intention was to go on to Cambridge and to follow in his father's footsteps through ordination as a priest in the Church of England, but this keen army cadet (he was colour sergeant in the O.T.C. at Ardingley) had decided to apply for the Reserve Army as well. In June 1914, he applied to join the Army as a supplementary special officer in the Royal Fusiliers. At the time he was still at Ardingley College, but Bournemouth School Headmaster, Edward Fenwick, joined the Headmaster of Ardingley in supporting Richard's application by attesting to his good character. After failing his initial medical, Richard appealed. On 3rd September 1914 he was deemed a "fit" young man "ready for appointment to the Special reserve of Officers". So having trained for the Royal Fusiliers, he was gazetted for his commission on 23rd February 1915.

The Royal Fusiliers was an enormous organisation – almost an army in its own right. When the war broke out, there were four Regular and three Special Reserve battalions as well as the first four (City of London) Territorial Battalions of the London Regiment (Territorials), which were affiliated to the regiment. By the end of the war there were more than forty-five battalions, and 235,476 of their men had fought in every theatre of the war, apart from Mesopotamia, in almost every major battle, and suffered 21,941 deaths as well as many other casualties.

In 1915, Richard was attached to the 3rd Royal Fusiliers Battalion, which had returned to the U.K. from India in December 1914. Part of 85th Brigade, 28th Division, it went to France, via Southampton, landing at Le Havre 19th January 1915. Richard would probably have received further training with the 6th Battalion at Dover before being sent out to replace an officer who had been lost in the fighting, and there were plenty of those needed for this battalion; in the first fortnight of February alone they had lost two officers and two wounded when the brigade was switched into the 3rd Division, and lost another two before the end of the month. Perhaps the order of his names confused the Army as well as, unusually, the medal rolls could only state that he was with the battalion in France "before the 12th October 1915". In fact, we know from the unit diary he was with them in the spring – but not precisely when he arrived to join them. Richard might not have arrived when the Germans launched their sudden gas strike at the Second Battle of Ypres, but if not, he was with them soon afterwards. His battalion fought tenaciously on Hill 60 from 23rd-28th April.

In the end, the Germans had won the Second Battle of Ypres despite the best efforts of the Allied soldiers, but they did not achieve the breakthrough or the division of the Allies for which they had hoped. They pushed the Allied line closer to Ypres, taking the village of Langemarck. As they did so, they actually shortened the Allied line, which could therefore be defended with fewer men, though Ypres itself became even more vulnerable to shell fire. The bitter fighting for the hill continued after the main battle had ended, and the Germans made continuing use of the gas. Richard's battalion was pulled back at the end of 3rd May 1915. From 1st May, the 1st Hampshire Battalion had supported them to stabilize the position. If we cannot be sure Richard was then involved, we do know that, within days, Harold Deans was back in action there, and Richard was certainly there soon afterwards.

Harold Deans had recovered from his wounds and from the sickness he had suffered in 1914 near La Bassée and returned to his battalion, the 2nd King's Own Scottish Borderers, on 25th April 1915, just after the battalion had fought to take Hill 60 alongside Eric Head and his friends. (*The Bournemouthian* made several errors in its account of Harold Deans, saying he returned in March 1915, and was with the battalion when it captured Hill 60 on 30th April – the battalion actually fought there on 17th April. On 30th April the battalion was resting from the battle and the control of Hill 60 continued to yo-yo between the belligerents.) When Harold arrived, the 2nd King's Own Scottish Borderers Battalion had moved and was in the trenches on the Yser Canal Line just north of Ypres, under German attack with gas shells. Over the next few days they supported the French in a counter-attack to the German gas attacks and took what rest they could in a wood north-west of Vlamertingue (north-west of Ypres). Then the battalion moved back to Hill 60. By then the Germans had regained the hill-top and Harold became involved in an attack on 5th May 1915, when the men assaulted the hill from what is now the line of the road to its north.

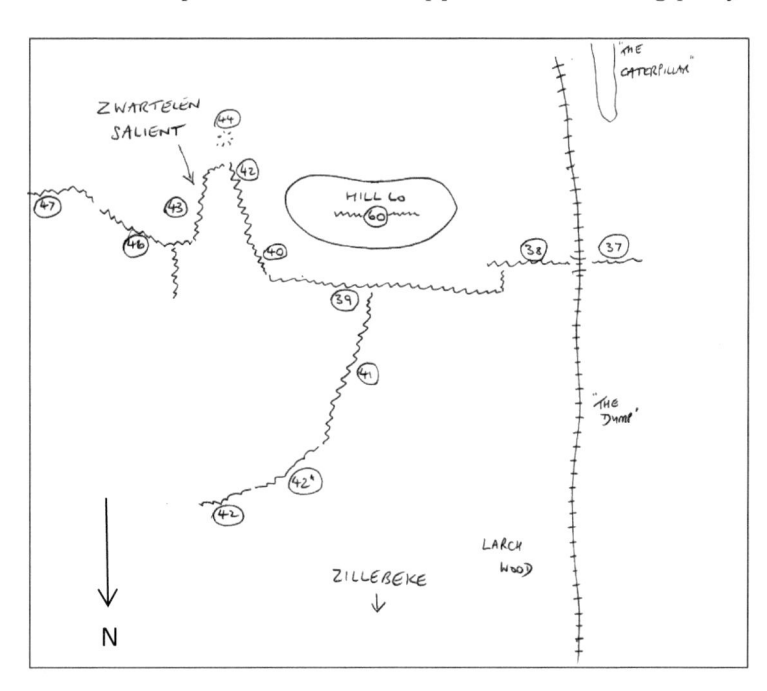

That day, at 1p.m., the battalion moved via dug-outs east of the Yser Canal to the main support area, the Larch Wood Railway Cutting, six hours later. "Orders were received to attack at 10 pm (subsequent to 20 minutes artillery bombardment) from trenches 38 and 39 the enemy's trenches facing. 'C' and 'D' companies to attack. A and C companies to furnish supports and working party. The battalion proceeded up the railway cutting under shrapnel and rifle fire to the entrance of trench 39 and scarcely had sufficient time for A and B companies to reach their appointed positions by 10 pm. 10 pm. C company attacked in face of a heavy fire both frontal and enfilade from both flanks and found the enemy massed in the portion of trench facing them. Heavy casualties were received, four out of five officers being lost. 10.45 pm. The remnant were withdrawn... 'D' Company found the trench opposite them evacuated by the enemy and occupied same but were enfiladed on both flanks and exposed to a number of bombs. Heavy casualties resulted including 2 officers and the remainder were ordered to withdraw shortly after 11 pm... The battalion held subsequently trenches 38 and 39, having relieved the Dorsets."[83] They then withdrew, being replaced by the 1st Cheshire Battalion. Hill 60 had not been recaptured.

Second Lieutenant Arthur Greg of the 1st Cheshires described how "At the allotted time they climbed over the parapet. The order was to go half right. They were met with a storm of rifle and machine gun fire from the hill. Our artillery had not yet stopped and soon theirs started. The poor Scots were simply blown back by lead. They started again and went half left. Their wounded were pouring into my trenches. The sounds were terrible, men shrieking, the fierce cackle of machine gun fire and the cruel shriek of the shrapnel. This was battle. When the next volley of star lights went up there were noticeably more bodies in No Man's Land. Wounded and belated Jocks were still returning, some helping other wounded back or bringing in the body of some comrade. These shattered remains of a fine regiment all found their way back to my already overcrowded trench and its continuation to the right."[84] One more officer was killed, and a further three missing believed killed; eight had been wounded. Although there is no mention of Harold Deans being wounded, or falling sick, the battalion war diary stated that he re-joined the battalion on 22nd July 1915. *The Bournemouthian* reported that arrival as starting his third tour of duty,[85] after he had been both wounded and gassed.

Three days after this bitter fighting, Richard Clark's battalion returned to the hill. We know that three un-named officers joined the battalion on 6th-7th May in time to suffer from further shelling and gassing. From 8th May, the battalion supported the East Surreys and 3rd Middlesex Battalions in their attempt to regain some lost trenches and was hit by gas and heavy shelling. The Germans not only held on to their gains but advanced their front line to a hundred yards from the 3rd Royal Fusiliers, taking advantage of a weak area on the right to push round them and to snipe at them. On 10th May, a further four un-named officers also joined them, and two more the next day. By this time Richard was most certainly with the battalion, as some time between 8th and 12th May he was wounded for the first time in these attacks.

Richard had been shot with a bullet hitting him on his buttocks. It was too serious for him just to have been patched up at the casualty clearing station, and for him to continue with the battalion. He was sent back down the line to Rouen, where he was admitted to the 2nd Red Cross Hospital. The wound was serious, and so he wasn't discharged from the hospital and sent back to duty with his battalion until 31st May. This meant, however, that he missed a dreadful onslaught on 24th May when the Germans attacked through gas, killing four more officers, wounding and capturing four, and wounding eight others. Five hundred and thirty-six men were killed, wounded or went missing. Only one officer of the seventeen with the battalion when the attack began was still in action, and just 160 men were left. "This was probably the worst loss in a day's battle of any Fusilier battalion during the war."[86]

As Richard re-joined the battalion, there was a rapid infusion of new men and officers to recreate it

---

[83] War Diary, 2nd King's Own Scottish Borderers, May 5th 1915.
[84] Quoted in *Ypres Hill 60* by Nigel Cave, Pen and Sword, 1998, p. 68.
[85] *The Bournemouthian*, July 1915.
[86] *The Royal Fusiliers in the Great War*, H.C. O'Neill, London William Heinemann, 1922, p. 74.

– on 5th June, 300 new men were added, together with thirteen new officers, whilst forty-five men re-joined the battalion from hospital. The battalion must have seemed very different. That summer it remained in the Ypres Salient, south of Ypres near Mount Kemmel. There were no more major battles, but sniping and shelling from both sides meant there was a steady trickle of continued casualties.

Slightly further west, in the early months of 1915, the 1st Honourable Artillery Company Battalion, including Eric Quaife, Arthur Hame and Leslie Gilbert, occupied trenches opposite Spanbrokmolen and later at St. Eloi.

Eric (born 1893, at school 1904-1909) worked in the Union Assurance company. On 6th February 1911 he enrolled as a private in the Honourable Artillery Company, citing his experience in the school O.T.C. as his former military experience. His training was augmented by attending training camps each summer between 1911 and 1914. In February 1912 he enrolled as a student at the University of London Engineering School. He received his mobilisation orders on the second day of the war – 5th August 1914. After a training spell with the 2nd Battalion, Eric landed in France on 14th February 1915 and re-joined the 1st Battalion on 18th February.

Here they heard the sounds of the battle for Hill 60 and the attacks made by the Germans east of Ypres in the second battle. Casualties were steady and quite heavy. On 24th May, "In the evening about 5pm all trenches reported the men were suffering with extreme irritation of the eyes... By some it was attributed to some powder having been dropped by enemy aeroplanes. There was a peculiar sweet smell noticed in air in late evening... we later heard it was caused by the use of asphyxiating gas against troops on our left in neighbourhood of Ypres. Many... men in trenches were rendered momentarily useless owing to their eyes being made to smart & water so much."[87]

Meanwhile, another group of Bournemouthians had arrived together to join the 1st Dorset Battalion. These young men were George Turner, Ralph Drayton, Wilfrid Fuller and John Nethercoate. After John Turner's death in October 1914, the battalion had seen a lot of action. In early November 1914, it had been moved to Ploegsteert Wood about the time Jesse Atkin had been killed there with the 3rd Worcesters, and afterwards further north again into the Ypres Salient proper. George Turner, born 1895, at school 1905-1911, arrived to join his brother's old battalion, disembarking on 11th May 1915. You can't help wondering what his parents might have thought. The 1st Dorsets Battalion had fought hard to capture, and to try to recapture Hill 60, and the battalion was still in its vicinity.

Ralph Drayton had left school on 26th November 1914, perhaps inspired by the reports reaching Bournemouth and the school. A school photograph taken to record his success in gaining First Class Honours in his senior exams shows him as looking almost like the officer into which he was to turn. Indeed, on 14th August 1914, he had applied for a commission. He had been in the O.T.C. at school for six years. He was just about old enough to serve as an officer, having been born in December 1896. The Army had taken its time to consider his application but he was medically examined and judged fit on 25th November, so left school the next day. Writing in support of his application on 15th August, Captain Sewell of Bournemouth School O.T.C. had written, "He is very

---

[87] War Diary, 1st Battalion, Honourable Artillery Company, 24th May 1915.

keen & has done very good work indeed as Col. Serg."[88] After training with the 3rd Dorsets he too was sent to the 1st Dorsets, landing in France on 13th May 1915, two days after George.

Wilfred Fuller's early history was slightly different. He was born in San Francisco in 1896, the son of a journalist. His mother, Alice Fuller, moved to Britain, and after attending Wimborne Grammar School for two years he joined Bournemouth School in January 1912. He left when term ended on 29th July 1914. Almost immediately he was in the Army – the school records report his commission to the 3rd Dorsets as his occupation on leaving school, and he was made 2nd lieutenant on 14th November 1914.[89]

John Nethercoate, born in Bournemouth in 1894, had attended the school between 1905 and 1909. After he left the school, he continued his education at King's College, Taunton. His father was an Alderman of Bournemouth. John went to France on 16th May 1915, and also probably joined the 1st Dorsets whilst they were still at Hill 60 or later that month. He remained there with the battalion when they moved to the Abbeville area in July 1915, going into billets at Pont Noyelle.

This group of school friends, junior officers together in the same battalion, joining over a period of a couple of weeks, was the nearest the school had to a 'Pal's Battalion' on the Western Front, though larger groups from the school served together in the Middle and Far Eastern campaigns.

Soon after they arrived, Cecil Hughes also came to the trenches near Ypres. Born in 1895, Cecil was at school only for about a year, 1908-1909, though this overlapped with the time of his older brother Sydney, who served in the Navy during the war. He volunteered after the outbreak and was posted to the 2nd East Surrey Battalion, a Regular unit. By the time Cecil joined it, it had been in France since January, and had seen a lot of fighting in the Second Battle of Ypres, taking heavy casualties. He landed in France on 18th May 1915, and was probably in the draft of one hundred and thirty four men who reinforced the battalion on 21st May.

Two days later they were in trenches at Potijze near Ypres, being heavily shelled. On 24th May at "about 3am the whole line held by the battalion was heavily gassed with asphyxiating gases and the right near the railway attacked. 'C' Company on the right with two companies 8th Middlesex retired and no trace of the Company (about 100 men) has yet been found… Enemy gained some trenches south of the railway held by the 3rd Royal Fusiliers. Enemy active on whole front but no further attack was made. Casualties: Other ranks killed 5; wounded 19; missing 157; suffering from gas poisoning 24. At dusk 3rd Middlesex Regiment reinforced our right."[90] The next day was a "Quiet Day" according to the war diary – even so, one officer and seventeen men were killed; one officer and forty men wounded; whilst forty-four men were missing. Four more were killed and four wounded the day after. A few days later, Cecil had a brief respite at Poperinghe before experiencing a less dreadful trench tour and then for most of June a training routine incorporating the arrival of a team of machine gunners. Cecil survived his fighting in the Ypres area from May 1915. His next experience of battle on a large scale would come that autumn at Loos. On the 'Quiet Day' for Cecil, however, another Old Boy, Douglas Hazard, lost his life.

---

[88] Army File, Ralph Drayton, WO 339/30754.
[89] *The London Gazette*, 7th May 1915.
[90] War Diary, 2nd East Surrey Battalion, 24th May 1915.

Sanctuary Wood and Hooge Crater

Douglas was a Boscombe boy. He left Bournemouth School in 1910 at the age of sixteen, having been a member of the O.T.C. and was articled as pupil with the law firm, Mooring, Aldridge and Haydon. He maintained a commitment to the Reserve Army and in 1912 was commissioned into the General Reserve of Officers and was mobilised on 5th August 1914 and appointed to his battalion immediately on the start of the war, joining the King's Shropshire Light Infantry. After training at Pembroke Dock he was attached to the 2nd Battalion King's Shropshire Light Infantry, 80th Brigade and 27th Division, which had landed at Le Havre on 21st December 1914. Douglas arrived in France the following May. He joined the battalion on the front line just east of Ypres in Sanctuary Wood. (It had been nicknamed that by soldiers in October 1914 when the trees appeared for a very short time to present the prospect of cover, and therefore sanctuary to pressurised troops. However, it was not long before it became synonymous with danger and death.)

Douglas Hazard

Sanctuary Wood lies on the slope below a hill which the British maps designated as Hill 62, east from Hill 60 and south of the Menin road at Bellewarde. The Germans held Hill 62 and from it targeted the British. On 25th May, "about 1am [the] Battalion was ordered to advance and assault enemy's trenches in vicinity of Bellewarde Farm. Attack failed. Battalion held line of wood west of Whittport Farm and entrenched itself."[91]

Douglas died in this night-time charge against the Germans entrenched at the top of Hill 62. Another subaltern also died, and seven other officers were wounded, whilst 192 men were killed, wounded or went missing. At first, once the attack was repulsed, there were doubts as to whether he was alive and prisoner or dead, but after a short while the truth emerged. Major R. T. Toke, 1st Welsh Regiment, writes: "On the 25th May we made a night attack about three miles east of Ypres. We attacked through a small wood and up a hill. I led my men amid a murderous fire and charged the trench at the top and took it. The Germans retired to a trench about 15 yards further back and fired very heavily on us. While lying there a Company of the Shropshires, who were supporting us, came charging through the wood led by an officer (probably Lieutenant Hazard). He was at the head of the Company shouting to them to 'Charge.' I got up and shouted to my own men to 'Charge.' I then saw the Shropshire officer fall, but it was too dark to see whether he was killed or wounded, and the fire was so heavy that I could not get near him. We hung on until dawn, until I had only about 30 men left. We then retired under a most murderous fire. Your son fell within 15 yards of the German trenches. We tried to get back through the wood after dark to bring in the wounded, but could only get half-way up, as the Germans were again in position. The Shropshire officer was splendid in the way he led his men and I wrote about him to the Colonel of Lieutenant Hazard's Battalion."[92] He is commemorated on the Sanctuary Wood Cemetery Memorial.

---

[91] War Diary, 2nd King's Shropshire Battalion, 25th May 1915.

[92] *The Bournemouthian*, March 1916; a very similar account was included in *The Bournemouth Visitors' Directory*, 29th January 1916.

After the Second Battle of Ypres, the fighting in the area rumbled on but neither the Germans nor Sir John French made any serious attempt to break through in this sector of the Western Front, though the fighting rumbled on. On 5th June, Arthur Hame's luck changed.

The 1st Honourable Artillery Company Battalion had been in reserve billets on the Ramparts. The "town [is] in a terrible state of destruction though fairly clean as far as bodies go owing to work done by engineers & cleaning parties. A great deal has been burnt down by them and in places burning is still going on... the Ramparts were shelled – a normal occurrence in the afternoon. Several shells fell near the billets & one into house in which the stretcher-bearers were. Pte Pilgrim P. (B Coy) killed, & wounded Pte. Lemmon M.H. (B Coy) (died 8/6/15), Pte. Hame A.W. (C Coy) & L/Cpl Charles L.P. First 3 named were stretcher-bearers & the first casualties among this section."[93] Arthur had been badly wounded by a shell fragment which struck him in the shoulder and was admitted to the IBRC Hospital at Le Touquet on 6th June 1915. He returned to England on 10th June 1915.

Leslie Gilbert survived the heavy fighting, even when the battalion lost two thirds of its effective force on 16th June 1915 whilst attacking at Bellevarde. Later, on 27th January 1916, Leslie was to be promoted to lance corporal, and on 3rd September 1916 to shoemaker sergeant (for which he was paid a farthing extra per day from March 1918). In King's Regulations, governing the rules for infantry, the rule stated that "In each battalion to which a sergeant-shoemaker is appointed, at least four men per company will be instructed in the rudiments of shoe-making, so as to be able to carry out minor repairs when on service." Leslie, a fighting soldier, had the skills to sort minor problems with the men's boots, and the responsibility to train up other men. On 7th February 1916, Alexander Simpson (born 1897, boarded at school 1906-1912) arrived in France and joined Leslie in the battalion. He was placed in 'B' Company. He went on to celebrate his birthday on Armistice Day!

Meanwhile in the spring of 1915, further south, the British renewed the attempt to break through.

The Battle of Fromelles (Aubers Ridge – Festubert)

Even before the Battle of Neuve Chapelle, the French city of Lille had been designated a necessary target to be captured, as the fourth biggest French city and the most important in the north. Its capture would allow the British from La Bassée and Ypres to link and to advance eastwards across to the north German plain. First the Aubers Ridge would have to be captured, a target in the Battle of Neuve Chapelle that had not been achieved. Its capture would allow the direct observation of the railway lines leading from the east and south-east of Lille and of the city itself. A second attempt to capture the Aubers Ridge was therefore made on 9th May 1915 with the British 8th Division attacking at Fromelles in the north and the 1st Division attacking in the south near Neuve Chapelle again. At the same time the French would attack Vimy Ridge, near Arras. The hope was that a British pincer attack preceded by a heavy bombardment might this time succeed, whilst the French capture of Vimy Ridge would be a double set-back for the Germans. In the event, the French colonial troops were driven back just below the summit at Vimy, and the British attacks failed with the loss of 11,600 casualties.

Henry Budden was in the Battle of Fromelles. Born 1895 and a boarder at the school between 1907-1911, Henry was a sergeant in the 'Corps' and won cricket colours in 1910. On 18th August 1914, he volunteered for service and applied for a commission two months later, supported by the

---

[93] Both extracts from War Diary, 1st Battalion, Honourable Artillery Company, 6th June 1915.

Mayor of Bournemouth. On November 1st 1914, he was commissioned into the 3rd Dorset Battalion, but when he left for France in March 1915, instead of fighting in the Dorsets, Henry and some other young officers were attached to the 2nd Lincolnshire Battalion and on 10th June was promoted to lieutenant.

On 9th May 1915 they were placed in the second wave of the attack and on the left flank. Henry was one of the most junior officers in the battalion to take part in the attack. The attack began with an artillery bombardment, at 5a.m., after which the battalion attacked in support of the 1st Royal Irish Rifles. "The enemy at once opened a heavy artillery and rifle fire. The leading companies of the Battalion were able to advance as far as the trenches immediately in front of our own fire parapet and there found further advance impossible, heavy flanking fire from rifles and machine guns being brought to bear on them. Before this position was reached 2nd Lt Ayres (3rd Dorsetshire Regt) and 2nd Lt Nisbet were killed and Clifford wounded. The Royal Irish Rifles who preceded the Battalion were also unable to reach the German trench. The 2 companies of the Battalion on the second line had by this time reached our own parapet and as a further advance from this point was impossible the G.O.C. 25th Inf. Bde. issued orders for these two companies to endeavour to work down the sap leading towards the mine crater on the left and after gaining possession of the German trench to work westward and join up with the left of the 2nd Rifle Brigade. At this moment the Brigadier was killed... Captain B.J. Thurston was sent forward with the left party. He sent on first a blocking and bombing party under 2Lt E.O. Black who succeeded in gaining the German trench and clearing 300 to the west but running out of bombs could advance no further. The remainder of the party followed close behind, but came under an extremely heavy fire from their right and left front especially the latter." The bombing party of the Scottish Rifles went forward and cleared the trench to the east of the mine crater. Men were sent across to occupy and put in a state of defence the cleared trenches but heavy casualties were suffered and only a small proportion of the men reached their objective. Two German machine guns firing from beyond the crater were causing many casualties, but were overwhelmed by five British machine guns. Communications were very difficult because the area between the trench lines was swept by other German machine guns from the side, so the captain in the captured trench was ordered to bring his men back. "As this was impossible during daylight he waited until 8pm at which time he was attacked on both flanks and rear, the enemy bombing and rushing in from the crater on the left first. Seeing the situation and having no machine guns or bombs and being so hard pressed Capt Thurston gave the order for the party to get back to their own parapet, which they did."[94] Of the twenty officers who had been in the attack, including Henry, three had died, three been wounded and one gone missing.

A month later, when he helped to command a battery of trench howitzers for the 8th Division, Henry wrote: "It is the German machine guns that do the damage. They are awfully clever with them, as we found the last time this Battalion attacked. I shall not forget it for a long time. They also seemed to find a lot of big gun ammunition, but their shells, and especially their shrapnel, are not a patch on ours, but nevertheless one of them blew up 20 of my platoon, and my escape was marvellous. I was right in the middle of a group of 25 men, 14 of whom were killed and seven wounded, but I was only knocked down by a sod of earth and was not one whit the worse for my fall."[95]

---

[94] War Diary, 2nd Lincolnshire Battalion, 9th May 1915.
[95] *The Bournemouthian*, July 1915.

Behind the front line of this battle, Richard Barfoot was also involved, with the 24th Field Ambulance near Sailly. By 4p.m. "work became very heavy, many lying cases… at midnight we were nearly cleared… During the past night all cases… were collected. A large part of this was done by 2 Bearer subdivisions, one each from 1st and 2nd West riding Field Ambs, & a detachment of 2nd Lincolns, our own Stretcher Bearers being tired out."[96] By noon on 12th May they had treated forty-five officers and one thousand and fifty-eight men. Later they classified the types of wounds – five hundred and sixty-one from rifle fire; four hundred and ninety-five from artillery; eleven with bayonet wounds; five from grenades; and thirty-one "accidental (Barbed wire etc.)".

The Battle of Festubert

The Battle of Festubert, fought about three miles south of Neuve Chapelle on 15th May, was the last phase. Haig ordered the first night attack of the war using British, Indian and Canadian divisions. It lasted from 15th to 25th May and cost an additional 16,000 casualties.

The bombardment began on 13th May and the assault began at 11.30p.m. on 15th May. Casualties became heavy and the 3rd Canadian Brigade (attached to the British 7th Division) was brought in at noon on 17th May. For several days they attacked, though again having problems with the Ross rifles jamming. All the attacks were called off on 25th May after Sir John French had agreed instead to strengthen French attacks at Vimy by extending the British lines south of La Bassée Canal. He was aware that British ammunition was running out. The French lost 102,000 at Vimy and the Germans lost 50,000.

Philip Tollemache had probably joined Alexander Sandbrook and the 8th Canadian Infantry Battalion on 7th May. On 17th May, the battalion moved forward on a miserable day spent under heavy rain, followed by a night in which most of them had somehow to bivouac in the pouring rain, though their adjutant claimed "the men's spirits remained undampened".[97] On 19th May they took over trenches from the 2nd Wiltshire and 8th City of London Battalions. They found the German shelling "pretty hot" as "Every conceivable kind of Shell & Calibre were thrown at us."[98] By the time they were relieved they had lost four officers and twenty-seven men, and another three officers and 127 men had been wounded.

The battle had failed to achieve the longed for breakthrough.

By 23rd May, the 1st Canadian Field Artillery Brigade, including Basil Keogh and the 2nd Canadian Field Battery, had taken up new positions north-west of La Bassée and were pleased when a week later were allowed an increase to firing fifty shells per gun to support infantry. The 2nd Battery HQ was hit but fortunately there were no casualties despite the loss of four limbers and ammunition. They were then positioned near Festubert. On 6th June, triple telephone lines were laid to the batteries in preparation for a renewed attack but they were instead moved under cover of a ground mist followed by a heavy thunderstorm south-ward on 8th June. Two days later the rain had flooded these positions so "officers and men rather uncomfortable".[99] On 14th June they bombarded the German first and second line trenches at La Bassée and in the evening two guns were moved up

---

[96] War Diary of the 24th Field Ambulance, May 10th-11th 1915.
[97] War Diary, 8th Canadian Infantry Battalion, 17th May 1915.
[98] War Diary, 8th Canadian Infantry Battalion, 21st May 1915.
[99] War Diary, 1st Canadian Field Artillery Brigade, 10th June 1915.

by hand to a front line trench with 150 rounds of ammunition for each to fire in support of an attack the next evening. "Parapets screening these 2 guns were torn down and effect was a complete surprise to enemy. First few minutes the right gun smashed 2 machine guns and the left gun smashed one machine gun which were in the German trenches. Wire cutting next received their attention with the result when the Infantry assaulted at 6pm they reported these entanglements completely removed. The enemy's parapets and trenches were then badly smashed." One gun fired its entire one hundred shells but the other went out of action after forty rounds. "As a signal for the assault a British mine was exploded at 6pm but it was either too heavily charged or laid too close to our trenches, the result being nearly all the infantry in front trench were killed or wounded. Casualties included bombing party all of whose stick of bombs exploded. This disaster eventually frustrated object of the attack."[100] The two officers in charge of the front guns, and another soldier, were wounded and two men killed. Over the next days Basil Keogh's 2nd Battery kept up the shelling.

Summer and Autumn 1915 in the Ypres Salient

In the north, after leaving Ypres, the Menin road reached a junction which the men named "Hellfire Corner", today a busy roundabout. From there various roads radiated out like the spokes of a wheel. The most famous of these roads is the road to Menen (known as 'Menin' to the British), and it heads almost eastwards. The front line bisected the Menin road near a notable feature, which was a chateau just north-east from the road at Hooge. On 2nd June 1915, the Germans bombarded the British from 5a.m. to midday and then attacked with infantry. In this assault the British lost control of the ruins of the chateau. The British retaliated: at 7p.m. on 19th July 1915, the 175th Tunnelling Company RE exploded a large mine there, under a German trench. The spoil from the detonation threw up a lip 15 feet high, around a crater 20 feet deep and 120 feet wide. After the firing, it was immediately occupied by two companies of the 4th Middlesex (8th Brigade, 3rd Division). British artillery quelled all signs of German attempts to recover the crater. Soon afterwards, Bertram Ball and Richard Smith arrived there.

Bertram Ball (born 1890; at school until 1905) was in the 14th Division, a soldier of the 8th Rifle Brigade Battalion, a Service battalion formed at Winchester on 21st August 1914, placed alongside the 7th Rifle Brigade Battalion in the 41st Brigade, the 14th (Light) Division. They had landed at Boulogne on 20th May 1915 and arrived in the Ypres Salient at about the time the British extended their front to Boesinghe, taking over from the French immediately north of Ypres on 7th-8th June 1915. The British now had complete responsibility for the salient. Because of the shortage of war supplies, Sir John French issued general orders to the First Army that operations should be limited to "'small aggressive threats which will not require much ammunition or many troops" as he was hoping to build up his resources for another battle he planned to fight further south at Loos.

Bertram's battalion was given the role of holding the Hooge crater lip on 29th July 1915, although "all ranks were quite strange to the trenches".[101] The battalion had five machine guns and spread out in companies along a line which included the southern edge of Zouave Wood. "The weak point of the position were as follows:- (1) There was no wire to speak of in front. (2) The front line trenches deep + narrow and communication along them very difficult. (3) The communications to

---

[100] War Diary, 1st Canadian Field Artillery Brigade, 15th June 1915.
[101] War Diary, 8th Battalion, The Rifle Brigade, 29th July 1915.

the rear also difficult and inadequate. (4) Trench howitzers of the enemy daily blew in parts of the support trenches and although these trenches are shown on the map hardly any of them were habitable consequently too many men were crammed into the front line and there was not enough depth. (5) The crater divided the front line as the part blown up there was not held though bomber posts were established on each side."[102]

On 30th July, Bertram's battalion was attacked by the first German use of flamethrowers. Just after 3.15 a.m. "part of the front trenches was subjected to an intense bombardment which lasted only about two or three minutes, then suddenly sheets of flame broke out all along the front and clouds of thick, black smoke. The Germans had turned on liquid fire from hoses apparently which had been established just in front during the night. Under cover of the flames swarms of bombers appeared on the parapet and in rear of the line. The mass of them had broken through at the crater and then swung left and right. The fighting became confused and the machine guns were soon out of action."[103]

On the extreme flanks, the battalion stood their ground – but these had not been attacked by the new flamethrowers. In the centre, the companies were forced to retreat despite intense fighting, and the Germans were able to bring up machine guns of their own. Between 4a.m. and 5a.m. the British attempted to counter-attack but were beaten back by the machine guns and intense rifle fire. When they regrouped only one company remained intact, and after a brief British artillery bombardment this company bravely went into yet a further counter-attack of an almost suicidal nature: "At 2.45pm exactly the counter attack started. ¨D¨ Coy on the right advanced as if on parade. The enemy's machine guns and rifle fire had apparently not been in any way silenced by the bombardment. The whole ground was absolutely swept by bullets. The attack was brought to a complete standstill halfway towards its objective and no reinforcements could reach it."[104]

The remains of the battalion were relieved that night. They had lost six officers killed, three missing (presumed dead), ten wounded, whilst of the ordinary soldiers like Bertram, known as the 'Other Ranks', eighty had been killed, 132 missing, and 267 wounded. Four of their five machine guns had been lost. "The men fought without rations or water throughout the day." There is no record of whether Bertram was wounded that day – certainly he was reported wounded by the autumn.[105] However, he was to survive and go on to many more interesting and dangerous experiences in the war.

Richard Smith was not directly involved as his 6th Somerset Light Infantry Battalion, also 14th (Light) Division, but 43rd Brigade, was in reserve. He was young, born in 1897, and had left school in 1912. Only 17 when the war broke out, it did not stop him volunteering as a 'boy soldier'. He was just 18 – still officially a year too young to be in the trenches – when he landed with them on 21st May 1915. The division suffered from a lack of rifles and artillery ammunition, as British production simply could not produce enough resources, so initially the battalion was given the work of digging support trenches and was then given further, practical instruction by men of the 5th North Staffordshire Regiment, who "were full of praise of the bearing and behaviour of the

---

[102] War Diary, 8th Battalion of the Rifle Brigade, 30th July 1915.
[103] ibid.
[104] ibid.
[105] *The Bournemouthian*, December 1915.

Kitcheners who they saw for the first time".[106] They had deployed into their own trenches at Hooge for the first time on the night of 25th-26th June, coming under shell fire and taking casualties. Long-range German shell fire from behind Hill 60 pounded them, but on one occasion in mid-August British 'friendly fire' artillery hit them twice in one day, causing a lot of casualties, including a number killed. By September Richard was a sergeant, in "trenches everywhere in a deplorable state" due to incessant rain. On 4th September, Richard was hit on the wrist by a shrapnel bullet, though he quickly recovered from the wound. After convalescence he was moved from the 6th Somerset Light Infantry to join the Oxford and Buckinghamshire Light Infantry. He went to serve as a sergeant in Mesopotamia, where he was again wounded (on 21st February 1916). After recovering from that wound he was selected for officer training and was commissioned into the Gloucestershire Regiment on 18th December 1916. As a Gloucestershire officer, however, he was attached to the 2/5th Somerset Light Infantry Battalion, which was part of the Rangoon Brigade in the Burma Division of the Army which remained in India.

In mid-June Edward Hall and the 1/16th London Battalion (Queen's Westminster Rifles) had also moved to trenches north of Ypres, sustaining heavy bombardments. On 9th August they supported an attack on German positions to the east of Sanctuary Wood and on the Hooge Ridge as the British tried to force the Germans back to the east. That autumn they suffered a lot from heavy shelling. Edward was given extra pay from August 1915, and on his last day in France, 15th November 1915, he was commissioned 2nd lieutenant in the 3/9th (Cyclist) Hampshire Regiment. Once commissioned, he was sent to India with the 2/5th Hampshire Battalion, and later served as an attached officer with the 2nd Dorset Battalion. Sickness followed and when he had served in the 9th Hampshires, from which he was demobilised, he had served in Egypt and Palestine where he was shot in the arm. He was demobbed in February 1919.

John Snelgar was also in the Ypres Salient at this time. John, born 1887, was at school before 1905 and corporal in the O.T.C. He had studied science at London University. He volunteered on 15th October 1914 and his officer potential was immediately recognised. He was commissioned 2nd lieutenant in the 1st Battalion Wiltshire Regiment on 10th February 1915, a battalion, in 7th Brigade, 3rd Division, which had been one of the first battalions to land in France and had seen much fighting and heavy losses (fighting in the First Battle of Ypres and then at Neuve Chappelle – losing twenty-six officers and about a thousand men). John landed in France on 30th June 1915 and was sent to the Ypres Salient to join the battalion in trench duty and fighting where he began to experience trench life at Hooge and St. Eloi. On 29th July 1915 there was a near miss when the Germans exploded a mine – but it was ten yards in front of the trench, and only one man was wounded. In August it spent fourteen days continuously in the trenches at St. Jean, taking casualties, before moving back under fire to Hooge. On 27th August they were ordered to push the line forward "to occupy and fortify an old advanced trench running in front of Stables and connect up with 2nd S Lancs, who had to dig up to the stables... A bombing party occupied this trench after dusk and the working party commenced digging having reached the stables. A very heavy bomb throwing duel ensued, our grenadiers throwing some 500 bombs at the advanced German trench. Bombing activities hindered work on defences but the trench was occupied up to the stables."[107] By the end of September the regular shelling and fighting had taken its toll – the battalion fighting strength had been reduced to only four hundred and fifty.

---

[106] War Diary of the 6th Somerset Light Infantry, June 19th 1915.
[107] War Diary of 1st Wiltshires, 27th August 1915.

In the autumn he moved further south as 'A' Company Commander to the trenches at Ploegsteert. John distinguished himself in fighting in the wood. "September 2nd. Our artillery bombarded German line from 3.55a.m. Enemy retaliated immediately and kept up an intermittent fire throughout the day. Five trenches were blown in one or two places. Enemy's fire increased in the afternoon... At about 3p.m. our artillery opened a very heavy fire on the German lines. The enemy evidently expected an attack and concentrated an intense fire on crater and front trenches. The CTs were swept with shrapnel and in many places blown in by heavy shells. All lines were cut. C Coy were occupying crater trenches. A Coy the left Section with 2 platoons in support. These 2 platoons were moved up to reinforce the firing line and 2 platoons from B Coy were pushed up into crater. This adjustment was carried out without casualties. The men were moved up communication trenches in small parties. The dugouts in the crater were wrecked by trench mortars and heavy casualties sustained here. The fire trenches on the left were obliterated and the main CT completely blown in many places... Heavy rain all night. Very little rifle fire. Casualties, other ranks 14 killed 38 wounded 2 missing, believed killed. (These 2 platoons were moved up by 2nd Lieut Macklin with great skill, under heavy bombardment, suffered no casualties. 2nd Lieut Snelgar was in command of A Coy). September 3rd. Heavy rain all day. Enemy's infantry very quiet. Following message received from General Haldane:- 'Convey to Wiltshire Regt my appreciation of stout hearted manner they stood bombardment yesterday. Regret heavy casualties.'"[108]

In the middle of September they suffered a particularly gruelling week of fighting culminating in a battle at Hooge on September 25th which became very desperate. By the end of the day the battalion was reduced to only four hundred riflemen, "the majority of whom were in a very exhausted condition. There had been very few opportunities of getting any sleep during the past week."[109] John was mentioned in dispatches by Sir John French for his "gallantry and distinguished service". In the aftermath of this fighting, the battalion was temporarily withdrawn and placed under 8th Brigade orders, though within days John and the others were back in trenches near Zillebeke. On 17th October, General Haldane, their former divisional commander, gave a speech praising them as he said farewell, "I am very sorry to lose you although no doubt you are not sorry to leave the 'health resort' Hooge. I have been with you for eleven months and well remember the first time I met you when you were marching back after that heavy fighting round Ypres last November reduced to less than one third of your war strength. Since that time your Battalion has always distinguished itself in fighting, work, vigilance and other soldierly qualities. You made the defences of Hooge when we took over the trenches there. You have had more fighting than any other Battalion in the Division... On each occasion you distinguished yourselves and proved yourselves second to none. I have always felt that, when the Wiltshires were holding the line that portion of the line was secure. Whilst I have been in command of the 3rd Division no trench has ever been lost until the other day a small portion in Sanctuary Wood was lost, that solely owing to the exhaustion of the troops. Your Battalion has won more honours than any other Battalion in the Division." The battalion continued to man the trenches at Ploegsteert Wood until late January 1916 when, moving south, they began to prepare for the battles to come.

That autumn Frank Cox arrived in the area. Francis and Edward Cox, brothers, were so keen to serve that they added years to their age in order to be accepted into the army. Francis, known as Frank, was born in 1897 and was at the school initially as a boarder, from 1907 to 1910. He had

---

[108] War Diary, 1st Battalion Wiltshire Regiment, September 1915.
[109] War Diary, 1st Battalion Wiltshire Regiment, 25th September 1915.

emigrated to Canada before the war and volunteered on 16th November 1914. In order to be accepted he was not entirely accurate about his details. He said that he had been born on 28th April, which was true, but moved the year forward five years from 1897 to 1892. This meant he also needed to adjust a few other details of his life so far: in the autumn of 1917 when he switched to the R.A.F. he said that he had worked as a commercial traveller for Etons Ltd of Winnipeg from Jan 1908 to Aug 1914, although he was actually still at school for part of that time. Perhaps he forgot that he had told the Canadian infantry recruiters that he was a farmer! He also told the Canadians that he had served four years with the 4th Hampshire Volunteers – which might be a sort of a gloss for membership of the school O.T.C.? He named his brother Edward as his next of kin, rather than his parents – perhaps because he knew that Edward too planned to adjust his own age? Finally and unusually, he cited his junior school headmaster from Middlesex as his educational referee rather than Dr. Fenwick of Bournemouth School. He joined the 31st (Alberta) Canadian Battalion, part of 6th Canadian Brigade, 2nd Canadian Division.

(His younger brother Edward, born 1898, served in the R.A.M.C. as a hospital orderly, with the B.E.F. from 11th April 1916. In 1915 he had told them he was over 19. He was to serve in the British Expeditionary Force from 11th April 1916, and continued on the Western Front until 1919. Although he was able to transfer to the R.A.F. in 1919, he was not fit enough for front line service.)

After training in Kent (and being inspected on 2nd September by the King) Frank had sailed aboard the *Duchess of Argyle* steamship from Folkestone to Boulogne on 18th September 1915. On 26th September his battalion reached Kemmel in Belgium, where they would be in and out of trenches for the rest of the year. On 13th October, an officer and nine were killed with seventeen more men wounded. The battalion was not impressed that no fewer than 138 of their Ross rifles jammed after only between ten and twenty-five rounds had been fired. Two stretcher-bearers "calmly and nobly went into the midst of falling shells and brought all the wounded safely out of danger." A German shell buried five signallers in their dug-out, but "they dug themselves out and within seven minutes had re-established the signal station, and continued work on the signal wire which was very much in requisition at the time."[110] Frank was in and out of the Kemmel trenches through November and December, and then just north of Spanbroekmolen, facing the Messines Ridge.

Alexander Sandbrook and several other Canadian Old Bournemouthians were also there. For the rest of the year after their fighting at Festubert in May 1915, Alexander, Philip Tollemache, and the 8th Canadian Infantry Battalion had rotated in and out of the trenches. In the autumn they were in the Ypres Salient. During the night of 2nd November, "trenches fell down in many places as result of heavy rain and no revetting. Dug-outs caved in and things generally in a most fearful mess. Rain continued all day and matters did not improve at all, companies being kept busy keeping trenches clear. Some communication trenches caved in for a hundred yards or more... Sniping and machine gun fire was active on account of amount our men had to expose themselves by reason of trenches falling in."[111] Impressively, on Christmas Day they were visited by Canadian Major-General Currie who came to wish them 'Merry Christmas' – he managed to visit every trench in the front of his division, a feat which took him more than six hours to complete. Such actions, however, did wonders to build ésprit de corps amongst the Canadians.

---

[110] War Diary, 31st Canadian Infantry, report on fighting of 13th October 1915.
[111] War Diary, 8th Canadian Infantry Battalion, 2nd-3rd November 1915.

Arnold Whitting also experienced these conditions. Born in 1894, he had left school in 1911 where he too had been in the O.T.C. He volunteered on 8th September 1914 for the 2/3rd (City of London) Battalion (Royal Fusiliers), part of an enormous and complex military body. The London Regiment was an entirely Territorial force, of ninety-four battalions – including Reserves. Each battalion really should be identified as a regiment and each had a number of battalions of their own but not all were trained and ready to be sent into action. Further to confuse the nomenclature, each battalion/regiment of the London Regiment was regarded as a corps in its own right and had three sub-battalions of which – as was customary – the 3rd Battalion was a recruitment and basic training unit. At one stage in 1915 the 4th Battalion even had its own fourth battalion, which became its reserve unit. The first four battalions of the London Regiment were allowed to call themselves Royal Fusiliers and to be described as the City of London, Royal Fusiliers.

Arnold had left England and was on Malta from December 1914 until April 1915, then at Khartoum, to 22nd June 1915. However, Arnold Whitting was gazetted 2nd lieutenant on 23rd June 1915 to the 4/2nd City of London Regiment, the depot battalion, from which he would expect to be deployed to a fighting unit. In the event he was sent to join the 1/2nd City of London Royal Fusiliers, 17th Brigade, 6th Division. This was a Regular Army division and from June 1915 was based in the Ypres Salient, serving at Hooge, Sanctuary Wood and at Zillebeke. In October it became part of 24th Division on the Messines Ridge.

Arnold described travelling by train at two miles an hour into Poperinghe and struggling up to the line.[112] "I found a small limber waiting to take me to the battalion headquarters in a little village three miles further on. On the way I could see where the firing line was owing to the many star-lights that were sent into the sky. These present quite a pretty sight and look rather like a firework display. From where I was it appeared as though I was completely surrounded, for these star-lights could be seen in every direction. It is really because, in this part, we are on a salient which makes a full semi-circle. The next day I was told to go up into the trenches with the transport which takes up the rations. It was pouring with rain, and we had a walk of seven miles. The Belgian roads were in an awful state and we were continually treading in shell-holes. By the time I arrived at the Battalion Headquarters I was absolutely drenched through and through. My Company was in the trenches at the time, so I had to go straight in as I was, and there I remained for two more days.

"The trenches were the last word in mud. Several times I was stuck and had to be pulled out, and, to a spectator, it would present rather a comical sight no doubt. When a party of men are detailed for a fatigue, they often have to stop while someone is pulled out. I remember seeing one poor chap have to leave his gum-boots stuck in the mud and push along in his socks! I shall never forget one little incident. I was in the fire-trench, and just behind me were some men working at a dug-out. Presently a very irate sergeant-major came stumping along to tell them they were not doing it to his liking. Suddenly he stuck in the mud and couldn't move. There he was, purple in the face, and condemning everyone to most unpleasant places! I had to turn away: it was really too funny for words. To add to his discomfort one of his boots refused to move, and he eventually stumbled away with one boot on and one boot off. Although some of the men can hardly feel their feet owing to the wet and cold, they still remain cheerful. I think that was what impressed me most. Whatever were the conditions they always made the best of things. I think while I was out here I experienced some of the worst weather they have had at all. In several places the trenches were falling in, which,

---

[112] These extracts are taken from his letter, *The Bournemouthian*, December 1915.

naturally entailed a great deal more work. There are fatigue parties detailed night and day, and they usually have to work four hours at a stretch. There has been no real fighting near our quarter for some time, although artillery has been pretty active. Unfortunately German snipers are very smart, and have secured many victims who shewed themselves only for a moment."

He temporarily left his unit on 15th November to go to grenade school. On 17th November 1915, near Ypres, he was undertaking instruction in bomb (grenade) throwing using a catapult when unfortunately the trigger of the Mills bomb caught in the catapult mechanism and exploded. A fragment hit him on the inside of his left calf, exiting about four inches lower than the entry wound. At Le Touquet he had an operation to remove a blood clot. On 28th November he was sent back to England on the *Stad Antwerpen* to recuperate at Endsleigh Palace Hospital, Euston. When he reached Endsleigh Hospital he could not flex his ankle.

He came to the hospital at an inauspicious time. It had originally been a hotel with a nursing home in the top apartment but had been requisitioned by the War Office for use as a hospital for officers. In October 1915, the matron, a Miss Florence Tubbs, had been summarily sacked without real explanation – possibly because discipline amongst the recuperating officers was deemed by some to be insufficiently tight. In protest, all the nursing and domestic staff had left and had appealed to Lord Kitchener to intervene, and a delegation had even visited the Under Secretary of War, Harold Tennant, with a petition from fifty-two injured officers appealing for the matron's reinstatement. However, the government refused to intervene. This dispute had been publicised in the *British Journal of Nursing* on October 30th, describing the regime the hospital committee desired as being more of "Prussia in St. Pancras" which the newspaper maintained should be "treated with the contempt it deserves".[113] So Arnold's stay there must have been at a time of unpleasantness.

In contrast Arnold described in glowing terms the hospital at Rouen where originally he was treated as "absolutely the best they have. It belongs to the Duchess of Westminster, who comes in every day and visits the patients. I was told the place used to be a casino, and the ward I was in was actually the gambling room."[114] On 27th January 1916, the doctors judged he would need another three months before he could be available for General Service, though it was reckoned he might be able to cope with Home Service after another two months if he started with light duties. He reported to the 4/2nd London Battalion at Salisbury on 30th March 1916. He was finally declared fit again on 23rd May 1916, though for the time being his service was not on the Western Front.

Perhaps out of the worst of the mud though not the weather, Basil Keogh's 2nd Canadian Field Battery was positioned on top of a ridge between Messines and Ploegsteert. On 5th July they had been given wireless apparatus to contact planes and started working that way two days later, though they could not fire in cloudy or stormy weather as the planes could not get up to guide them. They remained there until early April 1916. From 29th May 1916, the 2nd Battery was taken out of action to be refitted as a howitzer battery over the next fortnight and a new 'A' Battery added. It is not currently clear in which battery Basil Keogh ended up, though he might well have remained with the 2nd Battery, now equipped with howitzers. The brigade moved to the Somme to support the Canadian operations around Courcelette and Mouquet Farm in September 1916.

---

[113] *The British Journal of Nursing*, October 30th 1915, pp. 354-355.
[114] *The Bournemouthian*, December 1915.

La Bassée, Summer 1915

In the summer of 1915, Robert Tyson served near La Bassée. He was an English-speaking Welsh man. Born in Flintshire in April 1889, he had attended Hawarden County School before going on to train as a teacher. He joined the teaching staff of Bournemouth School in September 1914 as Form Master for the 2nd Form and to teach the range of maths, English and geography. With the growing international crisis, he volunteered for the Dorsetshire Regiment Territorials, and served two terms as a private. His time at school, though well spent, was brief, as he was promoted 2nd lieutenant on 6th March 1915 and left the school. Shortly afterwards, on 26th May 1915, he went to France as a member of the Dorsets, but on 31st May was one of three Dorset officers to be attached to the 1st Royal Berkshire Battalion, a regular battalion which had been in France since 12th August 1914. The battalion position was precarious. "We were shelled heavily in the trenches for several days and the 'souvenirs' (as Tommy calls them) fell most frequently round about my Platoon and near my dug-out, which was a very safe one, though dark and low… Whilst in the firing line of these last trenches I had about two hours sleep per night, so that all the spare time during the day was used for sleeping." Later he described how their colonel, Lieutenant-Colonel Charles Glencairn Hill, had been killed on 26th June with two other officers, and a servant, when a shell hit their position. This artillery accuracy he attributed to an enemy agent: "Several headquarters have been shelled—another instance of the work of spies. One spy was caught driving a white horse round various fields in the daytime, whilst a blue light sent signals by night (from the top of a cottage chimney)."[115] The battalion war diary account suggests rather that it was all part of a tit-for-tat artillery engagement: "In the evening at 10.20pm our guns were to shell the enemy officers billets near La Bassée. The enemy replied to their fire. The first few shells fell short of our billets, but they lengthened, and got very near to where the officers mess was. Lt Col C G Hill, Lieut Green, 2/Lt Colbourne, Captain Large RAMC and Captain Isaac were in the mess at the time. The Commanding Officer Captain [sic] C G Hill said 'Come on boys we will go down to the cellar'. All the Officers started off. Captain Isaac was the first to get down. Just as Lt Col Hill and Lieuts Green and Colbourne were going down the steps, a shell burst with disastrous results. Lt Col C G Hill CMG DSO was killed. Lieut C W Green seriously wounded. Died following day. 2/Lieut E K Colbourne seriously wounded. Died following day."[116]

In these La Bassée trenches, Robert also had to "paddle along trenches which were in most parts 6ins. deep in water, other parts being very sticky or very slippery, as it was a clay district—some very famous brickfields. The rain was very heavy at times—now the heat is quite oppressive… We experienced much shelling in the trenches this last time and tons of 'hate' came over spasmodically every day, especially when we did some damage with a big mine."

By August 1915 he had charge of the battalion trench mortars. On 23rd August, "our snipers and Trench Mortar Battery under 2/Lt Tyson obtained direct hits on an enemy working party at 3.30pm. No further movement observed."[117] On 8th September, he was transferred from the 1st Royal Berks back to the 1st Dorsets as he had to be invalided to England where he had cartilage successfully removed from his leg in an operation. That winter, instead of returning to the Royal Berks or to the Dorsets in the trenches, he was sent to a training course, with a view to becoming

---

[115] Letter of 4th July 1915, *The Bournemouthian*, July 1916.
[116] War Diary, 1st Royal Berkshire Battalion, 26th June 1915.
[117] War Diary, 1st Royal Berkshire Battalion, 23rd August 1915.

an officer in the transport section of the Army Service Corps, which he joined on 27th March 1917, taking up a post in the Mechanical Transport Section. He survived the war.

The Battle of Loos

By July 1915, amidst a grim military and political situation, the B.E.F. had grown to twenty-one divisions, and so a third army was formed, under the command of General Monro. This 3rd Army was separated from the first two British armies by the French 10th Army. The 3rd Army held fifteen miles of the line between Arras and the Somme, whilst the other armies remained further north round Ypres.

On the Eastern Front the Russians had unexpectedly collapsed and pressure needed to be applied in the west to relieve them. Italy had entered the war on the Allied side, but its war against Austria-Hungary had already started to go badly. British and French troops needed to cooperate to break or at least batter the Germans on the Western Front, so German reinforcements could neither be sent east to finish off the Russians nor to support the Austrian successes. The British Eastern Strategy in Gallipoli and Thessalonika had also gone badly awry.

They might need to cooperate, but the French and British commanders were not in a mood to appreciate each other. The French commander, Joffre, saw the British as essentially cannon fodder to support the glorious French breakthrough which he planned to achieve in Champagne. Sir John French was minded to support it with artillery but not with further costly infantry attacks. From London, where in May 1915 the Liberal government had changed to a coalition, Lord Kitchener unrealistically could only see the need for British advances. Therefore, pressure from Kitchener and the ministry required Sir John to cooperate with Joffre when he called for another British attack north from Lens to the La Bassée Canal. The British were again to be supported in their attacks by another French attempt to capture Vimy Ridge on their left. And so the Battle of Loos was initiated.

Haig was not impressed. He had recognised some of the shortfallings of Sir John's approach. That summer he had employed a French teacher, and spent several hours every day learning French – in the end it was said that he could speak French more clearly and accurately than he could speak English! Not only had he began to doubt Sir John's ability to coordinate with their French allies, but also he was hostile to the new military plans, which, to be fair to Sir John, he also had doubts about. In his diary for 7th August, Haig wrote that Joffre "now wishes the British army to attack between the Canal to La Bassée and our Right opposite Loos with the object of taking Hill 70 and the ridge to the north of it near Hulluch. This will cover the left flank of the 10th French Army in its attack on the Vimy plateau. Sir John has decided to comply with General Joffre's wishes, even though he disagrees with the plan. I am therefore to work out proposals for giving effect to the decision, but my attack is to be made chiefly with artillery and I am not to launch a large force of infantry to the attack of objectives which are so strongly held as to be liable to result only in the sacrifice of many lives. That is to say, I am to assist the French by neutralising the Enemy's artillery, and by holding the hostile infantry on my front."[118]

Haig realised that this mining territory – unlike the planned French attack ground of Champagne – was full of natural and man-made obstacles. (As elsewhere, here the Germans held the high ground

---

[118] Haig, Diaries and Letters, op cit, 7th August, p. 134.

and could see and bombard any attackers.) He insisted that no attack should take place until the British scientists had supplied his men with poison gas of their own to send ahead of them against the defending Germans – who meanwhile, anticipating a much talked of attack, had a month to strengthen and prepare their defences. This battle was to see the first significant use of the new 'Service' Army.

For ten days, the French fought an expensive, but ultimately unsuccessful campaign in Champagne. As August drew into September, French pressure meant Haig had further to revise his plans to allow for an infantry assault. Several Old Boys of Bournemouth School fought in this battle, with very varied experiences. These included Reginald Fairley of the East Kents ('the Buffs'), Arthur Bolton and Henry Hollies of the 15th London ('Civil Service Battalion'), Joseph Henry of the Middlesex Regiment, Harold Deans of the King's Own Scottish Borderers, Maurice Hellier of the 6th Shropshire Light Infantry, and Joseph G.C. Jones of the Wiltshires.

Meanwhile, the British had worked up their response to, and potential to use, poison gas.

David Lever was probably involved. David was born in 1895, and he and his older brother Abraham (known as Abie) were both briefly members of the school from November 1908 to March 1909. In Glasgow, David continued his studies and became a chemist. After the German use of poison gas at the Second Battle of Ypres, there was an urgent need in the Army to develop both counter-measures and also a gas capacity for the British forces. Consequently, chemists suddenly found themselves much in demand. In July 1915 he joined the Army at Chatham in Kent. The circumstances were unusual. His papers were marked. "Chemist. Enlisted for promotion forthwith to Rank of Corporal @ 2/6 per day plus 6 per day Engineers Pay." Within days he was in France; he left Chatham on 11th July and arrived in France the next day. His Army file stated that his military character had been "Very good. Conduct very satisfactory during his 148 Days service". Presumably the urgent need for him was to act as a chemist with the new chlorine gas the British were preparing to use. He returned to the United Kingdom on 10th November, and two weeks later was discharged on 26th November under King's Regulations (Number 25) which stated "his service no longer required".

As a result of the work of chemists, gas was available to the British by early September, though not in the quantities which Haig had earlier stipulated. Haig then had to wait for the wind to shift to an easterly direction to blow the poison gas onto the Germans – not swirl back westwards onto his own men. Gas masks were very much in their infancy, and terribly difficult to see or hear much through, let alone to fight in to deliver an assault. Doubts continued about the wind direction to the last moment. Even when, on 25th September, the wind was suitable – measured by the steady trail of cigarette smoke at 05.45 – Haig and Foch could not agree on the time of the assault. Haig decided to start the attack at 06.45. But Foch, whose artillery was meant to be a decisive element covering the British advance, refused to start until his gunners had had several hours of daylight so that they could be sure of their targets. Foch and Haig did agree that Sir John French's decision to hold the reserve sixteen miles further west, out of danger from the Germans, was too far back to be help. To compound the fault, Sir John chose as his battle headquarters a place from which he could have no telephone contact with Haig, to whom the conduct of the assault had been entrusted.

To distract and confuse the Germans it was decided to launch a diversionary attack a little further north near Armentières. Henry Budden went back into action in that attack. This attack was intended to mislead the Germans in the unsuccessful hope that they would not reinforce their defences at Loos. This attack began with four days of artillery bombardment, and then the assault was made on 25th September, the same day that the main battle began. Henry's 2nd Lincolnshire Battalion was tasked for an attack "as an adjunct to the Battle of Loos. The aim was 'to capture about 1200 yards of the German front line system opposite the re-entrant and link them up with our own line at the Well Farm and Le Bridoux salients, thereby both shortening and strengthening our position'... A four day bombardment was used. By day three it was noted that the German retaliatory fire had increased."[119]

The war diary of the 2nd Rifle Brigade Battalion (which attacked alongside Henry's battalion) described their objectives as "the line of forts, on a twelve hundred yard frontage" and explained how Brigadier-General R.B. Stephens "in addition to the artillery... brought up two trench mortar batteries into the Well Farm and Bridoux salients, and caused six 18 pounders to be dug into the front line parapet – two in the Bridoux salient; one in the Well Farm salient; two west of Well Farm and one east of Le Bridoux – to fire direct on the enemy's parapet."[120] The brigadier "rejected the idea of gas, but arranged for smoke to screen the flanks, and laid two shallow mines which, when exploded, would facilitate the digging of a communication trench to join up with the captured trenches."[121]

The weather was bad all day – mist and rain. When the 2nd Lincolnshire Battalion lined up, Henry was in 'Z' Company at the front left of the attack. Unfortunately, "The assault force got forward at 3.30am on the 25th... Smoke discharges on the flanks were ineffective because of the wind. Two mines were blown but did not break the surface, so they too were ineffective... At 4.25am, the barrage increased. The 18-pdrs also began firing at the German parapets. The infantry kept forward under cover of the bombardment then leapt to the assault when the barrage lifted."[122] The barrage was an intense five minutes shelling of the two front German trenches, and stopped at 4.30a.m., a minute before the whistles had blown and Henry and the others went over the top.

"The assault was carried out as follows. At 4.30am Z Company moved forward and rushed the Bridoux Fort opposite, immediately obtaining a footing in it and bombing parties were sent forward to take the 2nd line trenches, which was done."[123] This second line "was heavily manned by the Germans and a protracted bombing engagement ensued."[124] The problem was "a 200 yard section of trench between the Rifle Brigade and Berkshire companies that remained in German hands. It was linked to a communication trench through which the Germans could funnel forward counterattack troops."[125] "The pressure on Z Company became severe."[126]

At 6.30a.m., the captured second line had to be abandoned under pressure from German counter-attacks, particularly as they used their communication trenches to get grenade throwers up close to where Henry and the others were fighting. The British 'bombers', however, were having

---

[119] Official History of the 8th Division.
[120] War Diary of the 2nd Rifle Brigade.
[121] ibid.
[122] Official History of the 8th Division.
[123] War Diary, 2nd Lincolnshire Battalion, 25th September 1915.
[124] War Diary of 1st Royal Irish Rifles.
[125] Official History of the 8th Division.
[126] War Diary, 2nd Lincolnshire Battalion, 25th September 1915.

difficulties with re-supply and with the rain, which was affecting the fuses. On the right and in the centre, the German attacks were held. Pressure increased on the left but reinforcements of two companies from the 1st Royal Irish Rifles were fed into the left sector and later three grenadier platoons of the 24th Infantry Brigade were sent up at 8a.m. as reinforcements, but despite this the situation deteriorated as the morning advanced. The supply of bombs gave out completely.

At some point early in the attack, Henry was wounded in the right hand and, after being temporarily attended to, was told to go to the first aid station. Instead of that he "pluckily returned to his men".[127] Henry's company tried to hold a line on the outside edge of the German fort, but when their grenades had run out and German reinforcements had increased it could not be held.

Henry had refused the chance to go back to where men like Richard Barfoot and the 24th Field Ambulance were in action in support of such first aid stations. Richard's unit established an advanced dressing station, a divisional collecting station, and a dressing station even as the preliminary bombardment began. On 25th September, the first wounded began coming in, "a steady flow of wounded till 9.0pm." By midnight they had treated nine officers and three hundred and fourteen men, some of them their own men. "Work here was carried out under heavy shell fire… Many casualties among troops while retiring from German trenches… Our work very hard because of water formed in trenches." [128]

The British centre gave way under increased German pressure. Although the right flank held out longer, reinforced with two trench mortars, once contact with the centre companies was lost, it too withdrew. The battalion had tried to hold out against six separate German counter-attacks. At some point in all this fighting, Henry was killed. His body was recovered, and he is buried at White City Cemetery, Bois Grenier. In the school magazine that December, Henry's life was summed up, "He was a credit to the School, a splendid fellow, so thoughtful and considerate for everyone, and loved by all who met him."[129]

Maurice Hellier was also involved in this diversionary attack. Maurice, born in 1896, left school in 1913. By that time he had been a member of the school since 1906 and a member of the O.T.C. for over five years. He had been a school prefect and a sergeant. On 8th August 1914, Maurice applied for a commission in the Army and on 17th September 1914, with no requirement for further training, he was commissioned and joined the 6th King's Shropshire Light Infantry Battalion, 60th Brigade, 20th Division. On 21st February 1915, Maurice was promoted to lieutenant, and landed with the battalion at Boulogne on 23rd July 1915, after a rough crossing. From 11th August, the battalion began their experience of the trenches and suffered their first casualty, from a German trench mortar. When more men of the battalion went into the trenches two days later, two fell dead with gun shots to the head, whilst a third was wounded in the neck. These were the normal casualties of battalions entering the trenches for the first time, not remembering the importance of keeping their heads down. Soon they moved to Laventie, north-west of the Aubers Ridge where, after trench defence and supplying working parties for manpower to support the Royal Engineers, they took part in the diversionary assault.

They were to support the 12th Rifle Brigade, and to dig a communication trench to link the British

---

[127] *The Bournemouthian*, December 1915.
[128] War Diary of the 24th Field Ambulance, September 25th 1915.
[129] *The Bournemouthian*, December 1915.

front line with the German one, which had been occupied by the assault battalions. This they tried to do, but were under heavy rifle and machine gun fire, as well as severe shelling. Two half companies were even hurled into the action against a strong counter-attack, under very heavy fire, without much support – and held their ground for some time under difficult conditions. "The K.S.L.I. company and some men of the R.B. held their ground for a short time, under difficult conditions shooting down many of the attacking Germans. At about 12.30 p.m. they were forced to retire. This withdrawal was covered by detachments of the K.S.L.I. and R.B. from the reverse slope of the German parapet, these men held until the Germans were only yards away. They got back by working along ditches which ran by the side of Winchester road. The sap was also used by the retiring troops, and helped reduce casualties. Major Wood of the 6th K.S.L.I., who spoke Hindustani, managed to rally some 300 men of the Indian Division."[130] Maurice survived, though three officers and sixty-three of their men had been killed or wounded. The other Old Bournemouthians involved fought in the main battle itself.

Despite the diversion, the Battle of Loos turned out to be a disaster. In the northern sector, the wind swirled round and blew gas back at the British. Medical officer Captain J.C. Dunn of the Royal Welsh Fusiliers described the confusion: "Our artillery treated the German front line with rapid fire; the shooting was good – but the garrison had been withdrawn to the support line. At the same time the Special Gas Company opened the cocks of the cylinders. The unfavourable wind had been reported earlier to the Brigadier, and he applied to have the gas countermanded – without avail. What wind there was caused it to drift along the line from right to left and to fall back into the trench. Men in the front line got mouthfuls of it, and some became panicky. Gas helmets were adjusted. While the wearers were being stifled in them, the German artillery opened on the crowded trench with well-aimed fire which caused casualties. The first rearward stream of walking wounded began, and the scared, including many of the gas merchants, went with them. Some disorder had been caused, but the Old Line steadied itself. Scaling ladders were put into position, and other final preparations made. The infantry assault was not to start until 6.30 – 'to let the gas act'. During the time of waiting to go over German shells were bursting on the front line and communication trenches. A portion of the Middlesex climbed out of their trench ahead of the timetable to escape the gas, and began a forward movement. The Argylls climbed out on time from both front and

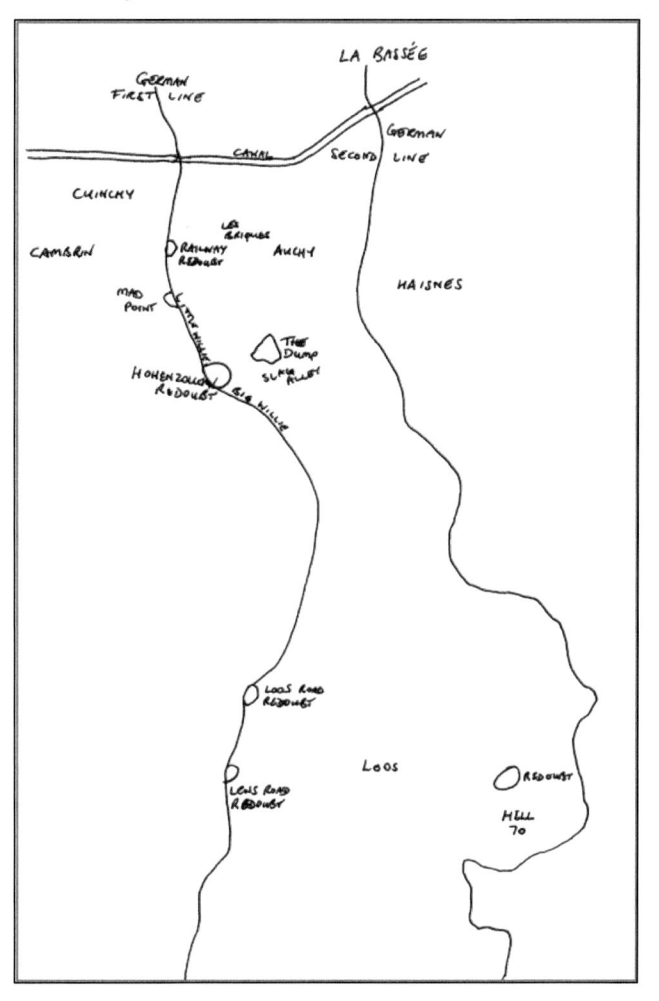

---
[130] War Diary, 12th Rifle Brigade, 25th September 1915.

support trenches; the cover given by craters let some of the first wave get to the German wire; the second wave dashed forward and was checked by their own front line and wire.".[131]

On the left wing, around La Bassée and north of the canal, the British made little impact on the German defences. In the centre there were some patchy successes. At the heart of the northernmost part of the battleground was a German redoubt, the Railway Redoubt. A hero to emerge from fighting in front of this redoubt was Second Lieutenant Joseph ('J.L.') Henry, of the Middlesex Regiment.

Curiously, almost all the records seem simply to refer to Joseph Henry just as J.L. Henry. This must be because he preferred (like his father) to use his initials rather than his forename. In 1922, when the *British Book of Jewry* was published, Joseph was listed amongst those Jews to be honoured for serving since 1914, though on his Army forms he stated his religion as Protestant. He was born in Argentina in 1896, the son of a consulting engineer and at the school from 1905 to 1906. On 27th August 1914, he had enlisted in the 14th London Battalion. He embarked from Southampton on 19th March 1915, joining his battalion in the line on 23rd March but on 22nd April 1915 he was sent away with the 'flu. He was sent via 275 Field Ambulance from 1st Casualty Clearing Station and was taken to 14th General Hospital at Boulogne the next day. He was then sent to Marlborough. He re-joined his battalion on 17th May 1915. He was formally gazetted 2nd lieutenant on 11th September 1915 to the 1st Middlesex Battalion, otherwise known as 'the Duke of Cambridge's Own' which he joined on 23rd August. This battalion was in the 19th Brigade, 2nd Division.

From 6th to 11th September, the battalion underwent 'special training' for the coming attack, followed by a quiet spell in the trenches near La Bassée. On 23rd September they moved into the Cambrin trenches near Loos to ready themselves to attack. J.L. was in 'C' Company, one of the three companies designated to attack at 'Zero' hour. The 1st Middlesex occupied the right-hand side of the brigade attack: "At 5.50 a.m. a gas attack was opened on the German trenches for 40 minutes. This was not, however, very successful, and did not have much effect."[132] Although the gas did not drift back onto them in the same way as onto the Highlanders on the far left of the brigade front, it did drift into the many craters which pitted No Man's Land in front of the Middlesex men.

When the whistles blew at 6.30a.m., Companies 'A' to 'C' of 1st Middlesex went over the top and almost instantly were met by a tremendous storm of bullets from the German rifles and machine guns. So confident were the German defenders that there are reports of some even standing on their parapets in order to fire with greater force and accuracy. They got about one hundred yards forward but the surviving Middlesex men had no choice but to lie down in whatever cover they could find. The fourth company, 'D' Company, and their support battalion, 2nd Argyll and Sutherland Highlanders, tried to reinforce them but suffered heavily.

Some Middlesex bombers, assisted by remnants of 'D' Company, did reach forward craters – only to be fired upon by their own, British, artillery. It is hard to think of a more horrifying set of circumstances than being smashed by machine guns, risking poison gas when taking cover, and then to be hit from your own side. A desperate message sent from the 1st Middlesex Battalion Headquarters and received at Brigade Headquarters read, "7.30 a.m. Reported casualties probably 400, but impossible to tell – have observed an enormous number fall." Despair escalated. "7.55.

---

[131] Captain J.C. Dunn, *The War the Infantry Knew*, pp. 153-154.
[132] War Diary, 1st Middlesex Battalion, 25th September 1915.

Must shell German first line – Our men are all out in front – Almost all must be killed or wounded – Please shell first line." [133] J.L. Henry was in the thick of this. About 8a.m. Battalion HQ received a dramatic message from Lieutenant A.D. Hill, commanding 'C' Company: "Enemy very strong in front with machine-guns and rifles. 'C' Company strength only about 30 or 35 men. Impossible to advance on account of machine guns. Mr. Henry and 3 men alone remain out of two platoons. Can we have reinforcements?"

At 8.12a.m., Colonel Rowley in charge of the 1st Middlesex responded: "Hang on where you are until reinforced." The diary contains a scrap of paper which is muddy and blood-stained with the despairing message, "8.30 a.m. 'B' Company attack held up 100 yards out of own trench... few men stand fast."

The artillery was ordered to bombard the German trenches at 9a.m. in an attempt to restart the assault, partly in response to the desperate messages which the attacking officers were sending back to battalion and brigade HQs. The new plan was for the 2nd Royal Welsh Fusiliers to send in two companies to help out the 1st Middlesex. As these men also were smashed by the defensive barrage of machine gun and rifle fire, that plan failed as well and the attack had to be abandoned.

Eventually, what was left of the battalion crawled back and the battalion was withdrawn from the battle. Initially, the roll call listed only eighty-four men fit to answer their names to the surviving officers, though others managed to crawl back under cover of the darkness, including the heroes of the grenade group and 'D' Company who incredibly had even tried to push on forward and reached the German wire before their officer was killed. They had managed to set up, and use to good effect, a machine gun at the crater, but had to stop when the machine gun officer was himself wounded. That night, and the next day, men crawled in and stretcher-bearers were able to recover more men, and there was some optimism that others might have been recovered through the casualty dressing stations of other brigades. Ten officers had been killed and another died of his wounds two days later. Seven officers had been wounded. Of the ordinary soldiers, seventy-three were killed, two hundred and eighty-five wounded, whilst sixty-six were missing. In addition, seven more had been gassed and two were suffering from concussion from the shells. There is no surprise in the fact that the battalion took no further part in the Battle of Loos, but were sent into brigade reserve instead, whilst some new men were drafted in as replacements for the lost. Joseph, however, though he had survived the battle apparently unscathed, was about to suffer unexpected consequences, and his military career to change radically.

After the battle, Joseph had gone on leave. On 1st January 1916, Sir John French mentioned him in his final set of dispatches: "30th November, 1915. In accordance with the last paragraph of my Despatch of the 15th October, 1915, I have the honour to bring to notice the names of those whom I recommend for gallant and distinguished service in the field." [134] J.L. Henry was included in that list.

But for Joseph, still on leave, life had changed dramatically. "He came home on ordinary leave from France, and while at home he had a severe nerve break down: very restless; could not concentrate; and was very emotional. He is now better of these symptoms." [135] Joseph actually had two problems. The nervous breakdown he had experienced whilst at home did gradually improve; but

---

[133] War Diary, 19th Brigade, 25th September 1915 (appendix).
[134] *London Gazette Supplement*, 1st January 1916, citing dispatch dated 30th November 1915.
[135] Army File of J.L. Henry, WO 339/39789, including Medical Board report, 19th January 1916.

examination had shown up congenital health problems which were unresolved. For a time he was at the Hospital for Officers, Tidworth, until at least March 1916. Officially his breakdown, classed as neurasthenia, meant nervous exhaustion and debility, did slowly improve. However, he had severe headaches and vomiting. His consultant warned that the effect whilst on active service could be fatal; the medical authorities were worried about him undergoing physical exertion, such as route marching in England or active service in France, though he was passed fit for light home duties, for which he reported to 2/5th Royal Warwicks on 14th May 1916, and as his nerves improved he was on 1st August passed fit for Home Service, but as permanently unfit for General Service. A few days later on 6th August 1916 he was posted as O.C. No.8 Eastern Command, Non-Combatant Corps.

Almost immediately, Joseph began to look for a way to get back into action. In late August he began the process of asking for a transfer to the Royal Flying Corps. In September 1916 he was actively searched for by the School of Wireless of the Royal Flying Corps (R.F.C.). They wanted him because he had knowledge of the work of an adjutant, having acted as one for a month or so, and was also a wireless operator. Then followed a period of negotiation within the Army: His services as Officer Commanding No.8 N-C Corps were valued, and there was delay until the Army decided that he would be better employed within the R.F.C. On 6th November 1916, he was posted as Acting Adjutant at the School for Wireless Operators, R.F.C. On 1st January 1917, he was promoted to full lieutenant and went to Hendon on 9th May 1917, having – the day before – been passed as medically fit to be a pilot. As a flying officer in the Royal Flying Corps, with effect from 21st September, his new allegiance was to the newly formed Royal Air Force in which he was a flying officer until the end of the war, and on the R.A.F. list published that year his position was confirmed as Lieutenant (Aeroplane and Seaplane Officer) from 1st April 1918.

Meanwhile, on the right, southern, end of the battle there was more progress – at first. The 47th Division (London Territorials) and 15th Division (New Scottish Army) successfully attacked under cover of shells and gas, capturing the town of Loos. Old Bournemouthians Arthur Bolton and Henry Hollies were part of this initial success. They had enlisted in the Civil Service Rifles, the 15th London Battalion. For the Battle of Loos, this battalion was part of 47th (2nd London) Division and its 140th (4th London) Brigade.

Arthur Bolton (born 1897, at school from 1907-1911) and the older Henry Hollies (born 1890, at school 1903-1905) had both joined the Civil Service, and then had joined the Civil Service Rifles. This battalion had mobilised in the heart of government, at Somerset House in August 1914. Henry Hollies landed with the battalion at Le Havre on 18th March 1915. It was brigaded alongside the 8th London Battalion – the Post Office Rifles - and the 6th and 7th London Battalions on 11th May. Arthur arrived to join Henry in France on 18th August 1915. They had had a lively time in the trenches as the battalion took casualties from many 'aerial torpedoes' before being withdrawn to prepare for the Battle of Loos. Arthur was promoted corporal.

These 'aerial torpedoes' were heavy German explosive shells which could do a lot of damage. The term 'aerial torpedo' was commonly used to mean large shells fired by heavy trench mortars or by howitzers. Their impact could be dramatic: "27th August… aerial torpedoes… did a lot of damage… We had some 50 land within 100 yards of Battalion Headquarters which were in a sort of crater and up to this date thought to be safe from shell fire. But these torpedoes appear to fall at an angle of 80° when they are fired from 400 yards range. Their explosives are very powerful & big pit props were displaced & thrown a distance of over 50 yards."[136]

As they prepared for the battle, their battalion found itself on 18th-19th September "carrying gas cylinders into the new gas trench and placing them in position. It required a good deal of organisation but the men did well and it was successfully carried out without incident."[137]

The 47th Division was placed on the front line, at the southern end of the battle front with the objective of capturing the town of Loos itself. The weather conditions were daunting: "More rain and the trenches awful. A bad look out for tomorrow's attack."[138] Yet the division managed, in conjunction with the 15th Scottish Division immediately north of them, to take all its objectives on the first day with relatively light casualties. The division not only took Loos but stormed through to capture Hill 70 beyond.

The 15th London Battalion was in support – and suffered badly considering the overall success of the day: "We supplied a party of 25 men to carry over bombs. They had a bad time crossing and only 4 were neither killed nor wounded: immediately they left our front trench they came under a heavy fire from the right. A most striking event of the attack was the absolute silence of the German guns as our first 4 lines went over. There was also not enough wire cut. The Germans had machine guns concentrated on all places where it was cut and our men lost heavily at these points. The gas seemed to do no actual damage and not a single dead German killed by gas was found opposite us though without doubt it frightened many: the prisoners who were brought in certainly did not appear to be in any way effected and except for a very few oxygen respirators the only thing they had was a wad of cotton wool."[139]

The trenches the battalion held were too shallow – only five feet deep in places and this left them vulnerable to German shelling, and they were on the receiving end of gas shells themselves. Their smoke helmets were useless, and men gained relief from fresh air and by putting cream on their eyes. They suffered again when they advanced under heavy shell fire to consolidate the captured old German front and support trenches, and as they tried desperately to place new wire for the trenches and to bury their dead. After a brief period of relief, they returned to the trenches, first digging new communication trenches and then going back into support on the old German lines. Once again the shelling was very heavy and things became even more difficult when they took over the new front line from the 14th October. When the Germans heavily bombarded their trench on the afternoon of 16th October 1915, Henry Hollies was wounded badly enough to be sent home to recover.

On 21st October, Arthur too was wounded – less seriously (the wound was regarded as 'slight'). He described it later as having been incurred whilst repelling a strong German counter-attack. By now he was acting company sergeant major. His 'slight wound' was a bullet which hit him in the left shoulder and travelled downwards before exiting several inches below. Every British soldier carried a first aid kit in his pack, which included bandages and two patches – one for the entry and one for the exit wound. One of his comrades bandaged Arthur up, and asked if he should call for support to help him back to the advanced dressing station. Arthur – rather unwisely, but certainly

---

[136] War Diary, 1/15th London (Civil Service) Battalion, 27th and 28th August 1915.
[137] War Diary, 1/15th London (Civil Service) Battalion, 18th September 1915.
[138] War Diary, 1/15th London (Civil Service) Battalion, 24th September 1915.
[139] War Diary, 1/ 15th London (Civil Service) Battalion, 25th September 1915.

bravely – said he felt he could cope alone. "I knew the way over the top, but not by trench, but I hadn't gone 100 yards before the Huns started sending over shrapnel. I took no notice of this until a shell burst quite close, whereupon I took to the trench. To make matters worse it began to rain. It was about midnight and the trench was filling with water. Both my arms were wrapped inside my coat, which—owing to my wound—I could not wear in the usual way, and it was quite dark, so I found it very difficult to get along. After wandering about for an hour, wet through and altogether in a pitiable state, I somehow got in the reserve trench which was occupied by another London Battalion. Explaining my plight to the sentry, he got their stretcher-bearers out of 'bed.' They were jolly decent chaps, and did what they could to ease the pain, taking me to their dressing station where I arrived about 4.30 a.m. absolutely 'done' and quite ready to faint. However, 'All's well that ends well.' The bullet is a fine souvenir to bring home. I have the satisfaction of knowing I killed one or more of the enemy, and when I am quite well I shall try my luck again."[140]

Meanwhile the Scots had pushed on further to the town of Lens, causing near panic amongst the German defence who prepared to retreat if their hastily scratched final defence should break. It didn't because there were no reinforcements to swell the battered numbers of Highlanders who had come so near to victory. (Sir John did not give permission for the reserve to advance until 1.20p.m. and when they did move forward it was at half normal speed because of congestion behind the battle). The Scots were smashed when the Germans counter-attacked.

One of those who were sent in to try to deal with the counter-attack in the northern sector was Reginald Fairley. Born in 1890, with his brother Gerald (who became an officer in the Merchant Navy) he was at school about 1904 to 1906. Like his younger brother, before the war he was a mate in the Merchant Navy, but when war broke out he joined his father's old regiment: the 2nd East Kent Battalion (the 'Buffs'), 85th Brigade, 28th Division. He landed in France on 1st June 1915. On September 27th his battalion moved up to support the attack..

By this stage at Loos, the German counter-attack had regained Hill 70, giving the Germans excellent scope to observe the British efforts and to bombard them with their artillery. Haig threw in fresh troops to try to regain lost ground. "We left Béthune for the trenches on the 27th September at 8a.m. We had arrived at that place by a forced march of 20 miles the day before, and as we had not had much sleep that night were none too fresh. Off we started and every step seemed to bring the thunder of the guns nearer and by the noise and continual stream of ambulances full of wounded we knew that we were in for a hot time of it. Three miles from Béthune we began to come across the remnants of the regiments who had taken part in the first attack. They were bivouacked on either side of the road. In one place a couple of hundred of one regiment, in another place a hundred odd of another. They were quite a contrast to our men. Their faces were haggard and unshaven, their clothes smothered in mud. They must have been through a terrible time, poor fellows. Later we met a transport wagon driven by a man wearing our 'Buffs' badge. Our fellows called out to know what battalion he belonged to. I could hear the fellows murmuring in the ranks behind me: 'By Jove! There must have been something doing.' At noon we reached a village, where a road turned sharply to the left at right angles to the main road. The traffic here was congested, and was being regulated by a sergeant of M.M. Police, and a fine job he must have had, for there was a continual stream of empty limbers, and general service wagons, ambulances, and big mechanical transports, full of wounded, coming from the firing line down both roads, whilst

---

[140] *The Bournemouthian*, April 1916.

another stream of full transport wagons and empty ambulances was coming from Béthune. The scene was one of general uproar, the transport drivers cursing and cracking their whips, the horses snorting and plunging. In the midst of it the mounted policeman sat as cool as if on point duty at home, stopping one stream of traffic with one uplifted hand, while with the other he waved on another. Over all sounded the thunderous roar of the artillery, as close on the left of the road the continual bright flashes showed one of our batteries blazing away at the enemy. We turned into the road on the left, and marched into a field, piled arms, and got ready for the mid-day meal. Then two companies of ours, and two of another regiment were sent up into the reserve trenches. I and two or three others were sent for by the Adjutant, and were told to go up and find out the general lay of the trenches we were to take over. At that moment the whistling scream of a shell was heard, and the Adjutant yelled: 'Lie down every one.' Down we went, being pretty used to shell fire for four months in various parts of the line in France and Belgium. The shell burst close beside our field cooker, killing the cook and wounding four men and the Company Q.M.S., and incidentally smothering myself and the other fellows in dust and earth.

"We had hardly regained our feet when we heard the sound of another shell. Down I went again, and as I dropped I glanced at the roadway along which the stream of waggons were still passing At the top of a loaded ration limber I saw a bright flash, followed by a burst of black smoke. The limber disappeared, and I ducked my head to avoid, if possible, the flying fragments. When the danger was over I looked again along the road. All that remained of the limber was a few scattered fragments of wood and four wheels. A few yards farther along were the motionless forms of two drivers, the horses had disappeared, goodness knows where. A few moments later another shell burst close and our transport horses started to bolt; the field cooker went into a ditch, and the horses galloped away with the broken pieces of shafts hanging to their harness. One of the battalion water-carts near me turned completely over, the horse attached to it began lashing out in all directions, but the driver stuck to his charge, and succeeded in getting it free from the cart, on which the horse made off across the field with the driver hanging to its head. He succeeded in stopping it, and our Colonel sang out, 'Well done, driver!' We slept that night on our waterproof sheets, with our overcoats for covering, as we'd done many a time before with a nice soaking drizzle to make things more comfortable. Our orders to proceed to the trenches were countermanded, and we went back to our respective companies.

"At 1.30 a.m. we were roused, and ordered to proceed at once to the trenches. The rain had stopped. It was a beautiful moonlight night, or rather morning, with only an occasional rifle shot to remind one that there was a war on. We followed the road for about half an hour, and then entered the communication trench leading to the particular trenches we were to occupy. We received orders from the trench headquarters that we were to make a charge as soon as we got into position, which was before 5.30 a.m., as we were to go 'over the top' at that time. Owing to our imperfect knowledge of these trenches we were not near our position till 8 a.m. In the meantime we halted for breakfast."[141]

Pivotal to the successful German defence in the northern sector south of Railway Redoubt was another, bigger, strongpoint known as the Hohenzollern Redoubt. This was their strongest defensive work on the whole battlefield. It jutted forward into No Man's Land, and its main purpose was to protect a flat-topped slag heap which the British christened 'the Dump', a twenty

---

[141] *The Bournemouthian*, December 1916.

The Hohenzollern Redoubt and the Dump

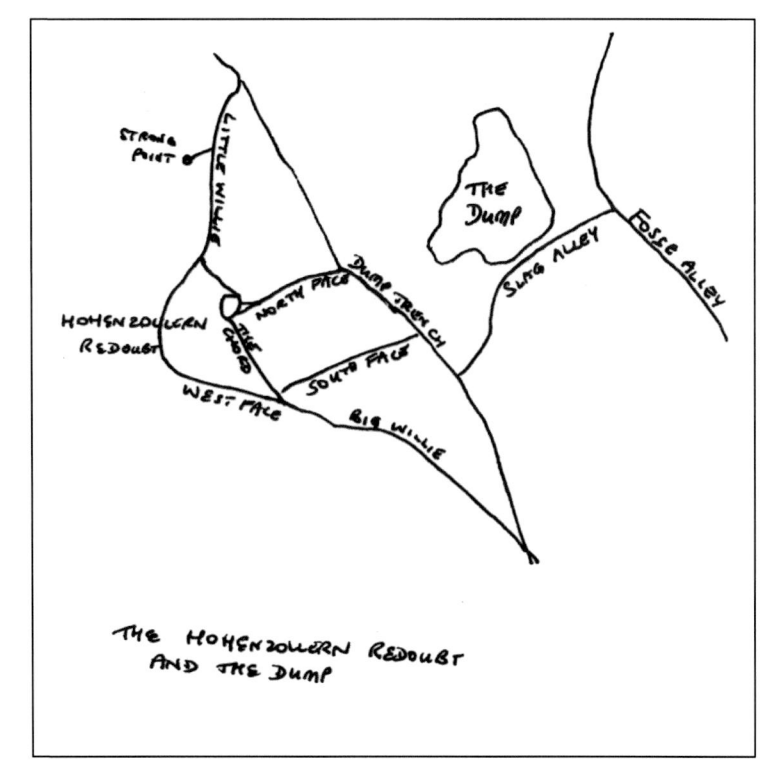

feet high vantage point. The Germans were determined to hold this redoubt.

The Scots of 26th Brigade, 9th (Scottish) Division had managed to capture both the redoubt and the Dump in the first hour of the battle, despite ferocious German defence, but the British were driven back off the Dump and back to the eastern edge of the redoubt on 27th September. The Germans then made repeated attacks to try to recapture the Hohenzollern Redoubt.

Reginald and his men were sent in to recapture the Dump. "Then came the order to 'Off packs and leave 'em in the trench; load rifles and fix bayonets.' We were to proceed to our position and be ready to charge at 9.30 a.m., after ten minutes bombarding by the artillery. We started off, and soon came across evidences of the earlier fighting. We had to pass under the German barbed wire by means of a trench which had been dug after the German first and second line trenches had been captured a few days before. Our troops were holding the second line of German trenches. The poor beggars had been in over 48 hours, and their water-bottles had given out, and as they were terribly thirsty we gave them a pull from our bottles.

"We were now told to get into a sort of ditch, about 4ft. deep, in front of the trench they were holding, and charge from that. We were to go straight ahead for about 20 yards, then wheel to the left, and clear the Germans off the top of a large heap of slag. We had to go in a crouching attitude to get into the ditch. An old Boer War man led the way, I was second. We were to make our way up the trench till our company was all in. That ditch was a sight: blood everywhere, great clots and splashes on the sides, and pools of it in the bottom.

"At last we were ready, crouched, waiting for the word; and how my heart beat. I peeped up to get a look at the ground in front, but a bullet kicked up the earth close to my face, so I got down again. At last a shout sounded from the right which acted like an electric shock. With one bound we were over the bank and racing across the open, yelling like only Kentish men can. The air was filled with a whistling sound, and the crackle of rifle and machine guns showed that the Germans were ready for us. Some of them ran out of their trenches, and started bolting to get behind the slag heap. I dropped on one knee and bowled one over. Our fellows were falling in all directions. A couple of seconds later I dropped again, and potted another German. Lots of our fellows were doing the same.

"Then we went for the slag heap. Up the steep ascent we went cheering like mad. The Germans didn't wait for us, but got down on the opposite side into a trench, where they waited for us with machine guns and bombs and grenades. We rushed across to the edge of the coal, and had to drop and take cover, for the Germans poured a heavy volley into us as soon as we appeared on the edge. I fired my rifle into the thick of them, and had the satisfaction of seeing one drop, so I told the fellow on my right as we lay on the coal. He said: 'I must have a pot at them.' 'For God's sake be careful how you look over,' I said, 'as they are waiting for us.' Up he got on his knees, gave a little sob, and pitched over backwards into a shell crater behind him. I peeped into the crater to see what was wrong with him. He lay head downwards. I never felt upset; I guess I was too excited. I now found time to look round me. Out of 200 men only about 30 had succeeded in reaching the slag heap, and some of them were wounded.

"I had a bullet hole through my pocket, and the strap of my haversack was shot away. We lay waiting for some of our bombers to come up and bomb the Germans out of the trenches in front of us. Only one officer was left with us. He crawled away to the right to see if there was any chance of us doing anything; I never saw him again. I expect he was killed. We then noticed a German peeping over the coal 30 yards away. The fellow on my left said to me, 'You shoot, and I'll see what effect it has.' So I waited, with my rifle trained on the spot. Up came his head again. I sighted carefully and pressed the trigger. His head gave a little jerk. 'Good shot,' said my companion, 'you got him dead between the eyes.' I felt quite delighted. Then I got another fellow farther away on the left. One of our bombers managed to reach us. He started lobbing bombs over the edge. We heard them burst, followed by shrieks and groans. It was then I got my first wound. A rifle bullet from a German sniper passed through my left hand and came out at the base of the thumb. The man near me sang out, 'I'm hit.' The back of his hand was torn across by a piece of shell. We crawled to a crater and bound each other's wounds up with our field dressing. While we were there another fellow crawled into the crater. 'Good heavens,' he said, 'isn't this awful. I believe we three are the only ones able to move. What shall we do?' So we held a confab. We agreed that the best plan would be to leave the slag heap and bolt for the trench that we had seen the Germans run out of. We got off the heap all right, and made a dash for the trench. Immediately we heard rifles crack, and I felt a stinging pain in my left thigh, and knew I was hit. I thought I would drop and take cover. Before I could do so I felt the shock of a bullet in my right arm; that caused me to drop my rifle. At the same instant two bullets struck me in the left shoulder, and as I flung myself to the ground a bullet coming from the right flank entered my throat just under my chin and exploded. My head went up with a jerk, and I felt the jaw-bones smash; then came blackness. I told you in my letters from Germany that it was a grenade that did the damage to my jaw, but that was because the Germans would not allow us to mention explosive bullets. They use them frequently, though they swore they never used such things. But I know what knocked me out. When I recovered consciousness I had a confused notion of someone talking to me. On looking up I found the trench in front of me was full of Germans, two of whom were covering me with their rifles, while a German corporal told me I had better crawl into the trench if I didn't want another bullet in me." Reginald Failey remained a prisoner of war until the end of the war.

Richard Clark was also there with the 3rd Royal Fusiliers, within yards of Reginald. When, on the morning of 27th September, the Germans had recaptured Fosse 8, the slag heap, and most of the redoubt, previous orders were suddenly changed at 2.30a.m. "to counter attack at once as this line had been retaken by the Germans. Orders were given verbally to Coy Commanders."[142] The battalion was split into its respective companies for this advance to the Hohenzollern Redoubt and even General Pereira threw himself into the battle – leading the battalion from the front until he was shot that afternoon. The brigade major also fell about the same time. So many men were wounded that the communication trench they were trying to use to reach the redoubt became

---
[142] War Diary, 3rd Royal Fusiliers, 27th September 1915, describing this battle (and subsequent extracts).

congested. But by midnight they had managed to regain three sides of the redoubt with the East Surreys holding the western side. Steady rain fell on them, and the casualties mounted.

These East Surreys included Cecil Hughes. In the early hours of 28th September, Cecil and the 2nd East Surrey Battalion pushed forward "attacking the enemy with bombs in an attempt to drive them out of the trench".[143] The next morning, 29th September, the Germans counter-attacked with grenades. They were held back by Number 3 Company of the 3rd Royal Fusiliers. In turn the British counter-attacked, with the Buffs and the Middlesex Battalions attacking the Dump, but this led to heavy German shelling which drove them back to the original British front line. As they retreated they streamed through the 3rd Royal Fusiliers who were holding the southern and western faces of the redoubt, followed by German assault troops. The Royal Fusiliers' own bombing (grenade) group and Number 2 Company tried to hold the Germans back, and forced the Germans back up the southern face of the redoubt, though they could not dislodge them entirely. The Germans then kept up a heavy shelling of the redoubt. A terrible fight followed, but Number 4 Company came forward to support the East Surreys. "The men being much shaken and owing to shortage of bombs began to retire. Lieut Fleming Sandes… rallied his men, jumped on the parapet and drove the enemy back and occupied the original position. Some men of the 3rd Royal Fusiliers took part in this counter attack. But this left the right of the battalion in the air, so two platoons of 'D' Company were pushed up in support. A counter attack was made on our right by York and Lancaster regiment which restored the original position."[144] German grenades thrown on their right down the south face of the redoubt and heavy shelling stopped the 3rd Royal Fusiliers getting very far forward.

Then the Germans attacked down the south face and forced the Middlesex Battalion back, leaving the flank of the Fusiliers exposed to enfilade attack.

Things now became even more desperate. The Germans attacked again, throwing grenades as they pushed down the western face and drove the Fusiliers back. An attempt to counter-attack was made by the 1st Company of the Yorks and Lancs Battalion who were in support, but this attack was repulsed by the Germans. The Fusiliers were taking heavy losses, but were able to drive the Germans back again and that evening managed to consolidate by blocking off the south face. The battalion soldiers on the western face, with the Yorks and Lancs, and Number 2 Company of the King's Own Yorkshire Light Infantry managed to extend the British position by pushing up and regaining touch with the Suffolks. The next day, 30th September, the surviving members of the battalion were able to repulse further attacks and hold on to the position until relieved on 1st October.

The 2nd East Surrey Battalion also continued to hold their position in the Hohenzollern Redoubt until finally relieved, at the cost of another ten killed, seventy-four wounded, and four more missing.

Cecil had emerged from this horror unscathed, but Richard was again wounded. This second wound was more significant than his first. He was hit in the right hand by gunfire on 28th September. Fortunately, the bullet passed through the hand between bones, so that the wound could recover without the loss of the hand. He was one of six 2nd lieutenants of the 3rd Royal Fusiliers wounded that day (a seventh had been wounded the day before); in addition a captain was wounded and a lieutenant and four 2nd lieutenants were killed (with a captain killed on 28th September, and another captain and lieutenant wounded both on the day before and the day after).

---

[143] War Diary, 2nd East Surrey Battalion, 28th September 1915.
[144] War Diary, 2nd East Surrey Battalion, 28th-29th September 1915.

Forty-eight men were found missing afterwards, whilst sixty-nine were known to have been killed and two hundred and twenty-four to have been wounded.

Richard was promoted to full lieutenant and sent back through the casualty system. It was decided to send him for recovery to Dublin. Accordingly, he disembarked on the hospital ship *Oxfordshire* at Dublin on 4th October 1915 and was assessed at the Red Cross Hospital at Dublin Castle. After initial treatment, Richard was granted leave to return home to Rowde Rectory at Devizes until, on 12th November, he was passed fit by a medical board at Devizes Military Hospital to return to active service, and he again reported to 6th Battalion at Dover on 13th November 1915.

The troops who had rushed forward to relieve the 2nd East Surrey Battalion and the 3rd Royal Fusiliers included Lieutenant Joseph G.C. Jones, generally known as Gwilyn Jones (born 1893 and one of the earliest members of the school). He had arrived in France on 21st May, and joined his battalion near Ypres on 4th June 1915. Although an officer of the 3rd Wiltshires, he and a fellow Wiltshire subaltern were attached in France to the 2nd Cheshire Battalion (part of 28th Division, 84th Brigade). Joseph had spent the summer of 1915 under fire in trenches in the Ypres Salient, especially near Mount Kemmel where he had been wounded. "Lieutenant Jones was injured in the left hand by a splinter from a shell, but it is stated that he is remaining on duty."[145]

Gwilyn Jones

At the end of September the battalion was hurried south to help. On 30th September they had hurried practices in throwing bombs and grenades before moving up to relieve the Royal Fusiliers and to try to regain the Dump where the Germans were clinging to the eastern side, and the British to the western edge. Two companies were sent forward to the west face of the Hohenzollern Redoubt, whilst the other two companies were held back in support. At this time Joseph had been given charge of the 'bombers' of the 2nd Cheshires, and he was in the thick of this fighting. The war diary records: "Trenches, Hohenzollern Redoubt. 5.30am 1st October... Heavy fire from Trench Mortars and Aerial Torpedos... 2/Lt Jones, bombing officer wounded."[146] Casualties were heavy with fourteen of the officers and three hundred and sixty-two men killed, wounded, or missing by the end, and the west face of the redoubt lost.

Joseph won the Military Cross for leading the bomb attack on the redoubt. First he had suffered the effects of gas poisoning – it is not clear if this was German or British-made gas. He was sent back to recover, but as he worked his way back, he was physically sick. This made him feel so much better that he decided to turn round and return to the firing line. Once he reached the fighting, he was shot with a serious wound in the leg. In the midst of the fighting it was not possible to give him immediate and suitable attention. When he was taken back to the advanced dressing station they passed him back further as it was not at all clear if he could keep his leg. Eventually, he was shipped back to convalesce in England, and the doctors decided that amputation would not be necessary. He was one of the first to receive the newly created Military Cross award. Bournemouth

---

[145] *The Bournemouth Graphic*, 2nd July 1915.
[146] War Diary, 2nd Cheshires, 1st October 1915.

School boys were given a half-day holiday in his honour to celebrate his achievement!

He and his parents had much to celebrate when he went to Buckingham Palace in July 1916 to be invested with his M.C. by the King. "If you ask these young heroes what the Decoration is for, they all tell you – Oh, it was nothing at all; somebody had to have a cross, and I happened to be there, and so I got it! and I couldn't get any more information than that till the official statement was published, and then it appears that 'J.G.C.' after being wounded, led his bombers three times into a well-known strong-hold of the enemy... The job was not one for a chicken-hearted chap. Bravo, we like our 'Joneses' to come out on top."[147] Joseph continued through the war and on 1st January 1916 was mentioned in dispatches for his gallantry. On 15th February 1918 he was seconded from the Wiltshire Regiment to be appointed as an equipment officer in the Royal Flying Corps and on 20th February 1919 he left the Army. He had survived the war, but died soon afterwards, on the Gold Coast of West Africa in 1922.

Behind and on the edge of the battle, John Winton played his part. John had been born in Wooler in Northumberland on 27th December 1897, and boarded at the school from 1908 to 1911. He was only 16 when the war broke out but volunteered at Newcastle on 23rd September 1914 and, as an under-age boy soldier, joined the 14th Northumberland Fusiliers Battalion. John lied to the recruiting officer, describing himself as a nineteen-year-old engineer. At just under six feet tall, and with a good physique, he was apparently also able to convince the doctor who examined him medically. He was made a lance sergeant on 1st November, despite his youth, and become a specialist bomber sergeant specialised in using, and training others to use, hand grenades and also the specialist mechanisms for discharging grenades from rifles (to get greater range). Bomber sergeants were in the forefront of any attack, clearing the way for others – responsible, and very dangerous, work. He was promoted to full sergeant on 8th September 1915, the day before they sailed to France.

The 14th Northumberland Fusiliers Battalion was one of those battalions essential to the war effort, a Pioneer battalion. Part of the 21st Division, for some purposes it operated almost as part of the 64th Brigade. Although it was not primarily a fighting battalion, the men were trained and ready to fight if needed, and so there was a need for a bomber sergeant. John had sailed from Southampton to Le Havre with the battalion on 9th September 1915 and was soon set to support their division when it went into the attack on 26th September, joining in the Battle of Loos. Their task initially then had been to improve the road system leading to the battlefield, but even in this they came under enemy shrapnel fire and received casualties. Indeed, that afternoon their Pioneers were hurriedly brought in to man support trenches by an anxious brigadier. Later they had the task of helping to clear the battlefield after the fighting had moved on, "gathering the dead together and burying them and collecting stores and materials left on the battlefield."[148]

The Battle of Loos continued unsuccessfully until October 14th 1915. By then Haig was in near rebellion with his criticism of Sir John French, and Joffre had secretly ordered the French to ease off their part in the battle "taking care to avoid giving the British the impression that we are leaving them to attack alone."[149] In the recriminations that followed, many blamed Haig for being

---

[147] *The Bournemouth Visitors' Directory*, 12th August 1916.
[148] War Diary, 14th Northumberland Fusiliers (Pioneers), 1st October 1915.
[149] C.R.M.F. Cruttwell, *A History of the Great War*, p. 168.

too eager to throw men into a futile assault, and defended Sir John French, who admitted he could not control Haig. Whoever was to blame ultimately, it was mostly the ordinary soldier who had paid the price.

Soon after it finished, Alfred Gould arrived in the area with the 2nd Royal Sussex Battalion. Alfred (born 1889, at the school from 1902-1906) was a solicitor's articled clerk. On 24th February 1915 he was commissioned 2nd lieutenant in the 3rd Royal Sussex Battalion, the depot unit of the regiment. On 19th October 1915, he landed in France and on 22nd October joined the 2nd Royal Sussex Battalion, 2nd Brigade, 1st Division. From 15th November, Alfred experienced trench warfare including the impact of another wet winter: "December… owing to the inclement weather, much work had to be performed by Companies, in keeping the trenches free from water & mud, by removing trench boards and digging deeper sump pits."[150] So strenuous was the period that the battalion was only able to celebrate Christmas Day a fortnight late, on 3rd January, when they were safely back in brigade reserve. However, the respite was brief and the attrition of killed and wounded continued, except that rain and mud was temporarily replaced by freezing conditions with ice and snow.

In March 1916, Alfred's fortunes changed. The battalion was still near Loos in an area 'South Maroc to Double Crassier'. On 20th March, the Germans made a localised attack. "About 7pm the Germans sent up a green rocket signal, which was closely followed by the explosion of a mine at the end of the Southern Crassier. Part of our front line trench was blown in, otherwise no damage & no casualties. During the shelling of our trenches which followed the mine explosion, Lieut Gould & one other rank were wounded."[151] This marked the end of his active service with the battalion. Alfred did recover and on 1st June 1916 he was transferred from the Royal Sussex Regiment Special Reserve List to become a 2nd lieutenant in the Army Service Corps. He survived the war and remained in the corps into the 1920s.

La Bassée and Northern France, Winter 1915-1916

Thomas Lonsdale served north of La Bassée. Born 1894, he and his older brother Joseph attended the school between 1905 and 1911. Thomas was an O.T.C. sergeant in the school, a rank he also attained in the University of London O.T.C. He volunteered immediately on 6th August 1914, asking to join the Dorsetshire, Devons or Somerset Regiment, so following its own special logic the Army placed him in the adjacent western regiment, the 7th (Service) Battalion of the Duke of Cornwall's Light infantry, as a 2nd lieutenant. This was in the 61st Brigade of the 20th (Light) Division. On 25th July 1915, Thomas (known as 'Doggy' Lonsdale to his friends)[152] and the battalion landed at Boulogne.

Twice in September 1915 Thomas was recommended for the Military Cross.[153] On the night of 18th-19th September, Captain O.L. Hancock was leading a small patrol, consisting of himself, Thomas (then a lieutenant) and two sergeants. "About 11 pm Capt. O.L. Hancock whilst on reconnaissance

---

[150] War Diary, 2nd Royal Sussex Battalion, December 9th-14th 1915.
[151] War Diary, 2nd Royal Sussex Battalion, March 20th 1916.
[152] See letter from Walter Cutland, *The Bournemouthian*, July 1917.
[153] *The Bournemouth Visitors' Directory*, 26th August 1916.

outside the parapet was wounded in the leg and ankle (since amputated)."[154] Indeed, when the patrol had gone out, "they were discovered by the enemy and fired upon. The Captain had his foot shot off, and one of the sergeants was wounded. The two non-commissioned officers helped the Captain back to the trenches, whilst Lieut. Lonsdale stayed behind and guarded them with his revolver, drawing the enemy's fire, and thus enabling the others to reach our trenches."[155]

These were testing times but "during this spell of bad trench weather, this battalion of men who are for the most part young and immature townsmen behaved exceedingly well. The writer with 21 years' experience of soldiers drawn from hardy peasantry considers it admirable and entirely due to the liberal dietary and good clothing the army now enjoy. He attributes the disease resistance of the men mainly to these improved supplies."[156] Christmas was endured in heavy rain, still in trenches in France, with mutual artillery shelling. Despite the wet weather, there was only one instance of trench foot in December.

Thomas Lonsdale

Herbert Short also helped man this northern sector of the line in France after the failure of the Battle of Loos. He was born in 1895 and won a scholarship, funded by the Chairman of the Governors. After passing his exams he left to become a clerk with the railways. On 9th September 1914 he volunteered for military service with the Royal Field Artillery, in which he became a gunner. On 13th February 1915 he arrived in France. He clearly did well, and on 24th October 1915 was commissioned directly from being a R.F.A. gunner to become a 2nd lieutenant in the 7th Suffolk Battalion, a Service Army battalion, 35th Brigade, 12th (Eastern) Division. On 9th December, the battalion assisted in a round-up of spies and other suspicious characters in the streets of Béthuneand and the next day took over trenches north of La Bassée Canal at Givenchy. In 1916 he was wounded three times, but each time recovered. Unfortunately, the battalion war diary is extremely vague about casualties and rarely names anyone, so it is very hard to be precise. At the start of the year, the battalion was based on Festubert, between Béthune and La Bassée. On 20th February they were in the front line where they had to repulse some tentative German grenade attacks. At this time, there was a mutual explosion of mines by both sides, jockeying to gain advantage. Trench mortars and grenades, with sniping, kept up a degree of pressure in an otherwise relatively quiet spell.

As Herbert was moving into the La Bassée Sector, Maurice Hellier was moving out of it. On 1st October 1915, he had escaped unharmed when the Germans exploded a couple of mines under the front line and sent across gas shells. For the next month or so the 6th Shropshire Light Infantry had been in and out of the trenches, and taking casualties. In November, Maurice's luck turned. He was with a working party near Neuve Chapelle when he was shot through the arms. Not only was he wounded in both arms, but he also had to survive a very dangerous crossing of the channel. "Lieut.

---

[154] War Diary, 7th Duke of Cornwall's Light Infantry, 18th September 1917.
[155] *The Bournemouth Visitors' Directory*, 26th August 1916.
[156] War Diary of the 7th Battalion, Duke of Cornwall's Light Infantry, October 1915.

M. J. Hellier, 6th Shropshire Light Infantry, had a marvellous escape. On November 8th a bullet pierced one of his arms, then made a surface wound across his chest and emerged after damaging his other arm also. He returned on the hospital ship Newhaven at the same time as the 'Anglia,' and had the terrible experience of seeing that and the 'Lusitania' go down feeling that it might be their turn next. Being wounded in both arms and so unable to swim we can understand what an awful time it must have been. Fortunately no bones were broken, and though the flesh wounds are severe, he is doing wonderfully well. He is now in the Royal Free Hospital (Military Section), Gray's Inn Road, London."[157] Maurice had sailed from Dieppe to Dover. (This was not the famous liner *Lusitania* which had, of course, been sunk off Ireland the previous May, but a smaller collier of the same name which had gone to try to help the *Anglia*, a hospital ship which hit a mine and sank near Folkestone about midday on 17th November, and which itself then sank about fifteen minutes later. Over a hundred and fifty had died, many of them bed-bound patients returning from the front.) Maurice's right arm had been badly damaged and required a long time to mend, but the left arm wound was more superficial and cleared up quite quickly. After a period at the Royal Free Hospital he was transferred to the Mont Dore Hospital in Bournemouth, one of several military hospitals in Bournemouth, and today is more familiar to residents as the Town Hall.

After the rather miserable task of burying the dead from Loos, John Winton and the 14th Northumberland Fusiliers worked near Armentières, where for several months they were employed "sapping – construction of large underground rooms for the purposes of the RAMC – Dug outs on a large scale – construction, repair and alteration of trenches – Tunnelling under roads – Roadmaking."[158] In the autumn, the machine gunners had sometimes been detached to support the brigades. On 1st January 1916, "13 men, one Sergeant and 2nd Lieut M F W Dawson proceeded in the darkness to occupy the 3 sap heads running out to the craters caused by the German mine explosion opposite the Mushroom. The grenadiers were to cover the working party of the 10th Yorks & Lancs Regiment who occupied the trenches opposite the Mushroom and who were digging an advanced fire trench... Several grenades were thrown and the enemy was successfully kept in hand." They continued with the same task for the next two days, but "one of our grenadiers was accidentally killed and one wounded owing to a grenade exploding in the former's hand."[159]

John was posted to a special cadet school at St. Omer after which he was promoted to become 2nd lieutenant in the 9th Northumberland Fusiliers Battalion on 6th May 1916. John was posted to 'C' Company, and although for a brief spell returned to the trenches near Armentières, most of this time as an officer was spent training with his men for the coming actions on the Somme.

For the cavalry regiments, the winter of 1915-1916 was a frustrating time. Among them was Herbert White (born 1891, at school 1905-1906). He joined the cavalry, and was placed as a lance corporal in the 12th Reserve Cavalry, one of seventeen reserve cavalry regiments formed in August 1914 to reinforce the active regiments. Herbert's regiment supplied men to both the 11th and 13th Hussars as well as to three Yeomanry regiments (Leicestershire, Lincolnshire and Staffordshire). Herbert was sent on 17th October 1915 to join the 13th Hussars, which had been operating in France with the 2nd Indian Cavalry since December 1914.

---

[157] *The Bournemouthian*, December 1915.
[158] War Diary, 14th Northumberland Fusiliers (Pioneers), 30th May 1916.
[159] War Diary, 14th Northumberland Fusiliers (Pioneers), 1st to 4th January 1916.

His time on the Western Front was a period of frustration. Instead of fighting as cavalry they were forced to divide their time between training as cavalry, training as potential infantry, and manual labour doing such tasks as digging reserve and support trenches. "November 25.-'You can see what it is trying to make us do two jobs at the same time, Cavalry and Infantry. The men are simply worked off their legs and haven't a minute all day... We do all our Cavalry parades, all these Infantry ones, route marches, afternoon parades, fatigues, evening classes, &C., &C., and they complain if the men don't turn out smartly on parade. In spite of all this we are to organise games, and let the men train for cross-country runs and so on. Whenever can they possibly have the time? And... I must help the country people in their farming in my spare time." However, "Dec 27th... 'We are all very well and flourishing, and are managing to get a lot of football, &C., arranged for the men now – so their life won't be so bad. This is rotten weather for the trenches. Wet is the worst for them, nearly always up to their knees, and often deeper in places. Cold weather they don't feel nearly so much, owing to the depth of the trenches.'"[160] After a miserable winter 1915-1916, "on the 17th day of June... the Thirteenth Hussars, who were at that time digging trenches for cables behind the lines in France, received orders to get ready... great excitement prevailed... leaving for Mesopotamia. Everyone was in the best of spirits and glad to be leaving France, where Cavalry were inactive... and though no doubt there had been much disappointment among officers and men with the fact that in France 'Cavalry were inactive,' it would not be easy to find among all their letters and diaries bearing on this time a word of murmuring or regret at the prospect of turning their backs on England again, and entering upon another term of distant Eastern service. The universal feeling was one of satisfaction at being sent to some other theatre of war where Cavalry would come into its own."[161] Herbert left the Western Front. We know from regimental records he fought with the regiment in Mesopotamia. However, on 18th August 1918, he was discharged from the 13th Hussars. His Army record card lists him as having been a lance corporal in the 15th Hussars, which had remained in France. The medal roll states he joined the Dorset Yeomanry but the *London Gazette*, in recording his commission states he was sent to join the Dorsetshire Regiment.[162] He survived.

The Somme in 1915-Spring 1916

When Harold Deans re-joined the 2nd Battalion, King's Own Scottish Borderers on 22nd July 1915, it was at Steenvoorde, west of Poperinghe but soon, promoted to captain, he was in trenches on the Somme, in most unpleasant rain and mud (knee deep in the trenches) from which he contracted trench fever, which left him permanently weakened. On 15th September 1915 he was even sent to hospital.

From the spring of 1915, Wilfrid Fuller, John Nethercoate, Ralph Drayton and George Turner were with the 1st Dorsets in the Ypres Salient, but on 30th July 1915 they too had left the Ypres Salient and Hill 60 and gone south by train to the Somme Sector, first south-east of Albert and on 9th August 1915 into the trenches near Fricourt.

---

[160] *The Thirteenth Hussars in the Great War*, the Right Hon. Sir H. Mortimer Durand G.C.M.G., K.C.S.I. K.C.I.E., William Blackwood and Sons, Edinburgh and London, 1921, pp. 86 and 88.

[161] *The Thirteenth Hussars in the Great War*, the Right Hon. Sir H. Mortimer Durand G.C.M.G., K.C.S.I. K.C.I.E., William Blackwood and Sons, Edinburgh and London, 1921, p. 92.

[162] *The London Gazette*, 24th October 1918.

George was the first of the trio to leave the battalion. "By command of Brigade Headquarters a trench was named after him, 'Trench Turner,' in recognition of reconnoitring work done by him when he crept up to within ten yards of the German lines and obtained some valuable information."[163] But George wanted a new challenge and on 11th September 1915 left to join the Royal Flying Corps. He wrote a comedic letter: "I wanted to buy some tooth-paste, and I had to gaze for many minutes into the window of a chemist's shop before I completed this masterpiece. 'Je desire quelque chose à laver mes dents.' Before I was word perfect a girl pounced on me. She was so animated that I was terrified and nearly fled. However I bubbled out my little phrase, and subsequently many more little phrases. —was quite jealous I'm quite braced with the pronunciation of French à la Bournemouth School. — 's pronunciation is appalling: he was at — School. However he doesn't come near to —. He jumped into a cab at Havre and shouted with much gusto to the cabby chap 'A la guerre, à la guerre, vitement!' meaning, of course, 'à la gare'."[164] Two years later, George was mentioned in dispatches by Sir Douglas Haig.[165]

Ralph, John and Wilfrid remained with the battalion. Although German gunfire was bothersome, casualties were relatively light. In October they were near Bray. "During this tour of duty in the trenches (October 6th to 17th inclusive) active patrolling was carried out nightly by ourselves and the Germans. One of our patrols saw a German patrol of about 4 men accompanied by a dog. The Germans were active with their light field guns and especially with rifle grenades and it was very difficult to obtain adequate retaliation from our own Artillery."[166]

It was not only the Germans who had pets in the trenches. One photograph was published on 28th October 1916 – presumably taken some little while earlier – shows Wilfred and a colleague with pets – a cat, tortoise, dog and a rabbit! This was taken by a ruined cottage behind the lines by a local, so perhaps these animals belonged to the photographer, though the original caption to the photograph described them as "regimental pets". The photographer was trying to make a living from creating personal postcards for the men to send home.

Wilfred Fuller (on the right)

On 13th October 1915, John Nethercoate was sent to hospital by field ambulance.[167] It is not clear if John was sent off in the ambulance because he had been wounded or because he was ill. Then, on 25th October, the battalion took part in an honour parade before their king, George V and the French President Poincaré, each of the three brigades of the division being represented by two battalions.

---

[163] *The Bournemouthian*, December 1915.
[164] *The Bournemouthian*, December 1915.
[165] Reported in *The Bournemouth Visitors' Directory*, 3rd March 1917.
[166] War Diary, 1st Dorsets, October 1915.
[167] War Diary, 1st Dorsets, Casualty Report dated 15th October 1915.

Things became more intense at the start of December. Wilfrid was wounded on 10th December. "Second-Lieut. W. R. Fuller recovered from his wound after two months in hospital. He was hit in the arm by shrapnel last December."[168] After his recovery, Wilfrid was posted to a different battalion within the Dorsetshire Regiment in which he remained for the duration of the war. Ralph continued to serve with the 1st Dorsets before following in George Turner's footsteps.

Bernard Clough shared some of the suffering that winter on the Somme, though in his case as a private soldier. Born in 1887, the son of a Wesleyan minister, he was an early member of the school and probably a boarder. When war broke out he joined a newly-formed 'Pals' battalion – the 16th Northumberland Fusiliers (otherwise known as the 'Newcastle Commercials'). This battalion was the first to be formed by civilians in the north of England entirely from the wave of enthusiasm: on 6th August 1914 – just two days after war was declared – a group of Newcastle businessmen began to discuss raising their own troops as a volunteer force, which could then drill at Newcastle Grammar School. With the support of the mayor and council the whole battalion – including Bernard – was recruited within a week between 8th and 16th September.

Bernard was in 12 Platoon under Lieutenant Wake, within 'C' Company commanded by Captain Lindsay. Their channel crossing was rough and landing at Boulogne on 22nd November came as a relief to many. "The sound of the guns was very loud: rifle and machine gun fire could be heard distinctly; the semi-circle of light was much more vivid; Véry lights shone brilliantly as they sank slowly to earth. During the night two or three shells burst in Dernancourt, the first seen by us at close quarters. At that stage, however, they were more objects of curiosity than shedders of fear."[169] Their welcome was not universal. One woman, with whom officers billeted, would not allow them to use her front door – they had to come and go through the window.

They were placed within 96th Brigade, 32nd Division, but for their initiation to trench warfare they came under the patronage of two battalions of the 54th Brigade (18th Division) – the 7th Bedfords and the 11th Royal Fusiliers. For a week, the battalion, divided into pairs of platoons, experienced the trenches – though in one place the two front lines were only twenty metres apart, and then the 'host' battalions left them to man the trenches for themselves. "We learnt that these particular Huns were fairly quiet people and most regular in their habits. Each day at the same times they shelled the same places and rarely put any 'stuff' over during the night. Their snipers were our chief trouble and, although we had practically no casualties, we soon learned not to be too curious and anxious to peer over the top. Very few Germans were ever seen to show themselves, which was rather disheartening to our scouts and snipers... who spent many a long day gazing through telescopes from their observation posts."[170]

In Albert, just behind the front line, "the houses in the square near the cathedral were the most damaged. The cathedral itself was in ruins, but the tall spire still stood surmounted by the gilded figure of the Virgin holding her child. This figure had been struck by a shell and was hanging over, suspended by one or two steel supports. It seemed as if it might fall to the ground at any moment. It was said that some of the inhabitants believed that, when it fell, the war would come to an end. [It did not fall until 1918 when the town was captured by the Germans]. Most of the inhabitants

---

[168] *The Bournemouthian*, April and July 1916.

[169] *Historical Records of the 16th (Service) Battalion Northumberland Fusiliers*, published by Newcastle and Gateshead Incorporated Chamber of Commerce, 1923, author C.H. Cooke, p. 26 (So proud was the Chamber of Commerce in its battalion that soon after the war they commissioned C.H. Cooke to compile this history of the battalion.)

[170] ibid, p. 28.

had evacuated the town, but a few of the poorer people still remained. They kept tea-shops and sold picture postcards and other souvenirs to the troops. They appeared to be quite unconcerned about shells although plenty dropped in the town every day."[171]

After Christmas the battalion relocated to a new section of the trenches slightly further north of their original positions. "The front line system ran along the top of the east bank of the River Ancre, which was thickly wooded. The river turned in a big bend and crossed the line to the left of us, the trenches running right down to the water, the river being more of a swamp than a well-defined river at this point. Opposite and slightly to the left of us were the ruins of Thiepval just behind the German front line. A part of the château still stood and could be seen from our line."[172] "B.M. Clough, Northumberland Fusiliers, was badly wounded early in 1916, but after spending six months in hospital he writes to say he is doing well."[173] He was discharged from hospital as unfit for further active service and discharged from the Army the following year. On 13th May 1918, he was awarded a 'Silver War Badge' to wear so that misguided folk back home should not accost him and accuse him of cowardice for not being at the front.

Another clergyman's son, Edwin Hill, was also on this front in 1915-1916. Edwin was born in 1894 and attended the school from 1910 to 1913. He excelled at football, cricket, and athletics as well as being a member of the O.T.C. Horrified by reports of the atrocities perpetrated by the German troops who invaded Belgium in August 1914, he volunteered for the Royal Sussex Regiment on 3rd September 1914 at Brighton. He was commissioned on 7th November 1914 and on 24th July 1915 landed in France at Le Havre with the 8th Royal Sussex Battalion. His was a Pioneer battalion, 55th Brigade, 18th Division, carrying out essential work behind the lines or in construction and repair work on the front lines. Their training with route marches to harden the men and in fighting with grenades and bayonets reminded them all that they were indeed soldiers even if their main role was in technical support. From August 1915 they had varied work helping to prepare and improve defensive positions around Albert on the Somme, and from 25th August began to take casualties.

Edwin had the chance to meet up with George Turner and Ralph Drayton, but also to experience the horrors of war for himself. "Being a pioneer battalion we do not go up into the trenches except to do work there. Of course, I have been up into the front line trenches several times, and the day before yesterday I saw (through a periscope) the rifle of a German sniper who had established himself only 15 yards from our trenches. He and one of our own snipers were exchanging shots all the time I was there… It is rather trying work digging trenches close to the firing line at night. The Germans send up very brilliant 'star shells' at frequent intervals during the night. The only thing for us to do is to go flat on the ground until they die out. The officer who was sharing my billet with me was unfortunately hit, along with three of his men, by a rifle grenade yesterday morning, so I am now by myself."[174]

The weather conditions could make their life and work as difficult as it did for the fighting Tommies. "Weather. Very wet all day. Ground is becoming very heavy making transport of material anywhere except on metalled roads slow and difficult. The same applies to digging. The soil sticks to the shovels and makes digging very slow."[175]

---

[171] ibid, p. 29.

[172] *Historical Records of the 16th (Service) Battalion Northumberland Fusiliers*, published by Newcastle and Gateshead Incorporated Chamber of Commerce, 1923, author C.H. Cooke, pp. 30-31.

[173] *The Bournemouthian*, December 1916.

[174] Letter of September 17th 1915, printed in *The Bournemouthian*, December 1915.

[175] War Diary, 8th Royal Sussex Battalion, 28th October, 1915.

4: 1916 on the Western Front

Training

1916 was a momentous year on land, in the air, and at sea, and Old Boys were involved in all three aspects of the war. Until 1916, hundreds of the Old Boys of the school had mostly been in training, but those who had already served were now to be joined by something of a deluge of warriors.

In 1915, three teachers were required to join the Army. Music and geography teacher Archibald Rogers was the oldest, born in 1880. He taught at the school from 1st May 1911 and had held a commission as 2nd lieutenant in the Cadet Corps since 1906 when he was teaching in Mansfield. He left in July 1916. French teacher Victor Allen was born in 1887, started work at Bournemouth School in May 1914, went off to war at the end of February 1916 and returned to the school in January 1919. Harold Kerr taught maths. Born in 1888, he started at Bournemouth School in 1910 and went off to the Army in February 1916. In 1915 all three attested under the Derby Scheme: Archibald joined the 12th Northumberland Fusiliers; Victor joined the 6th Wiltshire Battalion; and Harold joined No. 1 Platoon, A Company, of the 1st Officer Cadet Battalion.

The government had become concerned that the number of volunteers had been reducing. In May 1915 they raised the upper age limit from 38 to 40, but as this was still insufficient, in July 1915 parliament passed the National Registration Act. At this point, Asquith's Liberal government still wanted to avoid compulsory conscription, but this Act paved the way towards it. All men between the ages of 15 and 65 not already in the forces were required to register and give details of their employment. The process was complete by September, and it became clear that whilst over one and half million were employed in work regarded as vital to national interests, there were about three and a half million men whose employment was deemed less essential. In October, the new Director-General of Recruiting, Lord Derby began a new scheme for recruits officially known as the Group Scheme, but generally known as the Derby Scheme, whereby men aged between 18 and 40 were allowed to choose between volunteering to enlist, or registering with the Army (known as 'attesting') with the understanding that they would be obliged to join the Army at a later date if the war continued. Anyone not voluntarily attesting under this scheme would know from publicity that the last day to volunteer was the 15th December, and compulsory and immediate (within a month) conscription was likely soon to follow.

Harold had to come to terms with the regime of training, which even to be an officer was rigorous. "Our day starts at 6 a.m., and at 7 a.m. we go on first parade for drill, usually without arms. This lasts until 7.45 a.m., when we breakfast off porridge, and either bacon or fish. At 9.30 a.m. comes physical exercise for three-quarters of an hour, and having tired ourselves out at this, we are allowed half-an-hour's rest, which is generally occupied in cleaning boots and rifles, after which we drill with arms until 12 noon. As soon as we are dismissed there is a lecture for three-quarters of an hour on topography, company accounts, musketry or visual training. Lunch follows, and then parade again at 2 p.m. for another hour's drill. Our time is then supposed to be our own, but as there is a scheme of work drawn up for each week we are not really free till about 8.30 p.m. This leaves about half-an-hour's leisure before bed, for which by that time we are quite ready… When I came here I expected to find mostly O.T.C. men, but was very much surprised to find that nearly 80 per cent were men in the ranks, and that more than half of these had already been at the front. But, as all are ready to help, there is never any feeling of being an outsider… Although most of the men here were non-commissioned officers, and some indeed were sergeant-majors, no stripes are allowed, and all start level as Cadets."[176]

Archibald found himself unexpectedly interested in grenade throwing when he trained. "I intended to show no enthusiasm over this branch, but when I came to throwing one it was so much like bowling a cricket ball that professional pride prevented me from shirking it, consequently I much fear that I may have to become a member of the 'Suicides' Club,' as they call the bombers' detachment… The lectures are really interesting, and the sergeant adds to the interest by telling us chatty little anecdotes of 'Sergeant So-and-so, who had his hands blown off when fixing a detonator, and Lieut. So-and-so, who was blown to pieces while taking charge of a bombing practice,' etc. All this adds to the interest. To-morrow night we are having night operations with live bombs, and the experience should be exciting. When I have finished my bombing I'm supposed to be a trained bomber and ready for the Front."[177]

On 6th July 1916, he was gazetted 2nd lieutenant in the Dorsetshire Regiment. After an attachment to a battalion of the King's Royal Rifles in Salonika, he was promoted lieutenant and posted to the Northumberland Fusiliers (though always remaining a Dorset officer), but by or soon after end of the war he had been sent to France, and may there have served with a Dorset battalion. Soon after the war ended he returned to the school where he became the Officer Commanding the School O.T.C. He died in 1970.

Archibald, too, applied for a commission, but the brigadier rejected him on the grounds of his age (36) though he was promoted to lance corporal on 19th October 1916. He was sent out to France on 22nd December 1916, initially to join the Northumberland Fusiliers: first with the 12th Battalion, but later also with the 8th Battalion. He remained on the Western Front until 29th March 1917, finding life very different from training: "We travelled in horse boxes— 26 to a box! and our journey lasted for 30 hours! As they did not ration us at the base, the food question became serious, but fortunately we struck a Y.M.C.A. place up the line. We fairly raided it! On reaching our destination late at night, we slept once more under canvas in an ocean of mud and slime, and next morning, without breakfast, marched in full pack to our billets five miles off. Full pack out here is different to England, as you carry a tin helmet, leather jacket and waterproof sheet, and 120 rounds of ammunition, in addition to the rest. Oddly enough we felt none the worse for our experience, though we were wet through and chilled to the bone most of the time… The men in the regiment are rough diamonds, but very good fellows, and they made us welcome when we arrived. It was amusing to see them sitting round the fire in the barn which is our billet, killing lice in their clothes. Everyone abounds in lice here, but so far I've not suffered though I'm assured by the old hands that I must have them on me by now. We are expected to clean buttons and badges though all our cleaning tackle was taken away from us when we came out and none of us have anything at all."[178]

Once trained, Victor Allen embarked at Southampton for Rouen on 9th August and joined his battalion, the 6th Wiltshire Battalion, 58th Brigade, 19th Division. The battalion was in the trenches on the Spanbroekmolen and Wytschaete Line, a few miles south-west of Ypres. They responded to German *minenwerfer* (a class of short range mortar) attacks by firing rifle grenades but took

---

[176] *The Bournemouthian*, July 1916.
[177] Letter of 12th October, published in *The Bournemouthian*, December 1916.
[178] *The Bournemouthian*, April 1917.

casualties. Victor was promoted to corporal. After a spell training some Canadians from the 73rd Regiment they left their trenches to the Canadians and relocated at Armentières on the French frontier, and at the end of October they moved down to the Somme. But Victor was suffering with his eyes. Twice he was sent to hospital, and on 18th January 1917, in Amiens, his defective vision was diagnosed as dacryocystitis, an inflammation of the lacrimal (tear) sac, often as a result of infection. Three days later he was transferred to another hospital in Boulogne, but could not be restored to full health. From the end of March he was employed as a cashier at the base camp and later formally transferred to the Army Pay Corps. On 17th December 1918 he was sent back to England to be demobilised, in time to resume teaching French at the school the following January. What a massive change to his system that must have been! He stayed on for many years until he retired at the end of July 1947.

La Bassée

Clermont Grantham-Hill had been in and out of the trenches, despite being in a cavalry regiment, throughout 1915. On 7th February he was severely wounded whilst serving with the new 4th Dismounted Battalion in trenches further south, near La Bassée. (The school magazine erroneously rendered the date as a week later.) He had suffered multiple gunshot wounds, probably from a machine gun. One major wound was in his left thigh; another two in his left buttock; two more – in his right thigh and his right calf. At first his wounds became septic, making recovery slower. He left Calais for Dover on 13th April and began a series of medical boards and a prolonged time in hospital. After prolonged treatment in England he was demobilised on 12th October 1917 (still bed-ridden after corrective surgery) and finally discharged from the Army on 24th August 1918 as no longer physically fit enough for service, although at the start of March 1918 the Army had concluded he was never going to recover enough to serve again, and so had advised him (after he had asked) that he could resume his medical studies. Even by 1920 it was a matter of some relief that he could now walk without a limp.

A few days after Clermont was hit, teacher John Day was also wounded near La Bassée. John had taught geography, commercial subjects and maths at the school between 1903 and 1909 before moving on to become a lecturer in geography at St. Andrew's University in Scotland. Born in 1880, he had joined the school as a young teacher and taught younger pupils for over four years. Whilst teaching he gained a degree in geography from London University in 1908 and took charge both of geography but also the Cadet Corps as its captain (later attached to 4th Hampshire Battalion). When war broke out he had volunteered and was posted as an officer in the 12th Durham Light Infantry Battalion, 68th Brigade, 23rd Division. By May 1915, he held the rank of captain.

The battalion crossed to France in August 1915 – John was in the advance party, crossing from Southampton to Le Havre on 25th August. After practical up-to-date training from the King's Royal Rifles and the Oxford and Bucks Light Infantry, they took up position in the trenches near La Bassée. They stayed there, in and out of the trenches, normally inter-changing with the 13th Battalion, Durham Light Infantry, but sometimes with the Sherwood Foresters. John was mentioned in dispatches by Sir Douglas Haig for his gallant and distinguished service in the field in the list of 15th June. Casualties gradually grew, and things really heated up on 12th February 1916 when the Germans bombarded them for three solid hours, using both high explosives and trench mortars.

Three were killed and a further sixteen wounded. After a lull the shelling restarted on 19th February and John was wounded, whilst another man was killed and two others wounded. His wound was to his right arm and was quite serious. He was taken back through the casualty system and onwards from Boulogne to Southampton, and then on to Dorchester House, Park Lane Hospital. He had several operations to try to save the use of his arm. His doctor decided he was not fit even to appear before a medical board on 4th April, but slowly his condition improved. However, his bone was shattered – a gap meant he effectively lost the use of his right arm so he was formally struck off the list of the 12th Durham Light Infantry on 16th November, but kept in the Army on light duties in a wide range of units and capacities until he was demobbed on 29th December 1918. Sadly, the Army ruled that the effective loss of an arm was not worth a permanent gratuity. He even enlisted the help of his MP, Winston Churchill, but without success.

Meanwhile, another teacher, Thomas Searls, was also in these trenches about this time. He was born in 1890. His time as a teacher at Bournemouth School was rather brief – two terms in 1913, from January to July but during that period Thomas gave up a lot of his time to coach sport amongst the younger boys. When war broke out Thomas was swift to volunteer. On 6th September 1914, he volunteered to serve as a private in the Field Ambulance of the Territorial Royal Army Medical Corps, in a unit meant to serve the medical needs of the three volunteer cavalry units of the 1st South Midlands Mounted Brigade. In spring 1915 his unit served on Gallipoli, but Thomas did not go with them. Instead he was re-trained, gaining his commission as 2nd lieutenant on 6th May 1915 in the 2nd South Staffordshire Battalion (a Regular battalion), 6th Brigade, 2nd Division.

Thomas landed in France on 28th November 1915 to join this battalion, which had been there since 13th August 1914. He joined the battalion on 4th December, along with five other junior officers, just in time for a practice drill in which they were required to move through a gas-filled chamber wearing smoke helmets. Within days Thomas was with the battalion when they relieved the 1st Hertfordshire Battalion in trenches at Vermelles, south of the La Bassée Canal and south-east of Béthune. At first their main concern was of having to stand in rising water in soggy trenches. On 14th December, he was selected to assist in a raid with another officer and thirty men, each with ten grenades. "An artillery bombardment from 10am to 2pm was to take place, in the course of which gaps were to be cut in the German wire opposite certain points. Bombing parties were to make raids on the German trenches. For a quarter of an hour previous to the advance of the bombing parties, gas was to be turned on from emplacements at various parts of the line… The entire party was to be equipped with steel helmets. The whole enterprise was to be contingent upon a favourable wind. All arrangements were made and the men sent down to Factory dugouts to rest for 24 hours… The artillery bombardment was carried out and wire was cut just north of the Auchy-Vermelles Railway, at which point our patrol was to enter the German lines. From the position in which the wire-cutting battery (17th Battery, Royal Field Artillery) was placed it was apparently impossible to cut the wire very satisfactorily. One small gap, however, was made. About 10pm orders were received that the enterprise was postponed owing to the unfavourable nature of the wind. Shortly after these orders had been communicated, fresh orders were received that the Battalion was to stand by to carry out the original programme, in which the gas was to be turned on at 12 midnight, the raiding parties to advance as soon after cessation of the gas as was considered safe. This was to be determined by a patrol sent out immediately the gas cylinders had been entirely emptied. Just before midnight orders were received that the operations were definitely cancelled…"[179]

---

[179] War Diary, 2nd South Staffordshire Battalion, 14th-15th December 1915.

It is hard to imagine the emotional turmoil that Thomas and his comrades went through as they repeatedly prepared for this raid, which then did not happen: excitement, fear, maybe even relief or disappointment.

After Christmas celebrated near Béthune, he was promoted lieutenant on 1st January 1916, when they were in a period of training, route marches, boxing and football competitions, and even concerts. In one of those, on 14th January 1916, in front of the three divisional brigadiers and the commanding officers, a one act play was performed – *Box and Cox* – and Thomas, along with 2nd Lieutenants Whitehead and Beech, played one of the three characters. The next day, the battalion returned by train to Béthune, to take over the trenches at Givenchy, opposite La Bassée and north of the canal. In this tour they were shelled and bombed with grenades and trench mortars, and some RE engineers were entombed when a German counter-mine exploded, trapping them underground. The adjutant also noted that with the rigours of trench warfare and the constant call for replacements to battalions holding the line, this battalion was down to only about half-strength. A series of such tours followed but in February the battalion was re-located a short distance south to hold the Festubert Line. By early 1916 on the Western Front, a short distance could mean significant differences, and the war diary describes the very different (and dangerous) nature of this part of the front line: "The front line in this section consists of 'islands' or isolated breast-works with a garrison varying from 7 to 13 men in each. The remainder of the Battalion occupies Old British Line (i.e. the British Line before the offensive of May 1915) almost 600 yards in rear of the Islands. The latter are only accessible at night, and all relieving too is done across the open, the garrisons taking their rations and water for 24 hours. The distance of the German front line from the Islands varies from 150 to about 300 yards. The Old British Line is a continuous breastwork."[180]

Then they moved on south to various trenches, to the front line at Bully-les-Mines at the start of March, where they suffered from both dilapidated former French trenches and unpleasant amounts of snowfall. At this time Thomas was wounded, but not seriously enough to be sent back to the UK and soon he was back in the trenches with the battalion.

About that time, Joseph Cornwall also moved into the trenches near La Bassée. Born in 1891, Joseph was another of the earliest Old Boys, from 1903 to 1905, and was a member of the O.T.C. By the end of 1914 he was a private in the 2nd Royal Sussex Battalion. He did not go to France initially but served as a musketry instructor in England. As a result of this he was singled out for officer training.[181] He was commissioned 2nd lieutenant in July 1915 and given further training in southern England before himself instructing in

THE LATE SECOND-LIEUT. JOSEPH CORNWELL.

---

[180] War Diary, 2nd South Staffordshire Battalion, 14th February 1916. One of those islands was at that time commanded by Irish Nationalist M.P. William Redmond, a moderate Nationalist whose father John Redmond had campaigned successfully for the Irish Home Rule Bill in 1914.

[181] *The Bournemouth Visitors' Directory*, 10th June 1916.

musketry at Tring in Buckinghamshire. He was re-assigned to the 13th Royal Sussex, a New Army Service battalion. On 15th April, about the time Joseph joined the battalion, they were on the front line near Givenchy – in almost the same trenches where John Turner had been killed in 1914, so little movement had there been in the front line in that sector. For an apparently 'quiet' sector, the battalion began taking regular casualties – from shelling, machine guns, and rifle grenades. They were similarly 'quiet' when they shifted front a little to trenches near Festubert, where machine guns and 'whizzbangs' took their toll.

On 29th May they suffered more losses. Their war diary describes it laconically: "Heavy enemy bombardment and raid. 6 casualties. Enemy captured an NCO and several rifles."[182] Joseph was shot through the head by a sniper. "He only had eight days in the trenches and was looking forward to a rest."[183] He never regained consciousness, and was taken back down the line to 33rd Casualty Clearing Station where he died, and was buried the next day, in the cemetery at Béthune. At 24, he left a young widow to mourn him.

Meanwhile, Alan Markwick had got his first taste of fighting in the vicinity of Neuve Chapelle. Alan was born in 1892, and he too was an early member of the school. After Cambridge University he went off to Ceylon (Sri Lanka) to become a rubber planter. There, unfortunately, he contracted malaria. On 13th December 1914, he reached London from Rangoon having embarked at Colombo with about thirty-five members of the Ceylon Contingent Volunteer Reserve – all "ordered to Recruiting Office Scotland Yard by War Office". The same day he attested as a private in the Royal Fusiliers and was posted to the 17th Royal Fusiliers (Empire) Battalion, which had been formed in London at the end of August by the British Empire Committee. (Alan's two sisters also 'did their part' – one serving a winter in a French military hospital and the other as a V.A.D. at Haslemere in Surrey.)

Two weeks after joining up, on 30th December 1914, he was made a lance corporal, and after another week a full corporal, on 7th January 1915. At the end of January he first applied, unsuccessfully, for a commission in the infantry but on 22nd April 1915 was discharged to a commission having been specially requested for service by the commander of the 18th Lancashire Fusiliers. Alan's new battalion was a Bantam battalion.

Bantam battalions were originally formed in Cheshire when a local MP, Alfred Bigland, gained War Office permission to form a battalion of under-sized men (shorter than five foot three or with a chest less than thirty-four inches) because so many were incensed that they were not being allowed to join the Army. Initially, the War Office refused to fund the battalion. By November 1914, three thousand such men had arrived in Birkenhead which forced the formation of a second battalion. They took their name 'Bantam' from the feisty little chickens which became their adopted emblem. Soon the idea had spread across the country and to Canada. One unfortunate and unintended consequence was that in the early years it was easier for underage boys to get into these battalions, which became renowned for their keen, fighting spirit and bravery.

On 29th January 1916, Alan and the 18th Lancashire Fusilier Battalion mobilised for war and sailed from Southampton to Le Havre that night as part of the 104th Brigade, 35th Division. The battalion was not yet ready for action: twenty out of its thirty-four officers were sent to cadet school at St.

---

[182] War Diary, 13th Royal Sussex Regiment, May 30th 1916.
[183] *The Bournemouthian*, July 1916.

Omer, whilst some others went for instruction by officers of the Guards Brigade. Soon, however, this phase was over and from 20th February the whole battalion was attached temporarily to the 115th Brigade, training by experiencing the trenches near Neuve Chapelle, under instruction. In the second week of March 1916 they were in Reserve trenches at La Couture, west of Neuve Chapelle and north-west of La Bassée and suffered their first casualties. The next week they began to man the front line for themselves, conducting their first raid on 24th March, after which they rotated regularly in and out of the Neuve Chapelle zone trenches. On 30th May, they came under an intense barrage which almost broke the line. It began at 7.30p.m. and their war diary pays tribute to the swift and decisive actions of a number of NCOs and privates whose work helped rescue the situation. The battalion adjacent to them seems to have withdrawn from about four hundred yards of the front line trench, leaving it deserted, but the battalion was able to extend to cover this significant gap. Their diary includes an interesting reflection on why they received relatively low casualties: "owing to the fact that the men instead of crowding into dugouts lay under the fire step."[184]

On 20th June, Alan's name appeared on the published casualty list. According to a letter from his father he was actually wounded twice, though both times he was able to remain with the battalion near Neuve Chapelle. This might have been because of an attempted raid carried out on 10th June that failed, with relatively heavy casualties, which the war diary attributed a bit ambiguously to "fact of shells bursting in no man's land".[185] Presumably these were British shells falling short. No other casualties were recorded in the diary before the national papers recorded him as one of the wounded. For some of this time Alan worked as the battalion bombing officer, as well as serving in a trench mortar battery.

The Ypres Salient 1916

It is always tempting to assume that all the fighting, and suffering, of 1916 for the British centred on the Somme. But although that terrible battle was the main 'action' of 1916, the Army fought across the whole British front, holding the line, making patrols or forays, occupying the enemy. Old Bournemouthians were engaged in the Ypres Salient and also in the area around Vimy Ridge and Arras.

Thomas Lonsdale was one. In January 1916, the 7th Duke of Cornwall's Light Infantry Battalion had come under the command of General Plumer and the Second Army in the Ypres Salient. At the end of February they were in trenches on the canal bank, north of Ypres, near to Essex Farm and the Yorkshire trench. On 29th February, a 2nd lieutenant called Eric Lailey was working on improving the barbed wire in front of his post when he was killed by German machine gun fire. At that point the German front line was only about fifty yards away. Despite the heavy fire from the constant enemy action of their trench mortars and aerial torpedoes, Thomas went out and recovered Eric's body, which was found to have been riddled with machine gun bullets. To add to the problems caused by machine guns, snipers, trench mortars and enemy artillery, the men also had 'flu to contend with to add to their woes, and it was only at the end of March that the battalion was issued with waders to try to combat the soggy trench conditions. The ubiquitous mud caused machine guns and rifles to jam at crucial moments. By May, Thomas had been promoted to full lieutenant, and as Acting Captain of 'D' Company.

---

[184] War Diary, 18th Lancashire Fusiliers, 30th May 1916.
[185] War Diary, 18th Lancashire Fusiliers, 10th June 1916.

Another of those in the salient was John Bennett. John, born 1894 and a boarder at school from 1910-1911, joined the Border Regiment and on 24th August 1915 was commissioned 2nd lieutenant. He left for France in January 1916, joining the 1/5th Border Battalion on 13th February 1916. The battalion was a Territorial battalion, 151st Brigade, 50th (Northumbrian) Division.

On the day John joined them they came out of the trenches after an arduous six days, and were told by their brigadier that they needed to rest and recuperate, but that evening the battalion received an urgent message that there was an S.O.S. from Hooge, and that they should be ready to move back to the trenches at half an hour's notice. They rushed to get ready, but were stood back down. A few days later, on the night of 18th-19th February, the battalion relieved the 5th Yorkshire Battalion in close support, in position across Glasgow Cross, Sunken Road and Larch Wood. The battalion then engaged in a mix of grenade throwing from a sap and sniper firing using rifles with periscopes to pin down German snipers. On 22nd February, they moved forward again to Mount Sorrel, Hill 62, relieving the 6th Durham Light Infantry. Despite it snowing heavily on them, they managed to put out a lot of extra barbed wire to reinforce the position. They were in turn relieved on 26th February.

On 2nd March, the battalion came under heavy German bombardment when the Germans counter-attacked against an action by the 17th Division. At the time, they were again in support to Mount Sorrel, occupying trenches at Blauwepoort Farm and at Railway dug-outs. Four platoons re-inforced the 9th Duke of Wellington's Battalion in the right sector trenches, advancing through the enemy barrage. "Your men were splendid. They came through the barrage in perfect order and behaved throughout with great gallantry. I hope your losses were not too severe. My men appreciate your help."[186] John and his colleagues endured this pattern of trench rotation through March, coping with heavy snow and German "rifle grenades, sausages, and trench mortars".[187]

Ernest Snelgar, brother of John, was also there. He was born in Bournemouth in 1888 and was at school between 1902 and 1909. He had had four years' experience with the Hampshire Territorial Force before he decided to go out to Canada in 1911. He maintained his military interest there, serving three years as a trooper in the 9th Mississauga Horse Militia while working as a carpenter in Toronto. In September 1914, his regiment voluntarily mobilised and offered its services to the government, but that offer was declined. However, the commander of the 4th Mississauga Horse was authorised to raise a mounted rifle regiment, which became the 4th Canadian Mounted Rifles and Ernest volunteered to join it on 28th November 1914.

After initial training at Niagara, in May 1915 the unit was asked to volunteer for overseas service as a dismounted unit. They agreed though it meant the disappointment of leaving behind their horses. The battalion sailed from Quebec aboard the SS *Hesperian* in July 1915. After final training at Shorncliffe Camp they sailed from Folkestone to Boulogne on 24th October 1915. Once inducted into trench warfare, they were sent into the trenches by Hill 63 near Ploegsteert and south of Ypres, and from 1st December began to take casualties. In January 1916, with the creation of the 3rd Canadian Division, the battalion was formally re-designated as infantry, though retaining its cavalry title. They were now in the 8th Canadian Brigade. This meant a fresh period of intensive training, because they had previously been organised and trained as cavalry, and now they were

---

[186] Letter from Major in Command of the Duke of Wellington's Battalion included with the War Diary, 5th Border Battalion, March 1916.
[187] War Diary, 5th Border Battalion, 18th March 1916.

re-organised into the model of an infantry battalion.

They entered the trenches at Sanctuary Wood amidst the misery of wet snow on 20th March 1916. "Machine guns raked the roads, shells of all descriptions enfiladed this strategic death-trap, high explosives crashed on the pavé or fell in the town of Ypres. The night was made more unreal by the flares and Verey lights which seemed to surround the mysterious darkness. During the days in the front line, the men's lives were menaced by bombs and grenades. Dodging minnenwerfers and repairing their damage occupied many hours on duty."[188] A week later, at 4.15a.m. on 27th March, there was excitement when the 1/5th Border Battalion heard a mine explode about a mile south of them, followed by a heavy bombardment. John Bennett would not have known, however, that Hubert Dinwoodie from his school was involved.

Hubert's main call to fame came later, in 1946 in Lübeck as Hubert Dinwoodie, O.B.E., M.C, who won the George Cross for defusing eleven 110lb. bombs after a twelfth had already exploded, killing a dozen people because the bombs had faulty, experimental shock-sensitive fuses. But these top military and civil honours began on the Western Front.

Born in 1896, Hubert was at the school from 1907 to 1912. With the outbreak of the war he joined the Sherborne Volunteer Training Corps of which he was a member from August 1914 to May 1915. On 20th May 1915, he volunteered for the Dorsetshire Regiment and was gazetted 2nd lieutenant on 8th June 1915. He arrived in France on 10th October 1915 as a 2nd lieutenant attached to the 1/76th Trench Mortar Company. This meant that he had been specially trained in the use of light trench mortars which the British had only begun to develop at the end of 1914 (responding to their development by the Germans). Hubert's unit was the 43rd Trench Mortar, renamed on 1st April 1916 the 1st Light Trench Mortar Company, 76th Infantry Brigade (3rd Division). Hubert was in the main fighting in the Ypres Salient that spring, known as 'the actions of the St. Eloi craters'. The aim was to capture a minor mound east of the village of St. Eloi, which the Germans held very strongly. On March 27th 1916, the action had started: a two pronged attack by 4th Royal Fusiliers and 1st Northumberland Fusiliers, preceded by the explosion of five mines, which John Bennett's men had heard. The enemy position was captured and held in the face of ferocious counter-barrage, although the Germans managed to hold one of the craters. Desperate fighting continued over the coming days, and on March 30th, 76th Brigade took over the struggle. Conditions were grim. Despite good weather and the drainage work of the Royal Engineers, "there are in many parts however 2 to 3 feet of water and mud."[189]

On 2nd April, Hubert Dinwoodie's brigade launched a successful attack which his mortars would have supported. So desperate was the fighting that even the divisional general got involved: "We saw our Divisional General mid-thigh in water and splashing down the trenches," says an observer. "I can tell you it put heart into our weary men."[190] "At 1.30a.m. the artillery opened an intense bombardment on the enemy's position. This lasted until 2a.m. when the 8th K.O.R.L . [King's Own Royal Lancaster] Regt. assaulted. Owing to the very thick mist and the thick clouds of smoke, it was almost impossible to keep the right direction, and it is unlikely that there will ever be an accurate account of the action. The results were however that the assault was completely successful and

---

[188] *The 4th Canadian Mounted Rifles*, Captain S.G. Bennett, Murray Printing Company Ltd, Toronto, 1926 pp. 13-14.

[189] War Diary, 76th Brigade, March 1916.

[190] Quoted in Arthur Conan Doyle, *British Campaign in France and Flanders, Volume III*.

that the 8th K.O.R.L. Regiment captured the line."[191] Even then the Germans kept counter-attacking, and on April 4th the division handed over the ground to the 2nd Canadian Division, who resisted a major German assault on April 6th-7th. In the end, two of the Eloi craters could be held by neither side. Frank Cox – in the 31st Canadian Infantry Battalion, and in the 2nd Canadian Division, also served in the battle.

On 3rd April 1916, as they entered the forward trenches at St. Eloi, Frank and his comrades were finally issued with steel helmets and rubber boots. They were certainly needed – their doctor noted that men had to stand in water for 24 hours at a stretch. One assault on the craters was cancelled because it was felt that the mud would only suck the rubber waders off the men if they tried to advance. The Germans bombarded them so heavily that many men suffered shellshock, not helped by being unable to sleep for several days and nights. It rained heavily. However, they were able to repulse German attacks, trying to gain the craters they held. Between 3rd and 9th April, six officers were wounded, and twenty-nine men were killed, 141 wounded, with four missing. One hundred and eighty out of a total strength of just over seven hundred had fallen or been wounded: Frank survived and the battalion remained in the salient, mainly at St. Eloi.

In this fighting at St. Eloi, Hubert Dinwoodie had distinguished himself. During an enemy attack his trench mortar emplacement was destroyed by a shell and the mortar gun was partially buried. Nevertheless, Hubert got the mortar firing again, and "after firing till his ammunition was exhausted, removed the gun into safety. He then, though partly incapacitated, led parties with ammunition and bombs up to the firing line."[192] For this he was awarded the Military Cross, and was promoted to a temporary post of lieutenant whilst working with trench mortar batteries. He had, however, been injured, and was redeployed as assistant instructor at the Fifth Army School of Mortars and further promoted to the rank of acting captain on 7th November 1916. (In December 1917 he was confirmed in the permanency of his position as full lieutenant whilst remaining seconded from the Dorsetshire Regiment. By then he was changing his role as he became interested in switching to take to the air.) His final posting was to the R.A.F. and at the end of the war he was permitted to retain the rank of captain. He was demobbed on 11th June 1919 – but volunteered again for the Officers' Emergency Reserve on 24th May 1937.

At this time, young Cyril Cooper arrived. He was born in October 1897 and was at the school between 1907 and 1915, where he was a keen member of the O.T.C. and reached the rank of sergeant. At school Cyril was a "genial and popular youth".[193] He only left school on 31st March 1915 and went straight to the Royal Military Academy, the training school for artillery officers. He was gazetted 2nd lieutenant in the Regular Army, and arrived in France on 1st March 1916 at the age of 18. If he had been in the rank and file, this would have made him a 'boy soldier', but as an officer he was allowed to serve in France at a year younger than the usual permitted age. He joined 132nd Heavy Battery of the Royal Garrison Artillery on April 5th 1916. He was immediately set to work. At about 4.00a.m. the next morning he was working as orderly officer in the battery commander's shelter, working out a new range for his gun. Several enemy high explosive shells smashed into the shelter. When the rescuers dug out the debris, they found Cyril dead. He had not lived to see his first dawn in the line. His parents were left only with messages of sympathy from

---

[191] War Diary, 76th Infantry Brigade Headquarters, Account of St. Eloi fighting, 1916.
[192] Citation in *The London Gazette*, 31st May 1916.
[193] *The Bournemouth Visitors' Directory*, 15th April 1916.

men who had known him in training, and the 'standard' condolences from his battery major, who can hardly have met him. He was buried at Vlamertinge Military Cemetery, five kilometres west of Ypres off the Poperinge road.

Next, John Bennett of the 5th Border Battalion fought at St. Eloi. "On the 6th, 7th and 8th April there was much activity on our immediate left held by the Canadians and the craters in front of St. Eloi changed hands several times. 'C' Company, who were on the left, received the edge of the enemy's shelling, but casualties were not severe, though our parapet was breached in several places."[194]

After a brief respite in reserve, John returned to St. Eloi. "Practically the whole time the Battalion occupied this position, the enemy shelled trenches… evidently searching for our mine shaft which is near; on one occasion they succeeded in placing a shell directly in the mouth of the shaft. Trenches were breached in several places, but were repaired by working parties at night… During the time the battalion was in the area occupied from 3/4/16 to present date, it has been found most difficult to carry out reliefs or to bring up stores expeditiously owing to the fact that there are only two communication trenches in this sector, namely the P & O CT and the Chicory CT. Owing to heavy bombardment the P & O was impassable almost the whole time."[195]

At last, from 21st April to the end of the month, the battalion was withdrawn far back to Boeschepe, south-west of Poperinghe and just inside the French frontier, where John and the battalion were inspected both by Sir Douglas Haig and by General Sir Herbert Plumer, who commanded the 2nd Army, and distributed a large number of gallantry medals and spoke warmly to the division. But during a spell of battalion training, "at about 4.15pm on the 25th May, a bombing accident took place in the Bn. Bombing Pit causing twenty casualties, five men dying from the results. Three officers were wounded, 2 Lieut J.P. Bennett, 2 Lieut J. Mackay, and 2 Lieut L.O. Stocken, attached from the 10th Middlesex Regiment."[196] John was treated for a significant injury through the casualty system and on 1st June returned to England. Fortunately, he was fit enough to return to service elsewhere the following August.

Thomas Lonsdale was not so lucky. The 7th Duke of Cornwall's Light Infantry was in trenches at Potijze Wood, immediately east of Ypres on 24th May, when he was shot through the stomach by a sniper. Ironically, several days later the *London Gazette* recorded that on 3rd June 1916, he had been awarded, in the King's Birthday Honours list, the Distinguished Conduct Medal.[197] He had previously been mentioned in dispatches and verbally complimented on his work by the divisional general. He was sent back along the chain from the dressing station to the 10th Casualty Clearing Station, then all the way back to the 10th Stationary (Field) Hospital at the huge British base at St. Omer, but he could not be saved, and died on 5th June. His commanding officer wrote of him, "He was such a good officer, and his men were devoted to him" and the company captain who had commanded him whilst he was a lieutenant said, "I think I can say no man was more loved in every sense of the word by all ranks. He was a very gallant man, and a most efficient officer." Thomas was also awarded the Military Cross, though the ceremony to present it had not happened before he was killed – his father wrote in November 1916 to accept the Army's invitation to accept the medal

---

[194] War Diary, 5th Border Battalion, 8th-11th April 1916.
[195] War Diary, 5th Border Battalion, 14th-19th April 1916.
[196] War Diary, 5th Border Battalion, 25th May 1916.
[197] *Supplement to The London Gazette*, 29th June 1916, p. 6450.

in a military parade in London on behalf of his son. The school magazine summed up the feelings of the school in an obituary to him: "So passed a fine young soldier, whose career has been in the highest degree creditable to himself and to the School."[198] His father wrote to say that he had five children, all serving their country – three sons and two daughters. One daughter was a nursing sister, and the other was "represented by her husband". Though Thomas had been killed, his brothers C.Q.M.S. Joseph Lonsdale of the 28th London Battalion and Sergeant Henry Lonsdale of the 3rd Canadian Mounted Rifles survived the war.

Thomas had been taking photographs and his father wrote asking for the return of his leather kit bag and his camera. This elicited the comment from the Assistant Financial Secretary at the War Office, "With regard to the camera I am to observe that the Military Authorities at the Base point out that the carrying of this article is strictly prohibited by General Routine Order 1137."[199]

A few days after Thomas died, Douglas Collingwood also in the Ypres Salient, needed medical attention. His father was the retired Major-General Clennan Collingwood of the Royal Artillery. Born in 1887, he was a very early member of the school, and had already left for university when the first *Bournemouthian* magazine was published in 1905. His younger brother Gordon was also a member of the school. When the war broke out, Douglas was living in Halifax, Nova Scotia, and working as a mining engineer, where – by 1907 – he had worked for a degree in mining engineering. By 1914 he already had some military experience. He had been a sergeant in the Cadets and at Dalhousie College in Nova Scotia he had joined the Engineering Corps, initially as a sapper. From August to November 1914 he had served as a lance corporal in the 10th (Fort) Company of Canadian Engineers and in December 1914 was a commissioned lieutenant, serving within Canada.

On 30th November 1915, he was taken as lieutenant onto the strength of the 2nd Canadian Pioneer Battalion, Canadian Expeditionary Force (C.E.F.). His battalion drew on skilled men from western Ontario and his company was 'C' Company. (This battalion was sometimes also known as the West Ontario Battalion, though that name can be confusing as it was also used by an infantry battalion.) The battalion sailed from Quebec on 4th December and landed at Le Havre on 8th March 1916, after spending three months in final training in Devon, and received their first casualty four days later, in Belgium. Many more were to follow. They were divisional troops in the 2nd Canadian Division from March 1916 onwards.

Pioneer battalions were not the same as Labour battalions. Pioneer units had come into existence as the result of an Army Order of December 1914. To qualify, men had to have A1 fitness. They received extra pay compared to infantry, as the men had had extra training and skills. Their training included weapons like rifles and the Lewis gun. Pioneer battalions included a mix of men. Some were men experienced with using picks and shovels like miners or road makers. Their duties were varied: whilst a lot of the time they worked on trench construction and maintenance, including the creation of dug-outs, Douglas' men also used their different skills for a wider range of tasks such as bridge building, putting up buildings, canal maintenance, roadworks, and even creating the hard standing for new railway lines. In the battalion would be specialised tradesmen. Some might be experienced in working with wood or metals, such as smiths, carpenters and

---

[198] *The Bournemouthian*, July 1916.
[199] Army File, Thomas Lonsdale, WO 339/20804.

joiners. Others had building work experience, such as bricklayers and masons. Some battalions – though not that of Douglas, had more specialised skills yet, including working on the railways, perhaps as engine drivers and fitters. To enable them to fulfil their duties, the pioneer battalion would carry a wide range of materials and equipment, often of a technical nature.

Soon after arriving in France, on 25th March 1916, with two other officers and ninety-three men, Douglas was attached to the 31st Canadian Infantry (Alberta) Battalion (in which Frank Cox was serving) for three days "for instructional purposes"[200] as part of the battalion-manned trenches north of Spanbroekmolen, west of Wytschete, on the western edge of the Messines Ridge, and the rest at St. Eloi on the northern edge of the ridge. They remained in these positions to the end of the month, experiencing a period of active defence as the infantry raided and bombed the German lines.

On 20th May, he was sent with another officer and about eighty men for attachment to the 3rd Canadian Division under their chief engineer. When the battalion was working near Poperinghe, on 7th June he was transferred sick back to the Canadian Training Division H.Q. at Shorncliffe where Canadian hospitals had been established. (At Shorncliffe the Canadian Medical Corps had transformed a number of schools, hotels and people's houses into hospitals.) It is not clear how long he was away from the battalion sick, so he might have missed being with them in close support of the front-line infantry during the later stages of the Battle of the Somme.

There are familiarly designated three Battles of Ypres – October 1914; April 1915; July-November 1917; and some would add a fourth, in April 1918 against the major German offensive. However, when the Germans launched their major attack on Verdun in the spring of 1916, they left a substantial reserve force at Ypres, and they used this to attack the British in June. This was really an attempt to pin down the British to stop them weakening their lines to help the French further south. At that time Ernest Snelgar and the 4th Canadian Mounted Rifles Battalion were holding Mount Sorrel (otherwise known as Hill 62) above Sanctuary Wood, east of Hill 60. On 2nd June, after five hours of ever-increasing ferocity, a German bombardment virtually destroyed their trenches. Later, artillery officers estimated they might have received as many as 180,000 German shells. At the start of the afternoon, the Germans launched an assault and captured the Canadian trenches. The Canadian remnant fell back, but only three or four officers and seventy-three men from the front line had survived. One British general had been killed, and another wounded and captured along with the commanding officer of the battalion. The battalion was reduced to its headquarters and a single company, including Ernest. The whole brigade had to be withdrawn and reformed with new drafts, though remarkably it was deemed to be back up to strength after only two weeks.

Alexander Sandbrook and the 8th Canadian Infantry Battalion were amongst the troops sent in to recapture Mount Sorrel. From reserve, the battalion was committed to the attack to regain the hill on 13th June. It was a bloody fight – the battalion took over a hundred casualties. Amongst the dead and wounded were a number of their senior officers. What made things worse for them was that the British artillery seemed to have miscalculated the positions and for two days they were firing onto the Canadian trenches. These resorted to sending messages like "How[itzers] are firing short right into our trenches. For God's sake get an FOO to watch things." "Our own shells falling short

---

[200] War Diary, 31st Canadian Infantry Battalion, 25th March 1916.

combined with the almost continuous enemy shelling made conditions very trying indeed."[201] In the end, their colonel – though himself wounded and "in a weak state" – went back to sort it out. By the time they were relieved, one officer had been killed and five wounded, whilst sixty-four men had died, 195 wounded, with two missing. After withdrawing to train and reorganise, in September they moved down to the Somme.

When the fighting for Mount Sorrel was at its height, William Challis, Walter Bailey, and Frank Wellum were fighting in Ploegsteert Wood, south of Mesen. William was an interesting boy to join Bournemouth School. Born in New York in 1892, he was the son of an American lawyer. He joined the school in 1904 when he and his sister lived in Bournemouth with their aunt. He was at the school from 1904-1908. After leaving school, he became a lawyer. In April 1914 he applied for British citizenship (attained a year later). When the war broke out he joined the 23rd Royal Fusiliers Battalion, but soon was selected for officer training. He was commissioned into the 12th Hampshire Battalion, which had already left for Salonika, but was soon moved into the 15th Hampshire Battalion instead. He landed in France on 25th May 1915 and reported to the battalion at Ploegsteert Wood.

Walter Bailey

Walter Bailey was only a comparative youngster, born in Boscombe in 1895 and attending the school from 1910 to 1914. Walter briefly left school in the spring of 1911 but things changed, and he was able to return to school that April and resume his academic career. By the time he finally left in 1914 he had an impressive set of school achievements under his belt: a school prefect (1913-1914); 2nd XI and house football player; and sergeant in the school O.T.C. and he had attained a place to study at Queen's College, Cambridge. He joined the Cambridge O.T.C., and after just a term at Cambridge, in January 1915 he left and, at the age of 19, was commissioned into the 15th Hampshire Battalion in June 1915. Cambridge had to be put on hold, Walter hoping to return after the war.

Still only aged 19, he was rapidly promoted to full lieutenant on 1st July 1915, and soon after to captain. This was a remarkably fast series of promotions – to captain of a company within a year. The battalion was brigaded to 122nd Brigade and the 41st Division. Before they left, the entire division was inspected by King George V and Field Marshal Lord French on 26th April. They arrived in France on 1st May 1916.

Another fellow officer in the 15th Hampshire Battalion was Frank Wellum who had been born in 1887. He had been in the Cadets at school from 1902-1904, and played football for the school in 1904. He continued his military interest whilst at the Winchester Teacher Training College and was a member of the 1st Volunteer Battalion of the Hampshire Regiment (just before the formation of the Territorial Force). By 1911 he was an elementary school teacher with a special qualification in Swedish Drill (the origins of P.E.). On 16th January 1915, he applied for a commission, passed his medical four days later, and was commissioned 2nd lieutenant into the Shropshire Light Infantry on 9th February but transferred to the 15th Hampshire Battalion on 21st November 1915. On 18th March 1916, he was promoted to lieutenant and went to France with Walter.

---

[201] War Diary, 8th Canadian Infantry Battalion, 14th June 1916.

Soon the 15th Hampshire Battalion was in the trenches at Ploegsteert Wood. On 6th June 1916, the Germans renewed their assault in the salient, accompanied by the explosion of mines, and managed for a fortnight to capture the front line trenches at Hooge until driven back by the Canadians. They tried again between 26th and 28th June 1916 but were held off by British artillery fire. Then, "from July, 1916, to May, 1917, the Ypres sector remained comparatively quiet. There were few attacks on either side, but the guns thundered day and night. It may be said that the British were 'trying their hand'."[202]

For the 15th Hampshire Battalion this fighting was very real. As the Commonwealth War Graves Commission explains (describing the memorial at Ploegsteert), "Those commemorated... did not die in major offensives, such as those which took place around Ypres to the north, or Loos to the south. Most were killed in the course of the day-to-day trench warfare which characterised this part of the line, or in small scale set engagements, usually carried out in support of the major attacks taking place elsewhere."[203] William Challis was killed. His friend Horace Tollemache afterwards wrote to William's sister Mary, "You have heard of the death of your heroic brother. All the Regiment feel the deplorable loss. As we were at the Bournemouth School together I thought you would like an account of his brave deed prior to his death. He volunteered to go and fetch in the wounded in spite of heavy shell and machine gun fire. The other officer who accompanied him was killed. Challis managed to get back safely, only to be struck next day by a rifle grenade. He was killed instantly." His lieutenant colonel also wrote, "He was one of my best officers, and the Adjutant and I feel his loss very much. Only 24 hours before his death he did a most gallant deed in assisting to save the lives of wounded men in 'No Man's Land' under a very heavy fire of all kinds. His name has been asked for by the Division, and the conduct of this officer and a few men who accompanied him was gallant in the extreme." We are told that he had written home a few hours before his death, describing the bringing in of wounded men from No Man's Land – but he had not mentioned that he was the man who had done it.[204] What they did not mention was that William was accidentally killed at 1a.m. on July 14th 1916 by gas fired by the British as part of an attack. He was buried in the Berkshire Extension Cemetery on the edge of the wood. A few days later, his friend Horace Tollemache took his place as a 2nd lieutenant in the battalion.

The Germans were pushed back, and when Ernest Snelgar and the 4th Canadian Mounted Rifles Battalion returned to the trenches on 23rd July, it was to those of Sanctuary Wood from which they had previously been driven. These they held again whilst the Germans were preoccupied further south, not only with Verdun but also with their defence against Haig's attack on the Somme. (On 23rd August 1916, Ernest and his comrades left the Ypres Salient and began to prepare to join the bloodbath of the Somme.)

About 3rd August 1916, sick, Frank Wellum left his battalion and the salient. He was suffering from dilated action of the heart as well as septic tonsillitis – which led to an operation for the removal of his tonsils. On 8th August 1916, he arrived at Dover aboard the SS *Cambria* and, hospitalised, went before a sequence of medical boards. He was required to relinquish his commission on 6th December 1916 on the grounds of ill-health. He remained in Bournemouth until his death in 1964.

---

[202] *Michelin Battlefield Guide*, published soon after the end of the Great War.
[203] Commonwealth War Graves Commission description of the Ploegsteert Memorial within the Berks Cemetery Extension.
[204] These letters were quoted in his obituary published in *The Bournemouthian*, July 1916.

Coming the other way, Reginald Lapthorne of the 1st Hampshire Battalion moved north into the Ypres Salient. He was born in 1891 and at school from 1905-1906. After leaving school he trained to be a dentist and became the sole owner of a dentist service with multiple branches, though he based himself in Bournemouth. A single man, on 4th March 1912 he attested for the 9th Hampshire Battalion – the Cyclist Battalion of Territorials, based in Bournemouth, which so many Old Bournemouthians joined. When the war broke out, the Territorials were called to the colours, and Reginald was embodied on 5th August 1914. This gave him a professional problem with his dental practice, which he could only solve by closing down some branches, and leaving the Boscombe branch in the hands of his assistant. (This problem intensified when the assistant was called up in May 1918.) Reginald was made corporal. On 13th May 1915 he was commissioned 2nd lieutenant in the 13th Hampshire Battalion, a reserve battalion for the Service Army. When it was formed on the Isle of Wight the previous autumn its members might have thought they were joining the 'Isle of Wight Pals'. On 31st May 1916 he was promoted to lieutenant and on 15th August 1916 switched to become an officer of the Regular Army. He disembarked at Rouen on 11th July 1916 and eight days later joined the 1st Hampshire Battalion in which Victor Martin was serving as a private. The 1st Hampshire Battalion was in the 11th Brigade, 4th Division and had already seen considerable action on 1st July and in the opening days of the Somme.

At this time the battalion was at Beauval, north of Amiens. From there, they went by train and narrow gauge railway to Poperinghe and into dry, but weak, trenches on the east bank of the canal opposite Boesinghe, where they suffered from machine guns, trench mortars and sniping.

Several members of the school were in the 2nd Hampshire Battalion: Eric Rey, Andrew Peden, Howard Farwell and Russell Prichard. (This battalion had already had a glorious history in the war. Initially brought back from India to England in 1914, it had received 231 additional men before going to Gallipoli in 1915. Their landing under fire at Cape Helles on 25th April became almost legendary for the valour shown and casualties suffered – one 15-year-old soldier was wounded three times that day. After hundreds of losses, they had only withdrawn with the final evacuation on 8th January 1916. Part of the 88th Brigade of the 29th Division, they landed in France at the end of March 1916.) They were in the trenches in front of Potijze, north-east of Ypres near Boesinghe, where they worked hard to consolidate and strengthen the defences.

Eric Rey was a boy soldier. Born in Ilfracombe in May 1899, he was only at the school for the year in 1913. He volunteered at the age of 15 in April 1915 for the Cyclists' Corps of the 9th Hampshires. Almost as soon as he was seventeen, he was sent to France, attached to the 2nd Hampshire Battalion, landing in France in April 1916. Andrew Peden was born in 1894 and was at the school from October 1907 until December 1909. The son of the Christchurch Baptist minister, Andrew had volunteered for the Hampshire Regiment at the same time as his older brother Alexander and younger brother Fergus who may not have been members of the school. (Older brother Alexander served with the 9th Hampshire Battalion, and younger brother Fergus was listed as a lance corporal in 11th Hampshire Battalion (Pioneers). Fergus died of wounds on 27th September 1917 whilst fighting for the 14th Hampshire Battalion alongside Cyril Howard in the Third Battle of Ypres.)

On 8th August, the alarm was sounded as a gas cloud was observed approaching from the north-east. The wind was light so when the gas reached them it had a deadly impact – and was accompanied by a terrible German artillery bombardment. The battalion had already been under German rifle grenade bombardment, sniping, and machine gun fire. "As soon as the gas cloud was observed to be approaching our line the alarm was taken up and due precautions made. The cloud took about an hour to pass and came in two waves. During this time our supporting artillery opened a barrage of shrapnel fire and the enemy made no attempt to leave his trenches. The enemy at the same time opened a fairly heavy shrapnel fire onto our front line system and main communications, a few large howitzer shells being directed at our reserves. The gas seemed to be of a particularly deadly kind and penetrated a considerable distance the effect being felt some distance in the rear. It was noticeable that the gas corroded all metal that it came in contact with and killed many rats and birds."[205]

Howard Farwell

Four officers died and six were wounded; one hundred and twenty five men were killed and a further hundred wounded in this attack. It was phosgene gas that was killing rats and birds as well as the men over a wide area. Howard Farwell did not survive it. He died the next day, at the Potijze Advanced Dressing Station which was located at the battalion reserve base, and was buried there. He had been born in 1888, and was at the school from 1903 to 1905. When he volunteered in October, 1914 Howard was the foreman of a large farm in the east of Hampshire. He was a good, keen sportsman, and as captain of the Mudeford Cricket and Football Club he was well known and very popular. He enlisted in the Hampshire Regiment and started with one of their battalions for India, but he fell sick and was in consequence left in hospital at Alexandria. He went on to land on the Dardanelles 5th August 1915 where he joined the 2nd Hampshire Battalion. He had survived the Battle of the Somme only to die in an equally awful place, the Ypres Salient. The others had survived. The battalion was subsequently withdrawn into the reserve, and set to work strengthening the second line of trenches, and reinforcements were brought in on 12th and 17th August. During the rest of the month they remained in reserve, but a steady stream of men were sent back sick to hospital – sixty- one by the end of the month. In September and October, despite some spells back in the trenches, including some raids, it was sickness that continued to wear down the battalion but still the battalion went back to the Somme.

1st Hampshire Battalion also was hit by this gas attack, which the battalion had anticipated from the north-easterly wind direction. Here, the Germans followed up with a raiding party which had to be driven off by heavy rifle fire and grenade throwing. Their major, in temporary command of the battalion, recognised a number of deficiencies in the defensive measures shown up by the gas attack: warning gongs from old shell cases were useless with all the noise of battle; a klaxon horn was out of order; most of the red S.O.S. rockets were damp and would not go off; and the stokes and other mortars did not manage to fire.

Later in the month they took over a section of trenches stretching south from Hooge and east of Zillebeke. "Position rather unpleasant on account of being overlooked from all points of the salient… strafed for about an hour with field guns – heavies and 'Minnies', on both Front and Support lines. Our casualties were Capt C C Smythe, wounded, 2/lt N Prynn suffering severe shock, both buried. 5 men killed and 15 wounded, all C Coy. During the Enemy's bombardment 10

---

[205] War Diary, 2nd Hampshires, entries of 4th and 8th August 1916.

Germans tried to get into the Sap on A Coy's left but were dispersed by the rifle fire of Sgt Clark, a Corpl and one Pte, the last of whom was killed by a shell."[206] That month the battalion lost twenty-three killed; thirty-eight wounded; two missing; forty-six gassed; and ninety-one sent to hospital.

That autumn 1916, Eric Rey also suffered some kind of poisoning. The continual sickness rate of the 2nd Hampshire Battalion makes it difficult to be sure quite when he left, but in any case, after considerable questioning and debate in parliament about the presence of boy soldiers like Eric, he was sent back to England along with hundreds of boy soldiers under 18. He was transferred to the Reserve Battalion Royal of the West Kents and put into camp at Tunbridge Wells. Many boys in this situation bitterly resented being sent back to what they saw as a form of school, designed to occupy them until they grew old enough to be sent back to war.

Arras, Loos and the Vimy Ridge, Spring 1916

Percy Robertson, who had been pulled out of the trenches in May 1915 suffering badly with his health and with shellshock, again served for a time in the trenches in the northern part of France. Once invalided to England and then recovered, he was discharged from the King's Royal Rifles on 6th September and the next day was made a 2nd lieutenant in the 6th Welsh (Glamorgan) Battalion.

Percy joined the battalion in France on 29th October 1914. It was part of the 3rd Brigade in the 1st Division. This period of active service was often described with some humour by the adjutant writing up the battalion diary. For example, whilst Percy and the battalion were in old German trenches at Loos, on 31st March 1916, "Huns started strafing our front line between Harts & Harrison's Crater. They evidently appeared to have a grudge against this part of the line as they poured in shells, two at a time, until after midday. At last our artillery replied but it did not seem to intimidate the Huns... The front line resembled a badly metalled road in a very short time. Tried to get up to the front line but got caught by two shells. Our 'tin-hats' saved us again, as about three pieces of shells hit my hat! Doctor considered that this was getting a bit too much of it! His stretcher bearers did very good work in getting the wounded men down from the front line. The weather was really glorious – just the sort of day to be in England. Sergt. Powell was killed by a sniper's bullet on Harrison's Crater. Must interview that sniper tomorrow. Major Carrington, Commandg the 115 Battery, visited the HQs during the afternoon & expressed his views on everything in general. In the evening, the Doctor took our 'liaison' officer up to the front line to shew him what the Huns had done. A fairly quiet night except for some rifle grenades on our front line. However we gave them more back than they wanted."[207]

Cecil Tollemache, one of Horace's brothers, also served in this sector of the line. Born in 1889, Cecil was not the oldest brother, but he was the oldest to attend Bournemouth School, followed by Horace, Philip and Archibald. (Their three other brothers also fought in the war, but did not attend Bournemouth School.) His childhood was unusual and gave him a range of experiences: between 1896 and 1900 he had lived and attended school in France and then was at Bournemouth School from 1903 to 1906, where he was a very early member of the Cadet Corps. Later he went abroad again, living and working in Cuba from 1910 to 1914. These experiences allowed him later to claim qualifications in banking, and sugar and banana planting. He had returned to England a few days

---

[206] War Diary. 1st Hampshires, 23rd to 26th August 1916.
[207] War Diary, 6th Welsh Battalion, 31st March 1916.

before war broke out and initially activated a commission he had been granted in a Territorial battalion, the 7th Hampshire Battalion. A large number of Old Boys of the school had joined this battalion and later several were to express their frustration when it sailed to Karachi on 9th October and remained in British India until it was moved to Aden in January 1918. For the men involved it made for a relatively comfortable life in India, but one that frustrated their desire to serve by fighting and perhaps earn glory – which in joining the Territorials before the war many had thought they might be doing. Cecil, however, took a bold decision: he resigned his commission in the 7th Hampshire Battalion and on 31st August 1914 enlisted in a regiment which still had vacancies – the Southern Cavalry Depot at Bristol. He could already ride, and on 3rd September was posted to the 4th Hussars. However, although he was not on his way to the exotic East with the 7th Hampshires, neither was he serving at the front. Instead he had been sent to Curragh, near Dublin, in Ireland, for further training and to be part of the British military presence in Ireland. So, still frustrated, he tried again to get to the Western Front. On 3rd November 1914 he re-applied for a commission, expressing a preference for the infantry.

On 5th January 1915, he was commissioned 2nd lieutenant in the 11th Hampshire Battalion, then stationed near Dublin as part of 16th (Irish) Division. Just as he was posted to the battalion the Army re-designated it to be Divisional Pioneers rather than Brigade Infantry. Whatever he thought, there could be no fourth switch for Cecil. On 18th December 1915, Cecil and the battalion landed at Le Havre.

Cecil was with the battalion for just two months, through the winter of 1915-1916. They frequently operated in places vulnerable to German artillery, and even rifle or machine-gun fire. On 11th February 1916 he was wounded near Loos. A shrapnel shell burst at close quarters near him. Two or three men with him were killed. One shrapnel fragment smashed into his right shoulder whilst a second fragment hit him on the calf of his right leg. He fell, and was taken to the advanced dressing station. Two days later he went to the hospital at Le Tréport, an important centre for hospital services, encompassing No. 3 and No.16 General Hospital, No.2 Canadian General Hospital and No.3 Convalescent Depot. He stayed there for over a week before being sent back to Dover from Dieppe on 21st February 1916. From Dover he was sent the same day to the newly opened Princess Christian's Hospital for Officers which only opened in March, with thirty-five beds designated for the convalescence of officers. There Cecil stayed for a few more weeks. He returned to the Western Front in May 1916.

In March 1916, the British had taken over an additional twenty miles of former French trenches in order to release the French for their battle to defend Verdun. This section of the line ran south from Loos to Ransart, and included the strategic sector known as Vimy Ridge. There, the Germans held the high ground above the scarp slope, which meant the British could not see behind the Germans down to the coalfields at Douai with their supply routes and distribution points. On the other hand, the Germans could look down the dip slope, over the British trenches all the way to Arras. The trenches which the British had taken over were in a very poor condition, with few redoubts or dug-outs, and poorly dug and maintained. The British also realised that the Germans had dug deep and long tunnels under the British trenches, so the British immediately attempted to strengthen the trenches (having considered pulling them back) and began shelling the Germans and counter-tunnelling. There was a period of bitter fighting above and below ground level. John Snelgar of the 1st Wiltshire Battalion was there. On 20th January 1916, he had written to Dr. Fenwick at school that "I have been lucky to escape all bullets and shells so far, but have seen some since I came out. We hope soon to finish the war now."[208]

On 11th April 1916, John Snelgar and the 1st Wiltshires had moved into trenches at La Targette, just north of Arras. John and the others were soon fighting in and around the tunnels and craters in a spell of operations based around active mining and the holding or capture of craters on Vimy Ridge. For example, on 24th April, "At 7.28pm the enemy sprang a mine on the left of the outpost line by a former crater at the top of the Grange CT and considerable bombing ensued for over an hour. The 10th Cheshires Regt on the left was more deeply involved and sustained several casualties. In the course of this bombing 2nd Lieut Maybrook the Battn Bombing Officer was killed by a bullet shot through the neck. His body was not discovered until the next morning as it was out in advance of the outpost line by the craters."[209] Each day seemed to bring more casualties, but John emerged unscathed. His unit began to receive training in using the more mobile Lewis machine gun, which was to become the main attack gun of the infantry by 1918, as well as in practising bayonet fighting.

In May 1916, the British defence in the area was weakened as five divisions were moved south to prepare for the Battle of the Somme.

After further serious fighting on 3rd May, John was tasked to help to consolidate one of the crater defence positions. The enemy "was very quiet but at 8pm sprang two mines, one to the right of Common CT, the other to the North of Birkin CT. The former did no damage to the trenches, the latter blew up a bombing post of the left company and three men were missing. The near lips of both craters were consolidated and rifle fire from the Common Crater accounted for several of the enemy. They retaliated with bombs and later with rifle grenades, only. Neither side opened artillery fire."[210] These were tense days, with men being lost to sniping or the explosion of mines on a regular basis. On 8th May "at 8.13pm we sprang a mine NE of the top of Grange CT between the two existing craters. This had the effect of obliterating both craters and forming a crescent shaped crater about 45 yds across and 80 yds in length. It was at least 60 feet deep. After the explosion a Lewis rifle was rushed up and enfilading fire brought to bear upon a German working party which was fixing loopholes in the northern lip. Good execution must have been done as work ceased and was not resumed. A sap was run in continuation of Grange CT to the lip and a side cut was made to command the right flank. A further sap ending in a Y shaped fork was run out to the Southern extremity and two loophole plates place in position."[211] So, by blowing a mine in No Man's Land they were trying to eliminate a German advantage and create one for the British. These were difficult days. German high explosive artillery shells mixed with tear gas, grenades, machine gun and rifle bullets, aircraft bombing, and underground explosions all added up to weeks of tension and casualties.

Thomas Searls, who was nearby, shared these hazards. On 14th May, the 2nd South Staffordshire Battalion carried out a raid from its trenches at Calonne. Thomas was involved in the preliminary stage: with a Corporal Sadler, he went forward from the British front line at 10.30p.m. with the object of finding out if the Germans had established a forward listening post which might disrupt

---

[208] *The Bournemouthian*, April 1916.
[209] War Diary, 1st Wiltshire Regiment, April 24th 1916.
[210] War Diary, 1st Wiltshire Regiment, May 3rd 1916.
[211] War Diary, 1st Wiltshire Regiment, May 8th 1916.

the raid following on the German 'Road Sap'. The two men got some cover by staying close to the edge of a road which crossed No Man's Land until intercepted by the German front line and the Road Sap, which came out forward of it. They got to within twenty-five yards of the German sap and were able correctly to report the absence of a listening post, although they could not clearly make out the condition of the German wire. They returned safely and Thomas made his report, after which the raiding group went out successfully.

For John Snelgar and the 1st Wiltshire Battalion the problems continued. On 21st May, the Germans bombarded the British trenches on their front to a depth of eight miles using massive artillery resources assembled out of sight of the British. The Germans mixed tear gas with massive quantities of high explosive. After twelve hours, that evening the Germans blew a mine and launched a major infantry attack. This smashed through the front lines and took the support trenches as well. Then, having taken a considerable area, the Germans dug in.

Henry Hollies was involved. Henry had been wounded in the aftermath of the Battle of Loos. And when he was fit enough to re-join the 15th London Battalion in France on 27th January 1916, they were only a few miles from where he had left them: still in position near Loos. But from March they were a little further south, holding trenches on the spur of Notre Dame de Lorette, where today the French have a National Sepulchre, an extension of Vimy Ridge. This too was a war of mines and craters, of sudden attacks and desperate defences, but on a relatively small scale most of the time. In April, Henry was granted leave, and visited Bournemouth. Then, on 22nd May, Henry and the 15th London Battalion were involved in the fighting at Cabaret Rouge between Souchez and Vimy. Here, what was meant to be an advance turned into a desperate fight to hold their positions, which they managed – but at the loss of two officers wounded and missing; eight men missing; nine killed; and seventy-three wounded. (Henry was then promoted to corporal. His battalion moved south towards the end of August to the Somme.)

Haig ordered a counter-attack for 23rd May. John Snelgar and the 1st Wiltshire Battalion defended their craters and trenches whilst three brigades made the attack. The Germans were expecting them – their counter artillery bombardment hit the 7th Brigade twenty-five minutes before the planned attack. The 99th Brigade was smashed even before they got started by German shells and intense machine-gun fire. Modest gains were made by the counter-attack, but overall the divisions had lost about 2,500 soldiers. Both sides then dug in and concentrated on other sectors of the front. In the middle of June, John and the 1st Wiltshire Battalion also moved south to prepare to support the Battle of the Somme.

Thomas Searls and the 2nd South Staffordshire Battalion were also caught up in this counter-attack. The battalion had moved onto Vimy Ridge, taking up their new position on 25th May. "The trenches in all this sector were in an awful state owing to the hostile bombardment... The enemy was particularly active with minenwerfer and rifle grenades. We replied vigorously with Stokes Mortar bombs and organised rifle grenade fire so that the German fire was effectively silenced on the 27th instant."[212] On 26th May, Thomas was again wounded. He received a shrapnel wound to his right foot, "inflicting a rugged wound about 2 inches long by one"[213] wide. The damage reached down to the inner side of his foot, down to the metatarsal bone. He was evacuated to No.2 General Hospital

---

[212] War Diary, 2nd South Staffordshire Battalion, 25th-27th May 1916.
[213] Army File, Thomas Searls, WO 339/34918.

at Le Havre. From there, although the wound was classified as serious but not severe, he was sent back to the United Kingdom, and admitted on 2nd June to the 1st Southern General Hospital at Edgbaston. He remained there until 7th July and was promoted to be a full lieutenant.

Shortly afterwards, boy-soldier Lewis John Gosschalk fell in action near Arras. The school records list him under two surnames, Gosschalk and Kent, yet he actually served using a third variation, 'Barton'. He was born in 1897. His father had already died, and his mother, whose maiden name was Barton, remarried to Edward Goss-Chalk. Lewis was known by his second name, John, and was a member of Bournemouth School from 1909-1912. At school he was a member of the O.T.C. It was probable that John's stepfather was German in ethnicity, Holman Gosschalk.

As soon as war was declared, he tried to join the 7th Hampshires, but was told that he was too young. So he tried again a month later, attempting to join the Hampshire Cyclists. Again he was rejected because of his age. Undeterred, he went to London where he disguised his identity and his age (becoming 'John Barton'), so that he was accepted by the 2/14th London Battalion (the London Scottish). It was

John Gosschalk (Kent)

a common practice amongst under age volunteers to use their mother's maiden name to disguise their true identity. He spent 1915 in England, training. "He was very keen in his work, and had refused a commission preferring to remain with the pals he had trained with."[214] At the end of April 1916, a strong detachment of nine officers and three hundred and three men from the battalion was sent to Ireland to help quell the security alarm following the 'Easter Rising'. As the battalion continued its training and prepared for imminent departure abroad, it was inspected by the King on 31st May. Finally, the battalion embarked at Southampton on 21st June and crossed the channel to Le Havre.

On 6th July 1916, they moved into trenches near Arras for instruction by the Gordon Highlanders. Immediately they started to take casualties – the first men killed died on 7th July. On 12th July John and the others moved into the firing line trenches near Arras, supported by the 2/16th London Battalion. Another man died that day. The next day, 13th July, John was killed and another three men were wounded.

Part of the problem had been that Lewis and his pals lacked enough grenades (then known as 'bombs'). "On the right the London Scottish were holding on to their redoubt, building barricades, and beating off the German bombers. But as the hours passed ammunition became scarce. The supplies of bombs here and there were almost exhausted. The London men went about collecting German bombs, and for some time these served, but not enough could be found to maintain effective fire. The position became more ugly. But the men did not lose heart. In those bad hours there were many men who showed great qualities of courage, and were great captains whatever their rank."[215]

---

[214] *The Bournemouth Visitors' Directory*, 19th August 1916.

[215] *The Bournemouth Visitors' Directory*, 19th August 1916; this article also quoted from the captain's letter to his mother.

John's body was taken back behind the lines and he was buried on the north-western outskirts of Arras at Maroeuil. He was only just nineteen when he died: just old enough to be abroad. His company captain wrote to console his mother: "It will perhaps be some consolation to know that his death must have been absolutely painless, and that he was not in the least disfigured. I visited his grave in the British cemetery here yesterday (August 1st)... Be assured that the grave will be taken care of so long as we are in the neighbourhood."

The Build-up to the Somme

Another Old Bournemouthian, Eugene Holland, was also discovering that the war in the trenches at the start of 1916 was an ugly business. Eugene was one of the earliest Bournemouth School boys, at the school between 1902 and 1907. After an active school life he emigrated to Jamaica, but he returned from there especially to volunteer after the outbreak of the war, gazetted 2nd lieutenant in the Special Reserve on 25th April 1915 and joining the Regular, 2nd Border Battalion, 20th Brigade, 7th Division. He went to France on 1st October 1915 and joined his battalion on 6th October when it was at Cambrin, west of La Bassée. Soon afterwards, on 28th October, the battalion was inspected (alongside other elements of I Corps) by King George V.

In February 1916 his battalion went into trenches near Fricourt on the Somme. Here they drove off a significant German raid. Eugene Holland was in command of a group of men on the left hand of the Tambour Salient. "22nd February 1916. Between 5 and 5.15 pm at night the enemy opened a heavy fire with every description of artillery and trench mortar on D3 sector which was held by the Battalion. The heaviest projectiles came from N.N.E. and were mainly directed at the Tambour salient on the right of the front line. A frontal fire was directed all along the whole of the front line trench. The two Companies in the front line were 'A' Company (left) and 'C' Company (right). By 5.30 pm the bombardment was very intense and it was felt certain the enemy meant to attack. At 5.40 pm it was found that communication between the right forward company (C Coy) and Battalion Head Quarters by telephone had been cut. The bombardment continued to about 6.45 pm when the hostile guns lifted from the Tambour but continued on the trenches further back. At 7.25 pm a report was received that the enemy had attacked the Tambour. Two enemy parties succeeded in getting into the front line in two places but were driven out. At about 8.40 pm the hostile artillery fire slackened and by 9 pm had almost quieted down. The estimated number of Germans who attacked were some 80 all ranks of whom 20 dead were counted from our fire trench next day. The enemy succeeded in throwing a bomb down one of our disused mine shafts before they were turned out and in their flight they left behind a lot of bombs and 3 pairs of wire cutters. A German corporal was taken prisoner and on being questioned he stated that they had moved forward in three parties of about 28 Other Ranks each: one between the two southern craters and two round the north of them. The flank parties had orders to take prisoners, the inner one to destroy mine heads by bombing them with special large bombs. The prisoner belonged to the 99th Reserve Regiment. Our Artillery retaliation seemed splendid and was most effective."[216] Casualties continued over the next months, as Eugene and the battalion had plenty more experience in the trenches followed by training and preparation for the Battle of the Somme.

The 1st Dorset Battalion had moved from Hill 60 to the Somme in July 1915. Here they shared in digging mines, despite the fatal danger of foul gases. After their experiences on Hill 60, however,

---

[216] War Diary, 2nd Border Regiment, 22nd February 1916.

they found this sector "exceptionally quiet"[217] and suffered only intermittent casualties. Raids were made by both sides, mines exploded, snipers were active but overall it was an easier time than in the Ypres Salient. The battalion manned trenches initially opposite La Boiselle and later slightly north, opposite Thiepval. Ralph Drayton, Wilfred Fuller and John Nethercoate also paraded before the King. On 22nd December, Ralph was promoted to temporary captain and at the end of the year the battalion transferred to 95th Brigade – almost immediately on to the 14th Brigade – both in the 32nd Division, a newly created division of the New Army. The idea was that experienced battalions like the 1st Dorset Battalion would provide enough experience to strengthen the new division that it could take its part in the front line. In this period, the Somme was still a relatively quiet British sector, though shelling by German artillery or trench mortars did take a regular toll.

On 12th January 1916, Ralph led a patrol in the direction of Thiepval and tried to ambush a German patrol, but it moved off without the two coming into contact. After that he remained in and out of front line trench duty between Thiepval and La Boiselle until 7th May. The 1st Dorset Battalion had returned to the trenches, relieving the 16th Lancashire Fusiliers. At first the situation seemed quiet, and until 3p.m. there were no casualties. However, at 11p.m., a German bombardment was followed by a raid in force. "At 11.30 pm three parties of the enemy (each about 35 strong) attacked the left of the sector (19th L.F on our left; 10th Inniskilling Fus[iliers] on our right); two parties entered 'D' company's trenches; third party attempted to enter trenches occupied by 'C' Company but was repulsed by Lewis gun and rifle fire. The whole of that portion of the line occupied by 'D' Company (extreme left of the battalion) was practically demolished by trench mortar bombs and artillery fire before the enemy raided. Germans were eventually driven out leaving one of their dead and one prisoner in our hands. At 1.45 am 8th May the situation again became normal. Our casualties were 2nd lieutenant Bayly killed, 2nd lieutenant Drayton wounded. 12 other ranks killed, 28 other ranks wounded, 23 other ranks missing, 1 other rank wounded and missing and 8 other ranks suffering from shell shock and effect of gas shells."[218]

Ralph Drayton

Ralph was awarded the Military Cross for his part in the defence, though the citation in the *London Gazette* on 24th June placed him with the 2nd Battalion, which at that time was recovering from its losses incurred in the capture of Kut-el-Amara in Mesopotamia: "Award of Military Cross - Second-Lieut. (Temp. Captain) R. Drayton, 3rd Bn. (attached 2nd Bn.), Dorset Regiment. For conspicuous

---

[217] War Diary, 1st Dorsets, 7th September 1915.

[218] War Diary, 1st Dorsets 7th May 1916. It later corrected the German numbers to 36, 25 and 25; explained that the trenches concerned were right and left of 'Hammerhead'; that they had been there 15 minutes; and several were killed in the trench. It criticised British howitzers for how slowly they responded to the German bombardment though the British field guns had returned fire quickly.

gallantry. When, after a heavy bombardment, the enemy raided our trenches, although wounded, he collected a few men and repulsed all attacks on his portion of the trench. He set a fine example to all around him."[219] "It appears that in this case Drayton was dazed and partly buried by a shell explosion. On extricating himself he found that he was surrounded by five Germans, who tried to capture him alive. Drayton shot three of these, and, though wounded by a bullet in the point of the shoulder, he made good his retreat to a neighbouring wood. There he found and rallied some of his men, and, returning with them, recaptured the trench out of which they had just been driven."[220]

For the time being, however, Ralph was out of the war with the wound in his left shoulder needing attention. This meant he missed the dreadful casualties the battalion incurred on 1st July 1916 as it joined in the attack on the Somme. Ralph was sent to hospital, and then invalided home where he was well received: "Fortunately his injury is not serious. He is making excellent progress towards recovery, and his friends in Bournemouth are delighted now to be able to congratulate him on such distinguished official recognition of gallant and efficient conduct. Bournemouth, we may add, has something also to congratulate itself upon, – in that it was at Bournemouth School he received the training which enabled him to obtain a commission in the Army, and at a very early period of the war to join the fighting forces on the Continent."[221] The culmination of these celebrations was his reception at Buckingham Palace on 8th July when the King presented him with his award.

Ralph had been buried alive and fallen unconscious for some time. Over the following year, the effect of the gunshot wound to his left shoulder (when he had been shot with a revolver) was compounded by the memory of being buried, and this led him to develop nervous shock.[222] Later, while weakened, he twice caught influenza whilst at Chesil Beach Camp with the Third Battalion – something not helped when a series of high tides flooded the camp. For much of the second half of 1917 he was attached to the 35th (Young Soldier) Training Battalion, which until the end of October 1917 had no regimental affiliation but then became the 53rd (Y.S.) T.R. Battalion of the Devonshires, and in January 1918 moved to Rollestone in Devon while Ralph was still a member of it.

Meanwhile, James Sinton joined the battalion. Born in August 1896, he was a few days short of 18 when war was declared. A member of the school between 1909 and 1912, initially his declared aim was to become a boy clerk in the Admiralty Civil Service. He worked there from 1912 to May 1914, but left work to return to school in order to study to take higher exams and so to improve his career prospects in the Civil Service. However, on 5th September 1914, he applied for a commission as a Reserve officer with the 3rd Battalion of the Dorset Regiment. The Headmaster, Dr. Fenwick, and the Head of the O.T.C., Mr. Sewell, both supported the application even though he had only been in the O.T.C. as a private, studying for his 'Cert. A' for three months. He passed his medical board at Weymouth on 9th September and his application was endorsed by the colonel of the 3rd Dorsets at Wyke Regis on 11th September. This was indeed a fast track response – and when he was gazetted on 7th May 1915 to the 3rd Battalion, the Dorsetshire Regiment, he was granted seniority as a 2nd lieutenant dating back to 15th August 1914. This, of course, was the Reserve and Training Battalion. In 1916, he was promoted full lieutenant with seniority from 27th March and two months

---

[219] *The London Gazette*, 24th June 1916.
[220] *The Bournemouthian*, July 1916. The wood would have been probably Thiepval Wood or, less likely, Authuille Wood.
[221] *The Bournemouth Visitors' Directory*, 1st July 1916.
[222] Army File, Ralph Drayton, WO 339/30754.

later, on 25th May 1916, he left to serve with the 1st Dorset Battalion in France, joining them on the Somme. By the middle of June 1916 they were attempting to build a new trench forward of the line opposite Thiepval, to be used as a 'jump off' trench for the battle, and this attracted a lot of German retaliation using shells, mortars and machine guns.

Two other members of the school were wounded that summer as the Army prepared for the battle: Edward Wroth, a former teacher, and Frederick Furness, a former pupil.

Edward Wroth (b. 1884) was a temporary master at Bournemouth School for the autumn term of 1908, when he served as form master of the 'Remove', and taught history and English. He landed in France on 3rd May 1915 and joined the 1/5th Royal Warwickshire Battalion (143rd Brigade, 48th (South Midland) Division) as a 2nd lieutenant soon afterwards. Frederick Furness was an early pupil of the school. On 30th April 1915 he joined the 1/14th London Battalion, commonly known as the London Scottish, and, after training, was sent to France to join 1/14th London Battalion, 1st Brigade in the 1st Division, arriving at the battalion on 22nd November at a time when it was training and resting – the battalion having been in the thick of the fighting in 1914 and 1915.

Edward and his battalion were in and out of trenches at Foncquevillers, overlooking the German strongpoint at Gommecourt. On 1st June 1916, the battalion relieved the 4th Gloucestershire Battalion in the trenches and almost every day suffered casualties – and then on 6th June they pushed forward with new saps the front line towards Gommecourt. The next day he was wounded. The injury was serious and they brought Edward back to England. He did recover but could only be posted as a lieutenant to the 51st (Graduated) Battalion, Royal Warwickshire, a training battalion, though after the Armistice it went to Germany as part of the Army of Occupation on the Rhine.

Three days after Edward was wounded, Frederick was probably a few miles further south, a little north of Beaumont-Hamel. Frederick's wound on June 10th was a gunshot through his buttocks, a typical result of a machine gun firing sweeping shots across the battlefield. He was taken away by the 2/1st Field Ambulance Unit attached to the 56th Division. This unit was based at Hebuterne, close to the battalion, and was staffed by four officers and one hundred and ten other ranks. It had established an advanced dressing station in a cellar protected with elephant shelters and with ambulance cars available. He was only with them a relatively short while before passing via Number 41 Casualty Clearing Station at Doullens to the 2nd Canadian General Hospital in Le Treport. On 19th June he was sent back to England, to the Territorial Force depot whilst he recuperated on light duties. That autumn, encouraged by his colonel, Frederick applied to take a commission, and on 3rd January 1917 he was nominated to be commissioned into the 4th (Reserve) Royal West Surreys. On 6th February he was transferred to the 4th Officer Cadet Battalion for officer training.

Further south at Heilly, Thomas Chaffey (b. 1898, at school 1906-1911) had landed in France on Christmas Day 1914, as a member then of the 7th Divisional Cyclist Company, though at that time legally he was too young to serve. He was an army cyclist.

The main role of the cyclists was to conduct reconnaissance and help to maintain communications by carrying messages. He and his comrades would be armed as infantry, in which role they could also be required to fight if need be. They were designated by the Army as 'Mounted Troops'. Once the war became bogged down in the trenches, the cyclists' role diminished, although numbers were held in reserve to help with the expected war of movement once the phase of trench warfare was over. However, even during that phase they might be found even, sometimes, cycling down communication trenches, especially if it was suspected that German use of their Moritz receiving stations meant that the security of the trench telephone system could not be relied upon. Elsewhere they might be used on security patrols – for example along the railways and canals (both in Britain and in France) – to act as a check against sabotage. At the earliest stage of the war, they might even be used as scouts (sometimes even directly fighting their German opposite numbers).

On 11th May 1916, the "11th. The 7th, 21st & 39th Divisional Cyclist Companies assembled at Heilly to form the XV Corps Cyclist Battalion, 376 strong, under the command of Major A.J. Hay."[223]

Heilly is on the northern bank of the Somme, mid-way between Amiens and Albert, west of the southern end of the battlefield. There was not enough work to engage a cyclist unit so men were sent off for all sorts of purposes – typically to assist signallers, to dig or to labour. Men of his unit were sent to help dig out the 21st Divisional Advanced HQ dug-out or to help the Labour battalions on various fatigues. They also provided labour to man the Heilly narrow gauge railway station. In preparation for the Battle of the Somme they were briefed with the mounted troops – presumably to be ready to carry messages once the anticipated breakthrough had occurred. Heilly became a communications centre and had medical facilities which were to prove important to several Old Bournemouthians in the coming battle.

---

[223] War Diary, XV Corps Cyclist Battalion, 11th May 1916.

5: The Battle of the Somme

At the end of 1915, Sir John French had been given little choice but 'voluntarily' to resign his leadership of the B.E.F. and to accept the rank of Field Marshall in charge of the Army within the United Kingdom. He was replaced by Douglas Haig.

Haig had forged an uncomfortable alliance with David Lloyd George, Minister of Munitions, with the intention of building up a much greater range of weaponry and ammunition. Although Haig has fashionably been portrayed as stubborn and unimaginative, wasteful of men with his belief in attrition as a strategy to wear out his opponents, this is by no means the entire story. Haig was also very interested in the use of the best technology he could acquire to support his troops. In September 1915, he tried the first use of poison gas to support the attack at Loos. In spring 1916, he had become very interested in the development of the tank. He pushed for greater use of narrow gauge railway systems to move men and materials, and he pressed hard for an increase in the number and scale of artillery pieces to be made available, and for the ammunition to use in them. He recognised even before the summer of 1916 that his army remained short of high explosive shells, relying far too much on shrapnel – useful for firing over men in the open, and for a limited number of trench situations, but not really what was needed to break the German defences.

In the summer of 1916 he was to fight the Battle of the Somme. This was originally conceived to be part of a much wider offensive by all the major Allied powers to squeeze the life out of the Germans and their allies. The French were fighting a defensive battle at Verdun, but under General Brusilov the Russians opened what seemed likely to be a promising eastern offensive.

It is all too easy to forget that never in British history had one man attempted to deploy so many troops over such a wide area, and to do so without most of the benefits of modern communications. Haig had to rely on field telephones, carrier pigeons, and runners to send information between units and back to the various levels of headquarters. The main battle was to be fought in the Somme department on a twenty mile front, roughly from Serre in the north to the French Army at the south. The northerly half of the British battle line ran roughly north-south, after which the line bent west to east before turning south again. The River Somme was south of the main battlefield. To distract the German defenders, Haig ordered an attack at Gommecourt, just to the north of the main battleground, hoping that this might confuse the defence and draw off significant resources which would not therefore be available to the Germans on the actual battle front.

Before the battle began, Sir Douglas Haig and General Rawlinson, to whom (entrusted the direct conduct of the battle) ordered the greatest artillery bombardment of the German trenches which the Army had ever known. The object of this bombardment was to destroy the German front line defences and to wipe out their front line forces, so that afterwards the British could advance and occupy them. Amidst the explosives of this bombardment was to be mixed the release of poisonous gases. Even at the time Haig had misgivings at Rawlinson's optimistic plan, but both men were faced by a number of seemingly intractable problems. Haig wanted the attack to begin whilst it was still dark so that the German machine gunners would have to fire blind, but the French insisted the attack must start at 7.30a.m. to allow their men to see what they were doing.

The battle was originally conceived as a British support action helping the bigger French Army advance to its south. This would have been launched in conjunction with the Russian offensive under

General Brusilov in the east. But whilst the Russians were ready and able to make their attack (though after initial successes it petered out) the French role was reversed to become a supportive action with the British divisions to make the breakthrough attempt, because the French were fully occupied further south trying to hold off the massive German assaults in the Battle of Verdun.

A major problem for Haig and Rawlinson was the need to make great use of the Reserve or New Army. Many of these soldiers were as yet relatively un-blooded and undertrained, and so Rawlinson decided that the only way to get units intact to the German trenches was to ensure that they moved across No Man's Land as organised battalions which would not lose structure and formation on the way. Rawlinson's answer to this was to direct that instead of running and taking cover across the gap, the men must walk over in lines – marching as if on the parade ground – to reform in the German front line. This decision has been much pilloried and much misunderstood. We need to remember the consensus current at that time: that given the communications available, and given that it was believed (or at least hoped) the Germans in the front line would have been obliterated by the artillery, it seemed a reasonable way of keeping the men, including those only semi-trained, in their correct units. To make sure that that solution would not be a slaughter, Rawlinson and Haig required the artillery to pulverise the German front line so that it would effectively offer no resistance. They were aware that for this they needed huge quantities of high explosive shells and that, despite repeated urgings on the British government and the Minister of Munitions David Lloyd George, they had to accept that the British factories simply could not produce enough. Therefore, the artillery would largely be firing shrapnel shells, which were really designed for sweeping aside infantry exposed on the surface, not an enemy sheltering within trenches or in dug-out shelters. They were also to be disappointed that so many of the shells that had been produced simply did not explode because of the poor quality of their manufacture. (Later, disagreements between Haig and Lloyd George may be dated from this difference over shell quality and shortages and became a most damaging rift in British leadership.)

If you can believe his war dispatch after the battle, Haig did not underestimate the strength of what opposed the British. He said that he recognised that the Germans had prepared well: "During nearly two years' preparation he had spared no pains to render these defences impregnable. The first and second systems each consisted of several lines of deep trenches, well provided with bomb-proof shelters and with numerous communication trenches connecting them. The front of the trenches in each system was protected by wire entanglements, many of them in two belts forty yards broad, built of iron stakes interlaced with barbed wire, often almost as thick as a man's finger. The numerous woods and villages in and between these systems of defence had been turned into veritable fortresses. The deep cellars usually to be found in the villages, and the numerous pits and quarries common to a chalk country, were used to provide cover for machine guns and trench mortars… These various systems of defence, with the fortified localities and other supporting points between them, were cunningly sited to afford each other mutual assistance and to admit of the utmost possible development of enfilade and flanking fire by machine guns and artillery. They formed, in short, not merely a series of successive lines, but one composite system of enormous depth and strength. Behind his second system of trenches, in addition to woods, villages and other strong points prepared for defence, the enemy had several other lines already completed; and we had learnt from aeroplane reconnaissance that he was hard at work improving and strengthening these and digging fresh ones between them, and still further back."[224]

---

[224] Sir Douglas Haig, Second War Dispatch, 23rd December 1916.

The bombardment, which was meant to minimise the challenges of this defence, cost Percy Pean his life. Percy Pean had worked as a temporary junior maths and science teacher at the school from September to December 1915. Born in 1886, Percy had taken up a long-term residential post at the Royal British Orphan School in Slough from 1907 to 1915 and had arrived at Bournemouth School to fill a war vacancy. He had left in December under the Derby Scheme, initially to become a soldier in the Civil Service Rifles (15th London Regiment) but almost immediately transferred in the spring of 1916 to be a Pioneer in the Royal Engineers. He was placed in a specialist chemical unit, the Special Brigade (Chemists).

These specialist companies of the R.E. were originally formed, in great secrecy, in the summer of 1915 so that the British could develop the means to retaliate for the German use of poison gas at Ypres the previous April. In early 1916, the original four special companies were expanded by the compulsory transfer of suitably qualified personnel from other units to form a special brigade of five battalions. Percy was placed in the 1st Battalion. Their main purpose was to dispense poison gases from special cylinders for both offensive and defensive gas measures. A few men were also, briefly, given the task of developing flame throwers. The brigade also launched smoke screen barrages and fired thermite bombs.

Since the first use of chlorine gas at Ypres and Loos in 1915, new and deadlier versions had been created. The Germans had regained the technical advantage in December 1915 with their creation of di-phosgene gas mixed with a small quantity of chlorine. Phosgene was reckoned to be several times more deadly than chlorine. The inclusion of a small element of chlorine in the mix was meant to make the gas mixture easier to disperse. The Germans also hoped that, because it did not initially irritate, the British and French might be fooled and only feel the effects some hours after inhalation.

The British used a mass gas attack from cylinders as part of the final 'softening up' of the Germans before the planned attacks. In this gas phase of the main barrage, Percy lost his life – "killed in action" on June 26th. It is possible that he might have been killed fetching gas cylinders or Livens projector tubes from the front line, but it is more likely that he was killed in an accident or in an attack that went wrong. When they described the gas releases of the pre-Somme bombardment, the war diaries of all five gas battalions showed that the men spent days and nights of feverish and concentrated activity. Their hard work was interrupted by shrapnel injuries, shattered emplacements, gas-related accidents, not least because the gas equipment still did not work reliably. Gas leaked from joints in the piping. Wind eddies and changes of direction blew gas back into British trenches. German shells and shell fragments sometimes ruptured gas pipes. The system which, one way or another, killed Percy was afterwards analysed for effectiveness by both sides. Both sides recognised that releasing gas by cylinder and letting the wind blow it across was not an efficient way of destroying their opposition. With men on guard to give the alarm, troops had time to put on masks. The wavering wind meant that the gas was likely to hit the originators' side almost as badly as the intended opposition. For the Germans there was also the recognition that the prevailing wind blew west to east, against them.

Percy was buried at the 10th Brigade Cemetery, which was afterwards renamed Sucrerie, at Colincamps. He was by no means that last Old Bournemouthian to suffer or die from gas. "Though Mr. Pean was here a very short time he made no enemies, but many friends, by whom his memory will for a long time to come be held in affectionate regard."[225] Percy had died in the preliminary bombardment, and after five days of the heaviest bombardment then known, Haig remained unconvinced that Rawlinson's plan would work because it was still not certain that the German wire was cut and their front line trenches smashed. Instead of attacking on 28th June, two more days of artillery bombardment were ordered.

The First Day of the Somme

Then, on 1st July at 07.20, a series of mines, which had been prepared over the previous months, was exploded in an attempt to destroy selected German strongpoints. The bombardment finished ahead of the assault, to give the British soldiers time to prepare without danger of being hit by their own artillery as had happened at Loos in 1915. But, unbeknown to the ordinary soldiers, the artillery had failed to destroy the enemy and the Germans swarmed up from their deep dug-outs to man their machine guns and prepare to repel the coming attack. A few days after the initial attacks, an officer of the 10th Royal Fusiliers, of which William Mitford and Stanley Birdseye were members, described those German dug-outs first-hand after some had been captured: "The outstanding feature of all the captured German trenches so far seen is the very little damage done to dugouts by our artillery fire whereas the trenches are practically obliterated. Most of the dug outs are about 30 feet deep and are fine examples of expert workmanship, some of them being luxuriously furnished & in a number of cases fitted with electric light installation."[226]

Over twenty miles of front line British soldiers attempted to swarm forward at 07.30. Generally they were expected to advance in brigades of four battalions. Typically, one brigade would make the initial assault: the lead battalions were meant to walk across and occupy the German first trench; a few minutes later the second wave battalions were meant to follow, and then either replace the first battalion or leap frog on to the second line trench. The second brigade would develop the attack, either taking the German second or third line trenches, or occupying trenches so that the lead brigade could again move forward. The third brigade would act as a reserve to support and meet any emergency the division encountered. In the event, the first battalions almost inevitably bore the brunt of the enemy's fury, but sometimes the second brigade's lead battalions fared as badly – or even worse. The remaining battalions sometimes fought to recover the wounded from the first two or to consolidate such gains as had been made, and the reserve and support brigades sometimes did not come into action.

As is well known, 1st July was the single most disastrous day in British military history with almost 60,000 casualties, including nearly 20,000 killed. Yet even on this most dreadful of days, fortunes varied. Overall, the further north of the British line an attack was made, the less was its success.

The Diversionary Attack at Gommecourt

A little beyond the northern limit of the main attack, a diversionary assault was made on the village of Gommecourt, about eight miles north of Albert, British headquarters for the battle. The assault was designed to achieve two things: to pull some German reserve troops away from the main Somme offensive further south, and to straighten the line by capturing a fortified village which

---

[225] *The Bournemouthian*, and *The Bournemouth Visitors' Directory*, 22nd July 1916.
[226] War Diary, 10th Royal Fusiliers, 14th July 1916.

formed a German salient sticking out into the British front line. The German defences were in multiple lines which were particularly strong from the Schwalben West Redoubt and Gommecourt Wood in the north to the redoubt at Nameless Farm in the south, with a very powerful redoubt in the centre. Against the British battalions, the German 2nd Guard Reserve Division had two regiments in line, four more in reserve, as well as the 19th and 20th Reserve Field Artillery regiments supplemented by some heavy howitzer batteries.

The plan was that Gommecourt would be attacked from two directions – from near Fonquevillers in the north and from Hebuterne to the south. This attack was to be launched by VII Corps, with the 46th Division attacking the north of the salient, and the 56th (168th and 169th Brigades) the south. The idea was that in the victory of capturing Gommecourt the two divisions would meet.

In the north, the 46th (North Midland) Division was to encounter great difficulties. The wire in front of the German trenches had not been cut by the barrage, and although a few men of the 1/6th South Staffordshires and 1/6th North Staffordshires did get into the enemy's front line trenches, they and the other attackers here (battalions of the Sherwood Foresters) had little success and could not get through the uncut wire (although briefly reaching the German front line) and were driven back with significant losses.

Several Old Bournemouthians fought in the attack on the southern of these flanks. The most northerly of those to attack was Bernard Richardson. Bernard, born in 1898, was still very much a boy when the war broke out. He had only briefly been a member of the school, in 1910. Early in the war he had volunteered and had joined the 5th London Battalion on 11th March 1916. It was in the 169th Brigade

Preparing for the attack they had made several practice assaults. On 26th June they were told that only twenty-three officers would be allowed to go into the attack, in case of heavy casualties, so that the battalion could be re-built. "28th. Weather very bad indeed and whether on this account or bad state of the trenches or other reasons, the attack was delayed 48 hours and we had orders to stand fast."[227] On 30th June, they moved up to their jumping off positions, lining up opposite a series of German trenches code-named by the British from north to south 'Fir', 'Fen' and 'Ferret', next to two other London battalions: 1/9th London Battalion ('Queen Victoria's Rifles') on their right and the 1/12th London Battalion ('the Rangers') beyond them further to the right and south.

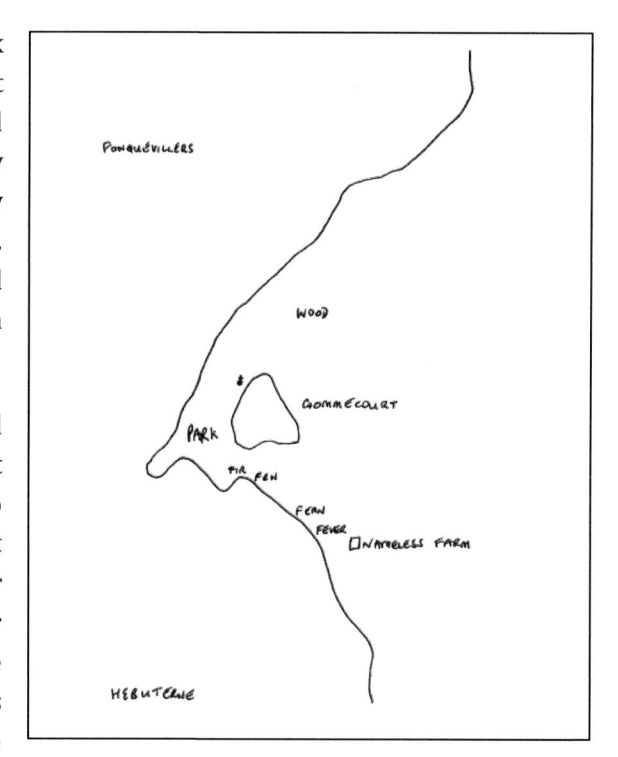

The 5th Battalion, Special Royal Engineers Brigade, fired mortars to try to create smoke screens to cover the assault. At 7.20 the British bombardment of the German front line stopped completely, and the artillery shifted their targets to German trenches further back. The idea was that in the

---

[227] War Diary, 5th London Battalion, 28th June 1916.

front line Germans were already destroyed, and the artillery now had to neutralise the German Support and Reserve trenches. But in fact the Germans in the front line had not been finished off by the bombardments.

"The smoke cloud, which was most effective, commenced at 7.16 am and at 7.27 am the 1st wave moved forward followed by the remaining ones exactly in accordance with orders. The lines advanced in excellent order and the movements went like clockwork, so much so that by 7.50 am all our objectives were reached. By 8.7 am the work of consolidation had commenced. Soon after this the first serious opposition was encountered in the shape of strong enemy bombing parties, whose advance was covered by snipers, some of whom were even up trees – heavy M.G. fire was also opened from reserve lines. Bad casualties began to occur and A Coy in Fir had to be reinforced by a platoon as they were having a hard fight in Gommecourt Park where hostile bombers were particularly active. Bombs now began to run short and German ones were freely used. Owing to the very heavy and accurate barrage across No Man's Land, the reserve Coy, although attempting it several times, were unable to get across with reinforcements and extra ammunition and bombs. The situation now became serious as our men were being driven out of the enemy's 2nd and 3rd line trenches by strong bombing parties, and finally men began to withdraw to our lines. Later our only hold on the German lines was in Ferret, but at dusk the men there were forced to withdraw so that at 8.45 pm we had no unwounded men except those who had been taken prisoners in the hostile trenches. It seems probable that although the actual attack was unsuccessful and was very costly, we killed a large number of Germans, but undoubtedly the attack failed on account of the lack of success by the Division on our left and also because we were unable to get the reserve Coy across with the supply of bombs that were so urgently needed."[228]

To Bernard's right, John May also attacked. John, born 1897, was at the school from 1910-1911. He volunteered on 17th July 1915 for the 1/12th London Battalion, known as 'The London Rangers', 168th Brigade. John had crossed to Le Havre on 10th May 1916 and joined the battalion on 6th June. The battalion had had to dig many of their new trenches in the face and view of the enemy, so that casualties were taken just creating their position, and the Germans were able accurately to get the range of the trenches into which the men must assemble before any assault.

Before the assault someone thought it would be a good idea to issue the men with pea soup to fortify them, as well as the usual rum ration. As they gathered in the jumping off trench they were hit by a ferocious artillery bombardment from the Germans, which caused many casualties and much confusion. Even so, at 04.30 they were ready to attack. They lined up opposite 'Nameless Farm' with the 14th London Battalion ('the London Scottish') on their right. Behind them were the Royal Fusiliers and the 13th London (Kensingtons).

Behind and in support of Bernard and John was probably[229] Reginald Winch, born in 1897, at school from 1907-1913. He had enlisted on 10th June 1915 and joined the 1/3rd City of London Battalion, Royal Fusiliers, 167th Brigade. They were supposed to dig the communication trench across No Man's Land after the attack had begun so that their trench would arrive at 'Fir' trench. However, unsurprisingly given the failure of the assault, this attempt had to be abandoned in mid-morning as a consequence of the heavy German shelling: one platoon of about thirty men was

---

[228] War Diary, 5th London Battalion, 1st July 1916.

[229] John's records do not show precisely when he joined his battalion, but it is likely he was with them by then.

reduced to just two men. Overall that day they lost three officers and about one hundred and twenty men.

The Germans had an excellent view and field of fire from their redoubt, the 'Garde Stellung', across the whole ground over which the battalion was to advance. Their machine guns could sweep the entire area. British aerial reconnaissance planes of the R.F.C. reported on 30th June that the wire in front of them was uncut. Some brave scouts crawled out that night to place Bangalore torpedoes (iron pipes containing dynamite, with electrical detonators) under the German wire, and it was also to be hoped that as the attack began these could blow the required holes in the wire. Although the British had been bombarding for days, a special 'hurricane' British bombardment started at 6.25a.m. It was clear that the Germans were well able to interpret what this meant. From 7.00a.m. German artillery concentrated on the British assembly trenches. At 7.20a.m. the great mine under the Hawthorn crater, a little to the south, was blown. The Germans knew that the attack was about to start.

John and the others began their assault, waved on by their officers who had decided not to use whistles. They had about seven hundred metres to cross to achieve their objectives, which optimistically included at least two lines of German trenches and a redoubt. When they finally reached the German wire, they found their nightmares (and scouts' reports) to be correct – the wire was uncut. German machine guns from the 'Nameless Farm' Redoubt smashed into them – all four company commanders were killed. In some places they managed to penetrate the first German trench, but even that was impossible for most. With such devastating losses and an intact defence to their front, the surviving men of the battalion began to retreat. Attempts to reinforce them from their support troops – the 4th London Battalion – failed. Hardly a man from the support companies survived the German artillery to get across No Man's land to reach them. By midday, only isolated groups of men from the two battalions still lived, trying to hold out or to get back. Those who tried to hold out nearest the enemy were killed or captured in the afternoon. As the regimental history put it, "From noon... Companies no longer existed."[230] It was effectively all over by 2.30p.m., when a fierce German counter-attack drove the remnants back.

Slightly further south again, William Hodges and 16th London (Queen's Westminsters) Battalion were in the attack line, part of the second wave. William had recovered from the effects of frostbite but few of the men with whom William had gone to France were still alive or with the battalion. In front of William stood Eric Head and the 9th London (Queen Victoria's Rifles), opposite Fern and Fever trenches. When the time came to attack, the Queen's Victoria Rifles and 5th London ('London Rifle Brigade'), followed by the 16th London, "moved forward steadily, as if on parade, across the 400 yards that separated our lines from those of the enemy."[231] But soon they found themselves under "galling machine gun fire".[232] By 0900, the situation was dire. They too ran out of their own grenades and there are reports of riflemen picking up German grenades from captured dug-outs and using them against their former owners. By 10.30, the German counter-attacks were ferocious and the official history reports that it was impossible for any reinforcements to survive crossing No Man's Land. Despite horrific fighting, the British were driven back to the German first trench. By

---

[230] *The Rangers' Historical Records*, edited by Captains Wheeler-Holohan and Wyatt, p. 56.

[231] The War History of the 1st Battalion, Queen's Westminster Rifles, 1914-1918 (16th London Regiment) p. 90.

[232] ibid.

midday the only men alive and well enough to get back to the British front line of William's Queen's Westminsters' assault were two wounded 2nd lieutenants and about one hundred men from the three assaulting battalions remained. The official history of the 1/16th Battalion records of these men, "These two officers, and the men who had responded so nobly to their leadership throughout a day of continuous fighting, had performed deeds of gallantry that the Regiment will always remember with pride. Gallant seems a poor epithet to apply to what they did, for indeed no words can sufficiently portray their courage, their grit and their devotion."[233] William was amongst those captured. He had been wounded. On 1st July ,"of the 750 officers and men who went into action, 600 were killed, wounded and missing, and it is believed that not a single unwounded member of the Queen's Westminster Rifles fell into the enemy's hands."[234]

Eric's battalion, the 9th London, had begun the assault in four waves, led by 'A' and 'C' Companies, but even those left in the British trenches came under an increasingly fierce German bombardment. His battalion lost six officers and fifty-one men killed; five officers and two hundred and ninety men wounded; whilst five officers and one hundred and eighty-eight men had gone missing, though Eric survived.

What was left of John May's 1/12th London Battalion was pulled back that night and a tally made of the survivors: only one of the sixteen officers in the assault was left, and only about 200 out of the seven hundred and forty-five ordinary soldiers. Somehow John May had survived, apparently unwounded but soon his situation was complicated by bouts of influenza and 'trench fever', which he could not seem to shake off. From 20th-22nd July, he was in the 2/3rd London Field Hospital and was back in hospital again (at 20th C.C.S.) from 29th July to 7th August. He was sent back to the 3rd General Hospital at Le Treport from the 4th to 26th August. He left France on 30th August 1916 to be attached to the 9th Reserve Battalion.

Bernard Richardson's 5th London Battalion also suffered horrific casualties. Of the ordinary soldiers, fifty-five had been killed; two hundred and twenty-four wounded; sixty-nine were wounded and missing; and a further two hundred and ten men had gone missing. Amongst the officers, seven had been killed; ten wounded; one seen to be wounded and now missing; and one missing, believed killed. The total casualties were five hundred and seventy-seven. The battalion had been destroyed.

The next day in the morning, German machine gunners made it difficult to rescue any wounded, but that afternoon there was an unofficial truce, and stretcher-bearers were able to bring in many dead and wounded. "It is satisfactory to be able to record this act of chivalry on the part of the enemy, but it is a matter of deep regret to know that many of our wounded, who were captured, were very badly treated on their way to the German hospitals."[235] Afterwards, the battalion was withdrawn from the line, and its numbers partly made up by two drafts of men from the 2/7th Middlesex on 4th and 5th July. Even so, from 8th July they were back in the line outside Gommecourt, putting in two companies at a time. By now the trenches were soaking – in some places waist deep in water. Most of the time it was a question of survival and trying to improve the trenches, and the fighting was limited to sporadic firing and the occasional raid. Although there was no specific

---

[233] The War History of the 1st Battalion Queen's Westminster Rifles, 1914-1918 (16th London Regiment) p. 98.
[234] ibid.
[235] ibid.

report of him being wounded, it is likely that Bernard had been one of the casualties of 1st July or soon after, as his service abroad with the battalion ended on 23rd July, and on that day no casualties occurred. It would also explain why there was such a long gap in his service abroad.

Nearly four and a half thousand men of the division had been killed, wounded, gone missing or been taken prisoner. The generals expressed satisfaction that the British had made the Germans suffer (German casualties were about 20% British) and that the war could soon by won!

The Somme: July 1st – The Disaster in the North and Centre

The fighting at Gommecourt was a failed, and costly, diversion, yet the failures at the northern end of the main battlefield have become even more famous. Several Old Bournemouthians also fought that day on the main battle front of the Somme. The most northerly of these was Arthur Stagg, and the attack in which he took part was supposed to have been eased by the assault at Gommecourt diverting German resources. In the event the Germans did not move a single artillery piece because of the Gommecourt attack, and when Arthur went into action things did not go smoothly.

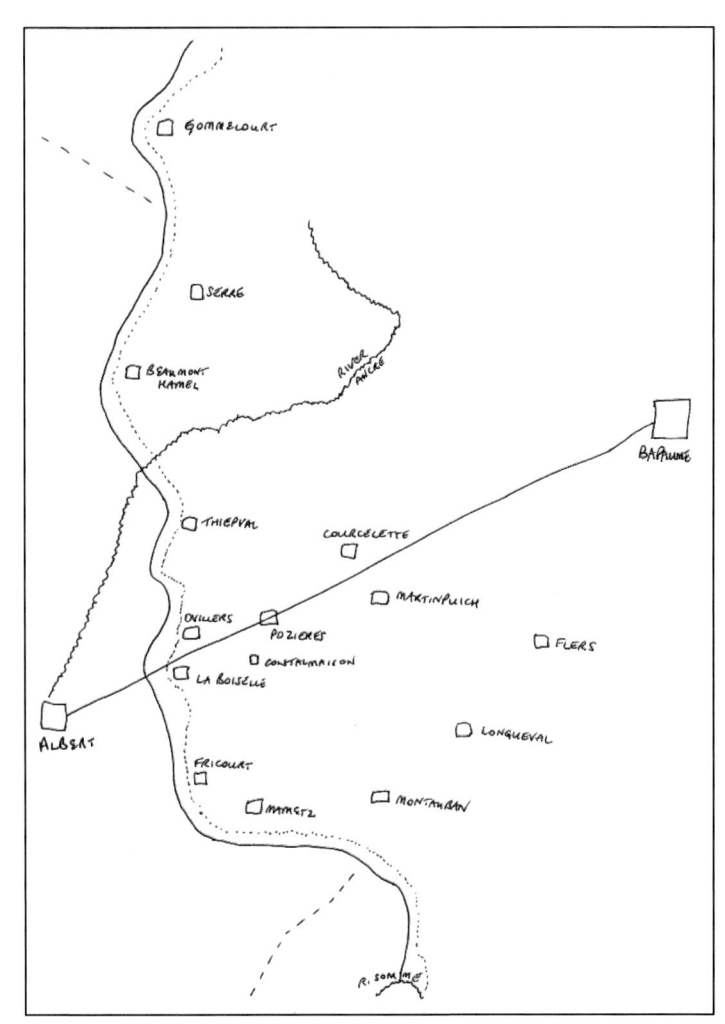

Arthur was born in 1892 and attended the school between 1904 and 1907. He volunteered for the Yorks and Lancaster Regiment on 5th June 1915. After a few months he was promoted to lance corporal, but soon asked to revert to the ranks – not an uncommon request as many men preferred to be one of a group of friends and comrades, rather to be separated out as a leader.

On 5th December 1915, he was posted to 'B' Company of the 12th Yorks and Lancaster Battalion. This battalion, originally known as the Sheffield City Battalion, had been formed in September 1914. It was a 'Pals' battalion' in the 94th Brigade of the 31st Division. It had been preparing to join the Mediterranean Expeditionary Force, to defend the Suez Canal, and Arthur had been with the battalion when it sailed to Egypt on 20th December 1915 and was there hospitalised with blood poisoning. But they did not stay long in the Mediterranean – they left Port Said on 10th March 1916 and he landed at Marseilles in France.

They lined up opposite the village of Serre at the northern end of the main Somme battlefield. Alongside them was the 11th East Lancashire Battalion, famously known as the 'Accrington Pals', which – with the 12th East Yorkshire Battalion (the 'Hull Sportsmen') and 13th East Yorkshire

Battalion ('T 'Others') – made up the 94th Brigade. Each night of the prolonged British bombardment, men of the battalion went out to check on the German wire, which the bombardment failed to break. At 3.45a.m., Arthur and the others were ready in the assembly trenches. From five minutes past four in the morning, a German counter-bombardment began to shell these trenches. For over three hours, Arthur and his friends endured this bombardment, and one can only imagine their feelings.

At 7.30a.m., they attacked. The smoke screen was too patchy, giving the German machine gunners a clear line of sight. The first two waves, which included Arthur, got into No Man's Land. The other two waves were cut down by half before they reached the jumping off line. Those getting across could find no way through the German wire – after a few minutes, Corporal Outram, a signaller, reckoned that only he and a fellow signaller were still standing – then the other man fell. On their right, the Accrington Pals took similar losses. The remnant of the battalion held on until they were pulled back on 3rd July – five hundred and thirteen men, including officers, had been seriously wounded, killed or fallen missing; seventy-five more were less seriously wounded.

Arthur Stagg had gone missing. He was lucky still to be alive but unlucky because he was badly wounded, and no one knew. He lay injured in No Man's Land. Later he gave an interview to a reporter of the *Huddersfield War Hospital* magazine, which was picked up and reprinted in the *Bournemouth Visitors'* newspaper on 18th November 1916 and later in the school magazine.

"It was on the 1st of July that we had 'to go over the lid.' At 4.30 am, we went across. The enemy were shelling us heavily, and, in addition, there was a heavy rifle and machine gun fire. I hadn't gone far, before I was hit, being shot through the chest. I immediately rolled into a shell-hole for better protection, and imagine I lost consciousness for a considerable time. When I came to, I heard a voice, and discovered that there was another fellow in the shell-hole, about 15 yards away, so I decided to join him. It was while crawling across that I got shot through the arm by a sniper. How long we were in that shell-hole I don't know, but it must have been several days—by then we were parched with thirst, and welcomed the heavy rain which came, and which we collected in our steel helmets. I had thrown off my equipment, and with it went all my food, so that you can imagine that I was feeling a bit hungry, especially as I was weak with my wounds. All at once the other fellow decided to crawl in, and off he went. That was the last I saw or heard of him. I decided then that it was impossible to stay out day after day, and started to crawl in myself. I found it an agonising and exhausting job, and have no idea how long it actually took me, but eventually I got into an unused trench. Here I discovered a dug-out, and turned in. All I wanted was rest and oblivion, and I slept—how long I don't know—but I think I must have been unconscious again for some considerable time. In the dug-out I came across a bag containing some bits of army biscuits, and these, soaked in rain water, were all the food I had. I was absolutely too weak to do anything but lie and sleep, and did not move except when I crawled to get water.""[236]

He had been shot through the chest, injuring his left lung, through his right arm, and in his right thigh. Trench foot damaged his right foot from which later an abscess had to be cut out. He was only found on 15th July having lain there practically without food and wounded. He was taken back to 16 General Hospital, one of several military hospitals at Le Trépot, on the French coast north-east of Dieppe. It had grown into a huge medical complex – with almost 10,000 beds by 1916. Urgent telegrams passed

---

[236] *The Bournemouth Visitors' Directory*, 18th November 1916.

home to Arthur's father near Bristol as Arthur's wounds caused the doctors great anxiety – he was described as "seriously ill" on 29th July, and then twice as "dangerously ill" on 10th and 13th August 1916. His father was even invited to visit his bedside in France, at public expense. He was not expected to live. But he did live and was sent back to Folkestone from Boulogne on 2nd August. He was taken north to Huddersfield to convalesce. That Christmas he was well enough to be granted leave from hospital for a week, and on 21st March 1917 was placed in the Reserve. He was never well enough to re-join his comrades – on 14th November 1917 he was discharged with a pension. He outlived the war which had so cruelly injured him.

Just south of Arthur, Victor Martin and the 1st Hampshire Battalion were also to face the ferocity of the German defence, in their case near the village of Beaumont-Hamel. Born in 1887, Victor was an early member of the school and a member of the football team in 1905. He had landed in France on 27th April 1915.

On 1st July 1916, half of the 1st Hampshire Battalion was to be in the second wave behind the 1st East Lancashire Battalion, and half in the front line alongside them. On their left were the 1st Royal Warwickshire Battalion, which was to make an attack on the Heidenkopf Redoubt across the Redan Ridge, a little south of Serre.

The Heidenkopf Redoubt, more commonly known as the Quadrilateral, was a strong German position which jutted out in front of the main German line, forming a small salient which could be attacked from the sides as well as the front. It had a small German garrison with a machine gun team and some engineers, and the Germans had taken the precaution of laying one of their own mines beneath it in case the British should manage to capture it. The German plan was that the retreating garrison would detonate the mine as they left. The redoubt was part of a series of strong trenches and dug-outs along the Redan Ridge. In the event, when the 1st Royal Warwickshire attacked the redoubt, the German machine gun jammed and their mine was set off with the result that the defending machine gun team and the engineers were killed before the British arrived. The explosion turned out to be more forceful than had been anticipated and as a result it blocked up many of the dug-outs, allowing the remaining garrison to be over-run.

On the right, the 1st East Lancashires and 1st Hampshire Battalion had a much harder time. The barbed wire they faced was uncut. As they advanced they too were cut down by heavy machine gun and artillery fire. They also faced enfilade fire on their left from the machine gunners at Serre and on the Redan Ridge. Both groups of the 1st Hampshires advanced and suffered terrible casualties. "As soon as our troops left their trenches heavy machine gun fire was brought to bear on them from all directions and it was impossible even to reach the German front line. Our casualties in Officers amounted to 100% and was also very heavy in Other Ranks. After lying about in shell holes all the day the men came back to their original front line."[237] The death or wounding of the officers had caused great confusion, which had been made worse because many Germans were able to emerge from their deep dug-outs behind the Hampshire men, and so to attack them from behind. Victor was very fortunate to have survived, but he might well have been wounded, as later he was switched to the 10th Hampshire Regiment which fought on Salonika. It was common, if a man had been wounded and hospitalised, to send him later to a different battalion and a different front depending on need. He survived the war.

---

[237] War Diary, 1st Hampshires, 1st July 1916.

Slightly further south, Howard Farwell and the 2nd Hampshire Battalion were also in the battle for Beaumont-Hamel. Howard and 2nd Hampshires had left Gallipoli in early January 1916. They had arrived in France on 21st March. After a short interlude of instruction (especially in dealing with gas, which they had not encountered on Gallipoli) they were brought into line at Beaumont-Hamel on 23rd April. Here they had held the line, repulsed German raids and tried a few raids of their own and prepared for the coming battle.

On 1st July, the actions of the 29th Division have become famous – especially because of the preservation of 'their' battlefield, now known as 'Newfoundland Park'. Fortunately for Howard, his 88th Brigade was the reserve brigade. Dreadful losses were experienced by the first wave of attacks made by 86th and 87th Brigades. For example, of the 86th Brigade, the 2nd Royal Fusiliers – who were supposed to take the crater formed by the Hawthorn Ridge mine explosion and then provide covering fire for the others – fought for survival as the detonation of that mine ten minutes early gave the Germans everywhere ample warning of the attack to come. In the 87th Brigade, the 1st Inniskillings did break into the first two German trench lines, but without adequate support. The 1st King's Own Scottish Borderers and the 1st Border Battalions did not even reach the German wire.

The 1st Essex and the 1st Newfoundland Regiments were meant to advance at 7.30a.m. in support of the attack. Both advanced late and both were slaughtered in the area which now bears the name of the Newfoundlanders (who suffered the second worst casualty rate of the entire battle on 1st July). The 2nd Hampshire Battalion was meant to follow them up. Victor and the 1st Hampshire Battalion had been devastated when they attempted to follow up the 1st East Lancashires, suffering losses almost as bad as those of the Essex or Newfoundland troops, but when the 29th Division General realised what had happened to the assault battalions, he halted the 2nd Hampshires and 4th Worcesters at the front line. He intended to launch a renewed assault at 12.30p.m., but fortunately for Howard and his friends, that order never got through because of the congestion and devastation in the communication trenches. So they remained, under German artillery barrage, for the rest of the day. Towards evening the Germans allowed some of them to go into No Man's Land to recover some of the wounded, provided they did not go too close to the German wire itself. The 29th Division had lost 5,000 men that day, but Howard had lived to fight again.

For the next ten days the 2nd Hampshire Battalion manned the line and tried to bring in the wounded and equipment from No Man's land. Although they left the front line on 10th July, they sent in a raiding party on 14th July which attempted to get into Y Ravine, but was driven back. Later they were pulled right out of the battle and on 29th July 1916 went north by train to the Ypres Salient, taking over trenches opposite St. Julien on 30th July.

Beaumont-Hamel, stands on the north side of the valley of the River Ancre. On the south side of that valley the skyline today is dominated by the Majestic Memorial to the Fallen on the brow of Thiepval Hill. In July 1916, this was yet another German strongpoint. John Nethercoate and James Sinton were with the 1st Dorset Battalion when it attempted to take this German position.

In the middle of June the 1st, Dorset Battalion had been pulled back west of Albert to rest and to prepare for the attack. On 26th-27th June, James and the men were issued with extra ammunition and equipment (including extra grenades and signalling equipment) after which they were given an opportunity to bathe and to rest. At 8.20p.m. on 30th June they left their rest area to move forward for the attack.

John, James and their comrades were soon in the thick of the fighting. The 1st Dorset Battalion was up against the formidable German Leipzig Redoubt, a German strongpoint of multiple machine guns, created in an old chalk pit opposite the corner of Authuille Wood, where the German front line turned slightly south-east towards Ovillers. The 96th and 97th Infantry Brigades had attacked the hostile trenches before the 1st Dorsetshire Regiment – the leading battalion of the 14th Infantry Brigade – left Authuille Wood. They had not, however, been able to attain their objectives; this fact was not known to the Dorsets until later although it was apparent that matters were not progressing quite as favourably as had been anticipated. "Capt. Kestell-Cornish and about ten other ranks were wounded by machine-gun fire as the Battalion was proceeding along Dumbarton track. After waiting about fifteen minutes in Authuille Wood the O.C. 'C' Coy (the leading company) received information from our liaison party attached to the 11th Border Regt. (97th Inf. Bgde) that the latter regiment had commenced its advance; 500 yards behind the rear platoon of 11th Border Regt. The leading platoon of 1st Dorset Regt. advanced from Authuille Wood in accordance with orders previously received. The remainder of the Battalion followed by platoons or sections. Immediately the leading platoon left Authuille Wood very heavy and extremely accurate machine-gun fire was opened by the enemy from some point on our right not definitely ascertained. As this fire concentrated mainly on the point at the edge of the wood where Dumbarton track ends – and past which the whole Battalion had to go – we endeavoured to find some other exit from the wood, but could not do so, barbed wire and other obstructions preventing.

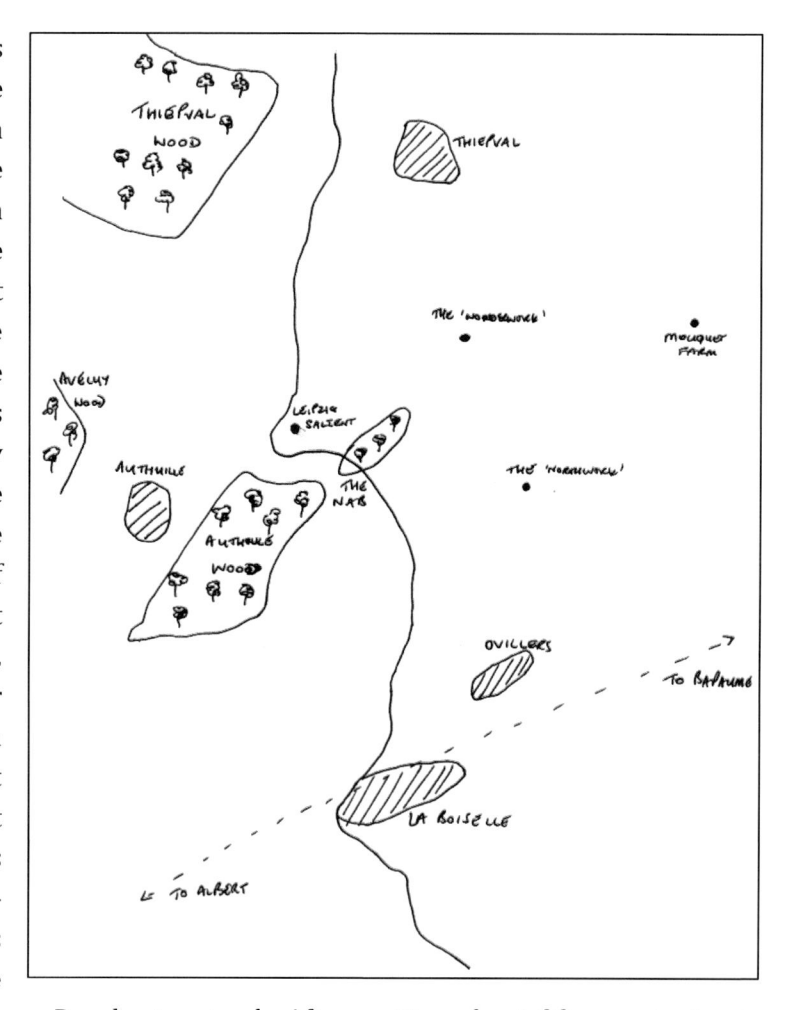

"The whole battalion, therefore, advanced from this point by sections and it was during the dash across country from Authuille Wood to our own front line trench about 100 yards ahead that at least half our total casualties were sustained. By the time half the Battalion had left the wood, the end of Dumbarton track and the ground up to our front line trench was covered with our killed and wounded; yet the men continued to jump up and advance over their fallen comrades as the word to go was given. Four Lewis guns were lost here by the men being wounded; other men following, who stopped in the endeavour to pick up the guns and take them forward, were also killed or wounded.

"On arrival in our front line Trench we found it to be already occupied by the 11th Border Regt. (numbering approximately 100 to 150 other ranks without any officers). Machine gunners, carrying parties and other details also occupied this trench and the shell craters in front and rear of it. Numbers of killed and wounded added to the congestion and lateral movement was practically impossible, except over the top, until we managed to organize matters somewhat and move the men further to the right. Six officers and about sixty men went forward almost at once into German front line trench. Part of this was found to be occupied by British troops and part by Germans. A few men of 11th Border Regt. were already there with a considerable number of 17th H.L.I. on the Left some of the 19th Lancashire Fusiliers reached the same place later. All these six officers were wounded – one very slightly who remained at duty – and out of the sixty men who went forward to the German front line trench only about twenty-five actually reached there. Parties were organised to bomb down the enemy trenches to the right and when further advance became impossible barricades were built. The enemy made several attempts to bomb our troops out of their trenches, and we lost some officers and men in this way, although the enemy were repulsed. Our bombs ran out and German grenades found in the captured trench were used.

"Meanwhile the Dorsets, Borders and Lancashire Fusiliers in our front line trench had become organised. Major J.V. Shute had been wounded and Capt. Lancaster being in the German trench (he had also been reported wounded), the Adjutant assumed command of both 1st Dorsets and 11th Border Rgt. Arrangements were made for a concerted attack upon the German position at a given signal; a patrol being first sent out to ascertain exactly which part of the German trench was in our hands and which was still held by the enemy. Also, as our own guns were still firing on the German Trench it was necessary to wait till this barrage lifted before we advanced. Before this plan of attack could be carried out the officer commanding the Right Column decided to withdraw the 19th Lancashire Fusiliers and 11th Border Rgt. from our front line trench, leaving the 1st Dorset Rgt. to hold the line. At that time we had – in addition to the adjutant – three 2nd Lieutenants and eighty-five other ranks actually in the trench. Soon after 1pm these men were sorted out into companies, a commander allotted to each company, and we became again a definitely organised unit. We were unable to get in touch with anyone on our right or left. During the early part of the afternoon, sixty more unwounded men rejoined – these having become detached in other parts of our trenches.

"The enemy's artillery bombarded us continuously all the afternoon and at 5pm his fire became so intense and accurate that our position became almost untenable. Thirty of the remaining men were either killed or wounded and the trench so damaged as to make communications very difficult. Soon after 5pm Major H.W. Thuraytes came up and took command; a message was received from Brigade saying that 15th H.L.I. would relieve 1st Dorset Rgt. and by 2 am on the 2nd July we were clear of the front line trench. The Party in the German trench was also ordered to withdraw."[238]

Amongst those who fell wounded was James Sinton. It is an ironic curiosity that the Army granted 'leave' when a man fell wounded, so that in his records his absence from 1st July onwards was officially listed as 'Leave necessitated by gun shot wounds received in action'.

James was passed back through the casualty chain and on 5th August was placed aboard the SS *Oxfordshire*. The next day he arrived at Southampton and was sent on to 3rd Southern General Hospital at Oxford. He had been hit twice, probably by the machine guns. His upper left leg had

---

[238] War Diary, 1st Dorsets, 1st July 1916.

been struck, and then a more serious wound to his right buttock from where the bullet exited on the inner side of his right thigh. Considering the seriousness of the situation he was lucky that no vital artery or part had been struck, and as early as 19th July the doctors reported that his "wounds have healed, he is still lame".[239] Released from hospital he was ordered to report to the 3rd Battalion at Wyke Regis for 17th August, the day after a medical board at Bournemouth's Mont Dore Hospital reported: "The wounds have quite healed and there is still some muscular stiffness remaining." Although the initial recovery was fast, he remained feeling very tired, and it was not until 24th October before a medical board held at the Nothe Hospital, Weymouth, could report him ready for general service. "The wounds are soundly healed without any apparent ill effects." Within days, however, he was attempting to transfer to a different regiment. In October he made abortive enquiries about switching to the Royal Engineers to work with a signalling section (perhaps wanting to stay alongside John), but in the end he was sent to India where he served in an attachment with the Indian Army from 1st June 1917. He was demobilised in September 1919.

John Nethercoate had also survived. On 27th October 1916, he was seconded from the Dorsets for duty with the Army Signalling Service, part of the Royal Engineers.[240] His new military role also took him east, and included a dramatic incident when his ship was torpedoed in the Mediterranean and he was in the sea, wounded and exhausted, for two hours before he was picked up by a destroyer. After the war he was a captain in the Royal Corps of Signals. (He was a colonel when he died in Algeria in 1943.)

Further south from Authille Wood the front line was crossed by the road which runs from the British fighting headquarters at Albert to the German fighting headquarters at Bapaume. The German front line was at the western end of the village of La Boiselle and its hamlet of Ovilliers immediately to the north. Many Old Bournemouthians fought here, though most not on the first day of the battle.

Life Guard Harold Pike was meant to be ready to exploit the anticipated breakthrough at this point.

Born in 1891, at school from 1904-1907, Harold joined the 2nd Life Guards on 16th November 1914. He arrived in France on 19th January 1916. His cavalry unit was in the 7th Cavalry Brigade, 3rd Cavalry Division. Almost as soon as he arrived, an outbreak of measles affected the regiment, and so for most of February and March 1916 the unit played no role in active service. In those days there were no antibiotics, so measles was a serious illness which had to be treated seriously. However, by April 1916, they were again preparing for the breakthrough and Harold and his comrades were tasked to improve their skills through practices – in mounted operations, bayonet and grenade training. On 26th June 1916, the regiment had moved up to the east of Amiens to be ready to exploit the breakthrough expected with the attack on the Somme. Conditions were far from ideal for cavalry movement: "We had a long trot to Flesselles and had to walk the rest of the way owing to hills… Reached our bivouac after doing the last ¾ mile in deep and slippery mud. Horses very closely concentrated & no cover whatever for officers and men."[241]

On 29th June, whilst Harold and the men fed and watered the horses, their commander joined others with General Kennedy in viewing a British smoke grenade attack (and German retaliatory

---

[239] Army records, James Sinton, National Archives reference WO339/26802.
[240] *The Bournemouth Visitors' Directory*, 3rd February 1917.
[241] War Diary, 2nd Life Guards, 26th-27th June 1916.

barrage on the British trenches) from the relative safety of a hill just west of Albert. The next morning, 30th June, the senior officers of the 2nd Life Guards were given their own visit to the site, to discuss the proposed line of their advance and to watch the British artillery shelling Thiepval, Pozieres, Ovillers and La Boiselle, and noting that there was little German artillery response.

At 7.30a.m. on 1st July, as the assault was starting, the 2nd Life Guards turned out, limbers and saddle packs ready, under orders to advance at half an hour's notice. They stood and waited until 11.00a.m., when they received their first communique and realised that all was not going according to plan. Even so, they remained poised to advance, as soon as the front line situation had resolved and the opposition dealt with. "3pm. Informed that it is unlikely we shall be used today. The opposition to VIII and X Corps attacking on our left has been very strong and they are unable to get on. Right of our attack has succeeded. Thiepval and Ovillers holding out. Sent 1 troop per Squadron out exercising (in full marching order) in immediate vicinity of camp. 7pm Regt put on 2 hours' notice: men not to leave camp."[242] In the end, of course, there was no breakthrough, and the 2nd Life Guards were not called upon to move forward into a break in the German line caused by the infantry assault. So, on 4th July 1916, Harold and the regiment were withdrawn westwards.

They had not made the anticipated move forward along the Albert-Bapaume road. To the north and south sides of this road the British had exploded a set of mines at 7.28a.m., the biggest of which was code-named 'Lochnager' and was blown up south of the village of La Boiselle; its crater is now preserved. The valley just to the north of the road was code-named 'Mash' whilst to the south the valley between La Boiselle and Fricourt was named 'Sausage' (the Germans had a well-known sausage-shaped observation balloon tethered there). The attacks here were made by the 8th Division (against Ovillers) and the 34th Division (against La Boiselle). The Tyneside battalions who attacked north and south of the road suffered appalling casualties (about 80% of the leading battalions) but gained very little ground, so on 2nd July the 19th Division renewed the attack. Although the British had managed only to get a toe hold into the German front line in La Boiselle village, these attacks had to be renewed to maintain the pressure and to ease the advance of the more successful British forces further south and also to prevent the Germans reinforcing crucial defensive positions like Thiepval further north.

Bruce Peake was in that terrible attack by the Tyneside Irish. Bruce had only been at school in 1913-1914. Originally from Madagascar, he had been born in December 1897. He had started as a sapper in the 2/5th Hampshire R.E., a Territorial unit, but his main Army service was as a private with the Northumberland Fusiliers. He enlisted on 18th October 1915 and was posted as a member of the 25th Northumberland Fusiliers Battalion, a 'Pals' battalion formed in Newcastle in November 1914, in the 103rd Brigade, in the 34th Division. It was otherwise known as the 2nd Tyneside Irish Battalion. The division was made up of similar 'Pals' battalions' – creating brigades including the Tyneside Scottish and Tyneside Irish. 'The Tyneside Irish' consisted of the 24th, 25th, 26th and 27th Battalions of the Northumberland Fusiliers. In January 1916, the brigade had crossed the Channel and concentrated east of St. Omer.

Bruce's 25th Northumberland Fusiliers Battalion was almost obliterated on 1st July 1916. They had been brought up the night before to their assault position opposite La Boiselle. Each man like Bruce was given two days rations, spare ammunition and grenades. They were in the trench line known

---

[242] War Diary, 2nd Life Guards, 1st July 1916.

as the Usna-Tara Line, west of La Boiselle, and expected to be held in reserve. In the event they went into the attack. "7.45am. Battalion ordered to attack German positions north of and adjoining fortified village of La Boiselle. Intensive bombardment from 6.20am to 7.30am when artillery lifted to second German lines. Mines exploded at 7.30am in La Boiselle, which was also subjected to intense trench mortar bombardment and thought to be obliterated. But when our advance began, La Boiselle was found to be strongly held with machine guns and rifles, which completely held up our advance. Battle order of the Battalion was 'B' Coy on right, 'D' Coy on left, each company in column of platoons at 150 paces distance whilst 'A' Coy (on left) and 'C' Coy (on right) advanced in similar formation in support of and 150 paces behind leading companies. Battalion Headquarters advanced in rear of last platoons. Heavy fire from machine guns & rifles was opened on battalion from the moment the assembly trenches were left. Also considerable artillery barrage at 3 places on the line of advance. The forward movement was maintained until only a few scattered soldiers were left standing, the discipline and courage of all ranks being remarkable. Twenty officers and seven hundred and thirty other ranks took part in this advance. 10.30pm. The survivors of the battalion were collected in British front trenches near Keats Redan NW of La Boiselle and the work of collecting wounded and stragglers went on all night. Bombing parties were posted on flanks and the trench held under heavy fire. 16 officers were missing and 610 other ranks, the remainder of the battalion being commanded by Captain T.L. Williams. Two battalions of the 19th Division arrived in the early morning (2nd, 6am) and the battalion received orders to return to reserve trenches near Tara Redoubt. The battalion was then moved to Bellenue Farm near Albert, to refit and equip. Stragglers from all parts of the battle field were collected here and the battalion held in reserve."

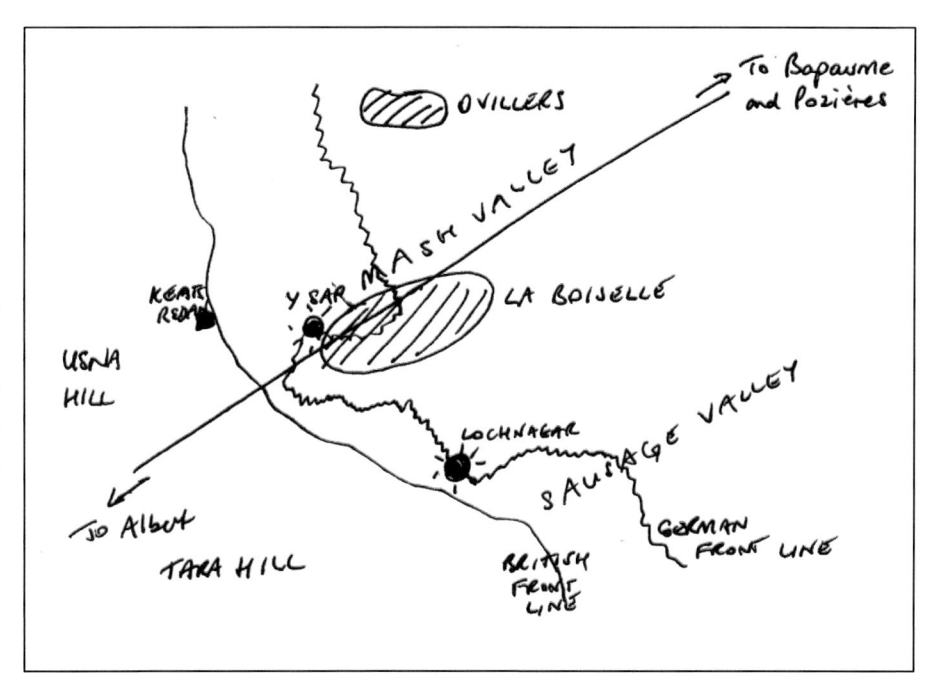

When the stragglers had joined and been counted, they found that the battalion had lost thirteen officers wounded, two killed, and one was missing. All four company sergeant majors had been wounded. Four hundred and sixty-seven men were missing. Two of the wounded officers died the next day. On 8th August, it was decided that temporarily the brigade could only operate with two battalions, and the men of the 25th and 26th Northumberland Fusiliers, including Bruce, were merged as a composite battalion, and went back into the trenches – but on Vimy Ridge to the north of Arras, which at that time was reasonably quiet, although both sides blew up mines, and a German raid had to be repulsed. For the rest of the year they recovered, taking turns in trenches (for a time at Martinpuich on the Somme, but mostly further north near Armentières). Only on 28th November 1916 were they sufficiently back up to strength as a single battalion, with new officers, and after training, to be able to re-join the 34th Division, which they did at Erquinghem, a suburb of Armentières.

South of this central part of the battleground and the road, the line reached the German defences at Fricourt. Here it turned eastwards south of Mametz before finally turning south again where French troops linked up with the British. Two Cecils, Goodall and Novarra, serving in the 6th Dorsetshire Regiment, fought at Fricourt that day.

Cecil Goodall, at 25, was the older. He attended Bournemouth School between 1905 and 1906. In July 1915 he received his commission into the 6th Dorset Battalion and for a time served as a musketry instructor. He had arrived in France on 18th March 1916. Cecil Novarra was younger. Born in January 1896, he was at school from September 1908 to July 1911. Unlike Cecil Goodhall, however, Cecil Novarra joined the 6th Dorset Battalion as a private, and embarked for France with the battalion on 13th July 1915. By then he was a corporal (and would eventually become a sergeant-major). This battalion was part of 50th Brigade, 17th (Northern) Division.

On 1st July 1916, their brigade had been detached from their normal division, coming under the orders instead of 21st Division. The plan was that the detached 17th Division Battalions would hold the British line opposite Fricourt whilst the 21st Division would attack Fricourt from the north of the salient with the 7th Division attacking from its southern flank. The German strongpoint at Fricourt formed a small salient, south of La Boiselle and 'Sausage Valley'. To bolster the position the Germans had heavily fortified it, taking advantage of some exploded mine craters (known to the British as the 'Tambour') by adding a complex network of supporting trenches and reserve lines.

This attack was to be helped – as at La Boiselle – by the explosion of three prepared mines laid by 178th Tunnelling Company beneath the Tambour. Then the infantry assault would take place. In the event, only two of the three planned-for mines exploded (though each had between 9,000 and 25,000 pounds of explosive). The Cecils' brigade was only supposed to advance when the Germans began to surrender so they were five miles behind the front at Ville-sur-Ancre. The 6th Dorset Battalion lacked training in open warfare attacks and they did not properly know the ground over which they were to fight. The 17th Division history records the measures taken to help the officers like Cecil to make up for these shortfalls: "Parties of officers were taken to points of vantage commanding good views of the German front, in order to obtain an idea of the general lie of the ground over which the advance was to be made. They saw the wide belt of trenches wrapped in smoke bursts, through which came the flashes of the explosions, and dark masses of stones were hurled high in the air. Mametz Wood was no longer green. Its leaves had been turned to brown and yellow by our high explosives. Fricourt village was crumbling into heaps of ruin. It looked as if the front line was being simply wiped out and that nothing could live under this deluge of fire."[243]

In front of the 6th Dorsets was placed the support battalion, the 7th East Yorkshire Battalion, whilst the 10th West Yorks and 7th Green Howards were the units actually to man the front line trenches whilst the two attack battalions were to make the assault. The 6th Dorset Battalion left their camp at 5.15a.m. and, being given breakfast, went forward. Fricourt lay "buried in a thick red mist of brick-dust thrown up by our shells" that morning, but out of that mist at about 10a.m. came "an evil-looking, unkempt crowd" of German prisoners. Soon "everybody felt the extreme heat moving up deep communication trenches with heavy loads, without a breath of wind… The trenches in the

---

[243] 17th Division History, July 1916.

valley were deep in mud and water." [244] Late in the afternoon the battalion was called forward to support the attack. In front of them, the 10th West Yorkshire Battalion had suffered the worst casualties of any battalion that day, losing 733 casualties, and the 7th Yorkshires whom they were sent to relieve had also suffered very heavily. Some of the village had been captured, and the Germans had been forced back to their second line of trenches. A follow-up attack in which the Dorsets were intended to join was called off, and the battalion remained to help to hold the front line.

These were exhausting days for the two Cecils and the battalion as they were carrying forward ammunition and other stores in order to consolidate the British position in Fricourt by building two new 'strongpoints'. Their battalion history recorded, "Fricourt was crowded with troops, the debris was being cleared, and dumps were springing up. The way passed the Crucifix and men stopped to gaze at the figure that looked silently down upon them in the dark, or rifled German packs for their brown bread, or hailed, in strong language, a great wire-bound mortar of wood, which had sent over many 'oil-cans'. Other parties had to dig posts on the edge of Fricourt Wood."[245]

Further south again, Eugene Holland fought in the 2nd Border Battalion, in the sector south of Mametz. Eugene, as the senior surviving officer from his company, wrote an account of his company in the action, mentioning himself only in the third person. He was adjutant to the battalion and his literary abilities may explain why this battalion overall left a really detailed account of the attack.

Though costly, the advance of the 2nd Border Battalion was quite different from the more familiar story of the disaster of that morning further north. The German counter-bombardment before the attack had damaged the British front line so much that the men formed up for the attack in a different section of the support line than had been planned. This turned out to be fortunate for them as the Germans continued to bombard the wrong place. The attack was then complicated by the need to turn the direction of attack once out of the trenches, in a manoeuvre to 'wheel' the line of attack so that the attack started roughly from south to north, but then turned from east to west. They attacked in line between the 22nd Manchesters on their right and with 1st South Staffordshires "in touch"; on their left was meant to be the 9th Devonshire Battalion, but that battalion failed to keep 'in touch' with the attack because when it reached the attack line heavy German artillery and machine gun fire killed all the officers of its leading waves.

The 2nd Border Battalion moved into position by 1.30a.m. on 1st July under heavy German bombardment, and "at 7.27 am the… advanced in 4 lines from our trenches… The Battalion… moved forward until it reached its first objective Danube Support trench when the lift was commenced. Up till now the casualties were small in the first and second lines and were caused by a machine gun firing from our right in the direction of Sap 'A' in hostile trench and also from one on our left in Danube Support. The wheel was now gradually completed and the advance continued towards our objective, Apple Alley, which was reached by our 1st line at about 8.30am. During this advance our line was broken up into a line of groups bombing and bayonetting the enemy, who when they found that their line had been entered formed a new front in shell holes and communication trenches facing us thus checking our advance.

---

[244] War Diary, 6th Dorsets, 1st July 1916.
[245] From *West Country Regiments on the Somme*, by Tim Saunders, p. 142.

"On reaching Shrine Alley the Battalion was temporarily checked through coming under heavy indirect machine gun fire from Fricourt and enfilade fire from Mametz, but on the 1st and 2nd lines being reinforced by the 3rd line the advance was continued to Hidden Lane. Here the line was again temporarily held up by fire from a machine gun and hostile party in Hidden Wood and another party at about the junction of Kiel Support and Bois Francais Support. The latter were bombed out without very much difficulty by our party working along Kiel Support but the former had to be attacked across the open as well as down Hidden Lane. This was done by a party organised and led by 2nd Lieut S J C Russell. The advance was now continued to Apple Alley by parties being pushed forward by the 1st and 2nd lines whilst the 3rd line consolidated Hidden Lane. At this time the right of the 4th Line moved up to Hidden Wood so as to strengthen that flank as it was found that the Devon Regt had not kept up with the advance of the Battalion and this flank was very exposed. The left of the 4th Line was still in reserve in Kiel trench, close up to that junction of Hidden Lane. The Battalion was now checked in Hidden Lane with posts forward in Apple Alley at junction of it and Pear Trench – ditto Bois Francais Support and also Bois Francais Trench. At 2.30pm the 20th Manchester Regt advanced across our front and bombing parties of the Border Regt worked along Apple Alley without any opposition.

"At about 5pm Apple Alley was occupied by 'A' and 'C' Companies of the Border Regt with a party of 8th Devon on the right. B and D Companies Border Regt held Hidden Lane as a Support Line. Head Quarters were established in an old Company dugout in Support trench at its junction with 75 Street. This position was maintained until about 8am on 3rd July when the Battalion changed its position to Bois Francais Support which was held by B and D Companies with A and C Companies in Bois Francais Trench. Battalion Head Quarters remained in the same position. Here the Battalion remained until the evening of 3rd July when it moved down to Post 71 South in Reserve.

"The casualties in the attack were not as heavy as they might have been owing firstly to the splendid way the wire had been cut by 'T' Battery RHA and secondly to the fact that the advance was very close behind the artillery barrage the whole time. During the latter half of the attack the Battalion was subjected to a heavy sprinkling of hostile shrapnel which in addition to rifle and machine gun fire and bombs caused the casualties mentioned. The whole battalion behaved with their usual steadiness and coolness under fire and all orders were strictly carried out. No mistake was made in the advance and the wheel was carried out without any gaps being left in the line which is entirely due to the care taken by all Officers in instructing their NCOs and men in all points regarding the operation and the interest taken by all ranks in it. The Battalion captured 3 machine guns, 2 Trench Mortars, 1 Projector, 5 Canister Throwers. The casualties were: Officers – 3 killed, 6 wounded, 1 Died of wounds; Other Ranks – 79 killed, 240 wounded, 10 Died of wounds, 4 Missing."[246]

We can also read Eugene's more personal account as surviving officer, and now in command of, 'C' Company, which, as we have seen, was in the forefront of the attack. "Report on the part taken by 'C' Company in the recent operations. For the attack which was launched on the morning of the 1st July the Company was put into position in Reserve Trench between 71 Street and Albert street, reaching this trench about 12.30 am on the 1st July without casualties. The order of platoons from right to left was No.11 platoon under 2nd Lieut E L Holland, No.9 platoon under 2nd Lieut L Mash, No.12 platoon under Sgt Knox and No.10 platoon under 2nd Lieut E W Shaw. There were two Lewis

---

[246] War Diary, 2nd Border Regiment, July 1st-3rd 1916.

gun teams with the Company. Captain A E Newton was in command of the Company, which was on the extreme left flank of the Division.

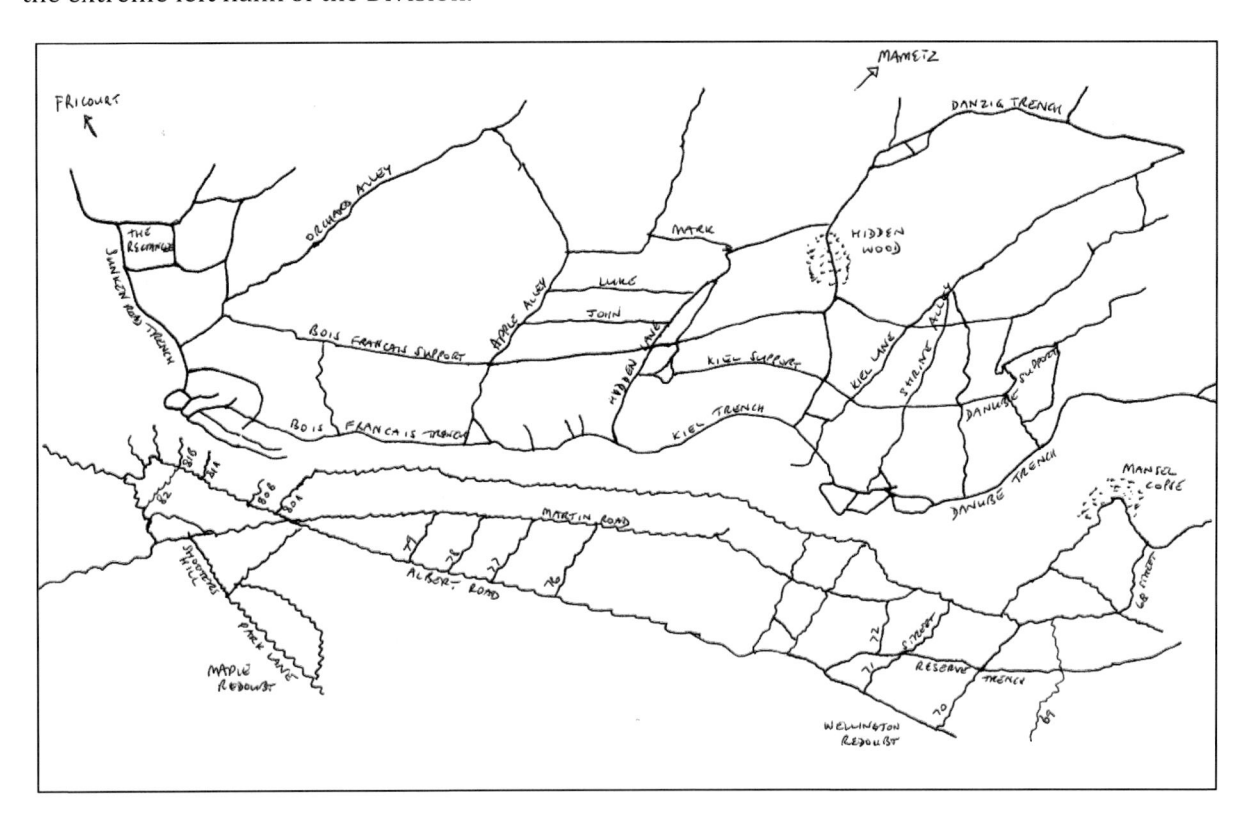

"At 6.30 a.m. began the intense bombardment of the enemies [sic] front trenches, which was to last an hour, and at 7.27 the two platoons on the right left Reserve Trench advanced over the open, followed at a hundred yards by the remaining 2 platoons, the Lewis gun teams advancing in the interval between the two waves. The forward end of a shallow gallery which had been mined towards the German parapet from our front line at 71 Street had been timed to be exploded at 7.30 a.m., and as 11 and 9 platoons reached our own front line this was blown, and the barrage lifted from the German front trench. It's attributed to the Company's having advanced so near its first objective under cover of our own artillery fire that up to this point not a single casualty had occurred. Machine gun fire, however, now opened from the right and a number of small land mines were exploded causing the first of our men to fall, but the first and second German lines were crossed with hardly any other opposition, and the leading platoons wheeled to the left making the line of Shrine Alley their new front. No.10 platoon, on the left of the Company's second wave wheeled to the left at the first German trench and drove out some hostile bombers who were throwing their grenades from behind the right craters. The Lewis gun under L/Cpl Clarke greatly assisted in this act, but unfortunately the entire team, coming under machine gun and rifle fire was shot down. Sgt Know also fell dead at the same spot, shot through the head. His platoon, no.12, following in rear of the other three, which owing to their wheeling were now in one line, came under the command of Sgt Gronow. All four platoons soon after became merged into one line.

"The first serious show of resistance by the opposing infantry began as the company attacked the two communication trenches, Shrine Alley and Kiel Lane, and from these onwards to our final objective enemy riflemen and bombers, hiding in the innumerable large shell-holes, put up a good fight, breaking up our line to a certain extent, but not checking our advance as the occupied shell-holes were worked round, and their holders shot or bombed. Captain Newton was well in the lead, encouraging a party of men to oust some Germans as above, and was in the act of shooting one of the latter when he was hit by a bullet in the left hand. The wound was a serious one, half the hand being blown away, and the command of the company fell to 2nd Lieut Holland. The advance of the line on the left was slower than on the right, German bombers made stubborn stands in Kiel Trench, but our bombers drove them out and some 25 of the enemy were captured as they emerged from dug-outs. Other dug-outs were bombed. At 8.45am parties of our men reached our final objective, Apple Alley, and smoke candle flares were lighted there.

"Bombing posts were established as follows: (i) At the junction of John Trench and Apple Alley under Sgt Gronow. The remaining 'C' Coy Lewis gun was placed here and did excellent work. (ii) At the junction of Bois Francais Support and Apple Alley, under 2nd Lieut Holland. It was attempted to block the Bois Francais Support trench forward, but this trench had been so badly knocked about by shell fire and had become so shallow that the men on this work were shot as they exposed themselves, and this post were [sic] employed in firing at the enemy who were holding the un-named trench joining Bois Francais and Bois Francais Support trenches about 40 yards to their front. (iii) At the junction of Hidden Lane and Bois Francais trenches, with a party of three bombers pushed up Bois Francais trench (which was blocked) under 2nd Lieut Marsh. This post did very excellent work and was made a target by aerial torpedoes and canisters. It constantly repulsed enemy bombers who attempted its dislodgement.

"In the meantime the remainder of the Battalion had reached Hidden Lane, which they were consolidating. Hidden Wood had not been captured, but 2nd Lieut Russel lead [sic] down a party of bombers who cleared the wood and a Lewis gun was put into position to fire down the Hidden Wood valley from Hidden Lane protecting the right of the trench. Touch with the Battalion on our right seemed to be lost, and it was decided to make Hidden Lane as strong as possible and to wait until our right was secure before holding Apple Alley in strength. At 2.30pm the 22nd Infantry Brigade attacked across our front, and while a party of the Border Regt advanced down Luke Trench and along Apple Alley, another party of 6 bombers and 10 men under 2nd Lieut Holland proceeded down Bois Francais Trench and along the un-named trench mentioned above. There was no opposition but about 20 Germans surrendered. Touch was now gained with the 20th Manchester Rgt... The un-named trench was watched by 2nd Lieut Holland's party and orders were issued for Apple Alley to be garrisoned... With the exception of apparently only one heavy gun which fired at our position at about one minutes interval till the next morning there was no molestation by the enemy. The Company remained in Apple Alley from its junction with Mark trench and Bois Francais Support until 8.0am in the morning of the 3/7/16 when it proceded to Bois Francais Trench and the same evening to the Citadel. I consider the bearing of the Company was at all times most praiseworthy. The casualties were: killed 31; wounded 40; missing 14."[247]

We learn from the account written by the Lewis gun officer, 2nd Lieutenant Russell, that Eugene had been the first to reach Apple Alley – the final objective – with just a few men to support him. He survived to fight again.

A short distance further east, Harold Martyn was in support for the action. He was a youngster who had gained rapid promotion. Born in August 1897, he had been at school from January 1913 to

---

[247] Eugene Holland's account as O/C 'C' Company, submitted 6th July and included in the War Diary of 2nd Border Regiment, July 1916.

December 1914 where he was in the Cadets and the 1st XI football team. Although only sixteen, he applied for a commission on 7th June 1915 and managed to persuade the authorities to accept him for military training at Sandhurst. On 21st May 1916, Harold landed in France as a 2nd lieutenant to join the 2nd Wiltshire Battalion, within 21st Brigade, 30th Division. On 24th June they had taken their place in trenches opposite Montauban, in the southern sector of the Somme battlefield. Here a patrol was sent out to see how effective the first day of bombardment had been, and came back with encouraging news: "24-6-16. 'W' Day... Bombardment of enemy's works begins. Artillery chiefly concerned in cutting enemy wire entanglements. Very little retaliation from the enemy. Weather good. During the night a patrol led by Sergeant Jolliffe reaches enemy wire entanglement and finds same to be cut in places."[248] The same good news followed on successive days. British aeroplanes over their heads were observed destroying German observation balloons. On 26th June, a raiding patrol reported "enemy works to be very much damaged, concrete machine gun emplacements blown in and dug-outs destroyed."[249] The news seemed consistently good. Smoke barrages to simulate an attack were made and elicited minimal defence fire. But on 28th June, just after they had received news of the postponement of the attack, a patrol probing forward suddenly encountered fierce, grenade-throwing resistance, and had to withdraw with casualties and in some difficulty, even though they too had noted the wire to be broken.

Harold and the 2nd Wiltshire Battalion were not in the attack on 1st July. Instead they provided support in reserve, and the men acted as carriers of water, rations and other materials. They were, however, pleased when the first wave captured the prime objective and the second wave went through to capture Montauban. Even so, one of their officers was killed in the former British front line. In the early hours of the next day they went forward to reinforce the 90th Brigade to hold newly captured Montauban, and suffered from heavy shell fire all day though they calculated that their casualties had been light – one officer and eight men killed with a further thirty-nine men wounded.

Also in support, Edwin Hill of the 8th Sussex Battalion (Pioneers) was mixed up with the fighting in this sector. As June 1916 had turned towards July and the Battle of the Somme, so their work, and the casualty rate of the battalion, increased. Then the battalion was given a dangerous role in support of the offensive. The different companies of the battalion were placed in different parts of the divisional battleground, essentially divided between the brigades, to open up communications, including digging new trenches across No Man's Land and opening up tunnel saps previously dug by the tunnelling companies and policing movements in them. These instructions anticipated the successful outcome of the infantry assault which the pioneers of 8th Sussex were to follow up. They were specifically required to maintain a one-way flow up or down the tunnels and communication trenches, and also to ensure that their company Lewis guns remained with the 8th Sussex Companies, and were not taken forward to join the assault troops.

Ten minutes before the attack commenced, they were supposed to begin firing flamethrowers from the ends of the sap trenches, and to blow open the sap tunnels three minutes before the attack. These sap tunnels were as close as twenty yards from the enemy trenches, making the assault across No Man's Land shorter and safer.

---

[248] War Diary, 2nd Wiltshire Battalion, 24th June 1916.
[249] War Diary, 2nd Wiltshire Battalion, 26th June 1916.

The flamethrowers were expected to be effective. Divisional orders, describing these British flamethrowers under their German name, 'flammenwerfer', explained their expected use: "The flammenwerfer... have a range of 100 yards and will be used against the German support trenches as well as the front ones for a few minutes before the assault. They will be situated 25 yards in front of the German entanglements. In addition to the above, two portable Flammenwerfer will be allotted to each Infantry Brigade. These will be used for attacks on strong points and communication trenches. Their range is about 60 yards."[250] However, shortly before the battle, revised instructions explained that these instructions had been cancelled – "Flammenwerfer will not now be available."[251] (An interesting entry in the battalion diary of 1st Honourable Artillery Company might help to explain this cancellation: "There was a demonstration of the effect of the German Flammenwerfer – a useless and messy contrivance – with a range of about 25 yards. Rashly, all the officers of the Battalion sacrificed their tunics by sitting in the trench to be played on, & came out spotted with oil."[252])

On 1st July, one company sent its bombers to assist the assault to help capture an enemy strongpoint known as 'the Loop'. The battalion had eleven men killed, three officers wounded and seventy-nine other ranks wounded (though eighteen were able to stay on duty). Two men were reported missing. (That was by no means their worst day: on 14th July three officers were killed; three more wounded; twenty-four men killed; and another eighty-five wounded. Eight men went missing that day.) In these days, Edwin learned to keep his men motivated and working despite the enemy action. Afterwards, the battalion returned to its work of building shelters, maintaining roads, improving trenches and similar work, but the casualty rate always continued at a higher level than before.

Behind the lines, but working hard, Richard Barfoot also experienced the horrors of that first day. In March 1916, Richard's unit, the 24th Field Ambulance, had begun to move forwards. Dug-outs were prepared behind British lines for wounded stretcher cases to be rested if they were being taken to the rear, and the unit was ready when the first salvos to be fired were recorded in their war diary for 03.00 on 24th June.

On 30th June they took up their battle positions – with the main dressing station in Henencourt Wood, a divisional dressing station in Albert, and an advanced dressing station behind British lines opposite Ovillers. Bearer parties were placed at various points in the British trenches. "1.7.16. 7.25am. Troops attacked. Many casualties in 'No Man's Land' from Machine gun fire. The wounded came in Main Dressing Station during the past night in a small stream, but a large number began to arrive about noon & continued during the rest of the day. The reception room accommodation was too little (4 stretchers & dressed patients filled the huts & about 200 were lying on straw outside wood. The wounds of chest & abdomen were sent to no.92 Fld. Amb. Warloy, but later in the day this was full & they were sent to whatever CCS was open. After nos. 38 & 36 CCS Heilly were full, cases went to nos. 3 & 45 CCS Fuchevillers about 12 miles away, so that evacuation went on very slowly."[253] Even severe patients had to be left on straw palliases in the open, and by 6p.m. the diary noted that they had had to withdraw the stretcher-bearers from the trenches as they were tired out; other field ambulances took over for the time being.

---

[250] War Diary, 8th Sussex, Attachment dated 14th June 1916.
[251] War Diary, 8th Sussex, Attachment dated 21st June 1916.
[252] War Diary, 1st Honourable Artillery Company Battalion, 22nd September 1916.
[253] War Diary of the 24th Field Ambulance, 1st July 1916.

From 0600 to 1400 (and again from 2200 to the following 0600) Richard was scheduled, under Sergeant Western and Lance Corporal Vincent, to work with fellow Private Merrifield nursing and feeding the patients at the main dressing station in Henencourt Wood.[254] Given the way events unfolded, it seems unlikely that he actually got his 'rest time' with the demands placed on them all by the colossal casualties of the first day of the Somme. The plans called for all soldiers to be treated the same, whether they be British, French or German.

After a few days of this, the field ambulance was pulled back nearer to Amiens to get some relief, and then was sent much further north to serve a sector of trenches near Bailleul, north-west of Armentières. This was because their division had taken such casualties they needed a respite from the fighting on the Somme. So in August, whilst they had treated three sick officers and five hundred and fifty five sick soldiers, they only had to treat eight wounded officers and two hundred and eighty-eight wounded men. They did not return to the Somme until the middle of October to support the attack in which Richard Clark and Reginald Lapthorne were to suffer (although Richard Barfoot's ambulance unit was supporting a different division). When that attack began the casualties were so great that the bearer section – which had been designated to be held in reserve – was brought into action almost from the start. Their work was exhausting. The ambulance remained on the Somme in support for the rest of the autumn, until in December when they got a short break before returning near Albert in January 1917. Later, they were moved further east to support the operations taking the British up to the Hindenburg Line, in the spring of 1917.

Cyril Horsey was probably in reserve as the disaster unfolded.[255] He was born in 1891 and attended the school as a boarder from 1901 to 1905, where he was a member of the school Cadet Corps. He decided to volunteer on 5th August 1914 for the 'Artists' Rifles', the 28th London Battalion. However, he was not long in the 1/28th London Battalion as on 17th September he was discharged on his appointment as a temporary 2nd lieutenant in the 10th South Lancashire Battalion, but later went to France to join the 7th South Lancashire Battalion, a Service battalion in the 56th Brigade and 19th Division. It landed in France at Boulogne on 18th July 1915. The battalion was in trenches north-west of Albert awaiting 7.30a.m. A quarter of an hour later they moved up to the Tara-Usna Line, where they again waited. "The day threw into vivid relief the antagonistic contrast between man and nature. Due west, the valley of the Ancre lay hot and perfect in the sun, its eastern slopes stained scarlet with massed poppies swaying to the breeze. Northwards, could be seen the trees of Authville Wood, unblemished in the distant view. South West, appeared the roofs of Albert and above them the gleaming figure of the Virgin Mother, brooding over the town and twisted life below. Overhead, the lark ascended to the sky with its morning song. But through the quietness of the day came the constant reiterating rush of shells, and on every hand in the trenches, which scarred hillside and valley, lay men waiting to kill and to be killed." They moved forward in the afternoon but "there were no guides at Ovillers Post, although these had been promised, and there was a tremendous congestion in Ribble Street, the trench being used for In and Out purposes, by fighting troops, stretcher parties, wounded men, orderlies, carrying parties. The heat was intense and the smell almost suffocating. The Germans were using 'Tear' shells and gas goggles had to be in readiness."[256]

---

[254] War Diary of the 24th Field Ambulance, Appendix concerning the 'Evacuation Arrangements'.
[255] Detailed records concerning Cyril and his movements have not survived – his Army File was gleaned down to details concerning events after his death, and his record card does not date his arrival in France.
[256] War Diary, 7th Loyal South Lancashire Battalion, 1st July 1916.

In the event, the battalion did not attack that day, but it did take part in the bitter fighting of 3rd to 9th July which led to the capture of Ovillers. One comment from the colonel stands out as he reviewed the action which, though successful, had cost the lives of most of his young officers: "I have no suggestions to offer as to how to overcome hostile Machine Guns. So far as my experience goes they had no flanks to get round, i.e., as soon as one tried to get round the flank of one gun, one came under close fire of another."[257] In the middle of August, the shortage of officers following their losses in the battle became acute: the war diary noted "not much patrolling was carried out owing to a shortage of officers".[258] Whilst not naming them, the war diary reported that on 28th August six new junior officers joined the battalion, and a further five the next day, so it is possible that that was when Cyril joined the battalion.

The assaults of 1st July had failed in the north and in the centre, though they had had been more successful in the south. The British made repeated attempts to remedy their failures with further attempts, particularly around Ovillers and Thiepval in the central part of the attack, with an idea of holding the line in the north and pivoting northwards from their southern successes.

More 'Boy Soldiers'

Before considering how the battle developed and the role of the Old Bournemouthians in it, it is striking to consider the desperate efforts of seven Old Boys, Charles Markham, John Wilson, Percy Pitfield, Eric and Harold Bott, Ernest Strudwicke and Stanley Feather, not to avoid the bloodbath but to be a part of it.

Charles was born in June 1899. He was a member of the school from 1908 to December 1913 – for most of the time as a boarder and he was in the Cadets. His parents may well not have known, but on the first day possible, 5th August 1914, Charles volunteered for the Hampshire Regiment, and was medically examined and accepted even though he was then just fifteen. He was posted to the 2/9th Hampshire Battalion, a Home Service Cyclist battalion, which was posted to Chichester and Bognor. In March 1916, Charles was promoted to lance corporal. He was in the machine gun group – the Maxim gun section. His parents must have known something of where he was and what he was doing, but their disquiet clearly increased when, on 27th July 1916, he was sent abroad to France.

Charles arrived in France and was attached on 28th July to the 1/4th Leicestershire Battalion. Just before he left for France, Charles had had some sort of an accident which he later admitted had affected his eyes. It is possible that the medical authorities with the 1/4th Leicester Battalion recognised something was wrong, as Charles was held at the base rather than being sent into the line with the battalion, which was in the 138th Brigade, 46th Division.

Behind the scenes, his parents (and probably those of another lad called Corporal Moast of the 14th Hampshire Battalion but also attached to the 1/4th Leicester Battalion) had been trying to get the Army to send him home as under-age. Officially, the Army insisted on accepting a boy's version of his age, and would not accept the proffered evidence of a birth certificate from distressed parents. Since the earliest days of the war, a political campaign to reverse this had been gathering momentum in parliament. The M.P. most associated with that campaign was, ironically, Sir Arthur

---

[257] Included in an appendix to the War Diary, 7th Loyal South Lancashire Battalion, July 1916.
[258] War Diary, 7th Loyal South Lancashire Battalion, 20th August 1916.

Markham. In October 1915, he had written to Lord Derby (when the Derby Scheme had been implemented): "Since I raised this matter in Parliament I have had quite a snowball of letters (up to 300 a day) from people all over the country saying that their sons have enlisted against their wishes, and in some cases boys of 14 have actually been enlisted... I do not think that any voluntary system which openly connives at taking young lads while others remain at home can be justified or defended... I hope now the matter of recruiting has passed into your hands, you will put a stop to this scandal."[259] Lord Derby agreed. His register of men eligible for service at last gave a method of checking names against lists, and he assured Sir Arthur Markham that the practice would stop. However, it would not apply retrospectively to boys like Charles even though government minister, Tennant, told parliament that the government did not want such boys, because they only filled the hospitals as they were too young to withstand war conditions.

Eventually, in June 1916, the government issued an order to release under-age soldiers from front-line duty. Boys began to be held back. Despite this, hundreds of boys died at the start of the Battle of the Somme – but Charles had only arrived in France after a process had begun to stop this tragedy. Boy soldiers like Charles were not told what was happening. The first they usually knew was that they were summoned before a court martial, and confronted with the accusation that they had exaggerated their age. Some tried to brazen it out, difficult now that the Army accepted birth certificates from parents. Others capitulated in face of the accusation. Many were relieved to be allowed to return to England; others angry.

At the end of September 1916 Charles suddenly found himself before a court martial. He was found to be under-age and ordered to return to Southampton aboard the SS *Arundel* on 28th September, and then to report to the Territorial Force Depot No.2 at Southampton, a holding base for the 2/9th Hampshire Battalion. He and Corporal Moast were immediately detached from the 1/4th Leicestershire Battalion. Once he reported in at the Southampton depot, Charles continued to argue to be allowed to return to the front. The officer in charge reported to the Territorial Force Record Centre at Exeter on 2nd October, "No 588 L/Cpl Markham late 2/9th Hants. The above named NCO reported at this Depot having been returned from the Expeditionary Force, under-age. He informs me he was attached to the 4th Leicesters but was retained at the Base. Will you please send instructions as to the disposal of this man. I have instructed him to obtain his birth certificate, but he states he does not wish to be discharged if it is possible for him to rejoin his old unit."[260]

Charles' parents had supplied his birth certificate, however, though Charles himself was not allowed to see it as his mother did not want him to know the details of his birth. After a few more days in the Southampton depot, Charles returned home to his parents in Boscombe, officially on the Army Reserve List from 18th October 1916. There he stayed until Christmas 1916. There must have been some tense conversations, and probably lots of tears. Charles was determined to play his part as a soldier. On 27th December, Charles wrote a remarkable letter to the Territorial Force Record Office at Exeter: "Sir, 588 L/Cpl Markham C W. On consulting your records you will find that I was transferred to the TF Reserve Class 'W' in the early part of September last. I have since been in communication with the officers of my old company and they would be very pleased if I

---

[259] From *Boy Soldiers of the Great War*, Richard Van Emden, p. 194, Headline Book Publishing, Bloomsbury Publishing PLC, 2012.

[260] Army File of Charles Markham. His mother did not want him to know that he was illegitimate and that his real surname was Walker. The Army agreed to withhold that information from him.

could get back to them. I have therefore obtained my parents' consent and should be very pleased if you could call me up for duty with my old Battalion as soon as possible. I am quite ready to report for duty at any time, the sooner the better, and my parents will sign any paper, if required, stating that they will not claim my transfer again. I should be very pleased if you could arrange for me to report sometime during the next week or sooner if required. Trusting that this will meet with your favour. Yours truly, C W Markham."

Two days later, on 29th December 1916, the Territorial Force Record Centre at Exeter wrote to his old battalion to say that should he be recalled he would actually be sent to 2/7th Royal Scots, but it did leave open the chance for the Hampshires to ask for him, which they did, stating he was category 'A' fit. (The 2/9th Hampshire Battalion officer responsible also let him know, sending the Exeter letter to him at Boscombe.) Charles then wrote again to Exeter, asking again to be allowed to return to the 2/9th Hampshire battalion but accepting 2/7th Royal Scots if that meant he could be called up at once. However, he then admitted that he had had an accident which had affected his eyes since he was last medically examined. That, he explained, rightly or wrongly, was why he had been retained at the base in France rather than going out on active service. He suggested he might be re-examined, and if necessary have a time on Home Service and then back to the 2/9th Hants. He presumed he would retain his rank as lance corporal. In the face of his keenness to serve and the apparent change in his parents' minds, on 3rd January 1917, the Territorial Force Record Centre at Exeter ordered his recall and attendance before a medical board. So he was recalled and taken back onto the strength of the 2/9th Hampshire Battalion on 7th January whilst the battalion was at Bognor. On the 11th January, a medical board at Chichester passed him as A1 fit to serve. He was still only seventeen, still two years too young to return to France.

So for the rest of 1917 and most of 1917 Charles sat out the war in 'B' Company, 2/9th Hampshire Battalion, helping to defend Sussex and the Isle of Wight from a German invasion threat, the threat of which was steadily diminishing. He was allowed to remain a lance corporal. Just before the end of the war he was promoted corporal and sent back to France from Folkestone. On 30th October 1918 he was at Rouen. It does not look as if he actually reached the front before the end of the war, as he was posted to the 15th Hampshire Battalion only afterwards, on 20th November. Two days after that he was before a medical board, and was "compulsorily & temporarily transferred to the Labour Corps & posted to Chinese Labour Corps Base Depot 11/12/18 for Benefit of Service at Infantry rates of Pay."

The Labour Corps – eventually 10% of the British Army – was manned by men like Charles Markham or men like Arthur Bolton who were not rated as medically fit enough ('A1') to serve in the front line. However, their role was similar to, but less technically skilled than that of the Pioneers. It was never easy and was frequently dangerous – for example they might be digging in No Man's Land, or doing salvage work near the line, or they could be doing road or railway repairs near or behind the lines. Some remained in the United Kingdom working in forests or on farms. They played an absolutely crucial part in the war effort, but where and when an individual soldier was employed is often almost impossible to tell because of the destruction of so many records later. For example, after being evacuated wounded in October 1915 from the aftermath of the Battle of Loos, Arthur Bolton had spent time in hospital. When he was released from hospital he was not regarded as fit enough to return to the 1/15th London Battalion. Instead, for a time he was attached to a London Headquarters unit, and afterwards placed with the less fit soldiers as a corporal in the Labour Corps. Although we know that Arthur was in 792 and then 787 Companies, as no war diaries were kept by companies, we cannot complete his story, except that he did survive the war, and spent the last phase of it with the Royal Fusiliers.

So Charles Markham's active service in France was with the 71st Chinese Labour Company for a few weeks before he was sent back early to England on 29th January 1919 to be demobilised. On demobilisation he was medically rated 'B2'. However, despite all his urgent and genuine efforts, including the sacrifice of all the years of the war, he had not served at the front, but he had survived, and he was deemed entitled to the War and Victory Medals for his service. He had certainly tried his hardest to be in the thick of it. It seems that his pal John Wilson made similar efforts, in his case with some success.

John Wilson's story is one of pluck. He and Charles Markham were of the same age, and must surely have known each other and even encouraged each other. John was born in 1898 and gained a council scholarship to attend the school, from September 1909 to March 1914. He too was a member of the 9th Hampshire, Cyclist Battalion for nearly three years. Despite his tender age, John may even have become a corporal in the unit. It seems, however, that he too was determined to get into the action on the Western Front.

In Bournemouth, on 1st April 1915, he attempted to join the Army Service Corps. Though at that stage he was aged sixteen, he claimed to be nineteen years and three months. He was accepted by a recruiting captain as a "Respectable man" and passed "fit" the same day after a medical examination. The enlistment forms were not the standard ones for recruit attestation, but rather a form used "for the special enlistment of a recruit" which could also be used for the retention of a man already serving. He was required to report to Aldershot where he was enlisted and began his career as a private in the A.S.C., but on 13th April was discharged as "having made a mis-statement as to age on enlistment".

So far, this seems simply to be the story of a young man, zealous to serve his county, but two or three years too young to do so. Somehow, however, he managed to re-enlist in the 10th Worcestershire Battalion, under the assumed surname of Watson. This time he remained in it for eleven months. John's records do not state when or where he served with them, though they show his promotion to the rank of sergeant, so that service must have been significant. John's name does not appear on the medal roll for men issued with the medals for service abroad, but in 1934 a card was produced which awarded him the War and Victory Medals for his foreign service before the end of the war, even though he would still have been underage until the end of the war. Two years after the war, he joined the R.A.F. and was made corporal on the day after his admission, showing they recognised his experience and previous training.

Another friend, Percy Pitfield, had at first very similar experiences to those of John Wilson. Percy managed to fit in two active service roles. Secondly, he was a 2nd lieutenant in the Royal Garrison Artillery. Before that, however, he had been a very successful soldier in the Army Service Corps (A.S.C.). He was born in 1898, and attended the school between 1910 and 1914. He was in the Officer Training Corps from April 1913 to July 1914. He exaggerated his age even more in order to be accepted for active service when he claimed his age was 20 years 5 months when he attested on 16th April 1915 at Grove Park in London. (His real age was seventeen.) Consistent lying about age is a tricky thing if you don't keep notes, and on 8th December 1917 he gave his age as 23 years 1 month when he wanted to be accepted for officer training. However, on an application form at that time he gave his date of birth as 26th November 1897 and in questioning said he was then nineteen.

There is no sign that the Army worried about such inconsistencies, and soon after he had enlisted he sent the headmaster a postcard to tell him the news. His father was a chauffeur-mechanic with a taxi company, and one of his older brothers also worked as a chauffeur, so car mechanics was something with which he was brought up, and something the Army was desperately short of in an age when horses were gradually giving way to the internal combustion engine. He had also claimed to be a chauffeur himself. He might well have been able to convince a sceptical recruitment team in Bournemouth with his ability to speak knowledgeably about car mechanics and about Army life (through Cadets).

He was quickly sent to France – on 26th May 1915, sailing from Southampton on the *Atalanta* to Rouen – and joined the Base Motor Transport Depot at Rouen on 30th May. This was part of 12 Divisional Supply Column. A few days later, on 3rd June, this 'boy soldier' was posted to the Railway Construction Engineering No.3 Abeele Station, but did not stay there long. On 2nd August he was brought back to Rouen and posted to 358 Company Motor Transport Unit within the 3rd ASC Repair Shop, where he was rated to be a 'very good fitter'. The next day he joined the Transport Directorate GHQ and by the end of the year had settled down into the role of an officer's clerk at the 3rd A.S.C. Repair Shop, part of 358 Company of the Motor Transport Arm of the A.S.C. Ironically, it was for his dexterity as a clerk more than for his mechanical ability that he became noticed. On 9th February 1916 he was with 358 Company when he was promoted to lance corporal.

For some reason he was admitted to a hospital in England on 29th February 1916 and only re-joined 358 Company on 17th March 1916. He was again promoted, to corporal on 26th September 1916, and given leave twice – a week in October 1916 and a fortnight in February 1917, at which time was reclassified as a fitter. By now, old enough at 18, he was interested in trying for a commission – he wanted to serve in the action, either with the Siege Artillery or in the Flying Corps. His colonel supported this ambition, rating him "Sober and very reliable and very intelligent. Good power of command and control, and tactful in his way of handling men."[261] So he was transferred to England and was ordered to report to Maresfield Park at Uckfield to join the 2 R.G.A. Officers Training Unit. He passed his course very successfully, passing out first of his company,[262] and was discharged from the A.S.C. and commissioned 2nd lieutenant in the R.G.A. on 8th December 1917. Unfortunately, in the winter of 1917-1918 he suffered increasingly with ill-health and on 9th May 1918 he relinquished his rank on those grounds. He was issued with a Silver War Badge on 6th May 1918.

Eric and Harold Bott also 'got away with it'. Eric Bott was born in 1899. Harold was slightly older, born in 1897, and he was at the school from 1908 to about 1912, whereas Eric joined from 1910 to 1914.

Harold had an excellent school record, gaining First Class honours in his Senior exams in 1912, and his school photograph, taken to commemorate his success shows a serious looking lad, still wearing the junior uniform with its very traditional taste in collars! Because he had volunteered for the 1/9th Hampshire Territorial Battalion, Harold found himself mobilised with this cyclist battalion in August 1914, but in England until November

Harold Bott

---

[261] This and other details are drawn from his Army File, WO 339/110389.
[262] *The Bournmouthian*, December 1917.

1915 when with three other cyclist battalions they were 'converted' to become infantry and sent off to India in February 1916. The battalion only returned to Europe in October 1918 and landed at Vladivostok on 28th November as part of the abortive British involvement in the Russian Civil War which followed the Revolutions of 1917. Harold survived the war, but never rose above the rank of private soldier.

Meanwhile Eric too joined up, possibly later. He managed to enlist as a private soldier in the 18th London Battalion, the 'London Irish Rifles'. He must have served under-age, as he would only have become nineteen during 1918. By December 1918, he was reported to have gone through several heavy engagements in France without hurt. The 18th London Battalion had landed in France on 10th March 1915, but it is unlikely he was with them then.[263] It is possible that he was with the battalion in the attack at High Wood on 15th September or later, during the Battle of the Somme in 1916 or in the fighting at Ypres in 1917. By February 1918 the battalion was in the trenches on the outskirts of Cambrai. On 21st March 1918, when the German Offensive began, the battalion took heavy casualties, and for five days they retreated, and ended up just west of Albert. At Bouzincourt north-west of Albert, on the Somme, they came under the orders of the 140th Brigade, until in mid-April they were pulled back into Army reserve to clean up and regroup, with more training, particularly for the benefit of the new replacements for those lost in the fighting. It is clear that in 1918 Eric transferred to the Machine Gun Corps alongside a number of fellow members of the 18th London Battalion and in the M.G.C. he rose to the rank of sergeant major, so his work must have been impressive. It is unfortunate that the details of his actions with the M.G.C. are unclear as this was a very hazardous branch in which to serve, and he was likely to have been involved in the counter-attack and advance to victory. He was discharged in December 1919.

Interestingly, Eric has also become known as one of the 'Moorland Poets' from Staffordshire, which makes him unusual and particularly interesting given his military career. His poetry all dates from the early years of his adulthood and reflects his early memories of his young boyhood in Leek, and possibly visits back there to meet his grandparents. Although Eric survived the conflict, he died young, in 1923. His only published work, *A Book of Children's Verse*, was published in the year of his death. In this the poems explore children's questions about the world around them.

Canadian Montague Strudwicke's brother, Ernest Strudwicke, also tried to serve. Sometimes even enthusiasm to join in was not enough. He left school in July 1916 at the age of sixteen, too young to join the British Army. Instead, he emigrated to stay with his sister Gladys in Canada, where on 24th January 1917 he volunteered. He tried to lie about his age – he gave his date of birth as 16th November 1898, which would have made him officially nineteen and therefore old enough to serve overseas, although afterwards his form was amended to show the correct date of 1900. He stated his previous military experience as the seven months he had spent in the school Cadets, the 'Officer Training Corps'. The doctor examining him apparently accepted he was aged nineteen and two months and certified him fit for overseas service. He was placed in the 176th Battalion, Canadian Expeditionary Force, and a few days later, on 14th February 1917, the excited young man wrote to his old headmaster to tell him the news. He embarked with his battalion at Halifax, Nova Scotia, on RMS *Olympic* on 29th April 1917. But Ernest never succeeded in following his brother onto the battlefield – instead he had to be discharged on 31st December 1917 due to sickness, and returned to Canada.

---

[263] Unfortunately, his Army File seems to have been destroyed in the Blitz of WW2. *The Bournemouthian* mentioned his war service in 1918.

Finally, Stanley Feather (born 1900 and at school in 1914) actually ran away from school to join the 2/1st Kent Cyclists in about November 1914, even though he was only fourteen! The headmaster, Dr. Fenwick thought that he had joined the 9th Hampshire Cyclist Battalion. However, on 7th July 1916, Stanley was discharged from the battalion when it was recognised that he was an under-age soldier. By then he had been a soldier for a year and eight and a half months. During 1916-1917 he attended a school of motor engineering in Bournemouth and was allowed to re-enlist on 16th November 1917 and was placed in the R.F.C., transferring to the R.A.F. when it was formed in 1918. He trained to be a pilot and gained his commission in 1919.

Stanley Feather

On the other hand, Thomas Chaffey did manage to get to the Somme battlefield. At Heilly, boy-soldier Thomas's 15 Corps Cyclist Battalion's first involvement with the battle came on 2nd July when some of their men were sent forward to assist in turning back stragglers – that is, men who had apparently become detached from their units and were individually turning away from the front line. A few days later, on 6th July, their duties were more dramatic: a group of twenty-four men were sent forward to help the Special Royal Engineers (presumably to move gas canisters), which led to two men being wounded (one fatally), and another group of thirty under an officer were sent to take up position in Marlborough Wood, in front of the main infantry position, to guard against a surprise attack. That officer was himself wounded and replaced. As the battle continued the cyclists were doing more carrying and digging than cycling. At the end of July most of them were used to help the Royal Engineers dig tunnels near Mametz Wood, and to help bury cables There was little glamour in their role. Sometimes they dug new communication trenches instead. One development by September was for details of men to be used to guard German prisoners. Otherwise the routine continued throughout the battle and into the winter, when sometimes frozen ground was a problem. The battalion was periodically moved around, but the work remained much the same.

The Battle Develops: July

The main road from Bapaume to Albert passes through the village of La Boiselle. This village was, and is, associated with its northern neighbour Ovillers as a single settlement, and seeing it today as a pretty modern village it is hard to imagine the carnage which occurred in both Ovillers and La Boiselle on 1st July, and in the weeks following it. The British made repeated attacks to capture these villages because they not only stood across the direct route to Bapaume, but also guarded the flank of the German positions at Thiepval. Although La Boiselle fell relatively quickly, it took several weeks before Ovillers was safely in British hands.

Herbert Short's battalion was involved in a major attack there on 3rd July. For Herbert and the 7th Suffolk Battalion, May and June 1916 had been dominated by training exercises, with a new concentration upon training for open warfare. They had moved to Franvillars, west of Albert, on 30th June and went into the reserve trenches at Henincourt by 8.30a.m. on 1st July. That evening they moved forward again as their division relieved the 8th Division opposite Ovillers-la-Boisselle. All day on 2nd July they remained in the support trenches and prepared to attack early the next morning. At 3.15a.m. they lined up with 'D' Company on the right, 'C' Company on left, supported by 'B' Company on the right, and 'A' Company on the left. On their right was the 5th Royal Berkshire Battalion, and they were supported by the Essex and Norfolk Regiments.

"Ten minutes before Zero the leading battalions advanced under cover of the bombardment and at the hour of Zero the Battalion assaulted in eight successive waves. The first 4 waves (D and C companies) penetrated to the enemy's third line and portions of them into the village itself, but owing to the darkness touch was lost with succeeding waves and with the 5th Royal Berks on the right, so that the leading waves were not supported closely enough, thus allowing the Germans to get in between the waves and cut off the leading ones at the 3rd line of resistance. It was at this 3rd German line that the chief casualties occurred, and the assault was brought to a standstill. The two companies of the Essex regiment moving up in support were too far behind and were practically annihilated by machine gun fire during their advance across the open. The casualties in the Battalion were 21 Officers and 455 O.R. killed, wounded and missing, though some of those missing eventually rejoined the Battalion during the following night."[264]

On 4th July Herbert was promoted to become a full lieutenant, possibly because he was a survivor of the awful onslaught and suddenly one of the more senior men. Despite suffering these heavy casualties in the area known as 'Mash' Valley, they had at least succeeded in capturing and holding the first and second German lines, close to Ovillers. With such casualties, however, it is unsurprising that they were withdrawn for reorganisation, training and to receive reinforcements of officers and men. Even so, on 21st July they were briefly back in the trenches, this time in the Auchonvillers Sector near Beaumont-Hamel before being again withdrawn for a few weeks to rest, train, and provide working parties.

Second Lieutenant John Snelgar, who had already distinguished himself with 1st Wiltshire Battalion at Hooge in 1915 and at later around Vimy Ridge in 1916, was now back in action a little further north, though still in the central sector of the battle. By the middle of June his battalion had been regularly practising for bayonet fighting and with the light, Lewis machine guns, with a particular emphasis on advancing across country into contact with the enemy – the open warfare Haig planned and hoped for. Indeed, this training was rather innovative for the Army (despite the views of some later critics!) including as it did, "particular attention [to] the development of initiative and leadership in section commander and to fire control by the junior NCOs. The advance to the assault and the assault itself were practised, first by single companies and then by the whole Battn, and the part played by specialists such as Lewis Gunners, Signallers and bombers and by carrying and wiring parties."[265]

On 2nd July, the battalion was moved up to assembly trenches in Aveluy Wood ready to assault the Leipzig Redoubt, a major German strongpoint to the south of Thiepval, from which the Germans had commanding views and machine gun fields of fire. The next day John and 'A' Company moved into a captured German trench which had been the front line before the redoubt, and they held this for two days despite intense German bombardment and infantry counter-attacks. At this point, on 5th July, John was wounded by a German bullet which, as he wrote later, "pinked me and made it very uncomfortable for me to sit down for some days."[266] This was a considerable understatement. From a later medical report we find, "A rifle bullet struck him on the outer and posterior aspect of

---

[264] War Diary, 7th Suffolk Regiment, 3rd July 1916.
[265] War Diary, 1st Battalion Wiltshire Regiment, 21st June 1916.
[266] *The Bournemouthian*, July 1916.

the right buttock and emerged about 1 inch further out, same level."[267] A bullet through the buttock was more than just being 'pinked', but as he said, as there were so few officers left, he just had to carry on. He stayed in the trench with his men.

On 6th July, the rest of the battalion joined John and his men in the forward trench. From there, two other companies, 'C' and 'D', assaulted the next German trench. 'D' was devastated by machine-gun fire and counter-attacks, but 'C' Company managed to gain and hold a foothold. However, all the battalion was under intense enemy shell fire – even the colonel, W.S. Brown, was killed. Yet by the next morning they had managed to reopen an old German communication trench to reinforce 'C' Company. Two companies of the 3rd Worcesters gave them assistance on the flank, in an area known as the Quarries.

On the next day, 7th July, orders were received that they should attack the strongest part of the Leipzig Redoubt, still holding up the British, roughly half-way between Ovillers and Thiepval. As they prepared they were subjected to violent enemy counter-attacks in the middle of the night in which the Germans even reached the edge of the British-held trench and were able to throw in their grenades before they were beaten back. Nevertheless, at 9.30a.m. the battalion made its attack, and John was in the forefront with 'A' Company. "At 9.30a.m., after 30secs intense bombardment by guns and Stokes mortars, the assault was made and the trench successfully captured. This was not accomplished without difficulty as the enemy did not seem to be taken by surprise, manning their parapet very heavily as our troops arrived. Previous to the assault our snipers had been placed in the shell holes in front of their line and fired 30 rounds of steel nosed bullets at the machine guns which had caused so many casualties in the previous attack by D Coy. Whether silenced by our snipers or by the bombardment, at any rate the enemy machine gun did not fire during our advance. During this advance Lieut Gosden was killed, 2nd Lieut Ross wounded and 2nd Lieut Sharpe wounded and missing believed killed. This left 2nd Lieut Clegg Commanding the trench, 2nd Lieut Snelgar being in charge of carrying parties in Quarries. 1p.m. In this attack a large number of Germans were killed and 23 were taken prisoner, 5 of them being wounded. The captured trench was consolidated but being very wide afforded very little cover. But for incessant bombing from the left flank, no great difficulties were experienced until about 1.30p.m., when the enemy opened a terrific bombardment with high explosive. There was practically no protection in any part of our position particularly in the newly captured trench and in the Quarries. The bombardment lasted for about 5 hours and our casualties were enormous: about 160. Two Companies of the 3rd Worcestershire Regiment who had been utilised as carrying parties were now put in to reinforce the line and suffered equally heavily. 2nd Lieut Clegg and 2nd Lieut Snelgar were both wounded and Capt Knubley was sent up to direct operations."[268]

When they recalculated the fighting strength of the battalion two days later, they found only two hundred men were left – and only thirty-two from 'A' Company which John commanded. But – though again wounded – John had survived. "My luck was extraordinary. During the morning three fellows were hit while talking to me and my helmet was several times struck by heavy pieces of shell and knocked quite out of shape. Yet it was not until the afternoon that a high explosive shell 30 yards away sent a small fragment into my thigh and compelled me to retire to my dug-out out of

---

[267] Army File of John Snelgar, G.O.C. District Medical Board, 8th August 1916 at Caxton Hall London. WO 339/34358.
[268] War Diary, 1st Battalion Wiltshire Regiment, 7th July 1916.

the rain and mud. As company commander I had had a pretty strenuous time for five or six days, and the rest in hospital was most welcome. There one heard from all sides that the Germans invariably lost in hand to hand fighting—in the case of the Wilts' attack on the 7th, Fritz was out and over his parados before our fellows reached his trench. Prisoners caught in dug-outs confirmed one another in stating they realised their fight to be a losing one. But the task before the British is tremendous, as Verdun has proved, and if we succeed in breaking the line the end will be in sight, otherwise a slow and battering form of advance will be necessary to compel the Huns to accept our terms."[269]

The medical board took a more sober view of this second wound: "On 7 July a splinter of HE Shell struck him on the posterior internal aspect of the right thigh middle third, and lodged, where it still remains. The wounds have healed now; but his thigh is somewhat hurt. He did not go for sick with the first wound, and it became somewhat septic and took a considerable time to heal. No important structures were wounded."[270] He was lucky that the septic wound had not become more serious in the mud of the Somme. John was sent back to England to recover from his wounds, leaving Calais on 14th July on the *Dieppe* hospital ship. Then he went to the same Endsleigh Palace Hospital that Arnold Whitting had been sent to six months earlier. However, now there were no scandals about the treatment of these young officers, and he was soon well enough to be sent home to his parents at Redlynch, near Salisbury, for two months leave after a medical board at Caxton Hall in London on 8th August. His wounds were judged to be serious but not permanent. He took the opportunity to marry on 10th August. (Presumably they felt that with life so uncertain it was best to take the chance of home leave, however it had been caused.) On 29th September, a medical board at Evelyn House, Salisbury, found him fit again for general service. He re-joined the war, as a full lieutenant in a different battalion of his regiment, fighting eventually as a captain and battalion adjutant of the 5th Wiltshire Battalion – but that further service was not on the Western Front, but in the Middle East. He was to receive the M.B.E. for his military service.

7th July was a bad day for the school. Near Contalmaison in the south, the school lost one of its younger casualties of the war – John Winton, now 2nd lieutenant in 'C' Company, the 9th Northumberland Fusiliers Battalion. His division, designated as the reserve division ready to support and exploit the anticipated breakthrough, had not taken part in the assaults on the first day of the battle. Now it too was needed as a relatively fresh force to break the enemy. They were heartened by the news of the advances made in their sector, including the captures of Mametz and Montauban, and later of Fricourt. The battalion, as part of the 52nd Brigade in the 17th Division, unfortunately had not had much time to train to learn the latest tactics and techniques which were supposed to characterise the new form of open warfare envisaged by the attack, because the battalions had mostly been trained and worked in defensive trench warfare and had only reached the Somme from Armentières in the second week of June.

On the night of 4th July, the men of the 9th Northumberland Fusiliers were expected, alongside the 1st Royal Welsh Fusiliers, 2nd Royal Irish and 10th Lancashire Fusiliers (a mixed group drawn from 22nd Brigade, 7th Division and John's 52nd Brigade, 17th Division), to creep forward from the British trenches between Shelter Wood and Bottom Wood (which had been captured at the start of the

---

[269] *The Bournemouthian*, July 1916.
[270] Army File of John Snelgar, G.O.C. District Medical Board, 8th August 1916 at Caxton Hall London. WO 339/34358.

battle) and move across a rain-soaked No Man's Land in the dark before Zero hour. They achieved this objective, capturing the German Quadrangle and Shelter Alley Trenches. This success was relatively uncostly to John's unit and John and 'C' Company, who were in reserve on 5th July, had not taken part. However, the British now needed to capture the Quadrangle Support Trench and associated trenches in order to open the way to attack the village of Contalmaison.

The battalion remained in the captured Quadrangle and Shelter Alley trenches the next day, when it was decided that a new attack would be launched at 2a.m. on 7th July. The assault companies were to be 'B' and 'C', including John. On the night of 6th July, they gathered in Quadrangle Trench as far as its junction with Quadrangle Alley. For thirty-five minutes, British artillery attempted to pound Quadrangle Support Trench. Then they attacked under flare lights, but the defensive German fire was intense. Communications back to the battalion and Brigade Headquarters had been cut by enemy artillery fire at 1.10a.m. so for a while the rest of the battalion was in doubt of the outcome, but at 3.15a.m. a runner got back to report that the assault had failed. Almost immediately a lamp message from 'A' Company, on the flank, confirmed that the attack had been held up by uncut wire. The ground had been sodden and, to make matters worse for John, in the front of the attack, the British artillery fire was falling short. Thwarted and forced to pull back once, they renewed the attack with the support of the 10th Sherwood Foresters. Still they were driven back.

Bravely, men from other battalions made the attempt amidst withering fire from three sides. It was futile. Amidst all this, John died. "It was subsequently learnt that the assaulting lines had met with severe opposition, the trench being strongly held by the enemy, probably in preparation for a counter attack. It was also reported that, in addition to intense rifle and M.G. fire, a heavy artillery barrage was opened as soon as our troops appeared on the skyline, about 300 yards from their objective. The timing of the attack was faulty... The artillery preparation was inadequate, the heavy artillery being very short."[271]

His Army file contains several descriptions of his death from eye witnesses. The version of which a modified account was eventually repeated to his father was the statement provided by his commander that "No. 10747 Pte. Davidson, F.H. states that he was on the left of Mr. Winton when he fell for the first time. That Mr. Winton got up again but was hit again almost immediately and fell face downwards. He did not see him again."[272]

An officer called Howard who described to John's father an account from another private called Greenberg who ended up in hospital in Rouen: "He maintained he [John] was seen lying badly wounded in a shell hole to the left of Mametz Wood. He said the attack began at 2 o'clock on Friday morning July 7th. The wires were not properly cut and they had to go back." Apparently they had intended to go back to help him after they had taken the trench. John's father took this to mean John might not have been killed outright, and to hope that he had been taken prisoner. The War Office made enquiries through the American Embassy, but decided on 6th April 1917 that he must have been killed. In fact, John's body had been recovered and buried on the battlefield, near the south-west outskirts of Mametz Wood, although the War Office never knew who had buried John. The body was found in December 1917. In 1920, as part of an effort to rationalise the battlefields, his body was exhumed and reburied "carefully and reverently"[273] at Ovillers.

---

[271] War Diary, 9th Northumberland Fusiliers, 7th July 1916.
[272] Army File, WO 339/61938.
[273] From a letter is his Army File, WO 339/61938.

According to the war diary of the 9th Battalion, in the four days from the 5th to 7th July 1916, the battalion had lost, killed, wounded, or missing fourteen officers and two hundred and ninety-nine men. His commander said of John: "Your son gave his life as a soldier should—in front of his men, doing his duty in the place assigned to him, giving all he had to the service of his country." [274] John lived and died a boy soldier, still only 18 when he died. His father concluded a letter of March 1917, in which he asked to have John's commission sent on to him: "I will be glad to have the commission. His mother and I grieve for his loss but feel proud that he considered it his duty to join the New Army in September 1914 at the age of 16 years & 9 months – He had reached the rank of Bomber Sergt in the 14th Battn North Fusiliers & got to France in time for the battle of Loos, after which he was recommended for a Commission, passing out of St Omer Cadet School in May 1916."

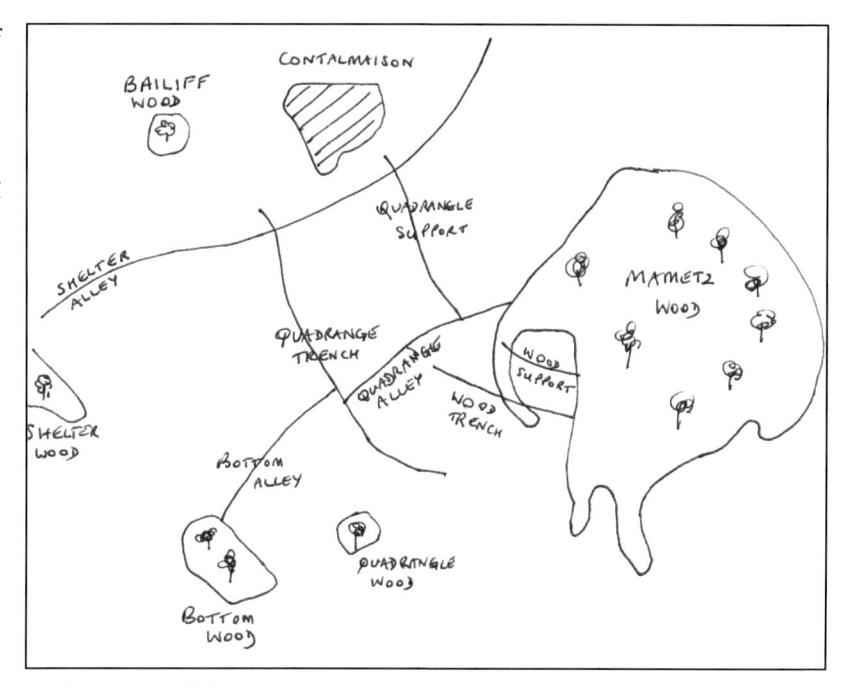

John had died on the western side of Mametz Wood. The two Cecils, Goodall and Novarra, fought close by. By 6th July, the 6th Dorset Battalion was occupying advanced trench lines in Fricourt Wood, 'Railway Alley' and 'Bottom Wood'. Fricourt itself was behind them to the south-west. They had received their movement orders at 2a.m., left their reserve positions at 8.00p.m. and were in the trenches by midnight. Pushing forward, 'C' Company managed to capture part of the German front line trench, code-named 'Wood Trench' by the British. This was an uncomfortable and dangerous night. The Germans were repeatedly shelling them, and killing numbers of them, and they were still there the next day, 7th July and "the line we were holding was a series of small pits on the northern edge of the wood, affording very little protection to shell-fire. A very heavy barrage was maintained throughout the day just behind this line, but casualties were surprisingly few." That evening Cecil Goodhall and 'B' Company, supported by a squad of regimental bombers, were ordered to attack the German 'Wood Trench' at 8 p.m. This line of attack passed along the western side of Mametz Wood, whilst their left would be exposed to fire from the Quadrangle Trench. "They came under very heavy machine gun fire from three different directions and were unable to gain their objective. Seeing that there was no co-operation whatever from the right [where 38th Division had been expected to launch a co-ordinated attack] the colonel decided not to involve a second company."[275] The 6th Dorset Battalion report to brigade, sent at 9.50p.m. was clear: "The Germans are still holding the S.E. corner of Mametz Wood. There is an enemy machine gun there. Five of our platoons attempted to advance towards Wood Trench and were mown down by machine gun fire from two directions. According to the report of one man who came back the whole of our leading company was mown down."[276]

---

[274] *The Bournemouthian*, July 1916.
[275] War Diary, 6th Dorsets, 7th July 1916.
[276] Appendix to War Diary, 6th Dorsets, 7th July 1916.

His commanding officer wrote the normal reassuring message to his parents that Cecil Goodhall died instantly – perhaps it was true, though it is hard to know how the colonel could be so sure. He was "killed in action on July 7th whilst gallantly leading his platoon in an attack. He was hit in the neck and killed instantly, so did not suffer in any way."[277] Later, the colonel recommended a survivor, Lieutenant Barton, for an award. His citation gives one a vivid picture of Cecil's last moments: "For coolness and great daring in reorganising 'B' Company under heavy machine gun fire, after it had sustained heavy casualties, all the officers having been killed or wounded; he himself had his clothing cut to pieces by machine gun bullets – July 7th." (The officer gained the Military Cross.) The 6th Dorsets remained in action in this area north-east of Fricourt until they had a brief rest from 11th July. For Cecil Novarra and the rest of the battalion the battle continued.

Cecil Goodhall

John Day and the 12th Durham Light Infantry faced the same machine-gun fire. John's battalion was brought into the line below Contalmaison. "This advance carried out across the open under heavy machine guns and rifle fire was made with the object of covering the right flank of the Wilts and filling up the gap between them and the 11th M.F.s... their first advance across the open was checked by enfilade and machine gun fire from Contalmaison but two platoons were eventually taken over by a covered way "[278] The men were exhausted. By the end of the day the men had had no sleep for forty-eight hours, and they were standing in mud – never less than knee deep. The rain seemed incessant. Enemy snipers wounded individuals and the Lewis guns replied to try to silence them. When they withdrew along Sausage Valley to Bécourt Wood the next day, they had lost five officers and one hundred and fifty-six other soldiers.

In the eastern part of the battle, on 7th July, Harold Martyn and the 2nd Wiltshire Battalion had moved up to prepare to assault Trones Wood, south of Longueval and Delville Wood. This was to be an attack in conjunction with the French on their left. "8.7.16. In the early morning we move, B & C Companies to Bernafay Wood, A & D Companies to Bricqueterie and assemble for the attack, our part being to follow the Yorks through Bernafay and Trones Woods, and spring from the SE corner of the latter and attack Maltz Horn Trench with two companies and gain connection with the French who are attacking on our right (A & D Companies remaining at Bricqueterie in reserve). On reaching the SE corner of Bernafay Wood, however, B & C Companies find the Yorks checked and driven back into the wood. Meanwhile the French attack has succeeded and their left flank is in the air badly needing protection and the French ask for support... A Company at once advanced across the open from Bricqueterie making for a point south of Maltz Horn farm and succeeded in taking trenches between this farm and the left flank of the French, thus protecting the French left. Meanwhile a re-bombardment of Trones Wood followed at 1pm by the assault by C & D Companies led by Lt. Col. Gillson succeeded in taking the southern half of the wood, clearing it of Germans, taking many prisoners and establishing a line on the south half of the eastern face of the wood. Col.

---

[277] *The Bournemouthian*, July 1916; his death was also reported in *The Bournemouth Visitors' Directory* on 22nd July 1916, with further details on 19th August 1916.

[278] War Diary, 12th Durham Light Infantry, July 7th 1916.

Gillson became wounded and handed over command to Lt. Shepherd. During the evening many counter-attacks by small parties of Germans are made from the north. These are all beaten off by our very thin line of men holding the ground taken. Reinforcements are called for and troops of the 19th and 18th Manchesters arrive before dark and reinforce. Capt MacNamara, who had been in reserve, now came up to Trones Wood and assumed command. About midnight the Germans make a strong counter-attack from the north, their only success being to capture a Lewis Gun and throw two grenades into our line. 9.7.16. In the morning the 90th Bde. make an attack on the northern half of the wood successfully, and eventually relieve us in the southern half... During the whole of our stay in Trones wood the Battalion was bombarded with heavy shells and considerable damage was done."[279] Five officers and twenty-eight men had been killed; eight more officers wounded with one hundred and eighty-six men; whilst fourteen of the men were missing. It was time for the battalion to be pulled back to be reinforced and to regroup.

In the aftermath of these attacks, a few days later on 11th July, Harold Pike and the men of the 2nd Life Guards were given a difficult, though less dangerous, duty to perform, very different from those actions so optimistically envisaged only just over a week before. They had returned to a position at Senlis-le-Sec, just west of Bouzaincourt at the western end of Aveluy Wood, north-east of Albert: "11th. 12.15am. Work commenced collecting & burying dead. 12.45am. Bombardment with small & medium HE shells started. Had to put C and C Sqdrns into old trench. Wounded 2 O.R. – 1 slight, 1 serious. 2am Bombardment stopped & work recommenced. Altogether 50 British & 15 German bodies were buried, mostly 10 days old. 3am."[280] That evening, the same grim work resumed.

Whilst men like Harold were trying to locate and bury the dead, three members of the school were there, in the 10th Royal Fusiliers Battalion. They were preparing for another assault – still trying to capture Ovillers. The partial capture, further north, of the Leipzig Redoubt made it seem possible to break the deadlock around La Boiselle and Ovillers. There were repeated attempts to capture Ovillers to the north of the road until finally it fell as a ruin into British hands after a mass attack on 16th July.

The 10th Royal Fusiliers Battalion had been formed in August 1914, initially as an independent unit, not part of the official War Department. The concept of the battalion had been suggested by Sir Henry Rawlinson who believed that there were many City employees who would join if they could be sure to serve with their friends. So initially, names and addresses of such men were collected after a letter was sent out on 12th August 1914, and when official recruiting was opened on 21st August two hundred and ten men presented themselves – and by the next day there were four hundred and twenty-five. By 27th August, one thousand six hundred men had come forward: William Mitford must have been one of the originals, as later his service seems to have been back-dated to 30th July! Despite the large numbers, there was actually a careful selection process. Once incorporated into the army it kept the nickname, 'the Stockbrokers'.

---

[279] War Diary, 2nd Wiltshire Battalion, 8th-9th July 1916.
[280] War Diary, 2nd Life Guards, 11th July 1916.

At school from 1912-1913, William was born in 1896. William served as a corporal in this unit and later with other battalions. William Moorey was also in the battalion. At the start of 1915, William Moorey's charismatic younger brother Frank had been killed, and his parents must have hoped that Will might make it safely through the war. Like his younger brother, William (known as Will) was a keen and able sportsman. He captained Christchurch Hockey Club for a time, and was also well known as a fine footballer and for his rowing prowess with the sculls. At school from 1905-1907, he was a member of the O.T.C. On 29th August 1914, he and Stanley Birdseye volunteered for this battalion. Will also became a corporal. Stanley was born in 1894 and was at the school for eighteen months from 1907 to 1908, during which time he was a member of the O.T.C. After school, he went to Germany for a short time to continue his education. He had been a signalling corporal but in 1916 was a signalling sergeant.

William Morrey

These three had landed with 10th Royal Fusiliers Battalion on 31st July 1915 at Boulogne. The battalion had been attached to the 8th Royal Fusiliers Battalion at Houplines near Armentières, on 19th August 1915, providing working parties and learning the business of trench warfare. On 24th August 1915, their period of instruction had ended and they parted from the 8th Battalion, which however set them an example by catapulting a message to the Germans about German naval losses in the Baltic. This began a tradition of the battalion for a time similarly to try to damage German morale by such messages – for example, on 10th December 1915 some members of the battalion placed a large noticeboard with a report of a peace demonstration in Berlin actually on the German wire.

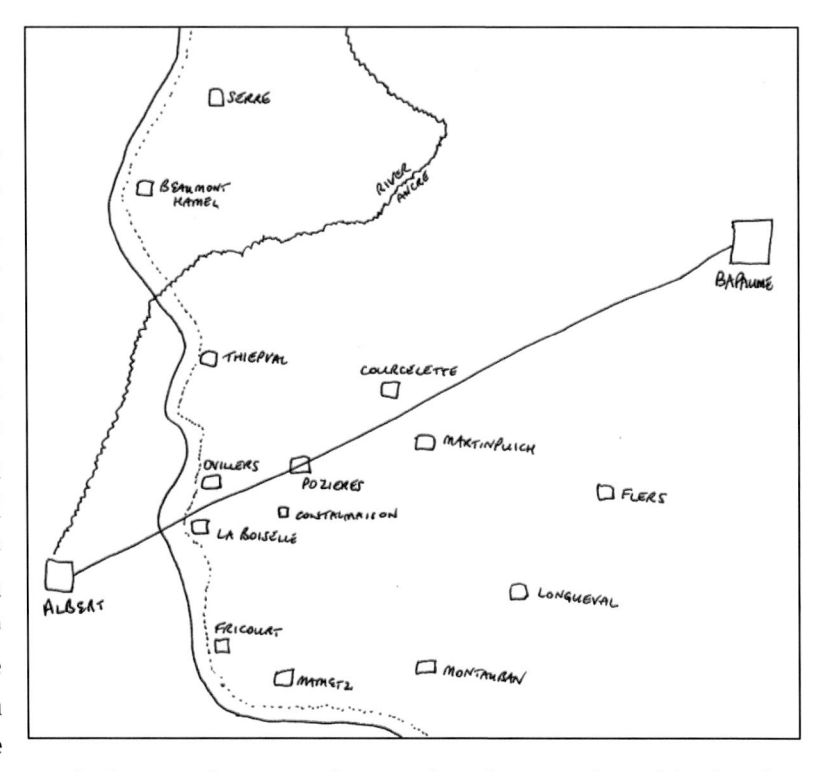

When the battle began, the battalion was positioned beyond its northern edge, but they could see and hear the explosions to their south at Gommecourt. They were moved up to help in subsequent actions. On 9th July 1916, whilst they were at Albert, their camp was heavily shelled, setting off the detonation of a massive dump of 50,000 grenades, which wounded an officer, and killed one man and wounded two more. Their 111th Brigade had been switched from the 37th Division to the 34th Division and was moved to the Usna-Tara Line opposite La Boiselle. When they arrived, the village had been levelled to the ground; the trenches were battered and exposed, and bodies lay about in plain sight in many places. That evening, two companies were pushed forward to relieve the 13th Rifle Brigade who had suffered heavy losses from the German machine guns when they had attempted to take the attack on towards Pozières. For two days the battalion lay in advanced positions suffering from heavy shell fire, and took significant losses. They witnessed the British artillery "intense bombardment [which] took place on Ovillers and ground N of La Boiselle as far as Contalmaison"[281] after which the 23rd Division attacked, reached, but failed to hold Contalmaison. In the aftermath they witnessed demoralised German prisoners ("Owing to the bombardment they had been deprived for several days of any supplies which might otherwise have reached them thro' their communication trenches") but also the destruction in La Boiselle where "the trenches in and about the village were full of German & British dead & the scene was one of devastation…La Boiselle… has been levelled to the ground by our artillery – not so much as a wall remaining."[282] On 12th July, at 10p.m., the battalion retired from its position, manning the line safeguarding the communication trench which ran up along Sausage Valley, to a 3rd line position "near the big crater immediately south of the village of La Boiselle. This position extended to the Right along the 2nd German Line as far as the Gordon Dump."[283] As they were pulling back just before midnight, Will Moorey was one of three men wounded (and one officer killed) when a piece of shrapnel flew at him, splintering the base of his right wrist. He was lucky not to lose his hand. After a short spell in the 6th General Hospital, in Rouen, he returned to England on 21st July for a prolonged period of hospital treatment (only being discharged on 18th October). After a period for his recovery, he was selected to be trained as an officer.

On 14th July, the British 25th Division renewed the attack on Ovillers. The plan this time was different. "In the early hours of the 14th July the attacking troops moved out over the open for a distance of from about 1,000 to 1,400 yards, and lined up in the darkness just below the crest and some 300 to 500 yards from the enemy's trenches. Their advance was covered by strong patrols, and their correct deployment had been ensured by careful previous preparations. The whole movement was carried out unobserved and without touch being lost in any case. The decision to attempt a night operation of this magnitude with an Army, the bulk of which has been raised since the beginning of the war, was perhaps the highest tribute that could be paid to the quality of our troops… The actual assault was delivered at 3.25 a.m. on the 14th July, when there was just sufficient light to be able to distinguish friend from foe at short ranges, and along the whole front attacked our troops, preceded by a very effective artillery barrage, swept over the enemy's first trenches and on into the defences beyond."[284]

The attack was part of a much bigger battle to push forward across the southern half of the Somme battlefield. Haig wrote of the battle of 14th July in his diary: "Very heavy artillery bombardment about 2.30 and then at 3.30am. I looked out at 2.30, it was quite light but cloudy. Just the weather we want. The noise of the artillery was very loud and the light from the explosion of the shells was reflected from the heavens onto the ceiling of my room… At 3.25 am today, after 5 minutes intense bombardment we attacked enemy's second line from west of Bazentin-le-Petit Wood to Longueval with the 21st, 7th, 3rd, and 9th Divisions. Attack went right through and by 9am we were holding the whole of Bazentin-le-Petit Wood and village, and the whole of Bazentin-le-Grand village and Wood.

---

[281] War Diary, 10th Royal Fusiliers, 7th July 1916.
[282] War Diary, 10th Royal Fusiliers, 8th-9th July 1916.
[283] War Diary, 10th Royal Fusiliers, 12th July 1916.
[284] Sir Douglas Haig, Second War Dispatch, 23rd December 1916.

Also all Longueval village except part of the north end. Most of Delville Wood. Trones Wood is all in our hands. At 7.40 am cavalry advanced to seize High Wood, but ground very slippery: it was difficult to get forward. General MacAndrew commanding the Division had two falls. So High Wood was shelled and infantry was pushed on to take it. Fierce fighting continued all day, and we increased our gains of the morning. Enemy retook Bazentin-le-Petit but it was retaken by the 7th Division. High Wood was taken by the 15th [Corps], and was connected up with Bazentin-le-Petit in the evening."[285]

In fact, the bombardment had not been as successful as hoped – "the outstanding feature about all the captured German trenches so far seen is that very little damage [has been] done to the dug outs by our Artillery fire whereas the trenches are practically obliterated. Most of the dug outs are about 30 feet deep and are fine examples of expert workmanship, some of them being luxuriously furnished & in a number of cases fitted with low electric light installation."[286]

Sir Hubert Gough had command of the troops north of the Albert-Bapaume road, and his men essentially maintained the pressure on the Germans there so that they could not be redeployed to assist further south, whilst Rawlinson had the use of the remaining forces to push eastwards and northwards from Mametz towards Guillemont, Longueval, Martinpuich, and then up to Pozières and the Leipzig Redoubt and German stronghold of Thiepval.

Percy Baker and Frank Forman were in that attack on 14th July. They were members of the 7th Royal Warwickshire Battalion. Both were significant in the early history of the school, as well as for their part in the war. Walter Percy Baker was one of the original boys to enrol at Bournemouth School, starting on its first day in January 1901. Born in 1888, he was generally known by his middle name, Percy. After leaving school he followed in his father's footsteps to work as a clerk in the Education Department of Bournemouth Town Council. He volunteered as soon as the war broke out. (Two of his brothers also volunteered for the Army, whilst a third served in the Merchant Navy.) He joined as a Hampshire Cyclist and served in France in 1915 before being commissioned into the Dorsetshire Regiment, but attached to the 7th Royal Warwickshire Battalion. When he joined them on June 28th 1916, the battalion was preparing for the battle. A day later he was joined in the battalion by Francis Forman, generally known as Frank, whom he would have known already through working so long for Bournemouth Education.

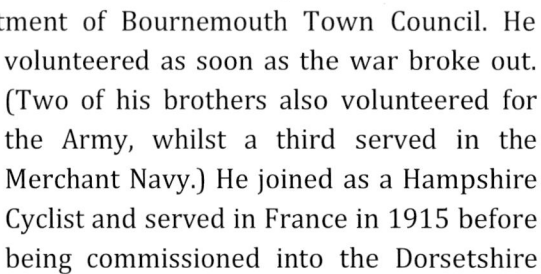

Percy (Walter) Baker

FRANCIS FORMAN,
Sec.-Lieut., Dorset Regt.
Killed in Action, July 14, 1916.

Francis Forman

Frank too had been born in 1888. He had been a teacher at Bournemouth School since April 1909. Frank taught French, as well as junior English, Latin and arithmetic. He lived and worked in Dr. Fenwick's boarding

---

[285] From *Douglas Haig, War Diaries and Letters 1914-1918*, edited by Gary Sheffield and John Bourne, p. 205.
[286] War Diary, 10th Royal Fusiliers, 14th July 1916.

house in Portchester Road where he would have known fellow teacher, Jesse Atkin. Before the war, Frank seems to have shown little interest in the Army or the Corps, but in the first September of the war, as school restarted, Frank joined the O.T.C. and was gazetted 2nd lieutenant on October 12th 1914 as an unattached officer of the Territorial Force. His forte seems to have been in map work and signalling rather than in drill and shooting, and in this he was successful – rapidly persuading eighteen boys to become signalling cadets in the O.T.C. At the end of the summer term, Frank left the school to take up his a position in the 3rd Dorset Battalion to which he was gazetted on July 31st 1915. Frank did not lose touch with the school however, and he visited it before he went out to France. On February 12th 1916, he acted as umpire and judge alongside Old Boy Jack New for the school O.T.C. Field Day. But the 3rd Dorset Battalion was only a reserve and training battalion and, like Percy, Frank was posted to the 7th Royal Warwicks to boost the number of junior officers available for the battalion and the battle. He went out to France a day later than Percy, on 29th June, just in time to take part in the Battle of the Somme.

Their battalion was part of the 48th Division, though their 143rd (Warwickshire) Brigade had been specially attached to the 4th Division for 1st July, within 8th Corps under General Hunter-Weston. The task of the 7th Warwickshire Battalion then was to hold the British trenches opposite Serre and Beaumont-Hamel – in the north of the battlefield – whilst the rest of the division attacked. In the event, this assault was a disaster despite the heroism of those who took part. The 7th Warwickshire Battalion remained holding the trenches until it was withdrawn from the front line for a few days.

The attack Percy and Frank were to make was intended as a diversionary attack – to distract the Germans from the north, by attacking La Boiselle from the north whilst the main attack went in from the south. On 13th July, they were taken by lorry to just outside Bouzincourt. "From there we moved in fighting order to Albert where we lay down in a field until midnight having had orders that the Battalion would attack N.E of La Boiselle at 7.30am… Moved into position in trenches and were heavily shelled going into La Boiselle. At 7.30am after artillery preparation A & B Companies proceeded to assault. They reached their objective. Many casualties were resulted chiefly from machine guns, the following officers being killed: Lt Bullock, and the following attached officers of the 3rd Dorset Regt: 2nd Lieut Jones, 2nd Lieut Baker and 2nd Lieut Forman. We held the trench for seven hours when we had to evacuate it on account of the enemy's extremely heavy enfilade fire both shell and machine guns."[287]

Afterwards, Frank's sister Mary wrote to the headmaster, Dr. Fenwick with a description of his death, which no doubt came from the letter informing her of it: "Frank lost his life while leading his platoon in an attack over open ground on the morning of July 14th in the face of very heavy fire from machine-guns and rifles. It was his first time in action, having been in the trenches but a day and a night since joining the regiment on July 1st."[288] "In Mr Forman Bournemouth School loses not only a highly valued member of the staff, but one who endeared himself by his courteous and obliging disposition to all the masters and boys with whom he came into contact."[289]

Percy died trying to help one of his sergeants: "The N.C.O.'s and men who were with him say how much they think of him. He was as cool and steady as if engaged on part of the ordinary day's

---

[287] 7th Royal Warwickshire Battalion diary entries, 13th and 14th July 1916.
[288] *The Bournemouthian*, December 1916.
[289] *The Bournemouth Visitors' Directory*, 22nd July 1916.

work... I have lost a staunch friend and can scarcely believe he has gone... Percy was with his platoon in the attack and his sergeant told me all about it. They worked a machine-gun as long as they could, and then had to leave that portion of the trench, and that is where Percy endeavoured to carry one of the platoon sergeants who was hit. He was carrying him when he was slightly hit. Sergeant Woodley then took the wounded sergeant from Percy who then just raised his head above the parapet, and was again hit. Everyone here joins in sincere condolences for one who gained everybody's affection and admiration."[290]

Sadly, identifiable bodies of neither Percy nor Frank were recovered and recognised, so their names were inscribed on the Thiepval Monument as those among the missing after the war.

Percy's death prompted a very special meeting of the Bournemouth Council. Having expressed their sympathy over the news of Percy's death (the first of the office staff of the Bournemouth Education Committee), the councillors then considered the deaths of Jesse Atkin, Percy Pean and Francis Forman, as well as those of teachers Mr. J.N.R. Taylor (St. John's) and Mr. E.C.F. Hart (Pokesdown) and started to debate if, after the loss of five Bournemouth Education staff, there should be a permanent Bournemouth Memorial to those Bournemouth citizens who had sacrificed their lives in the war. After this, Alderman Mate talked about Bournemouth School in particular, and said "he would like to call their attention to what that school had done. They had on record, though the record was not complete, over 420 old boys from the school who had joined His Majesty's Forces (applause). Twenty of the old boys had laid down their lives and thirty had been wounded. Four had been awarded the Military Cross and two others had been mentioned in despatches. That was a proud record for the town and it was illustrative of the general feeling of patriotism that had passed through the whole of the community. In conclusion the speaker said he trusted that when the proper time arrived they would see that some suitable memorial was erected to those and other citizens of the borough who had sacrificed their lives."[291] So the tragedy of Percy and Frank helped to start the process whereby Bournemouth Town Council moved to the creation of the war memorial at which still today the sacrifice of so many is remembered each year by the borough.

Sydney Thrift

Their attack was part of a huge operation involving many battalions. Whilst Frank and Percy had been attacking Ovillers from the north, Sydney Thrift and the 10th Cheshire Battalion's attack was launched south of Ovillers.

Sidney, known to family and friends generally as Sid, was born in 1890 and attended the school from 1902 to 1904. After leaving school, he too had first enlisted as a private in the Hampshire Cyclist Corps, and later as a trooper in the Royal Horse Guards, an élite cavalry regiment. This gave him some experience, but he only remained in the Royal Horse Guards for three years.[292] He bought himself out in October 1913, but was recalled to the colours when the

---

[290] Account by his friend Lieutenant F.C. Oxberry, *The Bournemouthian*, December 1916, reprinted from *The Bournemouth Visitors' Directory*, 22nd July 1916.

[291] *The Bournemouth Visitors' Directory*, 5th August 1916.

[292] I am indebted to Alexandra Thrift, his grand-daughter, for additional information about his family life, and for the photographs.

war broke out. On 13th April 1915, he was commissioned 2nd lieutenant in the 11th Cheshire Battalion; although when he went into action it actually was with the 10th Cheshire Battalion.

Sydney reported for duty in France when the 10th Cheshire Battalion, 7th Brigade 25th Division, was at Varennes, on 1st July 1916. He was one of nine new 2nd lieutenants who reported that day as the battalion prepared to enter the battle. They too were held in reserve but, on 2nd July, were called forward to trenches at Aveluy Wood, "which were extremely muddy, and not at all comfortable." Then "After spending the day resting we commenced to relieve the 19th Lancashire Fusiliers at 8.30pm in the front line trenches" in and around Authille Wood.

Under continuous rain they extending the line and collected bodies for burial from those who had fallen casualty on the first three grim days of the battle "Our artillery were pretty busy all day and the enemy retaliated with short, intense, barrages at intervals." [293]

On 7th-8th July, they moved via assembly trenches in Aveluy Wood to La Boiselle. The next day their bombers and 'B' Company helped the Loyal North Lancashires to resist a German counter-attack, but all of them were under heavy German artillery fire for two days before moving forward and at 11p.m.... "attacked and were successful in taking and consolidating three points."[294]

Sid wrote home a letter explaining, "I am writing this in a Hun trench which we took last night. We crawled up in the dark about 600 yards, and then rushed him and seized three of his strong points. We only lost two or three men. We bombed him out, and he ran like fury, shouting. We have since bombed him further and further away, and are blocking up his way back. He is kicking up a row and counter-bombing, but — Company is dealing with him now. We have been troubled by his snipers a bit."[295] *The Bournemouthian* reported that he had also said that he only had ten of his own men left because of this fighting.

Further fighting occurred on the 13th, and 'A' and 'C' Companies became isolated. That night, 'C' Company attacked to the northern side of Ovillers, but it could not get forward because of the heavy German machine-gun fire. After a quieter day, at 11p.m. on 14th July they gathered to attack.

The attack was made under a full moon and with no British artillery

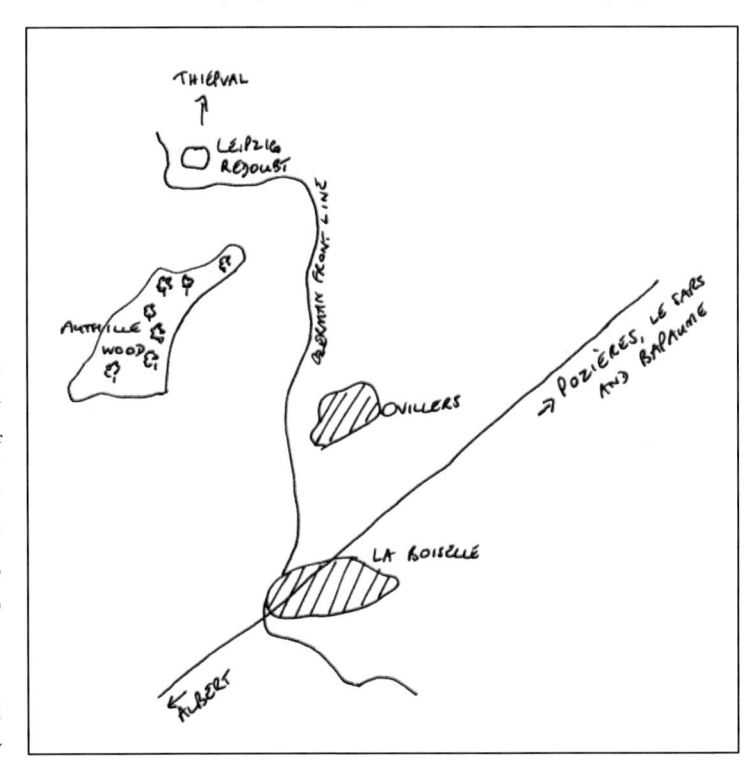

---

[293] War Diary, 10th Cheshire Battalion, 3rd July 1916.

[294] War Diary, 10th Cheshire Battalion, 12th July 1916.

[295] *The Bournemouthian*, December 1916, presumably quoting *The Bournemouth Visitors' Directory*, 19th August 1916.

support. Although initially successful, the Cheshires could seize, but not hold, some of their objectives. "A good many men reached the enemy trenches, but not in sufficient order or numbers to maintain their position. The loss in officers was severe."[296] "At 11pm we attacked the Trenches, S. of Ovillers in force, assisted by 8th Bn. Loyal North Lancashires. We actually got into the enemy Trenches in places only to be driven back by intense machine gun fire… By 2 am we had re-organized and with the assistance of the 11th Bn. Lancashire Fusiliers, we again attacked at the point of the bayonet but were again driven back by machine gun fire, and suffered very heavy casualties. A certain amount of ground was gained by 'C' Company (assisted by the Lancashire Fusiliers) in bombing up a trench on the right flank of the attack, but a very stubborn resistance was met with. 40 yards was gained and a block made."[297] Sydney died or was fatally wounded in one of these attacks. The remnants of the battalion were withdrawn from the line the following afternoon, very tired and feeling the strain of the last few days, according to the diary. When the survivors were checked no one who had survived remembered seeing what had happened to him after 14th July. There was no precise account of how and when he was wounded or killed. Between 3rd and 15th July, the diary noted that four officers had definitely been killed, four (including Sydney) were 'wounded and missing', and seven more wounded. Of the men, thirty-eight had been killed, seventy-two were missing, and two hundred and seventy-six had been wounded. As with Frank and Percy, Sydney's body, if it was eventually recovered, could not be recognised, and he too is commemorated as those with no named grave, on the Thiepval Hill Monument.

Ovillers and its vicinity had proved a most costly place for the school. The irony was that these three Old Bournemouthians had lost their lives in a diversion from the main battle further south. Whilst the generals would have liked to gain Ovillers that day, it was not their priority.

Eugene Holland took part in the main attack for the success of which these three had given their lives. Eugene and the survivors of the 2nd Border Battalion had only been allowed a few days rest in the 'Citadel' after their part in the attack of 1st July before being brought back into action on 13th July. The battalion assembled, tasked to attack Bazentin-le-Grand Wood, which the Germans had fortified and which was one of the series of strongpoints along the new German front. It had to be captured if the British were to push northwards towards the Albert-Bapaume road, and capture Ovillers and Pozières.

The battalion prepared under heavy high explosive and shrapnel fire. When the advance in preparation for the attack started at 2.20p.m., Eugene and 'C' Company were held back as the reserve, with 'B' and 'D' Companies leading the assault, followed by 'A' Company. That night the men crawled forward to within about thirty yards of the enemy, to make a swift assault once the barrage lifted. This enabled them to capture the German line and then to consolidate their gains. More men were needed for this consolidation, and 'A' Company moved to the front, whilst half of 'C' Company moved into support, leaving the rest with Battalion Head Quarters. Eugene's account in the war diary described the casualties as "few" but even so two officers had been killed and one wounded, whilst 23 other ranks had died and 136 fallen wounded. 58 more were missing. Once again, the battalion was withdrawn to rest, whilst new officers and men were brought in to fill up the gaps. Eugene was briefly acting captain for a few days at the start of August. The following January, 1917, Eugene was 'Mentioned in Dispatches' by Haig. Eugene's record for 1917 is hard to trace, but he joined the 1st Border battalion in February 1918.

---

[296] Regimental History of the Cheshire Regiment.
[297] War Diary, 10th Cheshire Battalion, 15th July 1916.

In the autumn of 1916, the battalion continued its involvement in the battle, including fighting in the battles of Delville Wood, Guillemont, and the attacks at the end of the battle on the River Ancre. They also fought in the Battle of Arras (around Bullecourt) in 1917 and in the Third Battle of Ypres.

The day after Eugene's battalion took part in the successful attack on Bazentin-Le-Grand Wood and Percy and Frank had died at Ovillers, Stanley Birdseye and William Mitford were again in action, trying to capture Pozières, reaching an orchard at its south-western edge. They had advanced at 9a.m. on 15th July up Sausage Valley in support of the main attack, but were hit by heavy German machine-gun fire about three hundred yards from Pozières. "Men were seen returning between these Roads and a large body of men of the Bedfords & other Regiments appeared to be blocked in the hollow road 200 yards S of the entrance to Pozières, on the Bailiff Wood Rd."[298]

It was clear that the main attack had stalled. Their colonel asked for an artillery barrage and permission to charge forward. "This permission being granted the 10 RF advanced in steady formation without any hesitation until the small orchard SW of the village entrance was seized by Lt F M Taylor (D Coy). Thence the line extended round towards the Contalmaison Road. A very fine effort was made to seize the… village, the outlying orchards of which were in some cases penetrated by parties of the 10 RF & other Regiments but the Enemy's Machine Guns carefully concealed & untouched by our bombardment maintained a fire so deadly that it was eventually found necessary to fall back to a line of trenches running through the afore-mentioned orchard at varying distances from 200 to 300 yards from the village."

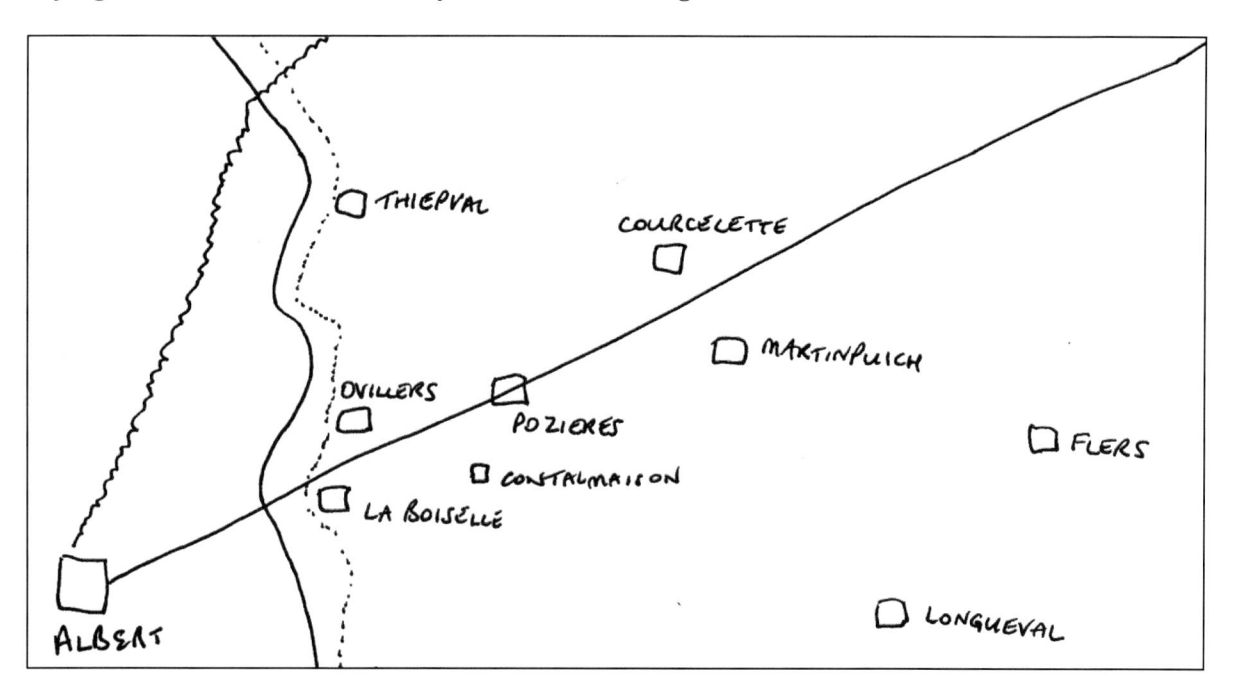

That afternoon, the divisional commander, Major General Williams, ordered a new assault to be attempted after an hour's bombardment from 5p.m. to 6p.m., drawing on the men surviving from the brigade. This would be an unsupported operation – the division on their right did not plan to attack at the same time – and it went wrong from the start. The assault should have been signalled by rockets, but these failed to fire because they were damp, so the attack was uncoordinated – some men went forward, others waited several minutes for the proper signal. As some men dashed

---

[298] War Diary, 10th Royal Fusiliers, 15th July 1916.

forward, others followed, but the German machine gunners knew their job and fired most effectively, inflicting heavy casualties and driving the battalion back again. "The enemy Machine Guns opened an even more destructive fire than that which had taken place in the morning."[299] All four companies lost their commanders, and the battalion losses were so heavy that they had immediately to be replaced in the line by the 10th Loyal North Lancashires, and the remnant of the battalion was pulled out of the battle. The initial casualty reckoning was that three officers and thirty-nine men had been killed; eight officers and one hundred and seventy-five men wounded; and twenty-four men were missing.

William Mitford was one of those wounded. He had been shot through the thigh as they had made their attacks, and had to be taken back through the casualty clearing system, after which he was lucky to recover quite quickly. By the late autumn he had fully recovered and could be sent back. Stanley Birdseye survived unscathed this time.

Two days after this attempt, John Day and the men of the 12th Durham Light Infantry tried their own assault. "At 8pm the attack took place as ordered. The Stokes mortars were however falling about 50 yards short and at 8.45 pm the attackers were all going forward. At this time the Enemy's M.G. fire was intense… cross fire of M.Gs made any further advance impossible. D Coy were only saved from annihilation by lying in shell holes where they remained until dark about 30 yards in front of their original line."[300] By the end of this attack, with no ground gained, they had lost another six officers killed, four wounded, twenty-seven soldiers killed, eighty-two wounded, sixteen missing, and four suffering shell shock. By the time the survivors were relieved by Anzac troops, some of them had been without water or rations for forty-eight hours. For the rest of the month they were given lighter duties, holding the line, or resting, whilst new officers and men were drafted in to make up the numbers of the lost.

As the casualties mounted, the generals debated ways to weaken the German defences. Gunner Albert Ing was caught up in a new diversionary attack at Fromelles, in an attempt to relieve the pressure on the Somme. Albert was born in 1898. He was at the school from May 1911 to April 1912. On 19th April 1915, he enlisted into the 3/4th London Field Artillery Brigade, at Lewisham and transferred to the Royal Field Artillery in April 1916, to the 306th Artillery Brigade. On 22nd May 1916, he landed in France. In 306 Brigade were four batteries – three field batteries and one howitzer battery. It was one of four artillery brigades (along with the 305th, 307th and 308th) in support of the 61st Division and was designated to fight in support of 61st Division in this diversionary attack. This had become urgent when the British learned that the Germans had withdrawn troops from the area around Lille to reinforce their Somme defences. Accordingly, a plan was drawn up to try to persuade the Germans that the British were preparing another major assault to try to capture the Aubers Ridge, with the villages of Aubers and Fromelles. This was soon modified to a narrower assault near Laventie, though with a heavy bombardment to give a similar impression, whilst the infantry would only try to capture the German front line along a four thousand yard corridor. One reason for this was that the designated artillery – including the Australian 4th and 5th Division Artillery – was newly formed and many units had not yet fired in battle. Six British and six Australian units were to bring to bear nearly three hundred field guns and howitzers, supported by seventy-eight heavier artillery pieces. This barrage – more

---

[299] War Diary, 10th Royal Fusiliers, 15th July 1916.
[300] War Diary, 12th Durham Light Infantry, 17th July 1916.

concentrated even than that of 1st July – was meant first to break the wire, then reduce German resistance, and finally support the assaulting battalions. Although Haig told his generals on 16th July that he no longer needed this attack, Lieutenant General Sir R.C.B. Haking decided to attack anyway since he was confident of success.

The main bombardment opened on 16th July. The weather was poor, but improved on 18th July. The German artillery retaliated with considerable force. Even so, the infantry attacked on 19th July and temporarily occupied parts of the German front line before being driven back with considerable losses – especially to the Australians – the next day. Men from Albert's artillery brigade were killed or wounded in the German counter-battery fire and in their overall counter-attack. The Australians viewed the entire assault as a catastrophe.

Later, this brigade (including Albert) was re-designated Royal Garrison Artillery. As part of VI Corps, Heavy Artillery, it was defined as a siege battery and saw action at the Battles of Messines Ridge in June 1917 and at the Third Battle of Ypres. According to the officer writing up Albert's record, he was judged by his commanders to be a fair, hard-working man. The war damaged his health, and he was returned to England and arrived back on Christmas Day 1917. He then spent the rest of his service time in England – in the Reserve Brigade from April 1918 until he was discharged early on 18th October 1918 as he was no longer physically fit for service. He was awarded a disability pension as he was diagnosed to be suffering from valvular disease of the heart, which was attributed to the conditions of his war service.

On 22nd July, back on the Somme, Alan Markwick was again in action with the 18th Lancashire Fusiliers. At the start of July the battalion had moved by stages from near Neuve Chapelle to the Somme, arriving at Bouzincourt on 10th July. Ten days later, after some practising further south, they occupied trenches on the south-western half of Trones Wood and at Maltz Horn Farm. Here they connected up with the French. The next day they beat off a German attack and retaliated with a mass raid the day after: "22.7.16. Ordered to raid enemy's trench at Maltz Horn Farm. Battalion less 100 men in reserve attacked north and south, passed through enemy front line trench and severely bombed support trench, then retired as ordered not to hold them. Lt Wood, L/Cpl Plant and twelve men with two Machine Guns established a post on the left killing three small parties of Germans making 15 and dispersing the attack but was then nearly smashed and forced to retire." [301] After a further month in the trenches on the Somme, they were moved up to Arras to man the front line trenches there.

Close by, Harold Martyn and the 2nd Wiltshire Battalion were also back in the action on 22nd July. They had not been allowed much time to rest after 7th July. They gathered between Bernafay and Trones Woods under heavy shell fire – one platoon of 'C' Company was virtually wiped out when a shell hit a passing lorry full of explosives. They 'dug in' in support of the 19th Manchesters and the next day 'A' Company joined in an unsuccessful assault on Guillemont. As they withdrew the next day, they lost the captain and the company sergeant major of 'B' Company and seventy-two more men wounded, and four men killed with nine missing. This time they were pulled much further back to refresh and train and relieved the 14th Hampshires on 11th August near La Bassée.

Here, Harold was briefly joined by fellow Old Bournemouthian, Eustace Chudleigh, born in 1890 the younger son of the Rector of West Parley and brother of Cuthbert. He had been an early

---

[301] War Diary, 18th Lancashire Fusiliers, 21st-22nd July 1916.

member of the school, around the years 1905 to 1907. Eustace was gazetted 2nd lieutenant and arrived in France on 17th August 1916. After a short time at base at Rouen, he joined the battalion near Arras on 24th August. Initially, Eustace was only with them for a few days before going on a musketry course at Camiers, near the huge British centre of Étaples. For Harold Martyn, being away from the Somme did not mean away from the action. In the early hours of 10th September "at 1am 2/Lt Martyn leads a patrol out towards the enemy's line south of the Red Dragon Crater and gains valuable information as to the enemy's position in rear of the high banks round this huge crater."[302] At some point, Harold too went off on a course, to learn more about Lewis guns.

Hard on their heels of these attacks, Harold Lambert, another former member of the school, was in action south and east of Pozières. His story is a good example of when the school magazine can be a little inaccurate, at least in understating events. It also gives an insight into the treatment of a mental wound.

Harold had been born in 1893, and gained a scholarship to the school valid from 1908 to 1912. After school, he went on to Queens' College, Cambridge with a scholarship. On 23rd September 1914, Harold had volunteered to be an officer, and was placed on the General List as a full lieutenant in the Territorial Force Reserve. Next spring, on 13th March 1915, he was placed as a 2nd lieutenant in the 12th Gloucestershire Battalion, a battalion formed at Bristol on 30th August 1914 by the Citizens Recruiting Committee and was sometimes known as 'Bristol's Own'. It was in the 95th Brigade and had sailed for France on 21st November 1915. On 26th December, they and their brigade were transferred to the 5th Division. In March 1916 they had moved with the division to take over a section of the front line in front of Arras, where Harold and the battalion experienced a lot of sniping activity, and also a mining war. Many raids were made on the enemy's trenches. Partly for this reason, their division, including the 12th Gloucestershire Battalion, was not initially expected to take part in the offensive further south on the Somme. Instead, they were held in G.H.Q. Reserve whilst they rested, trained, and re-fitted. However, the British, having made some progress in the southern sector of the battlefield, were now coming up against highly defended German positions based on the series of woods which dot that landscape.

On 14th July 1916, British troops had assaulted the village of Longueval, at the western end of Delville Wood and south-east of High Wood. This part of the battle is generally known as the Battle of Bazentin Ridge. That evening, attacks were scheduled to push on to capture High Wood. (The 12th Gloucesters were not directly involved.) Even the cavalry (squadrons of the 20th Deccan Horse and the 7th Dragoon Guards), armed with an anachronous mix of lances and machine guns, made a charge. Only part of the wood was captured, and the fighting for the rest took another two months, despite massive efforts by both sides. The task of the 5th Division was to draw off German defenders and try to turn their flank by attacking to the east between the wood and the village.

In the heavy fighting, Harold was wounded – mentally: he became a victim of shell shock. On 28th July, the 12th Gloucestershire Battalion had relieved the 1st Cheshires in the front line, west of Longueval. The next day they attacked, with the loss of two 2nd lieutenants and eight men, whilst a further twenty-three men were wounded, and seven were found to be missing. At the end of the day they were relieved by the 14th Royal Warwicks and were pulled back into reserve at Pommiers Redoubt though even there they lost eleven more men, with two officers and thirty-two men

---

[302] War Diary, 2nd Wiltshire Battalion, 10th September 1916.

wounded, and six men missing. Harold left the battalion on 31st July. The school magazine account understated what had happened to him: "Sec. Lieut. H.E. Lambert, Gloucester Regiment, was admitted to hospital at Rouen last July suffering from slight shell shock. He had been in the previous fighting, and a large shell burst close to him."

His Army file gives a more accurate and detailed explanation. "He went to France November 1915 – after 12 days fighting near Longueval he was knocked out by the explosion of a large shell on the 30th July. He has improved a great deal but has a little Tinnitus... and the hearing of the left ear is rather impaired but is daily getting better." On 3rd August 1916 he was sent back to England after a delay caused by the danger of German submarines. He was transferred to the Officers' Convalescent Home at Osborne on the Isle of Wight. As late as 23rd August, he was not well enough to deal with his own correspondence, but sleep, rest and time gradually worked a cure, and by 8th September he was again writing his own letters with confidence. On the day he was expected to be discharged he went down with a fever so bad that the drugs then available did not seem able to bring his temperature down. Twice he rallied, and twice the fever returned. In the end the fever left him, and he wrote asking to be re-examined with a view to a return to service. About this time, on 26th October 1916, he was promoted to full lieutenant. However, it was decided that so debilitated was he by the fever that he was for a long time only fit for light duties and home service, even though he had recovered from his original 'shell-shock'. It was not until a medical board of 24th April 1917 that the doctors were able to declare "He has recovered", but he never returned to the 12th Gloucesters. After a time in the reserve battalion, he embarked on a completely new phase to his military life when he was appointed to a commission in the 2nd King's African Rifles and took part in the East African campaign in Nyasaland against the German Army in Tanganyika. He relinquished his commission on 1st April 1919, but chose to make a life and a career in East Africa and was he appointed assistant district commissioner on Kenya's southern coast. Here he made a national and international reputation by studying and learning to speak Swahili fluently, earning the nickname 'Sheikh Lambert'. In 1939, he received an O.B.E. and began the Second World War as a senior district commissioner.

Percy Robertson had also recovered from the shell shock which invalided him in 1915 and had returned to the battlefield as a junior officer in the 6th Welsh Battalion. Although they had taken their share on the front line, on 15th May 1916 the character of Percy's battalion changed when it became the 6th Welsh (Pioneers) Battalion for the 1st Division. In the summer, the battalion was working on engineering tasks near Béthune, but moved and on 12th July arrived at Dernancourt on the Somme. Within hours a company was engaged in wiring to protect newly-won ground north-west of Contalmaison. Under heavy shelling (including gas) they worked, making and mending roads and to strengthen acquired positions and deepen trenches, but their casualties mounted. On 19th July "the four Companies left at 6pm to make a new front line trench between Poizier [sic, for Pozières] and Bazentin-le-Petit Wood. The work was successfully carried out. The 2nd and 3rd Brigades supplied the wiring parties. C Company fared badly in returning through Contalmaison. One shell killing 8 men and wounding 7."[303] Further men were wounded when they dug a new zig-zag assault trench between Gloster and Munster Trenches to provide a starting point for the men who were to assault Pozières.

On 22nd July, they were in more direct action to support "an attack on the Switch Line. 3 Companies

---
[303] War Diary, 6th Welsh (Pioneers) Battalion, 19th July 1916.

were attached to the 2nd Brigade and one to the 1st Brigade. Our part was to follow up the advance and dig communication trenches between Langs trench & the Switch Line. However, as the attack was unsuccessful there was very little consolidation to be done. Captain Fusley was wounded while waiting in the trench for the work to be done. 2/Lieut J Evans attached to the 10th Glosters reconnoitred Welsh Alley right up to within 20 yards from where the German front trench branched off. He then formed a barricade to prevent any surprise sortie of the enemy down this trench. 2/Lieut Baker Jones did meritorious work among the many wounded."[304] After days of work supporting the assault troops by digging trenches and working on communications, the battalion was withdrawn west of Albert for a few days' rest but, unfortunately, this did not help Percy very much.

On 1st August, he left the battalion to go into hospital again. Once again, trench conditions had damaged him. After being moved back through the casualty and hospital system, he was sent back to England, embarking from Le Havre on the New Zealand hospital ship *Marama* on 3rd August. The voyage was slow and he only arrived in Southampton on 6th August. Then followed a series of medical boards which continuously extended his period of sick leave until, on 3rd November 1916, he was declared fit again to go back to the service. On 4th December 1916 he was seconded to the Machine Gun Corps (like the Royal Flying Corps, men seconded to the M.G.C. retained membership of their own regiment) but on 1st February 1917 was back before a medical board and was placed on home and lighter duties. He was promoted to full lieutenant on 1st April 1917. It is difficult to be sure what he did in the M.G.C., and it is even possible (but unlikely) that he fought again on the front in 1917, but on 6th February 1918 he was declared unfit for the next six months. In the latter stages of the war he worked at the Machine Gun Base at Grantham, doing such good work that the authorities there resisted demobbing him. On 2nd January 1919, he formally relinquished his commission and then went out to live and work in Southern Rhodesia.

For other Old Boys in France, however, the Battle of the Somme continued to rage beyond July. The battles of July were about to give way to a renewed struggle in August.

August

The attack of 14th July had been a disaster for Stanley Birdseye and the 10th Royal Fusiliers. "Every Company commander & Cy Sergt. Majors & majority of sergeants had been casualties."[305] The battalion had been pulled back west of Albert and rapidly re-built. As soon as 22nd July, classes for Lewis gunners, bombers and junior NCOs were started. These were desperately needed: almost all the Lewis gun sections had been wiped out during the attack. Experienced NCOs like Stanley must have been vital. As they started to recover on 23rd July, there was another shock with the news that their divisional general had been killed by shell fire in Mametz Wood. On 25th July, the reformed battalion was again training to attack. "In view of recent experience, troops now being trained to advance close up to the barrage when attacking."[306] That afternoon they were inspected by III Corps Commander, Lieut. General Pulteney, who told them that their sacrifices of 14th July had "contributed materially" to the subsequent capture of Pozières by the Australians and Territorials.

---

[304] War Diary, 6th Welsh (Pioneers) Battalion, 22nd July 1916.
[305] War Diary 10th Royal Fusiliers, 16th-19th July 1916.
[306] War Diary 10th Royal Fusiliers, 25th July 1916.

Hundreds of reinforcements now joined Stanley and the 10th Royal Fusiliers. Training and practices continued all day long. A quick bathe in the River Ancre at Ribemont, south-west of Albert, whilst on route march to build physical fitness, was the greatest relaxation they experienced. Ready or not, a few days later, on 31st July, they were back in support trenches at Mametz Wood. Although they could see the German front line, it was, fortunately, some 2,500 yards away, so they were able to strengthen the support lines and dig an additional strongpoint. Visibility was unnervingly good because, "It is safe to say that literally every tree in this very large wood has either been destroyed by shell fire or has suffered from rifle fire. During the whole of the time that the battn has been off & on in Mametz Wood the enemy has kept up a heavy shell fire."[307]

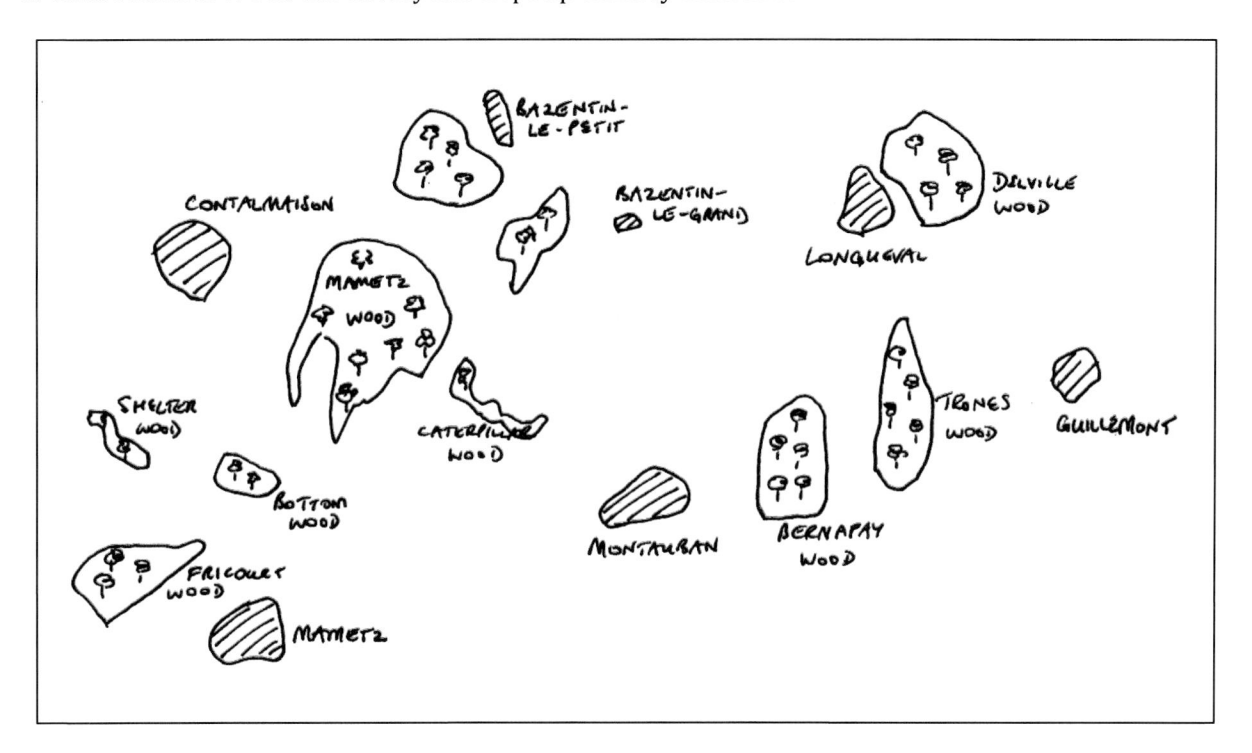

On 3rd August they moved closer to the Germans to a new support line east of Bazentin-le-Petit. Two young officers were seriously wounded. On 6th August they moved back into the front line itself. This was a difficult position – in some places the trench was only two feet deep and two feet wide, and had no fire step. Whilst they dug frantically to improve this trench, they also constructed some saps and four machine gun positions in addition to six Lewis gun posts, whilst the brigade behind them dug out a communication trench, despite heavy German shelling. Two companies were able to pull back for rest in the support trench on 9th August, but two were needed to reinforce the relieving battalion, the 13th Rifle Brigade, which had taken casualties coming up into position. As a signalling sergeant, Stanley worked in the hazardous role of communications within the battalion and beyond it to brigade. He benefited when eventually they were pulled out of the battle sector completely and sent to ten miles south of Abbeville to train and to recuperate. When they moved on to Estaires, south-west of Armentières, it was "the first occasion on which the Battn has been stationed in an unshelled town since arrival in the Country in July 1915".[308] The battalion was no longer fit to fight and was withdrawn from the brigade and division whilst re-training, and when they were sent back into corps reserve, north of La Bassée, at the beginning of September, temporarily they were attached to

---

[307] War Diary 10th Royal Fusiliers, 2nd August 1916.
[308] War Diary 10th Royal Fusiliers, 20th August 1916.

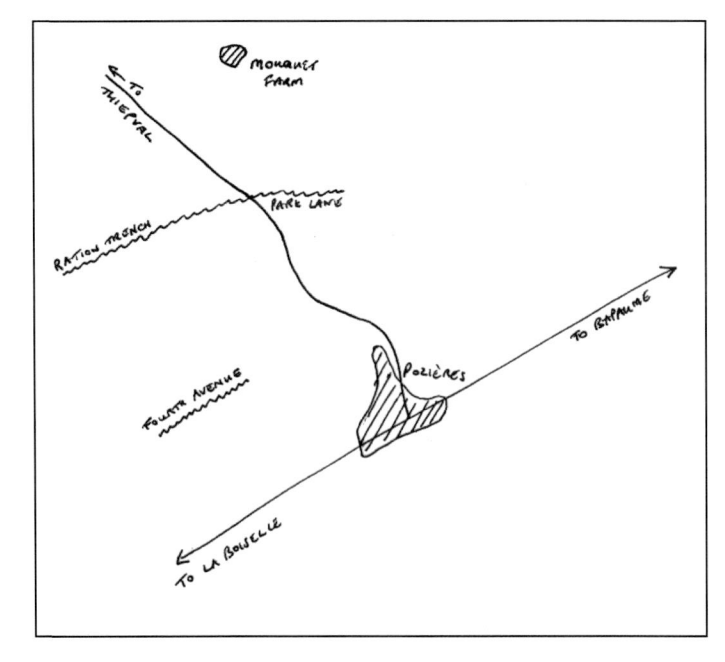

the 63rd (Naval) Division and the 190th Brigade. (Soon they reverted to the 111th Brigade of 37th Division.) Here, two companies were temporarily detached whilst, in the middle of the month, the others inducted the 10th Royal Dublin Fusiliers into trench life with a spell in the front line trenches three miles west of Lens, where the Germans were only one hundred yards away. Inevitably, more deaths and wounded were sustained, particularly from trench mortars, shell fire and machine guns.

In another battalion of the Royal Fusiliers, Richard Clark was a temporary captain.[309] After recovering from his second wound, in July 1916 he had been sent back to France to join the 8th Royal Fusiliers Battalion. This was a Service battalion which had fought on the fringes of the Battle of Loos as part of 36th Brigade, 12th Division. By the summer of 1916, this battalion was crippled by losses. Although it was held back in reserve on 1st July, it had played its part in the disastrous attempt to capture Ovillers on 7th July. "Every officer engaged was either killed, wounded or missing… The battalion had gone into action 800 strong; they mustered 160 at night, but held on until relieved on the following day."[310] Richard was sent across with these urgently needed reinforcements. Almost immediately he went back into action as commander of 'A', 'B' or 'C' Company.

On 20th July, the 8th Royal Fusiliers were back in the trenches. The unit war diary noted that the new men "behave well under fire"[311] and they were certainly tested by shelling, mortar and rifle fire. When they came back out of the line they worked hard on practising for future attacks.

This practising was for a purpose. On the evening of 3rd August, they prepared to attack a German trench system north-west of Pozières, known as 'Fourth Avenue'. The division had moved back to the Ovillers area and the operation was designed to attack from Ovillers northwards and northwest from Pozières to weaken the enemy position at Thiepval. By 8p.m. they were in position. "The plan of attack was that 2 Coys should attack by frontal assault with 2 platoons each in the front line and 2 in support and that a flank attack should be delivered against the enemy bombing block by 2 platoons of a third Company. A and B Coys were to attack from 3rd Avenue and C Coy was responsible for the flank attack, D Company to be in reserve in 2nd Avenue and to move into the place from which A and B attacked." The artillery had been firing all day, and now intensified the barrage. At 11p.m. the men crawled forward to form up their attack line. "They took the enemy completely by surprise and entered the trenches with little resistance to encounter from the enemy who in many instances had no time to seize their rifles."[312]

---

[309] Mentioned in his obituary in *The Times*, 7th November 1916.
[310] *The Royal Fusiliers in the Great War*, H.C. O'Neill, London, William Heinemann, 1922, pp. 116-117.
[311] War Diary, 8th Royal Fusiliers, 21st July 1916.
[312] War Diary, 8th Royal Fusiliers, 3rd August 1916.

"The Germans sent up phosphorus red flares which lit up the storming troops; and they fought very well. Colonel Cope, commanding the Buffs, personally reconnoitred the ground during the attack, and owing to his prompt decision, part of the 5th Avenue trench was also seized and held. By midnight the position was being consolidated, and the two battalions had captured 2 officers (one wearing the Iron Cross) and 89 other ranks."[313]

The fighting continued, sometimes hand to hand, but gradually the companies linked up. "A party of A Company was working up the trench to the right with the bayonet and eventually came into touch with C after making between 20/30 prisoners. Meanwhile B Company had gained touch with the 37th Infantry Brigade on our left who had captured the strong point... Thus by midnight the line was completely in our hands. The success of the attack was down to the fact that the assaulting troops were close behind the barrage and ready to charge directly it lifted thus taking the enemy by surprise." Two officers had been killed and a third wounded, whilst about one hundred and fifty men had fallen casualty, the majority wounded. The next day they pushed on forward. "Eventually the 8th R Fusiliers took over the trench... and the reserve Company was sent up to occupy it. This Company (D) extended the gains by about 150 yards and established a bombing block which was successfully held by Capt S.H. Clarke with a bombing party, in spite of two attempts of the enemy to rush it supported by trench mortar fire and accurate sniping."[314]

"The darkness made it difficult to determine the positions with accuracy… Night attacks have their own peculiar difficulties and terrors. Even in broad daylight actions could rarely be carried out exactly as they were planned. So severe and constant was the bombardment by both sides that even villages were difficult to recognise, and trenches appeared to be little different from the pitted lines of shell-holes. In the attack on Ration Trench on August 4th many circumstances conspired to add to the strain on the men. The battalions engaged advanced on lines which might have led to hopeless confusion and did, in fact, result in isolated encounters of almost unimaginable horror."[315]

That evening they continued the attack, losing another officer killed and one wounded, and about thirty more men falling as casualties. The next morning, 5th August, they realised that in between the captured trenches were about a hundred Germans: "After dawn it was found that a large body of the enemy were between Ration Trench and 4th Avenue – the assaulting Bn. having charged through them during the attack. Such a body was a serious menace and we lost several men by snipings. It was feared that if they were allowed to remain for any length of time they would escape towards Pozières Trench to the W under cover of darkness. Machine guns were trained across the Pozières flank to prevent them. At about 2.20 pm they were subjected to rifle grenade and Stokes mortar fire. After this Lance Cpl. Camping and one or two other men who could speak German crawled out though exposed to constant sniping and explained that if the enemy did not surrender they [would] be subjected to a severe bombardment, but that if they chose to come in they would be well treated. This had the desired effect and parties began to come in and finally the whole party surrendered. They numbered 110 NCO's and men and 2 officers. They proved to be a part of the 9th Jaegar Bn. who had been brought into the trenches the evening before the attack and who had no idea of their whereabouts. They had intended to break through Ration Tr. the same night (5th) in order to get back to their own lines." After a quieter night, on 6th August, "In the early morning the

---

[313] *The Royal Fusiliers in the Great War*, H.C. O'Neill, London, William Heinemann, 1922, p. 125.
[314] War Diary, 8th Royal Fusiliers, 3rd-4th August 1916.
[315] *The Royal Fusiliers in the Great War*, H.C. O'Neill, London, William Heinemann, 1922, pp. 125-126.

enemy attacked the rt. Flank of the 9th R. Fus. on our right with 'Flammenwerfers', with little success. The day was quiet and passed without incident. The work of consolidation was carried out with success. At 11.20 pm the enemy artillery again opened on 3rd Avenue. Our artillery retaliated."[316] "The assault was made by flammenwerfers, supported by bombers using smoke as a screen. The flames burst through the clouds of smoke from various directions, and all the conditions of panic were present. The fumes alone were sufficient to overpower some of the men. But no panic took place. The situation was handled very coolly. The attack was made on the north-east end of Ration Trench, and about 20 men were extended in the open on either side of the trench with two Lewis guns. The attack was thus beaten off with a loss of only 40 yards of trench."[317]

The British assault had been a success: they had launched successful attacks to capture German trenches and beaten off German counter-attacks, including flamethrowers. Despite considerable casualties, this time Richard had come through unscathed. The 8th Royal Fusiliers Battalion were relieved and given some respite in training behind the immediate front line. On 22nd August, they were switched to the Arras Sector for a quieter time, with trench raids to keep them up to the mark. Recognition of their efforts was impressive: combining the actions against Ovillers on 7th July and near Pozières on 3rd-4th August, four Military Crosses were awarded; six D.C.M.s; and 25 Military Medals.

Herbert Short and the 7th Suffolk Battalion were ordered to sleep in clothes and boots to be ready to support Richard's sister battalion, the 9th Royal Fusiliers, within an hour. On 7th August, they took over these trenches west of Pozières, under heavy shelling. Herbert had been made brigade bombing officer. Within hours of returning to the trenches, they were fighting to repel a German assault which managed to capture part of one of the trenches. They counter-attacked on 9th August, supporting an Australian attack the next day. Further raids were made later in the month. On 25th August, *The London Gazette* announced that Herbert had been awarded the Military Cross: "For conspicuous gallantry in action. As brigade bombing officer during an attack he showed the greatest courage in maintaining the bomb supply and directing carrying parties under heavy artillery and machine-gun fire."[318] Later in August they were pulled away from the Somme and sent to the sector around Arras, initially relieving the 6th Border Regiment. Here they continued to be active both in making raids and in supporting the raids done by other battalions within the brigade. Herbert was invested by King George V with his Military Cross on 4th November. Soon afterwards he returned to the front as a captain to command a company. The boys at the school were pleased to have a half-day holiday in honour of his Military Cross.

The battle continued to rage through August and into September in different phases. As the British attempted to sweep northwards to capture Thiepval and Beaumont-Hamel from the south, they also tried to attack eastwards in the south in the hope of breaking through the Germans nearer to Bapaume.

Behind the line, Harold Pike and the 2nd Life Guards had moved back to Corbie, on the Somme between Albert and Amiens. They helped to build a cage as a temporary pen for prisoners of war,

---

[316] War Diary, 8th Royal Fusiliers, 4th-6th August 1916.
[317] *The Royal Fusiliers in the Great War*, H.C. O'Neill, London, William Heinemann, 1922, p. 127.
[318] *London Gazette Supplement*, 25th August 1916.

and soon after discussed the news of the fate of the Indian Cavalry which had charged to disaster near High Wood. By the end of July, all hope had faded of using them in a breakthrough, and they were pulled back west of Amiens. At a divisional leaders conference on 3rd August, General Vaughan expressed his frustrations as well as his hopes for a breakthrough in 1917: "General Vaughan compared us to the Grand Fleet, & told us to try and keep the men up to showing some enthusiasm for 'individual training' (cavalry) which is to commence forthwith: he admitted the natural disappointment of such an anti-climax – but was sanguine about next year."[319] So, once again they trained, though detachments were sent off periodically to act as pioneers in support of the infantry – probably not the role Harold envisaged when he volunteered for the cavalry back in 1914. Twice, a working of party of fifty men was sent forward to Bouzincourt to lay cables within range of the German guns, taking casualties. Eventually, on 14th December, Harold was admitted to a field ambulance, suffering from jaundice, and he was sent on to the 26th General Hospital at Étaples, where the British had their main base. It was not the largest of the hospitals, but even so it could accommodate 2,600 patients, staffed by eighty-three nurses in a combination of huts and tents. After a month at Étaples, Harold was shipped back to England suffering from jaundice and synovitis of the right knee (inflammation of the membrane).

Also behind the lines, Edward Harlow, with the artillery, was in support of the some of the British attacks. He was born in 1898 and only briefly a member of the school from the end of February to the end of July 1909. Edward enlisted on 28th September 1915 into the Royal Garrison Artillery, initially as a member of the 3rd Kent R.G.A., before he was posted as a signaller and a telephonist with the 109th Siege Battery in March 1916. Despite the battery being formed at Dover, it was sometimes known as the 'Northern Scottish Siege Battery' although only a proportion of its personnel came from that region. During his time with the 109th Siege Battery he specialised in observation post work in which he looked for opportunities to advance his knowledge and skill. He was promoted to bombardier and, with his battery, was posted to France on 7th June 1916 to join the 30th Heavy Artillery Group. He fought in this battery over the next six months, in the southern sector of the Somme battleground in the summer of 1916, armed with 6-inch howitzers. Another member of the battery, a fellow signaller called Fred Tomlinson, kept a private diary, which would have been illegal – but was very interesting afterwards. In it Fred mentioned the awful stench from partially buried bodies and limbs, and the troublesome swarms of flies, in the area around Contalmaison and Mametz Wood. The battery was shelled by counter-battery fire when they were situated near Fricourt, but when they tried to move the battery, the road on which they had to move the big guns was itself shelled.[320]

As August rolled into September, British disappointments at the limited successes achieved on the Somme led to a determination amongst the command staff that September would see the real breakthrough to victory.

September

September 1916 marks a turning point in the history of the school on the Western Front. A large number of Old Boys were now involved. One of these was an American, Harold Brooks.

---

[319] War Diary, 2nd Life Guards, 3rd August 1916.

[320] The information about this diary is derived from his grand-daughter's comments posted on the Great War Forum, www.greatwarforum.org.

The Canadians were allotted a part of the front line in the south, west of the village of Courcelette. In the weeks before the Battle of Flers-Courcelette, 15th September, the Canadian Corps took another two thousand six hundred casualties. The village of Courcelette was at that time still in German hands, but Pozières had fallen to the Australians after bitter fighting in the last week of July, the way having been cleared by the capture of Ovillers on 14th-15th July. Canadians had been involved in the capture of Pozières and subsequent fighting in August to try to secure the areas to its north by the German strongpoint at Mouquet Farm and eastwards towards Courcelette, which had to be captured if the British were to push on towards Bapaume. Harold and the men of the 1st Canadian Division were used at the end of August to secure the line between British-held Pozières and German-held Courcette, in preparation for the attack planned for 15th September.

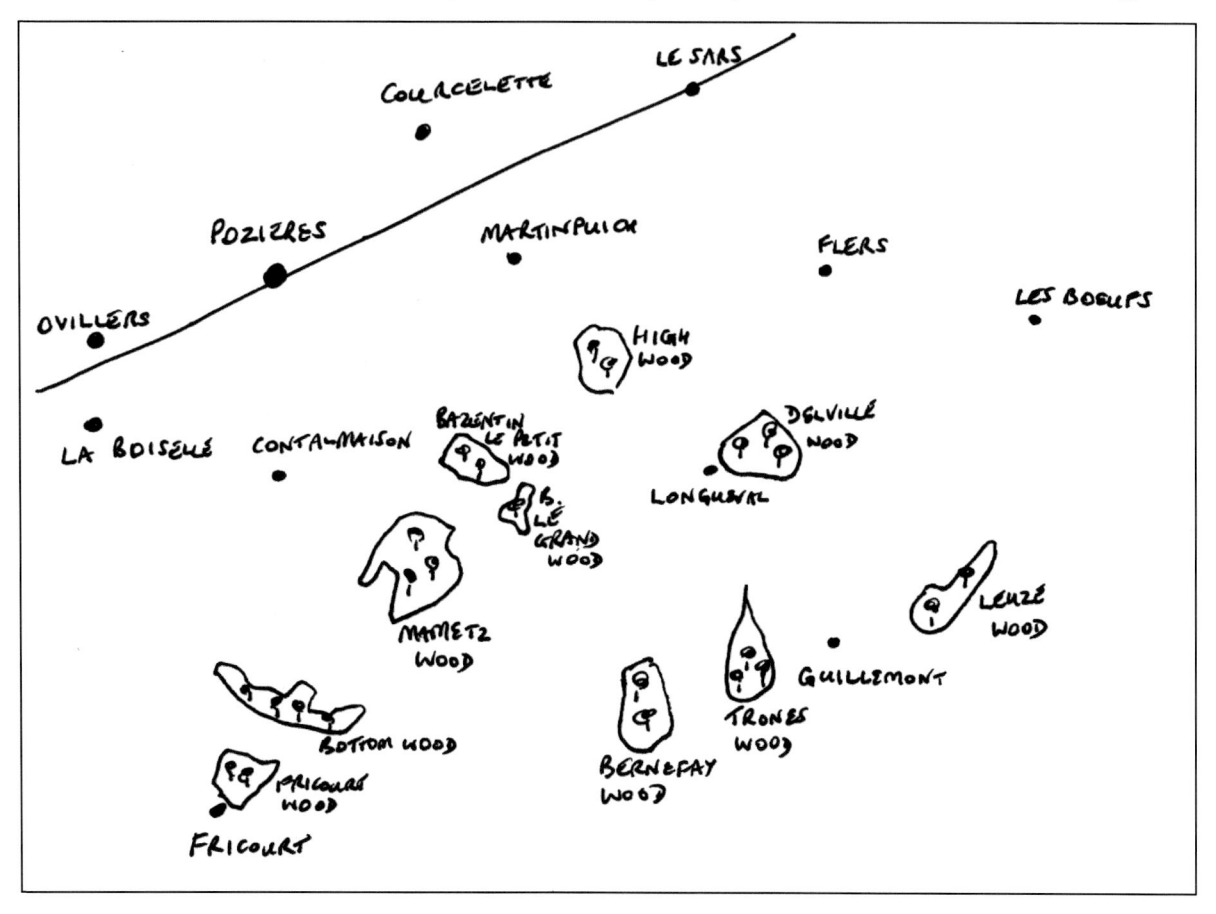

On about 6th September 1916 he was wounded in the legs, with a gunshot wound to his right knee. He was taken back through the casualty clearing system until he reached Number 5 General Hospital at Rouen. His wound was not life threatening (unless infection took hold) but it did require some surgery and the removal of part of some part of the knee structure, which was carried out in France. As soon as possible, on 12th September, he was sent back to Folkestone and was treated at a number of hospitals in England. Although his knee wound was judged to have healed by 25th October 1916, he then almost immediately went down with 'flu from 7th November to 11th December, a dangerous illness in the days before antibiotics and a real set-back to his recovery. Then he was judged to be suffering from D.A.H. ('Disordered Action of the Heart'), which was something of a 'catch-all' diagnosis covering a number of possibilities. In Harold's case it was noted that he suffered headaches and chest pains when he exerted himself. He was also noticed to be nervous with a visible tremor. He was sleeping badly, had a rapid pulse, and did not seem to be very well nourished despite the hospital care. Clearly his spell on the front line had damaged his nerves and mind as well as his knee. Very slowly, however, he did recover and he was able later to return to the Western Front.

Whilst Harold helped to hold the line near Courcette, Noel Clayton was in action a few miles to the south-east.

South African, Noel was born in December 1896. He was a boarder from 1909 to 1913. He had volunteered on 12th March 1915 and was rapidly promoted lance corporal in the 3/14th London Battalion (London Scottish); by March 1916 he was a sergeant. With some pride, *The Bournemouthian* reported in July that he had repeatedly been asked to accept officer training, but had stated his determination to remain in the ranks.[321] On 13th August 1916, he was transferred to the 1/14th London Battalion, in which Frederick Furness and John Kent had served. This battalion, part of 168th Brigade, 56th (London) Division, was then training for the Battle of the Somme, to "get fit for more mobile warfare, including marching and the attack after very short reconnaissance, followed by a limited pursuit and then rapid consolidation of the ground gained."[322] In strict secrecy they were preparing for a new kind of warfare, "practising the attack following the advance of caterpillar tanks."[323] When he joined the battalion he was given the substantive rank of corporal, but asked to act as unpaid lance sergeant.

At 3p.m. on the 5th September they moved two miles north-east of Maricourt where they left their packs and moved up to the front, relieving the 2nd West Surreys in Leuze Wood. (The battalion HQ was established on the old German second line, half a mile south-east of Guillemont.) The battalion was a short distance south-east of Delville Wood, but the continued German occupation of Ginchy created a salient which, whilst making the Germans vulnerable, also weakened the British line by jutting out between Delville and Leuze Woods.

Their new position was far from ideal. Two companies (A and B) went forward into Leuze Wood itself whilst 'D' Company was two hundred yards south of the wood with 'C' Company just to the east of Battalion HQ. The trenches were inadequate – only two feet deep, so immediately they began digging to deepen them whilst under heavy German shell fire all day.

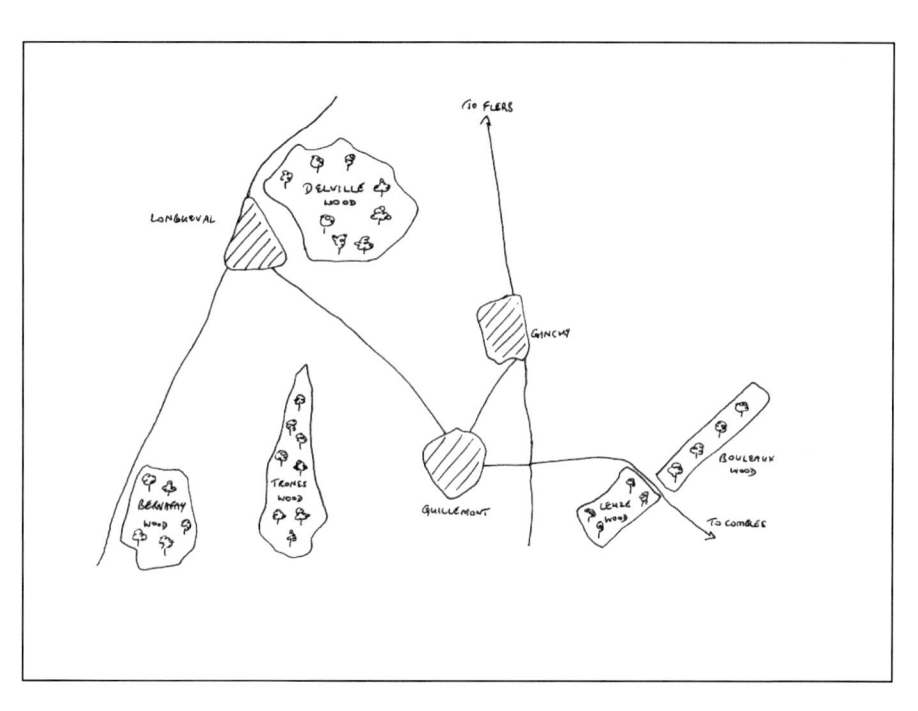

---

[321] *The Bournemouthian*, July 1916.
[322] War Diary, 1/14th London Scottish, Appendix II to August 1916.
[323] War Diary, 1/14th London Scottish, 1st September 1916.

To make matters worse, when the British artillery opened up a bombardment to support a French attack on their right against Combles, most of the British shells fell short onto their own men in Leuze Wood, the 1/14th London Scottish and the Royal Irish Rifles, with the latter battalion suffering heavy casualties. In vain, Very lights were sent up to alert Battalion HQ, but unfortunately these messages were not understood so the shelling continued causing the Royal Irish Rifles to evacuate their forward positions, leaving the 1/14th alone in the front line. Runners had to be sent back with increasingly desperate messages. As the note from Captain MacGregor of 'C' Company put it, "Our shrapnel is still bursting short. They appear to think that the Huns are just on the edge of Leuze wood, whereas they are at least 200 yards further north." Sometime later he was still reporting, "I am waiting for the artillery to stop shelling the front line before occupying it. They are firing on the edge of the wood... and sometimes on my trench inside the wood." As a further note put it, "please send as many stretcher bearers as you can. There are 8 wounded R.I.R. in the trench, which is very cramped. Don't forget the artillery – it is the limit – heavies and shrapnel going short, especially the latter."[324]

At 9p.m. the next day, 6th September, the Germans counter-attacked with grenades and drove in the remaining Royal Irish from their central and right positions. 'A' Company manned its trench whilst 'B' Company split – sending a platoon each to the right and to the left to guard the flanks, whilst the rest of that company manned a defensive position at the south-west corner of the wood after the retreat of the Royal Irish and 7th Inniskilling Fusiliers. 'B' Company then moved forward and took the line to the right of 'A' Company, whilst 'C' Company stood in support and 'D' Company moved to the western edge of the wood. At 11p.m. 'C' and 'D' Companies moved forward to relieve the remaining Royal Irish Rifles, but found only about twenty survivors. Already two of their officers had been wounded, and sixty-four men were killed, wounded or gone missing.

At dawn on 7th September, 'C' Company held the left of Leuze Wood, forty yards from its northern edge, and 'B' Company held the adjacent line up to a grenade post established on an old German communication trench. 'A' Company manned a strongpoint behind the left of 'B' Company whilst 'D' Company was in support, two hundred yards south of the wood. The battalion consolidated its hold and took opportunities to snipe at Germans and even to take three prisoners, despite intermittent shelling. Eventually they were relieved by the Queen Victoria's Rifles that evening and retired to brigade reserve.

At some point in this fighting, probably during the night, Noel was wounded in the arm by a shell (according to the school magazine) and had to be evacuated through the casualty clearing system. (Army records state his wounding to be a gunshot wound on 6th-7th September.) By the end of 7th September he was at Boulogne having his left elbow examined and was sent back to England on 10th September. His recovery took a couple of months, but by December "He has almost completely recovered, and is now marked for two months light-duty at home" remarked the school magazine.[325] At his own request, on 27th December 1916, he reverted to the rank of private, and was posted to the 2/14th London Scottish Battalion on 5th February 1917. After this he served in Salonika, Egypt and in Palestine until his demobilisation in January 1919, after which he returned to South Africa.

---

[324] Appendices IV, VI, and VII, War Diary of 1/14th London Scottish, September 1916.
[325] *The Bournemouthian*, December 1916.

That day, 7th September, Eric Head and the 1/9th London Battalion relieved Noel's 1/14th London Battalion in Leuze Wood and two days later "assaulted and captured trench 300 yds E of Leuze Wood and SW end of Bouleaux Wood... Captured position maintained. Battalion relieved by 13th Composite Brigade at 11.0pm & withdrew to Citadel Fricourt."[326]

Whilst Noel and Eric were fighting in Leuze Wood, Maurice Hellier had also gone back into action. After several months recovering from the wounds to his arms which he had received in November 1915, he was at last able on 19th July 1916 to embark from Folkestone to re-join the 6th King's Shropshire Light Infantry. The battalion had returned to France on 24th July, and four days later had entered the trenches on the northern edge of the Somme battleground for a sobering period, rebuilding the front line trenches, salvaging war materials, and bringing in the dead for burial. Between 3rd-7th September they were on the front line at Guillemont close to Noel and Eric, taking heavy casualties despite not making any assaults: seven officers were wounded (and one missing, believed captured whilst on patrol); eleven men were killed and a further twenty-three wounded.

The crucial Battle of Flers-Courcelette followed, in which several Old Bournemouthians took part, helping to make history. One of those involved, albeit in his case briefly, was Harold Froud. He was another of the original boys of Bournemouth School, arriving a very short time after the school first opened and attending from 1901 to 1906. At school he specialised in athletics at which he was very skilful – helping the school to beat Winchester. For his last three years he also played for the school football team and, needless to say, he did very well in his public exams. On 18th May 1915, he enlisted in the 28th London Battalion, the Artists' Rifles and on 29th October 1915 was commissioned 2nd lieutenant (later promoted to full lieutenant) with the 5th Durham Light Infantry Battalion. He arrived in France on 15th July 1916, at which time the battalion had already seen a lot of fighting in the Ypres Salient, and was being transferred to support the attacks on the Somme, as part of 150th Brigade of the 50th (Northumbrian) Division. The division was not involved in the earlier stages of the battle, but came into its own in September. By now, the Germans had been pushed back by some determined and bloody fighting on their south flank, so that the British had taken and secured a line from La Boiselle to Bazentin-le-Grand, Longueval, Ginchy and Guillemont.

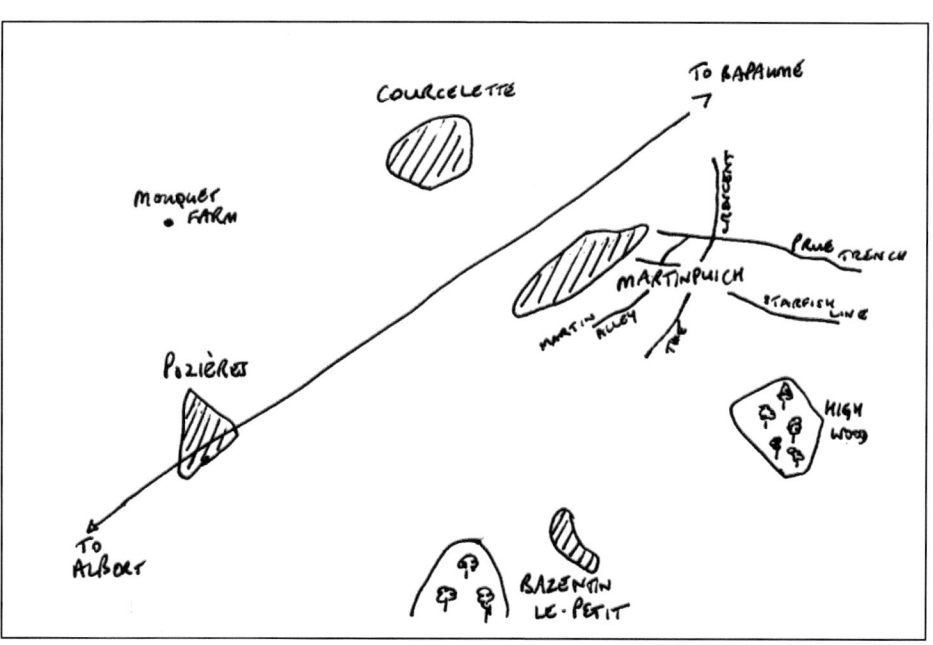

In the attack of 15th September, sometimes known as the Battle of Flers-Courcelette, the British sought to roll up the Germans from the Pozières Ridge and to capture the line from Courcelette in

---

[326] War Diary, 1/9th London Battalion, 7th-10th September 1916.

the centre to Flers further east. Haig was to make use of tanks, but they did not appear on the part of the battlefield over which Harold fought. The 50th Division, including the 5th Durham Light Infantry, was given the task of capturing the line east of the village of Martinpuich: "14th September. 7.30 pm. Battalion about 650 rifles strong went up to take part in offensive operations and proceeded via Contalmaison and Mametz Wood to Bezantin Le-Petit where we assembled in the old German lines... We remained here until 6.20 am the following morning which was the time fixed as Zero Hour. 15th 6.30 am. At this hour the bombardment commenced & the assault took place. The first assaulting line was followed up by A Coy under Capt. Hill & the second by B Coy under Lieut. J.K.M. Hessler. C Coy under Lieut. F.D. Brown went forward to the third objective. D Coy in regimental reserves under Capt. P. Wood moved up with Battn. HQs at 7.20 am into Swansea Trench."[327]

On the day of the assault, 15th September, Harold he was shot in the left forearm (not earlier, and not in the leg, as erroneously reported in *The Bournemouthian* that December) but fortunately the wound, though significant, did not produce any major, permanent, injury. He was evacuated from the battle the same day, and was sent back through the casualty clearing system until, on 19th September he embarked on the *Stadt Antwerpen* from Calais to Dover, and then to the Duchess of Rutland's Hospital in London. On 23rd October he re-joined the 5th Durham Light Infantry Battalion.

Thomas Searls was in the same action, on Harold's left. In the spring of 1916 Thomas had twice been wounded in the fighting in the Arras Sector but on 10th September, as he finished his recuperation, Thomas was attached to the 8th Yorks and Lancaster Battalion. On 12th September it was bivouacking in Bécourt Wood by La Boiselle. It was temporarily attached to the 15th Division, 45th Brigade. (Normally this was a division of Scottish soldiers, and this was only a temporary attachment.) Men were then sent forward on working parties to assist the 73rd and 74th Royal Engineers Field Companies, and to dig advanced trenches in front of the front line, after which the battalion became the reserve battalion for the 45th Brigade. In the battle of 15th September, under cover of an intense barrage, the brigade, including Thomas' battalion, attacked the Germans at Martinpuich, capturing the German front line at 6.21a.m., completing the occupation of the village and the trenches north-east of it by 3p.m., and taking about five hundred prisoners. The battalion's role in this was to take up rations and supplies to the advancing troops, and they were relieved to suffer only one man killed and fourteen wounded, most of them only with slight wounds.

North of the road, Canadian Ernest Snelgar Ernest of the 4th Canadian Mounted Rifles, 8th Brigade, 3rd Canadian Division, was also in this assault. On 11th September they were at Albert and that evening moved up the Bapaume road through La Boiselle to Pozières, after which they entered the maze of muddy trenches which were so difficult to navigate in the dark. Soon they were struggling in gas-filled trenches and shell holes, and on the night of 12th- 3th September entered the front line trenches, just east of the German strongpoint at Mouquet Farm. They were supposed to capture the German first and second line trenches, by attacking in two waves at five minute intervals, and then to build a communication trench to link them to the British front Line.

The attack went in on 15th September. Some accounts mention the presence of two tanks, but these were not mentioned in the battalion war diary. The lead companies in the attack, 'B' on the left and 'C' on the right, immediately encountered massive problems. 'C' Company lost nearly half its men

---

[327] War Diary, 5th Durham Light Infantry, 14th-15th September 1916.

just advancing to the start line when it found its communication trench cut and the decision was made to cut across the open – only to be smashed as "two platoons were practically wiped out by machine gun and shell fire".[328] Even so, they 'dribbled men across' No Man's Land and later were integrated into the fighting force of 'B' Company. Meanwhile, 'B' Company had attacked (not knowing what had happened to 'C' Company) and suffered casualties by being too close up to the British artillery barrage. However, "when the barrage lifted they rushed forward and charged the enemy's trenches, encountering some wire in front of the trench." The second wave followed close behind the first, "although suffering casualties from enfilade rifle and machine gun fire, from the direction of Mouquet farm, and passing over the first line, charged the second German Trench which was heavily manned."

Having reached these trenches, the 'Fabreck Graben', the battalion bombers began to bomb their way left and right along the trenches and managed to make contact with the 7th Canadian Infantry Brigade on their right flank. Many Germans were killed or taken prisoner, whilst others fled down the trench in the direction of Mouquet Farm and across the open to the Zollern Graben Trench. The Canadians then managed to start to dig a communication trench on the left side of their front.

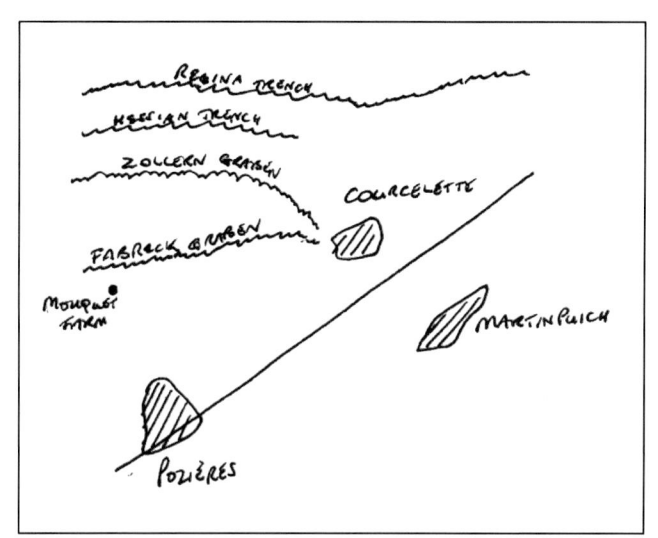

Over the next two days the bombers made steady use of their grenades. Overall, they captured fifty prisoners, including three officers, two machine guns, as well as a "quantity of ammunition". But casualties had been heavy, particularly amongst the bombers as the Germans had been able to inflict significant losses from their Mouquet Farm stronghold in particular, including some unpleasantly accurate trench mortar fire. The battalion had lost thirty-three killed, one hundred and sixty-two wounded, and sixteen were missing. Two officers had been killed (and another died of wounds) and another two emerged wounded. Their colonel paid tribute to his men like Ernest: "I feel it my duty to call to your attention to my appreciation of the way all ranks of my Battalion, carried out the above operation, not only reaching the objectives ordered but anticipating the orders issued, and for their coolness and steadiness which enabled me in less than 4 hours to assemble my Battalion and march them to a point, 2 hours distant, through an exceptionally heavy barrage, and crowded trenches and possibly a still more important feature, was the work of consolidating and building a new trench which latter was carried out, in the face of heavy shelling and rifle fire and sniping. Every man working steadily until relieved… the trench completed."

Frank Cox and the 31st Canadian Infantry Battalion also took part in attacking Courcelette on 15th September, and again on 22nd September. The casualties were enormous, but Frank's name does not appear on any of the lists. Then, early in October, they were shifted north again, this time to the Loos Sector to take over a quiet section of trenches at Souchez near Arras, where they remained, in and out of the front line, for the rest of the year. Here some of the trenches were so waterlogged

---

[328] Account of operations of September 11th to 17th 1916 contained in the War Diary, of the 4th C.E.F. Battalion. The following details are also derived from this account by their colonel.

that the adjutant noted that they were only of use for taking up battle positions – or for bathing!

Corporal Henry Hollies was also fighting again that day, slightly further east. He had returned to the front early in 1916, having recovered from his wounds of September 1915. Henry's battalion, 15th London, (140th Brigade, 47th Division) was one of those designated to right a deficiency in an earlier part of the battle: the failure to advance beyond High Wood. When, on July 14th, the British had reached this wood, General Rawlinson had hesitated as to whether to order them to continue their advance into the wood, and the Germans had reoccupied it. When the advance had been renewed it had driven the British back. On 14th July, two cavalry squadrons (the 20th Deccan Horse and 7th Dragoon Guards) had been slaughtered trying to take the wood, together with the infantry which had been sacrificed in their support. Two more months of bitter fighting had not yet succeeded in allowing the British infantry to claim the wood for their own, although some parts of the wood had been captured. The Germans resisted from a very strong set of trenches focussed on their Hook Trench, which still held the north-west corner of the wood, reinforced by the Starfish Line and Prue Trenches further north. By this stage, of course, the wood had been reduced to charred trunks rising from a sea of churned up mud.

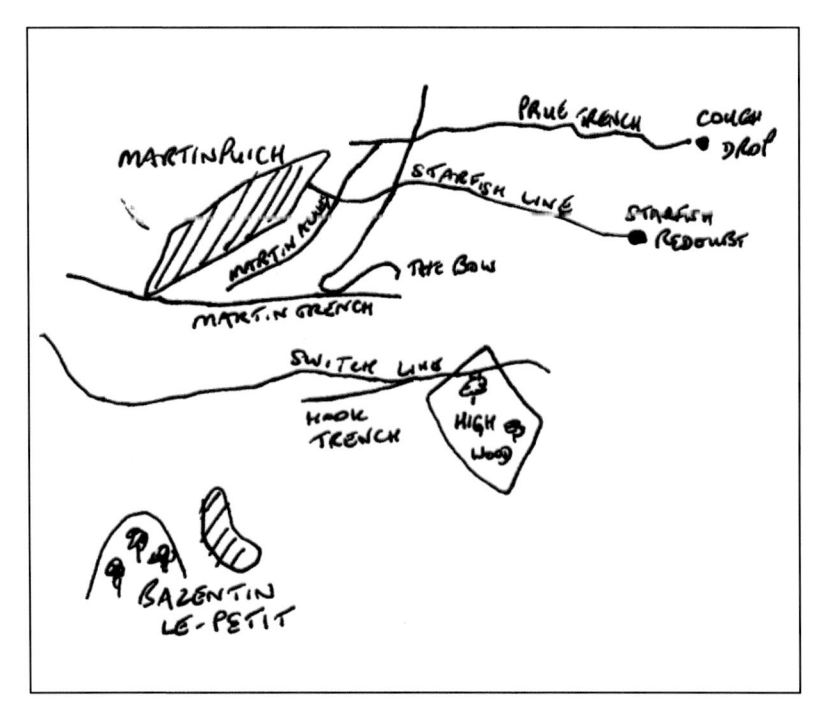

As the 47th Division had arrived on the Somme "we walked into a new world of war. We passed through Albert for the first time under the Virgin, holding out her child, not to heaven but the endless procession below. Fricourt, where the line had stood for so long, was now out of range of anything but long-range guns, and we could see freshly devastated country without being in a battle. All round the slopes were covered with transport of all kinds, and whole Divisions of cavalry waiting for their opportunity. Farther forward in Caterpillar Valley heavy howitzers stood in the open, lobbing their shells at a target miles away. Up near the line by Flatiron Copse and the Bazentins the ground was alive with field guns, many of them hidden by the roadside and startling the unwary."[329]

Henry and the men of the 47th Division were given the task of completing the capture of High Wood. On the left, the 141st Brigade was to attack and capture the Hook Trench, whilst on the right Henry's 140th Brigade was tasked to capture the 'Starfish Line' which ran south-east from Martinpuich, some distance north of High Wood. Once captured, the 140th were meant to link up with the New Zealand troops who would be attacking to their right, then to join up with the 141st Brigade and push onwards to capture the German 'Prue' Trench beyond the 'Starfish' Trench, so

---

[329] 47th Division Official History, London Amalgamated Press (1922) Ltd, London, 1922.

squashing the Germans between the western attack and this attack from the south. In support of the attack, four tanks were given the impossible task of driving through the forest of broken tree stumps through the muddy, broken, ground. The decision to use these tanks was only taken at the last minute. Two major mistakes were made by the divisional general – to order the tanks to drive straight into the wood, and to advance down corridors without artillery barrage support. (This made them easier targets for the German defence, but was intended to make things easier for the tank commanders.) One broke down before the start of the battle, and the other three struggled to find their route before eventually grounding to a halt, stuck just inside the wood or trying to cross the trenches. To make this awful start worse, one of the tanks had become so confused that they had actually opened fire, not on the Germans but on the Londoners and New Zealanders who were about to make their charge into the attack.

So, on 15th September, the two brigades attacked, with neither artillery nor tank covering fire. Almost immediately their attack was smashed by German machine guns, rifles and grenades. The Germans had constructed concrete machine-gun bunkers in their part of the wood, and the British had no way to break through them. Survivors took cover as best they could in the shell holes. The battalion war diary described the uneven results: "Zero 5.50 am. 'A' Company on right immediately successful and pushed through the support line. 'B', 'C' and 'D' Companies were cut up by Machine Gun fire and were unsuccessful. 7th Battalion on right entirely successful. 17th on left entirely unsuccessful on account of machine gun fire."[330] Reinforced by the second wave, some progress was made, but all would have been lost but for covering fire from the 140th Trench Mortar Battery which managed to fire 750 Stokes mortar bombs into the wood in their support in fifteen minutes. Some of the men tried to dig a trench eastwards towards the New Zealanders. "As you know High Wood was our objective, and our Trench Mortar Batteries… really saved the situation, as the Tanks were not worth a d-n there, and never did anything except spoil the show."[331] "11.00am. Enemy front line bombarded by Stokes Mortars. As a result of this and progress of Divisions on right and left, enemy surrendered and by 12 noon we were in possession of whole of High Wood and Switch Line and in joining up with 17th Battalion on left and 7th Battalion on right. Meanwhile 6th London Regt pushed through 7th on right & occupied E half of Starfish and Cough Drop."[332] Suddenly the entire picture had changed because, when they had tried another attack, the defending Germans stood up and surrendered, and by 1.00p.m. the wood had been captured.

About 250 men and fifteen officers had been killed or wounded. Henry died at some time in all this carnage. The school mis-recorded his death as having occurred on 16th September. To put this into perspective, one of the other battalions – the 21st London Battalion – had only two officers and sixty soldiers left unwounded out of the seventeen officers and five hundred and fifty soldiers who had attacked that morning. No wonder the reserve brigade, the 142nd had also been brought up to the wood at 6.00p.m. that evening to support the survivors against a German counter-attack. In four days the division lost about 4,500 men.

Eventually Henry's body was recovered. He was buried in the London Cemetery, which was begun when forty-seven men were placed in a large shell hole on 18th and 21st September. Later they

---

[330] War Diary, 1/15th London (Civil Service) Battalion, 15th September 1916.
[331] Captain Frank Deverill, Transport Officer of 8th London, quoted by Malcolm Brown, *The Imperial War Museum Book of the Somme*, p. 191.
[332] War Diary, 1/15th London (Civil Service) Battalion, 15th September 1916.

added more burials of other men found who had been killed on 15th September. That original cemetery is preserved within the extended cemetery near Longueval on the Somme.

Stanley Seymour was in action in High Wood the next day, having been in reserve when Henry died. He was born in 1898 and from 25th February 1909 to 16th December 1910 Stanley was a boarder at Bournemouth School. On 29th August 1914, he enlisted for one year with the Sussex (Fortress) Royal Engineers at Newhaven, Sussex. At that stage he was a seventeen-year-old clerk, living in Birmingham. The following May he was promoted lance corporal. On 7th January 1916, he joined the Inns of Court O.T.C. but was posted as a lance corporal to the 1/23rd London Battalion, part of the 142nd Brigade arriving in France on 26th August. On 11th September they went into reserve at Mametz Wood, but immediately went forward and reached High Wood on 14th September. On 16th September the battalion, less 'B' Company but with a company from 22nd London attached instead, was switched from 142nd Brigade and placed under the 140th Brigade and attacked that morning, being expected to advance 1,500 yards without a preliminary reconnaissance due to insufficient time. "At 8.55 am the leading platoons extended and moved forward over the crest in line, the other platoons following at proper distance. The Battn reached the crest in 4 waves, followed by Bombers, in good order, without casualties. East of High Wood they were subjected to heavy barrage fire. At 10.25 am reports came back that the attack was going well. Bn was subjected to heavy machine gun fire on reaching sunken road. After dark, patrols were sent out encountering German posts and patrols and made prisoners, among them an officer. Casualties very heavy, being brought in from neighbourhood of sunken road."[333]

The next day the situation deteriorated - having handed over their position to the 6th London Battalion, they pushed forward. Whilst they were in low ground, things were satisfactory, but "after that the attack was exposed to very heavy enfilade fire from both flanks and must also have suffered from our own artillery. The trenches were obliterated and the ridge is far from being a feature of the ground."[334] Yet the depleted battalion, combined now with the 24th London Battalion, attacked again two days later in the early morning, capturing the Starfish Line. After that, heavy German machine-gun fire, and their barrage, held them up for forty-five minutes, after which they were able to advance again and to start to consolidate a new line. However, "about 10.00 am a very strong bombing counter-attack was launched from a strong-point on the left of the captured trench, which drove the garrison out. A position was taken up about 100 yds from where the bombing attack took place and 23rd & 24th Bns were engaged the whole day (10 am till dusk) in very heavy hand-to-hand bombing and fighting. Official records of orders, messages, etc., were buried by the Adjutant... as soon as he saw the attack develop."[335] After they had been relieved at 10.30p.m., it was calculated that the battalion casualties had been sixteen officers and 565 men.

John Bennett also fought in the follow-up attacks on 16th September. By August, John had recovered sufficiently from his wounds after the bombing pit accident to be able to re-join the 5th Border Battalion on 13th August 1916. On 15th September they moved forward in stages to Shelter Wood, and then the south-west corner of Mametz Wood, to become part of the attack on the Star Fish Line and Prue Trench, beyond High Wood. These two trenches were the second and third objectives of the 151st Brigade in the battle, 15th September.

---

[333] War Diary, 1/23rd London Battalion, 16th September 1916.
[334] War Diary, 1/23rd London Battalion, 17th September 1916.
[335] War Diary, 1/23rd London Battalion, 18th September 1916.

"About 6.30pm Battalion was ordered to move up and attack and capture with the rest of the 151st Infantry Brigade, the second and third objectives, namely Star Fish Line and Prue Trench... Darkness set in before passing the Brigade Headquarters at the Quarries where guides were provided. The guides however, in moving forward lost their direction and the Battalion did not reach the assembly trench... until about half-an-hour after the time laid down. About 11pm the Battalion was ordered to its objectives and got in touch with the 6th and 9th D.L.I. some of whom had already gone. Owing to the darkness and general state of the ground the Battalion did not reach its objectives but moved forward about 6 to 700 yards and dug themselves in in the Bow CT owing to the advancing daylight. Some HQ details had been ordered to move forward in support of the rest of the Battalion and they eventually got in touch with part of 'B' Company and part of the 6th D.L.I. getting up almost to the Star Fish Line on the left of the Bow but were driven back by M.G. fire, joining up with the rest of the Battalion and digging in between the Bow and Crescent Alley." During these operations the battalion lost six officers and about 100 other ranks killed and wounded.

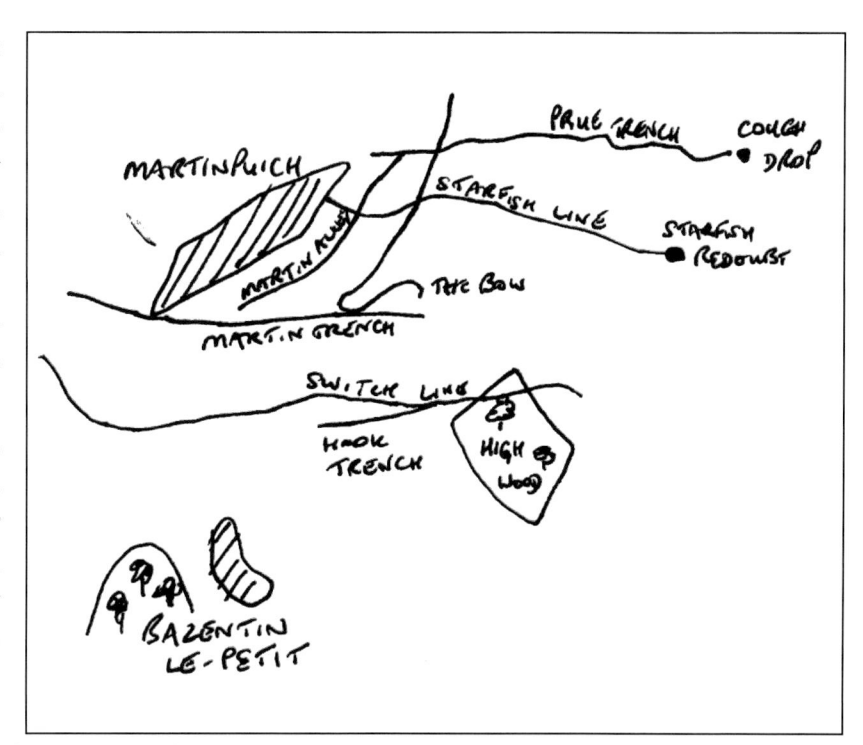

The next day the battalion stayed put "and improved the trenches. Capt. M.R. Inglis (R.A.M.C.) was killed whilst attending to the wounded in the field during the night. On the night of the 17th/18th 'A' Company was withdrawn to the Hook Trench. 18.9.16 The Battalion was ordered in conjunction with the rest of the Brigade to attack Star Fish Line about 5.50am. At the appointed hour Companies in the front line left the trenches for the attack but they did not reach the objectives owing to the sodden condition of the ground and again heavy machine gun fire... The Battalion was relieved in... and moved to trenches S.W. corner of Mametz wood. The following letter was received from the B.G.C. 151st Inf. Brigade: 'I have been asked by the Divisional Commander to convey his warm thanks to the four battalions of the 151st brigade for the whole hearted efforts they have made during the strenuous operations of the last few days and for the success which they have achieved... For myself, I should like to add that I am full of admiration at the soldierly spirit displayed by all ranks of the four Battalions in the attack and their endurance under very considerable hardships, privation and exertion lasting nearly a week. Signed N.J.C. Cameron, Brigadier General, Commanding 151st Infantry Brigade. 20th September 1916.'"[336]

For the rest of the month they alternated between manning these trenches and 'resting', though 'A' Company had to be withdrawn into isolation for a few days due to an outbreak of dysentery.

---

[336] War Diary, 5th Border Battalion, 15th-20th September 1916.

For persisting in such attacks, Haig is often criticised for an apparent lack of imagination but he had intervened to make changes – for example remonstrating with, and altering the plans of Rawlinson to prepare for the more successful attacks of 14th July. He was making the best use he could of modern technology, such as the narrow grade railways in use to bring up ammunition and supplies to behind the battle line. Elsewhere on the battlefield, on 15th September, Haig decided to use the latest invention – the landships (coded and now universally known as 'tanks'). He had asked for hundreds of them, but the British factories could only produce about fifty Mark I tanks, and, despite security, there was always the danger of the Germans discovering the true nature of the 'water tanks' which the British tried to mislead them into believing were being brought up to the battlefield. There were not enough tanks to use them everywhere, and so several Old Bournemouthians were not on the part of the battlefield where they were to be deployed for the first time.

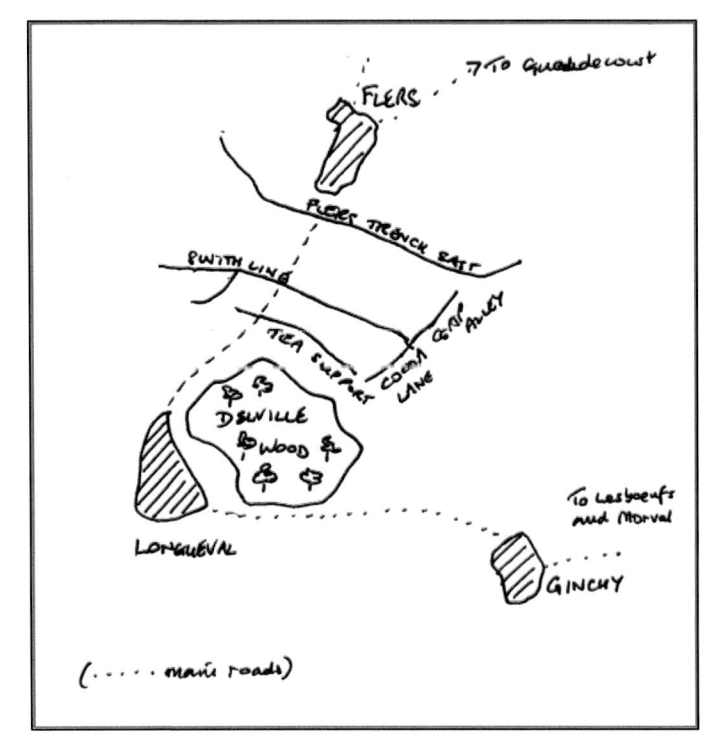

In his private war diary, Robert Mackay, who served with the Scottish regiment the 11th Argylls, described his first sight of the tanks: "Went along to a park after tea to see our latest form of frightfulness about which mystery hangs, namely, the tanks. They have not been used against the enemy yet." [337] That was about to change, and several Old Bournemouthians in the battle that day had direct experience of these tanks and the difference they could make.

Having arrived in England with Canadian forces on 11th February 1915, Horace Tollemache had gone on to land in France. Then, possibly at the battle of Neuve Chapelle, Horace had been wounded in the leg, which required medical treatment and time to recuperate. On 14th July 1916 the *Gazette* announced his appointment as 2nd lieutenant in the Hampshire Regiment with seniority dated back to 14th August 1915, the date he arrived in France with the British Army itself. He joined the 15th Hampshire Battalion in France and after the fighting in July, was with the battalion when it had been withdrawn from the line to west of Bailleul, and then to Villers-sous-Ailly north-west of Amiens for training in August. This was also Walter Bailey's battalion. In September they arrived at Dernancourt, south of Albert, ready to be deployed to the infamous Delville Wood – already nicknamed 'Devil's Wood' in recognition of the bitter fighting that had meant it had taken two months for the British to secure. They were positioned on the northern edge of the wood, facing the German front line, 'Tea Support' Trench.

The 15th Hampshire Battalion was in the front line of the attack, on the left half of the wood, with the 18th King's Royal Rifle Corps on its left and the 21st King's Royal Rifle Corps to its right.

---

[337] Private war diary of Robert Lindsay Mackay, 10th Argylls.

"The 18th Battalion made an unfortunate start, which might well have affected the whole operation. Just as the attack was about to commence, the Commanding Officer (Lieut.-Colonel C.P. Marten, West Yorkshire Regiment), the Adjutant (Captain F. Walton), the Signalling Officer (Lieutenant W.S. Mathews), and the Trench Mortar Officer (Lieutenant D.S.D. Clark) were all killed by one shell. It speaks volumes for the training and discipline of the Battalion that, after this catastrophe, the attack was carried to a successful conclusion." [338]

The 15th Hampshire Battalion, including Walter and Horace, attacked at 6.20a.m., "moving across No Man's Land, just behind the barrage. The barrage in front of this Batt. was excellent – just what the men had been trained to expect, and came up to expectations so far as keeping the enemy quiet. Things were not so satisfactory on our left however, for a full 10 mins was taken up before three machine guns were silenced. These guns took heavy toll of the left platoons – of Coy Commanders – no less than three being fatally hit before the first objective was won – Capt. H.E. Carrington, Capt. S. Thompson and Capt. H. Stapleton. One of these guns was put out by two men who walked along the trench and shot the team. The second objective was taken with less trouble, many of the enemy running towards Flers without equipment or arms. The armoured 'cars' did not up to this point, do much except perhaps [to] cause alarm in the second enemy line, owing to their having dropped behind. The Batt., with the 124th Bde. on our right, and the 18th K.R.R.B. on our left swept on to Flers which was entered, more or less cleared, and passed. It was during this period that one of the armoured 'cars' did most useful work smashing in the enemy's strong points and without doubt demoralizing them. It also gave the men great confidence.

"Meanwhile losses had been fairly heavy owing to the heavy barrage put up by the Germans. By the time troops had passed through Flers organised attack had ceased owing to formations having been broken up and to heavy casualties among the officers. This appears to have resulted in men either strolling back through Flers, getting into dug-outs, or digging in around and beyond the village. They were isolated and disorganised, and little or no information came back to Batt. H.Q. Heavy barrages of Gas and common shells made communications difficult and at first when men were seen coming back it was thought a counter-attack was in force. And every man available was turned in to assist the parties building strong-points. Two of the enemy's machine guns were mounted on the parapet and with the two left behind, prepared to defend the trench. The batt. H.Q. during the above period moved by bounds from the original trenches to the first objective after the second objective had been taken and again to the second objective after Flers had been taken. It did not subsequently move from here but 2nd Lt. Hall was sent forward to clear up the situation.

"Messages, however, began to come in after 11 am but it was not then known, or indeed until the evening, that all four Coy. Commanders were fatally hit and our Coy. Sergt-Majors wounded. The fourth Coy commander Capt. W.G.W. Bailey was killed in front of the second objective. These casualties all occurred before the second objective was taken. Meanwhile the 124th Brigade appeared to advance without difficulty and I should think have suffered less from shell fire generally during the day than the 122nd. The valley between the two was kept full of gas by gas shells fired about every twenty minutes all through the afternoon. The first indication of the partial evacuation of the village was the withdrawal of the New Zealand Division on our left, who retired for a short distance and then started to dig in. Small bodies of men occasionally went back into Flers and again others came out. But during the whole of this time every messenger sent forward

---

[338] Divisional History, quoted in www.greatwarforum.org.

was hit in one or other of the barrages. After orderlies had eventually got into the village it was reported that no men of the battn, except 30 men under Lt. Smith, were there, and these could not be located.

"...With reference to the artillery, the creeping barrage was perfectly done. The accuracy of the heavy barrage however was nothing like as good and the captured trenches showed little sign of active hits. In the enemy line opposite where the regiment attacked were captured two enemy machine guns. The trenches were supplied with Mineral Waters, Cigars and Bread. There were also a large number of Bombs, both Egg and Cylindrical stick. It was noticed in the second objective that the dug-outs, 20 feet deep, were half full of equipment and rifles. 2nd Lt. Smith, 2nd Lt. Menzies-Calder, 2nd Lt. Tollemache and 2nd Lt. Hall all behaved with great gallantry and determination, particularly the former who did his best to keep in touch with Bn. H.Q. to furnish reports, which had they been received earlier would have been invaluable. 2nd Lt. Tollemache, although wounded, remained with his men, and took them forward to beyond the village. Casualties: Officers – killed 8; missing – ; wounded 5, including M.O. Other Ranks – Killed 31; Missing 60; Wounded 188."[339]

So, Walter did not live to see the success. He had died leading his company – "the smartest officer I have ever seen" according to his colonel. When his body was later recovered and recognised for burial, the battle was over, and he was buried further north at Serre, close to Clarence Goodall. Horace, however, had come through, though not unscathed. Wounded, he had led on the men to their third objective at the northern end of the village of Flers. Afterwards, he was specially picked out for congratulations by Sir Douglas Haig: "The G.O.C. wishes to place on record his appreciation of your great gallantry in leading and inspiring your men, though wounded, and remaining in the captured trench for 14 hours."[340]

Cecil Hughes fought in the same brigade as the 15th Hampshire Battalion. For Cecil, after the Battle of Loos in 1915, things had been quite varied. Pulled back into reserve or support to lick their wounds, the 2nd East Surrey Battalion had had only a few days to rebuild. Then they were put on a train for Marseilles where, on 24th October, they had embarked aboard the SS *Transylvania* and the SS *Royal George* to sail to Alexandria in Egypt, which they reached after a brisk voyage on 30th October 1915. On 25th November, they embarked from Alexandria aboard the SS *Hororata* and arrived at Mudros and then Salonika where – despite a scare when a British submarine was sighted and for a moment not recognised – they arrived on 1st December. About this time Cecil fell ill. Perhaps this was after 16th December when everyone apparently became soaked in the heavy rain as they moved up to Lembet. The men had all been vaccinated against cholera whilst they were in Egypt, but Cecil went down with what they then called 'enteric fever' but which is now more commonly called typhoid. This was extremely serious. For six months he was in hospital and he was brought back to England, including a welcome period of convalescence in Bournemouth. In the spring of 1916, his brother feared that he would be permanently invalided by the illness. However, instead he recovered slowly and was temporarily posted to the 12th East Surreys (which Alex Copp was to join in 1917).

This battalion only landed at Le Havre on 2nd May 1916, and had been sent up to the Ypres Salient in the 41st Division and the newly-formed 122nd Brigade, alongside the 15th Hampshires, 11th Royal

---

[339] War Diary, 15th Hants, 15th September 1916.
[340] *The Bournemouthian*, December 1916.

West Kents and 18th King's Royal Rifle Corps. Cecil's battalion was in the second wave of the attack: "The battalion advanced at 6.15 am and took the enemy's 1st and 2nd line trenches. Although it suffered heavy casualties, it continued to advance to about 200 yards in front of Flers and occupied enemy trenches there. Casualties: Officers 16; O.R.'s 286."[341] Cecil survived and was commissioned on 17th Dec 1917 into the Northumberland Fusiliers. After the war he was commissioned as a lieutenant in the Indian Army. He died on war service on 30th May 1943.

These men had fought alongside the new tanks. At least two members of the school, Harold Head and Claud Couch, however, were working with these tanks. One was actually in one of those tanks in the battle, and was one of the original tank commanders, though both of them had started off as ordinary privates within the Hampshire Regiment.

Harold Head, who was born 1895, had left school in 1910. If anyone's war might be described as 'dramatic' or 'exciting' it was Harold's, even if it seemed to start quietly enough. In December 1914, like a number of his Bournemouth School friends, he enlisted as a cyclist in the 9th Hampshire Battalion. Harold, however, was clearly not content just to patrol on his bike. Harold had joined the 9th Hampshire Maxim Gun Section – a unit within the battalion which had specialised training with heavy machine guns. He clearly showed promise and was allowed to apply for a commission, and was gazetted 2nd lieutenant from the Hampshire Regiment into the Motor Machine Gun Service, on 17th October 1915. He would not have known it then, but he was on the brink of making history.

The tanks were developed in great secrecy. The original machines, code-named 'Little Willie' and 'Mother' had been developed in 1915 and two manufacturers, Fosters of Lincoln and Metropolitan of Birmingham, were awarded a most secret contract to build one hundred and fifty Mark I tanks. Also in great secrecy, a core unit of men with an aptitude and interest in machines of war, as shown by commitment and intelligence in the use of machine guns, had been assembled on 16th February 1916 at Bisley in Surrey, under the command of Colonel Swinton, and training had started on the Monday following the Easter holiday. They moved in late May to Elveden in Norfolk. At this time, to help preserve the secrecy, the unit was first designated as 'The Armoured Car Section, Motor Machine Gun Service' and by May as 'The Heavy Section of the Machine Gun Corps'. (It became the Tank Corps on 28th July 1917.)

LIEUT. HAROLD GEO. HEAD,
Harold Head

Elveden is a little west of Thetford and even today contains a large expanse of woodland. In 1916 this was the estate of the Earl of Iveagh. To ensure secrecy, a large area (from Icklingham in the west to Barnham, south of Thetford, in the east, and centred around North Stow Farm) was cordoned off. Farmers and local residents were evacuated from the area. A complex training ground was created, including trenches and obstacles which were supposed to simulate the conditions on the Western Front, although because they were on the much drier heathland of south Norfolk they were only partially accurate. The soldiers were placed in a tented camp. Before May

---

[341] War Diary, 12th East Surrey Battalion, 15th September 1915.

1916, they had not even seen the new tanks. These began to arrive from Lincoln, fitted with sponsors (but not yet with guns) on 4th June.

"Early one morning we were awakened by a rumbling and rattling. In great excitement everybody rushed out and there they were – the first of the tanks passing our tents to the practice driving ground. We were almost too excited to bother about any breakfast."[342]

In June, the Heavy Section of the M.G.C. was organised to operate as six companies, to be designated A to F. Harold was in 'D' Company. Each of these companies would have four sections, each with six fighting tanks and one spare tank. Therefore, the original order for one hundred and fifty tanks was quickly increased to one hundred and sixty to allow for the spare tanks. Each section would have three 'male' and three 'female' tanks. At Elvedon, the men like Harold continued to train – relying a lot on theory since few of the actual tanks were as yet available. About this time, Harold's story became inter-woven with that of Claud Couch who, though older than Harold, had only joined the school after Harold had left it.

Claud and his twin Wilfrid had been born in Oxford in 1893. From September 1911 until July 1912 they were at Bournemouth School. After this they went together to Queens' College, Cambridge. At Cambridge their ways divided slightly, as Claud was commissioned 2nd lieutenant on 28th December 1914. (It is possible that Wilfrid Couch was the W.C. Couch who was a private in the Tank Corps; or he may have been the Wilfrid Charles Couch who was ordained and served with the YMCA in India from May 1917.) On 17th April 1916, Claud had transferred from the 13th Hampshire Battalion to the Machine Gun Corps (Heavy Section). On 1st July 1916, Claud was promoted to be a lieutenant. He therefore also became one of the original tank commanders, in his case in 'C' Company. Conditions of great secrecy were maintained – seven hundred sentries were deployed in a series of three cordons around the tank park – those on the outer ring had no idea of what they were guarding! As part of the deception, Claud's tank originally had been given a Russian Cyrillic inscription at the factory, reading 'With care to Petrograd', but once they arrived at Elvedon the inscriptions were obliterated and replaced with a serial number – though even these were designed to confuse any spies who got to see them: the 'male' numbers started at 701 and the 'females' at 501 in order to give the impression of a collection of hundreds being amassed.

Over the summer months, Harold and Claud trained hard, but also had to show off their secret weapons first to Prime Minister Lloyd George and to King George V in July 1916 when they visited the secret base. It was realised in early August that the production schedule for the tanks had not included provision for the production of any spare parts until the first one hundred and fifty tanks had been completed. Compromises and adjustments to tanks and plans had rapidly to be made, so after one hundred and ten tanks had been delivered at the end of August, a three-week production line change rushed through spare parts.

On the 13th August 1916, four tank companies, including Claud's, began to prepare to embark for France. This was Operation 'Alpaca' and the initial company to be sent to France was 'C' Company[343] which began embarkation from Southampton on 20th August. Individual tanks were sometimes coded as 'armadillos'. It is most likely, however, that by then Claud had been switched

---

[342] Private W.T. Dawson; Quote displayed at the Tank Museum, Bovington.

[343] His initial membership of this company is confirmed by the original membership roll, now held at Bovington Tank Museum.

into 'A' Company as Claud's record card shows he arrived in France in September. Harold Head's 'D' Company followed 'C' Company across the Channel.

'A' Company, twenty-five tanks commanded by Major C.M. Tippett, together with eight spares and a mobile workshop crossed a little later than 'C' and 'D' Companies, arriving in mid-September. Half of them sailed 13th-14th September, and the other half 15th-16th September. It had been planned to ship them across earlier, but German submarines in the channel, naval capacity, and refusal of personnel on the docks to work overnight (secrecy meant they could not know the urgency) delayed them. It was decided to leave 'B' Company in England, and use its resources for the spare parts and personnel urgently required after 15th September. As Brigadier-General J. Burnet-Stuart of the General Staff put it in a secret, undated letter from the end of August, "As at present arranged 2 Coys (C & D) should be ready to enter battle on Sept. 15th – a third Coy (A) should be ready to enter the battle at the end of Sept. The arrival of the remaining 3 Coys is problematical – we have no forecast, but they will probably be too late for this season's fighting."[344]

Therefore, 'A' Company was not deployed in the original tank action of 15th Septembers at Flers-Courcelette though it moved down to the Somme where their tank crews reinforced the men of 'C' and 'D' Battalions in the Battle of the Ancre. (Three tanks of 'A' Company, of a different section from Claud's, did attack on 13th November in support of the 39th Division, though one was lost in the mud, one broke down, and only one reached the German front line where it crashed into a dug-out and had to be rescued by the infantry after a fierce fight.)

Later, Harold described leaving the estate at Elveden on 13th August and travelling to France from Southampton, whilst the tanks were secretly transported via Avonmouth. To fit them onto the trains, they were partially dismounted as the sponsons made them too wide for the stations and tunnels. Special trucks carried the sponsons separately. Men and tanks were reunited at Yvrench, near Abbeville, where the sponsons were refitted and the tanks camouflaged. After getting them back into working order, the unit moved up to the Somme, where they gathered at an assembly point, identified as 'Happy Valley', on the eastern edge of Mametz Wood. There, a mass of men and materials gathered ready for the attack – infantry, limber wagons, and of course the tanks.[345]

Haig might well have preferred not to use them as soon as they were available, but the Battle of the Somme developed its own political imperatives, and he decided he must use them as a means to gain a victory and to minimise the further loss of British blood. For the sake, too, of his own reputation, Haig needed a success.

Harold had charge of one of the new Mark I tanks, designated D3, number 728. His company, 'D' Company Number 1 Section, was allocated the task of assisting the 14th Division in its attack northwards from the edge of Delville Wood against Flers: the same part of the attack in which the 15th Hampshire and 2nd East Surrey Battalions were involved.[346]

Mark I tanks designated with numbers between 501 and 557 were 'female' tanks – that is, their

---

[344] WO 158/843 TNA file, Documents relating to the Heavy Section, Machine Gun Corps, May-Sept 1916.

[345] Taken from Harold Head's account, quoted in *Tanks and Trenches*, edited David Fletcher, 1994.

[346] For some of the details of the tank movements, I have used the accounts contained in the website, https://sites.google.com/site/landships/home, created by Stephen Pope, which is itself based on a number of excellent primary and secondary sources which it lists.

armament was machine guns designed to shoot down the enemy as they broke cover when their defensive positions had been shattered by the 'male' tanks, armed with cannons, designated 701 to 775. Harold's tank therefore was a 'male' tank, armed with cannon and with four rather than six machine guns.

Harold described halting at 'Happy Valley' for three or four days, waiting for the weather to improve. Before they could move off "the engineers had the job of laying white tapes for the destination or kicking-off point for each tank. The engineers, not knowing the capabilities of the tanks, laid the easiest route they thought along the edge of trenches, which was a big mistake as a tank must really cross as near right angles as possible. So we found our way to our kicking off points and through the sunken road. The site of my destination was Delville Wood."[347] "We started at 8.30 the night before, but the ground was so bad that by the time we had traversed half a mile it was 5.30 am."[348]

His section of four tanks was led by Captain H.W. Mortimore in tank D1, which he had christened 'Daredevil I'. In the plan Captain Mortimore with his tank D1, 765, alongside number D5, 540 'Dolphin', would attack to the east of Delville Wood to eliminate a German pocket from two sides. These tanks were planned to start about a quarter of an hour before Harold's tank. Harold's tank, D3, 728, with Tank D4, 516, were planned to start fifty-three minutes before Zero hour and move along the line of Cocoa Trench (the British name for a German communication trench to reach the German front line (Tea Support Line)). Harold's orders were to pause at the German Tea Support Line and clear it of its German defenders. Then he was supposed to resume his advance on Flers in front of the British assault infantry as far as the objective 'Green Line', which he would help the infantry to capture and consolidate. After this he was to advance to 'Gap Trench' on the designated 'Brown Line'.

Inevitably, the plan did not precisely work out. As the tanks moved up into the wood, number 540, which was supposed to support the attack on the German 'pocket' east of the wood, ditched. Harold's crew managed to tow it out of its rut, but this meant that D5, 540, under 2nd Lieutenant A.H. Blowers, started his part of the attack late – behind, instead of in front of, the infantry attack.

Some of the difficulties of the advance to the start line were caused within the wood by unexploded mortar shells. To start with, Harold's crew kept stopping to move these shells out of the way, but as Harold put it, "We tried to pull them out of the way, not knowing if they had been detonated or not. Eventually the Germans sent over some tear gas shells, on came our masks, but you couldn't see a thing so we had to do without. It would have taken all night long moving these bombs so I had a conflab with the fellow following me and we decided to go over them. We tested the ground and realised it was soft so the bombs sank in very, very gently and that was that. At the very edge of the wood we had to turn at right angles and pass along the front of the wood and wait for dawn. The fellow following me unfortunately got in the wood too far and got his tracks suspended on the stump of a tree. The stumps were not more than four feet high with continuous shelling for weeks on end and we manoeuvred into such a position to tow him out, which we did just before dawn. Dawn, I think, that morning was at half past six and we made our way very slowly towards Flers."[349]

---

[347] Harold Head's description, quoted in *Tanks and Trenches*, edited David Fletcher, 1994.
[348] *The Bournemouth Visitors' Directory*, 23rd December 1916.
[349] Harold Head's description, quoted in *Tanks and Trenches*, edited David Fletcher, 1994.

Despite the delay in getting D5, 540, underway again, Harold's tank reached the start line on time. The tank which was supposed to support him, number D4, 516, reached Delville Wood, but here it ditched badly and its crew abandoned it. (It was never to be used again.) Harold and his crew were on their own without the machine guns of D4 to support them. Nevertheless, he started the attack on time, crossed No Man's land and engaged the Germans. However, instead of following the line of the abandoned part of the German 'Cocoa' Trench, he seems to have veered to the left and attacked 'Tea Support Line' near the point where it crossed the Longueval-Flers road. "Three cars were detailed for the job; one broke down before it had gone far, one got hit, and only mine got through to the Bosche's second line. Then we were hit and we were put out of action for 10 hours, and during the whole time we were under incessant shell fire… It fairly got my 'wind' up and I don't want another time like that."[350] "On the outskirts of Flers, unfortunately, the tank got hit and that was the end of me for that day."[351] Although his tank did not quite reach Flers, it had played its part in assisting the infantry assault and the capture of the German front line. The infantry went on with the few surviving tanks to capture Flers.

Harold and his men managed to recover the tank and on the evening of 25th September he was ordered to take his tank into Flers to support tank D4 in the attack on Guedecourt the next day. Unfortunately, his tank broke down when one of its tracks snapped before the attack began, and so he was unable to assist in the assault. This was a disappointment because, whereas Haig had been able to allocate forty-eight tanks on 15th September (even though only thirty-four actually started, and only twenty-three managed actually to engage the enemy), on 25th September only six tanks could be allocated – of which only three started and only two were able to engage the Germans. Harold tried again to get into the action, but "at Guedecourt on 28 September I was unfortunately hit again and that was that."[352]

Why did these tanks keep ditching? They had a number of flaws which were to be ironed out over the following year, but three in particular caused problems that first autumn. A major flaw was their steering system, which depended on a tiller pushing out at angles a double 'steering wheel', which was attached to the back as a rudder is on a ship. These wheels readily bogged down in thick mud and either immobilised or made it impossible to steer a Mark I tank. Also, their engines were really not powerful enough to move such heavy machines – they could move them on reasonably solid ground, but laboured in the mud. Finally, they were relatively low-slung, and if they caught on something like a sizeable tree stump this could lift a caterpillar track off the ground, and so the tank would lose traction. Needless to say, they were tremendously heavy to shift back onto solid ground – something impossible under fire. Whilst they were immobilised, as the Germans quickly realised, they were vulnerable to artillery fire. (This problem only increased when the Germans developed special anti-tank armour-piercing shells. These could even be fired from rifles by early 1917.)

The day after these momentous events, 16th September, Maurice Hellier of the 6th King's Shropshire Light Infantry was back in the trenches, this time at Les Boeufs. The next night they repulsed, with difficulty and significant losses, a German bombing raid on their advance post. The rain meant the SOS rockets failed to ignite, and the eventual success of the repulse was credited to the actions of

---

[350] *The Bournemouth Visitors' Directory*, 23rd December 1916.
[351] Harold Head's description, quoted in *Tanks and Trenches*, edited David Fletcher, 1994.
[352] ibid.

the lance corporal in charge (who was killed) and the superior distance which the British grenade throwers could achieve compared to the German bombers. Even so, twenty had been killed and forty-two wounded. Casualties mounted. However, although they manned and worked on the Somme trenches through the autumn, winter and the next spring, they were not involved, except in a support role, in the major attacks, and consequently suffered less than some of the other battalions.

Elsewhere, on the northern side of the battlefield, September 1916, action, drama and despair affected several Old Bournemouthians fighting in the sector dominated by Thiepval Hill and the Schwaben Redoubt. One of these was Wilfred Omer-Cooper.

Wilfred and his brother Joseph Omer-Cooper had had an unusual education experience. Joseph was two years older than Wilfred, who was born in 1895. They joined the school in March 1903 but they were withdrawn in July 1905 and for the next four years were home tutored. However, in September 1909 they re-joined the school. Joseph then remained until May 1911, whilst Wilfred continued until the following December.

After leaving school, Wilfred began to make a name for himself. "Both he and his brother displayed a remarkable talent for Natural History, and in the short interval which elapsed between his leaving school and entering the Army he had achieved fame, of a very uncommon degree in one so young, as a naturalist… a student of science who was rapidly approaching the dignity of master in the narrow, circumscribed branch of research he had made his own. He was a keen and accurate observer in zoology, and without the advantages of that training only to be acquired in the lecture rooms and laboratory of a University, had accomplished much work that was of a high order. His particular study was the Isopods, a group of crustaceans, some land, mostly marine, popularly best known as common wood-lice. He added two new species to the British Fauna… He contributed several papers to zoological journals."[353] As a result of the reputation he had gained in this field, in February 1916 he was elected a member of the Linnean Society on the proposal of a member of the British Museum. He had also begun to make a reputation for himself for his research into Gipsy life and the study of the Romany language, as well as by various literary compositions. Wilfred showed no inclination or interest in joining the Army! In the end he joined under the Derby Scheme, becoming a private in the 12th Middlesex Battalion. (His brother Joseph had volunteered on 14th September 1914 to join the Royal Army Medical Corps. His entire war service was spent with the ambulances within the United Kingdom.)

Wilfred went out to France in August 1916, joining the 12th Middlesex Battalion ('the Duke of Cambridge's Own'), 54th Brigade, 18th Division. At the end of August the battalion was training. By 23rd September, it was a few miles north-west of Albert, ready for the next great 'show', the capture of Thiepval and the Schwaben Redoubt.

Thiepval has sometimes been described as the fulcrum of the Battle of the Somme. Today the great British monument at Thiepval dominates the countryside. In 1916, only the ruins of an old chateau were visible. These ruins and a smashed village lay on the crest of a great slope from which the Germans could see – and fire down upon – the whole British position from Beaumont-Hamel across the valley of the Ancre to the north to Ovillers and Albert to the south and west. Repeated attacks from west and north had failed to dislodge the Germans who had the formidable Leipzig

---

[353] *The Bournemouthian*, December 1916.

Redoubt to the south and Schwaben Redoubt to their north. Although the British artillery fire had smashed the German front line trenches, German accounts show that instead of making them ready to give up, it had only made them more determined than ever to repel the British. But, by September that formidable German position was looking more vulnerable. The 180th Würtemburger Regiment had bravely held the position for perhaps two years, but their defence was based on depth, with the anticipated attack from the old British front line, down the hill to their west. By September 1916, the British axis of battle had changed. The old front line was still in more or less the same place to the west of the Germans, but to their south, instead of the security afforded by huge defences stretching south to Ovillers and beyond, they faced the prospect of attack from what was effectively their old flank. The British battles from July to early September had captured the southern half of the German position and the British were now ready to assault Thiepval from the south rather than from the west.

"The troops were trained to the minute; attack formations had been practised till it could be expected that the advance would push through to its final objective as a drill movement, whatever the obstacles or casualties. It was known, too, that the artillery preparation had been terrific. As our men took their places in the assembly trenches it was whispered that before 'zero' 60,000 rounds of field artillery and 45,000 rounds of heavy stuff would have been fired by the 2nd Corps alone and that a big dose of gas was being put into the village overnight. Clearly the Prussians and Würtemburgers who held the place were having a thin time."[354] Wilfred's Middlesex Battalion was to be the assault battalion to attack the Chateau Redoubt and village, with the 6th Northants in close support.

The sight which would have met Wilfred's eyes as he looked beyond the British jumping-off line was an 1,800 yard space to cover – "the toughest job in the Division".[355] The Germans not only had deep dug-outs in the Chateau Redoubt (which so far had resisted the impact of the British artillery shells) but a further 144 deep dug-outs across a front of only 300 yards. We know that in the previous April, engineering Major Hans von Fabeck had ordered that the dug-outs in the Leipzig Redoubt had to be deepened to over seven yards, and they were connected by tunnels, with multiple entrances. Although this formidable strongpoint had been captured by Highlanders on 1st July, the chateau was similarly fortified.

The 54th Brigade, and Wilfred's 12th Middlesex Battalion, was placed on the extreme left flank of the attack line. They faced several complications – to their left were the original German front line trenches; in front of them was Joseph Trench, stretching west-east in front of the ruined chateau with its own defences; behind that were the German defences based on the Schwaben Trench, Zollern Trench, and the huge Schwaben Redoubt.

Zero hour was set for 12.35p.m., 26th September. At 12.15p.m. heavy German shelling hit the jumping-off line. This was probably a coincidence. At 12.35p.m. the British artillery opened up with a ferocious barrage designed to cover the attack. "With the first shell we were over the top, and had gone several yards before the barrage had really started. When it did start — my word! It came with a fearful ear-splitting crashing and rending, thousands of shells bursting almost simultaneously. We met Bosches running about, scared out of their wits, like a crowd of rabbits

---

[354] *The 54th Infantry Brigade, 1914-1918; Some Records of Battle and Laughter in France*, p. 51.
[355] ibid, p. 53.

diving for their holes. Men were rushing about unarmed, men were holding up their hands and yelling for mercy, men were scuttling about everywhere, trying to get away from that born fighter, the Cockney, but they had very little chance."[356]

As Wilfred and the battalion advanced they were met by a tremendous volley of machine-gun fire from the chateau ruins. This might have stopped the attack, but at that moment two tanks trundled out of Thiepval Wood having timed their advance perfectly. They destroyed the German machine guns, allowing the Middlesex men to continue their advance into the ruins, although both tanks were brought to a halt by the ruins and so could not help to consolidate the attack further.

On the right the battalion was succeeding, but on its left the German opposition was more determined. Together with the Fusiliers, the left companies were suffering considerable losses. Middlesex Colonel Maxwell took command of the two battalions and held the line close to the ruined chateau. German snipers seemed to be everywhere, using the shell holes and old dug-out entrances. Two Victoria Crosses were won that day. The Middlesex men suffered the worst casualties of the day: ten officers (including two majors) and sixty men were killed, with a further eight officers and 233 men wounded. Wilfred lost his life amongst them, but his body was never recovered in a condition to be recognised, and his name is commemorated where he fell, on the Thiepval Monument. He was 21 years old.

Wilfred had been a celebrated and outstanding young zoologist and his death was not only a great loss to his family but also to the scientific community. "The rolls of honour of the Universities and Public Schools are largely lists of men whom the State can least spare, and whose deaths are a double loss – a deprivation of manhood, and of what is no less important, character and intellect… the sympathy of many friends will go out to her [Wilfred's mother] in the loss of a dear son and of a young man of high character and much intellectual promise."[357]

Royal Fusilier Leslie Hands fought alongside Wilfred against the trenches of Thiepval that day. Initially he had joined the same battalion as Stanley Birdseye and William Mitford, the 10th Royal Fusiliers. Leslie had been born in 1896, and was at school from September 1911 to December 1912. He was a member of the 10th Royal Fusiliers Battalion on the Western Front only from 16th to 29th August 1916, after which he was transferred to the 11th Battalion for the rest of his service. On 24th September, the battalion moved into the trenches south of Thiepval, and into the support trenches the next day.

The 11th Royal Fusiliers attacked alongside Wilfred and the rest of the 54th Brigade across only a three hundred yard footage, which meant that the battalion and its brigade were very compacted. "Owing to recent successful fighting it was now possible to attack from the south, the jumping-off point for the 54th Brigade being a trench running east and west, about 500 yards south of Chateau Redoubt, and at a distance varying from 100 to 250 yards from the German front line. The old British front line, running roughly north and south, enabled the artillery to enfilade the German position from the west."[358] When the 11th Royal Fusiliers lined up for the assault, 'C' Company on

---

[356] *The 54th Infantry Brigade, 1914-1918; Some Records of Battle and Laughter in France*, p. 54.

[357] *The Bournemouth Visitors' Directory*, 18th November 1916.

[358] *The 54th Infantry Brigade 1914-1918; Some Records of Battle and Laughter in France*, Gale and Polden Ltd., Wellington Works. Aldershot, London and Portsmouth (Printed for private circulation only), by 'E.R.' of the Headquarters 54th Infantry Brigade, March 1919, p. 51.

the right of the battalion's position was deliberately mixed with the assaulting companies of Wilfred's 12th Middlesex as they were meant to assist them by clearing dug-outs when the men of the Middlesex reached the German positions. 'D' Company lined up to the left of the 12th Middlesex to play their own role in the assault, with 'B' Company in support and 'D' in reserve. So it is possible even that Leslie and Wilfred might have stood side by side in those last anxious moments before the whistles blew.

The German position that Leslie and the battalion was attacking was far too strong for German panic to last more than a few minutes. Very soon the battalion was encountering fierce opposition, and the attack became a blood-fest of individual fighting. Like Wilfred and the 12th Middlesex Battalion, all the companies found themselves mired in the assault. The 11th Royal Fusiliers were meant to be capturing the left flank – the original front line trenches and dug-outs, whilst the Middlesex men were meant to capture the chateau. Leslie was in the thick of it.

"The Fusilier companies were necessarily rather scattered. 'D' Company... with two machine guns and two trench mortars, was detailed to clear the enemy's front-line trenches. 'C' Company... was sent over with the Middlesex to 'mop up', a job so well done that practically all Germans left behind the leading waves were silenced, and there were no cases of the assaulting battalion being shot in the back as it advanced. The other companies were sent over in support."[359] This summary understates the horror that Leslie would have faced that day. For example, "'B' Company had suffered considerably getting through the barrage and from Machine Gun Fire, and on reorganising it was found that 2nd Lieut Goddard had been killed, 2nd Lieut Walker wounded, all the full rank NCOs except 1 Sergeant and 2 Corporals were gone, and nearly half the rank and file... Practically every inch of the ground had to be covered as in addition to the organised defence there were snipers in every other shell hole... L/Cpl Tovey of 'B' Coy captured a Machine Gun single-handed, bayoneting both the men who were working it. Another machine gun was accounted for... in this way we reached the line... meeting a stubborn resistance all the way. 'D' Coy cleared altogether 25 Dugouts in the front line and in many of them the Germans showed fight. In one of them [in] particular there was a large number of the enemy with two machine guns and as they could not be got out peaceably the place was set on fire. Several are believed to have perished in the flames and 11 men were killed as they came out; an additional

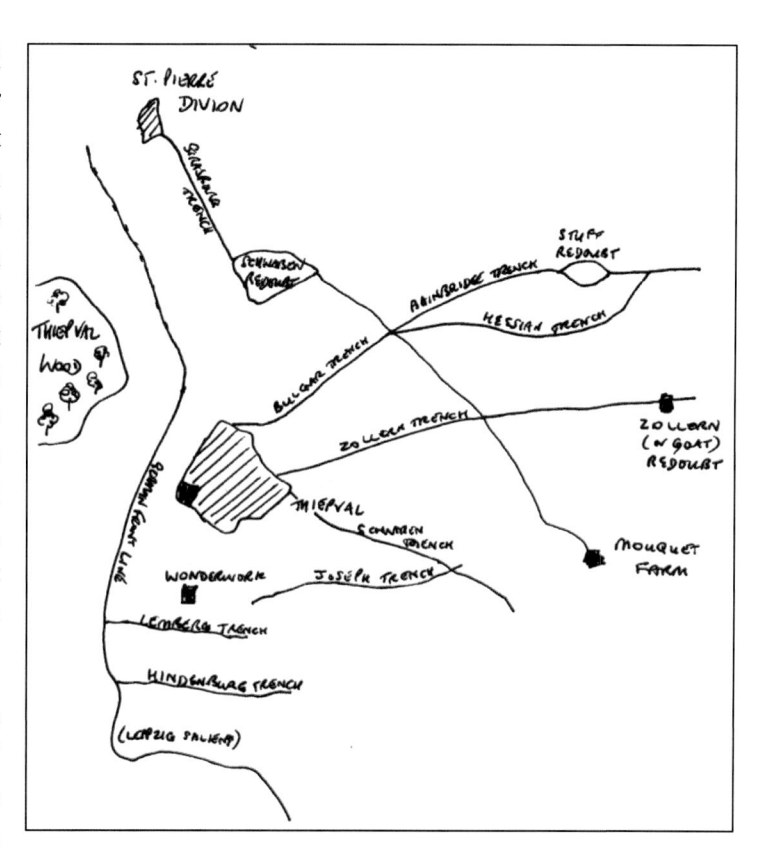

---

[359] *The 54th Infantry Brigade 1914-1918; Some Records of Battle and Laughter in France*, Gale and Polden Ltd., Wellington Works. Aldershot, London and Portsmouth (Printed for private circulation only), by 'E.R.' of the Headquarters 54th Infantry Brigade, March 1919, p. 52.

14 who were only wounded were sent to the rear."[360]

By the middle of the afternoon, the 11th Royal Fusiliers had got well north of the chateau and even established posts in the north-east part of Thiepval village, but on the right the Middlesex line was skewed round trying to cope with the German strongpoints. One feature of this confusing fight was that almost all the officers were killed or wounded. This showed up a weakness in British military training, which was partially to be remedied for the successful fighting a year later: the fact that only officers had been entrusted with plans and maps, and so it was tricky for the brigadier to deploy his supporting battalions to best effect. "The reports reaching headquarters were largely contradictory. Most of them were sent by N.C.O.'s, as the officers were out of action; and, without maps, their references could not be expected to be more than approximate."[361] The Germans continued to put up a strong resistance. "It was not unusual to see from 12 to 20 German stick bombs in the air at the same time, and the whole area looked like a firework display owing to the number of egg bombs the enemy showered on us." Nevertheless, the brigadier was able to deploy his support, the 6th Northamptonshire Battalion, and by dusk most of Thiepval village had been captured by the three battalions, with the rest captured the next day by the men of the reserve 7th Bedfordshire Battalion. The 11th Royal Fusiliers dug in to form a strongpoint round a stranded tank from which the machine guns were removed.

By that evening, the Northamptonshire men who had come in as support were reduced to being led by two 2nd lieutenants and two sergeants, all the other officers directly involved in the assault having been killed or wounded. Leslie might have heard of the experience of a certain runner from his battalion who was reputed to have annoyed their colonel that night. "For some hours during the night Colonel Maxwell was writing diligently page after page—it was supposed popularly to be a letter to his wife. Shells were passing over and dropping all the time, and one runner who had the wind up gave a groan every time one came. Suddenly Maxwell got up from his writing, saying, 'I can't stand this any longer—send that man here.' He then told everyone round to stand in a line, said, 'I'll give him the first kick—the rest of you pass him along,' and the runner was passed out into the dark."[362]

The devastation was terrible. A story is told that afterwards a casualty first aid post was placed on the ruins of the chateau. An officer came up to a stretcher-bearer and asked him where the chateau was. "Sorry, Sir, you're standing on it," was the reply. The brigade had lost nineteen officers and one hundred and seventy-six men killed, twenty-eight officers and five hundred and sixty-three men wounded, with a further one hundred and ninety-eight men missing. On the other hand, it was estimated that the Germans had lost over three thousand, and four officers and six hundred and six men had surrendered. Leslie, though, had survived to fight again soon after. We don't know if Leslie had even known that Wilfred had fought and died alongside him that day.

Cecil Harbord also died that day, a short distance to the right towards the eastern end of the attack line. Cecil had been born in 1896, and attended the school from 1907 to 1911. Aged 18 in 1914,

---

[360] From an account within the War Diary, 11th Royal Fusiliers, September 1916.

[361] *The Royal Fusiliers in the Great War*, H.C. O'Neill, London William Heinemann, 1922, p. 140.

[362] From an original account by a Royal Fusilier, 11th Battalion, quoted within *The 54th Infantry Brigade 1914-1918; Some Records of Battle and Laughter in France*, Gale and Polden Ltd., Wellington Works. Aldershot, London and Portsmouth (Printed for private circulation only), by 'E.R.' of the Headquarters 54th infantry Brigade, March 1919, pages 55-56

Cecil had also joined the 9th Cyclist Battalion of the Hampshire Regiment, alongside other Bournemouthians like Richard Hodges and Percy Baker. By 1916, Cecil had become a private in the 5th Dorset Battalion. From his regimental number, 22119, it may be supposed that this switch was made after the Dorsets had retired from Gallipoli, but it is possible he was sent there. He was promoted to lance corporal.

His battalion had arrived at Marseilles on 9th July 1916, and was moved north to St. Pol where it arrived on 14th July. So the battalion was not involved in the early attacks of the Battle of the Somme. It was part of the 11th Division, 34th Brigade. In September, the battalion was brought up, moving to Bouzincourt on 7th September. On 8th September, they took up positions in the area to the south of Thiepval, and formed the 34th Brigade's reserve for its attack on the German Wunderwerk Redoubt, which took place on 14th September. Fortunately, they were only the reserve in the fighting to capture this formidable obstacle to British progress, as casualties were heavy.

Cecil Harbord

However, their time was to come on 26th September. The Leipzig Redoubt had already fallen; the Wunderwerk disposed of, but the German position was still defended by formidable obstacles including the Schwaben Redoubt and the redoubt at Mouquet Farm to the south-east. The 34th Brigade was separated from Wilfred Cooper's 54th Brigade by the interposing 33rd and 53rd Brigades. So the 34th Brigade was at the extreme right flank of the British assault, facing the Schwaben and Zollern Trenches, with the Schwaben Redoubt behind. The chateau and the original front line trenches were off to their left.

On 26th September, the main target for 34th Brigade was the German redoubt and formidable defence position at Mouquet Farm (known as 'Mucky' Farm to the British, and 'Moo-Cow' Farm to the Australians!), and the 5th Dorset Battalion was to play a considerable role in this attack, even though it is generally regarded as an Australian battle ground. The Australians had fought hard to try to capture it from 8th August to 3rd September, but without success despite considerable casualties. This had really been as an extension to the Australian efforts at and around the key nearby village of Pozières. The 1st Australian Division had attacked it on 23rd July and had quickly taken most of the village. The 2nd Australian Division had renewed the assault on 29th July but was beaten back. Another attempt on 4th-5th August had pushed the line beyond the village, and the 4th Australian Division had then extended the line north towards Mouquet Farm. In six weeks the Australians had suffered 23,000 casualties, almost as many as at Gallipoli.

The Canadians had then taken on the task of holding that part of the line near the farm, but the farm had to be captured if Thiepval was to fall, and 34th Brigade was given the job. The 5th Dorset Battalion was to help by attacking from a line centred on the southern edge of Mouquet Farm. This was to be their first action after leaving Gallipoli. As with the Middlesex and Fusiliers to their left, Zero hour was set for 12.35p.m. The attack was to be led by the 8th Northumberland Fusiliers and the 9th Lancashire Fusiliers, with the 5th Dorsets in support. The farm they were to assault held German snipers and machine guns as well as men with trench mortars.

Their attack was to be assisted by two tanks, which were supposed to advance ahead of the attack, and be at the farm, about zero hour as the men left their trenches. The tanks were meant to neutralise the German machine guns from the farm and minimise the battalion's losses. Unfortunately, both tanks 'ditched' – one right by the farm (its crew left the tank and assisted in the infantry attack).

"The Battalion suffered heavily from enemy's barrage before reaching the 1st Objective, also suffered heavily from bombs, machine guns and snipers from Germans who were still in Mouquet Farm. Could not get any messages back. All Coy Commanders and Coy S Majors were knocked out early in the advance. Casualties amongst NCOs were heavy."[363] At 8p.m., the 5th Dorset Battalion received a command from the brigadier to move up from the second to the third objectives, and to move their Battalion HQ onto the line of the second objective – which was an impossible order as they had no safe connection even with the troops that had reached the first objective – most were stuck less than a third of the way to that objective with the Germans in Mouquet Farm causing massive problems. A plan to attack with grenades had to be called off as it was realised that these had already run out. Nevertheless, they managed to establish a position on the edge of the Zollern Redoubt. In the dark, despite German flares and machine guns, some additional trench communications were dug to help them forward, but an attack onwards towards the Stuff Redoubt was thrown back by German machine-gun and sniper fire. Eventually, Mouquet Farm was reported fully taken, when the remaining defenders (who had held out underground) were forced to surrender by a mixed party of Lancashires and Dorsets led by 2nd Lieutenant Dancer who threw smoke bombs into the dug-outs.[364]

The next day, 27th September, was not much better. The men were pinned down by German artillery and machine-gun fire, and were short of rations, supplies and ammunition. It was not until the late afternoon of 28th September that the battalion began to be relieved and pulled back to Ovillers. By the end of the battle, the battalion had helped to capture most of Thiepval (and to neutralise the Zollern and Stuff Redoubts). But the fight was costly. Five officers had died, five more were wounded, and three more were missing. The battalion had lost about four hundred and ten men, including one hundred and twenty-two men killed in action. Cecil Harbord had fallen. Many of the Dorset dead were later found well forward in German positions. On 30th September, the Dorsets were still scouring the land looking for survivors. Cecil's body was not found in a recognisable condition, and so he is commemorated on the Thiepval Monument, with the date of his death set as 26th September 1916.

Although we cannot be certain of his actions, it seems appropriate at this point to mention Cecil's friend, Henry Friendship, who might well have shared Cecil's war experiences, and his last months. Henry Friendship was also in the 5th Dorsets, with a similar regimental number. He probably joined the 9th Hampshires at much the same time – maybe the same day – and gone through the same experiences as Cecil. Henry (or Harry as he was sometimes known) was a little older, being born in 1890 and at school in its early years, including 1905 when he performed in *HMS Pinafore*. At some point, Henry moved from the 5th Dorsets to the 1st Dorsets. Unfortunately, we have no record of precisely when that happened. Henry was a private, and his Army record was largely destroyed in the 1940 blitz. If he remained with the 5th Dorsets in the summer of 1916, he would have shared

---

[363] War Diary, 5th Dorset Battalion, 26th September 1916.
[364] *History of the Dorset Regiment 1914-1919*, with information provided by contributors to the Great War Forum, www.greatwarforum.org.

Cecil Harbord's experiences on the Somme, including the action by Mouquet Farm. On 4th November, Henry was struck in the wrist by a piece of shrapnel. The wound was, however, not considered to be particularly serious and was probably incurred in the battle, as the diary mentions no casualties in the month or so following it. By July 1917, he had recovered and had returned to the firing line but we do not know in which of these battalions Henry was then fighting. It is possible he was already with – or about to join – the 1st Dorsets that summer. On 1st July 1916, the 1st Dorsets had been reduced to a fighting strength of four officers and eighty-five men, and although that situation had improved as stragglers and missing re-joined, and lightly wounded recovered, the battalion had been reduced to two companies in the aftermath. On 17th July, they received a mass reinforcement of nearly three hundred additional soldiers, and Henry Friendship might well have been one of these.

On 26th September, some of the Canadians, including Philip Tollemache and Alexander Sandbrook of the 8th Canadian Infantry Battalion, fought close to Pozières not far from the 5th Dorset Battalion. At 12.35p.m., following an intense artillery bombardment of the German forward positions which had gradually lengthened out over and beyond the Zollern Trench, the "first three waves of the attack went forward under cover of our barrage and occupied the first objective, with the exception of 'B' Coy on our exposed flank."[365] The company in difficulties was supported by artillery and also reached the objective. However, the German machine gun and artillery defensive fire was intense and two platoons of the 10th Canadian Infantry Battalion helped 'B' Company to move further forward. Because the Germans continued to hold Stuff Redoubt on their left they were able to inflict severe casualties upon 'A' and 'B' Companies with their machine guns. In the end four officers and forty-two men were killed, seven officers and 233 men wounded, whilst 171 men had disappeared as 'missing'. However, once again, there is no record that Alexander was amongst the wounded. Perhaps it was at this time – we cannot be certain – that Philip Tollemache was invalided home after being wounded and suffering from shell shock.[366]

Three days later, Thomas Searls, who had survived the attack on Martinpuich two weeks earlier, was back in action. They had been doing some gruelling work – recovering for burial the men of their battalion who had died on 1st July – eight identifiable officers and twenty-nine other men, and it must have been a considerable relief when – although in relatively forward positions – the whole battalion was able to bathe and change clothing on 23rd September. On the evening of 28th September, they relieved the 11th Sherwood Forester Battalion in front of Le Sars, on the main road not far from Martinpuich. Half an hour later, one company of the 11th Sherwood Forester Battalion attacked Destrement Farm but was driven back by intense German machine-gun fire. At midnight, "Orders were received to take the above named farm without delay. C Company were detailed… The attack was launched promptly at 6.0 am & was entirely successful, despite the fact that almost 800 yards of open ground had to be traversed by our men. The men charged with great spirit, cheering when just approaching their objective. The Enemy offered very little resistance & fled in disorder, leaving a number of dead & one machine gun which was brought back by our men. The farm was immediately consolidated & one platoon commanded by 2nd Lieut. J.V. Medley left as a garrison. The farm was heavily shelled during the whole of the day & caused several casualties among the garrison. During the day 2nd Lieut. Medley was wounded. Lieut. T.H. Searls then took command & he too was seriously wounded."[367]

---

[365] War Diary, 8th Canadian Infantry Battalion, 26th September 1916.
[366] *The Bournemouthian*, December 1916.
[367] War Diary, 8th Yorks and Lancaster Battalion, 27th September 1916.

Thomas was indeed seriously wounded with a "very severe" gunshot wound in the right shoulder; his third rib, and the outer end of his clavicle were fractured, and damage to the spine end of his scapula was feared. He was taken to the casualty clearing station at Durnancourt, and from there to Rouen General Hospital. Soon he was back at the 1st Southern General Hospital at Edgbaston, having crossed from Le Havre to Southampton aboard HMS *Panama* on the night of 4th-5th October 1916.

By the autumn of 1916, of the more than five hundred Old Boys who had joined the Army or Navy, about thirty had been killed and about a further hundred had been wounded,[368] and the battle continued with an emphasis again on the southern sector.

October

On 28th September, Ernest Snelgar and the 4th Canadian Infantry Battalion were back in support trenches just west of Longueval, spending their days clearing the fields of their harvest of death. On 1st October, they went into attack again, this time against the formidable German Regina Trench line, close to where they had fought in September. This line was on the reverse slope, and could not be directly viewed by the British artillery. The wire was tremendously thick in front of it – with at least two bands of wire. "9.45am Telephone communication with G.O.C., when he ordered the attack to take place whether the wire was cut or not."[369] That wire had not been touched by the shells – scouts saw the barrage had gone "clean over the trench". 'A' and 'C' Companies were designated to make the attack in two waves with machine guns and the support of the battalion light mortars.

They assembled in the captured Zollern Trench to make the attack in the afternoon. 'D' Company on the right was annihilated almost immediately in a blizzard of machine-gun fire as the artillery had misjudged the range and laid down the covering barrage behind rather than in front of the German line, so that the Germans had a clear line of sight and fire against the attacking Canadians. A few men reached the enemy trench where they were killed by the defenders; others huddled in shell holes in No Man's Land, trying to snipe Germans. They "were finally wiped out. Very little information can be obtained that is reliable as very few of the Company were not casualties." It was not much better on the left for 'A' Company. "As ordered the first wave of 'A' Company crept up behind the first band of wire, and got into position, but as soon as our two minute barrage lifted, the enemy was seen standing up in their trenches; machine gun fire... criss-crossed our first wave, and wiped them out. Capt. Mackenzie and a few of the men crawling into shell hole... Our attack had now been reduced to a bombing attack, supported by 'A' Company, second wave, after advancing and retiring several times; enemy's advance being marked by the small red flares, feet high, and his retirement by two green flares, and his position by a board placed on the parapet, his barrage being accurately placed across the C.T. and moving backwards and forwards in accordance with signals... Captain Mackenzie succeeded in getting a machine gun forward... The Imperial Troops on our left reinforced us, lending us a machine gun, bombing squads, and supplying us with bombs. After repeated attempts to dislodge us by the enemy from this point, he ceased his counter-attacks."

---

[368] *The Bournemouth Visitors' Directory*, 18th November 1916.

[369] Account of operations of 1st October 1916 contained in the War Diary of the 4th C.E.F. Battalion. The details following are also derived from the diary.

For a short time, two platoons managed to dig in on the German Hessian Line but the only real success of the day was that the battalion managed to repulse a German counter-attack late in the afternoon; otherwise the bloodbath had resulted in no tangible gains. The remnants were withdrawn from the battle: Ernest lived to fight again. By the end of October, the battalion had lost over a thousand men on the Somme, and was unrecognisable from the men who had left Ypres a few months previously. At the end of the month they moved north to Arras to rebuild and to prepare for the next battle.

In the north of the battleground, the 1st Honourable Artillery Battalion, including Alexander Simpson, Leslie Gilbert and Haswell Shears had moved into trenches on the Somme near Beaumont-Hamel. They had been moved south from near Arras at the start of October and on the way had encountered tanks, near Albert: "For the first time we saw the famous tanks – and they certainly created almost as much interest as the first time we saw an aeroplane on Salisbury Plain – that must have been a 100 years ago."[370] When they went into the trenches of the 'Redan Sector' near Beaumont-Hamel, Haswell's company was placed in the front line, with one section in support. Alexander's company was in the support line. There was a considerable period of bombardment and counter-bombardment over several days in the middle of the month. One poignant moment came when one of Haswell's comrades, a Private Freeman, was discovered killed by the bombardment near a communication trench – but a kitten, which he carried as a mascot, was found unhurt, curled up asleep on his chest. There is an interesting observation on the conduct of men like Alexander and Haswell who had replaced the earlier members of the battalion, as they marched forward to Puchevillers on the Somme: "The men jogged along thinking a lot no doubt. They do not sing as much as the old 1st Battn did – but there is no doubt their courage burns with a steady flow and they will not be denied."[371]

Elsewhere on 1st October, after a brief respite, John Bennett and the three companies of the 5th Border Battalion not affected by dysentery had also been back on the attack, providing the first and second waves in an assault on the Flers Line, supported by the 8th Durham Light Infantry. This attack began at 3.15a.m. after a prolonged artillery bombardment. "When the bombardment lifted at the time stated the first wave left the assembly trench (North Durham Street) and followed close-up to the barrage line, followed by the other three waves at intervals of 50 yards. The two lines were captured before the enemy realised that we were in possession. A very small number of the Battalion on our right reached the final objective, the result being that the composite Battalion of 5th Border Regt & 8th Bn. D.L.I. had a very strenuous… time in clearing their right flank and forming blocks there to. An enemy machine gun was captured in the first objective just as it was beginning to cause trouble. The position was held and consolidated until the following night, Oct. 2nd when we were relieved by the 4th Bn. N.F. and withdrew."[372] On 14th October 1916, John was promoted to captain in command of a company.

Unusually, the war diary also included a copy of a report from the R.F.C. of the view of the battle from the air. "At 3.15am the steady bombardment changed into a most magnificent barrage. The timing of this was extremely good. Guns opened simultaneously and the effect was that of many machine Guns opening fire on the same order. As seen from the air the barrage appeared to be a

---

[370] War Diary, 1st Honourable Artillery Company Battalion, 4th October 1916.
[371] War Diary, 1st Honourable Artillery Company Battalion, 18th October 1916.
[372] War Diary, 5th Border Battalion, 1st-2nd October 1916.

most perfect wall of fire in which it was inconceivable that anything could live. The first troops to extend from the forming up places appeared to be the 50th Division who were seen to spread out from the sap-heads and forming up trenches and advance close up under the barrage, apparently some 50 yards away from it. They appeared to capture their objective very rapidly and with practically no losses while crossing the open... The tanks were obviously too far behind, owing to lack of covered approaches, to be able to take part in the original attack, but they were soon seen advancing on either side of the Eaucourt L'Abbaye – Flers Line, continuously in action and doing splendid work. They did not seem to be a target of much enemy shell fire. The enemy barrage appeared to open late, quite five minutes after the commencement of our own barrage, and when it came it bore no resemblance to the wall of fire we were putting up... 30 minutes after Zero the first English patrols were seen entering Le Sars. They appeared to be meeting with little or no opposition, and at this time no German shells were falling in the village. Our own shells were falling in the northern half."[373]

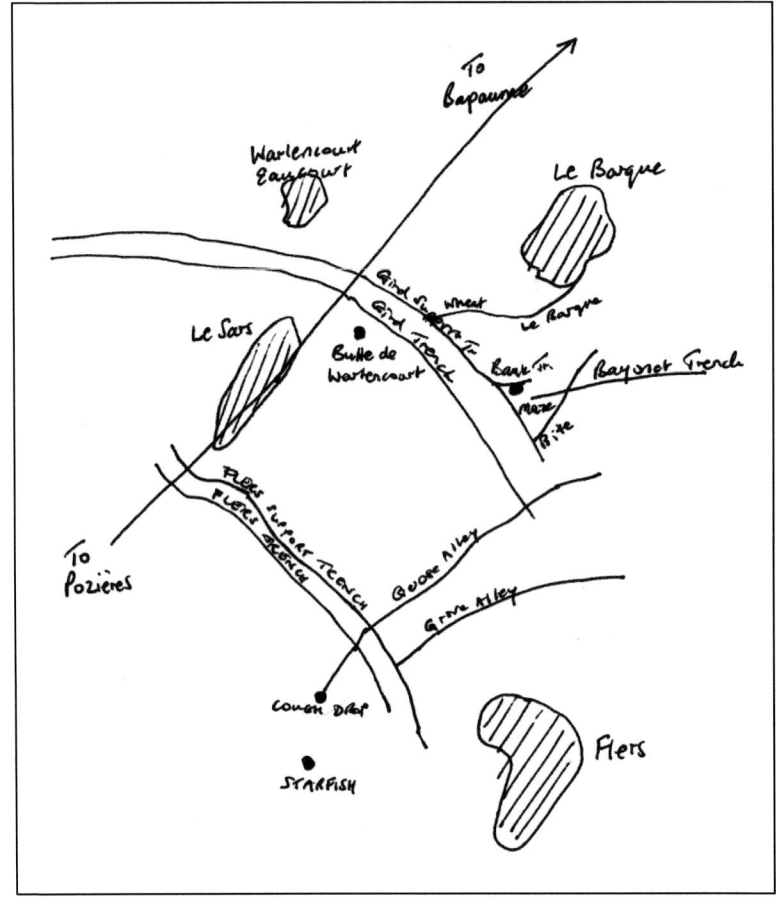

Slightly further west, Stanley Seymour was also fighting again. On 1st October, Stanley and the 1/23rd London Battalion were re-deployed to the Quadrangle where they were placed at the disposal of the 141st Brigade. Three companies then went forward to Prue Trench, whilst the fourth company was detached to carry grenades up to the British forces in High Wood. The next morning, whilst it was still dark, they moved up through congested communication trenches and then attacked, making their assault in four waves at 6.45a.m. The attack was unsuccessful as they encountered heavy machine-gun fire, and at the end of the day they withdrew to High Wood, where they were placed under 142nd Brigade. Casualties were heavy: five men had certainly died but seventy-five were missing, some presumably killed, and eighty-three had been wounded (including seven officers). So the next day the battalion had to be reorganised.

Stanley arrived back in England on 19th November 1916 where he was attached to the Territorial Force Depot. Why he returned at this stage is unclear, but it is likely that he had been amongst the wounded and was sent to the depot to complete a period of recovery and convalescence.

---

[373] Report of J.F. Channier, Major Commanding 34th Squadron R.F.C., included in the War Diary, 5th Border Battalion, 6th-16th October 1916.

The respite for Richard Clark and the 8th Royal Fusiliers Battalion also came to an end towards the close of September when they were sent back to the Somme. At the start of October they were moved to the new support line north of Flers. Immediately the casualties caused by intense and almost continuous shelling mounted – thirty-three were wounded and two were killed on the first day back near the front, with eleven more wounded (and one missing) the next day. On 5th October, two 2nd lieutenants were sent back down the line suffering from shell shock, and were followed the next day by a captain in the same condition. That day, Richard and his battalion moved forward from the support to the front line trenches.

There was little shelter from the remorseless shelling. In the whole of their trench system there was only one dug-out. The death toll of officers and men continued. These were awful days. Then word came that they were again to attack.

By now Haig was considering concluding the battle, and he was facing severe criticism for the dreadful casualty rate. On the other hand, French diplomatic and military pressure was pushing for the British to continue. So the battle continued until the weather eventually made it impossible to continue. Richard and the 8th Royal Fusiliers were caught up in a huge effort to take the British to the 'finishing line' at the Butte de Warlencourt.

On 7th October, the battalion went to fight in what is known as the Battle of Le Transloy. Richard and his men found themselves trying to advance against heavy shelling and hard-hitting machine-gun fire, to try to capture 'Bayonet Trench'. This was supposed to open the way to Le Barque, which in turn would help the British push on towards Bapaume. At 1.45p.m., "the battalion were ordered to attack at this time in conjunction with the whole of the Fourth Army, Reserve of the Fourth Army, and the 6th French Corps: the 9th Battn were now on our right and the 32nd Batt R.F. were on our left. The objectives were two: the first being a line… in Bayonet Trench; the second objective… in Banley Trench. The order of attack was two Platoons of each of A, B, Coys in the front line, two Platoons of each in the second line, and D Coy following in one line of support. The attack was not successful owing to the very heavy casualties suffered through enemy's machine guns and artillery, and owing to the fact that an enemy's Relief was taking place at this time with the result that the enemy were at double strength in this part of the line."[374] Richard was amongst the wounded.

As the battalion came to terms with these losses, and still suffered from shelling in the reserve area, they received a consolatory message from their brigadier, which was read out to the men: "Will you please thank all ranks of your Battalion for their magnificent gallantry they displayed yesterday. They advanced steadily under a very heavy fire which only the very best troops could have faced; though unfortunately unsuccessful, their gallant conduct has added to the fine reputation which you have already won for yourselves."

Richard was unlikely to have heard the message. He was taken back with another gunshot wound to his buttocks. For maximum impact, defensive machine guns were frequently trained at this level to cut down great swathes of men. This time Richard was not to survive. He had not gone back to a permanent hospital but had been kept at Number 38 Casualty Clearing Station at Heilly station, Mericourt-l'abbé, about ten kilometres south-west of Albert, and it was in the cemetery next door that he was buried. These casualty clearing stations were the most forward places where

---

[374] War Diary, 8th Royal Fusiliers, 7th October 1916.

operations could be performed. On 10th October, at Rowde Rectory in Wiltshire, his mother received the telegram she must have been dreading: "Deeply regret to inform you Lt. A.J.R. Clark 8 Royal Fusiliers died of wounds 9 October. The Army Council express their sympathy." His commanding officer wrote: "He died of wounds received in action while leading his men through the heaviest fire on October 7. He was a most gallant officer and a great favourite with both officers and men."[375] By an accident of history – a confusion of names and details – his name was not recorded by Bournemouth School as one amongst the fallen, and his name did not originally appear on its War Memorial.

John Day and the 12th Durham Light Infantry also attacked that day near Le Sars in the face of heavy machine-gun fire and managed to push the line forward. The next day, 8th October, Reginald Winch and the 1/3rd City of London Battalion attacked the Transloy Heights. Both battalions took heavy casualties, but both John and Reginald survived.

A couple of weeks later, on 18th October, Harold Head got tank D3, 728 into the action. His tank seems to have been the only one even to have managed to start and engage the Germans. Once again the accompanying 'female' tank (number 523) had broken down behind the start line, back in Flers. Harold, in D3, reached the start point near 'the Maze' north of Cobham Trench to assist the 21st Brigade (30th Division) in an attack north-west from Flers, but he reached the assembly point after the infantry had begun their assault (Zero Hour had been 3.40a.m.). "We went over at 4.30 in the morning, but one of the cars broke down and I had to do the job of both of them myself. We took the Bosches completely by surprise and we saw the German dead in piles. Some of them had their boots and socks off and their morning coffee beside them. When we got to the Bosche's front line we sat on their strong-point for twenty-three minutes. When the Bosches saw the car they ran from their trench down a communication trench into a sunken road. We then swerved to the left and went along their front line about 400 yards. As we went along the Bosches ran out of their trenches." By this time the Germans had repulsed the attack, and the infantry had already retreated to their assault trenches. Harold straddled the German line for twenty-three minutes, destroying a German machine gun and killing German defenders. Harold became frustrated – the British infantry still had not renewed the attack to reach him, so he climbed out of his tank and tried in vain to persuade the infantry to come forward again. Finally, he climbed back into his tank, and moved it forward along the German front line, firing at the fleeing Germans. For ten minutes he stayed on the German lines driving out the German defenders, but, still unsupported, he had no choice but to turn round and return to the original British assembly point. "I brought my machine back and reported what I had done. Unfortunately, two of my men were killed. My driver was a splendid fellow and he was driving for fifteen hours without a stop. I gave orders to him as to what directions we were going to travel and he worked. Well, when I got back and reported to the Commanding Officer what I had done. He seemed to be very pleased and communicated with Brigade Headquarters and afterwards I was invited to dinner by the General Commanding."[376]

On 4th December, Harold's parents received a letter from the general stating that "The General Officer Commanding-in-Chief has, under the authority granted by H.M. the King, awarded the Military Cross to Temp. Lieut. H.G. Head, Heavy Machine Gun Corps, for gallantry in the field. The

---

[375] Obituary in *The Times*, 7th November 1916.
[376] *The Bournemouth Visitors' Directory*, 23rd December 1916.

Corps and Divisional commander wish to convey their congratulations to the recipient."[377] The school magazine reported that "Lieut. Head paid us a welcome visit during the Christmas holidays, and spoke very modestly of his performance."[378] The official gazetted citation for his Military Cross is very clear: "Temp. Lt. Harold George Head, M.G.C. For conspicuous gallantry in action. He handled his Tank with great courage and skill, remaining out for over an hour under heavy fire, and accounting for many of the enemy."[379] The boys at school had a new hero and an extra day's half-holiday on February 15th 1917.

Despite the difficulties with these tanks if they broke down, even in battle something could be done if the men were sufficiently determined. Harold was quoted in the same *Bournemouthian* article explaining how once he had repaired his broken tank in the face of the enemy: "On one occasion when he was in action, and his tank in 'No Man's Land' it was struck by a German shell, which destroyed the clutch. Unable to move the machine, he and his men were obliged to abandon it and retire to their own trenches. When night came they returned to the 'Tank' with the tools and spare parts necessary to do the repairs, but they were 'spotted' by German searchlight and, the neighbourhood having become 'unhealthy,' they were obliged to discontinue their work and again retire. They by no means gave up hope of retrieving their derelict, however, and the next day, under the cover of a friendly fog, they went out again, completed the repairs, and brought back the Tank in triumph. We understand that, though barely 22 years old, Lieut. Head has been recommended for a 'Captaincy'. For this, and for the brilliant exploit which earned for him his decoration, we most cordially congratulate him."

Reginald Lapthorne and the 1st Hampshire Battalion had returned from the Ypres Salient to support the fight in this part of the battle. "18th. After a very wet night the 1st Rifle Brigade and the 1st East Lancashire Regt attacked the German system of disconnected lines to their immediate front. We supplied carrying parties and working parties on advanced Brigade Head Quarters. News most meagre during the day but apparently we did not have much success which was not surprising in view of the bad state of the ground. 19th. A very wet day, moved into support behind les Boeufs. Reinforcements went back to Transport. We occupied wet, muddy trenches with no dugouts in them."[380]

On 22nd October, they moved forward and relieved the 1st Somerset Light Infantry in the line at the eastern half of the front between Morval and Les Boeufs. The next day they attacked. "23rd. After a fine clear night the day broke very misty and zero hour was postponed from 11.30am to 2.30pm. The Brigade was disposed with the Hampshires in the front line and the Rifle Brigade in support on the right, and the Dublins in the front line and Warwicks in support. We were in close touch with the French on our right. Our objective was an imaginary line on the map known as the Brown line and the objective of the support was an imaginary line known as the Green line. Our guns, both Field and Heavy, were falling short most of the morning. At 2.30pm our intense barrage opened and the infantry commenced their advance. We had 'C' Company on the right and 'A' Company on the left in the leading wave, 'D' Company in support and 'B' Company in reserve. Immediately the assault commenced very heavy machine gun fire was directed on us and the right flank was

---

[377] *The Bournemouth Visitors' Directory*, 16th December 1916.
[378] *The Bournemouthian*, April 1917.
[379] *Supplement to The London Gazette*, 10th January 1917.
[380] War Diary, 1st Hampshires, 18th and 19th October, 1916.

scarcely able to advance at all as the French who were also attacking failed at the outset. The right, although suffering heavy casualties managed to get into the first German trench where they remained for a few hours but eventually had to retire owing to want of ammunition. Eventually the whole line had to retire to its normal position and the situation became normal once more. The Dublins on our left were successful in taking a strong position known as 'Gun Pits'."[381]

The next day, they calculated that their casualties had been ten officers and one hundred and ninety-two men. Reginald was one of the wounded officers (three had been killed; one was missing; and seven wounded). He had been struck on the forehead by shrapnel and then buried. He was lucky that his head had not been split open, but he had lain unconscious for about twenty-five minutes. He was removed from the battlefield and taken that day to the 34th Casualty Clearing Station. Then he was moved on to reach the 20th General Hospital at Camiers, north of Le Touquet on the coast. On 31st October, he was taken from Calais to Dover aboard the SS *Dieppe* and then on to Bristol, to the 2nd Southern General Hospital, where he was assessed and treated. His recovery was very slow and he only returned to the battalion in 1918.

On the same day that Reginald was hit, Jack New was in action. John, known as Jack, was born in 1889. He was at school from 1902-1906. He volunteered early, trained as an officer, and was commissioned 2nd lieutenant in the Dorsets on 4th August 1915. It was not long, however, before he was attached to the new Machine Gun Corps. Formed in October 1915, initially the M.G.C. was formed by transferring the machine gun sections of the infantry battalions into newly-formed companies, and throughout his service with the M.G.C. Jack was officially in the Dorsetshire Regiment but 'attached' to the M.G.C. For most of 1916 Jack remained in England. Whilst in training, he visited the school for the O.T.C. Field Day in February, and alongside former teacher Frank Forman, Jack acted as umpire to the cadets. On 15th October 1916, Jack went to France and spent several days at the Machine Gun Base Depot, at Camiers near Étaples, the huge British wartime coastal base. Then he joined the 76th Brigade Machine Gun Company on 21st October 1916 which was then at Courcelles-en-Bois, near Serre and north-west of Beaumont-Hamel. "When I arrived I found my Company in the trenches, so you see I soon got my first experience of warfare. Well, I must say it was pretty lively, but of course there is no 'Range discipline' here is there? I am now enjoying a few days rest, but the weather is not at all pleasant, for it has poured with rain for the last day or two and washed us nearly out of recognition. However, one must not expect a feather bed on service... The spirit of the British Tommy is very remarkable – the more it rains and the worse the conditions the more he sings and whistles."[382]

The 'pretty lively' time he mentioned began on his very first day. According to the war diary of his new unit, 41,900 rounds were fired by its machine guns that day – at a variety of German trenches near Serre. The next day, the company fired another 27,660 rounds from eleven machine guns at similar targets. On 23rd October, they fired 36,100 rounds; 25,250 the next day. "October 25th. During part of the night, indirect fire was maintained on wire & defences of Serre, roads & tracks behind the German lines... October 26th. Our M.G.s were active at night & swept the enemy's wire, & enfiladed hostile roads & communication trenches. 27,525 rounds were expended. October 27th... During the night eleven guns fired 27,196 at Indirect fire."[383] Hubert Dinwoodie was there at the

---

[381] War Diary, 1st Hampshires, 23rd October, 1916.
[382] *The Bournemouthian*, December 1916.
[383] War Diary, 76th Brigade, Machine Gun Company.

same time – possibly still with the 76th Trench Mortar Company. Later, on 1st March 1917, Jack was promoted to lieutenant and that summer, according to the school magazine, "Lieut. J.G. New, – Dorsets (attached M G C) has been placed on the Instructional Staff of an Officer Cadet battalion."[384] This was probably the M.G.C. Depot and Training Centre which had been established at Belton Park in Grantham, Lincolnshire. After the war, he left the M.G.C. and the Dorsetshire Regiment, but subsequently joined the Hampshire Regiment, serving in the 5/7th Hampshire (Defence Force) Battalion. By the end of the war, Jack had become an acting captain, and as a captain he served in the Hampshire Regiment during the Second World War, gaining new honours.

By the early part of October, the 2nd Wiltshire Battalion had also gone back to the Somme. They took devastating losses in fighting from 18th to 21st October – losing fourteen officers and three hundred and fifty men. "Officers and men very fatigued" manned their "depleted companies."[385] Eustace Chudleigh and Harold Martyn had re-joined them about this time, and Eustace acted as battalion transport officer, which meant that he had a good deal to do with managing the horses and mules, which were needed to bring supplies and men up to the lines through the thick mud, where mechanised transport simply could not go.

Frank Hayes was also on the Somme towards the close of the battle. Frank was born 1891 and attended the school from 1902 to 1906, winning a prize in 1905 for his examination successes. Soon after the start of the war, he enlisted in the Royal Engineers. As a specialist 'relieving clerk' with the London and South-West Railway, he was a valuable man to keep at an R.E. base. There he was promoted to corporal. This base was probably a divisional one in France: it is known that he landed in France on 8th May 1915. Clearly Frank became frustrated in October 1916 and "feeling that he was not doing his 'bit' staying in an office",[386] at his own request was allowed to transfer as a corporal to the 12th Middlesex Battalion. This was a Service Battalion in 54th Brigade, 18th (Eastern) Division. It had landed in France on 26th July 1916, and already fought in several dramatic actions in the Battle of the Somme before Frank joined them, mostly recently in the attack at Thiepval where the battalion had been almost destroyed – it had been withdrawn in the aftermath to Prouville, north of Amiens, and most likely it would have been here that Frank joined them.[387] Frank probably joined the battalion in a group of thirty-three men who arrived on 11th October.

The battalion had moved forward to Bouzincourt, near Albert, on 18th October, and gone into the lines of Regina Trench and Stuff Redoubt, near Pozières, on 25th October. Here they had remained for several days under very heavy shelling which caused significant new casualties. Relieved on 29th October, it must have been a relief to be able to bathe in Albert two days later – but frustrating that they had to climb back into the same dirty, muddy clothes as fresh ones were not then available. It was not until 5th November that they got their clean clothing.

November and December

On the night of 6th-7th November, the 12th Middlesex Battalion had returned to Regina Trench in thick mud and where, at night, rockets were fired and artillery kept up its shelling. One small

---

[384] *The Bournemouthian*, July 1917.
[385] War Diary, 2nd Wiltshire Battalion, 20th and 21st October 1916.
[386] *The Bournemouth Visitors' Directory*, 7th April 1917.
[387] We know from the accounts both in *The Bournemouthian*, April 1917 and in *The Bournemouth Visitors' Directory* of 7th April 1917 that he joined the Middlesex Regiment in October.

consolation came when the Germans were observed to shell their own front line trench. However, two days later the battalion endured not only heavy rain but also their own British artillery shelling, though fortunately the British shells landed no nearer than a hundred yards from Regina Trench, possibly because the artillery observers could see so little. The war diary makes repeated references to the extent of the mud, so it must have been very bad. On 9th November, two trenches were judged to be impassable: "Trenches in a very muddy condition, but after dark it was possible to move men over the top… all ranks suffered considerably from standing in water & liquid mud – it being found necessary to evacuate several men from sickness."[388] In the circumstances it was a considerable success and achievement that in this tour on the front line only one man was killed with two wounded. Even so, some men had to be brought back to their billets in Warloy by lorry since after this tour they could, temporarily, no longer walk.

At the start of November, the 1st Honourable Artillery Battalion, including Alexander Simpson, Leslie Gilbert and Haswell Shears was in trenches at Hamel, and these were so wet that gumboots had to be issued, even when in many cases they were really a poor fit as the men had bigger feet than the issue allowed for! Conditions were foul. Mud was everywhere and cold rain made things miserable and difficult. It is unfortunate that on what was to be almost the last day for so many men, the brigadier made a terrible fuss because he saw them marching in overcoats! (All the odder as the brigadier had inspected them on parade the previous day and it had been "imposing" and the men "looked well and were very steady". To prepare, they had spent all the day before "cleaning and scrubbing their kit, getting their hair cut, & making themselves presentable."[389]) Perhaps the brigadier was trying to prove himself – he had only been appointed on 29th October when his predecessor had been wounded.

Just before the Battle of the Ancre, a significant number of men fell sick. An entry in *The Bournemouthian* magazine said that Haswell was wounded in October 1916: "H G Shears was wounded last October, but has completely recovered and returned to France."[390] This reminds us not to accept everything at face value. Actually, he was one of a number of men who were sent sick to hospital on 11th November 1916. There is no Army record of him being wounded. This sickness meant that Haswell missed the attack of 13th-15th November in which the battalion lost a huge number of casualties. Haswell's illness was, however, and on 16th November he arrived back in England from hospital in France. It seems that this marked the end of his time with the Honourable Artillery Company, though he possibly remained a member of it whilst serving on attachment to another infantry unit later in the year.

Meanwhile, the 1st Honourable Artillery Company Battalion had gone into the Battle of the Ancre, which began on 13th November in bad weather. Once again, sappers had tunnelled under Hawthorn Ridge where the Germans were using the old crater as a redoubt, and the British blew 30,000lbs of explosive at 05.45 hours, covering the German trenches with debris. (This part of the wider battle also saw the capture of St. Pierre Divion and Beaucourt-sur-Ancre.) Alexander Simpson's company advanced in thick fog, and there was considerable confusion, although they were able to capture the advanced German trenches relatively quickly. The day then became very difficult and by the end it was a question of digging in to hold the gains. On the second day, the

---

[388] War Diary, 12th Middlesex Battalion, 9th November 1916.
[389] War Diary, 1st Honourable Artillery Company Battalion, 9th-10th November 1916.
[390] *The Bournemouthian*, July 1917.

battalion moved ahead and captured the village of Beaucourt. "On reaching Beaucourt a large number of prisoners were taken & sent to the rear. We advanced through the village clearing Dug-outs on the way. The Dug-outs were all heavily manned, but presented little difficulty. Snipers & M.G.s fired from the flanks but not sufficiently to hold up our advance. We reached our line at the far side of the village & immediately started to make a trench. All the men were now very scattered and it was some time before the various units could be sorted… Snipers became active here, and the enemy shelled somewhat heavily with H.E. Most of the trench escaped serious damage, and the shelling was directed on to the main road. Digging was again very difficult owing to a lack of tools, but fair cover was obtained with entrenching tools. A Support Line was made 30 yds in rear of the Fire Trench."[391] Unfortunately, the first aid post was on the main road and suffered badly. When they were pulled back on 15th November, conditions remained poor – twenty-three men shared a tent, although this overcrowding at least helped the men to cope with the bitterly cold conditions. Alexander Simpson too fell sick, and was sent to hospital from which he returned on 12th December. At that time, the 1st Honourable Artillery Company Battalion was at Nouvion, just east of St. Valery sur Somme, not far from the sea, having been withdrawn again in order to rest, be restored in numbers, and train to return once more.

After several spells in the trenches, Stanley Birdseye and the 10th Royal Fusiliers had been pulled back and trained hard, with lots of long route marches as well as practising different methods of attack across open country, with an apparent emphasis on attacking in waves behind a rolling barrage. On 13th November, they reached an assault position in the forward trenches near Hamel, and attacked on 14th November: "At 8.15am in conjunction with a tank took 270 prisoners from Redoubt in old German Line… Not a shot fired. Released 60 English prisoners, who had been well treated. Redoubt had been passed in general assault on 13th by 63rd Divn (R.N.D.). We took 3 M.G.'s. Most of day spent in collecting wounded – both English & German."[392] After a further advance next day, and the capture of a few more prisoners, the battalion made a major attack on the 16th November: "Attack made at dawn failed owing to rifle and M.G. fire. At 3.45 pm 2 bombing parties reached the junction but had to retire – owing to enemy forces… foiled by enemy barrage."[393] For a day the battalion was poised, preparing for a fresh attack and then resumed the assault on 18th November: "Zero for 32nd Divn's attack was 6.10 am – at which hour our various parties stormed their objectives. All made good… Owing to failure of Right of 32nd Divn attack – our parties had to be again withdrawn… 19/11/16. Again ordered attack Triangle (night 18/19) – this time with 2 Coys in frontal attack. This plan eventually modified to 2 strong Officers' patrols under 2/Lt RC Bambridge & 2/Lt Heywood – with previous artillery bombardment. This bombardment was ineffectual – owing no doubt to the Artillery having had no opportunity of ranging. The parties again reached their objectives, but were again forced to retire owing to the strength of the enemy."[394] For the rest of the month and most of December the pattern of trench occupation (and casualties) followed by training continued, though towards the end of the month they were switched north again to trenches near Neuve Chapelle. Although each attack had meant the battalion sustained casualties, Stanley had survived the battle.

Arthur Garrad was almost certainly also there. Arthur and his younger brother Harold both

---

[391] War Diary, 1st Honourable Artillery Company Battalion, 14th November 1916.
[392] War Diary 10th Royal Fusiliers 14th November 1916.
[393] War Diary 10th Royal Fusiliers 16th November 1916.
[394] War Diary 10th Royal Fusiliers 18th-19th November 1916.

enlisted. Born in 1895, Arthur attended the school from May 1908 until he left in July 1911, when he went on to be an organist's pupil – a music student. (Harold Garrad, four years younger, was at school from 1910 to 1916 and joined the Honourable Artillery Company after he left school, writing a letter about being a recruit which was published in *The Bournemouthian* in July 1918; he almost certainly did not get to serve in the war.) At school, Arthur was a member of the O.T.C. for three years. He volunteered for the 9th Hampshire Battalion at Southampton on 25th September 1915 and was accepted for training for a commission. He was sent to France on 28th July 1916 to join the 8th Somerset Light Infantry, of the 63rd Brigade, 37th Division. He joined this battalion when it was being re-built after suffering heavy casualties on the first day of the Battle of the Somme. During the time he served with the battalion it was involved in several bouts of fighting. In October 1916, it had manned trenches at Souchez where it came under heavy shell fire. Back on the Somme, the battalion fought in the snow and mist in the Battle of the Ancre in November 1916. The battalion took heavy casualties, especially from rifle fire but also from 'friendly' artillery fire. It tried to advance from shell hole to shell hole, but the attack was halted as casualties had become unsupportable. Even then, bombing patrols were sent out which captured twenty Germans. In this battle four officers were killed, including three company commanders, and about one hundred men were casualties. On 27th December 1916, Arthur went on a Lewis Gun course. This was about his last duty with the battalion. He left the battalion on 23rd January 1917. He was very ill. He had developed a nasty mixture of rheumatism (affecting his arms, hands, legs and back) with trench fever and quinsy (a peritonsillar abscess which is a rare and potentially serious complication of tonsillitis, and which can happen when a bacterial infection spreads from an infected tonsil to the surrounding area). He was hospitalised – sent from Calais to Dover on 23rd January 1917 to the Prince of Wales Hospital in Marylebone. Although *The Bournemouthian* school magazine reported in April 1917 that he was recovering, Arthur never really recovered fully. Regular medical boards found him unfit, but gradually a kind of improvement did set in, and before November 1917 he was switched to the role of messing officer at an R.F.C. camp at Yatesbury.

Ernest Parsons too was involved in these last days of the great battle. Ernest was born in 1897. He was only a member of the school for the first two terms of 1912. He served on the Western Front initially with the 7th Royal Fusiliers Battalion, from 23rd July 1916 to 23rd November 1916. He landed with them at Le Havre when they went to the Western Front, where they were attached to the 190th Brigade, 63rd (Royal Naval) Division – a brigade in which several Old Bournemouthians fought. In October, the battalion and its division had moved south to reserve positions behind the lines of the Somme battlefield and then moved into trench positions, initially on the Redan Ridge in the north, and later to positions overlooking the River Ancre near Mesnil. From there they took up trench positions at Hamel, adjacent to the river. On 1st November, Ernest might well have gone hungry when pack animals, which had been used to bring forward rations in sandbags had so jolted around that only the bully beef remained edible – the tea, sugar, bacon etc. having got so mixed up that it was unusable. The next day the men had hardly any food.

Ernest left the battalion on 23rd November. Before that the battalion had supplied men for an unsuccessful raiding party, and had then taken part in the major attack of 13th-14th November which had resulted in mass casualties – four officers and thirty-seven men killed, and twelve officers and three hundred and thirty-one men wounded, gassed or missing. Being wounded or going sick was often the reason why a man left his battalion, initially to hospital and then to base, before being allocated to another battalion that was short of men. He had probably been wounded. We know that he was wounded at least twice during his time in the Army, but unfortunately not the details of those events. When he returned to the front later that year, it was to a different battalion of the regiment.

Cyril Horsey too went back into action that November. At the start of the month, the 7th South Lancashire Battalion was in and out of three trenches north of Thiepval. These trenches, captured the previous month, were in a dreadful condition. The front line was in the area of Stuff Trench, the support in Bainbridge Trench and the reserve in Schwaben Trench, with Battalion Headquarters in Zollern Trench. Cyril's colonel railed against the conditions his men faced: "The condition of the trenches is still appalling. No material can be obtained from the R.E.; & little improvement to the trenches can be carried out. Most of these are almost indiscernible ditches, exceedingly hard to find, & Batt runners & orderlies have the greatest difficulty in reaching their destination. In addition to this, no communication by day can be obtained with the two coys in the front line, except by telephone, on account of the front line trenches being on the downward slope of the hill, & the only communication trench leading to them being impassable owing to the state of the trench & to the continuous shelling to which it is subjected to by the enemy. The enemy appears to realise this, and all the ground between the front & support lines is fairly heavily shelled throughout the day & night."[395]

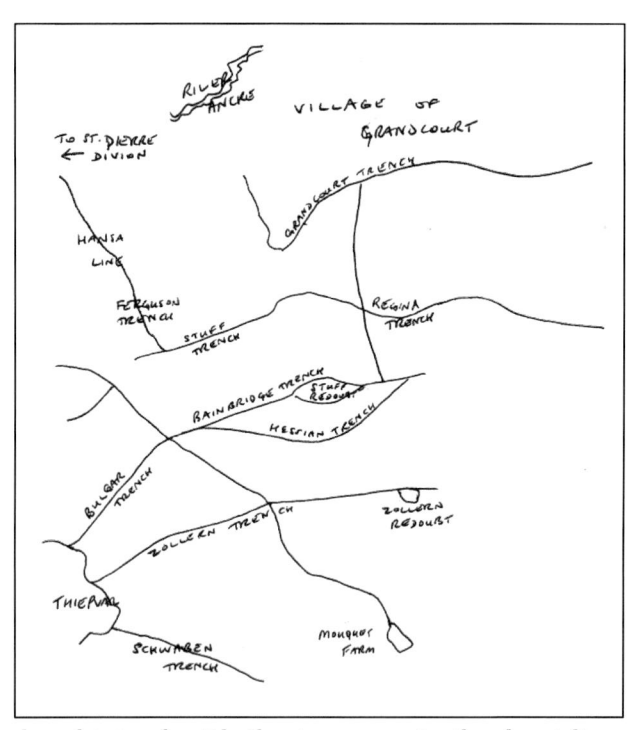

In November, diplomatic pressures, including French requests, kept the B.E.F. fighting. Much of the battlefield was now in British hands, but Haig could still target the elimination of the German salient between the road which stretched from Albert to Bapaume and the uncaptured village of Serre. Of especial concern was the capture of Beaumont-Hamel. To achieve this, Haig ordered Gough to push V Corps to lead the offensive, supported by II Corps south of the River Ancre. After bitter fighting, the battle was only a partial success: down by the marshy river gains were made, and higher up Beaumont-Hamel was captured by the 51st (Highland) Division and Beaucourt captured by the Royal Naval Division, but Serre and the northern part of the German line remained unconquered. Grandcourt was taken in the days that followed.

Cyril and friends got some limited relief when they moved back into support with their front companies in Zollern Trench, and the men were able to enjoy some "glorious weather" which put them into a cheerful mood even though there was nowhere really to rest even in the support trenches.

The battalion was ordered to make a raid in strength on 16th November into the outskirts of Grandcourt, which had not yet fallen to the British. The raid involved three of the four companies

---

[395] War Diary, 7th Loyal South Lancashire Battalion, 6th November 1916.

and was something of a bloody affair. Whilst most of 'A' and 'B' Companies made it back, 'D' Company had taken heavy casualties. The raid had been checked by encountering uncut German wire, and they (and the men of the 9th Welsh Battalion who also took part) had been unable to gain the German Grandcourt Line, and were forced back. The battalion had lost a lot of men. "11pm. Search party under 2nd Lt Horsey sent up in evening to endeavour to recover wounded and missing, and to find news of Capt. Honan & 2Lt. Morrison. Four missing men were discovered, but nothing heard or seen of the two officers."[396]

The battalion again attacked in the early hours of 18th November. By 7a.m. on 18th November, when they had captured the south-western corner of Grandcourt, "there were numerous casualties in gaining this objective from snipers and M.G. fire." Two strongpoints were created for defence. By the evening, matters were grim: "The three companies held on to their objective the whole day until 9.0pm, when A and D coys moved from the marshy ground... taking over a position of the 8th Gloucester R's line; B Coy remained to garrison the strong point. At this period there was only one officer left in the front line in command of all three companies, all the rest having become casualties by 9.30am."[397] Cyril was shot in the leg, and ended up in the No. 2 Red Cross Hospital in Rouen. Here his condition deteriorated. On 21st November, his mother was invited by the War Office to visit her dangerously wounded son. She embarked from Southampton the next day. Sadly, she arrived too late. At 1.15p.m. Cyril died at the hospital. His mother was in time to be given his effects. He was buried in the St. Sever Cemetery, in Rouen. His daughter Olive was born in March 1917, so he never saw her and she never saw him.

On 19th November, after one last day of attack, with rain mixing with snow and sleet, the battle was called off. Harold Finch and his comrades helped to hold the line in the south-east of the battlefield in a dangerous trench between Les Boeufs and Gueudecourt. Harold, born in 1896, had gained a scholarship from Bournemouth Education Committee to finance his place at the school as a day boy (1908-1911). On March 27th 1916, Harold was called up under the Derby Scheme and posted to the Hampshire Regiment. Fourteen days after arriving at the training camp he was promoted to lance corporal – which he attributed to his training in the school O.T.C. At the end of June he was promoted to full corporal and again by the end of October to sergeant. When he arrived on the Somme to join the 2nd Hampshire Battalion, the battle was drawing to its close.

The weather was bitterly cold. Enemy shelling added to the misery. Each day from 17th-22nd November the battalion took casualties. Harold was shot. "In one of the numerous battles which took place near the banks of the Somme in November it appears he was dangerously wounded in the legs and the body. As soon as possible, he was removed to the London Casualty Clearing Station, where everything possible was done for him, but he passed away—quickly and without apparent pain—early on Sunday morning, November 26th."[398] He was buried close by, at Meaulte, south of Albert. Harold was the last Bournemouthian casualty of the battle, and one of the last overall to die in the bloodbath that bears the name of the Somme.

As the winter drew on, tank warfare became almost impossible, though the tanks were there to add support. On 18th November, Claud Couch and 'A' Company, now renamed 'A' Battalion, was

---

[396] War Diary, 7th Loyal South Lancashire Battalion, 16th November 1916.
[397] Account included with the War Diary, 7th Loyal South Lancashire Battalion, November 1916.
[398] *The Bournemouthian*, December 1916.

moved alongside Companies 'B', 'C' and 'D' to the area around Bernicourt, and located in the villages of Humieres, Eelinieux and Bermieourt. (Harold Head's 'D' Battalion was at Blangy.) These tank battalions were later organised into tank brigades. Sections of the old companies were now in their turn known as companies. The number of tanks in each of these new companies was reduced to four to create a more manageable work load. On 12th April 1917, Claud and Harold Head were promoted to captain. (It seems then that in the summer of 1917 Claud served as Captain Commanding No.9 Section of No.3 Company, 'A' Battalion. The tanks and commanders for which he was then responsible were Autogophasta, A41, 2028, Lieut. G. Ingham; Aurora, A43, 2512, 2nd Lieut. J.B. Love; Ariel, A44, 2557, 2nd Lieut. A.E. Paxton-Hall; and Amphibian, A45, 2032, 2nd Lieut. G. Matthews). Whilst he probably fought at Arras, this is not certain. We know that on 22nd August 1917 Claud transferred to the Cheshire Regiment and on 27th January 1918 his appointment as a temporary captain in the Service Army was altered to that of one in the Regular Army. From the 1918 Army List it seems he was probably in the 1st or 2nd Battalion. He survived the war.

Behind the infantry attacks had stood the heavy artillery and, although we know few details, it is clear that Frederick Lonnen was there during the battle, playing his part. Frederick had been born in 1895. He attended the school from 1904 to 1906. He was an early volunteer, joining the R.G.A. as a gunner on 28th August 1914. He landed in France on 23rd October 1915 and spent twenty months on active service, posted to serve with a heavy battery. These were usually armed with five-inch guns, though some batteries had older howitzers. These could fire powerful shells and were used against German artillery. They were also fired upon key German positions such as communications like road and railway lines or on their defensive strongpoints or store and ammunition dumps. It is unclear with which battery he was first engaged, but eventually he was posted to the 136th Siege Battery, which arrived in France on 31st May 1916. "After spending about twenty months in the firing line in France, I am very thankful to write that I have been fortunate enough to arrive home in 'Blighty' again. The Battery to which I belonged was a time-serving one, namely the ---- Heavy Battery. I joined them in November, 1915. During the 'Great Offensive,' which commenced on July 1st, 1916, we were all kept very busy and were firing incessantly both day and night. Several of our fellows were awarded D.C.M.s, Military Medals, etc. After the taking of Bapaume, our Battery moved away to another part of the line nearer Béthune, Mazingarbe, Lens, and Loos. 'Fritz' tried very hard to break through here, but we pushed him back 'slowly but surely'."[399] He wrote "home in 'Blighty'" because, on 1st October 1917, the Army discharged him through his ill-health, suffering from shell shock. (*The Bournemouthian* erroneously stated this had happened in the summer, but at that stage he had been brought back to the R.G.A. Base for light duties.) He lived on until 1968.

Harold Martyn and Eustace Chudleigh were still with the 2nd Wiltshire Battalion. Eustace would have had time to get to know Harold although their responsibilities were quite different within the battalion. They were still in the trenches over Christmas time, in the front line, where Eustace found time to write a letter to his old headmaster. Perhaps he could find the time because the war diary reported that day as "Quiet day. Nothing of importance to report."[400] A regular and efficient postal service was one of the most impressively organised of the British Army's successes in this war. Even when men were in the front line trenches, the post could still get through. His letter began with, "I have just received your post card wishing me a Merry Christmas—thank you very much indeed for it." At the start of January, Eustace and his friends enjoyed a belated Christmas

---

[399] *The Bournemouthian*, December 1917.
[400] War Diary, 2nd Wiltshire Battalion, 27th December 1916.

celebration once they had pulled back into reserve at Bailleulmont: "The Battalion celebrated Christmas having been in the trenches on Christmas Day. An excellent dinner was provided for the men in the recreation room. In the evening the sergeants held a dinner in the recreation room which turned out a great success... The Commanding Officer Lieut Col RMT Gillson DSO... remarked that he hoped we would all meet again next Christmas but not in France. Three cheers were then given for the Commanding Officer. A concert was then given... with songs and... with a monologue... The proceedings were then closed with 'God Save The King'."[401] But "being out here makes one realise how good it is to be remembered by one's friends in England. I am glad the people in England seem to be realising, at last, what a big thing we are engaged in—out here that fact is forced upon one at every turn, and, in the face of everything, there is scarcely a despondent face out here. I came across a bunch of men a day or two ago laying bets on which plot of ground the next shell would pitch—it never seemed to occur to them that it might be the one they were standing on."[402]

Oswald Curtis, born in 1896, fought on the Somme after the battle, with the Honourable Artillery Company. He had left school on 29th July 1914 – just two days before the war started. In 1916, Oswald followed older Bournemouth School boys by joining the Honourable Artillery Company. With the patronage and support of his headmaster, he enrolled as a private in the 2/1st Battalion – commonly known as the 2nd Battalion in this regiment of three battalions, all classed as units of the Territorial Force. Despite its name, the H.A.C. had only five batteries of artillery in action and one in reserve, but three battalions of infantry known as the 1/1st, 2/1st, and 3/1st. The third of these battalions, as was customary, remained in England and supplied drafts of officers and men to reinforce the two fighting battalions.

Oswald enjoyed training at Richmond Park Camp. "Up to the present, I like the life very much. Of course, it is hard work, but then one expects that. I find that my O.T.C. training is of great service to me. After the training I received at school and at the annual camps it seems fairly easy to slip into the life here."[403] This training facility held a number of different army encampments. The area between Roehampton and Robin Hood Gate was designated for the Royal Naval Air Service, and this might have sown some seeds which later may have influenced Oswald's move to switch to the new R.A.F. towards the end of the war. Oswald's battalion landed at Le Havre on 3rd October 1916 and was placed in the 22nd Brigade of the 7th Division.

Oswald Curtis at school in 1912.

After experience in trenches at Steenwerke in Belgium from 7th October, initially under instruction and afterwards in their own right, receiving their gas masks and steel helmets and coming under fire, they moved south to the Somme, where they took over trenches at Beaumont-Hamel on 29th November. "Companies in front line had a bad time from shelling & sniping all day. Outpost groups suffering a lot with mud – Communication very difficult to maintain. Trenches obliterated in

---

[401] War Diary, 2nd Wiltshire Battalion, 1st January 1917.
[402] *The Bournemouthian*, April 1917.
[403] Letter in *The Bournemouthian*, July 1916.

places."[404] All four companies had men killed and wounded. "Front line, outposts & dugouts shelled continuously all day, especially during the relief. Sergt Peet killed and 7 wounded… Colonel Ward taken ill thro' effects of gas… Men very exhausted & fatigued – went into Hun dug-outs in support. Huge excavation – reached by 56 steps. Lighted by electricity. 3 wounded."[405] They were still there on Christmas Day.

At the start of 1917, the 2/1st H.A.C. assisted in the events surrounding the German withdrawal to the Hindenburg Line, and by 25th February 1917 the battalion was in action at Bucquoy. Later in 1917, it took part of the Arras offensive of April, in the grim fighting around Bullecourt, but by that time Oswald had been invalided out of the line with "a very severe attack of Trench Foot, brought about by long exposure to cold and wet. This was followed by other complications, resulting in a dangerous illness; but we are glad to hear that he is now progressing satisfactorily."[406] These experiences, as with others before him, seem to have convinced him to leave the mud of the trenches and try his luck in the air. He applied to join the air force. On 2nd July 1918, he was passed fit to become either a pilot or an observer for the R.A.F., and was then posted to the first of a series of units within the R.A.F. In September he was training at the School of Arms but his training was still incomplete when the war came to an end.

Arras 1916-1917

Whilst the Somme was full of frantic action in the second half of 1916, the Arras Sector was relatively quiet. Battalions which had been badly hit on the Somme were often sent to re-train and refresh at Arras or nearby at La Bassée.

Francis Holbrook was a member of the school whose initial experience of the war was to serve with the 2/15th London Battalion, holding the line east of Arras in the summer of 1916. Francis was the younger brother of Harold Holbrook, and both served in the 15th London (Prince of Wales' Civil Service Rifles). Harold was born 1894, and Francis in 1895. Both had won scholarships to the school, and both did well in their exams. (Harold was at the school from 1906 to 1909. When he wanted to join up, his Civil Service department for a time deemed him to be indispensable, so his enlistment was delayed. Eventually, however, he served in one of the 15th London Battalions, in France, from nearly the end of the war – from 4th October 1918 until his discharge on 14th June 1919.) Francis had been at the school from January 1907 until December 1912. He too joined the Civil Service and was allowed to enlist on 8th February 1916 when an official from the War Office wrote out a special certificate to allow him to serve in the Army. He trained as a private with the 2/15th London Battalion. Although the battalion was preparing to cross to France, the Easter Rising in Ireland caused a delay; for the first two weeks of May 1916 most of the battalion reinforced the situation in Ireland, before returning to England to work up to leaving for France, arriving at Le Havre on 23rd June 1916. Within days – on 26th June – Francis and the battalion were on the outskirts of Arras, and experiencing for real some of the emergencies for which they had trained in England: on 27th June, five German artillery shells hit 'A' Company's billets, wounding two men and destroying their field kitchen.

---

[404] War Diary, 2/1st Battalion, Honourable Artillery Company, 30th November 1916.
[405] War Diary, 2/1st Battalion, Honourable Artillery Company, 1st-2nd December 1916.
[406] *The Bournemouthian*, April 1917.

Over the summer, Francis and his colleagues suffered the rigours of trench rotation from east of Neuville St. Vaast to Vimy Ridge. On 9th August he might have seen King George V who passed by whilst the battalion was at rest, but positioned on the line of his route. In the early hours of 11th September, a raid was made on the German front line. Although the party of two officers and forty men lost one man killed and four more (and both officers) slightly wounded, they took four prisoners and learned that the Germans opposite them were neither confident nor content. "The morale of the prisoners was exceedingly low, and they were so terrified that it was only with great difficulty they could be induced to come out of their trench."[407] To be fair, 2nd Lieutenant Thompson had just thrown a grenade into the dug-out and threatened to follow it with others. Sadly, of two brothers who took part, a man called Alexander Small (awarded the Military Medal) had the melancholic experience both of being wounded and of returning to bring back his own, mortally wounded, brother.

Low morale or not, the Germans kept up a steady attrition of the men of 2/15th London, especially with artillery bombardments through October. It is to be hoped that Francis and his friends appreciated being inspected by Field Marshall Haig himself on 1st November. On 22nd November, Francis embarked at Marseilles, first for Salonika and later for Egypt and Palestine (where he was wounded). However, he, and the 2/15th London Battalion were to return to the Western Front in 1918.

Norman Fookes served in the 2/14th London Battalion, brigaded with Francis Holbrook's battalion. Norman was born in 1889 and was possibly one of the original students of 1901, and certainly there at least for the years 1903 to 1905. He volunteered for the 2/14th London (London Scottish) Battalion on 23rd June 1915. On 21st March 1916, he was rated as a 'First Class shot' and promoted to lance corporal on 19th April 1916. Norman left with the battalion from Southampton on 21st June 1916 overnight to Le Havre. The battalion moved up to Arras. Here, their first experience of the war was five days working on mining fatigues on the front line. They did repeated tours of duty in the trenches at Bray, north-west of Arras, just south of Mont St. Eloi. Most days there was the occasional casualty, though on 5th September they had a greater shock when the Germans exploded a mine near the front left of their position, killing four men and wounding a further eighteen. From 12th August to 9th September, Norman was in hospital either having been wounded or fallen sick, the records are unclear. Otherwise, Norman's experience was a drudge of repeated trench duties with no major incident or battle. In November, like Francis, Norman embarked for Salonika. He was to survive the war, but also not without incident and injury. He went on to campaign both in the Balkans and later with General Allenby in the Palestine campaign when the British captured Jerusalem from the Turks. He survived the war, though with a disability caused by one of the wounds which he received in Palestine.

Edwin Gunning was nearby at Neuville St. Vaast, in the 2/20th London Battalion, in a different brigade and division but holding the line close to his fellow Bournemouthians. He was on this front for only a short time. Born in 1892, he too was an early member of the school, whose records have largely been lost, though clearly he was still a pupil in 1905 and 1906. At some point, probably soon after leaving school, he took service at Maidstone with the 3rd Royal West Kent Regiment. For some reason, in February 1911, he volunteered to move to the Royal Sussex Regiment, but though this application was accepted, in November 1911 he was instead transferred into the Army

---

[407] Included within the War Diary, 2/15th London Battalion, September 1916.

Ordnance Corps. This does not seem to have suited him, for in July 1912 he was discharged at his own request, still a private. He had to make a fee payment of £18 (a lot of money for the time, but he did receive £9 back when, as a 2nd lieutenant he was appointed as a temporary full lieutenant into the 3/20th London Battalion on 15th February 1916).

Edwin ended up serving in the 2/20th London Battalion which was sent across from Southampton to land at Le Havre on 25th June 1916 and was soon in action. On 1st July they were at Agnières, just to the north-west of Arras, and here they practised the consolidation of mine craters and were instructed in rapid wiring techniques. From 11th July, the battalion manned 'P' trench line in front of Vimy Ridge. On 15th July, "there was considerable activity in the afternoon along the whole of the front, the enemy sending a large number of Rifle Grenades and Minenwerfers in Lassale Trench causing casualties from blown in parapet. We retaliated with Stokes Gun & 18 pounders. A little Machine Gun activity during night... Casualties: O.R. 5 wounded. 2/Lt Gunning removed to Hospital suffering from shell shock."[408]

Edwin Gunning

A report from a medical board held at Osborne on the Isle of Wight on 28th September described what had happened to him: "The Board find that a rifle grenade exploded close over his head and that, in addition to receiving numerous trivial punctured wounds of the head, he was rendered unconscious for an hour, blind for 6 days & had severe headache and pains in his neck. His general health is good. He is sleeping well and has no symptoms of shock." These wounds were judged to be severe, but not permanent.[409] That winter, the school magazine published a brief and dramatic version of the incident when it wrote, "Lieut. E.F. Gunning, London Regiment, was wounded on July 15th. He lay unconscious for 20 hours, and was blind for some days through shock. Writing on July 29th he says: 'My wound was not of a serious nature as I am already out of hospital and convalescent.'"[410] "In a letter the officer sent home he says he owes his life to the steel helmet he was wearing, for a German grenade struck the helmet and exploded, rendering him unconscious for twenty hours. The shock robbed him of his sight temporarily but we are pleased to say he is gradually recovering his eyesight."[411] The July 1917 school magazine reported that he had been "mentioned in dispatches".

He was initially treated in France and embarked for England on 27th September. There followed a prolonged series of medical boards as his recovery faltered. He never saw any further action but remained in England, and in January 1919 relinquished his commission because of ill-health caused by wounds.

William Ray was also nearby in the autumn of 1916. His battery served with the II Anzac Corps Heavy Artillery in the winter of 1916-1917 in the region of Armentières. William had been serving

---

[408] War Diary, 2/20th London Battalion, 15th July 1916.
[409] Edwin's Army records, WO 374 29777.
[410] *The Bournemouthian*, December 1916.
[411] *The Bournemouth Visitors' Directory*, 12th August 1916.

as a gunner with the Royal Garrison Artillery since 29th August 1916. He was born in 1896 and was at school from 1912-1915 (as was younger brother Frederick, 1915-1916). He had probably known fellow teacher Percy Pean at the Royal British Orphan School, Slough, from where in January 1916 he enlisted. He must have been in the school O.T.C. as his Army training was very brief: he trained from May 1916, attended a course in plotting and observing, was appointed bombardier on 17th June and arrived in France on 29th August with the 155th Siege Battery of the Royal Garrison Artillery. He wrote that "it is easy at night to follow the trenches, which are not very far off. Machine guns are constantly going and all along the line the star shells are sent up. These make rather a fine sight for they light up all the country like day. Another fine sight that we see nearly every sunny day is the shelling of aeroplanes. The little shrapnel clouds burst without any warning near the aeroplane, which flies very high. After a few seconds the explosion of the shell may be heard, and then other small clouds will appear generally nearer and nearer to the plane. It is not very often, however, that we have to shell German planes, for not many come over, but our own do a good deal of work. German aeroplanes are our chief worry, for we have to be very careful in disguising our positions to give them no information as to our position. Should they get an idea where we were they would very soon send over something and we would have to move—if there was anything to move."[412]

Waiting behind the siege artillery were the cavalry. As always they were meant to be ready to exploit the breakthrough when it should come whilst meanwhile training and waiting. Eric Trask was one of these cavalrymen. Born in 1896, he was at Bournemouth School as a boarder in Mr. Sewell's House from April 1909 to July 1911. When he left school at sixteen it was to go to live and work in Doncaster as an apprentice of the Great Northern Railway Locomotive Works, where he started in September 1911. As part of his apprenticeship he took and passed additional examinations in mechanics and heat engines. His apprenticeship was due to continue until September 1916, and he studied towards the Institute of Mechanical Engineers examination. In the course of this apprenticeship, having reached the age of eighteen, on 28th January 1914 he was proposed for membership of the Institute of Engineers by no less a person than Sir Herbert Nigel Gresley, the famous railway engine designer (subsequently creator of the famous *Mallard*). Yet even whilst he studied for his apprenticeship, Eric maintained an interest in the Territorial forces. In 1912 he had joined the Queen's Own Yorkshire Dragoons as a private trooper, probably beginning his military career in 'C' Squadron based in Doncaster, the headquarters for that cavalry regiment.

Eric and the Yorkshire Dragoons were mobilised for war after the outbreak, and like other units formed different sub-regiments depending on whether or not the men were prepared voluntarily to serve overseas. Eric volunteered to serve in the B.E.F. and was kept in the 1/1st Yorkshire Dragoons. In June, the regiment was split up with 'B' Squadron and the headquarters separated from the others. 'D' Squadron was too small to be of use so its members were added to the other squadrons. From 26th June 1915, Eric and 'C' Squadron were placed within II Corps and the 19th (Western) Division. At this stage they were a select group – six officers and one hundred and thirty-four men, with two members of the R.A.M.C. attached to them. On 19th July, the squadron split into two groups and went by train to Southampton, and across to Le Havre.

Eric then shared the frustrating experience of the cavalry. The squadron was employed in a number of very mundane tasks – guarding reserve trenches (which must have been far back, if only

---

[412] *The Bournemouthian*, December 1916.

a corporal and a couple of men sufficed!); checking out and relaying drains; guarding prisoners; and helping to prepare the rear areas for battle by helping to build casualty clearing stations and such like. They were told that these duties were "until they were required for duty as Mounted Troops for the Advance."[413] Humdrum work like clearing waterways continued, though in September 1915 there was a hint of what was to come when they received an instruction to "take part in a Scheme with Motor Machine Gun Section".[414]

They had been in France nine months before they had suffered their first casualty – a man who was shot in the wrist, receiving a slight wound at the end of March 1916 whilst helping to dig out and build defence works. The Army began to realise that this cavalry provision was an expensive luxury unless they could be given a broader remit. Consequently, on 10th March 1916, two NCOs had begun a course of instruction in the use of the British Maxim machine gun, and others followed. Meanwhile, the rest got some variety from occasional ceremonial duties or from being tasked to carry out traffic control on the roads. In May 1916, the regiment was reorganised to become the Corps Cavalry for II Corps. This took them to Hazebrouck, just across the French frontier from the Ypres Salient. They were present behind the scenes of the battles but they could not be used in the cavalry role for which they had trained. They were, however, often called upon to use their Hotchkiss machine guns to support the infantry in their attacks.

These Hotchkiss machine guns were of French creation, well designed, with a reputation for reliability and relative ease of maintenance. However, they were heavy to use, and by 1916 the British were increasingly turning to the more mobile Lewis guns for infantry use. Men frequently liked the 'stopping power' of the heavy machine guns. In theory they could fire at a rate of 500-600 rounds a minute, though that rate was rarely possible in the field and the magazines (improved in 1915) held a maximum of 249 rounds. Their range of approximately 3,800 metres was a positive factor, provided a line of sight was possible – tricky if the British infantry were advancing in front of the machine-gun position, so they were more successful in a defensive than in an aggressive role.

Despite being in the support role, Eric was eventually wounded by the explosion of a shell. He had been in France about sixteen months when he was hit – in about December 1916. He was sent to a war hospital in Norfolk. At this stage, Eric was optimistic that he would return to the cavalry but as an officer. For this reason he was posted to the 6th Reserve Regiment of Cavalry. This unit trained and held troopers to be available as replacements for the fighting regiments. However, the Army was facing a shortage of horses for the cavalry and a growing need to replace men and extend the numbers of other specialists. Consequently, instead of a commission into the cavalry, Eric was re-trained and on 14th September 1917 was commissioned as a 2nd lieutenant in the Royal Field Artillery. The R.F.A. also used many horses, but this appointment would also allow him to use his engineering skills and talents in a much needed and more active role and it was in this role that he survived the war.

On 7th July 1916, Leslie Gilbert and Alexander Simpson of the 1st Honourable Artillery Company had been joined west of Lens by Haswell Shears. Haswell was born in 1894, and attended the School from 10th March 1909 until 17th December 1910. On 9th November 1915, he enlisted as a private and was eventually sent to join the battalion on the front. When Haswell joined them the

---

[413] War Diary, 'C' Squadron, Queen's Own Yorkshire Dragoons, September 25th 1915.
[414] War Diary, 'C' Squadron, Queen's Own Yorkshire Dragoons, September 18th 1915.

battalion was being used for two purposes: to man trenches and carry out supportive duties, especially digging, but not in the front line; and to train men of promise to give them experience before they might apply for a commission, for which reason a great deal of training was carried out. Indeed, in this period they had a lot to do with the 1/28th London Battalion (Artists' Rifles) who were fulfilling a similar role. When, the next day, 8th July 1916, the battalion moved forward again towards Lens and action, they were led out of camp by the fife and drum band of the Artists' Rifles. A day later they came under the 190th Brigade of the 63rd (Royal Naval) Division.

On 4th August, "Two Companies, A and B, return to the Trenches. After nine months behind the lines, during which some 250 NCOs and men have passed through the ranks of the Battn and received Commissions in the Army, the Battn itself once more becomes a fighting unit and retakes its place in the Line. Most of the officers, many of the NCOs, and some of the men know well what this means & not a few who have been months in training are now to experience for the first time the realities of war. Some are glad to go back, others not so glad, but all are firm in one resolve to do their best whatever may befall them."[415] Alexander was in 'B' Company, so probably went into the trenches in that first wave. On the evening of 8th August, Haswell's 'D' Company went into the trenches for the first time, near Souchez, close to Arras. "Our first Casualties occurred in C and D Companies... They are the first but will not be the last. Lieut Reid (CO. D Co) speaks in the highest terms of the behaviour of the men. Nearly all are town bred and have had little outdoor life. Under conditions so different from any that the men had experienced it was surprising how rapidly and how well they adapted themselves to trench warfare. Calls for volunteers for any job were responded to by all and whatever work given them they carried out with keenness and energy. In trench life there is scanty sleep, and much labour, little comfort and much danger but there was no slackness and great cheerfulness. Tommy refuses to be depressed and never misses the humour of the situation."[416]

They needed this cheerfulness, for in this his first tour in the front line, Haswell's company came under fire from "Minnies, Rifle grenades and Whizz bangs". One day there was also a short exchange of artillery fire. Several men were wounded. From that time, the battalion was in and out of the lines, around Arras. Haswell went off to bombing school at the base from 7th to 15th September, but otherwise he was with 'D' Company as it had tours in the trenches and spells resting or training.

Eric Head left the Western Front at this stage of the war. The 1/9th London Battalion had received considerable reinforcements after the struggle in Leuze Wood on the Somme in September 1916. From 7th to 9th October they had been involved in an unsuccessful but bloody assault at Ginchy. After this the casualties continued to mount. It is not clear if Eric was still with the 1/9th London Battalion, which then was in the trenches near Laventie, north of Lens and south-west of Armentières. From his Army record, it seems he transferred to the Machine Gun Corps, perhaps on 13th December 1916. However, there is no doubt that he suffered: "Lance-Corporal E.K. Head was wounded on February 17th in France, when a piece of shell penetrated his right eye. He was removed to hospital in France, and, later, to the Royal Eye and Ear Hospital, Bradford. Here everything possible was done to try and save the eye, but without success, in spite of three operations. Finally it became necessary to remove the eye and provide him with an artificial substitute. The work has been done very well, and we

---

[415] War Diary, 1st Honourable Artillery Company Battalion, 4th August 1916.
[416] War Diary, 1st Honourable Artillery Company Battalion, 11th August 1916.

congratulate Head on his recovery after such a trying and painful experience."[417] It is unclear what followed for him, and whether he returned to France, though that is unlikely. Certainly he survived the war, and was demobilised in February 1919.

Replacing the Losses and Reinforcing the Battalions

Whilst the bloody battles of 1916 were being fought, the Army made an important alteration to the way in which it formed and trained men to replace the losses of the different battalions.

Before these changes, each battalion had maintained and recruited its own training and reserve unit, normally the 3rd Battalion for the infantry. However, now the casualty rate was so high these reserve battalions were frequently unable to meet the demands placed on them by losses in their front line battalions. This had meant that men who were recruited and trained by one regiment were increasing 'attached' to a completely different regiment for active service. This led to confusions, conflicts of loyalties, and in some cases disappointments. The system had also become cumbersome. Therefore, under the new system, introduced on 4th August, an additional and general 'Training Reserve' was created. The regimental Special Reserve battalions continued, but were kept numerically up to the required numbers from this overall Training Reserve. Whilst the intention was to have this tiered approach allocating men through the regimental system, if need arose drafts of men could also be sent directly from the Training Reserve to front line battalions that urgently needed reinforcements that their 3rd Battalions could not fulfil. Instead of wearing regimental badges, and so fostering regimental 'family' loyalties, the men (including their NCOs) in the Training Reserve, whilst officered by men wearing their own regimental insignia, would themselves wear only badges marked 'T.F.' for Training Force. This meant that some Bournemouth School boys were sometimes switched into the Training Reserve from regiments which they had chosen previously, or were placed in it if they volunteered, or were called up after its introduction. This partly explains the spread of Bournemouth School men ever more widely across the Army regiments, as these effectively ceased to have so much geographical significance.

Cartoon drawn by a Boscombe man and sent to *The Bournemouth Graphic*. Although this cartoon was published in February 1918, it could have been true of the way men were sent to battalions which had no connection with their home towns from almost any time in 1917-1918.

Prisoners of War

Some Old Bournemouthians had been taken prisoner. The issue of British prisoners of war, taken by the Germans on the Western Front, has sparked a good deal of controversy, with some

---

[417] *The Bournemouthian*, July 1917.

historians comparing their treatment unfavourably with that of prisoners taken in the Second World War. It is clear that there were certainly atrocities committed against British prisoners, but others did not suffer so badly. The conditions varied a good deal.

The British government established a branch within the Foreign Office to monitor reports of the treatment of British prisoners. A surprisingly large number of British prisoners escaped from German camps during the war, often because they slipped away from working parties and were able to cross frontiers into neutral countries. These men were questioned in the United Kingdom and provided evidence in London concerning how they were treated. In addition, Swiss and Dutch officials were asked to visit and report on the standards they found in the prison camps – and their reports also showed a wide variation in standards. One man who has left us a detailed account of his experiences as a prisoner was Reginald Fairley.

He had been hit several times at the Battle of Loos, including wounds in the right arm, the left hand, and in his throat which had knocked him out and left him incapacitated.

"…It was absolutely useless for me to attempt any resistance in my disabled state, so I crawled up to the trench, expecting a bullet for my pains. But to my surprise they were awfully decent to me, one fellow saying repeatedly: 'Poor Tommy! Poor Tommy!' Another got out a field dressing and busied himself trying to staunch the blood which literally poured from my throat. Another wiped the blood from my lips, and gave me a drink from his water-bottle. They took off my equipment, and improvised a couple of slings for my arms. The guard informed me it was well for me that it was a Saxon regiment that had taken me. I was lucky, as I should have had a different reception if it had been a Prussian or Bavarian regiment. When we reached the dressing station we found it packed full of wounded Germans, and the stock of bandages had run out. So we kept on till we got to a ruined village. We entered a garden of one house, and an officer came out of the cellar. He questioned me as to my regiment, battalion, brigade, and division. To all of which I replied by shaking my head, and pointing to my mouth. He cursed at me in German, and told the guard to take me away. We then went to another cellar, where I was properly bandaged; they had to cut the front of my shirt away to get at the wounds in my shoulder and right arm. I was then taken to another cellar, in which there were about eight English and Scotch prisoners, and two guards.

"The guards tried to make me a bed of sacks in one corner, but I couldn't lie down, as the blood clogged in my throat and I thought I would choke. So I sat with my head in my hands, and never felt so miserable and depressed in all my life, while the blood dripped from my throat to the floor, for it still bled, despite the thick bandages. After I had been there about an hour a corporal came and said that those who could walk could start for the dressing station behind the firing line, we should have our wounds dressed and be put to bed. So I decided to have a shot for it. We started about 4p.m., and got beyond the trenches by 6p.m. I cannot describe the journey. I was reeling along helped by a man of the Black Watch, who was only slightly wounded. We reached the first station about 6.30, but they would not take me in, but put me in a motor ambulance, and passed two more stations before the one where I was taken in. When the car stopped I was told to get out; and what a sight I must have been. My trouser leg had been slit up to get at the wound in my leg. I was plastered in mud up over my puttees. When I stepped out of the ambulance I saw a lighted doorway, and just had strength enough to make my way through it. I had a confused idea of a large room and a group of men in white jackets, then the whole place went round, and I started falling. One of the doctors rushed forward and caught me, and lowered me to the ground. I did not properly lose consciousness, but have a faint recollection of having my clothes cut off me, and of being sponged all over with hot water, and clean bandages being put on my wounds. The doctor squirted some liquid into the wound in my throat, which seemed to freeze it; it was deliciously cool. I was then given a cup of warm soup, and wrapped in a clean white blanket, placed on a stretcher, and carried out into a street. A few yards down the street we turned into a courtyard, and through a door into a long ward full of white cots, in one of which I was placed, propped up with pillows. The doctor asked me in English if I was comfortable, or was there anything more he could do for me. I replied 'No,' but I couldn't thank him enough for what he had done for me. By his orders my pockets had been emptied, and the contents placed on a little table by my bedside. I thought that ward must have been like heaven, it was so quiet in there, and the bed so clean and soft, and my wounds, now that they were dressed, no longer pained me. I hate the Germans, for I have good reason to. But I must say that doctor was a thorough gentleman, and as tender as a woman in his way of handling a wounded man.

"The food in Dulman Camp is vile, and the prisoners can do with all the parcels they can get. The parcels arrive safely enough, so no one need be afraid to send them on account of the prisoners not getting them. There is a staff of English sergeants, who receive the parcels from a party of prisoners, who fetch them from the railways in large waggons. These sergeants check them and distribute them, so there is no chance of them going astray. If there is any more you want to know, you must wait, as I am quite fed up with writing this letter and recalling those horrible times."[418]

Reginald was selected as being so injured as to be allowed to go to a special camp in Switzerland, "on account of my jaw being still broken". At the frontier, "we were… handed over to a Swiss officer and some Swiss soldiers. At last the train moved off, and in five minutes we were across the border. Then the fun began. The embankment was lined with people, who cheered and showered flowers upon us… All the inhabitants were at the station to see us and give us presents of tobacco, cigarettes, chocolate and huge bunches of flowers. Union jacks and Swiss flags were flying everywhere… Our first stop was Berne: the station was simply packed with people. We could not take the things in fast enough. Huge wreaths of flowers, Swiss and British flags, packets of chocolate and cigarettes, pipes, and tobacco, biscuits, cakes of scented soap, packets of stationery, patent cigarette lighters, combs, razors, folding scissors, huge bunches of roses and lilies tied with red, white and blue ribbons. The carriages were one mass of flowers, and tied on… were cards with 'Welcome glorious soldiers of England,' and 'May your noble country be victorious,' and 'God speed you brave soldiers,' and similar inscriptions. We only stopped about five minutes at Berne… At Montreux about 6 am… the people of this place were even more enthusiastic than the other places. We marched out of the station to the tune of 'Tipperaray,' with a full brass band, to the largest hotel in the place, the Hotel Suisse. The entrance hall was lined on either side with crowds of little girls, dressed in white with little black jackets and big black hats, who cheered us vociferously. Out on the roof garden large tables were laid out for breakfast, and hosts of ladies took charge of us. The hotel was hung with flags all over. After breakfast an old gentleman got up and made speeches to the crowd, finishing up by asking for three cheers for the most noble, the most gallant and heroic British Army, and they were given with a will. The band struck up our National Anthem, the Marseillaise, and the Swiss National Anthem; more cheering. We split up in groups and related our experiences to the ladies and answered their many questions. We took our departure to the railway station, the band playing the same tune as before… At last we reached Chateaux d'Oex.

---

[418] From the first letter to his father passed for publication in *The Bournemouthian*, December 1916.

Here, another reception was prepared for us, and more refreshments... It seems as if all my troubles were over. The valley is perfectly beautiful, surrounded by snow-clad peaks and wooded hills. The hotel at which we were quartered is very nice. Each bed has nice clean sheets, spring mattresses and feather pillows, so different from the prison camp. The night of our arrival a thanksgiving service was held in the Protestant Church. It is next door to the hotel, so we did not have far to go. The church was decorated with flowers and ferns. Large Swiss and British flags hung over the chancel steps, and two Union Jacks were crossed above the altar. The air here is simply wonderful: I feel the benefit of it already. We turn in at 10p.m., and I can assure you we sleep like tops."[419]

Reginald was unlucky to be allowed to go to Switzerland because it indicates the seriousness of his wounds, but lucky in that he went there! In February 1915, the American ambassador to Berlin had reached an agreement with the German and British governments to allow 'limbless and hopelessly invalided' British prisoners to transfer to Switzerland. In May 1916, about 350 additional wounded or disabled men were allowed to switch there from German camps. (Similarly, sometimes British prisoners were switched to Holland.) A British minister who witnessed such a transfer, Grant Duff, said, "...it is difficult to write calmly of it... for the simple reason that I have never before in my life seen such a welcome accorded to anyone..." and *The Times* newspaper reported, "Our men were astounded at the welcome, many were crying like children, a few fainted with emotion. As one private said to the British Minister, 'God bless you sir, it's like dropping right into 'even from 'ell.'"[420] In the end, twelve internment camps were established in Switzerland, and the Red Cross supervised a scheme whereby wives and mothers of those interned were allowed to visit them. Some of the prisoners made a remarkable recovery under Swiss care. Similar schemes were agreed for internment of prisoners in Holland, though somehow that does not sound quite as appealing as a stay in a Swiss hotel in the Bernese Oberland! He was lucky, as typically soldiers allowed such treatment and repatriation to Switzerland were mostly amputees. "Early in the year he took part in some winter sports at Chateau d'Oex, gaining 2nd prize in a Ski race and 3rd in a Luge race."[421]

Most taken prisoners did not get sent to such a welcome in Switzerland but endured the rest of the war as prisoners in Germany, sometimes in difficult conditions. Corporal William Hodges of the 16th London Battalion who had been taken prisoner at Gommecourt on 1st July 1916 had very different experiences.

British prisoners of war under escort in Germany. A photo published in *The Bournemouth Graphic*, 1918.

---

[419] From the second letter published in *The Bournemouthian*, December 1916.
[420] www.prisonersofwar1914-1918documents.com.
[421] *The Bournemouthian*, April 1917.

At the start of the war, the Germans had been taken by surprise by the number of prisoners they took. Their efficient war planning had been devoted to the logistics of driving forward their army to victory, not to how they would treat and manage prisoners. Consequently, the camps to which they were taken were constructed in haste and inadequately. The first prisoners seem to have been rounded up and held prisoner with nothing to do. By summer 1915, the Germans had started to organise their facilities for prisoners: they had set up work camps and begun to send British prisoners to work in mines, forestry, within factories and on farms. As the war continued, labour from prisoners of war formed a vital part of Germany's economy. Officers, including NCOs, were not required to labour like this, though sometimes mistakes happened and junior NCOs might have to argue strenuously for the right not to labour – particularly if their promotions had been made in the field and the paperwork had not caught up with their situation.

The whole process had become more structured by 1916. William would first have been taken to hospital for treatment. (Reports reaching England, and confirmed after the war, revealed that British soldiers were not always well treated in this phase, certainly not as well as in the case of Reginald Fairley.) Then William would have been sent to a prison camp within one of the new military districts set up in Germany, each corresponding to one of the German army corps.

Conditions in the camps varied greatly, largely due to the attitudes of the corps commander, the camp commandant, and their staff. Work details, known then as 'Commandos', were frequently a source of controversy: men were not allowed to work to support an enemy's war production according to the Geneva Protocols, but sometimes there were arguments – for example, if a local commandant tried to get men to work in a munitions factory. There were 'good' camps as at Friedrichsfeld, 'reasonable' camps, and 'awful' ones such as that at Minden. A camp inspector said the contrast was "the difference between day and night, between heaven, relatively, and hell absolutely." There was no centralised German War Ministry setting the standards, so that some commandants were justifiably disliked intensely, whilst others were liked by the prisoners. One commandant, for example, encouraged fraternisation so that a prisoner, Private Jeffrey, described Sunday football matches after which "the guards used to take us to the pub and we'd all have a drink."[422]

When William was taken prisoner, a system of inspections of the camps had been negotiated. National newspapers ran money-raising campaigns to send food parcels to prisoners in Germany, and in March 1915 the War Office had agreed to the creation by appointment of the 'Prisoners of War Help Committee' as a voluntary organisation to "...organise and provide a link between the various POW comfort groups." Different regiments had their own care committees, and every fortnight parcels were sent to Germany, so that each man would receive three parcels of selected food – and in each parcel was a postcard describing its contents to try to prevent stealing before the parcels reached the men. Nevertheless, the British Red Cross were later to report that, "A large percentage of the prisoners were getting too little food; a percentage too much; and it was discovered that parcels were being used for the transmission of prohibited articles... to Germany, and that information likely to be useful to the enemy was being conveyed through the same means."

This unsatisfactory situation led to the replacement of the 'Prisoners of War Help Committee' by a

---

[422] www.prisonersofwar1914-1918documents.com.

'Central Prisoners of War Committee', under the supervision of the Red Cross. This in turn led to a much improved system, and for the rest of the war prisoners usually received regular food parcels without the contraband which had worried both the Red Cross and the War Ministry. A postcard was enclosed for the prisoner to respond to the questions: 'Have you received your parcels regularly?'; 'Were contents in good condition and complete?'; 'Have you received your bread regularly?' and there was a place to write their name and address. Analysis of the returned postcards suggests that apart from the bread not always getting to its intended recipient, the rest of the system worked quite well.

Short article in *The Bournemouth Graphic*.

Local newspapers like *The Bournemouth Graphic* and shops like that of the Hudson Brothers of Old Christchurch Road in Bournemouth placed adverts not only for providing parcels for the troops in the trenches ("We have forwarded innumerable cases of goods [through the Post Office]… not one single case has been lost in transit."), but also for prisoners like William, though special arrangements were needed for Christmas deliveries: "Information has been received from Germany that owing to the great stress of work in the Post Office at Christmas, they will neither accept nor despatch parcels for prisoners of war from 10th to 25th December. If senders of parcels desire that parcels sent to prisoners of war before the 10th December should not be delivered before Christmas Eve, then 'Weihnachts-Paket' must be shown prominently on the parcel. Parcels thus marked (the contents of which should not be perishable) will be held over by the commandants of prisoner of war camps until Christmas Eve."[423] A few weeks later the same newspaper showed a specimen food parcel which had been sent by the East Dorset Guild of Workers.[424]

If he were lucky enough to be in a well-run camp, a soldier like William might even set up small enterprises such as printing camp magazines, postcards or paintings. There could be a canteen where prisoners could buy bacon and eggs, bread and butter, or tea or coffee. Sometimes there were even small 'shops' where prisoners became cobblers, tailors, or watchmakers. Theatrical productions could be produced, and in at least one camp, inmates formed a police force with their own police station. Currently, however, we do not know where William was sent or the conditions under which he was detained.

---

[423] From an advert in *The Bournemouth Graphic*, 17th November 1916.
[424] *The Bournemouth Graphic*, 15th December 1916.

Sometimes the British prisoners had a dreadful time – reminiscent of the worst excesses of the Second World War. Some were sent to punishment or retribution camps – not necessarily because they themselves had done anything, but because the Germans were angry about something the British had done. In such cases, men could be starved or even exposed to die in the harsh winter conditions of the German-Polish border. Sometimes the ill treatment seems to have been caused by acts of spite or barbarity. Although one must be cautious in accepting newspaper articles, not least in wartime, it is never the less grim to read in 1917 that "the camp guards took a fiendish delight in setting savage wolf hounds to attack unoffending men, and many were very seriously bitten. Another favourite pastime was to have the men shaved all over with blunt razors, which tore the hairs out by the roots. This kind of treatment was varied by assaults with rifle butts and bayonets, and one man, a petty officer belonging to H.M.S. Maori, was bayonetted through the spine. This story is made up of the evidence of officers and men who had been returned from captivity, taken by the Government Committee on the Treatment by the enemy of British Prisoners of War."[425]

One particularly notorious camp with a particularly awful commandant was at Holzminden. It was close to another bad camp at Ströhen, and in December 1917 it was noted that officers held there were only pleased that they were not at Holzminden. It was said that the commandant was "a German who has spent much of his time in America, is now at Holzminden. This man treats the prisoners as brutally as possible, and it was owing to their complaints that he was moved from Ströhen. The officers fear that any camp which is under him will be an uncomfortable place."[426]

Even with a system of inspections, poor conditions and even atrocities did continue. "I would like to tell you something of what our boys in Germany have gone through. I was in a batch of 20 men, 10 belonged to the Dorset Regiment. We were sent to an iron mine, and we wouldn't work. They took all our clothes from us, and fitted us in old rags. They made us stand in the open from 4am until 10pm without any bread or water. Then we were locked up for the night, and the same occurred the next four days. That was five whole days without a mouthful of bread or water. Then they put us in solitary confinement on bread and water for one month, then packed us off to another working camp. This was in 1916. They had stopped us from receiving our parcels and letters. We carried on for about nine months like this, and then we got sent all over the country in one's and two's. I eventually found myself at a Zeppelin shed. Of course, I wouldn't work there: more cells on bread and water. Whilst there I saw a Zeppelin, L29 I think it was, go up on a raid over England, but was very pleased it didn't come back. It came down in Essex."[427]

The Work of the Field Ambulance

Back on the Western Front, the work of the field ambulance was crucial. John Williams served in such a unit in 1916-1917. John, born in 1889, was an early member of the school (1903-1906). He had been a prefect and an athlete. After he left school, he and his family had emigrated to British Columbia, and there he studied medicine at Victoria University. When the war broke out, he

---

[425] *The Bournemouth Visitors' Directory*, 26th May 1917.

[426] From a letter by Adelaide Livingstone, Hon Sec. to the Government Committee on the Treatment by the Enemy of British Prisoners of War, 3rd December 1917, in which she enclosed a coded letter concerning these atrocities smuggled out from a Captain Tollemache via an escaped officer; FO 383/275.

[427] Extract from a letter from Private Banbury, a soldier of the 1st Dorsets, written from internment in Holland in 1918, read out at a meeting of the Dorset Guild of Workers by Lady Wimborne, and quoted in *The Bournemouth Visitors' Directory*, 31st August 1918.

"returned to help his motherland".[428]

The Army quickly put him to work in the Royal Army Medical Corps, in the 9th Field Ambulance which he joined in 1916, which was in the Guards Division.

A field ambulance was a mobile unit, working at brigade level in support of the fighting battalions. However, it was not a vehicular ambulance, like the modern use of the word, but rather something closer to an emergency hospital. Three were attached to each division. Each was under the command of a lieutenant colonel – in 1914, such an ambulance required ten officers and two hundred and twenty-four men. It would have been placed fairly near to where the men were fighting so that it could receive sick or wounded men who had been passed back from the front line first aid posts where they would have been given basic first aid treatment. When the field ambulance received such men, they had to make quick decisions whether, if the casualty was only slightly wounded or not very sick, they could treat him quickly and send him back to his unit. On the other hand, they might decide to give the casualties enough emergency treatment that they could then move them back to a casualty clearing station. They would do this by establishing a relay line ('Bearer Relay Posts') which could move men from the regimental first aid station through the advanced dressing station and on to the main dressing station.

Initially the ambulances relied on stretchers and wagons pulled by horses to move the sick or wounded, but by the end of 1914 they had a number of motor vehicles as well. In theory they were equipped to deal with up to one hundred and fifty men, but in times of crisis John and the rest could have to deal with more. As the unit carried out its task, John and the others in the field ambulance carried no weapons. They were not safe – shells bursting, or stray machine-gun bullets could hit them, but John worked unscathed for a time and rose up the hierarchy so that by 1917 he was a sergeant.

At the start of 1916, the 9th Field Ambulance was at Estaires, south of Bailleul, but it moved at the end of February further north to Herzeele, inside the French border, west of Poperinghe. Then, on 16th March, the ambulance moved forward to establish its dressing station in a convent in Poperinghe, and an advanced post of two officers and six men in dug-outs on the canal bank immediately north of Ypres, now known as Essex Farm. (This forward position still exists today as a major battlefield site for visitors. It was where, in 1915, the famous *In Flanders Fields* poem had been written by John McCrae). Sometimes, even in a unit as specialised as a field ambulance, they were given futile orders: at Poperinghe, an inspecting officer "suggested that an attempt be made to pump out the water from the one small cellar in the buildings occupied, so that it could be used as a place of refuge in the event of the place being shelled... the cellar was pumped out. It is impossible to take stretcher cases into it. It has no roof other than the wooden flooring of the room above, and is so small and low that it is considered to be more than useless."[429] Three days later the commander ruefully reported in the war diary that the cellar which they had pumped dry was again flooded with water.

The same day as they were ordered to pump the cellar, "Between 5.45 and 7pm the immediate vicinity of the dressing station was shelled... with what was probably an 8 inch gun; 68 shells are said to have fallen. There were about 25 patients in the dressing Station at the time. These were

---

[428] *The Bournemouth Visitors' Directory*, 30th March 1918.
[429] War Diary, 9th Field Ambulance, 10-11th April 1916.

assembled in the room facing S.S.E. on the ground floor of the convent. The personnel of the unit were cleared out of their billets in the upper stories of the convent. The 5th or 6th shell fell in the court-yard of the Convent among the motor ambulance cars. A Ford car was wrecked and the canvas of two Napiers was torn to pieces. About half an hour after the bombardment commenced, verbal messages arrived to the effect that about 5 stretchers were required to bring in men wounded some 250 yards along the main road from the Dressing Station. No. 1856 Sergeant F. Crowe RAMC and bearers at once went out voluntarily to collect these cases. As they were putting the wounded on the stretchers a shell exploded among them, killing or wounding every member of the party... This is another regrettable instance of what constantly happens. Whenever there is any idea of anyone having been wounded, the cry for stretcher-bearers is raised without any consideration being given to the severity of the wound which the patient in question is suffering from, or to the additional risk he is made to run by being brought from one place to another whilst the shelling is going on. On such occasions one finds most bearers only too willing to risk themselves in an endeavour to save others, but when they arrive where the wounded are, more often than not they find that their presence is not required, because the case is not a stretcher one, or because it has already died, or that the patient is in a sufficiently safe place to make his removal to a Dressing Station, whilst the shelling continues, unjustifiable. In the present instance 3 men had been killed and 2 wounded by a shell. The wounded were both in a comparatively safe house, and it was thus, in an effort to bring them from there to the dressing station that the above posted casualties occurred, and in addition, the Medical officer 1st Irish Guards and his RAMC Corporal were also wounded whilst attending to these same cases."

When they were withdrawn from the combat zone to Watou, the 'rest' that men like John enjoyed was to be spent on tasks such as road building and repairs, though there was perhaps some additional interest when the unit was visited by the Prince of Wales on 28th May. This 'rest' period was co-ordinated to coincide with a similar period for the whole Guards Division to which they were attached, and then, on 16th June, they returned to Poperinghe and the advanced dressing station in Ypres. The commander described the arrangements in place for the collection of the sick and wounded, something which John must have experienced: "Sick and wounded are collected from 3 battalions in the front line trenches, from 2 battalions in support and 2 in reserve. With the exception of those in reserve, the collection is done at Canal Bank dugouts, where 2 Officers and 40 Other Ranks are stationed. Eight of these other ranks are attached to Battalion Headquarters for conveyance of cases from Regimental Aid Post to Field Ambulance Dugout. Little or no collection is done from front line trenches in daylight. An Ambulance car is posted at Reigersberg Chateau for urgent cases. It is able to proceed to the dugouts in daylight. Ordinary cases are collected at night. Three cars leave here for canal bank dugouts – 5 ½ miles distant – at 10.30pm. Just before dawn (3am.), 2 cars proceed to make another collection. Except where there is an unusual number of cases, this is expected to be sufficient."[430] Another entry, at the end of July, reminds us that even men behind the lines suffered from some of the same issues as the infantry further forward: "Much damage has been done to kits and equipment by rats in the dugouts the men have occupied during the past 6 weeks."[431]

At the start of August, the 9th Field Ambulance moved, with the Guards Division, south to the edge of the Somme battlefield. There they served the men of their division, mainly behind the lines

---

[430] War Diary, 9th Field Ambulance, 17th June 1916.
[431] War Diary, 9th Field Ambulance, 28th July 1916.

north-west of Beaumont-Hamel, although at the very end of the month they moved to the south of Albert and moved into position to provide medical aid for the major attacks of 15th September in the south of the battlefield. At this time the men of the bearer divisions within the unit followed a three day rotation – working in the forward area on the infrastructure whilst acting as reserve bearers, then working as bearers to bring in the wounded to the advanced dressing stations, and the third day returning to unit headquarters for a rest. Their advanced dressing station was at Guillemont.

15th September meant a lot of work for the field ambulance as they managed to support the fighting units of their division. "Later – about 12.30pm – when the enemy's barrage had slackened off, all the available bearers were employed collecting cases. They continued almost continuously at work until nearly 4am, when, with the exception of a few wounded Germans few, if any, cases remained uncollected... Horsed ambulances kept the loading post... clear, and evacuated to the main Dressing Station by motor ambulance cars. Walking wounded followed the same route... The number of cases passed through was not recorded, it was estimated at over 2500, with a very large proportion of stretcher cases, and included great numbers from the 6th and 14th Divisions who operated on our right and left respectively."[432] A similar workload was carried through the next day, but there was a cost: "It is regretted that the casualties were heavy. No 9 Field Ambulance lost 6 killed and 13 wounded... The bearer divisions were all very much under strength when the work commenced, and sickness also diminished their numbers. The total stretcher-bearer strength when we were relived was under 150."[433]

When they returned to action a few days later it was to even muddier conditions because of the rain. The men had to carry the wounded out because even the horse-drawn ambulances could not get forward through the mud. They then prepared to support the attack of 25th September, even though a German shell hit their advanced dressing station, which had to be relocated in another part of an old German trench. As they tried to support this attack they found themselves unable to keep pace with the casualties, and wounded men had to be kept in the forward area, sometimes overnight, though they did their best for them, providing blankets and hot drinks and administering aid at the loading posts to the most urgent cases. All the bearers were committed and had to carry the wounded in across open ground. Fortunately, things calmed down over the next few days, but even so, when they were relieved the three ambulances which worked together had lost four killed and thirty wounded, of whom one killed and twelve wounded came from John's unit.

In October they were given a break, being relocated west of Amiens and away from the fighting. It must have been cheering news at the start of November when leave was re-instated – thirty-seven NCOs and men had been continuously in France and without leave since 1st November 1915, and one hundred more similarly since 1st May 1916, probably including John.

From 12th November 1916, however, elements of the 9th Field Ambulance were back clearing men from the vicinity of Delville Wood back to Bernafay Wood. Battalion stretcher-bearers would collect their own men and bring them in to the advanced dressing stations, where the men of the field ambulance picked them up and carried them back to the loading post for the horse

---

[432] War Diary, 9th Field Ambulance, 15th September 1916.
[433] War Diary, 9th Field Ambulance, 17th September 1916.

ambulances. Fortunately, there tended to be only about fifteen casualties to evacuate each day at this stage, which was just as well: the battalion stretcher-bearers had to carry their men about 2,500 yards and the ambulance stretcher-bearers about 3,000 yards – across open ground and with only partially duck-boarded access routes.

In contrast, despite deaths and woundings from German shelling, the unit had a quieter time for the rest of the month, and through December, though remaining for most of that time in the southern Somme Sector.

On 19th March 1917, as the guards advanced when the Germans retired to the Hindenburg Line, the field ambulance set up a series of relay stations to bring cases back to Combles. The nature of the unit war diary changed over these months, and the experiences of the ordinary personnel were mentioned less frequently than before, and John was not mentioned by name. Even so, for him, there was always another enemy lurking. On 16th April 1917, John succumbed to kidney disease whilst serving in France. Sick, he too had been taken back through the casualty chain, but he died in a hospital in Rouen. From there he was taken to a new extension to the St. Sever Cemetery, which had been opened up the previous September, and was buried far from Bournemouth and even further from his parents in British Columbia.

The Use and Development of Poison Gas

We have already noted that from 1915 both sides began the use of poison gas, starting with chlorine gas. Alexander Corbet's experiences in the latter part of the war illustrate how the use of gas developed.

Alexander had only left school in December 1915. He was born in 1896. He received notice to attest under the Derby Scheme at Bournemouth on 18th January 1916. His age was satisfactory and his height acceptable, but his physique was deemed 'poor' and when his eyes were tested they were found to be defective, and therefore he was not accepted for military service. He was issued with an armlet to wear to show that he was not shirking his duty and was placed in the Army Reserve. Alexander moved to Reading where he began a course in chemistry.

In January 1917, he received a notice offering him the chance to report for service overseas with the Royal Engineers. It was explained, "Men with training in Chemistry are required for service" and that "Ordinary standards of height and chest measurement will be waived, provided the candidate is organically sound and fit for service in the field. The eyesight test may be passed with the aid of glasses." It explained about the pay and rank, and stated, "If you are willing to enlist under these conditions, you are requested to take this circular to the nearest Recruiting Officer, who is hereby directed to medically examine you, and if you are passed fit, give you Army Form B.178 (Medical History Sheet) and a railway warrant to London." Alexander was anxious to play his part, and on 13th January 1917 he reported to the Royal Engineers at Whitehall and was enlisted despite his damaged left cornea. He was even officially rated medically 'A1'.

The Royal Engineers wanted him for the Special Gas Brigade. He was not in England long, as the Army bypassed most of the normal military training to smooth the passage of a specialist – on 21st March 1917 he was sent to France to join No.2 Special Company, 19 Special Brigade.

The Germans had been the first to switch from cylinders to delivering gas by shells filled with liquid gas. From June 1916, they had begun using 'Green Cross' shells filled with di-phosgene, initially against the French, and then also against the British. On 22nd August 1916, they had sent their new development, phosgene gas, by shells against Martinpuich on the Somme. The R.E. Special Brigades had begun to use Livens projectors (a crude, but effective, type of mortar) or their new 4-inch Stokes mortar to send gas across. Livens projectors were first used at Beaumont-Hamel at the end of October 1916 and were first used on a large scale at Arras on 9th April 1917.

In 1917, at the Third Battle of Ypres, the Germans would go on to deploy the most terrible of all the gases – mustard gas. Instead of mixing with moisture in the enemy's respiratory system, mustard gas (dichlorethylsulphide) acted on any exposed moist areas – most famously eyes, lungs, armpits or groin (particularly deadly for Scots soldiers). It created large burn blisters and could kill painfully over days. Heavier than air, it tended to settle in shell craters.

Alexander was clearly needed to help defend against such dreadful horrors and in devising British-made terrors to send against the Germans. In August 1917 he was to fall casualty, probably to gas in some form. He was admitted to No. 24 Hospital on 27th August 1917, at the huge British centre at Étaples, south of Boulogne. On 1st September 1917 he was transferred back to England where he was sent to the 2nd London (Chelsea) Hospital from 1st September to 2nd October – for treatment for ulcerated keratitis – an extremely serious infection causing ulceration of the cornea which can easily degenerate into blindness. From early in 1915 it had been decided to send all patients with badly damaged eyes to this hospital. By 1917 it could take 170 officers and 974 other ranks, all blinded or with severe eye damage.

Alexander was fortunate. The damage to his eyes was not permanent and eventually he was rated 'C1' and returned to duty. There continued, however, to be complications, and he was again in hospital at the end of the year – in the Military Hospital, Devonport, from 27th December 1917 to 15th January 1918, once again with corneal ulcer. After that he then spent some time at the Special Brigade Base Depot.

6: 1917 on the Western Front

On 6th May 1917, Gunner Harold Spicer died without getting to France, though he was preparing to go there. The younger brother of Henry, who was also a member of the school and who served in the Middle East with the Wiltshire Regiment, Harold was born in 1898 and was at school between 1910 and 1913. On 15th January 1917 he enlisted in the 15th Reserve Battery, Royal Field Artillery. As he was preparing to go to France on 28th April he contracted erysipelas and meningitis. He was taken to hospital in Salisbury, but could not be saved. After his death he was taken home and buried at St. John's Church, Moordown. He was just nineteen. Such an early death is always tragic. One could argue whether or not Harold was a victim of the war, but his illness was contracted whilst he was serving and preparing for the front.

The health of the soldiers, behind, and on, the front, was always an important issue for commanders. The conditions in the trenches caused physical and mental health issues, quite apart from the issues presented by enemy action. For example, the adjutant of Percy Robertson's 6th Welsh Battalion described conditions at Loos on 1st April 1916: "Owing to the hot weather, the trenches have already started to smell a lot. The C.O. was bad in the night – probably owing to the escape of acetylene gas from our lamp. We have now 'strafed' the lamp & use candles instead."[434] Leaking gas lamps, accidental poisoning, thick and slimy mud were bad enough, but there were so many other hazards: blood poisoning from rusty barbed wire; rotting body parts in the mud; rats and other vermin; trench latrines, and much more. Disease was a problem all through the war, and the Army recognised that one key to survival was to encourage good hygiene – very, very difficult in trench warfare. Therefore, all units were given opportunities to bathe or shower at least once a month if possible. The unit war diaries always make mention of these opportunities, which could require two days to get a whole battalion clean.

Bombardier William Ray described such bathing in April 1917. "We are near a village which is used for billeting and contains an old dye works, which has been turned into a bathing establishment. This is like the baths illustrated some time ago in one of the weekly papers. Clean underclothes are exchanged for one's dirty linen, and tunics and trousers are fumigated. Meanwhile the luxury of a bath in hot water is indulged in, and after the process is completed you feel like a different person."[435]

Mental health was a major issue. Too many men suffered from 'shell shock' for the problem to be ignored, and specialist hospitals were established to treat them. But prevention was better than cure, and for this reason some battalions, brigades or divisions encouraged positive measures to relax the men. These could include humorous trench newspapers like the famous *Wipers Times* but also included variety shows, often with men dressed as Pierrots. These were a popular form of entertainment (even being enjoyed back in Bournemouth). For example, Leslie Hands of the 11th Royal Fusiliers had the opportunity of seeing such a show in the training interlude between their services on the Somme: "Concerts were given by the 54th Brigade Pierrot Troupe and were well patronised by all ranks."[436] Perhaps the dressing up in clown gear gave men a welcome escape of

---

[434] War Diary, 6th Welsh Regiment, 1st April 1916.
[435] *The Bournemouthian*, April 1917.
[436] War Diary, 11th Royal Fusiliers, 9th January 1917.

from the reality and horrors of the trenches and of the battles. William Ray also mentioned such recent recreation: "Another feature of the neighbourhood is a 'theatre', in which concerts are given by a party of officers and men from the Division. A visit to this performance forms a pleasant break in the monotony of winter fighting."

Men's spiritual needs were catered for by the padres and organised church services. Physical needs were met when possible. Some days within a period when a unit was resting and training might be given over to games of football or to running or other athletic competition, sometimes within a battalion, and sometimes with a brigade or even a division.

Artilleryman Edward Ivamy was another whose physical ill health was impaired by service on the Western Front. He was born in 1892 and attended the school from September 1906 to October 1908, in receipt of a Bournemouth scholarship. At school he was a member of the O.T.C. He was mobilised on 22nd May. After a period of training in which he moved around the country and passed as a 1st class signaller and telephonist at Shoreham in September 1916, he was placed in 237 Battery R.G.A. and prepared to go off to the Western Front. In the autumn of 1916 he was promoted to bombardier. On 6th January 1917, he reached Codford where his battery received its guns: four 6-inch howitzers. They sailed from Portsmouth to Le Havre on 23rd January.

From Le Havre they had encountered difficulties moving up to the front. The roads were covered with ice and snow, which made the going hard. Eventually they reached Ypres, where for several weeks they were based at the convent buildings. Their position was heavily shelled, and three of their guns were destroyed. They moved their remaining gun to Brielen Farm to await replacements. On 2nd April 1917, they joined the 88th Heavy Artillery Group near Vlamertinghe. (A heavy artillery group was a flexible unit. The batteries in it could be moved between groups depending on the need as it arose. Their 6-inch howitzers fired 100-pound shells capable to hitting up to six thousand yards away.) Two days later, Edward applied for a commission and on 21st May 1917 he left France and returned to England – and never went back to the front. He was commissioned on 31st December 1917 as 2nd lieutenant R.G.A. signalling instructor with Northern Command. He remained with them into 1918 (and was promoted lieutenant) before eventually receiving his discharge (on the grounds of ill health – his asthma having been worsened by his service) in 1920.

Ronald Budden coped. Born in October 1897, he joined the school in September 1910. Although delicate of health in his younger years, he grew in strength and confidence and by the time he had left school he had spent four years in the O.T.C., becoming a corporal. He left at the end in July 1915, aged 18, to become an officer cadet at Sandhurst. He started there in August 1915. He was gazetted 2nd lieutenant in the 1st Worcestershire Battalion, on 7th April 1916. In his photograph as an officer he looks so much older than his eighteen or nineteen years.

Ronald Anderson Budden.

He landed in France on 21st September 1916 to join his battalion which had been in trenches outside Vermelles, just south of La Bassée. The unit was suffering daily from the bloody effects of German trench mortars. In the middle of October 1916, the battalion had marched down to the

Somme where they suffered heavy casualties. "The Battalion had a very rough time… as enemy's artillery was very active and trenches afforded little cover. The greatest difficulty was found in the matter of supply as all rations and water had to be brought up by pack animal and man handling 5 or 6 miles over an endless waste of shell holes, which in conjunction with the wet weather became a sticky mass of wet mud".[437] Ronald shared the danger in these later stages of the Battle of the Somme, even though his battalion was involved in no attacks, only in holding trenches. Officers and men were still killed by the shell fire, until in mid-November they were pulled out of the action to billets west of Amiens. Most of the winter months – especially December 1916 and January 1917 – were spent in training for attacks and in cross-country running to build fitness. Ronald and the rest suffered the bad weather as stoically as they could, and in February they were back in the trenches north of Peronne on the Somme as the Germans began to pull back to their formidable Hindenburg Line.

On 5th February, he wrote to his old headmaster describing these conditions: "I am writing this sitting on a bench by a brazier which is doing its utmost to smoke me out, and trying to balance the writing-pad on my knee in such a way that I get the light from the candle and keep warm, for it's bitterly cold, though much better than the rain and mud we had before. This time I did not go into the trenches with the Battalion – the first time since I've been out here – but was left out as O.C. Details, i.e. being in charge of the men left out, such as shoemakers, Regt. Police, and spare men to replace casualties. The other night I went up to B.H.Q. so as to know the way up in case at any time I was wanted. It took me four hours to get up to H.Q.'rs. – four miles of communication trench!! – and of course four hours to get back, so had quite an interesting walk as the view was miles of snow-covered ground. I was very interested watching Fritz bomb a small town a few nights ago. It's really very interesting when you are some way off."[438]

He was hoping later in February to go on a sniping course. However, he was soon back with the battalion, in the trenches, and in action. On 4th March he took part in a successful attack and the capture of two lines of German trenches, an attack which demonstrated how much was being learned by the Army in the effective use of both the creeping barrage and also the effective deployment of the light Lewis guns. Most casualties came from incessant German counter-artillery fire trained on what had been their own front line (and for which they therefore had accurate distances calibrated).

After the Somme: The German Retreat to the Hindenburg Line

Since the 1960s, because of the terrible casualty rate, it has become traditional to see the Battle of the Somme as a complete British disaster but in recent years historians have started to try to correct the imbalance of that judgement. After the war, some leading German generals wrote describing the battle as a decisive one in the path to German defeat. Certainly, at the end of 1916 the Germans decided that they could not afford to hold the line to which they had been forced back in the battle. Construction was undertaken of a new defence line, known to the British as the Hindenburg Line. This was several miles further east, beyond the range of anything other than British or French air attack. The Germans were able to build it with a measure of security for the men working on it, and they incorporated into it all the latest and most advanced techniques for

---

[437] War Diary, 1st Worcesters Battalion, 31st October 1916.
[438] *The Bournemouthian*, April 1917.

trench construction and defence. Their progress in the east against Russia had been surprisingly positive, and this strengthened their determination to create a defence line they could hold whilst they minimised their western casualties. This would let them release men for a major effort against Russia in 1917. Their problem was that once they had completed the new line, they needed to be able to extricate their advanced units with as few casualties as possible and pull them back to their new line. Any pursuit would need to be contained to ensure that the new line was not breached in the inevitable confusion of pulling their men back into it.

Leslie Hands of the 11th Royal Fusiliers Battalion had survived the Battle of Thiepval in September 1916 and the return in October to 'Regina Trench', a position a little north of Courcelette and east of Thiepval. The battalion was designated to assault Petit Miraumont, to their north, across the River Ancre. Though planned several times, in each case the attack was called off. According to one fusilier officer, this was a great relief, for "The weather was awful, and the mud beyond words. Fortunately, the attack did not come off. If it had it must have been a colossal failure. The first objective was, I believe, 1,700 yards away, and in that mud, and after going that distance, the men would have been dead-beat. The Brigade was to go on to the Ancre, cross the river, which was in flood and about 300 yards wide, and hold the crossings for the 53rd Brigade to go through. It was seriously suggested that trees might be felled across the Ancre, and the men might cross on them. The only implements for felling trees were bayonets, entrenching tools, and jack-knives!" The same officer explained, "Each time we went in for the attack the men were served out with a haversack ration of potted-meat sandwiches and a hard-boiled egg. Major Meyricke, on the telephone from battalion headquarters, used to inform the company commanders that the attack had been postponed again by the words, 'You may eat your sandwiches!' – for, if the attack was off, they could eat them whenever they liked, if they had not already done so. The men were soaked to the skin with liquid mud for days on end, and after ration-carrying fatigues, were dead-beat. It was a long carry, and the mud was appalling. On relief the men sometimes did not get back to Albert till 6a.m., and had no opportunity of getting properly dry before they went in the line again. The sick rate in the battalions at this time was the worst I have ever known. One morning each battalion in the Brigade had over 150 sick, and one had nearly 250. Eventually the attack was postponed till the New Year, and we were relieved by the Canadians."[439] Let us hope that Leslie Hands enjoyed boiled eggs.

On 17th January 1917, they were back at the Regina Trench, looking north towards Petit Miraumont. Though there was no new offensive, the Germans maintained intermittent shelling. The weather was an even greater enemy – a continual hard frost froze the water in the bottom of the trench. This, unfortunately, left only about eighteen inches of cover between the ice and the top of the parapet, so they had to keep low and cold. Yet even in such circumstances, the men looked for ways to make the best of it. Men from the different battalions in the brigade discovered that they could use their helmets for unofficial games of 'curling'. Apparently, sometimes even the Germans enjoyed watching these games, but then angered the British by deciding after a time to disrupt the games by firing trench mortars at them. In this period the duck-boards, usually a most

---

[439] From an original account by a Royal Fusilier, 11th Battalion, quoted within *The 54th Infantry Brigade 1914-1918; Some Records of Battle and Laughter in France*, Gale and Polden Ltd., Wellington Works. Aldershot, London and Portsmouth (Printed for private circulation only), by 'E.R.' of the Headquarters 54th infantry Brigade, March 1919, pp. 72-73; also quoted in *The Royal Fusiliers in the Great War*, H.C. O'Neill, London, William Heinemann, 1922, p. 142.

important and useful way of getting through the mud, became icy, wooden, skating tracks. The men took to wrapping their boots in sand-bags to help them keep their foothold; marginally to warm them; and to cut down the noise, as the Germans listened for the clicking of boots on the ice, and fired at the sounds.

On 9th February 1917, they went back into the front line, and 'A' Company launched a raid on a German trench the next night. Two 2nd lieutenants led the platoons in an attack on a German strongpoint. They managed to capture the position, but the Germans concentrated a very heavy machine-gun and grenade fire on the garrison. Both officers and the N.C.O.s became casualties, and the Germans recovered the position in a violent counter-attack. The few men remaining were forced back to the British line.

After a last three-day absence, Leslie and his comrades were again in the front line on the night of 15th-16th February, prepared to take part in an attack which the British were launching along both sides of the River Ancre. At that point, having briefly flowed roughly east to west between Thiepval and Miraumont, the river turned north again. The intention was to capture the high ground east of the Ancre to deny the Germans their opportunity to observe the British positions and to weaken the German defences at Serre, which the batteries on the high ground supported. The 54th Brigade was designated to attack: the 11th Royal Fusiliers were on the left, the 6th Northamptonshires on the right. "Just why the weather had such frequent pro-German moods during the war is a question to be discussed in a more scientific book than this. But the fact remains that the hard frost, which would have given us almost ideal ground to attack over, broke on the night of the 16th, and most of our troubles were due to the appalling mud which resulted from the untimely thaw."[440]

It was a dark and misty night. They formed up in front of a depression known as the 'Gully', from which a sunken road led to Boom Ravine. To get there they had to cross the German wire, and the Grandcourt Trench. All the way the land was filled with shell holes and the churned up ground was knee deep in mud. The forming up lines had been taped, despite hostile fire and shelling, between one and two hundred yards in front of the Gully. Before they had left their positions to form up, each man was given a hot meal, and in his mess tin carried his bully beef sandwich and his hard-boiled egg.

By 4.45a.m. the men were formed up ready. They had gone forward, either along the single communication trench or along the single duck-board. It was very congested. They were not aware that the Germans had learned in advance of the attack, and were waiting for them. "It must be remembered that the night was pitch dark and the duck boards and trenches were getting greasy and slippery. By 5.30am all Coy's were reported formed up and ready, but not before they had sustained heavy casualties, especially in the case of the right assaulting Coy who had three shells land amongst the platoons killing one officer and a lot of NCOs and men. The enemy had quite obviously spotted the attack, for from 4.30am onwards he kept up a steady bombardment of our forming up lines, and it was especially severe along the Gully and at Oxford Circus."[441] There was no shelter for the fusiliers and they were a compact mass offering an easy target. "It was in the pitchy dark hours before dawn, rain was falling, the ground was deep in slippery mud, and there

---

[440] *The 54th Infantry Brigade 1914-1918; Some Records of Battle and Laughter in France*, Gale and Polden Ltd., Wellington Works. Aldershot, London and Portsmouth (Printed for private circulation only), by 'E.R.' of the Headquarters 54th infantry Brigade, March 1919, p. 77.
[441] War Diary, 11th Royal Fusiliers, Special Report on battle of 17th February 1917.

were no trenches to guide to the forming-up line. One platoon of the Northamptonshire Regiment was almost entirely wiped out as it was led to the forming-up place; and of the total Fusilier casualties in the whole of the operation, one-half were suffered in the Gully and thereabouts. That the battalions were formed up at all, in this dark mouth of hell, was due very largely to their gallant and skilful handling by officers and N.C.Os., and to the courage and discipline of the men themselves, many of whom lay in the mud for hours under heavy shell fire, awaiting the order to go over the top. That, after the terrible ordeal before dawn, they fought their way forward so well as to snatch a very large measure of success out of what might so nearly have been utter disaster speaks volumes for their doggedness and dash."[442] Then "the Fusiliers leapt forward at zero as though no hour of horror had preceded it."[443]

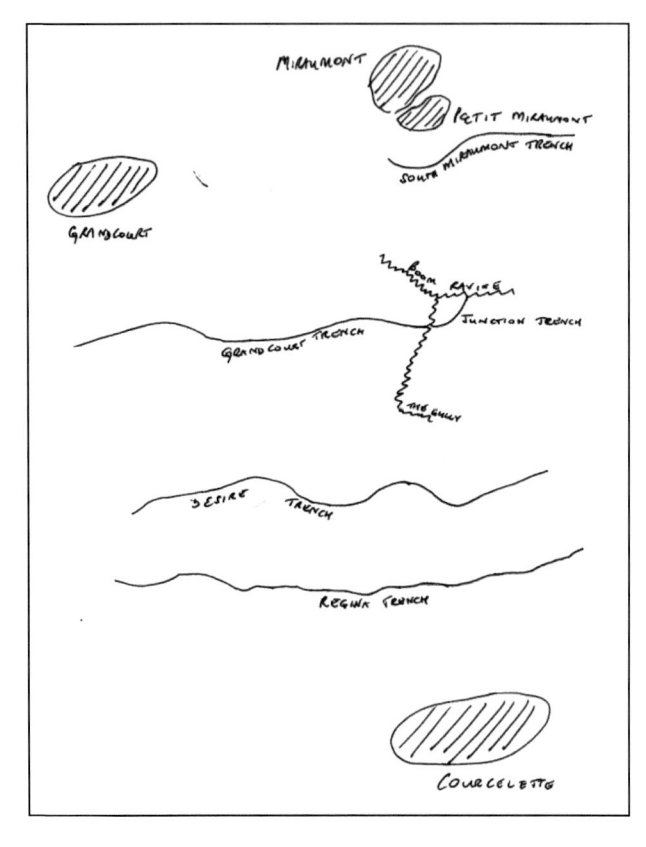

At 5.45a.m., the British barrage opened and the men went forward, as close to the barrage as they could manage. The battalion was accompanied by a single company of the 12th Middlesex Battalion. It was hell as they slipped through the mud in the darkness and drizzling rain, smashed by German bombardment, machine-gun fire and sniping, though their trench mortar battery and machine gunners did their best to put the heads of the Germans down. Fortunately, the German counter-bombardment was relatively short lived, perhaps because of the accuracy of the British bombardment. But "the sniping and machine gun fire must have been very heavy if only from the fact that not one of the officers got further than the wire of Grandcourt Trench, and of all those that started at 'Zero Hour', not one was killed or wounded by shells. Throughout the operations it was remarkable the high percentage of men that were hit through the head, showing beyond a doubt that these Germans who had to meet us were no mean marksmen."[444]

When they reached the wire of Grandcourt Trench it was found to be unbroken. The delay, whilst a way through was found, gave the Germans time to reorganise their defence, and led to further bunching and mixing up between fusiliers and Northamptonshire men, and a loss of direction. Eventually, they reached Boom Ravine. The NCOs alone were running the fight, managing there to take over one hundred prisoners, many of whom were immediately used as stretcher-bearers to help remove the huge number of casualties. 'A' Company was led by a corporal; 'B' by the company

---

[442] *The 54th Infantry Brigade 1914-1918; Some Records of Battle and Laughter in France*, Gale and Polden Ltd., Wellington Works. Aldershot, London and Portsmouth (Printed for private circulation only), by 'E.R.' of the Headquarters 54th Infantry Brigade, March 1919, p. 78.

[443] *The Royal Fusiliers in the Great War*, H.C. O'Neill, London, William Heinemann, 1922, p. 155.

[444] War Diary, 11th Royal Fusiliers, Special Report on battle of 17th February 1917.

sergeant major (who took overall command); 'C' and 'D' by sergeants.

C.S.M. Fitterer reorganised the battalion at Boom Ravine and brought under his command surviving men from both the 53rd and 54th Brigades. He was wounded, but even so the augmented 11th Royal Fusiliers went on, led by these NCOs, as far as South Miraumont Trench where again they found the wire to be uncut. Even worse, the British barrage was now too far forward, so that the German defenders in the trench were not under British shell fire, which fell behind them. C.S.M. Fitterer got his men to occupy shell holes and a few men reached the trench, but it and the shell holes could not be held in the face of a strong German counter-attack by a special unit of soldiers trained for this situation: excellent marksmen and machine gunners. The British found that most of their rifles and Lewis guns were now clogged up with mud, and such men as were able to fell back to a new defensive position near and across Boom Ravine. They managed to link with the Suffolks and even to dig in and put out some wire to protect them.

Some officers managed to come up and take control, and in the afternoon, the fusiliers managed to push up again towards the South Miraumont Trench and to set up some rifle and machine-gun posts short of it, reinforced by support troops of the Middlesex Battalion, despite German snipers doing deadly work from the shell holes in front of that trench. But it was the NCOs who had covered themselves with glory and shown what can be done when an army trusts capable men.

That day, the brigade had lost fourteen officers and one hundred and fifteen men killed; a further twenty-five officers and four hundred and twenty-three men wounded; and two officers and one hundred and sixty-one men missing. From the battalion, two officers and thirty-six men had died, with another officer still to die of his wounds; eleven officers and one hundred and sixty-two men were wounded; and sixty-nine men were missing. With some sang-froid, which grates today, the regimental history declared, "But, on the whole, it was not an exorbitant price to pay for an advance which carried the troops so near the defences of Petit Miraumont."[445]

Leslie Hands was wounded that day. The first aid system was at full stretch, and the use of captured Germans as stretcher-bearers was for many literally a life saver. The wounded were evacuated over a number of hours in appalling conditions. Wounded men like Leslie had first to be taken to a regimental first aid post. Then it was a distance of two thousand four hundred yards to carry stretcher cases from the first aid posts in Boom Ravine to the tram-head at Hessian Trench. Then they had to be pushed a further two thousand three hundred yards along the tramway to the advanced dressing station. All the way, the men were carried under fire, through deep mud and shell holes. It was grim indeed, but they got Leslie back to the advanced dressing station. From there he was taken back to a casualty clearing station, but his wounds were very serious. He was sent to a hospital near Rouen. There were a lot of hospitals there – eight general hospitals, five stationary ones, a British Red Cross hospital, a labour hospital, and the No. 2 Convalescent Depot. The records are unclear as to which Leslie was taken, but after a few weeks he died of his wounds, on 4th March 1917. He was buried nearby at the St. Sever Cemetery. One wonders if his mother would have agreed that his lingering death was not "an exorbitant price to pay" for an attack which failed.

Frank Hayes and the 12th Middlesex Battalion were also in this attack, alongside Leslie Hands and the 11th Royal Fusiliers. On 11th January 1917, they had begun their march, in heavy snow storms

---

[445] *The Royal Fusiliers in the Great War*, H.C. O'Neill, London, William Heinemann, 1922, p. 156.

and frost, returning to the Somme. From 19th January they had been back at Regina Trench and Stuff Redoubt, and the associated trenches, suffering from the intense cold as well as from intermittent German shell fire: "Night pretty quiet. Frozen duck board walks caused considerable trouble to carrying parties. The food containers are extremely valuable for keeping food hot in this sector, owing to the long, open communications from cookhouses to front line. Very cold."[446] When they returned to billets in Aveluy Wood for a day there seems to have been a lighter moment, as the war diary records men skating (and states two days later that the intensity of the cold was a record for that part of France), but any sense of fun would have been wiped out by a visit from the general who criticised the level of untidiness in the men's billets. Sometimes these generals seemed to lack any empathy with what men like Frank were enduring. It was not until over a week into February that conditions began to turn milder. One consolation was that the frozen ground meant it was almost impossible to order the men to form digging parties for trench maintenance.

With the amelioration in the weather came the order to return to the front line, initially to dig trenches across the now almost non-existent Grandcourt village. On the night of 11th February, the battalion attempted an attack on a part of the Grandcourt Trench still held by the Germans to the east of the battalion position. Two platoons were sent forward at 2a.m., but under bright moonlight they were easily visible and were beaten back with the loss of two men killed and an officer and two others wounded by German machine-gun and rifle fire.

The battalion moved up to the trenches again in the evening of 16th February to support the long-prepared for assault on the German trench system with Leslie Hands and the 11th Royal Fusiliers. "B and D Coys were told off as dug-out clearing parties and to follow closely the Royal Fusiliers and the Northants respectively, them being assaulting Battalions. C Coy acted as carrying party, while A coy remained in reserve with Battn HQ. Zero Hour, 5.45 am (17-2-17) found the weather foggy and full of thaw. The enemy, partly by reason of spies, and partly for other reasons, succeeded in barraging the troops, when forming up in the open, between 4.30 and 5.30 am some 200 yards north of the Gully. Some considerable casualties were suffered here. The objective, S. Miraumont Trench, was gained after some stiff fighting in Boom Ravine, a deep cutting 500 yards n. of Gully... At 10.15, A Coy, which had come up at 7.30 to reinforce, received orders to advance on a wide front astride the ravine to a line 200 yards n. of it and dig in, making sure they were in touch with the Suffolks on their left. This was done just as the 2 assaulting Battns were retiring from S Miraumont Trench followed by an enemy counter-attack... This was dealt with by the Right Platoon who drove the Boches back over the crest, capturing 15 prisoners. The Left was now clear, and as about 9 of the K.R.R. had been driven in on the right by a counter attack, A Coy was ordered to move from their position & form a defensive flank facing E.N.E., with their left on the right Northants post. Meantime B and D coys under the orders of Lieutenant Charlesworth (all their other officers having become casualties) had completed dug-out clearing in the Ravine and had reinforced the Fusiliers & Northants along a line of posts 100 yards n of Boom Ravine. Various conflicting reports continued to come regarding the situation on the right. A Coy at the east end of Boom ravine were now ordered to start a strong point at junction of Ravine & W. Miraumont Road (1 platoon & 4 L.G.S. garrison). The other platoons now began to dig in on the 1st Objective line, being close at hand if needed! B & D were rather in advance of this facing north. The K.R.R. line was now found to be about level with ours. At 3.30pm the Northants moved on to advance their line towards the crest. At 8.45pm A Coy received orders to relieve the Fusiliers, but owing to wet & fog and

---

[446] War Diary, 12th Middlesex Battalion, 22nd January 1917.

uncertainty of whereabouts, the relief was not complete till 5.15 am (18-2-17). 18 Feb. During the night the Northants moved their posts back somewhat thus bringing the line at dawn approximately 200 yards N. of Boom Ravine on the right, and about 100 yards N of it on the left. The G.O.C. now ordered this line to be pushed further forward, which advance in conjunction with a movement forward by the Suffolks on our left, was made, and this new line… was handed over to the East Surreys who relieved the battn and the Northants during the late afternoon. Snipers had previously been pushed up on to the crest and reached a position which enabled them to snipe the enemy in S Miraumont Trench. Our casualties in the action amounted to 10 officers and 135 Other ranks."[447]

The survivors were employed with fatigues in training. One moment of note was on 9th March when Haig himself, on a tour, took refuge in 'C' Company's cookhouse from a snow storm and met some of the men. Haig told the corps commander how struck he was by the cleanliness and tidiness of the cookhouse and its surroundings as well as how well turned–out and clean were the men he met. His remarks were passed down to the divisional general and the brigadier, and so down to the battalion commander, causing a good deal of satisfaction.

The attack, however, had only been one piece of the pressure which led the German Army to withdraw to the prepared Hindenburg defence line in February 1917. Near to where Leslie Hands was killed, Alexander Simpson and Haswell Shears were also in action, fighting as the Germans fell back to their Hindenburg Line. Alexander had been hospitalised and had only returned to the 1st Honourable Artillery Company Battalion on 12th December 1916.

The battalion had moved back into the trenches at Beaucourt at the end of January. Here, a dramatic German raid hit the men of an isolated forward machine-gun post – when help eventually reached them, the party found the Lewis gunner stunned, lying across the body of a German who had been almost cut in half by machine-gun fire. However, five men had disappeared – taken prisoner by the raiders. After a brief gap the battalion was back in the trenches by the River Ancre, near Beaumont-Hamel in early February. Following a daring reconnaissance, the battalion attacked and captured the Miraumont Alley Trench at Grandcourt, but, hours before, their colonel was killed and this shook them. Even so, the attack, and the repulse of counter-attacks, was a success, although Alexander's 'B' Company lost about twenty-five casualties, including the death of their captain. Conditions, especially communications, were made very difficult both by the intense cold and by German bombardments. "B Coy working with great good will and inspired by 2/Lts Garrard & Pollard completed the actual construction of the Barricade in the Sunken Road. They also established a listening post in Miraumont Alley to east of Sunken Road. Their casualties keep rising: the enemy began a systematic bombardment of our whole position. We are seldom in touch with the Artillery as our line is repeatedly cut. The Battalion Runners and Signallers & Linesmen show the utmost devotion throughout and have maintained communications under the most arduous conditions. The line was broken in 80 places during our operation of 7th/ 8th and has been broken an equal number of times since. The heavy artillery at 4.30pm commenced systematic counter battery work which in less than an hour had the effect of reducing the enemy's bombardment. On the HQ dug-out and approaches one 4.2" shells every 10 seconds had been counted during 5 hours – this began to pall, as much coming and going had necessarily to take

---

[447] War Diary, 12th Middlesex Battalion, 16th-18th February 1917.

place. Men were killed in either entrance."⁴⁴⁸ At this stage the men were exhausted and frozen, though morale was raised on 11th February when "first thing in the morning came in two Hun deserters – 1 Lieutenant and 1 Feldwebel. On being interrogated by the C.O. they stated they had had enough of it and had waited until their mail came in and then bolted. This version they varied later, when they came before the Divn, to a more dignified one of having lost direction in the mist."⁴⁴⁹

By 13th February, the condition of the men was described as "pitiable". With over a hundred casualties, reliefs were limited, and some men had had to remain in outposts for up to two days. So when relief came the next day it was most welcome – despite a walk of a few miles before lorries were provided to move them the rest of the way to camp, where hot soup and lighted braziers were provided. The brigadier singled out Alexander's company for congratulations on their conduct. When the medical officer held a sick parade, however, 220 men attended – the majority suffering the effects of exposure, though bad feet condition was also a real problem. This did not, however, excuse the battalion from trench duty, but they were pleased when, in mid-March, they left the Somme Sector to go first to La Bassée and then on to Arras. Haswell and Alexander's next experience in a major battle would come in the Battle of Arras.

A month later, Bernard Hame was involved as British units went forward to try to push the Germans back further and to break the line. Bernard was born in 1889, the cousin of Arthur Hame. He was probably a boarder at the school, which he attended from 1904-1907. He too was a member of the O.T.C. After leaving school he became an engineer. He gained sufficiently wide experience (with the family engineering firm in Plymouth and then as an engineer's assistant with Bournemouth Borough Engineering Department) to be awarded 'privileges of studentship' by the Institution of Civil Engineers (and to be elected to that institution in January 1919).

He was working as a student engineer with Bournemouth Borough, on 1st September 1914, when he enlisted as a private in the 7th Hampshire Battalion and promoted to lance corporal. He arrived in India on 7th January 1915. He was a member of 'H' Company, the 2/7th Hampshire Battalion. (Nearly forty Old Boys joined one of the three units which made up the 7th Hampshires, so Bernard clearly had familiar company. It must at times have been something of a 'Pal's Battalion').

Bernard had been recalled for officer training: as an engineer he had talents going to waste in India. He arrived back in England from India on 18th August 1916. "Second Lieutenant B.W. Hame, formerly of Hants Regt., now of R.E., took a course at Chatham with a view to getting a commission in the 'Engineers'. The test is severe, and only 18 (of whom Hame was one) were passed out of 40. He speaks of the eleven weeks' training as the most strenuous he ever spent."⁴⁵⁰ He was commissioned 2nd lieutenant on 23rd December 1916. In January 1917 he was sent to France and on 16th February joined the 5th Royal Engineers Field Company on the Somme, working out of Ovillers, on tasks such as building shelters and dug-outs.

On 10th March, they were tasked to assist the 99th Infantry Brigade in an attack on two German trenches on the German front line north of Warlencourt, defending the German base at Bapaume. The company was tasked to construct strongpoints and wire entanglement around them. They

---

⁴⁴⁸ War Diary, 1st Honourable Artillery Company Battalion, 9th February 1917.
⁴⁴⁹ War Diary, 1st Honourable Artillery Company Battalion, 11th February 1917.
⁴⁵⁰ *The Bournemouthian*, April 1917.

were also to dig a new communication trench to one captured trench and open up a second to the other. They carried out these tasks, including constructing a new 'jumping off' trench, whilst under heavy shell fire. Although new to the company, Bernard distinguished himself. "At 9.30am on 10/3/17 reconnoitring parties consisting of 1 officer 2 NCOs and a few sappers went up to reconnoitre the positions of strong points. ii Lt G H Dundon (5 Field Co RE) reconnoitred the three strong points on the Right, and ii Lt Hame (5 Field Co RE) the three on the left. These officers gave advice to the garrisons of the strong points and pointed out the best ways to carry out the work and assisted them as much as possible. They then returned to pick up their men at 1.30pm and returned to the posts in the evening to assist in improving them, and to wire the posts all round. This was done, and as there were no carrying parties available, the sappers had to carry up their own materials, having to make several journeys backwards and forwards from the strong points to the Dump, as well as construct the Entanglement. The condition of the ground made it very heavy going, the shelling was also very heavy, so it was not an easy task, but they carried out the work and put out all the wire that was available."

Bernard's contributions were not unnoticed. The divisional general wrote to the Commander of the Royal Engineers for his division that "He is particularly pleased with the way in which the consolidation of the strong points in front of Grevillers Trench was carried out, and also with the taping out of the line in front of these posts to provide a jumping off place for further operations."[451] Later it was stated that Bernard had twice in the early part of 1917 been recommended to his divisional commander for the Military Cross, and this would have been the first of those occasions.

Arthur Mosley was nearby. Arthur, born in 1895, had left the school in July 1911. He had spent three years in the O.T.C. at school. He volunteered on 26th October 1914 for the Cinque Ports Reserves – the 5th Royal Sussex Battalion. His officer potential was quickly realised and on 26th January 1915 he was re-posted to the Inns of Court O.T.C. for a very short period of officer training. On 11th April 1915, he was posted to the 4th King's Own Yorkshire Light Infantry Battalion. He was placed in a reserve battalion because it was felt he could particularly contribute as a training instructor and was sent to Aldershot to take a course in physical instruction and set to work as a PT instructor with Derby Scheme volunteers – which he did very well. At the end of December 1915 he was promoted full lieutenant, and spent 1916 training recruits in different camps in the Midlands and South of England.

On 16th January 1917 he arrived in France. His battalion (2/4th King's Own Yorkshire Light Infantry) was part of 187th Brigade, 62nd Division, which had been training in England for over two years. They arrived in time to experience the worst winter weather of the war. The picquets which were screwed into the ground at night in front of a trench to hold the barbed wire – a big improvement on the straight ones of the start of the war which had noisily to be banged into the ground, attracting enemy fire – could not be pushed into the ground because it was frozen. Yet, at other times the mud was so soft that men could not move. "January was at its worst when the Division arrived in France, and heavy rain, sleet and snow, with occasional hard frosts… roads were inches deep in mud… and men… wallowing… in slush and across sodden ground."[452]

---

[451] War Diary, 5th Royal Engineers Field Company, 10th March 1917.
[452] *The History of the 62nd (W.R.) Division*, Edward Wyrall, Vol. I, p. 10.

On 13th February, the battalion moved into the front line. "Trenches as such did not exist, for they had been obliterated by the concentrated fire of the guns... The front line was held by a series of posts and dugouts which somewhat resembled islands in a sea of mud. Shell holes pock-marked the ground, often overlapping one another and where pathways existed between them they were but a few inches wide. The holes were full of water and more than one man lost his life through slipping off the narrow pathway into the slimy mass which engulfed him. In daylight it was difficult enough to pick a way safely across such ground, but in the darkness of the night... It was a miracle if the relieved or relieving troops escaped without at least one casualty – through mud."[453] At the end of February, with his battalion, Arthur was at Beaumont-Hamel, advancing against some desultory machine-gun and artillery fire. The Germans were resisting, but not as they had the year before. They had already decided to pull back.

In February 1917, the Germans began their planned withdrawal, Operation 'Alberich', to the Hindenburg Line. This took the British by surprise – since the end of the Battle of the Somme, British troops had concentrated on holding on and consolidating the costly gains of 1916. As the Germans withdrew they destroyed anything they thought might help the British – for example, by blowing up houses or mining road junctions. They even cut down fruit trees to deny their produce for the following autumn, laid trees across the roads, and filled in wells – even poisoning some of them with arsenic. They left booby traps and mines of all sizes to try to catch unwary British soldiers. Following them up, British officers and ordinary soldiers alike died from artillery and shell fire, as well as from snipers and from sickness in the unhealthy conditions. Officer casualties were disproportionately heavy. Eventually, the Germans were able to consolidate on their new line whilst the British and French occupied the previously held German positions and tried hurriedly to construct new advanced lines facing the Hindenburg Line.

One un-named officer had a lucky escape: "When his battery entered Miraumont he had taken up quarters in a German dug-out which boasted a fire-place. His batman was about to light a fire when his officer told him he need not bother until the morning. Next morning as the man was laying the fire he noticed a piece of wire and on close examination found a length of quick match fastened to the wire leading to a hole under the dug-out in which was packed sufficient explosive to send the whole place sky-high."[454] Arthur seems to have coped with such hazards and the conditions and survived to be in action later that year at Arras.

Following up the Germans, on the evening of 12th March Frank Hayes and the 12th Middlesex Battalion returned to the front line from Thiepval and early the next day moved forward and occupied the Liupart Line, which was found to have been badly knocked about by British shelling, though it remained well wired. After a night of light shelling, the battalion again pushed forward. 'A' Company moved into touch with the Germans on the Grévillers road, with the other companies in support or reserve, despite heavy German shelling trying to hold the British back. Frank was not there two days later when the Germans abandoned Bihucourt Trench and the village during the night. "On March 15th, after being relieved from the front line and having almost reached the reserve trenches, he was hit in the arm by shrapnel and had an eight hour walk to the dressing station."[455] "The gallant soldier was returning to his dug-out with his comrades when a German

---

[453] *The History of the 62nd (W.R.) Division*, Edward Wyrall, Vol. I, pp. 15-17.

[454] *The History of the 62nd (W.R.) Division*, Edward Wyrall, Vol. I, p. 33.

[455] *The Bournemouthian*, December 1917.

shell dropped in their midst, and a piece of shrapnel went right through his left arm, fracturing it. After an operation he was brought to Southampton where he is progressing satisfactorily."[456] In December 1917, the school magazine could only report, "He has been in hospital ever since, but hopes to regain the full use of his arm." Frank was not finished, however and would return to the Western Front in 1918.

William Mitford had returned to the war after he had been wounded on the Somme. He did not rejoin his old battalion. Instead, he was sent to France to fight with the 7th Royal Fusiliers Battalion. This battalion, in the 190th Brigade, 63rd (Royal Naval) Division, spent the winter of 1916-1917 in line on the Ancre. William and the battalion saw the initial signs of the German retreat on 24th February 1917 and the battalion pushed forward strong battle patrols to scout out what was happening. On the next day, William and the battalion advanced in 'Artillery Formation' (a pattern of men formed to attempt to reduce casualties from defensive shell fire). They reached the eastern edge of Miraumont without encountering opposition, and there established a new forward outpost line. More scouts were sent ahead. When their reports were encouraging, the battalion again advanced, and they continued under a weak artillery fire for two miles, after which the task of following back the German withdrawal passed to a different battalion.

Later, Alan Markwick also followed up the German retreat. In 1917, his battalion, the 18th Lancashire Fusiliers, ceased to be a Bantam battalion, as bigger men replenished the losses. They had taken over old French trenches at Vrély, south of the Somme on 20th February. "These trenches were poor and extremely wet and muddy, the average depth of water and mud being 2 feet in front line and communication trenches. Men very exhausted. 2 companies in front line, one in support and one in reserve. It was extremely difficult to get up the communication trenches or to carry Lewis guns, ammunition or rations up. The rapid thaw had caused the sides of the trenches to fall in."[457] They decided that the only way to bring up rations and ammunition was to carry it over the top, relying on the darkness of the night to cover them. Conditions were made worse by heavy bombardments each day by German explosive and gas shells. On 17th March their sister battalion, the 17th Lancashire Fusiliers, took over the old German front line.

On 18th March, "Battalion parade 3am. Move in column through Chilly and down sunken road Chilly-Hattencourt into Whiskey Trench, German 6th line, arriving 6.15am. Moved on 7am into trenches west of Bois d'Hallu. No opposition encountered or enemy seen. Several patrols to front during day reported no enemy. Battalion advanced again in column of route at 6pm through Fonches and Fonchette into trenches ½ mile west of Curchy, with 20th Lancashire Fusiliers on right and 105th Brigade on left. No enemy seen. Rations brought up during night; also water as Germans reported to have poisoned the wells."[458] As the British advanced, the battalion was used to help repair railways, roads, and fill in craters. Eventually they found themselves preparing for their part in a mass attack.

This attack took place at Fresnoy-le-Petit, near St. Quentin, on 15th April 1917. "4.15am. Artillery bombardment of enemy trenches in and around Les Trois Sauvages Farm commenced. W and Z companies under command of Captain G.A. Duncan advanced to attack Les Trois Sauvages and

---

[456] *The Bournemouth Visitors' Directory*, April 1917.
[457] War Diary, 18th Lancashire Fusiliers, 20th February 1917.
[458] War Diary, 18th Lancashire Fusiliers, 18th March 1917.

establish themselves on ridge about 200 yards beyond the farm. They formed up on road East of Gricourt and advanced under shell fire. Trois Sauvages was found to be occupied by about 20 of enemy but this did not delay the advance, the Germans all being killed or taken prisoner by Z company, Sergts Francis and Owen leading the platoons which took the farm. Z Company then commenced to dig in, as ordered, about 300 yards east of the farm. W Company, seeing some Germans retreating, did not stop but pursued them up to and beyond the Le Catelet-St Quentin road and got into a trench there. Here they killed or wounded more than 100 of the enemy, using their bayonets, and also bombed enemy dugouts. As they had now (5.30am) got more than 500 yards beyond their objective and as their flanks were exposed, they were ordered to withdraw and consolidate in line with Z Company. The enemy consisted of men of the 453rd Regiment, 21 were captured. This retirement was well executed by small parties of 2 sections each and was covered by a Lewis gun, which had been sent to the right flank. L/Cpl Altham was in charge of the gun and ably carried out his duty. Unfortunately he and all his team were killed as they retired. As soon as all our men had come back across the Le Catelet-St Quentin road the Lewis guns of Z Company opened fire on this road and covered the retirement. Two German machine guns firing from a wood on our right front about 1000 yards away caused the casualties which we suffered during the retirement, and also those received while lying in the open, attempting to dig in. At 6.5am X coy was ordered to go up in support. They captured two German trench mortars to the East of Gricourt and established themselves North of Trois Sauvages. Our artillery fired on the wood (6.15am) containing the German machine guns but failed to silence them. 8.0am. Our machine guns… were brought up to the South East of Gricourt and pushed up the valley and at 8.30am the German machine guns ceased fire and did not trouble us again. W, Y, and Z coys remained in their positions all day but were ordered to withdraw West of Trois Sauvages at dusk. During the afternoon all three companies and both Gricourt and Fresnoy were heavily shelled."[459] That evening the companies withdrew to the east of Gricourt. Overall, three officers had been wounded and one had gone missing. Of the men, thirty had been killed, fifty wounded, and sixteen were missing.

From 21st June 1917 to 25th July, Alan was made acting captain whilst commanding a company. On 8th July, he was selected to accompany two other officers and a hundred and forty-one men to form a guard of honour to the King – but when they returned to the battalion on 13th July it was with the disappointing news of not having even seen the King. On 23rd July, he succumbed to trench fever, caused by exposure on active service, and was forced to leave the battalion. He landed at Southampton on 5th August. During this time he was running a high temperature, and so was immediately admitted to the vast military hospital at Netley in Hampshire, the Royal Victoria Hospital. By 16th August he was sufficiently recovered to attend a medical board which sent him to the Bassett Heath Auxiliary Hospital for convalescence, but his recovery was hampered by two bouts of the malaria which he had originally caught in Ceylon. Alan remained in the north of England for the rest of the war.

Edward Goddard and the 276th Siege Battery found that the poisoned wells affected them as they had Alan Markwick. Following orders received on 15th April 1917, they moved from 1st to 5th Army but it had taken a week to move the heavy guns to their new positions at Lebuquière, east of Bapaume on the Somme. From 26th April they were firing on fresh targets in the area of the Hindenburg Line, though because they were so far back they had to fire with maximum charges. Their position there was in an open field, but because the Germans had only recently withdrawn

---

[459] War Diary, 18th Lancashire Fusiliers, 15th April 1917.

the position was exposed and less than satisfactory. There were no gun pits and the ground was very muddy, making it difficult to bring up the ammunition they needed – a lorry could only get so far and much had to be done by the hard labour of the men like Edward. "All water locally had been poisoned by the enemy, & that used had to be treated with chloride of lime… Hostile Aircraft… were very active – stopping work for a considerable time on most days, & prevented ammunition in bulk going to the battery by day. Hostile shelling: The enemy's guns were fairly active shelling most of the village & suspected gun positions & Ops every day & during the night."[460]

Meanwhile, in January 1917, Archibald Rogers and the 12th Northumberland Fusiliers had moved into Belgium to be ready to support the Belgian Army should that be necessary. On 15th February, they had gone south again to the Quarry Trenches near Vermelles which were in a dreadful state, with the front line almost obliterated by enemy action and with badly damaged communication trenches. These had to be repaired, despite the rain, and despite German machine-gun and trench-mortar fire. On 22nd February, "at about 5.25am the enemy put a barrage of High Explosive and Shrapnel from 5.9", 4.2" and 77mm guns and howitzers and trench mortars on the entire length of the close support trenches… Almost immediately the enemy appears to have entered the unoccupied portions of the front line… From information gathered from a prisoner captured near the latter point the raiding parties totalled 2 Officers and 40 other ranks, but nothing like these numbers were seen by the garrisons of the strong points or the counter attacking platoons. At the hour of the attack there was a thick mist and a man would not be visible above 20 yds; the Battalion was 'Standing To' at the time, the front line platoons in their strong points and the counter attacking platoons in the close support line. One strong point however which is only held by a single platoon by day, but by two platoons during the hours of darkness… was being vacated by one platoon when the barrage was put on – this is a necessary precaution as no movement is desirable to and from this position in daylight – the officer in command… was moving this platoon in single file towards the junction of the close support line and Devon Lane, and promptly realising the situation regained the front line to the left of the strong point in time to capture one prisoner and see the remainder of this raiding party disappear into the mist across 'No Man's Land'. Doubtless the enemy mistook this for a prompt and strong counter attack and abandoned this part [of the] enterprise, for quantities of cylindrical stick bombs were thrown away by them at this point… A few minutes later the Coy Commander of the Centre Coy, having heard the rapid fire from the strong point and realising that the light Signals would be invisible in the mist (which they were) arrived in the front line with his counter attack platoon. All trenches in that area were at once searched but no trace of the enemy could be found except the remains of one or two Germans who had been blown to pieces by their own barrage. The fact that our own men were all wearing 'gum boots' made our advance rather slow over the masses of mud behind our front line. Meanwhile the raiding party which entered the trenches of the right Coy… had divided into two parties, one of which moved south along the unoccupied portion of the front line until it encountered the barbed wire gate on the left flank of the post… When a few bombs had been thrown by both sides, the raiders turned & withdrew across 'No Man's Land'. They were however caught by the fire of the Lewis Gun in this point… The other party which entered… were seen & fired on… by the Lewis Gun team in Dudley Dump, and bombs were thrown at them by a squad of Battalion Bombers posted at the junction of Dudley Lane and the close support line. This Lewis Gun was unfortunately put out of action by a piece of an aerial dart which smashed the mechanism

---

[460] War Diary, 276th Siege Battery, R.G.A., 29th April 1917.

whilst it was firing at the raiders. This party also withdrew too quickly for the counter attack platoon to overtake them; the right Coy area was at once searched by the counter attack platoon but no trace of the enemy except abandoned equipment could be found. The counter attack Coy was not called upon. The prisoner captured belonged to the Storm Truppe of the 26th I.R. (Prussian). Our casualties were 1 Sergt and one man killed by shell fire, no wounded or missing. The S.O.S. was not sent in, but the supporting artillery was called upon to retaliate and did so."[461]

In the late winter of 1916-17, as he had wished, Archibald was sent back to England to join an officer cadet school. The move was just in time as he was suffering badly from trench conditions. "I got my marching orders last Thursday, and, although I was due to go to hospital with trench feet. I begged the M.O. to let me travel. I had a 12 kilos walk to start with and then was 13 hours travelling to Boulogne (our train was only eight hours late to start with, but this is nothing in France) and eventually reached town at 8 p.m. on the Friday night, where all those who travelled were welcomed with open arms... Unfortunately the journey has made my foot much worse and I'm having it attended to here and am confined indoors with orders not to put a boot on, but I hope to get about in a week."[462] On 30th March 1917 he began his officer training. On 26th September 1917 he was sent back to the Western Front with No.4 Special Gas Company, as a specialist in gas warfare.

The Battle of Arras: Vimy Ridge and the First Battle of the Scarpe

The British failed to break the new German defence line as the Germans retired, so Haig resolved to make an effort to do so in the spring. In March 1917, the Tsar of Russia had been overthrown and there was considerable unease as to the fighting capacity of the Russians on the Eastern Front after their partial collapse during the winter of 1916-1917. Although at this stage there was confidence that a new, more democratic Russia would emerge, it was felt that it would help the new Russian Provisional Government if German attention was made to focus on their Western rather than on their Eastern Front. The French had changed commanders, and the new commander, General Nivelle, promised that under his control French campaigning would be far more successful. He wanted to attack south of the British sectors, in Champagne, but wanted the British to make an attack further north at Arras, to divert German attention. The new British Prime Minister, David Lloyd George, having been shocked by the casualty lists from the Somme, made it a controversial matter of principle (against reason in many ways) that British Army actions should henceforward be subordinated to, and under direction of, the French. Although that political aim was not finalised until the next year, in 1917 Lloyd George and the politicians were trying to push Haig in that direction. Consequently, it was planned that the British would attack at Arras in April 1917, and a month later at Ypres. The first of these campaigns, the Battle of Arras is commonly divided into a series of sub-battles, the most famous of which was the battle with which it started on the northern, left flank – the Battle of Vimy Ridge. This was the northern section of the First Battle of the Scarpe in which the British mostly fought further south, along the River Scarpe.

The part of the battle known as Vimy Ridge is commonly associated with the Canadians, who provided 80% of the initial assault troops (though not all of them, and not all the engineers and artillery by any stretch). It proved to be a massive step in the growth of Canadian self-

---

[461] War Diary, 12th Northumberland Fusiliers, 22nd February 1917.
[462] *The Bournemouthian*, July 1917.

consciousness and promoted the growth from Dominion status to separate nationality. Amongst those on Vimy Ridge in this battle were several Old Bournemouthians. Ernest Snelgar and the 4th Canadian Mounted Rifles had already distinguished themselves at Ypres and on the Somme. Now the battalion was to join the rest of the Canadians, forming one Canadian Corps to fight the battle.

The Vimy Ridge and the Souchez Ridge are parts of an escarpment east of Arras. The Germans had fought tenaciously to hold the top of this ridge since 1914. Their positions allowed them to look down over the dip slope across the British and French positions and on towards Arras. It also allowed them to protect the occupied French coalfields and the mining towns like Lens, which they were exploiting for their war effort. Further, it protected the important railways lines and communications which they used.

Both Germans and British had spent a great deal of time tunnelling the ridge. Mostly this was in order to blow mines, or to create counter-mines. When a mine was blown it was sometimes to try to destroy an enemy position, but more often to create new 'lips' which the infantry could try to hold and so advance their firing lines. Some of the mining was done to create huge shelters to conceal the soldiers, or to create underground communication trenches. Some of these long communication and shelter tunnels were built over the winter of 1916-1917 by the Royal Engineers, taking great pains to conceal their existence from the Germans. By April these tunnels and trenches on the Vimy Ridge were occupied by the Canadian Corps of four divisions with the British XVII Corps of two divisions to their south.

On the Vimy Ridge, the British line closest to the Germans was set a long way forward as an observation or jumping off line, supported by communication trenches or tunnels to a more orthodox set of trenches set further back. The British had begun to lay a number of big mines in tunnels up to the German trenches, but the Canadian Corps commander, General Currie, decided that, apart from three at the extreme northern end of the assault line which might help provide protection for the flank of the attack, these mines should not be exploded. He felt that it would be better to launch a completely surprise attack, and one unhindered by concerns about falling debris, the route to take after an explosion, or additional obstacles to tank deployment.

In February 1917, Ernest Snelgar was given special training as a signaller as the battalion undertook five weeks of intensive work preparing for the battle. By late March they were in the trenches on Vimy Ridge. "Headquarters were located in Goodman Tunnel. The trenches had become worse, some were practically filled with water; large working parties, however, soon drained and repaired the jumping off places."[463]

This was to be a different kind of battle. "No battle could have been prepared more thoroughly. Every unit from corps to platoon knew exactly what it had to do. Prior to the attack a stupendous bombardment was kept up day and night for a week along this huge front, flattening every obstruction and hammering the back areas (2,800 guns fired approximately 88,000 tons of ammunition, almost twice the amount expended in preparation for the Battle of the Somme). In Gun Valley, behind the Arras-Béthune road, artillery of all calibre stood almost wheel to wheel giving the Canadians the greatest moral and physical support they had ever had before going into action. Mines were laid under the German front line; one on the Battalion's front between Chassery

---

[463] *The 4th Canadian Mounted Rifles*, Captain S.G. Bennett, Murray Printing Company Ltd, Toronto, 1926, p. 49.

and Albany craters was to be blown, thirty seconds after zero hour. The many dumps were filled with consolidating materials, ammunition, water and every conceivable necessity. At least a quarter of a million men were to participate in this gigantic thrust. Each infantryman had his usual equipment as well as twenty-four hour's rations and forty-eight hours' iron rations, five sand bags, two flares, four bombs, flags and everything else that an emergency might demand. Apart from the previous training, everyone was made familiar with all the details of the attack. Four days in advance, preliminary instructions were circulated and on the 7th operation orders were received for the attack on Vimy Ridge."[464]

In preparation, in the middle of March 1917, there was another reorganisation for Basil Keogh's artillery unit. The 1st Canadian Field Brigade now grew to six batteries to support the attack. "Gun pits had to be built, and ammunition hauled… The congestion on the main roads was terrific, and the mud tracts were absolutely impassable. Drivers were on the road night after night, sometimes as long as for 14 to 16 hours, and the way in which these men carried out their duties under most appalling weather conditions, usually wet through to the skin, and under heavy shell fire is well worthy of the traditions of the Field Artillery, and is deserving of the highest praise. During the preliminary preparations for the attack an enormous amount of hostile wire had to be cut, and as many as 1,500 observed rounds a day were often fired by each Battery. The gunners were manning the guns all day, and at night had to handle the ammunition, as well as carry out harassing night shoots."[465]

As the battle approached, these preparations intensified. "April 6th, 1917. Today (Z-3) all preparations rushed for the coming attack by Canadian Corps on Vimy Ridge. Heavies up to 12" Howitzers concentrated on all towns immediately in rear of enemy's lines. A standard gauge railway has been built and is now completed up to the 2nd How[itzer] Battery. Bridges made and trenches filled in up to 500 Crater…" But, "many horses died during the past few days owing to so much hauling of ammunition and cutting down of hay and straw ration."

The 15th Royal Warwickshire Battalion, part of 13th Brigade was attached to the 2nd Canadian Division for this battle. In preparation, "13th Infantry Brigade have moved to present area for the purpose of practising the attack over a 'practice area' specially prepared, accurately flagged out, and to exact scale. Officers viewed the course today… Battalion practise offensive action 'over the course'. Ground very heavy owing to bad weather."[466] The Canadian troops, too, made similar practices over the specially-prepared practice terrain.

Then they moved into the tunnels and prepared for the assault. "The assaulting troops spent the early part of the night of the 8th in dug-outs and tunnels in and behind the front line. These concentrating points were necessarily crowded. Companies were squeezed into the ordinary accommodation of a platoon. The men could not lie down with comfort, so they sat around the light of a candle and dozed or played poker for unusual stakes, collecting paper credits which were given freely by the pessimistic members who sat in on the game. Early in the morning they moved out to the jumping-off points. The bombardment had ceased. There was a deathlike silence. An occasional shell would scream across the sky and accentuate the stillness. The rattle of equipment,

---

[464] *The 4th Canadian Mounted Rifles*, Captain S.G. Bennett, Murray Printing Company Ltd, Toronto, 1926, pp. 50-51.
[465] War Diary, 1st Canadian Field Artillery Brigade, Narrative included in diary for September 1917.
[466] War Diary, 15th Warwickshire Battalion, 3rd and 4th April 1917.

the muffled curses of the sergeants calling for less noise, added to the weird tension. All were hoping their movements would not be detected. Finally, the order to fix bayonets was given and a ripple of clicks passed along the line and died with the last obstinate rifle. An ominous whistle was blown somewhere in the German trenches, but nothing developed. The enemy seemed unaware of his impending fate. At 5.30 am Easter Monday, April 9th, the sharp bark of our barrage opened. Half a minute later the mine at Goodman tunnel sap was sprung and 'A' Company was on its way across the hundred yards of No Man's Land."[467] Within five minutes the first troops were inside the German front line and pushing on to their support line. In less than two hours the battalion had achieved its objective and reached their part of the top of the ridge, between L'École Commune and La Folie Farm.

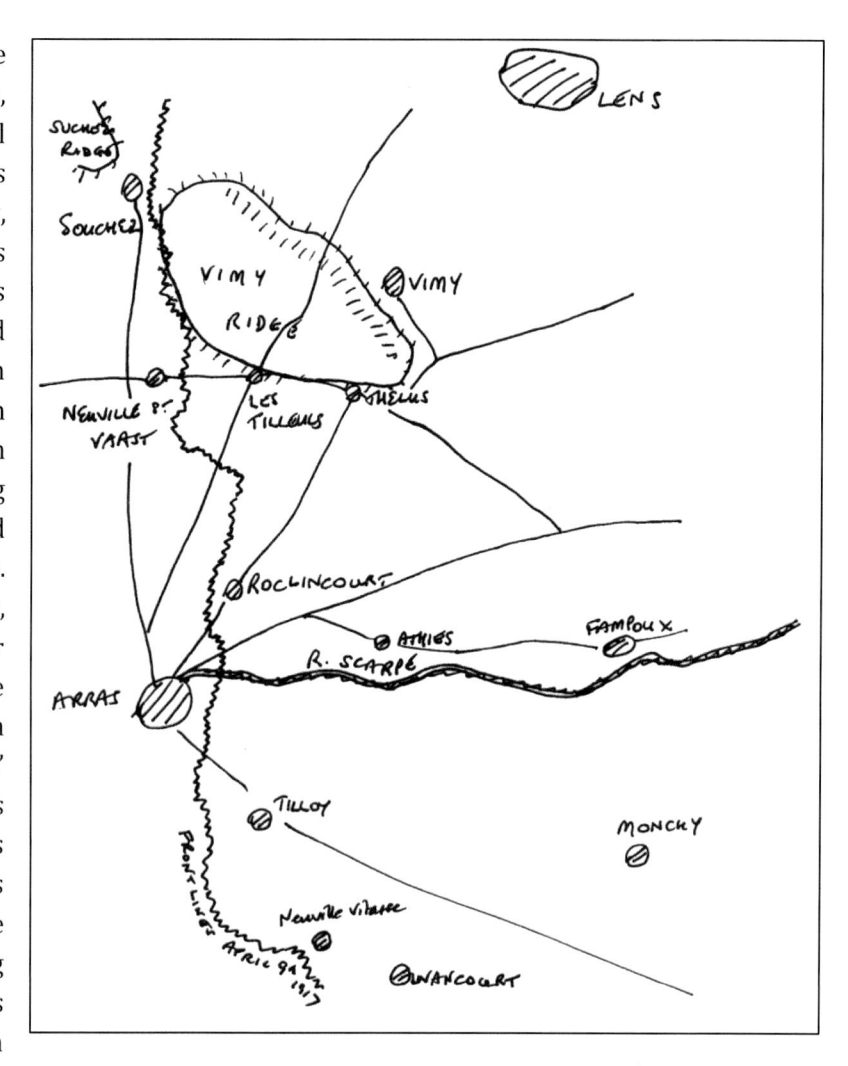

Ernest was a signaller. "The Signallers, under Lieutenant J.R. Woods, did excellent work following closely behind the infantry with their drums of wire and reported at 9.30 am that they had established a station in Zwishchen and connected it with Headquarters. This was the first wire available on this sector and was of invaluable assistance to the artillery."[468]

The speed of their success did not mean it was easy. The Germans resisted bravely and made various counter-attacks but these were comparatively weak. This has been explained as due to the severity of the bombardment they had suffered, which had obliterated trenches and normal dug-outs so that only the deep dug-outs remained intact. The battalion not only achieved their objectives but also captured hundreds of prisoners, including three officers, one of whom was a colonel. They also took seven machine guns and various trench mortars and other trophies of warfare. The cost was relatively light – one officer and forty-three men killed, whilst another officer later died of wounds received, and five officers and one hundred and thirty-one men were

---

[467] *The 4th Canadian Mounted Rifles,* Captain S.G. Bennett, Murray Printing Company Ltd, Toronto, 1926, pp. 52-53.

[468] *The 4th Canadian Mounted Rifles,* Captain S.G. Bennett, Murray Printing Company Ltd, Toronto, 1926, p. 54.

wounded. Most of these losses had occurred from sniping and counter-attacks rather than in the original assault, which had taken the Germans completely by surprise.

The later part of the battle was fought in a snow storm after unsettled weather on 9th and 10th April, and this was made worse for the men as they had left their greatcoats behind so as to be less encumbered for the assault. Ernest and his comrades endured sixty-three hours like that.

The Germans attempted to dig in half-way down the scarp slope of the ridge, but over the next days the Canadians and British launched a series of attacks to dislodge them and push them further back onto the plain. The battalion took some part in the attempts to push round Lens and drive back the Germans, although overall these efforts did not achieve the hoped-for results and the plain behind remained in German hands.

Arthur Lobley, brother of Owen, was a private in the 6th Universities (Overseas) Company of the famous Princess Patricia's Canadian Light Infantry. It is very likely that he was with the battalion when it launched its attack at Vimy Ridge on 9th April 1917. Born in 1890, and another early member of the school to perform in *HMS Pinafore* in 1905, he too had emigrated. In May 1916 he enlisted.

The Princess Patricia's Canadian Light Infantry Battalion held the line with two companies and battalion headquarters inside the Grange Sub-way Tunnel, which one can still visit today, and a third in the nearby Empire Redoubt. They had entered these positions a few days before. On Sunday 9th April, each man was given a tot of rum, and when the artillery barrage opened at 4.30a.m., the first wave started to climb up over the lip of the Canadian-held craters. Although it had been sleeting the day before, and was to snow quite heavily the next day, it seems that the day of the attack was relatively fine.

As with the 4th Canadian Mounted Rifles, progress was good. By 7.10a.m., Number 1 Company (which had been in the Grange Tunnel) had reached the German 'Famine' Trench with few casualties and had managed to keep in touch with Number 3 Company (also from the Grange) which was on their left and the Royal Canadian Rifles on their right. Number 4 Company had also achieved their objectives with light casualties by 7.30a.m. and pushed forward patrols into the woods in front of them. At 9a.m. the battalion headquarters was shifted from the Grange to the German forward trench. Whilst Number 2 Company suffered "pretty strong"[469] casualties, it too achieved its objective by 9.30. Their casualties came mostly from a German counter-bombardment on their previous front line. All companies had taken prisoners. Initially, the first two German lines had been taken with fewer than about forty casualties, but the number climbed later; particularly as Number 2 Company lost most of its NCOs. The battle continued with additional grenades and other ammunition being needed by the front sections. In the end, after three days of fighting, when they were withdrawn they had lost three officers killed and eight wounded, and sixty men killed, 142 wounded and ten missing. They had achieved their objectives and captured three trench mortars and three machine guns.

In this battle, Alexander Sandbrook and the 8th Canadian Battalion were in brigade support; the assault was made by the other battalions of the brigade (5th, 7th and 10th Canadians) but three parties of twenty-five men had joined the assault because their task was to create communication

---

[469] War Diary, Princess Patricia's Light Infantry. Narrative of events of 9th April 1917.

trenches to connect the German trenches and the Canadian trenches. After three-quarters of an hour the battalion moved forward at 6.30a.m. to support the advance and to bring up ammunition and four additional Stokes mortars. That afternoon, they moved forward to replace the assault battalions holding the new front line. A few days later, however, they formed the vanguard of an unsuccessful assault to take the advance beyond Willerval village, which foundered against strong German defences. Although their participation in the battle was limited, the battalion lost one officer killed, two officers wounded, and nineteen men killed and eighty wounded but had managed to capture three German machine guns, a trench mortar, a 5.9" naval gun as well as telephone and signalling equipment.

At the southern end of the Canadian assault, Frank Cox was in the attack from the first day. In mid-February 1917, in freezing weather, the 31st Canadian Infantry Battalion had moved south to Mont St. Éloi, west of Vimy Ridge and Thélus. Here, their trench line contained saps running up to craters, some of which were in British Imperial control, giving a degree of cover to the defending troops. From the middle of March the battalion was practising in a flagged area for the forthcoming offensive. For a day or two in the trenches, some of the men had the benefit of using the tunnels which were still being constructed – meaning that they had the benefit of bunks and electric lighting – luxury for the Western Front. Otherwise the trenches were cold and muddy, and when they rested in reserve they relied on tents and bivouacs. A raid at the end of the month brought them two German prisoners whom they interrogated to gain information to help in the upcoming assault.

On 7th April, the battalion bathed so as to be clean for the planned attack, and then moved forward the next day to the assembly area. The attack on Thélus followed. "The volume of our artillery fire was beyond description and the bursting shells all along the line as far as the eye could reach, was a sight to be remembered. The enemy put down a stiff bombardment just as the rear lines of the leading Brigades reached the front line German trenches, but all was going well… The leading battalions had to go through a heavy barrage of 5.9's and 4.1's when crossing No Man's Land, sustaining some casualties, but for the most part, the various sections moving in artillery formation were skilfully led through it. The appearance presented by these Battalions advancing was most striking, as they pushed forward over the shell torn ground, the going made all the more difficult by the snow and sleet falling at the time… On the way forward… Four 'Tanks', which had been detailed to accompany our attack on Thelus, were seen stranded about the vicinity of the German Support trenches. In spite of the most strenuous efforts, these had been brought to a stand-still by the exceedingly heavy going and deep mud."[470]

Unlikely as it might seem given the hilly nature of the northern part of the battleground and the deep craters which marked No Man's Land on Vimy Ridge, Harold Head was there at the southern end by Frank Cox, with his tanks. He had greater responsibility than he had had on the Somme. By now, the number of tanks had grown and their organisation adapted with that growth. Harold was in charge of 10 Section of 12 Company with four lieutenants as his tank commanders (tanks 795 with 596; and 595 with 580). This company was part of 'D' Battalion (part of 1st Tank Brigade) working with the 62nd Division (V Corps, 3rd Army). On 9th April 1917 his section was deployed to help on Vimy Ridge. His commander now was a Major Ward, DSO. 12 Company was split into two sections of four tanks. His section was expected to assist one of the brigades in the first wave of the

---

[470] Brigade Report included in the War Diary, 31st Canadian Infantry, 9th April 1917.

2nd Canadian Division's attack; they were the only tanks allocated to the assault of Vimy Ridge, which was not natural tank country.

The tanks in Harold's section were all the new Mark II tanks. Their deployment was itself something of a desperate measure. Originally, these tanks had been designed only for training and were not intended to leave England. Tanks were so much in need, however, that a number were sent to France and Harold's men were sent into battle with them – despite protests that they did not have the hardened steel plating of earlier (and later) models, essential as they risked coming up against the newly-developed German armour-piercing shells. In a letter of 12th March 1917, Stern (the man in London charged with many aspects of organising tank production and use) had written, "I consider it more than unwise to use practise tanks in action under any circumstances. They have all the faults that necessitated the design of last year being altered to the present design of Mark IV."[471] This advice was ignored.

The tanks assembled in a sunken road known to the British as Elbe Trench, in front of Neuville St. Vaast. However, the Germans spotted the gathering of these tanks and secretly placed the 204 Hahkampfsbatterie, an anti-tank battery, with four 77mm field guns, 500 yards in front of the Canadian lines at Les Tilleuls.

The plan was for the 5th Canadian Brigade to assault, after which some infantry from the 16th Royal Warwickshire Battalion would advance, screening the advance of the tanks. The 16th Royal Warwicks were part of the British 13th Brigade which had been attached to assist the Canadian 2nd Division. As the second wave, the British were to leapfrog through the 5th Canadian Brigade. Eight British infantry volunteers from the 16th Warwicks were split into four pairs of men, each pair attached to a tank. Their job was to walk behind the tanks, firing smoke grenades from their rifles. It was therefore hoped that this would provide the tanks with a mobile smokescreen. The idea was that the Canadians should take the first line; then the tanks would emerge, overtake the advance, and lead the fight to the second objective.

In the event, the preliminary artillery bombardment destroyed two of the German anti-tank guns, and the crews of the other two guns abandoned them within twenty minutes because the advancing Canadians had over-run their positions, so none of the tanks was hit by them. However, as they attacked, the tank drivers – who in any case always had a very restricted view – found themselves blinded by their own mobile smoke screen. The infantry with the tanks came under German fire and more than half were killed or wounded, whilst the survivors eventually took cover inside 'their' tank once their grenades had all been fired. The going was not easy for the tanks. They ran into a bog even before they reached the starting point. Still, they left the start line at 5.30a.m. and carried out a very successful attack round Telegraph Hill. Once in action, the tanks essentially worked alone, and – despite the reports from the 31st Canadian Infantry – some managed to remain in action until a long time in the afternoon, when they withdrew to refuel.

Two days later, 11th April, attacking slightly further south against Neuville Vitasse, Harold's 10 section tanks stayed in action for eight hours and took many prisoners. One tank even managed to fight for three consecutive days, helping the infantry in different pockets of difficulty. Unfortunately, although afterwards all eight tanks were recovered and made available for the next battle, casualties had been significant. The next day, 12th April, Harold was promoted captain.

---

[471] Quoted in *The Devil's Chariots*, p. 177, John Glanfield, 2001.

Reginald Gladney was almost certainly one of the Canadians. Born in 1897, he had attended the school from 1909 to 1913 when his family had emigrated to Canada. He volunteered at Niagara in October 1915, claiming to be aged nineteen (the normal minimum for overseas service). Like several others, he rated his four years in the school O.T.C. as former military service. The Canadians accepted him as an officer, despite the fact that he was still only eighteen. Later they caught up with him over his age. He was made to attest again – with no place of enlistment stated – on 15th August 1918, but on that occasion he seems to have exaggerated the truth even further as his birth year mysteriously was moved back two years earlier to 1894. On 13th November 1915, he wrote to Dr. Fenwick, in response to a request for news, to tell him that he held a lieutenant's commission in the 86th Overseas Machine Gun Battalion of Canada, which he said was the only such colonial overseas unit in existence. Although they left for Europe as a unit on 19th May 1916, they never fought as a battalion – when they arrived, some of the men were immediately sent as reinforcements to units of the Canadian Corps already fighting. The rest of the battalion was reconstituted to form the Canadian Machine Gun Brigade. The British Army was suspicious of the quality of the training they had received and indeed of the quality of the unit, and there was a delay sending Canadians into action specifically as a Canadian machine-gun brigade, rather than sending men off to various machine-gun units as they were required. For the next months, a British captain was attached to the school to assist in their training and selected men were also sent to British machine-gun schools. One cause of difficulty was that they were originally armed with Colt machine guns, which the British did not use. Spares for these Colts were in short supply, and there were compatibility issues: from 1916 the unit began to switch to using Lewis guns, and later the Colts were entirely phased out and replaced with Vickers machine guns.

In the last year of the war, Reginald served with a wide range of Canadian units including the later mobile machine-gun units, which included Canadian tanks. Eventually, he was promoted to lieutenant. In April 1918 he attended the R.F.C. Arms School, qualifying in June for using Vickers, Lewis, Colt and Hotchkiss machine guns. For a time then he seems to have served with the Canadian Arms School at their headquarters before rejoining his Canadian unit on 14th October 1918. After the war he moved for a time to the USA and he died in New Zealand in 1965.

Douglas Collingwood was in 'C' Company, the 2nd Canadian Pioneers, in 1917, supporting the fight at Vimy and the latter stages of the Battle of Arras. In the build up to the battle his company was hard at work excavating and timbering a new trench and dug-out (with the help of cyclists and prisoners) and preparing positions for the 119th, 120th and 121st Batteries, whilst another company worked on building a light railway yard for the Canadian Brigade command. In the battle, "'C' Company was allotted the task of burying the Northern Cable, which was to run from the 5th Brigade Report Centre, in Paynesley Trench, by sub-way and mine galleries to Litchfield Crater. As soon as the situation permitted, it had then to be pushed forward across No Man's Land to a former German tunnel codenamed 'Volker' and then by another tunnel and across the surface to the Cramer signal Dugout, about 150 yards West of the Lens-Arras Road. 'D' Company was allotted the task of burying the Southern Cable… It was necessary for 'C' and 'D' Companies to assemble at their starting points at 9:00pm on 'Y' Day (8th April)."[472]

Zero Hour was at 5.30a.m. on 9th April. "There was not a square foot of ground, between the British original front line and the Lens-Arras road, a distance of about 1000 yards, which had not been

---

[472] War Diary, 2nd Canadian Pioneer Battalion, 8th April 1917.

turned over by a shell. The difficulties encountered were great. Some of the craters were from 15 to 20 feet deep and from 30 to 40 feet across, these being made by the larger shells. All Mine craters were skirted. 'C' & 'D' Companies who were burying cable pushed out on their work shortly after the infantry had gone over in the attack. 'C' Company, by 3pm had got well into Volker Tunnel… Just before Major Galway with 'C' Company reached Volker Tunnel, it was reported to him by the infantry mopping up party that the tunnel was cleared of the enemy. This, however, proved to be untrue and it is probable that Infantry mistook some other Tunnel for the Volker. Lieut McGhie with a small party consisting of 2 officers of 172nd Tunnelling Company and Lieutenant Bend, CFA, proceeded to reconnoitre and soon came across 12 Germans in a recess. Pretending, by calling for bombers that he was accompanied by a large party, Lieut McGhie called on them to surrender. This they did. Placing some of his prisoners ahead of him he continued down the tunnel, which is some 500 yards in, length. His prisoners showing signs of fear, he questioned them and found that mines were set further on and that they could be fired from behind a subway barricade near the East end. Forcing his prisoners ahead, they pointed out the leads to two mines, the wires of which were cut by a Tunnelling officer. Going further, they came to a loop-holed barricade of sandbags, the defenders of which departed presumably at the instigation of the German prisoners. After removing the barricade the remainder of the tunnel was found clear of the enemy. Immediately in the rear of the barricade an electric battery and a button was found for firing the mine. The resourcefulness and presence of mind of Lieut McGhie undoubtedly rendered the capturing of this Tunnel an easy matter and prevented many casualties… 'C' Company stayed all night in Volker Tunnel. Lieut D M Collingwood, Sergeant B T Palmer and 1 OR were slightly wounded."[473]

Despite his wound, Douglas remained in the action. By the beginning of May the battalion had lost four hundred and seventy-nine men (killed, wounded, or missing) since coming to France, so although their losses were not on the scale of the infantry, they were still significant. After the battle, Douglas and the others were involved primarily in communications – working on roads and preparing light railway access to support the advance. The company to which Douglas belonged was reduced to three officers, one of them Douglas, owing to loss and illness. Things were not always easy: "'C' Company, while returning from their work… ran into a bad poison gas barrage in Farfus and along the foot of the ridge. Gas masks were put on, but as they had to leave the road and travel across country to escape the Barrage, great difficulty was found in making progress. When they reached their billets, 2 men were absent. These men turned up this morning. An inspection by the Battalion M.O. sent 5 men to Hospital as being gassed and ordered the Company 24 hours rest."[474] The sickness within the company got worse ("caused by living too much underground"[475]) but Douglas was one of the two officers who was able to keep working, almost as far as the front line.

At the end of May 1917, the battalion moved behind the lines to Camblain l'Abbé for training and recuperation, and then to Ablain St. Nazaire on the front line confronting Lens, for further work. A few days later, on 5th July 1917, they moved a mile or two further north along the front to Bully-Grenay. At some point that summer he temporarily left the battalion to attend the First Army School of Instruction, and on 13th July 1917 was promoted captain. He returned to the 2nd Canadian Pioneer Battalion on 10th August 1917.

---

[473] War Diary, 2nd Canadian Pioneer Battalion, 9th April 1917.
[474] War Diary, 2nd Canadian Pioneer Battalion, 7th May 1917.
[475] War Diary, 2nd Canadian Pioneer Battalion, 10th May 1917.

Almost immediately after the assault phase, Frank Cox and the 31st Canadian Infantry Battalion were deployed opposite the village of Vimy, holding the newly won trenches. The snow turned to rain, but it remained very cold. Unusually, "owing to the fact that the men show signs of becoming exhausted on account of the long exposure to cold and rain, and the hard work entailed in consolidation and lack of any facility for cooking anything hot, the Commanding Officer applied to the Brigade for relief."[476]

Looking back over the battle and the days that followed, their brigadier was cock-a-hoop: "It has been one series of successes only obtained by troops whose courage, discipline and initiative stand pre-eminent. Nine villages have passed into our hands. Eight German Divisions have been met and defeated. Over 5000 prisoners have been captured, and booty comprising some 64 guns and howitzers, 106 trench mortars, and 126 machine guns are now the trophies of the Canadians."[477] A few days after the battle, the Canadians of the 1st Field Artillery Brigade also reflected: "April 11th, 1917... O.P's established and used as Brigade O.P. These O.P's have a splendid view of a large stretch of the flat country east of Vimy Ridge."[478] The batteries were moved forward onto that plain, by 17th April being sited east of the Farbus Ridge.

Having pushed the Germans off the ridge, the Canadians had the further task of pushing them east towards the mining area. After a brief respite, Alexander Sandbrook and the 8th Canadian Infantry Battalion went into action in the effort to push eastwards off the Vimy Ridge from Willerval. They moved forward in the evening of 26th April at Farbus Wood to prepare to capture Arleux-en-Gohelle. After reconnaissance patrols, and work assembling dumps of ammunition and supplies, the assault began under cover of an artillery barrage at 4.25a.m. on 28th April. The three assault companies had mixed fortunes: 'C' Company on the left initially made progress as it broke through the German front line, but "met stiff fighting in the town and very stiff opposition from Machine Guns and Snipers in the Wood", but they did secure their objectives and linked up with the 10th Canadian Battalion. On the other flank, 'D' Company also reached its objective, despite the loss of its captain, and was linked up with the Oxford and Buckinghamshire Light Infantry. But in the middle, 'B' Company was in difficulties, and a gap opened between 'C' and 'D' Companies. "'B' Company encountered much uncut wire and considerable opposition in the German Front Line, chiefly from Rifle & Machine Gun Fire. On passing this line it was again held up by a strong-point... this being a sunken road about 15 feet in depth. At this point it was thought that all Company officers were casualties and the remaining men prepared to defend the position. They were found here by Lieut Still of 7th Canadian Battalion (1st British Columbia Regiment) who proceeded to organise the defence of the Line. Shortly after... Capt Michelmore arrived with a platoon; he collected all the 8th Battalion men who had attached themselves to the 7th Battalion and proceeded forward clearing the village and putting all 'B' Coy men under Lieut Patterson, into the Gap between 'C' and 'D' Companies."[479] Later, the line was moved forward a short distance to straighten it with the line established on the flanks. On the evening of 29th April, it was estimated that four officers had died and another been wounded; about fifty men had been killed, about two hundred wounded, and about fifty were missing. The next day they were relieved, after being subjected to further German explosive and gas shelling. Then they had a month and a half to rebuild and retrain before returning to the same area.

---

[476] War Diary, 31st Canadian Infantry, 17th April 1917.
[477] Included in the War Diary, 31st Canadian Infantry, May 1917.
[478] War Diary, 1st Canadian Field Artillery Brigade, 6th, 8th and 11th April 1917.
[479] War Diary, 8th Canadian Infantry Battalion, 28th April 1917.

Harold Austin was in reserve for the British part of this action. His new battalion, the 1st Duke of Cornwall's Light Infantry Battalion, was part of the 95th Brigade, 5th Division. His commander noted Harold's keenness: whilst he took up his duties on 19th November, he had only been ordered to report to the battalion the next day, 20th November. However, as early as 26th November, Harold was reported as a casualty, though this clearly did not amount to much as he was soon again serving with his battalion. The term 'casualty' could mean one who was wounded or one who was sick – the decision to use the term was in the jurisdiction of the battalion medical officer and the colonel. On 2nd December he was granted a form of leave (designated by the Army as 'Kit Leave') because he was suffering from scabies – an extremely itchy skin problem which must have been awful in the trenches. It was caused by a parasite, a mite which lives on the skin and burrows into it. Close contact with a carrier spreads it, so he would have picked it up from a comrade, and it was in the unit's, as well as his own, best interest to get it dealt with. His leave started and the same day he crossed from Folkestone to Dover and made his way home to his parents in Bournemouth, with whom he lived during this sick leave. He was treated at the Mont Dore Hospital (now Bournemouth Town Hall) and the disorder took some while to clear up – his original leave had to be extended on medical advice to 20th December, but he was back on the Western Front in time for Christmas. At that stage the battalion was still near Festubert in France, near La Bassée. Harold was promoted to captain.

Harold now commanded a company. On 3rd April, in a more relaxed moment breaking into the training regime, 'A' and 'B' Companies had so big a snowball fight that it earned its way into the unit war diary. Then the battalion moved further south and, when the soldiers became detached from much of their equipment, there was nothing for it but to hold a battalion tug-of-war. The sergeants easily out-pulled the officers, but the headquarters section won overall. The battalion stood ready to be involved at an hour's notice to support the Canadian 4th Corps at the northern end of Vimy Ridge, and was held in reserve close behind the fighting zone. The most dramatic aspect of the battle they observed directly was when a British sausage balloon broke loose in the wind. Although the two observers were seen to parachute to safety, British artillery attempts to shoot down the balloon failed and it drifted over the German lines.

Behind the infantry, of course, was the artillery, including Edward Goddard. Edward was born in 1898 and attended the school from 1911 to 1913. He volunteered to join the Territorial Army on 1st April 1914, and joined the Hampshire Royal Garrison Artillery. This unit had eight sections: two heavy batteries (at Southampton) and six garrison companies spread across the Southampton to Portsmouth area. Initially, Edward was in Number 7 Garrison Company, in Southampton. When the war broke out, he was sent to help to man the Cliff End Battery on the Isle of Wight. Although three times he agreed to serve abroad, for the first years of the war the only change in his position was to be sent to the warden battery. In these years he developed his specialism as a gun layer within the team. Then he was appointed to 276 Siege Battery, Royal Garrison Artillery. This battery was formed in December 1916 from a group of sixty-two men from the Hampshire Territorial R.G.A. and forty-one from various other R.G.A. units, who were gathered at Portsmouth for the purpose in November. On 15th December they were sent to Aldershot to train as a siege artillery unit, even though at that point their commanding officer had not yet been appointed. On 25th January 1917, three days into training and practice firing on the Lydd ranges, he was made lance bombardier.

Edward and the battery sailed from Southampton to Le Havre, 28th February-1st March 1917 aboard the SS *King Edward*, but it took another fortnight before the guns arrived, on SS *Huntscape*. The battery then moved up north of Arras, joining the 53rd Heavy Artillery Group and sited at the village of Mont St. Eloi, west of the Vimy Ridge. "The Battery position was one that had been partially prepared before, in a flat open field, close to the road with small parapets and Dug Outs, guns were concealed by camouflage."[480] By the end of March preparations were complete, and they opened fire the next day, targeting Thelus Mill with one hundred rounds. On 9th April they suffered their first casualties when a signaller was killed and five more wounded when a German HE shell burst near them, as the Germans retaliated. Edward's battery supported the 3rd Canadian Division, the Canadian Corps, targeting specific German trenches or strongpoints.

The Battle of Vimy Ridge was part of a much bigger battle, the First Battle of the Scarpe, fought from 9th to 14th April. The Battle of Vimy Ridge was fought by six divisions – the British 5th and 24th Divisions, and the 1st-4th Canadian Divisions but the associated First Battle of the Scarpe was bigger: eighteen British divisions. The assault on Vimy Ridge was designed to cover the northern flank of the main British assault. In its turn, the British assault was designed to assist (by occupying German troops with a diversionary attack) the major French offensive, the Nivelle Offensive. Nivelle had persuaded his government that he could break the Germans where his predecessors had failed. He had a massive force at his disposal, over a million men, and he believed that with such a force he could overwhelm the German defenders in the region of the Aisne on the Chemin des Dames, within two days at a relatively light cost of perhaps 10,000 French soldiers. By getting the British to attack earlier than the French, Nivelle's plan was that the British would draw up German reserves, allowing his army to punch through the Hindenburg Line. In the event, Nivelle's offensive, which began a week after the British attacks of Easter Day, April 9th, was a calamitous failure. The French lost 187,000 casualties in five weeks until Nivelle abandoned the attacks on May 16th amidst accusations that he was driving his 'lambs to the slaughter'. The French Army started to mutiny from May 3rd as a result of this calamity, further increasing the pressure on Haig and the British.

Overall, the British made a promising start to the First Battle of the Scarpe, despite the snow, the sleet, and the bitterly cold weather. While in the north, the Canadian Corps, with the British 5th and 24th Divisions, emerged from tunnels onto the jumping-off line and with blazing Lewis guns captured most of Vimy Ridge on the first day. British troops of the 9th Scottish and 4th Divisions, some also emerging from tunnels around Arras, were able to advance nearly four miles to capture the village of Fampoux, and, south of the river, the village of Monchy-le-Preux, a battle in which Stanley Birdseye fought.

When Stanley Birdseye and the 10th Royal Fusiliers began to file up to the British positions east of Arras on 9th April, they began to take casualties from enemy shelling – not least when a German shell hit a British ammunition dump. The next day, Stanley and the battalion "Advanced under slight enemy artillery fire & Machine Gun Fire until checked by intense M.G. fire about 600 yds west of Monchy-le-Preux. Our casualties this time were fairly heavy. Lt. Col Rice was badly wounded by shrapnel in right arm at this point. The Battn dug in for the night & reorganised & collected together stragglers. 11th 3am. Orders received to attack & take Monchy-le-Preux at 5.30am. Major R A Smith arrived at 4 am to take command. After a stubborn resistance the village was entered & occupied, the enemy placing on it a very heavy barrage. By 3pm were all entrenched about the western edge of village except for a small advanced post on eastern side of village. Enemy shelling of village very intense, & the Cavalry who entered the village about 11am suffered

---

[480] War Diary, 276th Siege Battery, R.G.A., April 1917.

severe casualties. At 11pm the Battn was relieved by the Queens (12th Div.)."[481] After they withdrew they spent one night in the tunnels under the Grand Place at Arras.

Bruce Peake, of the 25th Northumberland Fusiliers, who had survived the first day of the Somme at La Boiselle, also fought on 9th April 1917 in the area south of the ridge. That spring, Bruce and his comrades had been having a lively time, taking turns to man the trenches at Roclincourt, a northern suburb of Arras. The Germans regularly bombarded them with artillery shells and with pineapple mortars and trench mortars. Sometimes, the Germans raided their trenches, leading to fierce fire fights and multiple casualties. After a raid of their own in mid-March, the battalion was pulled back to train and to prepare for its part in the Battle of Arras. The instructions to the raiding party included the wonderful, "No officer, NCO or man is to know anything at all about anything, except his name, should anything happen to him." On 6th April, Bruce and the battalion had returned to the trenches near Roclincourt, just east of the village.

On the evening of Easter Sunday, 8th April 1917, the 25th Northumberland Fusiliers formed up – 'A' and 'B' Companies in the front line with 'C' and 'D' Companies in support in 'Spook Street' and by 3.30a.m. the next morning they were in their attack positions. At 5a.m. Bruce and the other men quietly left the trenches and formed up in No Man's Land, protected by a barrage of trench mortars. As soon as the barrage lifted, the first wave was able to occupy the German front line trench. The 'moppers up' were left there, and the second wave leap-frogged the first and took the German support trench. We do not know in which company Bruce was serving. These trenches were captured by 'A' and 'B' Companies with minimal casualties and then the other two companies moved forward to attack behind the creeping barrage and take the next objective, code-named 'the Black Line'. This was achieved about twenty-five minutes after Zero Hour, so the attack so far was very successful. "Many dugouts here were cleared and prisoners taken. 2 Maxim Guns were captured in the Germans' 1st & Support lines & one in the Black Line. There were 8 Minenwerfers captured in the Black Line including the Mittel Weg and one small one in the same line."

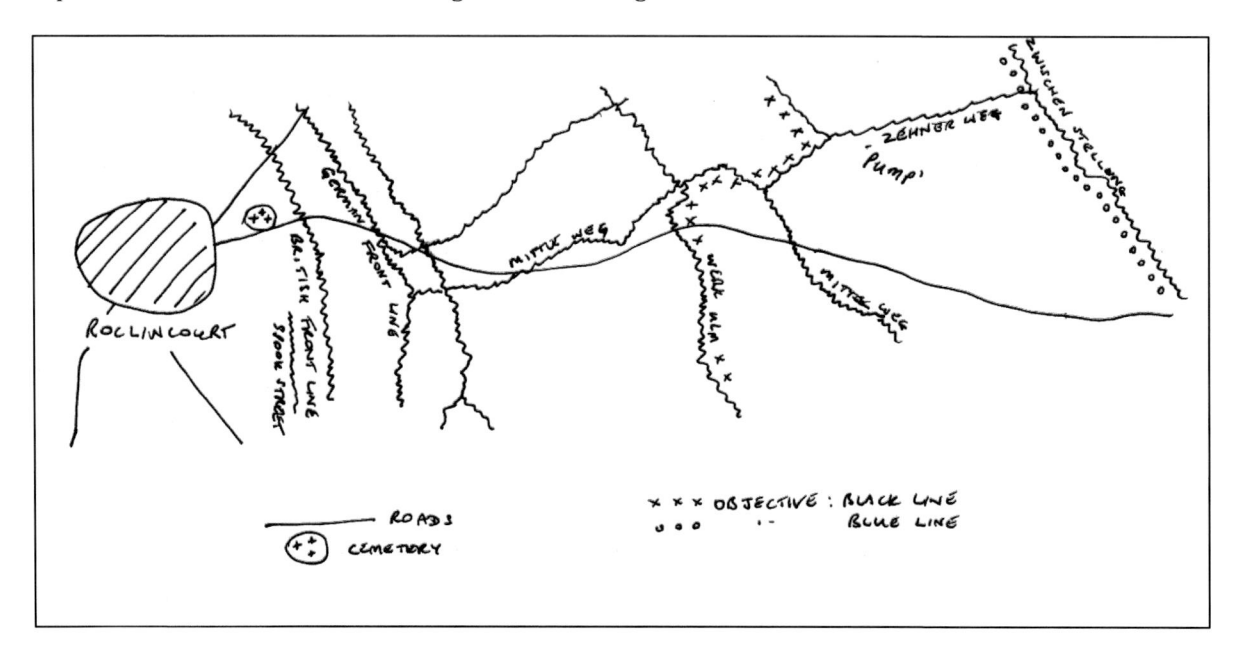

At this point, things started to go wrong. The different companies moved forward under cover of the continuing barrage to their next objective, code-named the 'Blue Line'. "All the officers of C & D

---

[481] War Diary 10th Royal Fusiliers, 10th-11th April 1917.

Coys were killed or wounded by the time the barrage lifted. These Coys were in the Black Line and its neighbourhood during this time consolidating. The other two Companies, A & B, advanced on the Barrage lifting, but B Coy was caught by Machine Gun fire coming from its left, owing to the Division on our Left not coming up. When they did, they advanced half right across our front & coming under Machine Gun fire came back. The confusion here was great owing to there being no officers left & units mixed up along the Mittel Weg. The troops were sorted out and the Highland Division made a new advance and got into the Blue Line. In the meantime 'A' Coy, supported by 'C' Coy advanced along the top and southern side of the ridge. Thus protected they escaped the Machine Gun fire from Pump or Zehner Weg. They were forced off their objective in the Blue Line owing to the Highlands pushing across our front ½ right. Of this party, 80 men, under 2nd Lieut J G Kirkup and 2nd Lieut J Snee, the only Company officers left standing, got into the Blue Line. On the left in the meantime I could only find 13 of our men under Coy Sergt Major R E Forster and 2 officers of other regiments and some Highlanders. Parties were sent up the Gaul Weg & Zehner Weg to bomb or turn out the German Machine Gun and get up to the Blue Line." [482]

The colonel reported the situation to the brigadier who sent forward the 26th and 27th Northumberland Fusiliers, who consolidated the gains on the Blue Line alongside the 51st Highland Division. At the end, only two officers and five sergeants remained unhurt. When the final tally was made that evening, the battalion had lost five officers killed and eight wounded. Nineteen men had been killed, sixty-three were missing, and one hundred and thirty-five men had been wounded. Bruce Peake had received a "severe gunshot wound in his right arm". He was taken back through the system and brought to a hospital in Whitstable, and although the process of recovery was slow and long, he was eventually released from medical care. Bruce was not fit enough to return for the action of 1918, and instead was posted to the depot for lighter duties. From there he was rapidly discharged at the end of the war, on 29th November 1918.

The 2nd Wiltshire Battalion also fought that Easter Monday. After a leave to England at the end of January, Eustace Chudleigh was back with the battalion in February 1917. On 7th March he gave up his role of battalion transport officer. German action, shelling with high explosives and with gas, was inflicting growing casualties again. A number of men were admitted to hospital, and on 17th March, Eustace was one of them, though it was more likely for illness than injury since he was able to return to the battalion a week later on 24th March 1917, in time for the build-up for the Battle of Arras.

Howard Stay was a private in this battalion, but unfortunately we know fewer details of his experiences than those of fellow Wiltshires, Harold Martyn or Eustace Chudleigh. Howard was younger than Eustace, having been born in 1898 and at the school about 1910. We do not know if he and Eustace were in the same company. Unfortunately, most of Howard's records are missing because of the 1940 Blitz, but we know that he was in the action in April 1917. Given his age, it is likely that Howard only joined the battalion quite late, perhaps like Eustace in 1916, either before or after they fought in the Battle of the Somme, or even in early 1917. (In 1916, Harold Martyn had attended a Lewis gun course. He had continued fighting with the battalion through the late autumn of 1916, apart from leave to England from 26th December 1916 to 9th January 1917 but as Harold was becoming something of a specialist in the new, lighter, infantry machine guns, at some time in the new year of 1917 he was given the delegated task of instructor in VII Corps Lewis Machine Gun School in France, where he remained until he re-joined his battalion on 1st August 1917, when they were in the trenches at Zillebeke.)

---

[482] War Diary, 25th Northumberland Fusiliers. Colonel's report on action of 9th April 1917.

At the start of 1917 they had helped pursue the Germans to the Hindenburg Line. Howard was wounded in three places by shrapnel just before, or during the assault. On 7th April they had moved up to trenches east of Mercatel. The next evening, without casualty, they took up assault positions in a sunken road south of Mercatel. On 9th April, Easter Monday, they fought in the battle. The first casualties came in the early hours when a preparatory attempt to clear a hazardous German strongpoint before the main assault went wrong. "At 1.30am a party of 100 O.R. of 'D' Company under the command of Lieut. Frisby went forward to attack the mill near the Henin-Neuville Vitasse Road. The attack met with considerable resistance, and the attackers were forced to retire, having sustained heavy casualties. Lieut. N Frisby was wounded and Lieut. S R Parsons killed, and 35 other ranks became casualties. Lieut. Bearne and one platoon moved forward to cover the retirement. It was ascertained from prisoners taken later that the garrison of the mill was at the time of the attack 120 other ranks and 2 machine guns." The main attack was a bloody affair. "At 5.30am the main attack on the Hindenburg Line commenced. Neuville Vitasse and St. Martin-sur-Cojeul, the villages on our flanks, were captured, and at 11.38am the 21st Brigade attacked with the 2nd Wiltshire Regt. on the right, the 18th king's (Liverpool) Regt. on the left, and the 19th Manchester Regt. in support. The distance between the assembly positions of this Battalion and their objectives varied between 2,000 and 2,400 yards. The Battalion advanced in artillery formation, the first wave being composed of 'A' Company on the right and 'B' Company on the left; the second wave composed of 'C' Company on the right and 'D' Company on the left; each wave consisting of 2 lines of 2 platoons per company. Considerable hostile shelling was experienced throughout the advance, which became intense as it proceeded, causing heavy casualties before the attackers came in sight of their objective. To reach the objective (namely the Hindenburg Line) two Sunken Roads had to be crossed, at which considerable resistance was offered but soon overcome, a machine gun and several prisoners being captured on the first. Between the first and second Sunken Roads the attackers came under fire from several machine guns, which together with the shelling formed a considerable barrage. The advance continued up to the enemy's wire, but by this time the ranks of the attackers were considerably depleted. The wire was found to be damaged but not cut sufficiently to allow troops to enter the trenches. The few unwounded men left took cover in all available shell holes, but eventually had to retire to the Sunken Road running from Neuville Vitasse to St. Martin-sur-Cojeul, where they dug in on the Eastern Bank. The enemy's artillery immediately commenced to shell this road heavily with shells of large calibre, causing further casualties. By this time most of the officers had become casualties, only three remaining." [483]

Afterwards, they calculated that on that day they had lost three officer casualties in the attack on the mill and two captains and twelve more officers in the main battle. Three hundred and twenty-eight men had also fallen casualties. The remnant of the battalion was withdrawn from the fight for a couple of weeks. Howard was sent back to a casualty clearing station and on to hospital. By July, the school magazine was able to report that "Two of his wounds have healed up and he is now able to walk, but the third – in his thigh – still gives trouble".[484] At the end of the year, the magazine stated, "H. Stay, Wilts Regiment, has gone to France on active service".[485] (In the reference copy held by the school, this was corrected to "returned to France".) In fact, the details are hard to trace, but his wounds were probably sufficient to make him unsuitable for participation in a fighting

---

[483] War Diary, 2nd Wiltshires, 9th April 1917.
[484] *The Bournemouthian*, July 1917.
[485] *The Bournemouthian*, December 1917.

battalion. At some point in 1918 he was placed in a labour battalion, whilst remaining a member of the regiment. In this he was clearly a success and reliable. On 12th November 1918, the day after the Armistice, he was commissioned 2nd lieutenant in the 2nd Battalion of the Wiltshire Regiment. So for the rest of 1917 Howard was out of the battle, but Eustace had survived, and for him the fighting went on.

On 10th April, along the line, both sides worked feverishly in awful weather – the British to try to overcome the issues of communications and re-supply, and especially to bring forward their field artillery to support the advanced troops; the Germans to reorganise and strengthen their remaining defences and to prepare a counter-attack. For the Germans there was the undoubted morale boost that the Hindenburg Line remained more or less intact. On 13th April, Harold Austin, commanding a company of the 1st Duke of Cornwall's Light Infantry Battalion, moved eastwards through Souchez and onto the north end of Vimy Ridge to reinforce the 46th and 50th Canadian Infantry. The terrain was badly damaged by all the explosions; aircraft from both sides flew over; and German artillery and snipers kept up harassing fire but "the Canadian troops deserve all the praise they can get, their work was magnificent."[486]

German resistance was hardening – British patrols were repulsed by machine-gun fire, and German artillery and aircraft were active. It was not until 15th April that the Royal Field Artillery was able to come up close enough to give support. For much of the time the heavy artillery shells of both sides flew over their heads as each tried to pound the other's support areas and the enemy's artillery, and it was difficult to get rations through to the front. On 17th April, "during the morning… shelled off and on fairly heavily."[487] This shelling then decreased in the afternoon and the rain returned. That night and the next day the shelling was lighter, and the rain stopped the German aircraft from flying over them. Later, Harold was to confess in a letter he wrote on 26th July that he had been stunned by the enemy shell fire of 17th April.

On 19th April they were relieved by the 12th Gloucesters and retired to the support lines. As they retired the German shell fire intensified and the headquarters dug-out took a direct hit which killed about twenty of the relieving Gloucesters. There was a lot of German aerial activity above and behind them, and German artillery was so intense that the Royal Artillery supporting them was for a time forced to abandon their guns and retire. The weather now was very clear and bright, but extremely and unseasonably cold. Despite heavy artillery shelling, on 22nd April the battalion again advanced to the front line. That night, two companies lay out in the open ready for an early morning assault.

At 4.45a.m. on 23rd April the battalion began its assault. They quickly took three "miserable specimens" prisoner, but "after topping the embankment 'C' and 'B' (the assaulting companies) came under heavy M.G. fire from Power Station and either flank. However, they pushed on and 'C' Company and 'Moppers Up' all cleared the embankment. 'D' Company following up just west of it with 'A' on right. 'A' and 'B' became rather muddled, and a combined assault was made on Callous, but owing to thick wire no one was able to get into trenches. Bombing from shell holes, and severe bomb fighting up Canine ensued but no headway was made. Posts were established at a point about fifty yards west of Callous and Canine… 'C' Company by this time had been completely

---

[486] War Diary, 1st Duke of Cornwall's Light Infantry, 13th April 1917.
[487] War Diary, 1st Duke of Cornwall's Light Infantry, 17th April 1917.

shattered and all that is [sic] known to remain are Captain Langdon and about ten men in cellar of house... and a few men who rejoined 'D' Company on the railway embankment. Our Heavies were now turned into the line Callous trench and into Power Station – Fosse 3 was reported by the 8th Sherwood Foresters to be held by them. The line now ran along railway embankment and slag heaps... Touch was never obtained with the Devons on our right, owing to the ground... being swept by M.G. fire. Therefore our artillery barraged Cité de Petit Bois – Bois de L'Hirondelle and the valley between the railway embankment and the Bois de L'Hirondelle. Several of our heavies fell short and it is feared that the men of 'C' Company lying out in the shell holes may have been killed. Our heavies continued all day, but the German artillery slackened off about 5pm, and were fairly quiet. The snipers made life very unpleasant along the main embankment line. At 9pm the 14th Royal Warwicks relieved the battalion, and we withdrew into the Vimy Angres Lines, two Companies North of embankment and two South. Battalion HQ under Brickstacks... The reasons for not getting our objectives were (1) wire in front of the first objective was not cut; (2) no proper artillery preparations; (3) the failure of regiments to our flanks to support."[488] In the early hours of the next morning, Harold got his company back into billets behind the lines, despite the fact that the roads were heavily shelled, with no new casualties.

On 25th April, Harold was sent off to hospital. Harold wrote a confused letter on 26th July from Bowhill Auxiliary Hospital for Officers, Selkirk, stating, "Whilst commanding a company in action at Vimy Ridge. 17th April 1917 Stunned by enemy shell fire. 22nd April 1917 Buried during bombardment and evacuated as battle casualty to Hospital No. 23 CCS suffering from Shell Shock wound, ultimately evacuated to England. 8th May I was examined by Medical board at No. 4 London General hospital and sent here for lengthy treatment as you will verify by Medical report." The medical report of 10th May from the 4th London General Hospital R.A.M.C. T gives a clearer view: "22/4/1917 or 23/4/17 stunned by shell explosion on Vimy Ridge when it burst by him; he carried on for two days, when he showed signs of nervous breakdown. When going into action he was blown up and buried by H.E.; dazed. After getting his men into billets, he collapsed and was found on the floor of his own billet. Sent to CCS, then to Calais. Thence he was sent here – arrived 27th April. On Exam: K.J. plus, insomnia, dreams, and frequent headaches. Better but has had bad nights."[489]

Harold was sent to Scotland for further examination and treatment, which originally was expected to require at least twelve weeks. Whilst he was there he appeared before a medical board at Craiglockart, Edinburgh, which found him unfit for further general service. He was probably still there when Wilfred Owen arrived in June, but probably gone before Sassoon arrived in August. He never returned to the front.

On the southernmost sector of the battle, April 10th had been a disaster. 20,000 Australians surrendered at Bullecourt when, having attacked despite the non-arrival of tanks, which were supposed to be breaking through the wire, they found themselves in the narrow salient of their own advance and unable to retreat. However, at Monchy-le-Preux, Stanley Birdseye and the British infantry of the 15th and 37th Divisions had captured the village with the help of six tanks; when the cavalry tried to advance beyond them they were annihilated by German machine-gun fire and accurately targeted artillery. An attack by the 2nd Seaforth Highlanders and the 1st Royal Irish

---

[488] War Diary, 1st Duke of Cornwall's Light Infantry, 23rd April 1917.
[489] Army File, WO 339/79518.

Fusiliers at Fampoux was similarly and catastrophically wiped out. At Monchy, on April 13th-14th, a disaster turned to valour (but not triumph) when one thousand Essex and Newfoundlander soldiers were killed by a ferocious German counter-attack as they tried to extend beyond the village, but the village itself was held against overwhelming odds by just nine surviving Newfoundlanders until reinforcements could reach them after five hours.

The Battle of Arras: The Second Battle of the Scarpe

After the first battle stalled, a second major initiative was made on 23rd and 24th April. This is generally known as the Second Battle of the Scarpe.

On 21st April, Stanley Birdseye and the 10th Royal Fusiliers were again in the trenches near Athies, immediately east of Arras. On the evening of 22nd they formed up into four waves of attack and attacked the next morning. "23rd. Report received from O.C. Coys at 3am that their Coys were in the attack formation. At Zero hour (4.45am) the Battn advanced in accordance with the Artillery Barrage programme until the German second line was taken and here considerable confusion arose owing to men of the 63rd Bde getting over too much to the Left. About this point it was found difficult to make a further immediate advance owing to enemy enfilade Machine Gun fire & snipers. The Battn on our Left was slightly in rear of us and we had to wait until they came up in line before the Machine Guns and Snipers were silenced. The advance then continued up to the road... At this point we were not in touch with the Battns on our left and right. A patrol was pushed out to find if Cuba Trench was occupied. The patrol returned and reported that Cuba Trench was clear of the enemy. The Battn then consisting of 3 Officers & about 502 O.R.'s occupied Cuba Trench at 9.30am. Men of the 13th R. Fusiliers and 13th KRRC arriving on our left about half an hour afterwards. Patrols were immediately sent out to get in touch with the 63rd Bde on our right, but returned having failed to do so. A defensive flank was then formed by Machine Guns on our right. Immediate consolidation of Cuba Trench was started. Patrols were periodically sent out to get into touch with the 63rd Bde but it was not until 9.55pm that we succeeded in doing so... At 1pm a patrol was sent out to reconnoitre the Cross Roads... but were unable to approach owing to very active enemy snipers. 50 Prisoners were captured during the day. Patrols were sent out during the night. All through the advance the enemy barrage was very intense."[490]

The trench they had captured was held despite heavy counter-attacks and shelling, but it was not until 29th April that the battalion was relieved. The casualties amounted to four officers killed and six wounded; forty-two men killed and one hundred and ninety-two wounded, whilst twenty-two were missing. On 23rd April, having survived so much and for so long, Stanley died in the midst of the battle. His body was never found, and today his name is engraved on the Arras Memorial to those without a named grave. Stanley's name did not originally appear on the school War Memorial, presumably because his sister and half-brother did not think to inform Dr. Fenwick of these events, perhaps because they might well have waited, anxiously hoping for some good news to trickle through to them; if so, it never came.

Harold Froud and Leonard Taylor were also involved that day. After recovering from his gunshot wound to the arm in September 1916, Harold had re-joined the 5th Durham Light Infantry Battalion and had spent the winter of 1916-1917 in the trenches. Harold was joined in the battalion by

---

[490] War Diary 10th Royal Fusiliers, 23rd April 1917.

Leonard Taylor. Leonard (who had been second master or deputy headmaster) had probably taught Harold when he had been at the school. He had begun to teach at Bournemouth School in January 1904. His subjects were English and history, with some classics, but he was one of those men who took on lots of extra responsibilities – founding and looking after the school magazine for five years, looking after the Old Boys Club and the library, and from 1909 serving as Captain to the School Officer Training Corps (O.T.C.). He had left in July 1913 to take up the post of headmaster at Darlington Grammar School. He had originally been commissioned as 2nd lieutenant on 18th October 1906 when he joined the Cadet Corps at a time of change (Captain Howarth having resigned and been replaced by Captain Day; 2nd Lieutenant Kelland being promoted to lieutenant). In those days, the School Corps was attached to the 4th Volunteer Battalion of the Hampshire Regiment. When, on 17th July 1908, the national reserve system had been reorganised, he and John Day had resigned their commissions in the Volunteer Force to be appointed to the Territorial Force on the Unattached List. By that stage he had been promoted to a full lieutenant, and later he was promoted captain to lead the Cadet Force at the school. So, at the outbreak of the war, he held a commission as captain on the Unattached List of the Territorial Force.

He had taken demotion when he volunteered for active service and was commissioned lieutenant in the Durham Light Infantry on 28th January 1916. He joined Harold in the 5th Durham Light Infantry Battalion. Leonard landed in France on 21st February 1917, at a relatively quiet time, south of Albert, with a big emphasis on training routines, though this was disrupted when two companies were isolated because of infection with scarlet fever at the end of March. They moved by stages north to Arras where they went into the famous subterranean passages which stretch for kilometres beneath the old city in mid-April. On 15th April 1917, he wrote, "Since [February] we have been on the march for a long time and now seem to have reached the hub of the universe as far as the Western Front is concerned. We are going up to the front line to-night, but at present we are living in a wonderful system of caves capable of holding 10,000 men. The atmosphere is very close and the roof drips continuously in all parts, so they are by no means comfortable. I have been for two days in charge of a Brigade unloading party in the big town near. As the trains did not come I had a good deal of time to myself and I have been wandering round. It is a very picturesque place, with abundance of cellar accommodation and troops were smuggled in in huge quantities for the push. Sunday and Monday they suffered a terrible bombardment, with the result that the Town Hall, a very historic old place, is in ruins, and the cathedral has no roof. In the square there are one or two holes 15ft. wide and 20ft. deep made by their delayed action shells, which have opened up the cellars underneath. Despite this the civilian population is returning, and yesterday I saw one or two shops open, and I even got quite a good lunch at a restaurant. On Thursday and Friday we had a little shelling, but since then nothing, though I still think we are up against a stiff proposition a few miles away."[491]

Harold and Leonard's division had been held in reserve in the First Battle of the Scarpe, about ten miles west of Arras. On 15th April they moved forward into the support area, known as 'The Harp'. Here there were deep dug-outs which had been captured from the Germans in the earlier fighting, and which had formed a bastion within the Hindenburg Line immediately south of the village of Tilloy les Mofflaines. Their battalion was not, at that stage, directly involved in the fighting.

On 20th April, their brigade, the 150th, moved up the hill through Wancourt and took over control of

---

[491] Published in *The Bournemouthian*, July 1917.

the new front line trenches on the ridge from the Wancourt Tower to the River Cojeul, which flows to the north of the tower past Guemappe and Wancourt villages. Three days later, the 5th Durham Light Infantry Battalion was in support alongside the 5th Yorkshires, whilst the 4th East Yorkshires and 4th Yorkshires were to assault eastwards to capture Cherisy and gain the far bank of the river as it meandered south from Vis-en-Artois. At 4.45a.m., eighty-four 18-pounder field guns, supported by thirty howitzers opened up a barrage on the German positions west of Cherisy. The German artillery retaliated and caught many of the assault battalion men in their assembly trenches. Even so, they attacked, supported by two tanks, but encountered disaster when the flank companies of the East Yorkshires encountered 'friendly fire'. The British support barrage was moving too slowly forward, and hit the East Yorkshires – killing or injuring every officer and NCO of those flanks companies! But the survivors still managed to occupy the enemy trenches by 5.25a.m.

To understand the disasters which were hitting the British assaults, including this attack, it is necessary to understand that when they retreated after the Battle of the Somme to the Hindenburg Line, the Germans had switched from a linear defence policy (strongly manned front line to be held or recaptured no matter the cost) to a defence in depth. The new German tactic was to designate three zones of defence: the Front Zone, Battle Zone, and Rearward Zone. The Front Zone was to be thinly held to minimise casualties from artillery, and to include scattered strongpoints behind the trenches. If the British attacked in strength, the Germans could withdraw to the second or Battle Zone, which could be up to two miles back from the Front Zone, where reserves were ready to counter-attack but were safer from the preliminary bombardment. At the back, in the Rearward Zone, were further reserves to support the counter-attack. The German theory was that the British would become disorganised and cut up as they advanced through the Front Zone, and then be smashed in the Battle Zone. The British supporting artillery would by that stage be in the wrong place, too far back, and be in the process of being moved forward, meaning that it was ineffective against the German counter-attacks. These German plans worked at Arras. It explains how even smashed advancing troops could have occupied the front lines, but it also explains how the Germans were able to hit back so strongly.

Later in the morning of 23rd April, the Germans launched a major counter-attack in force. The two support battalions, including Harold and Leonard, were rushed forward to reinforce the captured positions. However, the remnants of all four battalions found themselves effectively surrounded by the German counter-attack. By now, all the senior officers and senior NCOs were dead or wounded. The order to retire was given and junior officers or NCOs led the remnants back through the encircling Germans all the way to their original start line, where those that were left assembled by about 11.30a.m.

General Allenby sent through the order that, despite this reversal, the objectives "must be taken that day at all costs". At this stage there were so few men left that the four battalions combined to form a single battalion of men. According to the Official History, only 5th D.L.I. and 5th Yorks "could muster more than small parties of weary men".[492] Supported by 1/5th Borderers and 1/9th Durham Light Infantry, and with a new British barrage, they again attacked. This time it was the Germans who broke. "The steadiness and determination of the advance proved too much for the enemy. He

---

[492] Details of this assault have been largely derived from the Scarborough Maritime Museum website account, *1917 'At all costs'*, www.scarboroughsmaritimeheritage.org.uk/article.php?article=582.html.

was wearied out and beaten after a long 'slogging match'. Parties of his infantry surrendered freely, while others retreated under fire." according to the Official History. But they had lost four officers and twenty-three men killed, and a further three officers and one hundred and thirty-seven men wounded. Another officer and ninety-six men were missing. Harold and Leonard had survived, but the emotional and physical cost must have been enormous.

The same day, 23rd April, Eustace Chudleigh and the remnants of the 2nd Wiltshire Battalion moved to the original British fire trenches at Neuville Vitasse, south of Vimy Ridge. Earlier that day, the assault troops, supported by an effective artillery barrage, had opened up a new nine mile front. On the right of Eustace and his comrades were the 1st Middlesex and 2nd Royal Welsh Fusiliers, and on their left were the 18th Manchesters. The next day, 24th April, "about 11.0am the 2nd Yorkshire Regt advanced from their trenches in a North Easterly direction. Shortly after, parties of Germans were seen advancing from the South West corner of Vis-En-Artrois. Colonel Gillson at once communicated with Brigade Headquarters, and shortly afterwards ordered the Battalion to advance in support of the 2nd Yorkshire Regt. The Battalion advanced in artillery formation, 'C' and 'D' companies leading, followed by 'B' company and Battalion Headquarters. The enemy put down a considerable barrage and caused a few casualties, but in no way hindered the advance, which continued until we reached the Cherisy – Heninel road. The Battalion then dug in astride the road, and remained there until dark. The enemy continued to shell intermittently throughout the day, but being ignorant of our position caused few casualties. In the evening orders were received to proceed to the Blue Line and join up with the 33rd Division on our right and the 18th King's (Liverpool) Regt on our left... At 8.15 pm the Battalion moved to this position, 'D' company on the right, 'C' company in the centre, and 'B' company on the left, Battalion headquarters moving to the Sunken Road... Companies immediately commenced to improve their positions by consolidating the existing cable trench and digging 'T' heads out from the trench towards the enemy. Posts were pushed out in front of the cable trench... The enemy was quiet during the night on our front."[493]

For four days the battalion remained under intense enemy shell fire, and for a time ran short of food, since it was not possible to bring up new rations on at least one of these days, but eventually they were relieved and pulled back to lick their wounds, receive reinforcements, and to train for the next attack. On 10th May, Eustace was sent back to an army rest camp with eight men. The war diary does not make it clear whether he was sick, or had not recovered properly from his earlier hospital visit, or if he was simply the officer detailed to keep an eye on the men needing rest. Whatever the reason, he was back with the battalion, bringing back the eight men, on 26th May.

William Mitford and the 7th Royal Fusiliers were in position a little further north than that of Harold and Leonard or Eustace. They had moved into the trenches there on 14th April and spent the next few days trying to consolidate and to move the British front line closer to that of the Germans. First, they dug a new jumping-off line about two hundred yards from the German lines, only to see it smashed by a heavy German bombardment. This then necessitated the digging of a new line, after which the battalion took up position to launch an assault on 23rd April. That day, the battalion attacked north of Gavrelle, assisting other battalions to capture the village, which lies north of the river Scarpe and just a short distance to the north-east of Arras itself. "23rd. 4.45am. Zero. The artillery barrage commenced & that was the signal for the infantry to advance from the assembly trenches. They kept close up to the barrage and prepare for the assault – the enemy front

---

[493] War Diary, 2nd Wiltshire Battalion, 24th April 1917.

line. Great difficulty was experienced owing to the enemy wire not having been cut & our men could not get through. Many casualties were caused through this... They were met by enemy bombing parties & strong resistance was offered by machine guns etc. These caused a great number of casualties until a party was organised to attack and capture them. This they did taking 23 prisoners. They then reached the enemy's support line where the enemy were trying to bomb their way down Flabby & Falcon Trench. A party was pushed forward to hold the enemy at this point... A bombing party was organised, numbering 22 & started to force the enemy back up Flabby Trench as far as the Railway, with the help of the Bedfords on the right. The snipers & artillery were extremely active on the road & along our front... The casualties were said to have been very heavy & Captain Granville was reported to have been killed in the enemy front line... Report received from OC D Coy timed 8.20am stating 'My Company has taken enemy 2nd Line & have taken about 23 prisoners & one M.G. Our casualties are about 40%. I am in touch with the Bedfords on my right and 2nd Div on my left. 'A' Coy have lost all their officers & I have taken command. 8.30am.' Report received from an officer of B Coy to the effect that his party had reached German 2nd Line, but that things were not very satisfactory. Strong resistance in the form of bombing attacks had been encountered and machine guns & snipers were very active & holding them up. The runner also reported that OC 'B' Coy A/Capt Gush had been killed. According to information received it was evident that only a lane had been cut in the wire & that this caused the men to miss their direction. Consequently a stubborn resistance was put by the enemy on the left of the line 1st & 2nd & these lines could not be cleared. 9.20am. A verbal message received that the Germans were still holding the 1st & 2nd Line... & that we were suffering many casualties from machine gunfire & snipers. Only about 25 men left in D Coy party & that they were being held up 70 yards on the Left from the Railway. 9.40am. Report received from 2nd Lt Greenwood. 'We are consolidating our present position & have a party of about 40 consisting of all Coys of the Fusiliers still being held up by machine guns.'... 4pm. Hdqtrs move forward to new position in front line leaving signal post behind... Parties were pushing forward & it was hoped to dig the line along the Railway under cover of darkness. Several enemy contact aeroplanes were seen & these dropped red & green lights as signals on passing low over our line... 7.30pm. Report sent through the Bde, urgently for stretcher bearers to be sent up for carrying away the wounded lying in the trench & suffering very much from exposure... The Battn was withdrawn to the Green Line by daybreak. Enemy shelled the road very heavily about 5am. The attack had been very successful. The whole of the village had been captured & it was reported that 13 officers & 480 O.R. had been taken prisoner by the Division. Our casualties were rather heavy & amounted to officers killed 4; wounded 8. O.R.s during the tour in the Line, Killed 36; wounded 221; missing 84."[494]

Indeed, the cost was dreadful. At the start of the attack, the diminished battalion had eighteen officers and three hundred and fifty-eight men. When they were relieved the next morning, "the battalion had been practically wiped out."[495] William had been wounded again, hit in the thigh, this time by a shell fragment. Recovering was going to take some time, so he was sent back down the medical line, and back to England where he was sent to a hospital in Newcastle. By July, the school magazine was pleased to report, "when last heard of, he was doing well."[496]

Herbert Short of the 7th Suffolk Battalion was also wounded. From 19th November he was acting

---

[494] War Diary, 7th Royal Fusiliers, 23rd-24th April 1917.
[495] *The Royal Fusiliers in the Great War*, H.C. O'Neill, William Heinemann, London, 1922, p. 167.
[496] *The Bournemouthian*, July 1917.

captain in command of a company. In January, he had written of his satisfaction at being out of the trenches, "as about a week ago we had a fairly heavy fall of snow, and it has frozen hard every day since, so it must be jolly rotten for the fellows in the line now; and we are having a very cold rest. As usual during these so-called rest periods we are doing plenty of training and our time is fully occupied..."[497] His battalion, the 7th Suffolks, had moved north in 1917 and was in action at Arras in the First Battle of the Scarpe, and in two subsequent assaults. On 28th April, their brigade went into the attack at Pelves, adjacent to Roeux – about seven miles east of Arras. At 4.25a.m. the battalion moved forward from support in artillery formation and reached the front line at 4.45a.m. Faced by a heavy German barrage and machine-gun fire, their attack failed. "Captain H. A. Short has returned from France to England wounded, for the fourth time, but is now convalescent. His escape from death seems to have been little short of miraculous. In the great advance at Arras on April 29th, after penetrating about 600 yards behind the German front line, he was hit in the side by a bullet. He immediately took cover in a neighbouring trench – only to be buried by a German shell. In this condition he remained, inaccessible to rescue owing to the zone of fire, for 45 hours, when a relief party succeeded in reaching him and bringing him in."[498] Probably he remained in England at the Suffolk Regiment Depot, and so survived the war despite all his injuries. He served as a colonel in the Second World War.

Alexander Simpson of the 1st Honourable Artillery Company Battalion was with those who relieved William Mitford and the 7th Royal Fusiliers Battalion in this battle. Alexander's 'B' Company was in the thick of the action alongside 'A' Company. So fierce was the fighting that ammunition re-supply was a problem, and urgent messages had to be sent back for extra Stokes mortar shells and rifle grenades but once these had been brought up the companies were able to continue to push forward to support the 7th Royal Fusiliers Battalion.

Some lessons had been learned by the generals. Once the men had gained the German position, they were instructed to hold the new front line as lightly as possible with Lewis gun units, keeping back the rest of the companies to counter-attack (to avoid heavy casualties from German artillery and mortar fire on the old German line). In the afternoon of 24th April, the Germans did counter-attack in strength and, although this was beaten back after several hours, with the concession of some trench line, the fighting was just as intense over the next few days. Ammunition of all sorts again ran dangerously low. Early in the morning of 28th April, the Battalion Headquarters received a message that no rounds or cartridges remained, and grenades too had been sent for. Requests for the help of tanks seem to have gone unanswered, but Royal Marines did come in, themselves taking heavy casualties.

For days Alexander was in the thick of this battle. At one stage, on 28th April, the men of his company had no trench but a series of shell holes to guard to try to hold back German counter-attacks. They hoped to be able to move forward to occupy the German position if barrages of mortar bombs could drive them out. As they tried to move forward they found themselves mixing with isolated groups of marines as well as men from some Essex and Staffordshire Battalions. As well as German 'whizz bangs' to contend with, the British artillery 4.7" shells now began to drop short onto the leading groups of H.A.C. men. Ordered to construct a defensive trench, the company commander requested support, but even when some sappers were sent forward, it was only

---

[497] *The Bournemouthian*, April 1917
[498] *The Bournemouthian*, July 1917; it appears that the account has stated the wrong date in April.

possible to make a series of defence posts at fifty yard intervals. Meanwhile, the company had had no rations.

With or without food, the next morning they were ordered forward across the railway line to join up with the Bedfordshire Battalion. Things were still confused. One company commander reported from Oppy Trench when they reached it, "'8.40 Mixture of men – quite disorganised; practically without officers.' He suggests Vickers guns and engineers to help build strong point." After that, 'B' Company had further work to do: "Message from OC (B) 9.15 'Our line is established from a point 50 yds N of railway and extends for about 130 yards. We are in touch with 'C' Coy on our right & the Beds and RFs on our left'. 10 Message to OC (B) 'The Brigadier wishes you to push forward patrols on to the Sunken Road due East of your position. They are to bring back reports as to whether it is occupied or not. If it is not occupied establish a line of posts with the best field of fire available. Report result at earliest opportunity. Try to get people on your left to co-operate. 'C' Coy will reinforce you with a platoon.'"

In the event, Alexander and his friends had their hands full trying, successfully, to repel a major German counter-attack; at that stage, pushing forward seemed beyond their means. Later, in the late afternoon, they were again ordered forward to the sunken road. At 8p.m. that evening, his company commander, 2nd Lieutenant Pollard, reported: "Adj. Bedfords has orders to place himself under me for relief. Worded 'Step up quickly as HAC is responsible for trench.' I have fixed things up with him. My forward post has been relieved by 23 RF and all my Coy is together. 5 patrols have been pushed forward to Sunken Road at 6.30 and one down trench toward Oppy Wood... Left patrols report Huns in strength (almost 1200) extending in a line starting 150 yards beyond hut in trench and running in direction of Fresnes. If these gentry are going to attack us at dusk a little barrage might warm them up. I do not consider it advisable to establish line of posts as Oppy is obviously still occupied and our posts would be in danger of being cut off." [499]

Alexander's officer, 2nd Lieutenant Pollard, had risen through the ranks of the unit. He had already had been awarded the Military Cross and D.C.M., and for his part in this action he was awarded the Victoria Cross. The citation for it reveals the conditions in which Alexander was fighting: "The troops of various units on the left of this Officer's battalion had become disorganised owing to the heavy casualties from shell fire; and a subsequent determined enemy attack with very strong forces caused further confusion and retirement, closely pressed by hostile forces. 2nd Lt. Pollard at once realised the seriousness of the situation, and dashed up to stop the retirement. With only four men he started a counter-attack with bombs, and pressed it home till he had broken the enemy attack, regained all that had been lost and much ground in addition. The enemy retired in disorder, sustaining many casualties. By his force of will, dash and splendid example, coupled with an utter contempt of danger, this Officer, who has already won the D.C.M. and M.C., infused courage into every man who saw him."[500]

Alexander survived, and his battalion was pulled back from the front line to a quieter existence in support and reserve. After doing a lot of reserve work, including digging new communication trenches along the reserve line area, on 29th June 1917 the battalion was transferred out of 190th Brigade and became G.H.Q. troops. After this it becomes difficult to trace Alexander's experiences.

---

[499] War Diary, 1st Honourable Artillery Company Battalion, 29 April 1917.
[500] *London Gazette Supplement*, 8th June 1917.

The battalion – still as G.H.Q. troops – took part in the Second Battle of Passchendaele, losing a lot of men. Before that, several hundreds of them took part in quashing the famous mutiny at Étaples in September 1917, although it is not clear if Alexander was amongst those involved. On 5th July 1918, he left France to join an officers' cadet school, from which he was commissioned 2nd lieutenant in the Dorsetshire Regiment on 3rd March 1919. He died in Bournemouth in 1958.

Thomas Searls was in the thick of this battle, in the line next to Alexander. He had again recovered from being wounded on the Somme. After briefly being attached to the 8th Yorks and Lancaster Battalion, he was soon re-assigned to his own 2nd South Staffordshire Battalion. He may have re-joined them as a result of great battalion losses following participation in a failed attack, 16th-17th February on the Somme battleground: only one of the ten officers who participated in that assault returned unwounded, with six of them being killed. It was afterwards disclosed that a deserter had betrayed the details of the attack and the Germans had reinforced their line with additional men and machine guns. From 18th-22nd April, the battalion was in the British front line between the 1st Honourable Artillery Company and the 13th Essex Battalions, opposite the German positions at Oppy Wood. For those four days, Thomas and the battalion endured heavy German bombardment, but suffered relatively light casualties. Ironically, as they had withdrawn on 23rd April, on their flank the 63rd Division had attacked, and German artillery fire inflicted heavy casualties on the South Staffordshire Battalion. Even their commander was hit on the head and had to be replaced.

Then it was their turn to attack Oppy Wood. "27th. For the attack of the 28th ordered to be carried out by 5th & 6th Brigades on the Div. Front, this battalion was split up and allotted as follows: B Coy to 13th Essex (4 Officers 120 men); D Coy to 17th M'sex, (4 Officers 120 men); A Coy provided a carrying party of 1 officer and 68 men for the 13th Essex and C Coy a similar party for the 17th Middlesex. This Bn. on going into action consisted of 10 officers and 376 men besides 4 LG teams (16 men) lent to 13th Essex. Moves took place during the 27th. 28th. Zero time fixed for 4.25 AM and Z day 28th. The 5th & 6th Bdes reached their 1st & 2nd objectives but were obliged to retire to original positions owing to Div. on right (63rd) failing to reach its objectives. The British front was subjected to heavy and ceaseless fire all through the day. Our casualties were Capn. W.A. Simmonds, 2/Lts. H Johnson and J.S. Smith killed, Lieut T.H. Searls wounded, 2/Lieuts C.W. Bloomfield & R. O'Connor missing, and 186 other ranks killed, wounded and missing."[501]

Yet again, Thomas had been wounded. Once again his wounds were serious. A ricochet bullet had hit him in the upper part of his right arm, "making a jagged and dirty wound".[502] In addition, he had two superficial wounds to his right thigh above the knee. The arm wound was serious – after anti-tetanus serum had been given he still had a high temperature and an X-ray showed a metal fragment remained in his arm. This was removed by an operation delayed until 9th June to give his general condition time to improve. On 1st May, he had been shipped back from Calais to Dover and sent to the Royal Free Hospital. Recovery from these wounds took longer, but he was again fit for service on 24th September 1917. This time, however, he was sent not to the Western Front, but to the Italian Front. This time he joined the 1st South Staffordshire Battalion, sent to Italy in November 1917 to bolster the Italian Army after its defeat at Caporetto. On 15th June 1918, he was once more wounded – and again, seriously. This time he was again hit by a gunshot wound to his right shoulder blade. This fractured his scapula, with some bits reaching near to his dorsal vertebrae. He

---

[501] War Diary, 2nd South Staffordshire Battalion, 27th-28th April 1917.
[502] Army File, Thomas Searls, WO 339/34918.

was also hit in the chest on the left-hand side with a blast wound which caused a flesh wound only just below clavicle. In Italy these wounds were cleaned and the bits of shell and bone were removed. However, he needed further treatment and care, and so was evacuated through France to Le Havre and on 3rd July 1918 embarked for an overnight crossing to Southampton. The next day he was admitted to Reading War Hospital where, on 9th July, the shoulder wound was re-sutured (the flesh wound to the chest having already healed). On 7th August he was transferred to the Red Cross Officers' Hospital, at Bigadon, near Buckfastleigh in Devon. On 29th October 1918, he was deemed to have recovered, and was granted some leave – though for the next two months, before he was thought fit to serve again, he still required surgical dressings. By the time he had recovered he had heard the welcome news of a much deserved award. On 16th September, *The London Gazette* announced he had been awarded the Military Cross. The citation read: "T./Lt. Thomas Harvey Searls, S. Staff. R. For conspicuous gallantry and devotion to duty when in command of a platoon. He successfully completed an enveloping movement, with the result that none of the enemy garrison escaped death or capture. He showed conspicuous courage in hand-to-hand fighting, and personally inflicted several casualties on the enemy. He captured several prisoners single-handed."[503] Finally, he left the Army on 2nd March 1919. In a fulfilling life until his death in Winchester in 1960, Thomas went on receive the Order of the British Empire (in 1955 as Deputy Controller, Education Division, British Council) and to be made a Member of the Second Class, or Knight Commander, of the Most Distinguished Order of Saint Michael and Saint George in the New Year's Honours of 1959, a year in which he continued to work for the British Council, even going to Penang that July. Thomas was probably the most regularly wounded of the Old Bournemouthians who fought on the Western Front, and one of the most decorated.

John Bennett was also in the Battle of Arras in April 1917. Apart from a short spell in the front line trenches in November, for John Bennett and the men of the 5th Border Battalion most of the period of the latter part of 1916 had been spent behind the front line, repairing and improving roads, railway and tramway lines, despite horrible weather conditions. Whilst this was not glamorous work, it was important work and a message of appreciation from the brigadier was distributed amongst the men. The year had concluded with a move into support lines behind the 9th Durham Light Infantry, north of Mametz Wood. In bitterly cold weather, hampered by ice and snow, they moved by stages north again to Arras, and on 14th April were in position to support an attack made by the 6th Durham Light Infantry. For five days they remained underground in the tunnels, the 'caves' of Arras.

On 23rd April 1917, the battalion entered Nepal Trench to support the 150th Brigade in its attack near the Wancourt Tower position, south-east of Arras. At 4.45a.m., the 150th Brigade attacked and took its objective, about 1,000 yards east of Wancourt Tower but was driven back by a strong German counter-attack. Two companies of the 5th Border Battalion placed knife rests in front of the trench they were occupying and tried to consolidate that position. At 6p.m., with the 9th Durham Light Infantry on their right, the battalion attacked and re-captured the enemy position from which the 150th Brigade had been driven. They also captured five German machine guns and several trench mortars, about two hundred prisoners, and rescued many 150th Brigade wounded soldiers who had been taken prisoner in the German counter-attack. The next day, at 4p.m., they attacked again. Held up by German artillery and machine-gun fire, they launched a second, successful, attack at dusk and managed to reach their objective, dig a new line, and to consolidate. However, these

---

[503] *The London Gazette*, 16th September 1918.

actions were at some considerable expense. Six of their officers were killed and four wounded. Forty-five men were killed, and a further one hundred and thirty-one men wounded, with twenty-three more missing. After this battalion was withdrawn to recuperate, and the next month was spent behind the lines training and rebuilding. For some reason, John was struck off the strength of the battalion in July. It seems most likely he was one of the officers wounded in the attack of 23rd-24th April (none of whom were named in the war diary). He was promoted lieutenant on 1st July, and seconded for duty as an escort officer, Prisoner of War Company, on 16th July 1917, the sort of job given to an officer weakened by wounds. On 6th March 1918 he was appointed as a full lieutenant in the Labour Corps. His old battalion, the 5th Border Battalion had been re-designated a labour battalion the previous February, but it is not clear whether he re-joined them. On 2nd April 1918 he was again promoted to captain and only relinquished that rank and post on 31st April 1919. So John survived the war. He took up arms again in the Second World War, and on 1st February 1945 was created a Member of the Order of the British Empire (M.B.E.) "in recognition of his gallant and distinguished services in North West Europe" with the Pioneer Corps.

Arthur Mosley's brigade of the 62nd Division and his 2/4th King's Own Yorkshire Light Infantry Battalion was to support the others in the re-capture of Bullecourt. However, two companies of Arthur's battalion were required to join the men of the 5th Battalion in the assault line. When the attack went in on 3rd May, there were heavy casualties amongst the assault battalions, particularly from enfilade fire, partly made possible by a last minute change of plan by the Australians which left the Germans free to fire, and partly due to the sheer strength of the Germans who included one battalion with new, Swedish, automatic rifles. In addition to their heavy machine-gun fire, the Germans fired thousands of rounds of gas and explosive shells. Arthur was hit and was hospitalised to treat his wounds and his shell shock. He was six weeks in a rest camp recuperating.

As the British tried in vain to capture the Oppy Line, Bernard Hame once again showed his valour. By 2nd May, Bernard and the 5th Royal Engineers Field Company were near Farbus, east of Thélus and south of Vimy. Their job now was to prepare for another attack on the Oppy Line. That night, at "8.30pm... ii Lieut Hame RE and 7 Sappers of 5th Field Coy RE accompanied by an officer of 23rd RF taped out a 'forming up Line running from the Canadian Right Strong point... to a point in sunken rd due south... thence to Strong point 'A' in the Arleux Loop... This line was successfully taped out by 12.40 am on 'Z' Day 3rd inst.'"[504] Later that morning, with Zero Hour at 3.45a.m., this forming up line was used, but the attack failed, so they had to dig an emergency trench that evening/night to form a line to prevent counter-attack. Two days later, on 5th May, they were pulled back from the front line. On 23rd June the local papers were able to report that he had been informed that on the third occasion of being recommended for the Military Cross, the award was definitely being conferred upon him. The citation which gained him that high award was reported on 26th July 1917 in *The London Gazette*: "Temp. 2nd Lt. Bernard Whitfield Hame, R.E. For conspicuous gallantry and devotion to duty, in taping out the line from which an Infantry Brigade attack was to start. He was under heavy shell fire for three hours whilst so engaged."[505] According to the school magazine he was also "Mentioned in Dispatches".

That May, Harold Head and his tank men of 10 Section, 12 Company, 'D' Battalion were also in action, trying to help to recapture Bullecourt. If Bullecourt could be captured, a breach would have

---

[504] War Diary, 5th Royal Engineers Field Company, 2nd May 1917.
[505] Supplement to *The London Gazette*, 26th July 1917, p. 7629.

been made in the Hindenburg Line. At this time he had two lieutenants and two 2nd lieutenants whom he would send into action with tanks 795 and 596; and 785 and 580. The weakness in the armour plating, and the German use of armour-piercing shells would this time make a difference. The Germans against whom they were to be deployed had been armed with armour-piercing bullets, which the thin armour plating could not repel. Working with the 62nd Division, the plan was that two sections (eight tanks) would assist the infantry to capture the village of Bullecourt and its defence lines. They would then, in plan, advance and capture the village of Hendecourt. Zero Hour was set for 3.45a.m. on 3rd May. The attack started well; the counter-battery fire was very effective and the German artillery fire was suppressed. The first four tanks of the other section succeeded in reaching and crossing the German front line. Following them, the leading waves of the 185th Brigade (two Yorkshire battalions) captured Bullecourt – but with such heavy casualties that they could not hold it.

Harold's tanks had less initial success. One 'male', D46, 795, received a direct hit and was set on fire. Although wounded with three of his men, Lieutenant Smith and the other crew were able to evacuate the wounded men, and Smith was able to drive the tank back to the start line, having extinguished the flames. Meanwhile, its partner 'female', number D47, 596, reached the German front line where it co-operated with the infantry in engaging German machine guns. After much good work, however, the tank was so damaged by armour-piercing shells, and when it lost five Lewis guns it had to be abandoned. The survivors tried to fight on for a time with their remaining Lewis gun, before they retired to the British lines. Harold's other 'male' tank, 785, reached the German lines but found the British infantry struggling with unbroken wire and heavy machine-gun fire. Although it advanced on the German machine gunners, the infantry had lost heart – reduced to perhaps a third of their starting numbers and led only by a corporal, they retreated. With all four of his own gunners wounded, 2nd Lieutenant Chick pulled his tank back to the start line. Finally, its 'female', number 580, had also gone forward and taken out German machine gunners but suffered casualties and found the infantry had not come up to support the tank, so it too retired. All the tanks were back at the start line before 8.00a.m. Bullecourt had been recaptured by the Germans.

Harold was not himself with the tanks, but in reserve at Battalion Headquarters, near the ruins of Heinel. He was there when the battalion commander, W.H.L. Watson arrived. "I left the car by the dressing station outside the ruins of Heinel, which the enemy were shelling solidly, and walked forward. A few yards from Haigh's dug-out was a field-battery which the enemy were doing their best to destroy. Their 'best' was a 'dud' as I passed, and I slipped down, cheerfully enough, into the gloom. Haigh [who was Watson's second-in-command] was away at brigade headquarters, but I gathered the news that day from Head, whose tank had not been engaged. The tanks had left the neighbourhood of the destroyed dump well up to time. It had been pitch black at first, and the tank commanders, despite continual and deadly machine-gun fire and some shelling, had been compelled to lead their tanks on foot. They had discovered the 'going' to be appalling, as, indeed, they had anticipated from the reconnaisances." Watson went on to describe Harold's dejection and anxiety as the news of the fate of his tanks trickled back to headquarters. "Wretched Head, whose tank was in reserve, was waiting most miserably to know whether he would be called upon to start out alone and retrieve the battle. It would have been a desperate and foolhardy undertaking for one tank to attack in broad daylight, and I instructed Haigh strongly to urge this view. Luckily the brigade commander had never admired tanks, and now that his attack had failed, he distrusted them. Head's tank was not used that day."[506] Even so, Harold gained his captaincy, as the school

---

[506] From W.H.L. Watson, *With the Tanks 1916-1918*, William Blackwood & Sons, Edinburgh & London, 1920.

magazine recorded: "H. G. Head, M.C., has been promoted Captain for work done in a recent engagement. On that occasion two of his section officers were awarded the Military Cross and a number of his men received the Military Medal."[507]

On 3rd May 1917, Reginald Winch and the 1/3rd London Battalion went into the attack at Tilloy on the eastern side of Arras, in which three officers and ninety-nine men were wounded, two officers and fourteen men went missing, and eight men were killed. They were then back in the front line on 9th May when the German artillery scored a direct hit on one of their trenches, causing a further sixteen casualties. A significant casualty list continued over the fighting of the next week.

A week later, Joseph Lonsdale, older brother of Thomas, who had been killed the previous year, also fought at Bullecourt. Joseph was born in Montreal in about 1892. He was a member of the school in about 1905. On 25th January 1917, he went to the Western Front as a sergeant in the 2/5th London Battalion. During the course of 1917 he was promoted to company quartermaster sergeant – the second highest NCO of his company, with a specific responsibility to ensure the men got their supplies. They moved north to trenches south of Arras near Boisleux-au-Mont on 24th March. Joseph and his comrades took part in the next attack at Bullecourt on 17th May 1917: "Preceded by a hurricane barrage on trenches SW of village at Zero (2 am), Battalion attacked on a double coy frontage of 400 yards… Being formed up ready for the assault, about 300 yards from the trenches at Zero-1 hour: 'A' on right, 'B' on left, and 2 platoons of 'C' on left specially detailed to take strong points… 2 platoons of 'C' in support on railway line, 'D' Coy in reserve. The 1 platoon of 'C' detailed to relieve 2 Platoons of 'B' on railway line failed to reach the rendezvous in time owing to darkness, so that their place in the second wave on the left was taken by 1 platoon of 'C' Coy, finally leaving 2 platoons of 'B' & 1 of 'C' in support… All objectives taken: a number of Germans killed, 23 captured. In the evening the battalion took over whole of the village, relieving the 2/8th."[508]

A few days later, Bernard Bartlett was also at Bullecourt. He was born in 1894 and at the school for two years from 1908 to 1909. On 27th November 1915, he had enlisted in the 2/9th London (Queen Victoria's Rifles). Bernard crossed to France with the battalion, leaving Southampton aboard the SS *Maguerite* on 3rd February 1917 and landing at Le Havre the next day. At the end of February, after training elsewhere, they had entered the trenches in their own right, just south of Arras. The battalion was in the 175th Brigade of the 58th Division.

On 18th March 1917, a patrol discovered that the Germans had withdrawn from some front line and support trenches at Blaireville, south of Arras, which the battalion proceeded to occupy, and over the next few days to sabotage. On 24th March, the battalion, under the supervision of the Royal Engineers, had started schools to train Lewis gunners, signallers and bombers. Bernard trained and became a battalion bomber, a dangerous job, throwing grenades from the front line of an attack. On 6th May they had just come into the support lines. They moved up to the firing line on the evening of 8th May, relieving the 11th London Battalion, and serving there until they themselves were relieved on 12th May.

On 22nd May, they entered the trenches at Bullecourt. Here, the Germans shelled them heavily – on 23rd May they lost a man killed and another thirty wounded – and three killed and thirty-two more wounded the next day. On the last day before they were relieved, they lost an officer and another

---

[507] *The Bournemouthian*, July 1917.
[508] War Diary, 2/5th London Battalion, 17th-18th May 1917.

eighteen men wounded – the battalion was experiencing the horrors of the battlefield without, as yet, going onto the attack. In July they were to be back in trenches – briefly opposite the Hindenburg Line at Havrincourt, east of Bapaume and south-west of Cambrai, and afterwards back near Arras – but soon after they came back out of the trenches, Bernard fell ill with the influenza and spent three days in hospital with a field ambulance unit, from 21st July 1917. When he returned to the battalion, he was promoted lance corporal on 24th July. August for Bernard and his comrades was spent in assault training at various levels – in platoons and companies, as a battalion, and as part of the brigade. This was to prepare them for their entry into the Third Battle of Ypres.

Leslie Okey (born 1894) fought at Bullecourt with the 206th Machine Gun Company. He was one of four brothers, of whom two (Leslie and William) attended the school. Leslie left the school in 1908. (William, his older brother, was killed in Mesopotamia in 1916 and Harold died in England in the same year.) On 15th September 1914, Leslie had volunteered as a private in the 21st Royal Fusiliers Battalion, a battalion consisting of young men who had attended public school (of which Bournemouth School was one in 1914) or university. On 26th June, the battalion came under 98th Brigade, 33rd Division. Leslie landed in 'C' Company with the battalion in France on 14th November 1915. He spent the winter of 1915-1916 in the trenches with the battalion, but on 27th May 1916 he returned to England for officer training. Later he went on a machine gun course at Grantham and was commissioned 2nd lieutenant into the Machine Gun Corps on 25th September 1916.

Leslie Okey

On 18th March 1917, he returned to France attached to 'A' Company of the 206th Machine Gun Company, itself attached to the Royal Fusiliers and the 173rd Brigade. On 3rd May, when Harold's tanks had had such limited success, the 206th M.G.C. was still practising with the reserves for its part in the battle, though they heard heavy gunfire. Three days later, 7th May, the first three sections were detached to provide a covering barrage for the 7th Division's attack on Bullecourt. On 12th May the unit replaced the Australians on the right of Bullecourt in a newly-captured section of the Hindenburg Line. Over the next few days they endured heavy shelling and repelled a German attack, and shifted to the trenches west of Bullecourt towards the end of the month, where they remained for a couple of weeks, receiving occasional heavy shelling.

In a major attempt to take more of the Hindenburg Line at Bullecourt on 15th June, "attack made upon the Hindenburg Line & Ecoust Sector by 173rd infantry Brigade assisted by this Co's Machine Guns. One Section of 4 Guns were allotted to 2/2 Battn London Regt on Left, one Section of 4 Guns to Bttn on Right, and Eight Guns placed upon main line of defence, i.e. along Railway Cutting and Sunken Road. At 2.50am these 8 guns opened an intense barrage fire in conjunction with artillery & continued until the latter's fire slackened. During action 6 of the advanced guns reached their objective. Two guns were sent up to reinforce. Four Guns were lost during Action. During day Guns on the Sunken Road & Railway Cutting put down sharp bursts of fire at frequent intervals. Enemy put down a heavy barrage on our Front Line from 7pm to 7.30pm. Casualties: officers – 2nd Lieut L.A. Okey killed; 2nd Lieut R.A, Penman killed; 2nd Lieut T.A.N. Walker wounded; 2nd Lieut W.A. Stuart-Boyd wounded. Other Ranks – 2 killed; 5 Missing; 1 wounded & missing; 3 wounded."[509] So although the assault by the 2/3rd Royal Fusiliers succeeded in capturing part of the Hindenburg Line, Leslie had not made it. He must have been with the guns on the right of the attack. Afterwards, the officer commanding 'C' Company of the 2/3rd Battalion Royal Fusiliers, alongside whom Leslie had been fighting described how "he displayed great courage & bravery and carried on after he had been wounded, until he met his death a little while after."[510] His section officer, Lieutenant Whitby of the 206th M.G.C. described him to Leslie's father: "For months I have worked with your son and I can truly say that I never could wish for a better fellow, or a cooler man in action, and the men loved him, which is the highest compliment one can give." Leslie's body was not recovered, and today he is honoured on the Arras Memorial. At that time he was the third of four brothers to have been killed – the remaining brother continued on the Western Front.

Joseph Lonsdale and the 2/5th London Battalion made their next assault the next day, 16th June: "Orders received at 2 am to move to St. Leger at 6 am to be ready to support 173rd Brigade, who had temporarily lost part of Hindenburg Line E of Croiselles (gained previous day) by a counter attack. Battn moved on again from St. Leger at 9pm and took over Hindenburg front line from details of 173rd Bdge... June 17. Relief complete by 3 am. The following platoons... went forward as strong patrols to enter Hindenburg support line if possible and reinforce some elements of 173rd Brigade who possibly might still be holding out there. 2 platoons of 'D' Coy under Capt. T.L. Forbes and 2/Lt W.E. Green went forward on left: received with heavy fire and forced to return. 1 platoon of 'B' Coy under 2/Lt C.G. Brentford and 1 of 'D' Coy, the whole under Lieut W.E.O. Welch went forward on right, lost their way and finally discovered at 11pm in shell holes in rear of our front line. 'C' Coy on right pushed forward a platoon to a Mebus between the lines, which they consolidated & held during the tour, handing over on relief. Capt. T.L. Forbes, Lieut V.E.O. Welch & 2/Lieut C.G. Brentford wounded. 11 O.R. killed. 18 wounded, 3 wounded at duty... 18. 2/Lts L. Forbes, H.C. Lintott & M.C.K. McKenzie-Smith wounded. 8 O.R. killed, 33 wounded, 5 wounded at duty... 19. Lieut G.L. Harvest M.C. wounded (died of wounds 20th). 9 O.R. killed, 14 wounded, 1 wounded at duty. Capt F.L. Otter took over command of 'B' Coy. Relieved by 2/7th Londons commencing at 9.30pm, Battn returning to St. Leger."[511] Four officers had been killed or wounded; seventeen men killed, fifty-three were wounded. This was not Joseph's last experience of battle, but his part around Arras was over.

Frank Kent was a gunner with 290th Brigade's 'B' Battery. This was one of four batteries attached to the 58th Division, supporting these attacks. A boarder at the school between 1907 and 1912, he was born in 1898. Whilst at school, Frank was a keen member of the O.T.C. After leaving school he went to work learning to be a farmer, and in 1914, his father being seriously ill, he looked after the farm for the family. Because this was an employment crucial for the country, he was offered exemption from military service, but in September 1916 he decided to enlist as a gunner in the Royal Field Artillery, and in February 1917 was posted to 290th Brigade, which had been sent to France on 20th January 1917. It was what was known as a 'Flying' column, moving heavy guns into position to

---

[509] War Diary, 206th Machine Gun Company, 15th June 1917.
[510] Extracts from letters in the Army File of Leslie Okey, WO 339/64056.
[511] War Diary, 2/5th London Battalion, 16th-19th June 1917.

support the infantry. In this role he would have been firing shells throughout the battle, man-handling the guns closer to support the waves of infantry. He was in a six-gun battery, firing 28 pounder field guns.

On 12th April 1917, the guns of 'B' Battery were added to the other three batteries near Arras (which had already started to operate as six-gun batteries) to form a group of batteries which were in action laying down artillery barrages. (Since 7th April, the other three batteries had been used to lay down a barrage behind which the infantry had assaulted Henin-St-Cojeul and Croiselles as part of the Battle of Arras.) This action continued on and off, including a grand barrage laid down to support the unsuccessful infantry attack on Bullecourt on 3rd May, and, later in the month, 15th-17th May, they fired their guns to support the capture of Bullecourt. The 290th Brigade R.F.A. worked in tandem with the 291st Brigade, sometimes firing together, and sometimes relieving each other, although for 25th-26th July, Frank's battery temporarily came under the command of the 211th Brigade R.F.A. Periodically, they fired in action around Arras until the night of 26th-27th August when they were sent by train to Godewaersvelde, just inside the French border, south-west of Poperinghe.

The two Battles of the Scarpe had been intended by the British, if possible, to break through the German lines to allow the British cavalry to pour through. The authorities were only slowly learning the harsh lesson that strands of barbed wire were enough to render old-fashioned cavalry charges redundant. (The slowest to learn this lesson were the Russians who poured up to two-thirds of their resources into the cavalry, with the effect of clogging up and ruining their supply chain and rendering their army ineffective.) John Harlow was with the cavalry – a frustrated bystander to the Battle of Arras.

John had been born in 1896, and was a day boy at the school from 1906 to 1908. He volunteered for the Bedfordshire Yeomanry in September 1914. This was a cavalry unit within the Territorial Force, about half the size of an infantry battalion, with four squadrons. Since 1908, the unit, in 1914 based at Bedford, had trained as cavalry lancers, but they moved to France in June 1915 within the 9th Cavalry Brigade of the 1st Cavalry Division. John was certainly a corporal in France in 1917. Later he was appointed sergeant. The Bedfordshire Yeomanry were one of only four Yeomanry units to see active service with cavalry brigades in France.

In the Battle of Arras – April and May 1917 – the 9th Cavalry Brigade was part of the divisional element. Because the cavalry was held too far back in reserve, they were unable to take the opportunities provided by the initial successes of 9th April 1917. On 11th April, in the First Battle of the Scarpe, the 8th and 6th Cavalry Brigades were sent forward in a break in the snow storm, and the 8th Cavalry Brigade made a famous charge which eventually foundered in the bloody streets of Monchy. When their brigadier general went forward to assess the position for himself, he too was killed by a bullet. John's 9th Cavalry Brigade remained in reserve and did not take a direct part in the battle. The closest John got to going into action was on 9th April when he was "stood to" at 7a.m. and warned to be prepared to move at one hour's notice. The next day this was switched to two hours' notice. After that, the unit appears to have accepted that no action was imminent. Most of their days were spent looking after the horses, practising for action, making route marches, or being inspected.

John's experience of inaction in the battle was typical of the experience of cavalrymen throughout most of the war. Because cavalry units were so expensive to maintain, and the fodder and bedding for the horses alone used up a lot of the capacity for re-supply, with the development of newer and lighter forms of tank, the Army began to reduce and phase out the cavalry. By 1918, many were effectively superseded by mechanised units. In March 1918, they left the brigade and began to take on a number of new roles: first as a cyclist unit and then as a machine-gun battalion with the Essex Yeomanry. (As early as 18th June 1917, some members of the unit had been detached to create a new 4th Pioneer Battalion.) They were remounted and – briefly – returned to the 1st Cavalry Division, but soon they were been split up – their three remaining squadrons being placed within the 8th, 15th and 19th Hussars. At some point, possibly after the war, John joined the R.A.F. From the late 1920s to the 1950s, John took on a very different and significant role as a film director, making a number of well-known and popular crime and thriller films, including some *Sexton Blake* thrillers and two of the *Old Mother Riley* films.

Although the Battle of Arras was over, the line at Bullecourt still needed to be manned. Stanley Tucker was one of those who carried out that task. Stanley was certainly at the school by 1903 and probably before that, and he was one of the original members of the Old Bournemouthians Club. He was born in 1885. He enlisted on 20th May 1916, and was mobilised and posted two days later to the 3/7th Hampshire Battalion (renamed the 7th Reserve Battalion) which had been formed in Bournemouth in March 1915 as a 'third line' unit. On 17th July 1916, he was promoted to lance corporal, and was commissioned into the 3/4th Devonshire Battalion on 26th April 1917. The Devonshire Battalion had moved to Bournemouth from Exeter in August 1915. He served in Bournemouth with his battalion from 26th April 1917 to 2nd June 1917. Then he was transferred to the 8th Devonshire Battalion. This service battalion had been in France since July 1915, part of the 20th Brigade in the 7th Division. He disembarked at Boulogne on 5th June and spent a few weeks at Rouen before joining the battalion in the field on 25th June.

He joined the battalion at Ecoust, near Bullecourt, when it was resting, training and bathing. In the middle of July, Stanley and the battalion remained in the trenches at Bullecourt. The weather was hot and thundery. It was a period of consolidation – improving trenches and wire, accepting the impact of German shells, not a period of active patrolling nor assault. Casualties were limited that month – one officer wounded, four men killed and eleven wounded. More serious was the incidence of illness. Five officers had been away from the battalion sick, and, overall, eighty-three men had fallen ill. Stanley was back in Rouen for a week at the end of July on a machine-gun course, but returned to serve with his battalion at Bullecourt on 1st August. After a week there, in which the main work was improvement and wiring whilst the Germans used explosive and gas shells on them, they came back out of the trenches. He mourned the state of the country as he had begun to witness it. "It seems an awful shame that this glorious country should be blown to pieces. In nearly every case where the churches are ruined the crucifix remains standing, like a monument amidst all this destruction. Am writing this in an old ruined shed, which we use as a mess, rather different from the comfortable quarters we got in England. On active service one has to make the best of anything."[512]

Some Old Bournemouthians did crucial jobs within the Army which are not associated with any particular battle. Thousands served in the Army Service Corps. One of them, in support during this battle, was Alexander Miller whose contribution was made in the Motor Transport Section of the A.S.C. Alexander, born in 1891, was at the school from about 1904 to 1905. He joined the Army on

---

[512] *The Bournemouthian*, July 1917.

26th April 1916 at Grove Park in London, the centre for the Army Service Corps, and the Army wanted Alexander as an engineer and as a driver.

Alexander embarked from Southampton on 5th June 1916, arriving in Rouen the next day. He was attached to the 63rd (Royal Naval) Division's Supply Column as a driver, although on 29th June he was detached for service driving with the 3rd Field Ambulance of the 63rd Division. With this unit he suffered the first of two bouts of 'flu, and had to be admitted to his own field ambulance from 4th to 10th August, after which he returned to driving for the hospital. The 63rd Division had only landed in France from Gallipoli and the east in May 1916, but it then remained on the Western Front for the remainder of the war. The division fought in the later stages of the Battle of the Somme and then in the follow-up as the Germans retreated to their Hindenburg Line, and Alexander would have been there helping to move the injured. As the Germans retreated, in February 1917, Alexander returned from his detached work with the field ambulance and worked with the 63rd Division's Supply Column. These were not easy months, initially supporting the division in the Battle of Arras. After a leave from 28th August to 7th September, he was back with them, now in the Ypres Salient where they fought in the later stages of the Third Battle of Ypres and at Passchendaele in particular. Then he drove for them as the division tried to consolidate the gains in 'the Battle of Welsh Ridge' at the end of the year. It would be interesting to know if he was aware of fellow Bournemouthians like William Webber and Reginald Colborne, in the same division.

Cyril Brudenell also served in the Motor Transport Section of the A.S.C. His brother, Kenneth, may have done likewise. Herbert Cyril was born in 1894, and was at school from 1902 to 1909. His brother Kenneth (born in London in 1897, at school 1906-1913). At school, Herbert (known as Cyril) took part in athletics and as a 'cousin' of the First Sea Lord in *HMS Pinafore*. (Kenneth too performed in this 1905 production, as 'Tom Tucker, although at that stage he had not formally joined the school. "Brudenell was very clever as Tucker the midshipmite, and made a good deal of a very small part."[513]) From 1912 to 1915, Cyril demonstrated, and sold, cars. On 17th June 1915, Cyril enlisted into the Army Service Corps. Kenneth also joined the A.S.C. (Details of Kenneth's war service are incomplete: he remained a private soldier in the Army Service Corps to the end of the war.) Nearly a year later, on 16th April 1916, Cyril landed in France to serve in the A.S.C. Motor Transport Section, and was soon appointed to the 7th Corps Troops Supply Column.

The 7th Corps (III Army) fought at Gommecourt on 1st July 1916, and in the Battles of the Scarpe near Arras in April and May 1917 and, like Alexander, Cyril's role was to support the fighting troops, moving materials and sometimes men around behind the lines. The 7th Corps Troops Supply Column was based at Doullens, positioned so as to be able to support British troops both on the Arras and Somme battlegrounds. He remained on the Western Front for fourteen months before applying for a commission as a pilot in the Royal Flying Corps. Cyril spent the rest of the war as a cadet, and then a commissioned pilot in the R.F.C. (later R.A.F.) from December 1918 until he was demobilised in March 1919.

Charles Atlee of the Royal Medical Corps also served in support of these offensives until his health gave out. Born in October 1885, he joined Bournemouth School as one of the original, older boys – he was already fifteen when the school opened, possibly as one of the original boarders. By the time he joined up he was a qualified doctor, working in general practice.

---

[513] *The Bournemouthian*, July 1905, p. 8.

On 15th February 1916, though not yet in the Army, Charles applied to become a doctor in a Territorial Force unit, the 2nd London Sanitary Company. It seems as if he was already in contact with members of the force, since he wrote the application as if already assured of being a full lieutenant, and indeed a month later, on 25th March 1916, he was posted to that unit, commissioned as a Royal Army Medical Corps lieutenant. The 2nd London Sanitary Company, one of only two specialist units, was, despite its somewhat unlikely name, an active service unit with sections posted across the war fronts – such as the 46th Section which was posted to the Middle East or the 10th Section which was to go to France later that year. The company had many tasks, which included testing water quality to monitor the presence of bacteria and similar organisms. From the middle of 1915, sections of the 1st Sanitary Company were being deployed – attached one to each division, to work alongside the field ambulances. They were small sections and, until 1917, did not come directly under corps or Army control. Within each section there were jobs for architects, engineers, builders and medical men. It was not until 6th July 1916, that Charles was ordered to "report to the Colours" and at some point that summer, instead of the 2nd London Sanitary Company, he was posted R.A.M.C. lieutenant in the London Regiment.

Just before Charles joined them, it was re-designated the 2/2nd London Battalion, in the 173rd Brigade, 58th Division, when the original battalion with that numbering had been disbanded. Charles replaced the original R.A.M.C. Captain Yorke Moore as the battalion's medical officer, and on 30th September 1916, when he was deemed to have served sufficient time in the Army, he was promoted captain. On 21st-22nd January 1917, Charles and most of the battalion sailed from Southampton to Le Havre, and a few days later the rest of the battalion caught up with them at Ivergny, west of Arras. They then went into the trenches for instruction from various battalions of the West Yorkshire Regiment, and Charles might have seen his first significant introduction to the realities of the war when four men were wounded on 3rd February.

As regimental medical officer, Charles would have been in the danger zone of the front line. If a man was wounded, usually first aid was applied at a regimental aid post in, or very close to, the battalion's position on the front line. He would have had a small team of men trained as medical orderlies and stretcher-bearers. These would normally be formed from regimental bandsmen, though if pressure was great and others co-operated, he might have the assistance of men loaned from a nearby field ambulance. Normally, these battalion bearers would then take the wounded back to 'bearer posts', where they would be picked up by the stretcher-bearers and staff of a field ambulance unit, who would then take over the responsibility for the wounded, and take them back to the ambulance unit headquarters and on to a casualty clearing station, as most appropriate. Of course, Charles would also be dealing with less dramatic issues involving the health and welfare of the men – though all of great importance given the need to work to ensure the battalion was fit and ready to fight. In action in the trenches, he would be expected to work out of either the regimental aid post or an advanced dressing station, but when the battalion was not in action, he would have a camp reception station or a medical inspection room, which could even include the luxury of a few beds for those who needed just a short time of care.

If the battalion was in the trenches, the regimental aid post would be only a few yards behind the front line. A suitable spot would be chosen, which might be a dug-out, a widened part of a communication trench, a shell hole, or some ruined building or even its rubble if it was still stable enough to use. Because the role he had in battle was first aid, his post would be supplied from the advanced dressing station, and the equipment would be limited to anti-tetanus serum, bandages, dressings of various sizes and types, sulphur and boric ointments (antibiotics had not yet been discovered), and cotton wool. Beyond that he would have stretchers and blankets, a couple of stoves, and some limited supplies of items to help comfort the wounded – such as brandy, cocoa, Bovril, Oxo and biscuits. If he could not patch up the wounded, he had to send them onwards. The 'walking wounded', if they were not fit enough to return to their companies, were given a route to walk to the advanced dressing station and the relay posts. In some cases – to ease congestion – a different route might be designated for the men who needed stretchers (sometimes wheeled). In some situations, such wounded might have to be carried onwards for miles before they could be picked up by horse or motorised transport, or by light railway.

By March 1917, they were in the trenches near Arras, taking casualties. Later in the month they went onto the offensive and occupied some German trenches, though at a cost which would have challenged Charles and his team: "23.3.17 8.30am. Post… rushed by enemy & 1 section all casualties & 1 Lewis Gun left but subsequently recovered about 7pm. Casualties: 2 dead, 1 missing & 5 wounded."[514] The next day they lost two more killed and three wounded as the battalion withdrew on being relieved by the 2/5th London Battalion. After this initial period, Charles and the battalion had been moved south to the northern part of the Somme Sector, near Gommecourt.

Then they moved across to the eastern side of Bullecourt, where they came in for some very heavy fighting in the middle of May, having to beat off some significant German attacks and endure heavy shelling. Within six days, by 20th-21st May the battalion casualties were ten officers and one hundred and eighty-eight men – which must have been quite a strain for Charles and his team to deal with. In the war diary there is a sketch plan of the battalion dispositions in this fighting, and the regimental aid post in which Charles would have operated is clearly marked – right on the front line itself. A few days later, after a brief respite, back in the trenches on the western side of Bullecourt this time, the battalion suffered more casualties when an officer and soldier were killed and eleven more men wounded on 30th May. In June, the fighting was even worse but Charles was no longer with them. At some point, he had himself left the battalion, in his case through sickness. It is not clear precisely when he left the unit, but he was treated at a field ambulance at St. Leger, a few miles west from Bullecourt, and then sent back up the line to Le Havre where he embarked on 17th June, suffering from what was then diagnosed as influenza and a dilated heart. Having returned to England, for about two months he was in hospital at the 1st London General Hospital, St. Gabriel's College, Camberwell, where he was treated for trench fever and cardiac dilatation. The cause of his serious illness was put down to exposure to infection whilst in the trenches. It took him months to be strong enough to work again. At the end of August he was allowed a fortnight's leave, and then he had to report to London District, to his old unit, the 2nd London Sanitary Company, as he was regarded by the Army as fit only for light duties – classified fitness level 'C2', which meant he would not be allowed to return to the front. There he remained. By 1919, his condition was assessed to have improved to fitness level 'C1', but his disability was to be permanent, reckoned at a level of 50% when definitively assessed in March 1920. In August 1919, he was "brought to attention of the Secretary of State for valuable services in connection with the war", which was roughly the equivalent of being mentioned in dispatches. He resigned his commission (retaining the rank of captain) in September 1921. Though he lived on for many years, and returned to general practice, he never fully recovered his health.

---

[514] War Diary, 2/2nd London Battalion, 23rd March 1917.

In northern France, the Army kept up the general pressure. Alexander Sandbrook and the 8th Canadian Infantry Battalion were amongst the Canadians in action north of Lens at Hill 70, taking part in some fierce fighting between 14th and 17th August. "The operation was conspicuous for the initiative displayed by NCOs. Three small parties under junior NCOs pushed forward quite independently, and took up excellent covering positions. Two of these it was impossible to warn of the relief, and they, as a matter of course, went forward with the 5th battalion assault later in the battle... The defended shell holes were all disposed of by the gallantry of individuals; in one case by an officer, who was subsequently wounded, and in another by a very junior NCO. Over 70% of our Casualties (which amounted to 400 of the 720 engaged) were caused by bullet wounds.... Six Maxim guns, and three converted Lewis Guns were successfully assaulted by the Battalion".[515]

In support on 14th August, the 2nd Canadian Battalion received orders to assist in the Canadian Corps attack to force the Germans from Lens and Hill 70 at 4.25a.m. The battalion's orders were to open up communication trenches across No Man's Land to connect with the German front line. Douglas Collingwood, Captain in Command of 'C' Company, was to work on the appropriately named 'Combat Trench'. Their first tasks were to clear out and, in places, deepen the existing British trench and place signs to explain the planned use of the communication trenches being dug – 'In' and 'Out' and 'To the front line'. On 15th August, as they played their supporting part in the attack, two officers were wounded, four men killed and thirty-five more men wounded, including one who suffered from poison gas. They continued the work on the communication trenches over the next days despite heavy shell fire and the difficulties posed by having to remove the German wire blocking the way to the captured trenches. Only on 23rd August were they withdrawn for some rest and further training, and that period of recuperation would have been interrupted since the battalion was inspected by Sir Douglas Haig on 27th August, though Douglas might not have been there since the war diary reported his return on 5th September from leave. He was based again at Camblain L'Abbé from September, working hard to improve communication trenches. Sometimes Douglas had a hundred infantry, and even sometimes prisoners, to assist his company in the work. In the later part of October the battalion was sent north.

That summer, Charles Martin, born in 1890, also served in the Arras Sector. He had an older and a younger brother who also attended the school, and a couple of other brothers who did not. He was known as Charlie. He was at the school between 1904 and 1907. There, Charlie was a keen cricketer and footballer. He also joined the O.T.C. in its earliest days. After school he initially took up carving as his profession and remained in Bournemouth as an active member of the Old Boys' Club. Later he moved to London to study dentistry. However, on 30th November 1915, he volunteered and was posted to the second battalion of the regiment – 2/28th London Battalion ('the Artists' Rifles').

Sec.-Lt. C. S. MARTIN.
6th Batt. Leicester Regt.
Killed in action, 4th October, 1917.

Charles Martin

---

[515] War Diary, 8th Canadian Infantry Battalion. Narrative of the fighting 14th-17th August 1917.

As we have seen, in October 1914 this battalion had gone to France, and became an Officer Training Corps at Ballieul (and in April 1915, at St. Omer). So great were the numbers volunteering and being trained, the 28th Battalion actually split into three. Over the course of the war, 10,256 officers were commissioned after training with the Artists' Rifles and went into all kinds of regiments. In November 1915, the 2/28th was absorbed into the 1/28th, and the old 3/28th, which had remained at Romford, was renumbered as the 2/28th until being renamed again as No.15 Officer Cadet Battalion in March 1916 when it lost its affiliation to the regiment. Charlie was 'absorbed' into the front line battalion.

By 1917, Charlie had served on the Western Front as a private with the battalion for over a year. In April 1917, he applied for a commission. He was posted as 2nd lieutenant in the 6th Leicestershire Battalion on 3rd May. This battalion was in the 110th Brigade, 21st Division. On 3rd May, 1917, when Charlie joined his new battalion, it was in action attacking Fontaines-les-Croisilles, south of Arras, though afterwards they were holding the line, south-east of Arras, resting, or training. Later his lieutenant colonel wrote, "In July, when raiders were called for from the Battalion to raid the German trenches, he was one of the officers who volunteered. He worked very hard and patrolled many nights, and, if the raid had come off, he would have won an honour. As it was, he got the Major-General's honour card."[516] Despite this, the war diary of the battalion shows that this was a relatively quiet time, although concerns at possible enemy mining operations were proved correct when the Germans exploded a small mine on 22nd July 1917.

The raid which Charlie led was one of a pair (the other being attempted by the 7th Leicesters) and both were unsuccessful. The brigadier wanted information about the Germans opposite the brigade near Croisilles, north of Bullecourt. He also wanted to know how effective his medium trench mortars were at breaking the enemy wire to create gaps. On 23rd July, the two-inch mortars began firing at the German wire in designated target areas. Charlie's raid ('Raid A') was described in the brigadier's secret report: "Two Officers [according to the battalion only Charlie in the end], 3 NCO's and 17 other ranks, 6th Bn. Leicester Regt. left the new trench… at 10.15 p.m. and reached the enemy's wire… One German was seen wiring at this spot. Unfortunately one of our party dropped his rifle at this moment, and the German fell flat and disappeared. The wire in front of this point had been mended, and the officer in charge of the party did not feel justified in advancing through it. The party waited half an hour in front of the wire, and having seen no more enemy, returned to our trenches. Result:- No identification obtained. Casualties – NIL." The brigade intelligence report adds the comment that as "the enemy appeared to be on the alert, the party was ordered to return by C.O. 6th Battalion Leicestershire Regiment." The brigadier also commented that the raids had suffered from the darkness of a very dark night and that the ground and wire proved serious obstacles: "The enemy, had, however, partially closed all gaps with new wire about 1 bay in thickness. This obstacle appeared to be surmountable but not without noise. The enemy did not give any sign that he was suspecting a raid, but owing to the small number of Very Light sent up by him, it is practically certain that he had working parties out all along the front. The ground has proved itself unsuitable to stealth raids, as owing to its very broken state, silent movement is almost impossible… Both parties are anxious to attempt the raid again. If repeated, a little more wire-cutting, covered by artillery, will be required".[517] Charlie did not get another

---

[516] *The Bournemouthian*, December 1917.

[517] Intelligence Summary Report and Associated Diary, 110th Brigade, 25th July 1917. I am very grateful to Colin Taylor of the Great War Forum, www.greatwarforum.org for providing me with these documents.

chance, however, and the rest of the month was described in the battalion war diary as "uneventful" and largely given over to trench working parties.

Further south, Thomas Chaffey's role had briefly altered in spring 1917. They were north-east of Peronne. For a few weeks they seemed much more likely to be sent out on patrol than on fatigue parties, digging and carrying. Towards the end of March 1917, Thomas and others of the XV Corps Cyclist Battalion were used for reconnaissance. "21/3/17. One Coy Sergeant Major & 1 man (CSM Ros and Pte Cole) wounded whilst reconnoitring under 40th Division. This Company occupied Tincourt Village, being the first troops to enter the village. Lewis Guns were brought into action and did well at Longavesnes."[518] A few days later, 'B' Company was detached to 25th Brigade. The infantry were attacking the village of Fins near Guvencourt, just north of them. "This company took up its position between the two attacking battalions & kept up communication between them. It was held up outside Fins but managed to push forward again with the assistance of its Lewis Guns to cross-roads 2,000 yds NE of Fins on the Gouzeaucourt Road. Lewis Guns did good work & Coy captured 1 prisoner. Company casualties one man wounded (Pte Colley) remaining at duty."[519] The next day, two companies were sent out on patrol and another man was lightly wounded. But afterwards the battalion – actually really only two companies – was shifted round a lot and by May was in the front zone north-east of Peronne, and then moved in the middle of June, by stages, to the coast of northern France/Belgium, near Dunkirk. Here, the men were trained and acted as guides to other units moving forward. However, they do not seem to have been much affected by the start of the Third Battle of Ypres or its aftermath, spending their time training, on guard duties, and on fatigue duties such as digging new trenches. By April 1918 they were re-situated near La Bassée.

Frederick White was in the trenches near Arras at this time. He was cousin to, and great friend of, Edgar Ayling, who was fighting in the Royal Naval Division. The boys were brought up together by Frederick's mother and for a time were together at the school, which Frederick attended between 1903 and 1906. Born in 1893, Frederick never enjoyed great health, and his mother took him away to a school in Weston-Super-Mare in the hopes that he might grow stronger there. Aged 16, he went to live as a boarder at a farm near Blandford where he spent several years, but when he tried to take up motor engineering (at which, according to *The Bournemouthian*, he showed "exceptional skill and ingenuity")[520] his health again began to give way. So he returned to farming to live an open-air life. In March 1916, he enlisted but was graded 'C3'. This meant that the Army doctors reckoned him to be free from serious organic diseases, but not fit for active service. He was what was then known as a 'Category Man'. It was reckoned he would not be able to walk five miles and so was only suitable for sedentary work in an army garrison based within England. For some reason, perhaps through his keenness to copy his cousin or perhaps a measure of the growing manpower shortage, it was decided that, nevertheless, Frederick should undergo infantry training, which he did in a training unit with the Somerset Light Infantry. This did not work out because his health broke down under the strain. The Army moved him between various units until he ended up in the Dorsetshire Regiment.

He was placed in the 6th Dorset Battalion. Other Old Boys who were or had been in the 6th Dorsets included 2nd Lieutenant Clarence Goodhall (who had died at Fricourt on 7th July 1916), and

---

[518] War Diary, XV Corps Cyclist Battalion, 21st March 1917.
[519] War Diary, XV Corps Cyclist Battalion, 30th March 1917.
[520] *The Bournemouthian*, December 1919.

Corporal Cecil Novarra. Joining the 6th Dorsets in May 1917, Frederick arrived at a time when the battalion had been involved in some fierce fighting, which had meant that at the end of May, instead of four companies, 'A' to 'D', the battalion had reorganised the survivors into two temporary companies 'X' and 'Y'. it had also lost two commanding officers that month – one apparently sick or worn out, the other killed by shell fire when in the front line trench. At the end of the month the battalion had been withdrawn for rest and to recuperate, and the battalion diary reveals that on 8th June a draft of one officer and twenty-five men (mostly old 6th Battalion soldiers) arrived to help boost the battalion. It is likely that Frederick may have been with them or with another batch of forty-three who arrived on 14th June, or in a last batch of three on 21st June. The battalion recreated its proper company structure, even though its numbers were still limited. Frederick seems to have been placed in 'A' Company. On 20th June 1917, he had his first taste of the front line when the battalion moved back into trenches near Arras. The battalion was in and out of the trenches in July, and although no battle was raging, there continued to be individuals killed or wounded. Perhaps more significantly, a larger number of men were counted as casualties and had to be evacuated in the hot weather of July – presumably through ill health. In August, Frederick's weak frame could not cope with the rigours of trench life, and he was evacuated to the base hospital. However, whilst still not really fit, he returned to the trenches with the 6th Dorsets for the winter of 1917-1918. In March 1918, he was allowed to return home on leave, but was so ill that he spent most of the leave in a military hospital. This was not the end of his war service, however.

The Battle of the Messines Ridge

The Battle of Arras had started well, but petered out in the end into battles to capture small parts of a line, rather than a breakthrough. Even before it was finished, with Nivelle's offensive in the south a shambles and pressure growing to divert German attention from the French, Haig turned his attention further north to the Ypres Salient, where he was convinced the British had their best chance of making progress against the German line. Haig's big effort for 1917 was still to come: the Third Battle of Ypres. There were strong reasons why the British must fight, and clear strategic benefits from doing so, even though there was always the risk of a second Somme and the political fall-out of a second wave of such massive casualties.

The reasons why the battle must be fought were numerous. The Germans were strangling British imports with their policy of unrestricted U-boat warfare, even though it had brought the USA into the war on 17th April 1917. (No one seriously expected the American troops to make a huge change in the military balance on the Western Front until about 1920. Not only was their army small in 1917, it was untested in modern warfare, having only fought Mexican bandits and some Native Americans since their war against Spain in 1898.) Without sufficient imports, the war could be lost at home even if not on the battlefield. There was therefore a strong imperative to try to break the Germans on land if the Navy could not break their submarines at sea. In his diary for 30th June, Haig – who was visiting London and attending War Cabinet meetings – included a 'secret' account of one of these meetings: "At today's conference Admiral Jellicoe as First Sea Lord stated that owing to [the great shortage of shipping due to German submarines] it would be impossible for Great Britain to continue the war in 1918. This was a bombshell for the Cabinet, [and all present] and a full enquiry is to be made as to the real facts on which this opinion [of the Naval Authorities] is based. No one present shared Jellicoe's view, and all seemed satisfied that the food reserves in Great Britain are adequate. [Jellicoe's words were, 'There is no good discussing plans for next spring. We cannot go on.']"[521]

---

[521] *Sir Douglas Haig, War Diaries and Letters 1914-1918*, edited by Gary Sheffield and John Bourne, p. 301.

The French Nivelle Offensive earlier in the year had been an unmitigated disaster, and since then 90% of the French Army had mutinied or at least refused to do more than man trenches defensively. Unless the Germans were preoccupied with defending against British attacks they could break through the French lines and win the war.

Russia was in a mess. Although the British (and even more the Americans) welcomed the removal of Tsarist autocracy in the March revolution, Russian discipline was declining rapidly and, when the summer 'Kerensky Offensive' crashed after two days, mass Russian desertions followed and rapid German advances eastwards gave the prospect of a catastrophic collapse. There was the major danger that if the Germans in the west could sit tight for a few months, they could be reinforced from the victorious east and go onto the attack before the Americans arrived in significant numbers. Passive British trench lines opposing the formidable German defences would do nothing to win the war, and might even lead to copy-cat mutiny amongst the British if Communist agitators had their way.

More positively, if Haig could knock the Germans off the ridges to the south and east of Ypres then perhaps the much hoped-for cavalry advance to capture the vital German railheads supplying the German defenders might be possible. This in turn could allow the Navy to land additional forces at Ostend and Zeebrugge and by-pass the German line in the north. With German morale already troubled by having to retreat to the Hindenburg Line after the Battle of the Somme in 1916, and Germany also facing severe domestic shortages because of the British blockade, there was even a small chance that victory might be achieved within 1917.

The British had succeeded beyond the expectations of many at Vimy Ridge and in the first part of the Battle of Arras. With the improved tanks becoming available, Haig hoped that this time a crushing victory might be won. The British Cabinet was, however, much less sure. Too many times had they heard of the prospect of a big offensive to break through and win the war, and been both disappointed and shocked by the consequent casualties, so they were very much more cautious about the whole plan than Haig.

In preparation for the attempt to break through the German lines, General Plumer was entrusted with what today is normally separated from the main Third Battle of Ypres, and known as the Battle of the Messines Ridge. "General Plumer came to lunch today. Afterwards he explained his plan of attack and received my approval. I called his attention to the new German system of defence. The enemy now fight not 'in' but 'for' his first position. He uses considerable forces for counter attacks. His guns should be registered beforehand to deal with these. Our objective now is to capture and consolidate up to the range of our guns, and at once to push on advanced guards to profit by Enemy's demoralisation after the bombardment. No delay should take place in doing this.[522]

This battle was preceded by seventeen days of artillery bombardment. The assault by Plumer and the 2nd Army began on 7th June 1917 at 3.10a.m. with the detonation of nineteen huge mines along the German front line. Preparations had begun the previous year, and the attack was a huge success. In preparing, Plumer had adopted measures based on trusting his men: as before the Battle of Vimy Ridge, groups of officers and NCOs were taken to study models of the terrain and the men practised for their tasks with a clear idea of their objectives and the obstacles which they

---

[522] *Sir Douglas Haig, War Diaries and Letters 1914-1918*, edited by Gary Sheffield and John Bourne, p. 293.

would have to overcome. A series of mines was prepared along the German lines from St. Eloi in the north of the ridge, past the Bavarians opposite Kemmel at Bayernwald, and down past Wyatschate and Mesen. When these were exploded the carefully organised attack proved to be the most successful so far – and for the first time the British suffered fewer casualties (17,000) than the German defenders (25,000), and rolled the Germans off the Messines Ridge when a halt was called before attacking the Germans where the ridge turned north into the Passchendaele Ridge. The Germans were pushed back from the ridge and onto the defensive.

Edward Goddard's 276th Siege Battery was in the barrage. On 16th May, Edward's unit had received orders to move north via Abeele and Poperinghe to take up new positions on the Kruisstraat Road. Their position was south of Ypres, below the Messines Ridge, opposite the German position at Bayernwald: "The Battery position at Kruisstraat Road was in a line of trees near a Chateau called 'Belgian Chateau'. The two sections were about 90 yards apart and the guns screened as far as possible by trees and camouflage. Platforms were laid but the ground was very soft and a good deal of difficulty and delay was caused by the trails dripping into the soft ground in spite of the usual precautions of pit props and timber etc. behind them, and filling up with stones and rubble. Ammunition supply was by trench tramway in rear of the position – plus convenient also working parties from the British West Indians & other units were generally available to assist. Infantry working parties were of great assistance in helping constant cartridge reissues etc. Digging any depth is impossible in this soil owing to the presence of water, so all splinter props have to be built up. This is not so undesirable as might be imagined as there are usually plenty of trees to screen the work from the air. Both gun position and personnel came in for a certain amount of shelling by night (including gas shell) as they were on one of the main transport routes south to the forward area."[523] The war diary for this period, June to August 1917, is missing, but an anonymous letter, in which the writer gave his address as "276 S Battery RGA BEF", was found lodged in a second-hand book and this stated that the battery had had a "rough" time during the month of writing, August 1917.[524]

Frederick Furness was in this action. Frederick had already had a career as a private soldier in the 1/14th London Scottish, and on 27th May 1917 was commissioned 2nd lieutenant in the 11th Royal West Surrey Battalion, known as the Queen's Regiment. For the first week of June, despite being depleted, seventeen officers and five hundred and fifty soldiers, were in training to make the attack.

Frederick and the battalion went into action on 7th June, attacking approximately south-eastwards from St. Eloi, south of Ypres, at the north-eastern end of the battle front chosen by Plumer. "At 12.30am night 6-7 June the Battn moved on to tapes laid out behind our front line… a front of about 220 yards. The right flank was on the right of the Mud Patch and the left on the left of Triangular Wood. On the right was the 10th R.W.K. Regt and on the left the 8th Bn London Regt (47th Divn). In support – 20th D.L.I. Battalion Battle Order. The Battn formed up on a double company front with 'A' Coy on the left, 'C' and 'D' Coys in support on Right and Left respectively. Each company was in 3 waves and each wave in 2 lines. The distance between waves was 20 yards and between lines 10 yards. Company HQ were behind in rear of their last wave and Battn HQrs in rear of 6th Wave… 2.55 am. The front wave advanced to within 75 yards of the enemy front line and the

---

[523] War Diary, 276th Siege Battery, R.G.A., May 1917.
[524] The existence of this letter was reported on the Great War Forum, on 27th March 2013.

rear waves conformed to this movement. At this time the night was very quiet. The enemy commenced to put up a number of Golden-Rain lights from his front line on our right and a few minutes later did the same on our front. DamStrasse. 6.50 am At zero plus 3 hours 50 minutes the 122nd Inf. Brigade attacked through our line (Blue Line) accompanied by tanks and captured the Black Line (Oblong Reserve and Obscure Trench). This caused no hostile retaliation on our position… The ground attacked over was very much cut up by shell fire and almost all trenches obliterated so that some difficulty was experienced in recognising any particular portion of the enemy's lines… Casualties – killed – 4 officers and 29 Other Ranks." [525]

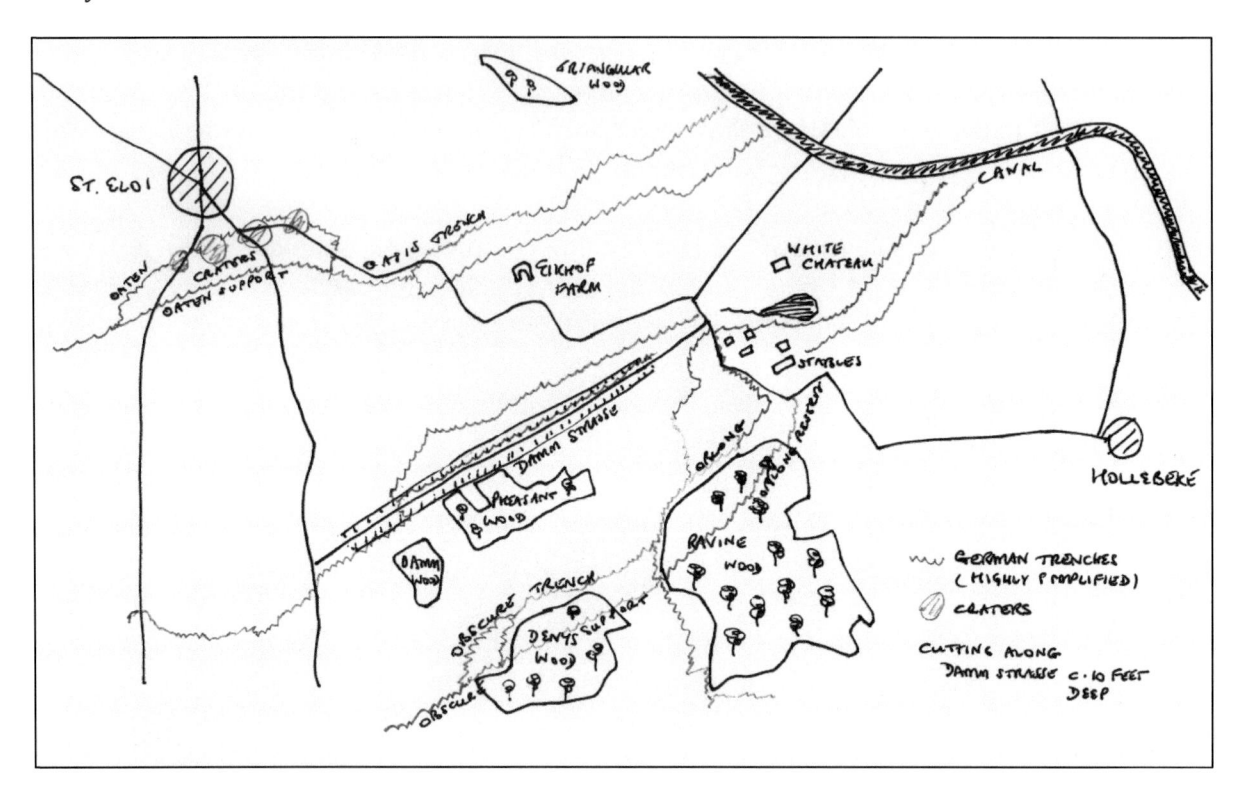

Although the next day the Germans shelled their position and tried to counter-attack, the battalion held its new line without further casualties.

Horace Tollemache was close by and on their right, in support. Horace had recovered from his wounds and had been able to re-join his battalion, the 15th Hampshires, after the Battle of the Somme had ground to a close. In January 1917, he had been mentioned in dispatches by Sir Douglas Haig for his part on the Somme. On 6th June, the battalion had moved forward at St. Eloi to the old French trench line. On 7th June, at Zero Hour (3.10a.m.), they watched as a large mine was blown under the German-manned craters at St. Eloi and witnessed the British artillery barrage open up. They saw the 123rd Brigade go into the attack, and two hours later they followed them by advancing in artillery formation as far as the Damm Strasse. They noted that the effectiveness of the artillery barrage did vary – rating it very effective on their right but ragged on their left and directly to their front.

They made their attack as the second wave at 6.50a.m. and suffered many casualties from the artillery which had remained intact on the German second line. Hurried messages were sent back to the British artillery to lift the bombardment onto those German trenches, which, once done,

---

[525] War Diary, 11th Royal West Surrey Battalion, 7th-9th June 1917.

helped to subdue the defenders.

At this stage, observers reported that the Germans were preparing a counter-attack party in the valley beyond. At 10.15a.m., five hundred more Germans pushed forward, and the battalion opened fire with Lewis guns on them as they broke cover, crossing a ridge line, and inflicted a number of German casualties. Even so, the Germans made repeated counter-attacks against Denys Wood at 10a.m., 3p.m. and 7p.m., each preceded by bombardments. The 15th Hampshire Battalion held 'Obscure Support' Trench, which ran through Denys Wood, until 3.15a.m. the next morning, when they were relieved. Losses were high: more than one hundred men (each one named in the diary) had been wounded whilst three were missing and about seventy had been killed. Of the officers, one had been killed and another had died of wounds soon after; six more had been wounded. After this, the battalion provided working parties and went in and out of the line, but, given the size of its casualties, was not called upon to make any further attacks in this battle.

Close by to Frederick and Horace, Ernest Parsons was also involved. After leaving the 7th Royal Fusiliers Battalion in November 1916, Ernest served with the 1st Royal Fusiliers Battalion in France from 28th February 1917 to 9th August 1917, and again from 12th December 1917 to 6th November 1918. When Ernest joined them they were part of 7th Brigade, 24th Division and stationed in the coalfields area near Lens. They were working in muddy and snowy trenches and had provided carrying parties in support at Vimy Ridge ("Men dead beat. They have had a very hard & trying time with carrying parties."[526]) and had even spent a few days at the end of the battle holding captured ground. In May, they had marched by stages north into Belgium, where for several weeks they trained at Brandhoek, between Poperinghe and Ypres, before they moved up into position for the attack.

On 7th June at Zero Hour, 3.10a.m., they watched the "Mines exploded by us at St. Eloi, Wycheate, Hill 60 & several other points. Simultaneously, hundreds of guns of all calibres opened up a terrific bombardment of enemy positions. The heaviest bombardment of the War I should imagine. Infantry advance under barrage. 4.30am. Aeroplane reports flares… 6am. Attack N of Canal; reported progressing favourably. 7.30am. First Objective taken by 41st Div. Streams of prisoners coming through, mostly Prussians. 7.45am. Damme strasse from Dome House to Canal in our possession. 8.45am. Hospice at Wychaete, our men seen crossing ridge… 12.20pm. Bn. moves forward in Artillery Formation, Front Coys 'B' on right, 'D' on Left, 'C' supporting 'D', 'A' supporting 'B'. Tracks to be used by Coys had already been marked out by small red flags. Several rather wide ditches had not been bridged but on the whole the going was fairly good. Bn. should have halted for a time at old French trench, but on account of orders arriving late all speed had to be made to get to Damme Strasse where Bn. was to reform and correct distances. 2.10pm. reached Damme Strasse. A sweltering hot day and not a breath of breeze. Five derelict tanks were stranded here looking like huge great tortoises floundering in the mud. 2.30pm. Assaulting Coys move from Damme Strasse still in Artillery Formation followed by supporting Coys."

Their advance was made twelve hours later. "Our Zero is at 3.10pm… 17th Bde attack on right, 73rd on Left. 3rd RBs right of our attack on a one Coy front, 1st RF left of attack on a two Coy front… Leading Coys advance in extended order at 4 paces interval. A & C follow in Artillery Formation. Barrage advances 100 yds in three minutes. Very little shell fire was met with until advance to

---

[526] War Diary, 1st Royal Fusiliers, 15th April 1917.

Green Line commenced. Fairly large amount of Shrapnel put over advancing lines, with very little effect. Country in an undescribable condition from our intense bombardments. Most strong points had been battered to pieces and wire everywhere on our front had been successfully cut by our Artillery. Enemy generally in a very demoralised condition. Our protective barrage was exceedingly effective, and attacking Coys through keeping close up under it avoided heavy casualties. Coys advanced to attack in perfect order, the lines being regular and intervals and distances kept as if on a drill attack. Little opposition was met with. 2nd Lt. Field and men of 'D' gallantly rushed a strong point containing two machine guns, capturing the two guns & 25 prisoners. These guns had caused a number of casualties. T. Capt. Stringfield was wounded when within about 100 yds of objective, 2nd Lt. Hepburn at once assumed command of 'D' Coy and captured final objective. 'B' Coy pushed on across Odyssey Trench and though encountering strong opposition, with the assistance of a platoon of 'A' Coy under 2nd Lt. Douglas-Crompton, they finally charged and captured strong point in front of Odyssey Trench. All Objectives were captured & consolidation commenced. 2nd Lts. Showsmith & Douglas-Crompton displayed the utmost gallantry in leading attack on strong point. Both officers were killed. 2nd Lt. Mander rushed his platoon forward and filled a gap between 'B' and 'D' Coys. Rev Studdart Kennedy proved a tireless padre and did excellent work with the wounded. Lt. Dic Verge RAMC attached, although his first time in action, did wonderful work in the collection & evacuation of the wounded also attending to the wounded under fire. He also performed an amputation quite successfully. All stretcher bearers did excellent work, no wounded were in too exposed a position, but they got them in. They collected wounded under great difficulties, and mostly under heavy MG and Artillery fire. Bn and Coy runners were all that could be desired. They kept communication between Coys & Bn HQ without a break during the whole operation. They had at all times to cross open and exposed country, which was continuously swept by MG & shell fire. All ranks behaved splendidly throughout attack and consolidation. Where all did so well it is exceedingly difficult to pick out any NCOs or men for special mention. Sergt. Haldane displayed great pluck and endurance. His two sections had become casualties from shell fire. Although badly wounded in the shoulder by shell fire himself, he carried all wounded to shelter, bandaged their wounds, and then reported to forward Bn Command post, where he fainted from exhaustion & loss of blood. 'A' Coy did excellent work in mopping-up and supporting 'B' Coy. 4.30pm. Coys reported objectives gained and in touch with RBs on right and 9th Sussex on left, enemy MGs active from Green Woods."[527]

After this, a counter-attack was thwarted. The assault had been a great success and the casualties relatively light, though still serious: two officers and fourteen men killed; three officers and eighty-two men wounded; thirteen men missing. On the other hand they had captured one hundred and thirty prisoners of the 156th Prussian Regiment, two machine guns and two 77mm guns, though these were not recovered as they were so close to the new front line. The next evening, after intense shelling, a further eleven men were killed, and two officers and thirty-three men wounded. It was only at 11a.m. on 9th June that they were relieved by the 12th Royal Fusiliers and so able to move back to the area around Damme Strasse. Even that relief was not without incident – their leadership (the colonel, the second-in-command, the adjutant and the medical officer) were all hit by a shell as they withdrew and two other men were killed; sixteen wounded; one shell-shocked and another went missing.

Soon they were back in the line, and found Hill 60 a gruesome sight: "Country in a very dilapidated

---

[527] War Diary, 1st Royal Fusiliers, 7th June 1917.

condition… Huge great crater at Hill 60 which was blown on the 7th inst. Still remnants of Germans lying about and smell is pretty vile just now. Scorching hot weather is being experienced just now. Enemy artillery very active, especially with 5.9s from NE direction."[528] Fortunately, they were not called upon to participate in the assault the next day, though 280 of them acted as porters carrying up ammunition and supplies to those in the attack. Even a week later, bodies of both British and German soldiers remained unburied, and artillery was active on both sides. German aeroplanes managed to strafe their trenches. It must have been a considerable relief when they were withdrawn behind the lines at the end of the month, when they were also reinforced.

The battle lasted several days on a wide front. Despite its success, Prime Minister David Lloyd George was unwilling to allow Haig to continue the battle. He feared risking another Somme and made Haig wait before permission was given to launch the main battle. This political delay also caused a military problem – while the Cabinet discussed whether or not to let the battle continue, the Germans were given time to rebuild their defences to the east of Ypres and on the famous Passchendaele Ridge.

In the lull between the Battle of the Messines Ridge and the opening of the main offensive, Eric Quaife's Army career reached its climax. On 3rd February 1916, Eric had re-crossed the channel and been discharged from the 1st Honourable Artillery Company Battalion on 15th February at the conclusion of the period of four years for which he had originally engaged, having clearly stated he no longer wished to serve. He was not allowed to stay out of the Army very long – experienced men were too much in demand. He was posted to the 18th Reserve Battery of the R.F.A. at Exeter on 21st June 1916. On 13th October, he was commissioned 2nd lieutenant in the Royal Garrison Artillery and left from Southampton with the 294th R.G.A. Siege Battery on 30th March 1917, arriving at Le Havre the next day. They were sent to the Ypres Salient. Almost immediately they were in action, with four six-inch howitzers based at Neuve Eglise bombarding the Messines Ridge. He was promoted to captain on 21st June 1917 and became second-in-command of the battery. For a couple of days he was acting major in command of the battery. Early in the morning on 30th June 1917, he was killed when he was in the battery observation post with another officer and some men. A German shell smashed into it, killing them all instantly. He was buried at Chateau Rosenberg Military Cemetery Extension, and reburied in 1930 a mile away at Hyde Park Corner – Berks Cemetery Extension, near Hill 63 and Ploegsteert Wood.

Harold Froud and Leonard Taylor were also in action during the interlude, though further south near Arras. After the Battle of Arras, Harold had suffered from trench fever and was sent to the south of France to recuperate but had returned to the battalion, rejoining Leonard and the 5th Durham Light Infantry Battalion in time for an action on the night of 26th-27th June. Two companies attacked in two waves and captured the German trenches, and the artillery broke up the German counter-attacks, but Harold was wounded leading twenty men towards the enemy trench. Attempts were made to save him, and he was sent back through

Sec.-Lt. H. W. FROUD
5th Durham Light Infantry.
Died of Wounds, 27th July, 1917.

Harold Froud

---

[528] War Diary, 1st Royal Fusiliers, 13th June 1917.

the casualty clearing system to a rail head at Achiet-le-Grand, south of Arras. Here he was treated at No.45 Casualty Clearing Station, but he died there on 27th July 1917. After the attack, on 1st July 1917, whilst they were still in the support trenches, Leonard was once again promoted to be acting captain, as now he had taken command of one of the companies of the battalion.

William Alder was a much younger man than Harold when he was killed the day before the Third Battle of Ypres formally began. It seems scarcely credible given what we know of the horrors of the war, but even in 1915 William was prepared to lie his way in to join the Army, and the Army accepted the untruths. So he became another boy soldier. Born on May 24th 1900, William only left school in July 1915. He was a keen member of the O.T.C., and his records described him as a "quiet, well-meaning boy, who never gave trouble and who could be depended upon to do to the best of his ability whatever duty fell to his lot."[529] The school probably knew what he intended, as his leaving record lists his occupation as a private in the Royal Engineers. Just 15 when he volunteered, the Army at least pretended to believe him when he said he was twenty, and suitable for training. When one looks at his photograph it is hard to believe that his deceit could not have been obvious.

W. A. R. ALDER
Pioneer, R. E. Signal Service.
Killed in action, 30th July, 1917.

William Alder

Perhaps he had been made keen by the enthusiasm of Francis Forman, for William became a signaller in the 55th Division Signal Company. He landed in France in July 1917 and was sent to the Ypres Salient to join his unit. At the time, after a comparatively quiet time in the salient (although still subject to enemy enfilade fire and artillery shells), his unit was preparing for the attack on Pilckem Ridge, the first phase of the Third Battle of Ypres. The division was positioning to make its attack near St. Julien. On the days before the attack he was posted with three others to help set up a forward communication point in preparation.

"On the 28th he was posted for duty with his section and ordered with three others to proceed to a forward test point of some importance. The journey was done partly by motor lorry, and partly on foot. In the latter stage the party being heavily laden with equipment, some boxes and bags of rations were left by the roadside. The distance to the new dug-out was not great, and, as all was quiet on arrival, the Sergeant sent back a small squad (of whom Alder was one) to retrieve the rations which had been dumped. Less than five minutes afterwards a shell burst very near them, and Alder was badly hit. Stretcher bearers were speedily summoned and he was at once carried off and well cared for, but he lingered only a few hours."[530] He died in the early hours before the battle started. His burial at Potijze was on the site of an advanced dressing station to which he would have been carried. The final poignancy is that the Army recorded his age at death as being 20, and so he continues to be commemorated by the War Graves Commission, but he was actually still only just 17. "Of all the sacrifices which the war has made so painfully familiar to us, surely none is more piteous than this – the spilling of the life blood of a boy, scarcely more than a child, of 17 years."[531]

---

[529] *The Bournemouthian*, December 1917.

[530] ibid.

[531] ibid.

7: The Third Battle of Ypres

The Battle of Pilckem Ridge

Meanwhile, Haig had taken the strange decision to switch commanders for the main battle. General Gough and his 5th Army replaced General Plumer for the first phase, known as the Battle of Pilckem Ridge, 31st July to 2nd August.

William had died trying to make sure the communications for the Third Battle of Ypres worked properly. Edwin Hill worked to keep open those communications. Since 27th February 1917, Edwin was a captain in charge of one of the companies of the 8th Royal Sussex Battalion, a Pioneer battalion, though he had been away for the first part of the year.

On 8th January, he was admitted to Number 2 Stationary Hospital, Abbeville, initially with suspected arthritis. Reports of this clearly frightened his widowed mother who telegrammed anxiously to try to find out what was wrong – she thought he must have been wounded. On 1st March, he sailed to Dover on the *Stad Antwerpen* and was taken to a hospital in Sussex. He was suffering from a septic arm and from pleurisy. Later, the cause of his unfitness was given as exposure and infection whilst on active service with the Expeditionary Force. On 12th March, a medical board at the 3rd Australian General Hospital in Brighton decided, "Capt. E.A. Hill was admitted from France on 2-3-17 convalescing from Pleurisy and suffering from an outcrop of boils. The notes did not state that there was a Pleural eppision. His chest is now clear. He is having an intagenous vaccine for the boils. His general condition is good."[532] From 12th March, Edwin was treated at Kitchener Hospital in Brighton, the largest of the three hospitals set up in Brighton, with over 1,700 beds and the capacity to treat an additional one thousand patients using tents or huts on the racecourse next door. It was originally established in January 1915 for the Indian troops. On 12th April 1917, a medical board ruled that his septic arm had recovered as had the pleurisy. He re-joined the 8th Sussex Battalion south-west of Ypres near Mount Kemmel on 5th July 1917 and assumed command of 'D' Company.

Edwin's role expanded with the scope of the responsibilities thrust upon him. 'D' Company was soon afterwards detached on 13th July to work on 7th Canadian railway construction; and on 25th July having brought his men back to the battalion, he took over 'B' Company.

We tend to think of the opening days of the battles in terms of the infantry assault, but the first day of the Third Battle of Ypres, 31st July 1917, was costly for Edwin's Pioneers as well. They did their best to keep open the communication trenches, create new track-ways to advance the artillery, and to maintain the infantry routes, but at a price: six men were killed and thirty-nine wounded (three from gas). As the battle continued into August and beyond, so did the casualties. They worked on a wide range of tasks: shelter construction; trench clearing; track reinforcement; camouflaging artillery sites; maintaining bridges; repairing roads; preparing ground for railway construction; and similar essential tasks. These often had to be done despite enemy shelling and sometimes in the teeth of machine-gun fire. On 1st September, the battalion was moved to the 58th Division, still within the Ypres Salient. All that autumn and into the winter they worked hard with very little rest. It was not glamorous work, but their relentless efforts made a great difference to the men making

---

[532] Army File for Edwin Hill, WO 339/389.

the attacks. They were allowed a day's rest for Christmas!

Edwin and his men had their work cut out on such a large battlefield. Although not as long a front line as that of the Somme in 1916, it nevertheless stretched several miles. At the southern end of the British assault line, the British right rested on the now captured Messines Ridge just east from Hill 60 and Mount Sorrel, and south of the Menin road from Ypres. From there the line ran roughly north-east to Hooge and then approximately north before returning back on itself westwards (forming the salient), turning again to a mainly northern direction about Boesinghe.

Richard Barfoot, still serving with the 24th Field Ambulance, was also there to help. At the start of June 1917, the 24th Field Ambulance had been sent north to Ypres. Their war diary included an interesting description of the planned evacuation route for the wounded from the battle. This gives us an idea of the sort of ordeal of jolting and travel a wounded member of the division (or of the school) would experience once they had been fortunate enough to have been brought off the battlefield to the regimental aid post. In the event, even this planned route proved impossible and even worse arrangements had to be made. "The Reg Aid Post is situated at Halfway House… & has only accommodation for 1 stretcher case. Cow Farm is in a ruined house & is at the head of the tram way. It has accommodation for 20 stretchers. From Reg Aid Post to Cow Farm carriage is by hand, a distance of 2400 yards (through a trench for 1600 yards and 800 yards is carried over the top). From Cow Farm to the Bund is 1000 yards. At the Bund there are 3 'Elephant' shelters each holding 12 stretchers – one is held by the 96th Fd amb, one we will take over and the third is held in reserve. Two M.O.s are stationed here. The tram may continue to Krusasstraat, a distance of 1½ miles where there is a 'Loading Post' where there are two shelters – one in a ruined house and one in an old concrete gun emplacement. The total distance from Cow Farm to Krusasstraat is about 2 miles. The motor ambulance run to the Dressing Station at Vlamertinghe Mill a distance of 6000 yards, hence by motor ambulance to CMDS at Brandhoek (3000 yards) & from there to Remy Siding where there are four CCSs – 10th & 17th, & 2nd & 3rd Canadians."[533] In late June, a move by the 24th Field Ambulance into a wood about two miles closer to Krusasstraat would still have left a long and painful journey for the wounded.

This planned evacuation route was abandoned by stages, even before the battle began. First, heavy German shell fire on Cow Farm forced the medical team there to move down to the Bund, where the lack of shell-proof shelter forced them to reduce the number of medical officers, reducing its status to that of a bearer relay post. Then both Cow Farm and the Bund received direct hits from German artillery, and the plan was changed to move men directly back from Halfway House[534] to Hellfire Corner instead – a route normally regarded as suicidal in daylight.

---

[533] War Diary of the 24th Field Ambulance, 13th June 1917.

[534] This Halfway House was an important reference point for men moving along the Menin road from Ypres. It stood approximately half-way between Ypres and the British front line at Hooge. At the start of the war, it was a large house whose size made it a prominent landmark. By 1916 no house still stood. But under its ruins was a large dug-out, with various galleries and chambers. It was big enough to house not only a brigade headquarters, but even to shelter a battalion and specialist troops. "The only spot with any pretensions to safety on the ridge. Below the atmosphere was appalling, and conditions were not improved by the constant drip of moisture and the presence of 2 inches of slimy mud on the floor. An engine used to pump day and night to keep the water down; it also lit some of the chambers with electric light. The dug-out was so crammed that men were sleeping in the passages and communication was difficult."

When the battle began, "the wounded commenced to arrive at 4.20am, 40 minutes after Zero, stretcher cases a little later. At about 1½ hours after Zero 'Mustard Gas' shells burst near the Menin Road ADS and interfered with the clerical work of stretcher bearing, but not much – a few stretcher bearers were slightly gassed; four knocked out of time. This inconvenience only lasted ½ hour… still raining, the going was so heavy that eight men were required to a stretcher case."[535] In the summary note and recommendations, there is the chilling observation: "a considerable number of wounded could not be got at in the front line captured and after our relief [on 3rd August] it required 500 extra bearers to clear the remainder of our division and the new division etc although we did not attack… Finally the whole evacuation was carried out under fairly heavy shell fire & the most adverse weather, making the ground almost impassable."

Richard and the 24th Field Ambulance continued, with brief interludes, to support the battle-fighting troops throughout the Third Battle of Ypres. They remained there until, in early March, they were transferred back to the Somme, near Lihons, south-west of Peronne.

Charles Austin, the younger brother of William and Harold, also supported this attack from behind the front line, though not from the start of the battle. Born in 1897, he was at the school for at least four years (during which he was in the O.T.C.) including 1906 and 1907. Unlike his younger brothers, Charles remained a private soldier. On 5th February 1917, was he posted to the Army Service Corps. He was tested out and three days later was approved as a "fair" lorry driver after a test at the A.S.C. Motor Transport Centre, Grove Park. From then on he was employed by the Army as a motor vehicle driver. From 13th March to 10th July 1917 he was posted to the 898th Company (Motor Transport) A.S.C. This company had been formed the previous January and was located in Liverpool. Its job was to man a depot to receive Holt tractors from the United States. In the Army jargon, they "erected agricultural tractors". This was important, but not glamorous work. Charles, posted to a new company, embarked on the SS *Huntsland* from Plymouth on 21st August 1917, disembarking at Le Havre two days later.

Initially, in August 1917, he worked in 344 Company A.S.C., which supported the 25th Division's supply column. (Each Army division was supported by a certain amount of motorised transport, although the division commanders did not directly command it. Responsibility for the supply of goods, equipment and ammunition from the divisional railhead to the divisional refilling point came under the divisional supply column companies. If possible, these companies also moved materials forward to the dumps and stores of the fighting units, especially if these were heavy loads. Originally, an A.S.C. company comprised five officers and three hundred and thirty-seven soldiers. These men looked after forty-five 3-ton lorries, sixteen 30-cwt lorries, seven motor cycles, two cars and four trucks of various types to serve the workshop and stores of the supply column itself.) Charles' role was therefore behind the scenes for the Third Battle of Ypres. In October he was briefly attached to 358 Company which was the Army's 3rd Heavy Repair Shop, servicing lines of communication troops under G.H.Q. command. Then, from October 11th, he worked under the overall umbrella of 814 Motor Transport Company (until 20th February 1919) but seems to have been detached from time to time: Between 15th October 1917 and 2nd November he worked with 315 ASC Motor Transport Auxiliary (Petrol) Company. These were not petrol tankers, but petrol-driven vehicles. 315 Company was the 3rd A.S.C. Company of this kind and was based at Étaples, the major British base on the coast south of Boulogne. It served under G.H.Q. command, serving lines of communication troops.

---

[535] War Diary of the 24th Field Ambulance, summary included with entry for 3rd August 1917.

Henry Footner also served in the Ypres Salient at this time. Henry was born in 1897 and attended the school from September 1910 until December 1916. He was keen to play his part and, as he put it in a letter to his old headmaster, he "had no difficulty in gaining admission". He was a skilful scientist, and was sent to a trench mortar company within the Royal Engineers Special Brigade of Chemists. The training his unit received in "an out of the way part of the country… about one hundred yards from the sea, on the cliffs, in a very wild spot, where we have snow every day" was infantry training, compressed into only about one month. "In joining this corps I have mixed with a good set of men, a good number of whom are schoolmasters."[536] Although the training for his unit was quickly completed, chance delayed their deployment – one of the men developed measles which led the Army to isolate the entire unit.

On March 21st 1917, he went to France as a Pioneer in the Royal Engineers. At first the unit was stationed at a major base camp, where they were immediately given basic training in defence against gas. After that, their work was boring – carrying timber or sweeping roads. This was a rather surprising use of specialised troops.

Henry and his unit went into the front line in May 1917. In a letter he described his journey of 26 hours "made in one of those delightful trucks labelled '8 chevaux, 40 hommes!'"[537] Based about four miles from Ypres, he fought at Messines and then also south of the salient at Ploegsteert. Their job was to fire gas, smoke and liquid fire shells as he explained in a letter from hospital in the winter of 1917.[538] In a third letter, written in the winter of 1917-1918, he explained, "The worst part of our job is the carrying in of the shells, as we have to carry three shells, of thirty pounds apiece, for anything up to two miles into the front line." They usually fired at night, attracting German counter-battery fire. They supported both the highly successful British offensive of the Battle of the Messines Ridge in June 1917 and the main battle. "Although… ours is far from a comfortable life, it is not so bad as that of the infantry, as we are never in the line for more than twelve hours at a time, and then go back to billets."

After serving in the Ypres Salient from June to November 1917 he developed jaundice and trench fever and was sent to a field hospital for three weeks. He was evacuated to England and sent to the Beaufort War Hospital in the Fishponds area of Bristol. On its busiest night, the hospital housed nearly 1,500 patients who were attended by an entirely female nursing team drawn from Queen Alexandra's Imperial Military Nursing Staff reserve, supplemented by women of the Voluntary Aid Detatchments or VADs (nicknamed the 'Very Adorable Darlings' by some of the troops). Perhaps the most famous man helping with this work was the orderly (and later war artist) Stanley Spencer who included several scenes from his experiences there in his famous set of murals in the Sandham Memorial Chapel (although most of these were focussed on the privations of the Salonika Campaign). Overall, the hospital treated 29,433 patients with considerable success (with only 164 recorded deaths, including 30 civilian victims of the 'flu in 1918). Spencer described the main gate of the hospital as "massive and as high as the gate of Hell". Spencer had volunteered for overseas service in 1916, and was in Salonika in 1917 when Henry arrived at the hospital. To Henry the gates might have been Gates of Hope instead. As Henry grew better he might have been allowed into Bristol as part of his convalescence. If so, he would have presented a somewhat ludicrous

---

[536] Letter dated 24th January 1917, in *The Bournemouthian*, April 1917.
[537] Letter dated 20th April 1917, in *The Bournemouthian*, July 1917.
[538] Letter published in *The Bournemouthian*, April 1918.

sight, as the men were required to wear a special blue uniform of lounge jacket and trousers, folded up into cuffs on the arms and at the ankles (and looking like badly fitted pyjamas) as splendidly depicted in Spencer's *Tea in the Hospital Ward* scene within the Sandham collection.

In 1918, Henry returned to France in time to face the German onslaught of that spring. As his file no longer exists, we cannot tell into which unit he was placed or precisely what he did that year. We know Henry survived the campaigns of 1918 and spent much of the inter-war years travelling for work across the empire and to the USA until his death in Chelsea in 1973. He became a respected chemist, for example publishing as co-author with Samuel Smiles *CCCC – Reactions of Organic Thiosulphates* in *The Journal of the Chemical Society* in 1925.

After the artillery barrage, the battle started on 31st July 1917. The main thrust was made by General Gough's men, east across the Pilckem Ridge, but General Plumer's 2nd Army was allowed to try to consolidate the gains made earlier on the Messines Ridge. Horace Tollemache was in Plumer's force, fighting on the first day. On 1st July 1917 he had been promoted to full lieutenant, commanding a platoon within 'C' Company of the 15th Hampshire Battalion. They were to be used to extend the British position on the Messines Ridge east of Wyatschate.

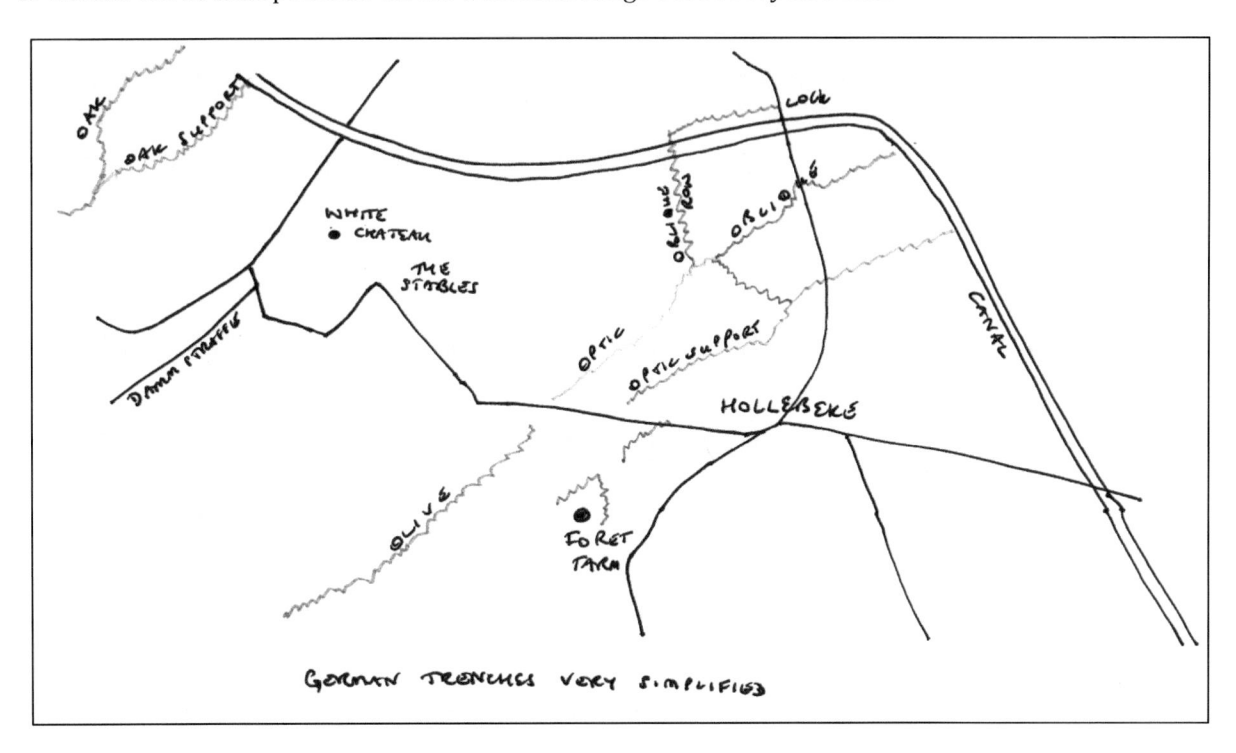

They gathered in the trenches at Bois Confluent, about two and half miles south of Ypres, and west of the village of St. Eloi. Their designated target was the village of Hollebeke. They were in support behind the attacking battalions (18th King's Royal Rifle Corps and 11th Royal West Kents) and saw them take their initial objectives on the first day of the battle, 31st July 1917, despite strong defensive machine-gun fire, particularly from Foret Farm. Horace and the 15th Hampshires advanced behind the assault troops under German shell fire, but their casualties were very light. Their main enemy at this stage was the heavy rain, which had begun about 4p.m. Within a day, though still in support rather than attack positions, casualties began to mount. They moved forward to a line from Lock Cellars via Oblique Row to Optic Trenches, leaving their reserve company behind in Oak Support. "Rain fell incessantly and conditions were extraordinarily bad, the men being in many cases up to their waists in mud and water. Casualties: OR – 8 killed, 30 wounded... Rain continues to fall and conditions are getting worse. The trenches are full of water and most of the men have been moved to shell holes."[539]

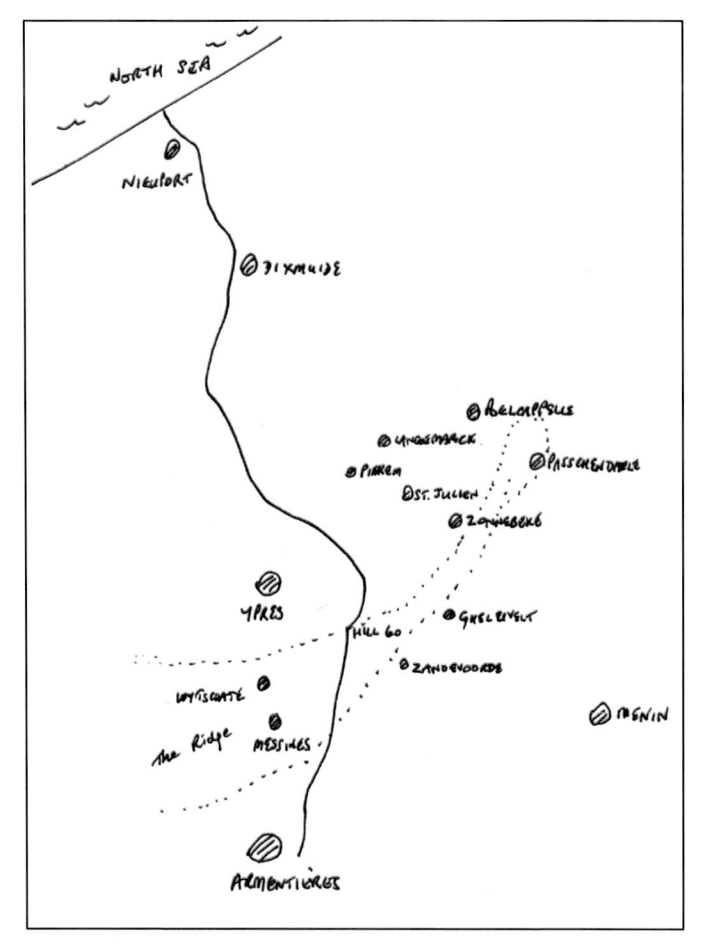

To add to their woes, the Germans opened up a massive bombardment on their positions, awful since they were not properly sheltered because of the flooded trenches. Then, at 4a.m. on 5th August, the Germans counter-attacked in heavy mist, trying to retake Hollebeke in a two-pronged attack and managed to capture a number of the Hampshire soldiers. The Hampshires, supported by some men of the 12th East Surreys, made their own counter-attack and regained the village. The war diary noticed that "in addition to the enemy divisions opposing us, some 100 'Sturmtruppen' specially selected for their physique and intelligence took part in this attack which was carried out on a large scale. But in spite of this and the fact that our men were wet through and tired out, the enemy gained no advantage whatever and had heavy casualties."[540] A further night attack, with the Germans attempting to crawl forward, was also smashed by machine-gun and rapid-rifle fire. A few days later they were able to withdraw from the line to train, recuperate, and prepare for the next round. This was just in time – in August one hundred and forty men had to go to hospital through sickness (fifty with trench foot from 4th to 6th August alone). No wonder some men speculated that the weather seemed to be better on the German side.

After three weeks of training behind the lines, in the latter part of July, Ernest Parsons and the 1st Royal Fusiliers Battalion had returned to the Ypres Salient to take part in the battle. Amidst the thundery rain they gathered in front of their trenches (to avoid the support companies being pounded by German counter-attack shelling) and two companies led the attack on part of Shrewsbury Forest, east of Sanctuary Wood. In this attack they lost fifty officers and men killed; 145 wounded; 78 missing; ten more, who had also been wounded, remained on duty. The remnant were reorganised into two emergency composite companies and remained at the front for another week before being pulled back, reinforced, sent forward again, and finally sent behind the lines for recuperation and working parties. We know that Ernest was temporarily taken off the roll of the battalion on 9th August. This was probably because he had been wounded. Whilst twelve men were killed and twelve wounded on 10th August, the days before that had only seen one man wounded – on 7th August whilst they were in the line near Bodmin Copse, just north of Shrewsbury Forest and

---

[539] War Diary, 15th Hampshires, 1st and 2nd August 1917.
[540] War Diary, 15th Hampshires, 5th August 1917.

east of Sanctuary Wood, so it is probable that Ernest had been wounded in the attack on Shrewsbury Forest, but only removed from the roll of active members of the battalion a few days later.

Frederick Furness and the 11th Royal West Surrey Battalion were also back in action on 31st July at almost the furthest south-west part of the battle line, with the intention of helping to drive a wedge into the German position in the south and to push south-eastwards. This attack had been anticipated and prepared for by the Germans, and a significant number of men were killed and wounded in the days before the assault, as the Germans bombarded the unit when it occupied the lines to be ready for the attack. It took two nights even to prepare the tapes marking out the attack, because the Germans strafed that part of No Man's Land with rifle and machine-gun fire. However, the final two days were quiet – a calm before the storm.

The Germans used their new defensive tactics. They deliberately left their front line lightly manned, hoping to draw the British deeper, beyond their supporting artillery's effective cover, and into a killing zone of concrete machine-gun posts. The 11th Royal West Surrey Battalion was ordered to attack from Imperial Trench, just south-west of Hill 60. The objectives for the brigade were to take the German trenches opposite them, and then to push through the complex of trenches and redoubts in Battle Wood, break through, and advance a couple of miles to capture the next line of German defences at Zandvoorde. The 11th Battalion were intended to get as far as the concrete emplacements in line with the trenches of Battle Wood and another brigade in the division was then designated to press on through to Zandvoorde.

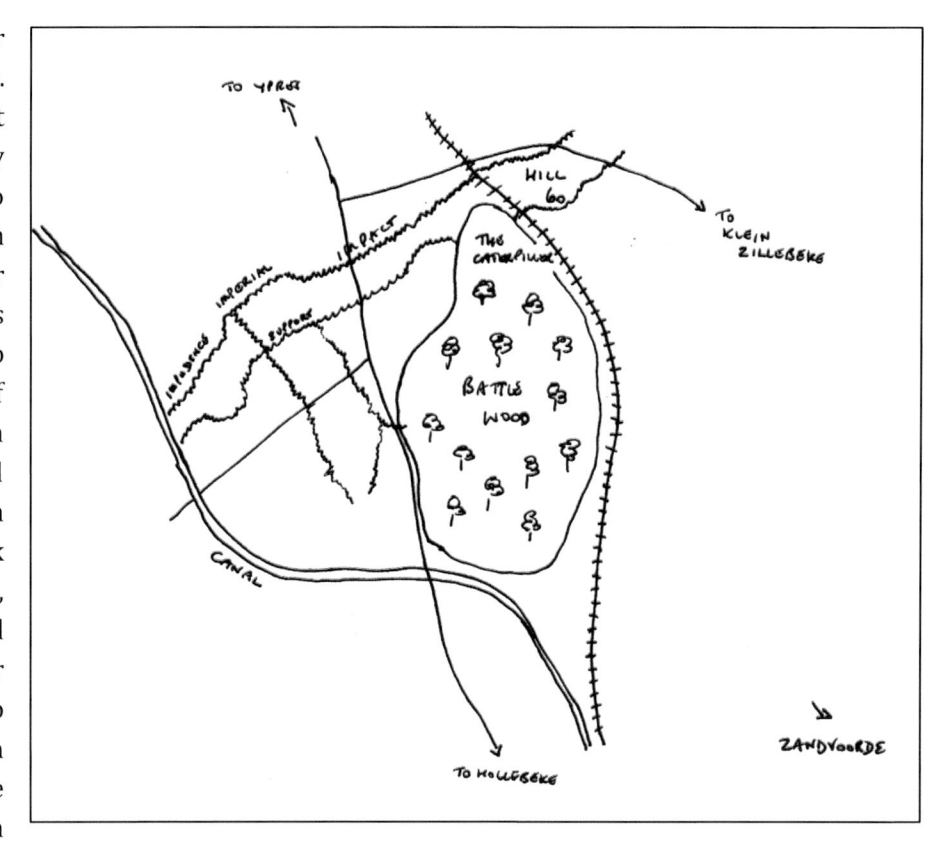

"The Battalion were in position about 1.30am without suffering a casualty of any description and without the slightest hitch. Zero hour was at 3.50am. The Battalion moved forward with the Barrage and experienced no difficulty in taking the first objective. It was found that, owing to the heavy state of the ground, the troops had great difficulty in keeping up to the Barrage which was gradually creeping away. At about 300 yards from the final objective three concrete shelters were found; these shelters were held by the enemy with machine guns and apparently picked rifle men. The Barrage, or the previous bombardment, had made no impression on these 'forts', and the taking of them by infantry bordered on the impossible. A party of 50 men... got to within fifty yards of these shelters.

These parties suffered heavily as it was impossible to stir without an enemy machine gun firing. During the night these parties withdrew, and joined the remainder of the Battalion at the second objective. Captain Bowden with C Coy had also been held up by these same concrete shelters and had linked up with the R.W. Kents also at the second objective. The casualties on this day were 2nd Lieutenant A.J. Smith killed, 2nd Lieutenant Kitchingman wounded and Lieutenant E. Apted missing. Other Ranks casualties were estimated at two hundred."[541] The next day the battalion lost two more officers wounded with forty other men, whilst forty-one more were reported to be missing. It was with some relief no doubt that on 2nd August the battalion was pulled back.

Further north-east at the point where the line stretched north from Hooge, Ronald Budden had gone into action. The 1st Worcestershire Battalion had undertaken intense training, working up from flags to indicate stages of a barrage to advancing under live mortar fire to get the men used to the horrors of the war. By mid-June 1917 they were back at Hooge, by the Menin road, encountering very heavy German shell fire. Fifty men were wounded on June 17th alone. As the weather improved, the training had intensified on the days they were not in the trenches, with specialist training in throwing grenades, working with Lewis guns, and hand to hand fighting with bayonets.

On the night of 27th-28th July, when they were still based in support rather than attack lines near Hooge, Ronald took men out on a night operation, to carry out a reconnaissance of the German wire. His patrol even entered the German front line trench, and he did so well with this patrol that his divisional general awarded him a Parchment Certificate for Gallant Conduct and Devotion to Duty, stating that he had carried out that reconnaissance with skill, judgement and determination and that he handled his men well and returned with valuable information. One man died and eight were wounded the day of that patrol. Later, the school gave the boys a half-day holiday on 18th October 1917 in his honour.[542]

The attack began at 3.50a.m. on 31st July, as light was just beginning to show in the east. The battalion advanced behind a creeping barrage of shrapnel. On the left were the 58th Canadian Regiment and on the right the 16th Manchesters. The battalion, suffering some casualties, captured Ignorance Support Trench. A good many dug-outs were bombed by the moppers up, who worked in prescribed areas, one platoon per company being 'moppers up'. The tunnel under the Ypres-Menin road was expected to give a great deal of trouble but turned out to be quite an easy matter to deal with: forty-one prisoners were captured there. However, the ground being traversed by the battalion had been very badly cut up by British shell fire and in places was very marshy. After Ignorance Support Trench had been taken, they attacked James Trench, still following the creeping barrage. Machine-gun fire continued to be encountered but to a great extent the Lewis gun sections succeeded in restricting the German gunners. The companies had got a bit mixed together but this did not prevent the battalion from capturing the strongly-held James Trench, which was situated on the edge of Chateau Wood onto which the enemy fired a heavy barrage that mostly dropped behind the front attacking lines.

Communication trenches leading from James Trench to the top of the Bellewarde Ridge were now cleared and the battalion started to dig in on the forward slope of the ridge, overlooking Westhoek. A protective barrage was put down some 200 yards in front. After a few minutes, the 2nd Battalion

---

[541] War Diary, 11th West Surrey Regiment, 31st July 1917.
[542] *The Bournemouthian*, December 1917.

East Lancashire Regiment passed through the Worcesters to attack the Black Line at Westhoek. A great deal of machine-gun fire was encountered from the right flank, where British troops were not progressing quite so well. 'A' and 'B' Companies dug in on the ridge and 'C' and 'D' consolidated Ignorance Support Trench. When it was certain that troops were well on their way towards Westhoek, 'D' Company was withdrawn to work as stretcher-bearers. The tanks now began to pass through to assist in attacking the Green Line (after the Black). But the ground proved too marshy for their successful use, and they were heavily shelled on their way up.

Ronald's company was now sent forward to attack the third German line. Enemy shell fire was heavy and machine guns and snipers were very active, trying to slow up the attack or drive it back. Ronald's men were checked for a moment by this machine-gun fire. Seeing it was hopeless just to rush across without cover, Ronald organised a small party from his platoon, and led them forward from shell hole to shell hole with a view to attacking and silencing the nearest of these machine guns. He needed to get a grenade onto the machine-gun position to silence it. But when he was within point blank range of the gun he raised himself onto the lip of the crater to throw a grenade, and was shot immediately. The men with him immediately rushed the gun and bayoneted the crew, including the man who shot Ronald. The gun was captured and the line went forward to its further objectives. [543]

Although his superior Captain Urwick later wrote glowingly to honour Ronald, it can only have been a marginal comfort to his parents, who had lost their only son, to know "I cannot hope to express the extreme value of such leading as was displayed by your son. Apart altogether from the personal gallantry of the deed, the initiative, the quick grasp of opportunity in the face of a momentary check are exactly those qualities which are needed to make the full use of the arms and equipment which are at last ours. The fact that the regiment fulfilled every task which had been set it to the letter, despite strong opposition, is in itself sufficient testimony to the value of the work done by him and other fine officers who leave such gaps in our mess. More immediately the fact that the men with him went on and completed the difficult little operation on which he had given them so splendid a start, speaks of the high quality of his example and of the devotion with which he was followed. The colonel and all his brother officers cannot speak too highly of him, while more important still, the men of his own platoon seem to miss him sorely… He lies in goodly company, in ground hallowed in all our memories, and on the occasion of an attack which the enemy newspapers have declared to be decisive in this great struggle."[544] The chaplain wrote, "He always proved himself a fearless soldier… He lived a good life and died a noble death in the greatest effort that England has made for the freedom of the world." Smashed by a machine gun, it was not possible later accurately to recognise his body, and today he is honoured on the Menin Gate at Ypres as one of those for whom the fortune of war has not allowed an identified grave.

Ronald had died alongside the Menin road and the others had fought to its south, but the first phase of the battle is known to history as the Battle of Pilckem Ridge, as the main fighting was north of the road. There, the British tried to regain the Pilckem Ridge, which had been lost to them and the French at the 2nd battle. This was where Cyril Howard fought, and where the British assault had to cross the Steenbeek.

---

[543] The description of the attack and his death was derived from combining the War Diary, 1st Battalion Worcesters, 31st July 1917 and *The Bournemouthian*, December 1917.
[544] *The Bournemouthian*, December 1917.

Born in 1892, Cyril was at the school from 1903 to 1909, and was a member of the O.T.C. He used his middle name, not his first name, Alfred. As a youngster he had not always enjoyed the best of health (illness made him miss both spring and autumn terms in 1904). Cyril volunteered for the Hampshire Regiment on 29th September 1914, and for a time served in the 7th Hampshire Battalion in India. On 24th January 1917 he was discharged to a commission for which he had applied from Chakrata. He was commissioned as 2nd lieutenant in the 14th Hampshire Battalion, the 116th Brigade, 39th Division. In his letter to *The Bournemouthian* of 5th July 1917, Norman Wragg, a 2nd lieutenant in the Dorsetshire Regiment, mentioned that he had met Cyril: "I have just run across one of our old boys – A.C. Howard, a 2nd-Lieut. in one of the Hampshire Regiments. We had a long talk the other night over things in general, including the war. This is the first time I have met anyone of the old school out here."545

The 14th Hampshire Battalion was the only Hampshire battalion involved on the first day in the Battle of Pilckem Ridge. On 31st July, "Its villages and farms had long ago been knocked to pieces and their ruins converted into 'strong-points', while of the woods only shattered stumps remained. It was largely open, barren or at best covered with weeds and rough grass, but bad going in rainy weather. Unfortunately the start of the Flanders Offensive of 1917 coincided with some unusually bad weather, including quite torrential falls of rain, and throughout its course the weather was a recurrent handicap, if at times the ground dried sufficiently to be no real hindrance, while in September dust was once actually reported. But in the Salient, with the streams often so damned up by debris as to have been converted into swamps or lakes, with the surface pitted with shell-holes which rain speedily converted into pools above a bottom of foul mire, with the natural drainage ruined by the shelling and the digging of trenches, even a little rain went a long way. The soil, if less glutinous than that of the chalk uplands of the Somme, had its own abominations; less adhesive, it was looser and softer, and if men slipped and slithered less, those who fell into shell-holes were hard to extricate. Those few battalions who went 'over the top' in 'Third Ypres' without finding the going a serious impediment were fortunate."546

The 14th Hampshires went 'over the top' that day. They had trained and prepared, and on 29th July moved up to the canal bank on the northern side of Ypres. The 116th Brigade was given objectives to attack east of the canal to the Steenbeek, south-west of St. Julien. The battalion was positioned between the 13th Royal Sussex on the right and the 17th Sherwood Foresters on their left. In front of them were the men of the 11th Royal Sussex. There was a clear view for over a mile eastwards towards their objectives – the same view that would give the Germans a chance to see and shoot them down.

It was still almost dark at Zero hour, 3.50a.m., when they attacked behind a tremendous barrage. The first objective line was taken relatively easily by the 11th Sussex. Then the 14th Hampshires 'leap-frogged' over them towards the next line, which was a ridge running south from 'Kitchener's Wood'. Although the Germans only lightly held their trenches, they had sited multiple machine-gun posts in pill boxes, including some made from the ruins of farm buildings. The battalion "captured and consolidated Black and Dotted Black Lines at Falkenhyn Redoubt. From there advanced onto Alberta and Dotted Green Line on East of Steenbeek which were captured… Captured 2 Field guns and one

---

545 Norman Wragg's letter of 5th July, in *The Bournemouthian*, July 1917.
546 *The Royal Hampshire Regiment, Vol. 2*, C.T. Atkinson, 1952, p. 228.

4.5 How., 17 machine guns (counted) and over 200 prisoners."[547] Of the three officers killed, one, 2nd Lieutenant Denis Hewitt, was posthumously awarded the Victoria Cross. He had reorganised his company when they had captured the Black Line. As he waited for the barrage to lift so that he could lead his men forward, a shell burst near him and hit him. More disastrously, it set fire to his clothing, and the fire caught the signal lights he was carrying in his haversack. He managed to extinguish the flares, at some personal cost in burns to add to the wound he received from the shell itself. Even so, he led his men forward into heavy machine-gun fire and helped to capture the next objective, the 'Black Dotted Line'. As he supervised his men consolidating that position he was shot and killed by a German sniper. Some units of the battalion, aided by two tanks, pushed further on across the Steenbeek, although as they were then exposed on the flanks they were ordered to pull back. Four more were wounded. Eighteen men died, forty-two went missing, and 156 were wounded.

The next day they re-occupied the line of the Steenbeek at a cost of four more men killed, twenty-two wounded, and one missing, though they withdrew again one hundred yards the next day to allow the British artillery to bombard the German defences at St. Julien. Even withdrawing into support cost a further eight killed, fifteen wounded, and another man went missing. The battalion returned to the trenches and came under fire, but was not directly involved in any further assault that August.

South of Cyril and north of Ronald Budden, Eustace Chudleigh also went back into action. On 1st July 1917, Eustace had been promoted to lieutenant. As they prepared for the battle, Eustace and his friends were treated to an address by the visiting Archbishop of York before whom they paraded on 23rd July.

On 28th July, they had moved into position near Zillebeke, though hit by German 4.2 shells and gas shells as they assembled. For the next two days they remained in their assembly position despite German shells and a barrage from German machine guns on 30th July. "Z day Zero was at 3.40am, and when our first wave, consisting of three platoons of 'B' company under Lieut L.C. Makeham, went over it was still quite dark. The enemy at once put down a barrage on our old front line trenches and on Crab Crawl. There was also considerable machine gun fire from the right, which somewhat hindered the 2nd Yorkshire Regt. However, the objective was captured and the trenches cleared by 6.15am. About 40 prisoners were taken from The Jam Support, Jeffery Trench and Jeffery Support. 'B' company HQ was finally established at the head of Jam Row near Green Jacket Ride… Three platoons of 'C' company, under Capt. W.B. Gardner, formed the second wave, and killed a number of Huns in Jam Row and Jam Lane, but took no prisoners… 'C' company HQ was established in a trench mortar dug-out… and the company astride of Jam Lane with 2/Lieut H.S. Starkey's platoon… 'A' company, under Capt. W.B. Wood, together with 2 platoons of 'D' company, met with a good deal of resistance from machine gun fire from the woods W of Dumbarton Lakes and Inverness Copse. About 12 prisoners were taken around junction of Jam Lane and Jar Row, and about the same number killed… 2/Lieuts F.R. Lewis and V.A.P. Bowen established a strong point with about 20 men… and strengthened the position considerably by Lewis guns taken from a derelict tank nearby. This position covered low lying ground and junction of Jar Row and Jasper Avenue. Later they were joined by men from other units… Heavy shelling continued around our reserve positions and 'No Man's Land' the whole day."[548]

---

[547] War Diary, 14th Hampshires, 31st July 1916.
[548] War Diary, 2nd Wiltshire Battalion, 31st July 1917.

The next day, Harold Martyn re-joined the battalion, having finished his work as a Lewis gun instructor. The battalion held their new positions despite heavy shelling and machine gun, surviving on iron rations since fresh rations could not be brought up for them, though they did receive some the following evening. Eventually, the weary men were pulled back on 4th August.

Stanley Seymour had been sent back to England towards the end of the Battle of the Somme. On 2nd April 1917 he had once again been promoted to lance corporal. He landed back in France on 21st July 1917, where he joined the 6th Northamptonshire Battalion. This battalion supported the assault by the 11th Royal Fusiliers and the 7th Bedford Battalions on 10th August against German defences in Inverness Copse and Glencourse Wood. Two of their companies acted as 'moppers up' behind the assault (and became involved in the front line); a third garrisoned the strongpoints whilst the fourth carried forward ammunition from the Dump for the assaulting groups. In the end the attack was driven back, and the battalion had lost one officer killed, six wounded with three missing. Of the men, twenty-seven were known to have been killed, 123 wounded, and twenty-six were missing.

Reginald Winch of the 1/3rd London Battalion fought at the end of this phase and the start of the next phase of the battle. After intermittently training and manning the trenches near Arras, they were transferred to the Ypres Salient at the start of August 1917 and from 12th to 16th August took part in the battle. They came under a German counter-attack on 14th August: "At daybreak 14th enemy put down heavy barrage on our right front and rushed two points causing casualties. All day our lines were heavily shelled. At dusk on 14th we re-established the line on our right, prior to relief. On our right front enemy patrols were driven off with loss."[549]

August 16th-18th: The Battle of Langemarck

The opening phase of the battle had been a major disappointment for the British. No breakthrough had been achieved. This added to Haig's problems. To placate Lloyd George, he had assured the Cabinet that a concerted effort could break the German line and allow the British to penetrate eastwards towards Zeebrugge. This was supposed to appease Jellicoe as it would endanger some of the German submarine bases. Haig also hoped that it would induce the Dutch to join in the war on the Allied side. But despite significant losses in terrible, wet weather, the British had only pushed the Germans back a relatively short distance and the German line seemed firm. Haig was forced to economise with reality in reporting to the Cabinet that the fighting had been "highly satisfactory". He claimed the losses had been "slight" when in fact there had been about 31,850 casualties and the maximum advance was only three thousand yards. The nine divisions of Gough's Fifth Army, which had attacked with two French divisions on their northern flank and five Second Army divisions to the south, had mostly, after serious German counter-attacks, not even achieved their first objectives. By the end of 2nd August, the battle had ground to an exhausted halt.

Then followed a pause in the assaults as Gough readied his men for another attack and the resources were brought forward to support it. Tanks had mostly been ineffective in such thick mud and knocked out, so the battle would have to be won by the infantry supported by the artillery. The next attack, the Battle of Langemarck (16th-18th August 1917) would be another determined effort to break through in the north and in the centre. Much was asked of the infantry around Langemarck.

---

[549] War Diary, 1/3rd London Battalion, 14th August 1917.

Reginald Winch and the 1/3rd London Battalion continued in action. "At dusk on 15th the Battalion massed for the attack. 'B' Coy were to act as 'moppers up' for 8th Middlesex Rgt. 'D' Coy were to act as 'moppers up' for 1st London Rgt. 'A' and 'C' Coys in reserve to take post in our original front line as soon as the attack went forward. The assembly for the attack was most difficult owing to the nature of the ground, the mixing up of units and darkness. At 4.45am the attack started and owing to the slowness of the barrage and the impetuosity of the men it appeared that all waves and moppers up joined in one thick line. For over an hour no reports came in, then both 8th Middlesex Regt and 1st London Regt heard that they were held up. The enemy barrage first started after the attack had gone three hundred yards. From 5.0am enemy shelled our front and support lines heavily with 4.2 and 77mm until nightfall… Our advance was checked by 5.15am by the swampy ground… This ground was impassable and was also defended by snipers and MGs on E and NE."[550] "An attempt was made to place duckboards across but these simply disappeared in the mud… The ground was impassable for troops even in small parties… After 9am on the 16th the enemy had complete control of the air and did exactly as he wished. None of our fighting planes were to be seen. He repeatedly flew about 300 feet up, along our trenches, more especially those in support, & freely used his machine guns. This takes the heart out of the men & also discloses their positions."[551] In this frustratingly unsuccessful attack, the battalion lost a lot of casualties: two officers and twenty-six men had been killed; four men had died of wounds; three officers and 195 men had been wounded; two officers and a further fifty-three men had gone missing.

Norman Wragg was there. In Norman we have an Old Boy whose history is more complete than for many of his contemporaries. This is because, as School Captain ('Head of School'), he was mentioned a lot in the school records, because he wrote several letters to Dr. Fenwick, which have survived in the pages of *The Bournemouthian*, and because his army record – though damaged by the Blitz of 1940 – is reasonably complete.

Norman joined the school at the age of eleven in 1909. He quickly excelled in his exams, and in 1910 was awarded a 'Thomson' Scholarship, meaning that his fees were paid by the current Chair of Governors who had generously established a fund to pay for suitably worthy boys. He very quickly established himself as a prodigiously able student, and was photographed for having gained First Class Honours in the Senior Exams in 1912. He continued by outscoring the national cohort in his Cambridge exams (despite his youth) both in 1913 and in 1914 – when he not only came first in the country in pure and applied maths but was awarded an exhibition to St. John's

Norman Wragg in 1912

College, Cambridge, though he was only aged fifteen. At that tender age he was appointed 'Head of the School'. Even then he was not satisfied – by the end of 1914 he had also passed his national science exams and in 1915 gained the highest entrance scholarship of £80 for St. John's College. Even so, he was far from a 'boring boffin' – he played cricket and football for the school (captaining

---

[550] War Diary, 1/3rd London Battalion, 15th August 1917.

[551] From a report of Captain Maunsell, O.C. 'B' Coy at Steenworde, within the War Diary, 1/3rd London Battalion, 15th August 1917.

the football team in 1914-1915), excelled at athletics, and was a member of the O.T.C., becoming sergeant in 1914. His parents must have been so proud of this remarkable young man.

He was 19 on 6th June 1916 and left school on 10th June. He had refused the opportunity to be exempted from military service (open to him as one whose education would be in the national interest) and on 11th July joined No.4 Officers' Cadet Battalion, stationed in Keble College, Oxford. Most of his fellow cadets were experienced men from the front. His experiences ranged from 'square bashing' and military training to sports such as swimming in the river or playing football and rugby. He particularly appreciated talks from officers back from the front, and also enjoyed viewing the propaganda film, *The Battle of the Somme*. He was gazetted 2nd lieutenant on 20th November 1916 to the Dorsetshire Regiment.

On 26th January 1917 he embarked for France to join the 5th Dorset Battalion. After a rough crossing he remained at the base for a month. In the first week at the base he had a 'refresher' course of a sort all officers arriving in France had to take. After that the 'Dorsets' (whether officers or other ranks) all had to wait a further three weeks, going repeatedly over the same materials until in the end he found that experience repetitious and tedious. Then he was able to join his new battalion who were part of 34th Infantry Brigade, 11th (Northern) Division.

His first duty was to act as 'Draft Conducting Officer'. This meant he had to help take one hundred and twenty men on a seventeen-hour train journey from the base, followed by two days searching out the battalion, which was on the move after a month's rest and training at Domqueur in France, after taking serious casualties fighting on the northern end of the Somme battleground. He arrived on 24th February 1917 in time to join in routine battle training, including the use of the bayonet.

Four days later he had caught the 'Rose' (now known as 'German') Measles so he spent over two weeks in a measles hospital attached to a casualty clearing station. Apparently, the illness had been brought to the battalion with the draft from England. He had little to do after a while except to go for walks and to play bridge whilst the rest of the battalion trained. The whole battalion was kept in isolation to avoid spreading the illness to other battalions. At the end of April, after further training in the battalion and working parties, he went into the trenches as the battalion relieved the 7th South Staffordshire Battalion. In June, the 5th Dorset Battalion moved to Kemmel in the Ypres Salient. They were troubled by planes and shells, and the casualty rate shot up high, with men being killed or wounded in sizeable numbers most days from 10th June. This led to a platoon reorganisation once they were relieved from the front as the commander and subaltern of 'A' Company had both been amongst those killed. The whole of July and the first half of August was again spent in training, as their 11th Division (in Maxse's XVIII Corps) was part of the 5th Army which General Gough had not used in the opening Battle of Pilckem Ridge, but kept back in reserve. On 14th and 15th August, they moved forward to fight in the Battle of Langemarck.

"We were also actively engaged in a show at the middle of August, when we were proud to be able to say our Brigade did everything it had to, and a bit more."[552] The battalion was in the thick of the action, attacking a line just south of the village of Langemarck. Their 11th Division formed up on the east bank of the Steenbeek, between the 48th and 20th Divisions at 2a.m. and their 34th Brigade formed the leading wave for the division – the 5th Dorsets were on the left and the 8th Newfoundland Battalion on the right with the 9th Lancashire Fusiliers and the 11th Manchesters

---

[552] *The Bournemouthian*, December 1917.

behind. In front of them, a shrapnel barrage crept forward over the German defenders. "No difficulty was met with on crossing the Steenbeek – the 5th Btn Dorsetshire Regt. on Y-Z night C.B Coys being the two leading Coys pushed across the Steenbeek with the assistance of guides from the 6th Yorks Regt. and occupied the posts on the east bank, that had that morning been evacuated to allow a heavy bombardment being put down on the strong positions close to them, and held strongly by the enemy, these posts were occupied without any casualties. A tape was then put down on the East bank and in the rear of our posts for the purpose of assisting the Btn. forming up. This being completed our two leading companies formed up with A and D companies formed up on west side of the Steenbeek supporting them… Zero 4.45 a.m. Our barrage started and our two leading companies moved off. Over the Steenbeek went A and D companies. Everything went in order. The strong points were in every case rushed and the whole of their garrisons either killed or taken prisoners. Two machine guns being captured during the period of these engagements on the strong points a small gap (120 yards) was made between B and C companies… D Company at once sent up troops to fill this gap. The fact of B Company having no trouble on the right and C Company keeping such splendid touch on the left and the opposition of the enemy strong points in the centre of the line of our advance having to be dealt with undoubtedly accounted for this very small gap. Our objective having been reached successfully, C Company found themselves in possession of Alouette Farm which was slightly to the left of our objective and on the right B company managed to gain communication with the Manchesters. Captain Wiltshire in command of B Company at once sent out a party to capture the Huts… which they successfully did, taking many prisoners. The posts on the right of B Company came down to the 'Langemarck' road. D Company in their rear dug their posts so as to make a defensive flank thereby assisting their comrades on their right. Our casualties up to this time had been very small. Consolidation of positions was quickly completed and the men during this process were troubled only by machine gun fire and snipers, these being engaged by our own snipers very successfully. During the afternoon of Z + 1 Day C Company brought down an enemy plane which was at the time very low over our lines. Throughout the whole of the operations the men were in high spirits, and splendid communication between companies and battalion HQ was maintained throughout – the liaison work was splendid. For this the battalion has to thank 2nd Lieutenant Elderkin and thanks to the work of Battalion runners. The liaison officer, three distinct and direct wires were in touch with the artillery from Battalion HQ and Francois Farm. As regards the pace of the barrage, everyone seemed quite satisfied with it, and not once during the advance was it lost. Our casualties numbered 3 officers, 143 O.R.s."[553] The next day they were relieved by the 33rd Brigade, suffering no further casualties.

Second lieutenant and fellow ex-School Captain, twenty-six-year old Brian New was slightly to the north of the line of attack of the 5th Dorsets. The younger brother of Jack, and better known to his friends as Barry, he was born in 1891 and was at the school between 1903 and 1909. He too had thoroughly immersed himself in school life: being in the O.T.C. as a top NCO, colour sergeant; school prefect; an outstanding captain of the cricket team; playing football for the school; and doing very well in his senior exams. In 1909, he was appointed Head Prefect (School Captain) and once he left school he became a well-known member of the Old Boys' Club. When Brian had volunteered he had not followed older brother Jack into the Dorsets, but instead joined the 7th Hampshire Battalion, which was sent to India. He was promoted to corporal, and then selected for officer training. So, in 1916, he was sent back to England to be trained in an officer cadet battalion

---

[553] War Diary, 5th Dorsets, 16th August 1917.

and was then gazetted 2nd lieutenant in the 7th Battalion of the Duke of Cornwall's Light Infantry, the battalion in which Thomas Lonsdale had served at Ypres in the previous year.

His specialism was to be signals officer. Brian arrived in France in March 1917. When he joined his new 7th Duke of Cornwall's Light Infantry Battalion it was at Le Transloy, near Bapaume on the Somme. That month, and again in April, the battalion was involved in fierce fighting to try to dislodge the Germans from the new positions to which they had retired after the Battle of the Somme. On the second occasion, on April 9th, they attacked Havrincourt Wood south of Cambrai. The British "advanced steadily under a light barrage of field guns. Enemy showed fight until our men were within 500 yards when the Germans took to their heels and were chased by our troops to the Northern edge of the wood and several enemy batteries were kept under fire as they limbered up. The Brigade then entrenched on a line running through the middle of the wood. We secured two wounded prisoners."[554] The attack had cost the lives of two men and a further seven were wounded, but it must have been an exciting day for Brian and his comrades. For the next months the battalion occupied trenches, suffering steady attrition from enemy shell fire from minenwerfer and other mortars, as well as machine guns and artillery.

Brian 'Barry' New

On 20th July they were sent north by train. After further training (including gas drills and observation of a terrain model of the battlefield) they ended up almost precisely where they had been the year before when Thomas Lonsdale had been with them, near Boesinghe, north of Ypres. On August 5th they returned to the canal bank, in trenches, receiving shell fire day and night, and once again under sniper fire.

Brian's Christian faith seems to have been important to him, and was remarked upon by the chaplain who recorded that he attended Holy Communion before the battle. At that stage the battalion was still based on the canal bank. The weather was dreadful – heavy thundery rain for much of the day as the battalion checked its supplies of ammunition, grenades, flares, tools, sandbags and so on, all under heavy enemy artillery shell fire. This made the canal bank where the men had to line up very greasy. Ironically, from about 10.30p.m., when they lined up in preparation for the assault, the sky cleared and the stars came out. Their target was to cross the canal and head for (and capture) the village of Langemarck. The battalion was expected to attack the third objective, building on the success of the first two waves. The whole attack was to be made under the protection of a creeping barrage. The expectation was that by the time the battalion made its attack, the village would already have fallen and they would be taking German positions to its east. Brian, as signals officer, was specifically directed to lay a telephone line forward from Brigade HQ by the canal to the forward positions where a battalion headquarters would be established.

The men moved forward quietly in the darkness across the canal before midnight, and then were allowed an hour and a half to lie down, have a smoke, and to receive a tot of rum. At 1.45a.m. they

---

[554] War Diary, 7th Duke of Cornwall's Light Infantry, April 9th 1917.

began moving forward again, reaching the Steenbeek stream west of Langemarck at 4.15a.m.

"Owing to the darkness, mud, and heavy shelling… which caused several casualties, the rear two and a half companies and Battalion Headquarters had lost touch and were some way behind."[555] This was just the start of communication confusions which hampered the advance. Nevertheless, the forward companies were able to cross the Steenbeek even though they were out of touch with Battalion Headquarters ("in charge of an inexperienced officer as Signal Officer"). Some signallers and runners did manage to report to the commanding officer about twenty minutes after Zero Hour. However, it became clear that some signallers "took shelter from the heavy shelling in the buildings about Iron Cross and Stray Farm". The battalion was taking heavy casualties (about 70) from the right of the advance and a German machine-gun post, known as 'Au Bon Gite'. Nevertheless, and despite delays from German resistance from concreted positions, progress was made. "About this time streams of German prisoners were passing Westwards; they were in such numbers that I thought they would disorganise my formation and after a short while stopped the sending of escorts back with them and directed them to the Railway line; they were only too ready to go and needed no escort; I believe many of them were taken by the 88th Brigade. I estimate that we sent back 150 and that there were about 400 altogether at this time."

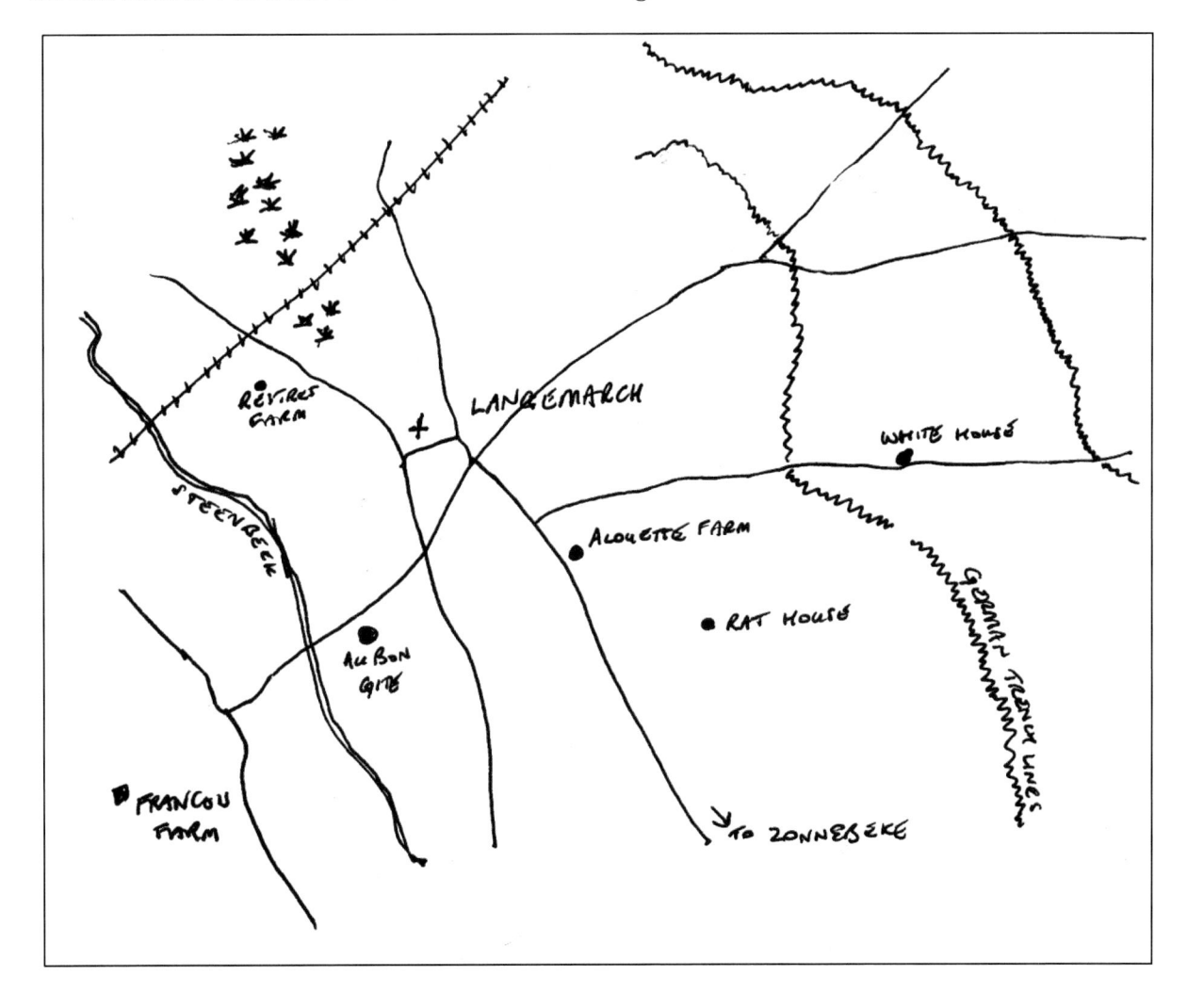

---

[555] The details of this battle, including those which follow, are included within the War Diary, 7th Battalion Duke of Cornwall's Light Infantry, August 1917.

The ground was wet and shell-torn, so the companies could not maintain their formations, but at least the second objectives were reached and the battalion began to dig in alongside survivors of the King's Own Yorkshire Light Infantry, which had preceded them. Langemarck was in British hands. The other companies joined the advance and the third and final objective was secured. Enemy aircraft duelled overhead with British, and it seems the Germans gained the upper hand that morning and they were able to harass the ground troops with machine guns from the air. The colonel established a forward battalion headquarters in the ruins of a concrete house in Langemarck which still had two walls standing. "About midday the acting Signal Officer, 2nd Lieutenant New arrived at battalion Headquarters with two or three signallers. It had previously been reported that the Signal Sergeant and some signallers were sheltering in one of the concrete buildings, near the east bank of the Steenbeek and that more of the Battalion Headquarter signallers were in another building about a quarter of a mile west of the Steenbeek; I sent 2nd Lieutenant New to collect his signallers and to try to establish a line to Brigade Headquarters." This meant that Brian was expected to criss-cross hundreds of yards of No Man's Land to round up signallers in clear view of the enemy defenders and their aeroplanes, and then to lay a line all the way from the canal to Langemarck, all in broad daylight. German gunners could see the temporary bridges across the Steenbeek so could concentrate their shells where British soldiers must cross if they were returning to the canal bank. "I heard nothing further until the following afternoon when a straggler from the Battalion reported that he had seen 2nd lieutenant New and his orderly killed by a shell between Langemarck and the Steenbeek – this was confirmed by the Signal Sergeant on the evening of the 17th; he stated that he had seen 2nd lieutenant New and his orderly lying dead in the same shell hole."

Brian's body was never recovered – at least not in a recognisable condition. Today his name is carved on the memorial wall at Tyne Cot Cemetery, one of the first of the dead with no known grave commemorated there as an 'overflow' to the inscriptions on the Menin Gate.

Close by, Maurice Hellier was back in the action. On 5th February 1917, Maurice had been promoted to captain, and from 15th April 1917 commanded 'B' Company of the 6th King's Shropshire Light Infantry. The battalion had remained, taking casualties, manning and improving trenches on the Somme through the late winter and spring of 1917 and at the end of June 1917 had withdrawn and entrained for the west, to Fieffes, near Doullens, where they began a period of intensive training. On 21st July they were brought up to Proven, near Poperinghe, on the edge of the Ypres Salient. Here, the division was transferred from 4th Corps of 3rd Army to 14th Corps, 5th Army in preparation for the coming battle. From 5th August they were employed on working parties (fifteen men died one day when a German plane bombed them), in final training, and in bringing up supplies to those troops already on the front line. Then, on 14th August, they were brought up to the canal bank.

On 15th August, the 6th King's Shropshire Light Infantry also crossed the canal and lined up on the west bank of the Steenbeek. They were between the 12th King's Royal Rifles on their left and the 9th Lancashire Fusiliers on their right. The two front companies were 'A' on the left and 'C' on the right; behind them were 'D', and then 'B' companies, with the Battalion Headquarters at the rear. However, since they had come under heavy German bombardment after crossing the canal, they were delayed even in lining up in the taped area. In position at last, they sheltered for an hour in shell holes under very heavy shell fire.

Finally, they too moved forward at 4.45a.m., crossed the Steenbeek and attacked through a patchwork of marshes and mud. Eventually, they reached the outskirts of Langemarck where they killed and captured many German machine-gun teams. The battalion was able to push on to secure Alouette Farm, which was turned into Battalion HQ. "At 7.30am the Battalion advanced with two Companies in front, supported with one Company in support as moppers up. The going was better, but against strong opposition from the Ferro-concrete forts, hedges and ditches. Intense machine gun fire was opened from the Mill, White House, and from a concrete fort due east of Rat House. After clearing the large concrete block-houses west of the salient, the three companies pressed on, killing scores in hand-to-hand fighting, and sending back batches of 26 – 32 – 19 – 11 – and 42 – unwounded prisoners. At 7.45am the final objective was captured, forming the cord across the two shoulders of the salient. The three Companies came into line and consolidated, throwing out a screen 150 yards in front, with three Lewis Guns. The enemy were driven out of Kangaroo Trench and shell holes, making for the small wood behind White House. This latter was dealt with by Rifle Grenades, and then rushed by one officer and eight men, who killed 9 Huns, sending back 5 unwounded prisoners."[556] Afterwards, the battalion lent two bombing sections, two rifle sections, two Lewis guns, two machine guns and the Stokes mortar to assist the 12th King's Royal Rifle Corps on their left, further north into Langemarck, as the Germans had counter-attacked in force and even gained a foothold in their trench. On the right, by 10.00a.m., the 9th Lancashire Fusiliers, who had not linked up with them at the White House, were seen to be in retreat some two hundred and fifty yards behind the position held by the 6th King's Shropshire Light Infantry but when, five times, the Germans made similar attempts to drive Maurice and the battalion back, each time they managed to annihilate the attacking Germans. However, that night they withdrew from the White House as their right flank remained exposed, creating a flanking arc of defence, assisted by two platoons of the 12th Rifle Brigade. "The enemy put an intense bombardment repeatedly on Battalion Headquarters at Alouette Farm, and from the Rat House concrete fort kept it continually under machine gun and rifle fire." Despite this, morale was high, and they held their new-won positions until relieved by the 10th Royal Welsh on the night of 18th/19th August. Five officers had been wounded (three dying afterwards), thirty-nine men had been killed, one hundred and forty-seven wounded, and five had gone missing but Maurice had survived. The battalion was then withdrawn from the front for almost a month to regroup, re-train, and prepare for their next intervention in the battle, which come in the middle of September.

Russell Prichard was also there. He was born in 1890. He had three younger brothers: Hubert, Cyril and Aubrey, and the latter two – if not all three – attended the school. Cyril and Aubrey both also served in the war, though Cyril's service was in the east. Their father was a nurseryman gardener, and their mother died when they were all young – in 1890. Russell was at school before 1911, but his records are lost. (Cyril was a member in 1909 and Aubrey, his youngest brother, was at the school from April 1909 to March 1913. Like his brothers, Aubrey's surname was rendered 'Pritchard' by the Army. Aubrey served in the 17th Royal Welsh Fusiliers Battalion, sometimes known as the 2nd North Wales Battalion, in the 128th Brigade, 43rd Division. At the end of the year the battalion was sent to the Western Front. His Army career is even less easy to trace than those of his brothers but we know he survived the war and died in Christchurch in 1969.)

Russell was in the 2nd Hampshire Battalion, though it is not clear when he joined the regiment. Given Russell's Army service number, 243191, it is unlikely that he served with the battalion in the

---

[556] Report contained within War Diary for August 1917, 6th King's Shropshire Light Infantry.

first years of the war. We know from an entry in *The Bournemouthian* magazine of December 1917 that he was "slightly wounded" in the left leg during August 1917.[557] On 9th August 1917, the battalion had moved forward, east of the canal line near Boesinghe to dig themselves in. They had almost no trenches to occupy, only a few former German block-houses, so they had to dig new trenches to take cover as a new support line. Most of their casualties started on 15th August as the battalion pushed up towards the Steenbeck and some men had to be pulled out of the quagmire by ropes and some men were wounded by German shelling as they moved into assembly positions for a major assault.

On 16th August the battalion attacked across the Steenbeck, at 4.45a.m. "The men got close under our barrage and never let it get away from them during the whole advance. All ranks are agreed that the accuracy and pace of the 29th Divisional barrage left nothing to be desired." Even so, the attack was held up by German block-houses and machine-gun strongpoints both north and south of the line of the railway, and the men acted heroically to capture these positions and to push further forward and to establish strongpoints of their own, under considerable defensive fire. "All the Coys in these two lines were subjected to heavy shelling throughout the day and the trenches they had made were repeatedly blown in and a good many casualties were suffered." The situation became more critical in the afternoon. Reports came in that in the area around Poelcapelle the Germans were massing for a counter-attack. "The inner Coys also dug strong points to support the flank Coys. During the afternoon and evening Bn HQ (Tuffs Fm) was very heavily shelled and a good many casualties received among the stretcher bearers and HQ personnel."[558] The shelling continued all night, but the battalion held its position, even though on its flank some British units were forced to pull back. The butcher's bill was, however, heavy. As well as seven officers (one killed, six wounded), the men had paid a price: "Other Ranks – 34 Killed; 148 wounded; 20 wounded (at duty); 9 missing; 10 sick to hospital." We cannot be sure that Russell was one of those wounded that day, but twenty wounded men remained at duty, and the school report described his wound as "slight", which sounds as if he might have been one who remained in the strongpoints. Only once, later in the month, was another wounded man able to remain at duty. Russell (like his brothers) survived the war, and in 1924 he emigrated to Victoria, Australia, where he died in 1953.

Ronald Paumier

Ronald Paumier was also in action that August. Born in 1897, the son of a travelling actor, Ronald lived first with his grandparents and then lodged along with his mother whilst he attended the school from 1909 to 1911. He then also became an actor, but when he was old enough he had volunteered to join the O.T.C. of the Inns of Court in London. After training he was gazetted 2nd lieutenant in the 5th Northumberland Fusiliers, but was not to serve with them. Instead, he became seriously ill and so was invalided out of the army. After a successful operation, he gradually regained health. He was called up for service on 27th February 1917 and certified fit. After that he was assigned as a private soldier to the 14th London Regiment, the 'London Scottish'.

---

[557] *The Bournemouthian*, December 1917.
[558] War Diary, 2nd Hampshire Battalion, 16th August 1917.

It must have seemed strange to have switched from the training he had received as a junior officer to being trained as a private, but his previous experience explains the speed of events. His training was from March to June, and on 9th-0th June 1917 he was sent to France, landing at Le Havre. He joined the 14th London Battalion on 13th July, just in time to take part in the battle. It was part of 168th Brigade and the 56th (London) Division. That July, the battalion received twenty-four new officers and three hundred and forty-eight new men – sixty three on 13th July alone. On 6th August 1917 they had moved into Belgium. Then, after training, they were placed in divisional reserve, and moved up for operational duties on 15th August.

They were to attack in the area where Ronald Budden had lost his life, just south of the main assault, east of Hooge between Inverness Copse and Glencourse Wood, and north of the Menin road. Inverness Copse straddled the road, and the brigade faced two lines of German trenches.

On 15th August, 'Y' Day, Ronald and the others were moved forward to support the assault. The next day, the other two "Infantry Brigades assaulted at 4.45am. The battalion moved forward at about 11 am from Chateau Segard to the southern edge of Etang de Zillebeke. No enemy shelling was experienced during the move. At 9 pm the battalion moved forward again to Halfway house area via Corduroy trench. The battalion suffered the following casualties during the move: 2nd Lt F H Laird wounded; 11 Other Ranks killed; 10 Other Ranks wounded. These casualties were all in the battalion carrying party."[559] Ronald was in the carrying party and was killed, presumably by German shell fire. He was buried close to Ypres at the Perth Cemetery, otherwise known as China Wall (from the communication trench named 'the Great Wall of China' which ran to Halfway House). He was aged 21. His active service had lasted just a month.

Although in the battle Langemarck had been captured, there was no breakthrough. Even Inverness Copse had not been secured (it reputedly changed hands eighteen times in August, ending up back in German control). In the face of this disappointment, British morale plummeted.

On 21st August, the 2nd Wiltshire Battalion, including Eustace Chudleigh and Harold Martyn, moved into trenches in the Messines Sector, near to Kemmel. After a day in reserve, they moved up to the front line to relieve the 45th Australian Battalion. There was hardly a trench line – more a shallow dip linking shell holes with little wire protection, and even its support line was a mix of old trench and shell holes. For the next few days it was impossible to move or be seen in daylight – and the Germans were well aware that the men had to go out at night to try to link up the shell holes and to add a barbed wire defence. In the early hours of 24th August, a soldier was captured by four Germans when he had stumbled a little ahead of the rest of his patrol. (However, the Germans in their turn had made an error, blundering into a Wiltshire out-post with their prisoner, with the result that the Wiltshire sentry had opened fire, rescued his comrade and captured three of the four Germans.) The next day, one of the captains was shot whilst out with a wiring party, risking the activity of German snipers and apparently random machine-gun bursts. The day after, about sixty German stormtroopers of their 179th Regiment attempted a silent raid on the Wiltshires, but were beaten off with heavy casualties. After another four days in these trenches the Wiltshires suffered from an intense German barrage followed by another German raid. This time, "after a stout resistance with Lewis guns under heavy shelling and MG fire the enemy penetrated some of our posts and took nine prisoners, one of whom escaped in no man's land & made his way back to

---

[559] War Diary, 1/14th (London Scottish), August 16th 1917.

our lines. Heavy losses are thought to have been inflicted on the enemy, who are identified as being the 22nd Pioneer Battn by dead bodies found near our wire. Our losses were 1 killed 14 wounded 9 missing."[560] That night the Wiltshires were relieved and Eustace and Harold were pulled back to 'rest', which actually meant more digging and carrying. On 4th September 1917, Eustace was one of a small group granted leave to return to England for a week or two. Afterwards, however, Eustace did not return to this battalion, nor to the Western Front. This suggests he had been wounded as, on 25th September, the War Office extended his leave and he was struck off the strength of the battalion. According to the Army List for 1918, he remained in the 3rd Wiltshires, but was employed by the Ministry of Labour. He survived the war. Harold Martyn remained with the battalion.

Plumer Replaces Gough, 25th August

The weather was foul that summer. The men called it 'Haig's weather'. The rain turned the low ground of the Ypres Salient to thick, slimy, treacherous, drowning mud. The artillery shells that were intended to smash the German defences also smashed the drainage channels. The rain had nowhere to go but into the churned-up soil. When photographs of men walking along duckboards between shell holes filled with water and putrefying flesh are viewed, they are likely to be of this battlefield.

Dissatisfaction with General Gough increased, including significant complaints from within his own staff. Ironically, even Gough now had little faith in his own plan and advised Haig to shut down the whole Ypres offensive. That was unacceptable to Haig, though perhaps the British Cabinet might have agreed to it.[561] On 25th August, Haig replaced Gough with Plumer as the general to continue the battle, now to be planned as a series of 'bite and hold' battles rather than a grand breakthrough across the front. The new tactic was to try for a series of more limited gains (the 'bite') after which the field artillery would be brought closer up to support the infantry, which were to consolidate upon the gains made (the 'hold'). Once one gain was secure, the battle could continue to bite and hold a new objective.

Doubts were widespread on both sides as to whether the battle could be won. Afterwards, in his memoirs, the German Commander in Chief, General Ludendorff, wrote, "The costly August battles imposed a heavy strain on the Western troops. In spite of all the concrete protection they seemed more or less powerless under the enormous weight of the enemy's artillery... Our wastage had been so high as to cause grave misgivings and exceeded all expectation."[562] On the other hand, at the British Staff College at G.H.Q., a tank specialist called Baker-Carr indicated British despair. He had been asked over lunch about the battle that August, and said that it was "dead as mutton". Afterwards, Baker-Carr was summoned by Brigadier-General John Davidson, Haig's Director of Operations: "When Baker-Carr arrived he found the general seated at his desk with his head in his hands. 'Sit down', he said. 'I want to talk to you.' Baker-Carr complied. 'I am very upset by what you said at lunch, Baker. If it had been some junior officer, it wouldn't have mattered so much, but a man of your knowledge and experience has no right to speak as you did.' 'You asked me how things really were and I told you frankly.' 'But what you say is impossible.' 'It isn't. Nobody has any idea of the conditions up there.' 'But they can't be as bad as you make out.' 'Have you been there yourself?'

---

[560] War Diary, 2nd Wiltshire Battalion, 30th August 1917.
[561] *In Flanders Fields, Passchendaele 1917*, Leon Wolff, p. 193.
[562] Ludendorff, quoted in *In Flanders Fields, Passchendaele 1917*, Leon Wolff, p. 197.

'No.' 'Has anyone in O.A. been there?' 'No.' 'Well then, if you don't believe me, it would be as well to send someone up there to find out.'"[563] It is infamous, though perhaps apocryphal, that when, eventually, Haig's information officer, Charteris, did visit the battlefield after the battle was over, he is said to have asked, "Good God! Did we really send men to die in that?"

Gunner Frank Kent of the 290th Brigade's 'B' Battery was engaged in the artillery preparations for the next phase. From 7th September, they were back in action, having just relieved the 102nd Brigade R.F.A. Frank was engaged in re-locating the field guns of the battery to support the bombardment which General Plumer planned to start on September 13th. The rains of August had given way to beautiful sunshine in September. The glutinous mud dried hard. The Germans could not believe the British had attacked in driving rain, but were not attacking in perfect conditions. They speculated that the battle might be over. Above their heads planes from both sides flew in great numbers – engaging in dog-fights (Richthofen scored his 60th authenticated victory that month over this battlefield) but mostly to try to see what the enemy was up to, and where their units were located. German planes would undoubtedly have seen the movement of the British guns. The Germans were always trying to destroy this field artillery. On September 11th, the Germans shelled Frank's gun pit with gas shells. There was no prior warning, and he had no time to put on his gas mask. Badly gassed, he was put into an ambulance but by then he was unconscious, and sadly never recovered consciousness. He was almost certainly taken to Duhallow Advanced Dressing Station, a few yards nearer to Ypres centre than the famous Essex Farm Cemetery, for he was buried there. He was nineteen when he was killed.

Plumer's new offensive, for which Frank had been preparing, became known as the Battle of the Menin Road, fought between 20th-25th September, and was followed directly by the Battle of Polygon Wood from 26th September to 3rd October. In these battles, British divisions assisted, but the assaults were led by ANZAC troops.

September 20th: The Battle of the Menin Road

Having suffered significant losses in August, the 11th West Surrey Battalion, including Frederick Furness, had been withdrawn to be rebuilt and re-trained. In September, he and they were back in action. Fortunately, the more limited 'bite and hold' tactic of General Plumer meant the men were less susceptible to moving beyond effective artillery support. The Germans had been forced back and their defence lines were now based on previous support positions. On 20th September, the battalion was in support, losing two men killed, and an officer and eight men wounded as twice the Germans counter-attacked. Over two hundred reinforcements joined them and the next evening they moved forward, losing another ten men, and with an officer and another thirty-six men being wounded. But, "50 of the reinforcements under one officer came up the line as Stretcher bearers and remain carrying wounded until the morning of the 23rd. The number of German dead is surprising."[564] (Then the battalion enjoyed what must have seemed almost a surreal episode: after a short period in reserve, Frederick and the others were moved north to the coast where they were for a short while given the role of coastal defence. In reserve, this was a pleasant time in round tents, playing football and even bathing in the sea – swimming lessons were given on the evening of 30th September. The main hazard was low-flying German aircraft which were driven off by

---

[563] *In Flanders Fields, Passchendaele 1917*, Leon Wolff, pp. 196-197.
[564] War Diary, 11th West Surrey Regiment, 20th-21st September 1917.

enthusiastic machine-gun fire. But when they were in the front line, even on the coast, things were less of a sinecure, and men were still wounded though the attrition was much lighter and they were out of the main battle. At the start of November the battalion moved to Italy to reinforce their Italian allies in the aftermath of the Italian defeat at the Battle of Caporetto. At some stage, Frederick went off to a French hospital. When and why is not recorded, and there is no reference to this stay in his Army file,[565] but he and another 2nd lieutenant re-joined the unit in Italy on 23rd January 1918.)

After a period of training and recreation following their earlier supporting role in the battle, Horace Tollemache and the 15th Hampshires returned to the fighting. On 20th September, they were the assault troops for their brigade, attacking along the Menin road on a two battalion front alongside the 18th King's Royal Rifle Corps to try to take the village of Gheluvelt and move the line east of the village to the German 'Tower Trench'. On the night of the 19th-20th September, they quietly assembled in the jumping-off line trenches without loss. At 5.40a.m., Zero Hour, they attacked – and got a shock. "The 15th Hants were checked by a strong point which had been untouched by the barrage about 5 minutes after the start, which was soon overcome by the gallantry of Officers and men in storming the position. After this the Blue line, which was the 15th Hants' objective was reached without difficulty. Casualties were heavy including all four Company Commanders. A counter attack was threatened from N.E. (on the Menin Road) but was dispersed by rifle and machine gun fire." [566] Because the follow-up attack by the 11th West Kents failed due to firm resistance in Tower Trench and from heavy machine-gun fire from Tower Hamlets, the 15th Hampshires were again ordered into the attack to take the Tower Line. One hundred and thirty men went forward and took the German position, capturing forty prisoners including a battalion commander and his adjutant, two machine guns and a field gun. They then held the new line, repulsing several counter-attacks, though for a time they were the victims of 'friendly fire' from British artillery, which was being fired "through false information."

When they had thrown back yet another German attack, including men with flamethrowers, and had again been shelled by their own artillery, the Hampshires decided the best thing was to move forward, but this meant they came under artillery fire from both sides. Only one officer and ten men survived to get back to the British line. Six officers had been killed and three more wounded; forty-nine men had died; three were missing; and two hundred and forty-eight were wounded. A further five more men were waiting assessment when the diary was written up, and thirty-one missing. The battalion was smashed by the experience, and once again needed to be rebuilt. So they were pulled back from the line to recuperate and retrain. On 25th September, twelve officers and three hundred and seven men of Hampshire Carabineers Yeomanry reported for duty with the battalion. (These cavalry Territorials were now reclassified as infantry, and the battalion renamed slightly to reflect their inclusion – the 15th (Hampshire Yeomanry) Battalion. The battalion also moved north to the seaside, in their case to Bray Dunes. On 8th October, one hundred and nineteen more men of the Hampshire Carabineers Yeomanry joined them.) Horace had survived and lived to tell the tale, but for now, like Frederick and the 11th West Surrey Battalion, he and the 15th Hampshire Battalion were sent to Italy. There, the division took the front line near the River Piave, north-west of Treviso. However, even before the Germans launched their offensive of March and

---

[565] All the surviving Army Files were substantially gleaned after the Second World War so there are many gaps in the records.
[566] War Diary, 15th Hampshires, 20th September 1917.

April 1918, British anxiety at the deteriorating situation, especially after the Bolsheviks had agreed an Armistice on the Eastern Front, releasing German resources to come west, had led to orders summoning the division back to France.

On 20th September 1917, Harold Head's tanks moved forward. After the Mark II losses sustained in the Battle of Arras, his section had a new set of tanks: one 'male', number D29, 2332 called 'Damon' and three 'females' (D16, 2576 'Derek'; D45, 2661 'Destroyer'; and D55, 2764 'Dragon'). The tanks planned to attack cross-country eastwards from Langemarck towards German positions south-west of Poelkappelle. With the increasingly thick glutinous mud, this was always going to be a difficult mission. From the start the attack did not go at all to plan. The crew of D16 'Derek' were overcome by gas almost at the starting line. The 'male', D29 'Damon' did move forward but before long was hit twice and burned out, killing two of its crew. 'Female' D55 'Dragon' ditched, almost certainly close to the wreck of D29. The most successful tank was 'female' D45 'Destroyer', which made good progress almost to the objective before it received a direct hit. With all the tanks from his section destroyed or derelict, Harold had to wait for replacements before further involvement in the fighting.

Joseph Wilkes and the 2/5th London Battalion had moved into trenches north of St. Julien on 8th September 1917, from which they took part in the attack, despite the fact that the depleted battalion had only 16 officers and 452 men. They prepared by advancing along slippery duckboards in the dead of night, heavy rain having started at 10p.m. the evening before. By about 4a.m. they were in position, but many men were so exhausted by the assembly walk they fell asleep immediately, and were not roused until about 5.20a.m. when they ate sandwiches which they had carried forward with them for their breakfast. The terrain around them was sodden mud and any landmarks had been obliterated, so their officers had to lead them by following compass bearings. Even so, they rose and advanced in formation at 5.40a.m. All four companies were committed to the attack on 20th September.

The Germans did not make it easy for them by sending down on them an increasingly intense artillery barrage. The 2/5th London Battalion veered left off course a little for a short time, confused by the nature of the country and by the loss of many officers. "Tirpitz Farm was only distinguishable by the hedges and ditches around it, and in the same way Stroppe and Genoa could only be guessed at."[567] 'A' Company lost all its officers. The machine-gun fire became very heavy, particularly hitting the right side of the attack but the British managed to keep machine guns working at the front of the assault line. Communications became very difficult. "The fact that so many Officers and Company Runners became casualties in the early stages, made it very difficult to get information back from the front line." Nevertheless, the survivors managed to consolidate their gains by defending a shell-hole position supported by outposts. That afternoon, they saw Germans assembling in the neighbourhood of Winchester Farm and on the ridge in the distance, and at about 6p.m. they beat off the counter-attack with their machine guns and help from the artillery. The next day, a couple more counter-attacks were similarly thwarted and the gains held. But nine officers and fifty-two men had been killed; two officers and one hundred and sixty-two men wounded; and twenty-five men were missing. The British had used Lewis guns to good effect, but three of the eleven which could be brought back were damaged.

---

[567] These extracts are taken from the battle account within the War Diary, 2/5th London Battalion, 20th September 1917.

On 19th September, Maurice Hellier and the 6th Shropshire Light Infantry had also lined up, this time near Alouette Farm, although as they did so 'C' Company took heavy casualties from shell fire. At 5.40a.m. they advanced. 'D' and 'A' Companies led the way, supporting the 12th Rifle Brigade and 6th Oxford and Buckinghamshire Light Infantry. 'C' and 'B' Companies (probably including Maurice) remained in the assembly positions. Both the assault battalions quickly took heavy casualties and so dug in, but 'C' and 'B' Companies were not immune – both suffered heavy casualties from shell fire. Then they too advanced one hundred yards, in their case to try to avoid the German barrage. That afternoon, just as the front companies were trying to move forward, the Germans counter-attacked strongly against the division to the right (south) of the battalion. As soon as he realised this, the battalion commander tried to halt the advance, and 'B' Company halted and turned right to face south to guard against being attacked. In the end they were not directly attacked, and 'D' Company was able to move the line a short distance forward and seize a German strongpoint called Louis Farm and part of the German Eagle Trench. The battalion consolidated its gains over the next two days, and sent out a couple of patrols, one of which encountered German stormtroopers, capturing eight of them and killing their officer. On 23rd September, they repelled two determined German counter-attacks before a thick fog came down in the evening, and the battalion was relieved by the Duke of Cornwall's Light Infantry. The battalion war diary writer considered that for these four days the battalion had endured the "most severe" bombardment anyone in the battalion had known.

Once relieved, Maurice and the battalion were again pulled back from the battle to rest, recuperate, and re-train. On 1st October, the whole division was moved out of the Ypres Salient and sent back to the Somme Sector near the old enemy base at Bapaume. For the next weeks they would man trenches, train, and rest. On one occasion, 14th November, they were observed by Sir Douglas Haig himself as they practised the formation for fighting alongside tanks (forming up behind them) – part of several days of special training for fighting in conjunction with the machines in preparation for the Battle of Cambrai.

The Battle of Polygon Wood, 26th September - 3rd October

Meanwhile, after the 'bite and hold' limited progress of the Battle of the Menin Road, General Plumer sent in the ANZACs for the next assault, known as the Battle of Polygon Wood, north of the Menin road, on 26th September 1917. This phase of the battle saw mixed fortunes. The initial assault and its bombardment allowed the ANZACs to occupy the wood with relative ease, but they discovered that the Germans had numerous garrisons in pill boxes throughout the wood, and clearing these turned out to be a messy and bloody affair. Bernard Bartlett of the 9th London (Queen Victoria's Rifles) Battalion was involved in the thick of it.

On 25th September, Bernard Bartlett and the battalion moved up to 'Clusters Houses' to prepare for an assault at dawn. This position near St. Julien had only just been captured (with the help of tanks) a few days before.

They attacked at 5.50a.m. and soon were able to send back fifty-eight prisoners, and to consolidate their advance, despite a German counter-attack and heavy German barrage. As Bernard went over the top, he was hit in the right groin with a rifle bullet which entered the middle of his right femur and exited through its back. He was evacuated through the field ambulance to the 61st Casualty Clearing Station. It must have been a difficult and painful journey – this casualty clearing station was then working out of Lozinghem, near Béthune in France. From there he was moved to a military hospital in Rouen on 11th October and on 16th October was transferred aboard the SS *Warilda* from Le Havre and taken to the Countess of Lytton's Hospital, in Berkeley Square, London. On 25th February he was discharged from the Army and awarded a disability pension – initially for 40% disability, though by 1920 the disability was reckoned at only 1%.

Whilst for Bernard the war was over and his personal battle with injury begun, for Cyril Howard and the 14th Hampshire Battalion the next challenge was to attack German defences situated on 'Tower Hamlets' Ridge, a flat-topped spur which ran south from the Menin road.

They would have to cross the Basseville Brook and then the soldiers would face a sharp climb without cover up to the German positions in 'Tower Trench'. The 15th Hampshires had tried valiantly to capture this position but they had not succeeded and the 14th Hampshires relieved them on 22nd September 1917. For two days, German snipers, machine gunners and artillery men fired at Cyril and his comrades trying to reach the advanced positions they had taken over on the eastern side of the Basseville Brook. Taking casualties they had mostly to sit it out until the attack planned for September 25th, although they were given one night to rest further back before the attack itself.

They too attacked at 5.50a.m. on 25th September and were immediately hit with heavy machine-gun fire. Very soon, the senior officers in the attack had fallen wounded, many fatally but they pushed on and reached the German 'Tower Hamlets'. Captain White kept the men as close to the rolling barrage as possible. After this attack, Cyril was awarded the Military Cross. "For most conspicuous gallantry, good leading and devotion to duty in the attack on September 26th and 27th. He led his platoon during the attack with determination and though a heavy mist made direction difficult, he led his men by compass bearing on his objective under very heavy shell and machine gun fire. In the advance he organised and led small bombing parties and cleared all the dug-outs in his advance. When the final objective was taken he assisted in organising his Company, and most valuable work in consolidating the captured positions. His energy, cheerfulness and contempt for danger were an inspiring example to all."[568]

By 7.30a.m., they had a group of 150 men consolidating at least the left end of the objective line, but just short of Tower Trench. German machine guns continued to trouble them. Subsequently they were reinforced, and relieved the next day. The cost had been heavy: four officers were dead and forty-one men killed and thirty missing, whilst a further four officers and one hundred and thirteen men had been wounded. Once again the battalion retired to recuperate and to man trenches in support. Even in 'rest', however, they were not safe – eleven men dying and fourteen being wounded by a German aircraft bombing raid. "Conditions were very bad, the 'line' consisted mainly of shell-hole posts in a sea of mud, in which carrying parties floundered slowly and stretcher bearers could hardly get along. If this quarter was 'quiet', to hold it even 'quietly' was a strain. To call the sector 'pestilential' was not libellous."[569]

---

[568] Version of the citation given in *The Bournemouthian*, April 1918. That published in *The London Gazette* was more concise but said the same things: "For conspicuous gallantry and devotion to duty when in command of his platoon during an attack. In spite of a heavy mist he led his men by compass bearing on to the objective under heavy fire. He organised and led small bombing parties and cleared all the dug-outs in his advance."

[569] *The Royal Hampshire Regiment Vol. 2*, C.T. Atkinson, 1952, p. 314.

Cyril went on to miss the final part played by the battalion in the Battle of Passchendaele when it attacked pill boxes on the Menin road because he went on leave at the start of November. This was intended to be a short leave, but he fell sick. He was examined at No.7 General Hospital in Boulogne and there a medical board decided he needed to be sent home on sick leave for a couple of weeks. He embarked from Boulogne to Folkestone on 30th November, but once home did not seem to improve. He reported to the military hospital in Boscombe who initially treated him as an outpatient, suffering from boils and being generally run down. In fact, he had a highly contagious viral infection which caused a whitlow on his right-hand index finger and he was told he must stay in at home, despite the expiry of his leave. This situation worsened when his temperature rose significantly just before Christmas, and he was admitted to Mont Dore Officers' Convalescent Hospital in Bournemouth on 28th December. There he remained for some time, and had to attend a series of medical boards before he was judged to be fit again on 24th April 1918. However, he did not return to the Western Front. In the latter part of the war he served with the 67th Machine Gun Company on Salonika and was there with them when the war ended. He was demobilised on 24th March 1919.

Sir Douglas Haig later called the Battle of Polygon Wood, 26th-27th September "most successful". "The assault was delivered at 5.50 a.m. and, after hard and prolonged fighting in which over 1600 prisoners were taken by us, achieved a success as striking as that of the 20th September." Whilst the Australians captured most of Polygon Wood, "North Midland and London Territorial battalions (59th Division, Major-General C. F. Romer, and 58th Division) captured a long line of hostile strong points on both sides of the Wieltje-Gravenstafel road."[570] Sir Arthur Conan Doyle later wrote, "There were no notable geographical points to be captured, but the advance was a fine performance which showed that the Fifty-Eighth was a worthy compeer of those other fine London territorial divisions which had placed the reputation of the mother city at the very front of all the Imperial Armies."[571]

Behind the front line, Edward Goddard had continued his work with the artillery to support the infantry. On 13th September, Edward had been promoted to bombardier. The war diary gives us a good picture of his living and working conditions: "Till the 11th one section was at Verbranden Molen and one at Elzenwalle. The 2 forward howitzers… [moved] to… a new position… on the Dollar Beek for the operations leading up to and including the attack on 20.9.17. In the 24 hours 5.40am 20.9.17 to 5.40am 21.9.17 1542 rounds were fired by the battery. On the 22nd the position in Ravine Wood… was taken over together with their guns. The position had very little cover and the old Elzenwalle position was kept for rest billets – only the minimum numbers required being with the battery. Rations & water were taken up by GS wagon & ammunition by light railway some 300x in rear of the position. This had been allowed to accumulate & a big dump had been formed there. The position was shelled a good deal & casualties occurred daily. The battery took part in the barrages of the successful attack on the 26th & on the 28th was transferred to the 9th Corps for counter battery work. Only one successful CB shot was carried out during the month – i.e. on the 30th."[572]

In October, operating from this new position in Ravine Wood, they went on to fire over eight and a half thousand shells, despite German counter-battery fire, and despite the rain making

---

[570] Sir Douglas Haig, Official Dispatch, 25th December 1917.
[571] Sir Arthur Conan Doyle, *The Great War British Campaign in France and Flanders, Vol. IV*.
[572] War Diary, 276th Siege Battery, R.G.A., September 1917.

communications so difficult – for a time the nearest point transport could reach being a thousand yards away. They certainly valued the help provided by a nearby labour battalion in bringing up shells for them to use. Casualties were heavy. "The Battery were not shelled quite so heavily as in September but were unlucky in having 66 casualties. This… includes one officer… and 3 OR killed, 9 OR wounded and 31 admitted to hospital wounded gassed. Every precaution was taken during the gas bombardment. The casualties must have been caused through gas fumes lingering in shell holes, dug-outs etc. 11 OR were gassed, remaining at duty. A few bombs were dropped on Battery positions, resulting in 5 casualties, 2 OR killed and 3 OR wounded, in ammo fatigue party from Labour Co."[573]

On 9th November, still firing from the same positions, Edward was wounded, but was able to remain on duty. *The Bournemouthian* described his battery as being located near Messines, south of Ypres.[574] In fact, the area of Ravine Wood, where they were situated, is south of Zillebeke by the 'Hedge Row Trench' Cemetery. Rather than firing south over the Messines Ridge, by this time they were directing their shells eastwards towards German positions such as the line at Zandvoorde and beyond that at German positions at Kruiseecke. Soon after, for the first two weeks of December, he was sick in hospital. From the middle of December 1917 his battery became part of 84 Heavy Artillery Brigade, and remained in this bigger unit until after the end of the war. He re-joined the battery on 12th December from hospital and his battery was finally pulled out of the line on 23rd December. Some of the guns were badly worn, and at least one was condemned as no longer serviceable. For a few weeks the men had a chance to rest and re-train, although the accommodation, at an old aerodrome near St. Omer, was unpleasant. Edward and his friends had to sleep in an old and draughty hanger, and the weather was cold. He was allowed some days leave to return to England in January 1918. (Although the war diary of the battery was lost after December 1917, we know that the battery was in action on the Somme in spring 1918 as a Major Watson from the battery died from his wounds on 2nd May 1918 and was buried at Doullens, on the Somme.) In the middle of June 1918 Edward was again sick and sent to the 1st Australian General Hospital. This time his illness was more serious and when he was discharged to the base, initially, not back to his unit, though on 28th August he was re-posted to the battery. After the end of the war, his battery was part of the Army on the Rhine, part of the Army occupying Germany, based at Gosdesberg. He was demobilised on 19th June 1919.

October 4th: The Battle of Broodseinde

The phase after the Battle of Polygon Wood was the Battle of Broodseinde. Plumer's objectives here were twofold: in the south to occupy the Gheluvelt Plateau, and to push on in the north towards Poelkappelle. The plan was that a major attack involving several divisions was to be made at 6a.m.

The weather on the previous day had turned from the bright sunshine of September to blustery winds and an annoying drizzle which soaked through the men's uniforms causing great discomfort. The assault troops gathered overnight. Forty minutes before the attack was due to start, a new and intense bombardment hit the centre of the British attack lines. At 6.00a.m. a furious British bombardment hammered the German positions, and the assault battalions led by the ANZACs plunged forward. What they did not know was that the Germans opposite them had also planned to

---

[573] War Diary, 276th Siege Battery, R.G.A., October 1917.
[574] *The Bournemouthian*, April 1918.

attack at 6a.m. the same morning, so there were many more Germans forward than anticipated. This led in the centre of the attack to a period of frantic fighting (which the British/ANZAC forces won and reached their objectives on the Broodseinde Ridge) but which sucked in support troops to consolidate the British front line, and eventually to move up to the captured German positions.

Stanley Tucker and the 8th Devonshire Battalion attacked alongside the ANZACs. They had been at Bullecourt near Arras for most of the summer. On 2nd October they were in trenches near Polygon Wood, near Charlie Martin. After the experiences of the Battle of Polygon Wood, it was recognised that the German defences in front of the 7th Division consisted of concrete pill boxes and fire pits, rather than traditional trenches and it was expected that the opposition would initially be light, as the Germans were now manning their forward line flexibly, with reserve and counter-attack groups further back.

Before the attack, in the night, pathways were cut through the British wire to ease the assault, and at 3a.m. 'A' and 'C' Companies crept forward and lined up on taped lines, pushing forward outposts to cover them. 'D' Company lined up behind them in support and to provide 'moppers up', with 'C' Company in reserve. On their right lay the men of the 1st South Staffordshire Battalion, and on their left the 4th Australian Battalion. They were meant to capture the German front line and advance beyond it to 'Objective 1' after which the 2nd Border Battalion and the 2nd Gordon Highlanders Battalion would leap-frog over their position and take the second, final objective, the high ground around the village of Noordemhoek. The assault was to be supported by both a creeping barrage and also a continuous machine-gun barrage firing over them and aiming to fall upon the German support troops.

In the event, the Germans seem to have been battered both by the initial barrage and also by the creeping barrage. The Devons advanced so close up that they took casualties from it themselves but they were successful with comparatively light casualties. The German morale seemed to have plummeted. As Captain Cooper of 'C' Company, attacking on the left, reported, "The enemy showed no desire to combat the ground, and was only too ready to come out of his pill boxes and put his hand up." Captain Roper of 'B' Company, mopping up, noted, "The majority of the men found, however, were simply sitting outside their pill boxes, shell holes and dug outs waiting to be taken prisoners. One machine gun opened fire… and the crew were at once killed by the moppers up attached to the second wave… To sum up the resistance offered by the enemy – it amounted to very little. The enemy was holding his line a great deal more strongly than we anticipated, as he had arranged to attack on a broad front at 6am on the 4th October 1917. His men were completely nonplussed by our barrage and suffered very heavy casualties from shell fire, and particularly from our machine gun barrage. The first line advancing closely under our barrage found very little resistance from the Posts and Pill boxes which they encountered. Any pill boxes that were missed by the first wave were dealt with quite easily by the moppers up and Reserve Company. Their garrisons appeared simply to wait until they were taken prisoners, and made no attempt to fire after the first line had passed them except in one or two places. Prisoners captured were estimated at 230 and 7 machine guns and 5 grenade-werfers." [575] Even so, four officers had been killed and ten wounded; fifty-three men had been killed, one hundred and seventy wounded, whilst eleven were missing. The battalion was withdrawn, re-organised, and fresh men brought in to make up its strength, ready to fight again.

---

[575] From a report in the War Diary, 8th Devonshire Battalion, 2nd-8th October 1917.

Charlie Martin of the 6th Leicestershire Battalion was designated to be in support for the attack. The battalion had been sent north from Arras to the Ypres Salient, and on 30th September replaced Australian infantry at Hooge on the Menin road. On October 1st, Charles Martin's company was ordered to reinforce the recently captured line in Polygon Wood north of the road. In doing so they were shelled heavily. We are told he acted with courage and determination, and was not hurt. This shelling was partially caused by German reactions to a new tactic General Plumer was using. To mislead the Germans, he had ordered a series of intermittent 'practice' barrages, which started on 27th September. The Germans took these to signal British preparations for a new assault, but they were unsure of timings. So they kept up counter-shelling to try, unsuccessfully, to disrupt the British preparations. That day, five of the officers of the 6th Leicesters were wounded. By the time they were pulled back to regroup in Scottish Wood, the battalion had lost four men killed and eighty-one wounded.

At 6a.m. on 4th October, the battalion began to move forward to relieve units of 62nd Brigade at Polygon Wood. As the battalion moved up to join this battle, Charlie's platoon was the lead platoon, and he was walking alongside his company commander. Although still some way from the front line fighting, a long range German shell landed on the platoon, and he was killed, together with the company commander and five others, whilst another five others were wounded. Charlie was buried south of Ypres in the Bedford House Cemetery, which at that time was by a country house complete with moat and park, and which was being used for a mixture of brigade headquarters and a field ambulance station.

Norman Wragg was in support for the action. In the middle of the night of 3rd-4th October, the 5th Dorset Battalion again moved up to the line. Their task was to occupy the front line vacated by the attack of the 11th Manchesters, which they did on 6th October after two days in the front line. Overall, in less than a week the battalion lost four officers and one hundred and sixty-four men killed, wounded or missing. Norman explained that "the Hun was well stirred up that time, for in addition to giving his beloved 5.9s and machine guns plenty to do, his airmen used to come and bomb the front line, a thing I have not heard of before."[576] Their relief by the 9th West Yorks Battalion must have been most welcome.

A German officer, Leutnant Hasse of the 12th Company Reserve Infantry Regiment No.46, later wrote, "The breathing spaces that the Tommies allowed us became ever shorter. On 4th October there was another utterly murderous major day of battle, but the British did not enjoy much success. However, they did not permit us much of a rest, because they still hoped for success before the onset of winter."[577] Although Hasse said it was not a success, overall this single day of battle had turned into a costly, but significant victory – the British lost three hundred men as casualties, the Australians 6,432 and the New Zealanders 892 casualties; but the Germans lost about 10,000 casualties and had a further 5,000 taken prisoners. There was considerable British excitement and optimism after this success. But once more the weather came to the aid of the defending Germans. The drizzle turned to rain, which set in dreadfully. The mud returned with a vengeance, not only making it hard for the infantry but also making it almost impossible to bring up the artillery in support. The men used desperate methods, even trying to float field guns on wood rafts over the glutinous mud, but it was almost impossible. Even when they could fire the artillery in support, too often the mud was so wet as to be almost liquid, and shells crashed into it and sank without exploding.

---

[576] *The Bournemouthian*, December 1917.

[577] Quoted in Jack Sheldon, *The German Army at Passchendaele*, p. 222, Pen and Sword Military Press, 2007.

October 9th: The Battle of Poelcapelle

Less than a week after the Battle of Broodseinde, on October 9th, General Plumer launched his fourth 'bite and hold' attack, known as the Battle of Poelcapelle.

Raymond Budden's battalion fought in this battle. He was born in 1893. He was at school from 1905 to 1912. He was awarded an Exhibition in Maths by St. John's College, Cambridge, though in the event when he left school, according to school records, it was to attend King's College, London instead, and he is listed in the O.T.C. of London University's Roll of Honour. There is a mystery about his record however: although the University Roll of Honour explains his participation in the war, and this is matched by relevant entries in *The London Gazette* for 1917, there is no mention of him in the Gloucester Regiment's Medal Roll or Medal Cards. He cannot have served under an assumed name, because the *Gazette* correctly describes him, but it is hard to understand why he had no medal entry, even if he had remained in England rather than serving in France, as his university record described. First, he had joined the university Officer Training Corps, and then he had joined the Training Reserve – on or before 22nd September 1915 (to which his seniority as 2nd lieutenant was back-dated when his promotion to that rank was published). He was commissioned into the 4th Gloucestershire Battalion, 144th Brigade, 48th (South Midland) Division. Raymond joined them in April 1917. On 1st July 1917 he was made a full lieutenant.

On 9th October, an advance party taped out their jumping-off line. When the battalion moved forward there was some chaos. The Buckinghamshire soldiers meant to guide them forward did not appear at the rendez-vous, and the colonel took his men forward but found three companies and a platoon of 'C' Company (which was at the front with him) had got lost. These missing men had to be found in a hurry and guided forward while the remaining men of 'C' Company lined up. The missing men arrived about 4.30a.m., just as the British barrage started. So the leading men, and as many of the others as had arrived, charged forward. They soon fell too far behind the barrage and "owing to the condition of the ground [it] was never caught up again." They came under murderous fire from three machine-gun posts. "The bulk of our men were held up... but a party of 1 officer and 6 men, the remains of a platoon, pushed on... Another small party under a sergeant... fortified a shell hole... Another party under a sergeant dug in... no advance appeared to be made on our left at all. 'C' Company formed a defensive flank facing North with three posts and one Lewis Gun post." The 6th Gloucestershire Battalion managed to silence one of the machine guns hitting them, and they were able to kill a number of Germans with their Lewis guns and rifles. The other machine guns were hit with their rifle grenades, though the Germans were able to bring forward a light machine gun as a replacement. At 5p.m., the 1/8th Worcestershire Battalion advanced through them, covered by a barrage, which came down on the men who had dug in forward of the main line (fortunately causing no more casualties). Eventually, the battalion consolidated the line attained, and the front men pulled back.

"Very few messages were received back from the line after the attack, owing chiefly to the fact that most of the officers became casualties and also that the heavy and accurate sniping made movement very difficult. This also greatly hindered the collection of casualties. The Germans sniped a great deal at our stretcher bearers on the 9th... on the 10th, however, they were left alone probably because large enemy stretcher parties were out collecting their wounded under the Red cross flag... in my opinion, the reasons why we failed to take our objectives were: (a) the exhaustion of the men, most of whom had been tramping over the heavy ground for the greater part of the night; (b) the sodden condition of the ground; (c) that the barrage was lost after the first lift and never caught up."[578]

Up to 14th October, Four officers were killed and six wounded (including the colonel). Thirty-two men went missing; 31 were killed; 3 more died of wounds; and 104 were wounded. The survivors went in to the support line.

On 21st November 1917, Raymond moved with his battalion to Italy for the rest of the war. Just before he left he met up with some officers from Norman Wragg's battalion when they were on a training course in France. He survived the war and eventually ended up in the Second World War as a senior R.A.F. officer in the Meteorological Branch.

Haswell Shears was involved on 9th October, and was probably wounded. After his spell in the Honourable Artillery Company and on the edge of the Battle of the Somme, Haswell's Army career becomes harder to trace. An entry in *The Bournemouthian* of December 1917 reads, "H.G. Shears, City of London Regiment, was wounded (October 9th) in the wrist and leg."[579]

This appears to be a mistake. In the Army records he had returned to England on 16th November 1916. If the school magazine was inaccurate by a year, and if it confused the H.A.C. for the City of London Regiment (a title used by various units), the wound might be the reason. When he was later deployed, it was as a sapper in the Royal Engineers. It is possible that he was with them if he was wounded that day. He was eventually demobilised on 31st December 1918. It was noted that he was scarred by a gunshot wound to his right leg and a separate gunshot wound to his left arm.

Edward Little was there, in support with the artillery. He has left us an excellent idea of the dreadful nature of the terrain and the defences with which the infantry and artillery were struggling. Born in 1887, Edward was much of an age with the older generation of boys who fought in the war. He was appointed to be junior science teacher on 14th September 1915. His career at the school was interrupted by war service when he left in July 1916, but he returned to teach in 1919. He was appointed Head of Maths in January 1945. Enrolled under the Derby Scheme, in December 1915, he was allowed to continue teaching for another six months, leaving in July 1916 to join the Army. By March 1917 he had been admitted to the Royal Garrison Artillery Officers' Training School in Uckfield, where he clearly enjoyed the very pleasant scenery and conditions, as well as the good food. He described the training as enjoyable hard work. It involved a lot of map reading and working out lines of fire. He seemed less keen on the nine mile cross country runs – the first of which was done in kit including army boots, though subsequent ones were at least run in PE kit. In June 1917 he went out to the Western Front and spent a lot of time in the Ypres Salient with his battery.

Afterwards, Edward wrote that "we have been very active indeed during the last three months, and so big has been the advance on this front that the Battery has moved forward four miles in that time. It is impossible to realise at home what that means! The advance has been over land which is naturally marshy, and into which thousands of shells have been poured, with the result that the ground is covered with craters partially filled with water, and consequently not suitable for the movement of pieces of ordnance. The roads, too, suffered considerably as a result of artillery

---

[578] War Diary, 1/4th Gloucestershire Battalion, 9th-14th October 1917.
[579] *The Bournemouthian*, December 1917.

activity, so that, when you search for a road marked 'First Class' on the map, you probably recognise it by the stumps of trees which once lined it, while you are standing in six inches of mud – and such mud! It seems to have been produced to delay progress, for it clings very closely to one's boots, and after a walk through it all signs of polish from toe to knee of the boot have disappeared, and you carry back several pounds of mud."

He also described German pill boxes, dug-outs, and observation posts: "The pill boxes are decidedly interesting, and provide excellent protection from shell fire and bombs. One I occupied for about three weeks was so small that though it was a very comfortable in which to sleep, one could not stand up, but had to crawl to get from one side to the other. The ceiling was only about four feet from the ground, so one had to sit on the floor to carry out the ordinary duties in connection with the battery. This pill-box was situated in a trench and could not be seen from outside, so it must have proved a formidable spot to our troops when they attacked the trench. Another pill-box I occupied for a few days was much more comfortable, having bunks for sleeping and a roof about six feet above the floor. The finest dug-out I've entered had two entrances which led to an inner room, fitted with bunks and cupboards, while a tunnel joined this to a third room. A ladder in this room led to an opening in the roof, which was used by the Hun as an observation post. I found another very clever observation post quite by accident a few weeks ago. That, too, was German. A tree on a hill had been cut down at about three feet from the ground and the inside hollowed out. A hole had then been cut facing what was then our lines. The observer had his post underground and a periscope was placed so that its object glass fitted the hole cut for it, giving the observer a perfect view of our lines, with no risk to himself. I saw yet another O.P., which I should not like to have occupied myself. A ladder, about 50 feet long, fixed to a tree, gave access to the top of the tree, which formed the observation post. Once there, the observer would have to stay till dusk, with no protection from shrapnel or other shell fragments." [580]

Partly due to the conditions, this assault failed in its significant objectives, and although the battle continued between the assaults, the main stage was set for the last two big attacks. These became so notorious that they have for many given their name to the entire battle. They were the first and second Battles of Passchendaele.

The First Battle of Passchendaele: 12th October

The First Battle of Passchendaele fought on 12th October was a costly disappointment. It similarly seems that no member of the school was directly involved in the costly infantry assaults which were hurled onto the Passchendaele Ridge, gaining relatively minor success, but Jack Phillips was another of the artillery gunners struggling to help the infantry in this battle.

Jack was born in 1892. He was the middle of four brothers at the school, which he attended for just over a year during 1906-1907. He volunteered on May 20th 1916. He could have evaded conscription because of the vital nature of his work as a farmer. He was sent to France with his battery as a gunner. Perhaps his school experience in the O.T.C. allowed the Army to speed up his initial training as he arrived at Boulogne on 9th September 1916.

Jack's battery, the 156th Siege Battery, Royal Garrison Artillery was armed with eight-inch howitzers, and was part of the 88th Heavy Artillery Group. The battery was divided into three

---

[580] *The Bournemouthian*, December 1917.

sections, each with two guns. These howitzers would fire high into the air, so that their large shells crashed down onto enemy gun pits. Their main task was to try to destroy, or at least neutralise, the German artillery. Additionally, they could be used to try to destroy enemy stores and dumps, break up their access roads, railway lines or bridges, or smash into German redoubts and strongpoints. The battery was sent wherever there was likely to be a battle and the need to suppress the enemy's counter-battery fire. Jack's battery was employed to support the Australians in the first Battle of Passchendaele. The rain that had made the Battle of Poelcappelle so difficult had continued and conditions had deteriorated even further. Once again the artillery struggled to get into position, and their shells often failed to explode. The assault was led by fresh troops – the 3rd Australian and the New Zealand Divisions. They were smashed by German shell fire – in some cases before their attack had even begun, and when they did seem to be making progress – some patrols even reached Passchendaele village on the top of the ridge – most of the troops who did get forward were hammered by German machine-gun fire, especially when the New Zealanders – finding the British artillery had failed to break the German wire – tried to get through a single gap. They alone lost 3,000 men that day. The survivors pulled back more or less to their start line.

Jack was killed three days later, on 15th October 1917. His body was exhumed from a battlefield site and reburied at the Divisional Collecting Post Cemetery in the north-eastern suburb of Ypres.

About two weeks later the second and last Battle of Passchendaele was launched in a desperate attempt to capture and hold the top of the ridge. The dream of a breakthrough beyond had already evaporated.

The Second Battle of Passchendaele: 26th October-10th November

Haig's men were demoralised by the hardships and terror of the losses from the battle so far, and the awful weather. The 2nd Australians who had played such a prominent part in September were for the moment finished. The Canadian Corps was fresher, so Haig decided to use them in a final attempt to break through the German lines and at least gain the top of the ridge. Haig might well have been encouraged by the telegram he received on 16th October from the Prime Minister, David Lloyd George. (Later Lloyd George made out he had always been against Haig's plans.) "The War cabinet desire to congratulate you and the troops under your command upon the achievements of the British armies in Flanders in the great battle which has been raging since July 31. Starting from positions in which every advantage rested with the enemy and hampered and delayed from time to time by most unfavourable weather, you and your men have nevertheless continuously driven the enemy back with such skill, courage and pertinacity as have commanded the grateful admiration of the peoples of the British Empire and filled the enemy with alarm."[581]

The weather had to be reckoned with, so this battle was postponed from 13th October to allow for further planning and preparations. General Plumer planned a series of assaults within the main attack, the repair of the damaged communications systems, and to move forward the artillery to support the infantry assault. Meanwhile, the British artillery was supposed to pound the German pill boxes and somehow to cut the German wire. The British weather forecasters looked anxiously at their charts and equally desperately the fighting men looked at the skies, hoping for some drier conditions. Instead, on 26th October, the rain poured down on the men gathered to make the

---

[581] Quoted in the article on Passchendaele by Richard Hargreaves in *Navy News*, October 2007, p. 46.

assault. In the centre of the attack were two Canadian divisions (3rd on the left or north and 4th on the right or south). On the left and north of the 3rd Canadians (next to the 4th Canadian Mounted Rifles of the 8th Brigade) was the British 63rd (Royal Navy) Division and to the south was the 1st ANZAC Corps, only the northernmost part of which took part in the assault. Will Moorey's battalion, the 1/3rd London (Royal Fusiliers) Battalion, was further north still, towards Poelcapelle, beyond the 63rd (RN) Division. Alongside William, in the 63rd Division, were fellow Old Boys Reginald Colborne and William Webber, although their battalion, the 1/28th London Battalion, was in reserve.

Will Moorey's 1/3rd Royal Fusiliers Battalion struggled to get into position for the assault. There were no communication trenches, because they could not be dug through what were effectively swamps, so the men covered the last part of their journey on duckboards placed round the numerous water-filled shell holes. Sometimes even these boards were submerged, on occasion as deep as knee-high. Moving up, the men were instructed not to stop to help anyone who slipped and fell from the narrow boards. Such men were in considerable danger of drowning, but the lines of men must continue to file forward, not bunch up unexpectedly and send others to their deaths. Several days were designated to ensure the troops got up into place, but there was little shelter for them when they arrived at the jumping-off line. For one day, however, they got some sunshine and a partial chance to get a bit drier before the rain returned with a vengeance.

The plan was that the Canadians would attack up two drier ridges while the British to the north would attack across the lower, swampier, ground. Haig and his staff were not oblivious to the task they were asking of these men. John Chateris, Haig's Intelligence Officer, who is often criticised for being over-optimistic, said of the coming battle, "It is impossible to forecast the result. The only certain thing is a big casualty list."[582] To try to weaken the Germans, and to confuse them as to the actual day and time of the attack, each morning and afternoon the British artillery fired a full barrage onto the German positions.

On the night of 25th-26th October, the men moved as silently as possible forward to their assembly points for the final attack. When they attacked at 05.40 it was under cover of a mist which turned to heavy and continuous rain. The infantry advanced under the cover of a rolling barrage – lifting fifty yards every four minutes, slow enough it was hoped for the infantry to keep up despite the mud.

Amongst the Canadians, Ernest Snelgar was at the southern end of the attack, beyond the 63rd Royal Naval Division. After the success of the Battle of Vimy Ridge, Ernest and the 4th Canadian Mounted Rifles had regrouped and trained. On 5th September they had been on the receiving end of the first use by the Germans of mustard gas, which caused many casualties. On 13th October, they were sent north to the Ypres Salient. Although the Passchendaele Ridge remained in German hands, one measure of the relative British success was that when they arrived at Ypres on 21st October their train was able to take them all the way to the city, because the Germans had been pushed back so far. As they moved north-east out of the city, they found "the roads leading to and from Ypres were jammed with all kinds of vehicles, from bicycles to gigantic caterpillar-drawn howitzers. The steady stream of men and animals never ceased: field kitchens, limbers, G.S. wagons

---

[582] John Chateris, quoted in the article on Passchendaele by Richard Hargreaves in *Navy News*, October 2007, p. 46.

and pack-ponies nose-to-tail made an endless chain. Troops from every quarter of the globe passed and repassed; black and yellow labour-corps worked unnoticed in the cosmopolitan medley of fighting and non-combatant troops."[583]

By 24th October they were in the front line. They had to cross 2,500 yards to assault Passchendaele. Although when they lined up they had the 63rd (Royal Naval) Division on their left, once the attack began it was impossible to maintain any pre-determined formation because of the squelching mud and dreadful conditions. Unusually, Vickers guns were to accompany the assault in an attempt to neutralise the fire from the German pill boxes or other targets as they might present themselves.

These pill boxes "were manned by picked resistance-troops who fought with courage and resolution, keeping their rifles and machine guns in action until bombed or bayoneted… Contrary to popular belief the majority of pill-boxes were not loop-holed fortresses from which the defenders fought. They were square rooms of reinforced-concrete with walls and roof about five feet thick with one door in the rear leading into a fire trench. Their walls were too thick to allow a field of fire through ports. During a bombardment and when not in action the garrison gained shelter within but as soon as an attack was launched the occupants manned the fire-trench which ran behind and extended on either side of the pill-box. They took the place of deep dug-outs which were impracticable in such a low-lying country, and were good rallying points giving moral support to the defenders. They were formidable, but with one weakness: their range of fire was limited, and unless covered by other pill-boxes on the flanks the blind points in the range of fire made it possible for individual attackers to crawl up under cover and bomb the garrison behind. This explains many of the individual acts of heroism in capturing or demolishing a crew defending a pill-box."[584]

The battalion managed to push forward to gain its intermediate objective, but at great cost. Eight officers were killed and nine wounded; three hundred and four men killed, wounded or missing. One "frail, delicate" youth, according to the description in the regimental history, Private T.W. Holmes, won the Victoria Cross for capturing a pill box by his own single-handed initiative in twice rushing forward to throw grenades into its entrance. In the midst of the carnage, Ernest would have seen their padre doing such fantastic work with the wounded that he seems to have inspired both sides: as he walked about apparently nonchalantly looking to care for the wounded, both sides spontaneously copied him. A brief Armistice just happened, and men from both sides went out to help the padre and to tend their own wounded. The Germans even helped wounded Canadians by carrying them to a pill box which had been turned into a casualty station, where the injured man would be handed over to his comrades. The medical officer also worked with determination and at great personal risk. "It was a rational paradox for the men in the line. But the unofficial truce did not last long. Some young, enthusiastic forward-observing officer of the gunners could not resist reporting the existence of so many targets and soon the guns opened on the weary missionaries who had to postpone their rescuing."[585] After the battle, both the padre and the medical officer, both called Davis, received the Military Cross.

The Canadians captured some of the German pill boxes with grenades and good use of Lewis guns.

---

[583] *The 4th Canadian Mounted Rifles*, Captain S.G. Bennett, Murray Printing Company Ltd, Toronto, 1926, p. 74.
[584] ibid, p. 80.
[585] ibid, p. 86.

The British got into greater difficulties. The Royal Naval Division became mixed up and fell behind – not surprising as their officers were being wiped out. Will's battalion also suffered; and amongst those men struggling hopelessly to run forward in deep mud against German machine guns in concrete emplacements, Will was killed. His body was never recovered for burial, and his name today is inscribed on the memorial wall to the fallen without a named grave at Tyne Cot just below the Passchendaele Ridge he died trying to reach.

The first attack, on 26th October, had quickly bogged down with huge losses and little to show. Even the most successful troops ended up being driven back almost to their starting points.

Further south the same day, Stanley Tucker was fighting a small way north of the Menin road. This was the second battle fought by Stanley and the 8th Devonshire Battalion within weeks. This time the battalion was expected to support the 9th Devonshire Battalion as they attacked north of the Menin road with the objective of capturing the chateau at Polderhoek and the village of Gheluvelt. The other two battalions of the brigade were meant to attack along the same south-easterly line, but south of the road and to secure the southern side of Ghelevelt and the Zandvoorde Ridge. It was known from aerial reconnaissance and scouts that the Germans were probably going to resist with a deeper concentration of machine guns than they had used when the battalion had attacked at the start of the month. This attack was in support of the main attack by the Army further north against the Passchendaele Ridge.

In the event the attack went hideously wrong. Even when they lined up the battalion to advance, the Germans shelled the start line, so before fighting the men had quickly to dig new positions. Their adjutant stated that this at least kept them warm and occupied before the assault. When the 9th Devonshire Battalion advanced in front of them, it quickly came under a murderous fire from the intense rifle and machine-gun fire directed at them both from in front and from the Tower Hamlets Ridge and the pill boxes on the southern side of the road – because the Scots battalions had not made progress in the face of the defensive machine gun which smashed them. Low flying German aeroplanes machine gunned the troops from the air. Very soon, almost all the officers of the 9th Devonshire attack had been lost, and the 8th Devonshires found themselves mixing up with the remnants of their comrades and with remnant troops of Gordon Highlanders. Even so they managed to keep some semblance of formation until, having passed over the position reached by the 9th Devonshires, the battalion was itself exposed to the full force of the enemy's fury.

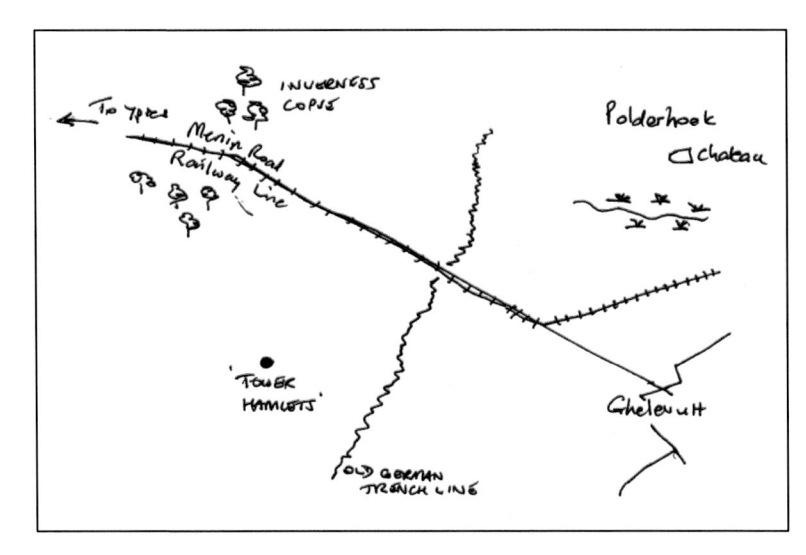

On the right of the advance, 'B' Company, under Captain Marshall, split; a large group led by a 9th Devonshire officer made an unsuccessful attempt to deal with the German pill boxes which were making such havoc from the south side of the road. The right-hand platoon broke into Gheluvelt but the men were never seen again. The rest, rallying under their captain, and joined by men from both Scots battalions tried to push north-east along the railway line and even managed to take some pill boxes until driven back by a counter-attack. They rallied and held a vital defensive position at a crater where the railway line met the Menin road. This became one of the only two organised parties of the battalion to survive the battle. On the left, 'D' Company, under Captain Girvan – who was wounded early in the advance – also split. Some tried to cross the railway line but were driven back; others headed more north-eastwards in the direction of the chateau and into the boggy ground. No more was heard of them.

The 'moppers up', 'C' Company, became mixed up with the attack companies and amalgamated with them. The reserve, 'A' Company, which had expected to be finishing off the Germans at the chateau and clearing the cellars in Gheluvelt, instead divided by platoons. "Not a single survivor has come back from the right or the reserve platoons... It is however clear from other evidence that these platoons in succession tried for the pill boxes on the south of the Menin Road, which were holding up our advance, and in the absence of a barrage were annihilated."[586] The centre platoon did little better and those not killed or incapacitated joined other survivors. The left reserve platoon also suffered heavily in an attack on a pill box, and those still able joined with men from the 13th Royal Warwickshire Battalion further north.

Only three officers and twenty-two men were killed, but eight more officers and two hundred and thirty-one men were wounded and a further four officers and one hundred and five men were missing. The battalion was in no state to fight again in a hurry, and was withdrawn to rest and to re-equip. Over the month, seven officers had been killed, fifteen wounded, four missing and one had gone sick. The figures for the men were almost as bad. Eighty-two had died, three hundred and thirty been wounded, one hundred and fifteen gone missing, and eighty-two fallen sick. The almost incessant rain and the cold had not helped.

Unfortunately, having survived the fighting, a few days later, on 5th November, Stanley succumbed to trench fever. This initially lasted three days, but he had a second bout on 11th November. He was taken from the battalion into hospital and the bout lasted for another three days. The illness was given three different descriptions by various medical boards – trench fever, influenza, or pyrexia. He was taken back through the casualty system and treated for a time at the 15th Casualty Clearing Station at Hazebrouck, just outside the salient. On 22nd November, he was brought back to England from Calais to Dover on the hospital ship *Brighton*, and taken to the Royal Free Hospital in London. Here he stayed for some time, though a medical board at Caxton Hall in London on 18th January 1918 recommended that, when possible, he should be sent to convalesce outside London. So he was transferred to the Mont Dore Hospital in Bournemouth, where on 6th February 1918 the medical board declared that with the pains in his legs and knees he remained essentially totally disabled. While at the Mont Dore he had a third relapse into the fever on 16th February 1918. He very slowly returned to health. He never returned to the Western Front, and remained with the 4th Battalion in Ireland until he applied for discharge in 1920.

Harold Ridout fought alongside Stanley on 26th October in the same brigade. Harold, born in 1895, attended Bournemouth School between 1904 and 1910. He was a member of the O.T.C. for three years. Before the war, on 9th June 1913, he joined the 2/9th Hampshires (Cyclists). On the second day of Britain's involvement in the war, 5th August 1914, he was embodied first as a cyclist, and then promoted to corporal. Soon afterwards, on 2nd November 1914, he was promoted to sergeant

---

[586] From a report in the War Diary, 8th Devonshire Battalion, 26th October 1917.

in 'D' Company. "Whilst the boys are naturally one and all longing to step on the other side of the Channel, their present work is of a character which must be described as quite as essential to the welfare of the country as that of those actually at the front. It is not too much to say that if the much talked of raid was made, our Bournemouth Boys in this company could now give the invaders more than that for which they would bargain. Their training has been strict, and they have long since realised that it was no matter of play. As a result, however, these young men never felt more fit than they do today."[587]

On 3rd November 1915, Harold had been made machine gun sergeant and was commissioned on 25th August 1917 as a 2nd lieutenant in the Machine Gun Corps. He was allocated to 20 Company, which he joined on 19th October 1917. The 20th Company, Machine Gun Corps was in the 20th Brigade, 7th Division, the same brigade as that of Stanley Tucker and the 8th Devonshire Battalion.

"BOURNEMOUTH BOYS" WITH THE 9th HANTS AT——
(See "Topics of the Week," page 3).

When the 20th Brigade attacked on 26th October, Harold was in the midst of the attack. The life of a machine gunner in this war was frequently short as they were obvious targets for the opposition. By 11.30a.m., all the machine guns of the 9th Devonshire Battalion had been put out of action.[588] By 12.30p.m., Stanley's unit was reporting 50% casualties. By 3.20p.m., the situation was dire: "3.20. Messages from 8th and 9th Devon Regt via 91st Inf Bde 'Our front line North of Menin Road now runs as it did before today's operations commenced... Asks S.O.S. barrage accordingly. Casualties by battalions 75%. Two Lewis guns or machine guns. In touch with West Kents on left.'" By late afternoon, the messages became even more dire: "5.45. 8th and 9th Devon R report that they are now back on the original line which is full of water and that the men cannot use their rifles."[589]

Fighting that day, Harold received what the medical reports described as a "Very severe wound". He was hit by a bullet in the chest which fractured his fifth rib and "penetrating right side of chest – superficial wound posterior aspect right arm also inflicted. He was transferred from B.E.F. with a jagged septic wound of right side of chest." After initial treatment at the first aid post he was taken back to the 3rd Australian Field Ambulance and then on to the 2nd Canadian Casualty Clearing Station. These medical stations must have done good work on him because, two days later, he was strong enough to be moved back to the 24th Field Hospital at Étaples. Here he stayed longer, but on 10th November was sent back to England on the *Stad Antwerpen*. His recovery took months. He did not go back into action so his war on the Western Front had lasted days, and his time in battle less than one bloody day.

---

[587] *The Bournemouth Graphic*, 12th December 1914.

[588] War Diary, 20th Infantry Brigade, 26th October 1917.

[589] ibid.

Behind the assault on the second day of the battle, but not out of danger, was Leonard Taylor. On 27th October, Leonard and the 5th Durham Light Infantry Battalion had moved up into trenches near the ruins of the railway and of Pascal Farm, about one and a half miles north-east of Langemarck. As they moved up they took casualties from a German shell which dropped onto a 'D' Company platoon. "Hostile shelling severe, especially as the only cover available was holes two or three feet deep scratched in the mud."[590] When they came out of the Pascal Farm trenches two officers had been wounded, thirteen men killed, forty-six wounded, five gone missing, and a further fifty-nine were suffering from gassing, sickness, or shell shock according to the war diary. Leonard and the battalion were fortunate, however, that this was their only involvement and that the battalion was in a supporting role in the Battle of Passchendaele, though they did return in mid-November.

Reginald Colborne and William Webber also went into action at this stage of the battle. Reginald, born in 1890, was another of the early members of Bournemouth School. He was the older brother of Douglas. He was a keen sportsman at school, in the football and cricket teams. When he left school in 1908 he began work as a journalist at *The Bournemouth Guardian*, a local newspaper which ran until 1921. He also found the time to be Secretary at the Wesley Sunday School in Holdenhurst Road and was a very popular cub-master of its boy scouts. He continued with this work in Bournemouth throughout the first years of the war and 'volunteered' under the Derby Scheme, in Bournemouth, on 11th December 1915. He chose to defer enlistment, and enlisted on 30th November 1916.

On 19th March 1917, Reginald had landed at Le Havre, and after further training at the St. Omer base, reported to the 1/28th London Battalion on 28th June 1917. This battalion was in the 63rd Division, the Royal Navy Division, in which London battalions (and Old Bournemouthians) often served. Whilst they were not the only army battalion in that division, most of the units were Royal Navy, fighting as soldiers in the trenches, but organised under naval units and naval discipline. The 28th London Battalion was part of 190th Brigade, a brigade entirely made up from army battalions, so the naval men of the division nicknamed 190th brigade members, the 'landlubbers'.

Reginald Colborne

He was not alone: another old boy, William Webber was in the battalion already and so shared Reginald's experiences. William, born in 1890, was at school from 1906-1909. He had volunteered for the 28th London Battalion in November 1914. Although many Old Boys passed through the battalion to become officers, in 1917 and 1918 the 1st and 2nd Battalions of the 28th London were very much fighting units. William remained in the ranks of the 1st Battalion. He had arrived in France on 14th February 1915, and had seen continuous service with the battalion in all their engagements.

In October, the battalion arrived in the salient to be briefed on their part in the battle. On 28th October they went into the series of defensive positions scraped into the mud which made up the

---

[590] War Diary, 5th Durham Light Infantry, 28th October 1917.

line. "There was mud to the right of us, mud to the left of us, with mud and slush as far as the eye could see... The most God-forsaken spectacle I had seen... the day's casualties, half-buried in the mud. Men and horses, half-submerged, eyed us with a glassy stare, and the brown water ran red with their blood."[591] The commanding officer of the 28th, Major Edlmann (their colonel having recently died and not yet replaced) gave them bad news: "Owing to the impossible state of the ground the Divisional front had not advanced so far as had been expected, so that what was to have been our jumping off line would now be our objective."[592]

Their brigade was held back in support reserve on the first day of the battle. With their comrades they had to hold on to the few hundred yards the attack troops had so painfully gained. General Gough called for the battle to stop – later commenting that with their rifles caked and clogged with mud, they could hardly advance any more. The position was actually untenable – either an advance had to be tried again, or a further withdrawal, since by day it was impossible to move up or down from the line with first aid or supplies except along duckboards which were in full view and range of the enemy.

On October 30th, it was William Webber and Reginald's turn to attack. "The story of the battle for the Passchendaele Ridge, so far as the Artists are concerned, is soon told. Other Divisions before us had been taking their share in the slow process of gaining ground in this waterlogged area, at tremendous cost. The 188th was the first Brigade of the 63rd Division to attack; and advancing under a terrific artillery and machine-gun barrage they, too, made some headway, but suffered severely. Early on the 30th our Brigade attacked, also under a very heavy barrage: the British artillery averaged one gun to every 9 yards of front. To reach our objective we had to cross the Paddebeek, on the map an insignificant streamlet, but in fact by this time a wide and almost impassable swamp."[593]

Witnesses later described the 28th London soldiers advancing through the mud at first "as if we were on the parade ground."[594] But their route was no parade ground – they were meant to advance over a quagmire. Their line of advance started south of Poelkapelle, from the direction of Wallemolen, across the swollen Paddebeek stream, and uphill against a German redoubt created from the ruins of Tournant Farm. The attack began to break up as they tried to cross the stream in the face of shrapnel bursting in their faces and mud covering them as shells exploded around them. Desperately, men tried to take cover in the shell holes. "The instant our attack started, the forward troops came under intense machine-gun fire from an almost invisible enemy who had taken refuge in their 'pill boxes' during our bombardment, and were now posted in carefully chosen tactical positions. Simultaneously our supporting troops suffered heavy casualties from enemy artillery, while the ground to be traversed was a deep sea of mud, which drowned wounded men and clogged rifles and Lewis guns in the first few minutes, rendering them entirely useless. Consequently it was not long before the attack was brought to a complete standstill, and the very attenuated Battalions proceeded to consolidate as best they could on our side of the Paddebeeke." The situation was desperate. "The enemy unexpectedly altered their barrage line on the morning of the battle, and our troops suffered cruel losses in the opening seconds. When after the initial

---

[591] Quoted in the article on Passchendaele by Richard Hargreaves in *Navy News*, October 2007, p. 46.
[592] The Regimental Roll of Honour and War Record of 28th London Rifles, 1922, p. xxiv.
[593] ibid.
[594] Quoted in the article on Passchendaele by Richard Hargreaves in *Navy News*, October 2007, p. 47.

disaster, the assaulting battalions were reorganized, they had lost the barrage… On the left of the front, the Artists Rifles, despite cruel losses, advanced on Source Trench, but were held up in front of it knee-deep in mud, by close range machine guns. Here, one company of this fine battalion was annihilated."[595] It is said that wounded men stuck their rifles upside down into the ground by their bayonets in a vain attempt to be seen by stretcher-bearers as the wounded sunk into the mud. German artillery fire, however, was said to have knocked over the rifles like skittles falling in a skittle alley. Many casualties who might have survived simply disappeared into the mud. Somewhere amidst this horror, Reginald lost his life. "The nature of the fighting precluded any attempt to give him help at the time, and it was hoped that he would find his way back to the dressing station."[596] "After the battle [he] failed to answer his name at the roll-call. Quite early in the action he was seen to be hit, but it was supposed that he was not seriously injured. It is conjectured that after being wounded he was hit and killed by a shell while on his way to the dressing station. Almost certain death leaves us with a keen feeling of personal loss, for he was a member of the journalistic profession and very much esteemed because of his excellent qualities in heart and mind."[597] Final confirmation of his death came only after the war when his body was eventually recovered, recognised (he had left letters, a photo and a religious book behind him before the battle, but his identity tag must have survived), and he was buried properly at Poelcappelle Cemetery.

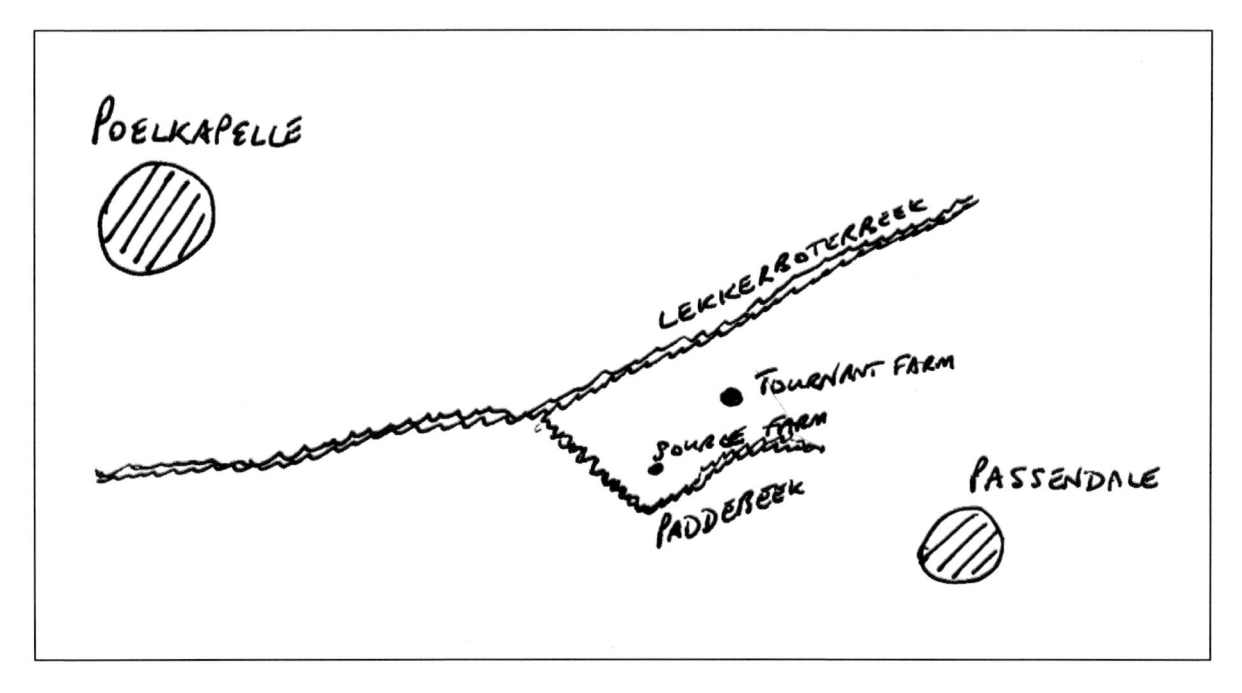

William Webber had survived. When they began the attack, the fighting strength of the battalion was about 500. By the end of the day, three hundred and fifty were casualties. Their division had managed to advance only a few yards, advancing the line almost halfway from its start line to the Paddebeek. The massacre of 30th October and the division's attack had been on the left or northern end of the assault, and it did help to draw off German resources from the Canadians to the south. The 78th Canadian Brigade lost half of its strength during the day but advanced Canadian patrols

---

[595] Douglas Jerrold, *The Royal Naval Division*.
[596] *The Bournemouthian*, December 1918.
[597] *The Bournemouth Graphic*, 7th December 1917.

did manage to reach Passchendaele, where they found the Germans preparing to withdraw.

The Princess Patricia's Canadian Light Infantry Battalion, including Arthur Lobley, was in one of the follow-up attacks. They had arrived at Ypres on 23rd October in heavy rain. A week later, 30th October, they went into the attack from Meetcheele towards Passchendaele. The assault started with the opening of the barrage at 5.50a.m. and they managed to take the top of the ridge with its pill boxes, but in this attack, over half of the battalion fell casualty: nine officers dying and eleven being wounded; of the men, ninety-six died, thirty-eight went missing and a further 200 were wounded. Desperate messages began to come back to Battalion HQ such as that of 5.05p.m.: "Message No. 9 received from Lieut. P.M. Puley No. 1 Company:- 'There are about 100 men out in front of Pill-Box... These are in charge of 3 Corporals and 1 Lance-Corporal. They are supported on right by party sent up by R.C.R. Position for fire is a good one. They have 2 Lewis Guns. Another party of 75 rifles command ridge and valley below on the left and join up with 49th.' We have Lewis Guns but a limited supply of ammunition. A party of Germans approached our trench at about 1.00. The artillery replied to our S.O.S. and had several direct hits, dispersing the party. At present they are moving around under cover of a white flag, picking up wounded." [598]

By the early hours of 31st October there were fewer than 180 men from the battalion in the battle. These were holding a line of shell holes and a pill box. With six Lewis guns they were holding positions on the crest of the ridge but the Germans were dug in about two hundred yards from them on the far side. They were short of ammunition but managed to hold on until relieved at the end of the day. Later, Arthur Lobley transferred to the R.F.C. He graduated as a flying and observer officer on 16th August 1919, and was later promoted to lieutenant in its Accountancy Branch. He remained in the R.A.F. after the war and became a squadron leader, still within the Accounts Branch, and later still in 1939 he was promoted to be wing commander.

The next day, Joseph Wilkes returned to the battle. After their participation in the Battle of the Menin Road in September, Joseph and the 2/5th London Battalion had taken a short time to recover. On 30th October 1917, they moved back up to the front line at Poelkappelle under heavy shelling and taking casualties. The next day they went back into action: "Oct 31. 'A' Coy having been ordered to push out their left post to get closer touch with the right of 'D' sent out a patrol which was fired on from an enemy post... It was decided to attack this post, 'D' Coy being ordered to make the attack with 'A' Coy co-operating in support. One platoon of 'D' under 2/Lt Stokes moved at 5pm from their right post and attacked from a NE direction. The ground was in very bad condition making movement extremely difficult. They met with strong opposition from machine guns in a line of fortified shell holes E and S of the objective and suffered a number of... Two or three men reached the post and killed 3 Germans there but were driven off again and the party withdrew... Patrols sent out to locate the wounded after the attack reported that the enemy were reinforced & the positions strongly held... Casualties: 2/Lt Stokes wounded and missing. 8 O.R. killed; 10 O.R. wounded; 1 O.R. wounded and missing; 4 O.R. missing."[599] Despite the low numbers now remaining in the battalion – so low that they were reduced to giving each company two strong platoons and two Lewis gun sections – they were soon back in the trenches, though for most of the rest of the year they were either training or providing reserve working parties as gradually their numbers were brought back up to strength.

---

[598] War Diary, Princess Patricia's Light Infantry. Narrative of events of 30th and 31st October 1917.
[599] War Diary, 2/5th London Battalion, 31st October 1917.

Behind the infantry, Douglas Collingwood and the 2nd Canadian Pioneer Battalion had arrived to support the Canadian troops. Conditions were grim and the work hard. Much of the time they were trying to build plank roads onto the battlefield as well as to drain the shell holes and pipe out the lying water from north of Zonnebeke towards the area south of St. Julien. For days, 'C' Company men seemed to be endlessly carrying forward planks to be laid as road sweeping from St. Julien south and then east towards Gravenstafel and Passchendaele, then returning to collect more. Endless numbers of sandbags had to be lugged up into place to try to fill in shell holes so that the road could be continued forward. Conditions when they were meant to be resting were insecure: "At 1.30am during a bombing raid, [a] delayed action aerial torpedo was dropped in camp burying 8 men of 'C' Company. None were killed but 3 men sent to Hospital suffering from shock and bruises."[600] Thirty of his men under one of his lieutenants had the task of carrying ammunition on pack animals to the troops making the front line assaults. When the battalion moved further forward to work near Zonnebeke, one group of men took over four Lewis gun positions to act as anti-aircraft protection to the battalion.

Even Canadian successes did not bring relief: "On the morning of 6th November at about 6am, 1st and 2nd Canadian Divisions attacked and captured Passchendaele Village. On account of this attack there was heavy shelling by the enemy of the Support Areas which seriously affected the work of the companies."[601] This also meant that their job the next day was to make a way forward passable for the advance of the field guns. As on subsequent days German shelling broke up the newly-laid light railway system, they had to work hard to make sure the plank roads could be extended, carrying everything by hand whilst themselves being shelled by German artillery. Relief finally came on 13th November after several gruelling and difficult weeks. They were moved south from the salient to France where they were again put to work on communication trenches near Thélus, and put into billets at Vimy.

By 10th November, the British line had partly straightened out – but the Germans still held the top of the ridge. Phillip Tollemache had rejoined Alexander Sandbrook and the 8th Canadian Infantry Battalion from September, having recovered from shell shock. They had arrived at Poperinghe on 4th November. On 8th November they went into the battle, in its last phase. As they advanced, their left flank – under the command of a very junior officer (its captain was wounded before the attack), got crowded off direction by the South Wales Borderers who seemed to get very mixed up and ran into British barrage, and retired, leaving the Canadian flank in the air. Casualties were extremely high. The reserve company was fully committed. Eventually they were relieved by the 10th Canadian Battalion.

William Ray was with the artillery and from the content of a letter in the autumn of 1917 it sounds as if his battery had been one of those trying to support these infantry attacks at Passchendaele. Commissioned on 2nd September 1917, he had returned to the Western Front, joining the 41st Siege Battery. The situation was much more difficult than that his previous battery had experienced. "My battery has been out here a considerable time and this part of the line is particularly unhealthy for all arms. There is not the slightest vestige of cover available, our guns stand in the open, and we have even seen our own shells burst. The latter is not a good state of things at any time and especially in the case of howitzers. My battery is a Siege Battery, R.G.A, B.E.F., and is of historic interest to gunners on account of facts which may not be disclosed."[602]

---

[600] War Diary, 2nd Canadian Pioneer Battalion, 31st October 1917.
[601] War Diary, 2nd Canadian Pioneer Battalion, 6th November 1917.
[602] *The Bournemouthian*, December 1917.

The allusion he made is probably to the fact that its original soldiers were drawn half from Regulars from Hong Kong, Singapore and half from Territorials from the Durham R.G.A. They had four 6-inch howitzers, capable of sending large calibre high explosive shells in a high trajectory arc, crashing down onto an enemy position. They were most often used to try to destroy enemy artillery batteries, but they could also fire down on German redoubts or other strongpoints, ammunition or storage dumps, and German communication links such as roads and railways. About the time William joined them they expanded (on 3rd November) to six guns. From December 1917 they joined the 23rd Heavy Artillery Group (later 23 Brigade R.G.A.). Having fought on through 1918, William, promoted to full lieutenant, was demobilised in January 1919. By the time William relinquished his commission in 1920 he had been promoted to captain.

George Hunt's experiences of the carnage of Passchendaele occurred shortly after the battle had officially concluded. Born in 1898, George had only left the school on 30th March 1917. He had been a boarder. After school, George went straight to an Army Cadet school to train to become an officer, claiming (like so many others) his School O.T.C. experience as a sergeant as previous military service. He enlisted on 7th April 1917 and was sent to France in early August, where he was attached to the 2nd Battalion King's Own Yorkshire Light Infantry, in the 97th Brigade and part of the 32nd Division, joining along with a large number of junior officers on 12th October 1917. He was posted to 'A' Company. This was a time when the battalion had been pulled from its duties helping to protect the devastated sea-port of Nieuwpoort and set to training and fitness tasks, so that they too could play their part in the battle. That training had come to an end on 22nd November when George and his comrades were sent by train from Poperinghe to Ypres, and then north-east to St. Julien. The next day they went into the line two kilometres south of Westroosebeke and one kilometre north-east of Passchendaele itself.

Just getting into line was hazardous. "The Battalion moved via No.6 Duck Walk track which was periodically staffed by the enemy with light calibre shells and the Battalion suffered about 30 casualties in completing the relief. The relief was completed at 8.10pm. Considering that the front line Companies had to wade through heavy mud which was knee deep and the weight of Battle stores carried (67 to 68 lbs per man) the relief was carried out very quickly and probably constituted a record for this Sector. On relief the dispositions of the Battalion was as follows: 'D' Company on the Right; 'B' Company on the Left in the line; 'C' Coy in close support and 'A' Company in Battalion reserve."[603] They had taken two days' supply of rations, 200 patrol cans filled with water and 100 home-made cookers with them, as getting food and drink to them by daylight was impossible and very hard even at night. They used petrol tins filled with hot tea or soup, packed into their packs surrounded by straw, to ferry hot sustenance to the front line men each night. Patrols were sent out to anticipate surprise attacks, and the British artillery did its best to pin down the enemy. Under severe German shell fire they managed to lay a telephone line between the front line and Battalion Headquarters, but casualties mounted. On George's first full day in the trenches, 24th November, by noon, eleven men had been killed, twenty-three wounded, and six gone missing. Unusually, there had been no losses amongst the officers. That night, George and 'A' Company moved into the front line as the battalion extended its line eastwards, taking over from the 2nd Middlesex Battalion. "The night was fairly noisy the enemy indulging in much promiscuous shelling of mixed calibre shells."[604] The next day, casualties were similar. George might well have

---

[603] War Diary, 2nd Battalion King's Own Yorkshire Light Infantry, 23rd November 1917.
[604] War Diary, 2nd Battalion King's Own Light Infantry, 24th November 1917.

felt some relief when told that the battalion was to be withdrawn that evening and relieved by the 16th Highland Light Infantry.

The Germans were unsure if a new attack was in preparation, so "put down a barrage on our front line and on the communications. Our artillery promptly replied and the situation became lively. When the heavy shelling had subsided the relief proceeded smoothly and was complete at 1.40am."[605] However, in the barrage George was one of two officers wounded, whilst ten men had also been wounded and two killed. "About 4 o'clock one afternoon he was in a dug-out whilst German shells were flying about and eventually one of them found his position, killed his brother officer[606] and buried him. This was observed by others who were near, and three of them came to dig him out. They succeeded in getting his head free when another shell burst amongst them and killed all the rescue party. Hunt received head wounds, was again buried, and this time he lost consciousness, his plight being much worse than before. About three hours later another rescue party came up, dug him out and saved him." [607]

George had been hit on the right side of his head by fragments of a high explosive shell, and although the bone was mercifully undamaged, the wound quickly turned septic. Another shell fragment had smashed through his nose from right to left. At this time, George was just over nineteen years old – a traumatic experience for anyone, let alone one so young. He was taken back to Calais and crossed to Dover on 1st December 1917. After initial treatment at Cannock and in London, he was sent to the Mont Dore Hospital in Bournemouth where he recovered enough to visit his old school. He remained deaf in his right ear, but otherwise, by May 1918, was judged to be fit again and was sent to join the 4th Battalion of the regiment, which was serving still on the Western Front. After such an experience of being buried alive, it is perhaps not entirely surprising that George, still only nineteen, applied to transfer to the air, and he was commissioned into the R.A.F. to train as an observer. Whilst flying over Wiltshire, the plane he was in crashed on 21st July 1918 and he was killed. He was really just a boy, first dreadfully injured, and then killed.

Another officer fighting in the R.G.A. (though not at Passchendaele) was John Sinclair, who was at school from 1908 until December 1916. In August 1917, John was with 145 Siege Battery R.G.A. and gave us a good impression of the hectic lifestyle of a junior artillery officer in the third of his letters to be published, though it was based on fighting experiences elsewhere: "The two weeks I have been out here seem like two months. I suppose it is because I have done such a lot during that time... I am greatly interested in my new hobby of strafing the Boche; it is very amusing sometimes. A Boche battery may be shelling Brigade Headquarters or some other battery. An urgent message comes down on the 'phone, 'Ten minutes' intense,' and the co-ordinates of the Boche battery. We sit in a cellar and work out a few angles, one sub goes down to the guns, and we 'ten minutes' intense.' The effect is marvellous. Although we cannot see his battery, and have no idea what size the guns composing it are, it is silenced for a time. Just as a congratulatory message comes down from Brigade the Boche starts again, and we have to give him a little more. It is a wonderful game. We are in a house, the fourth from the end of the road. This is lucky because the end house stops everything which the Boche sends over in our direction. Sometimes we have finished our 'soup' and are waiting for our 'fish,' watching the candle (stuck in a whisky bottle) start and flicker, as a

---

[605] War Diary, 2nd Battalion King's Own Light Infantry, 25th November 1917.
[606] The War Diary reported that Captain Hassell was wounded rather than killed.
[607] *The Bournemouthian*, April 1918.

gun nearby goes off. Suddenly there is a whistle, gradually getting louder, and then a crash. 'The end house,' we all murmur, and some wag adds 'Long may it live,' As the Boche has started again I expect we shall get some 'Intense' in a minute, so I will bring my letter to a close."[608]

The 1st Canadian Field Artillery Brigade, probably including Basil Keogh, supported the Canadian Corps in its campaigns, including the Battle of Passchendaele. On 1st November they relieved New Zealander batteries and were therefore positioned to support the 2nd Canadian Division assault on 10th November, in the later stages of the battle.

When Leonard Taylor and the 5th Durham Light Infantry Battalion returned in mid-November onto the now captured but insecure Passchendaele Ridge, they too spent an uncomfortable tour of duty: "Potijze. 16th... The tour was rather a trying one as the shelling was heavy. Getting rations to the front line was difficult owing to the darkness and the ration parties constantly lost their way, besides suffering casualties from shell fire. The total casualties were 7 killed, 28 wounded and 16 sent down sick. During the tour enemy aeroplanes were very active and flew so low over our posts that in one case the observer could be seen trying to locate the exact position of the posts. They also used their machine guns freely as our Adjutant discovered when he attempted to perform an operation of nature outside the pill box used as battalion Headquarters."[609] December and January 1918 also brought hard times for Leonard and the men. In the latter part of the month, much of their time was taken up with carrying and laying down fresh duck boards, or using railway sleepers to try to create an artillery track up towards the ridge. They mostly had only tents to rest in, which had to be sand-bagged to try to provide protection from enemy aircraft or artillery.

The Battle of Cambrai

It is understandable, but perhaps ironic, that the dreadful costs of the Third Battle of Ypres, and especially the Passchendaele phase has caught the attention of many people more than the strides towards victory which tentatively began in 1917, and which were to come to fruition in the summer and autumn of 1918. Yet, in the spring of 1917, the British undoubtedly knocked German confidence with their initial successes at Arras (especially at Vimy Ridge) and at Messines in the early summer. These added to the troubles which the grim and hard-fought British victory on the Somme had caused the Germans – forcing German retreats at great human cost. The Third Battle of Ypres had been an awful struggle, but once again the Germans had been pushed back. True, that was only a tiny distance, and the costs of the limited success were dreadful for the British, but once again it had been the Germans withdrawing and losing men they could not afford to lose. As that titanic struggle came to a close, a smaller but extremely significant battle took place further south which was to presage the victory of the following year, even though at the time it was a bitter disappointment to the extent that a court of enquiry was later convened to enquire into its failure: the Battle of Cambrai.

Unlike other major offensives, limited time was spent on planning for the Battle of Cambrai though enthusiastic Tank Corps and artillery officers had been sharing ideas for such a battle since at least the summer. As the Third Battle of Ypres developed, they increasingly stressed the advantages which could accrue from a determined mass tank attack, supported by artillery and infantry. The

---

[608] *The Bournemouthian*, December 1918.
[609] War Diary, 5th Durham Light Infantry, 16th November 1917.

enthusiasts argued that it was ridiculous to squander resources in the thick mud of Ypres where tanks had bogged down or simply sunk deep into the mud, drowning the occupants in the slime. That argument was generally accepted. Instead, they rapidly created a plan to attack on the drier ground further south where the front rested opposite Cambrai. However, although they could release considerable artillery (more than 1,000 guns and howitzers), the High Command could only release six infantry divisions – not enough to follow through properly on any success which might be gained. (The Germans used about twenty in their counter-attack.) Instead, there was a forlorn hope amongst the planners that cavalry could rush into any breach and somehow occupy or destroy the railway centres and routes in and out of Cambrai. The plan called for the artillery to open a surprise attack with a lightening barrage made possible by technical improvements – air observations making accurate mapping of German defences possible; improved shells and improved systems to fire them accurately; improved technical training of artillery crews, especially in teaching the maths needed for accurate calibration and precision firing. The success of this enterprise was reckoned to depend on surprise as the tanks would launch against the German lines in huge numbers: for this battle, the Tank Corps assembled 476 tanks, mostly of the new Mark IV variety, which could move more quietly than earlier versions, whilst the R.F.C. had flown extra missions over the lines to try to stop the Germans realising the tanks were being brought up to the front. The expectation was that the infantry would follow the tanks as they broke the Hindenburg Line instead of the more familiar movement in line abreast across No Man's land. The cavalry were then to pour into the gap, rush forward and secure the victory.

So the Battle of Cambrai was a risk and a gamble. Two Old Bournemouthians involved were John May and Arthur Mosley. In 1916, John had been a private in the 12th London Battalion, and had been invalided home, sick with trench fever. For three weeks, from 3rd to 29th September 1916, he had been treated at Ballymena, in County Antrim, for influenza. Even as he recuperated, John decided that it would be worth his while to apply for a commission. On 27th June 1917, he gained his commission as 2nd lieutenant in the prestigious 1/9th London Regiment, the 'Queen Victoria's Rifles'. The 9th London, Q.V.R. was part of John's old brigade – 169th Brigade, 56th (London) Division – so he returned as an officer to France amongst people whom he knew (if they had survived).

John returned to France on September 6th 1917 and joined the battalion when it was resting and training after fighting at Inverness Wood by the Menin road on 15th-16th August. Soon after he arrived, the battalion moved into the trenches near Doignies, closer to Cambrai, at Louveral. In between trench tours they rehearsed for the tank attack. On 22nd October, an un-named officer was wounded whilst leading fifty men in an unsuccessful raid. In November, they had two spells back in the trenches, and in between working parties were repairing roads – so that at the last minute the tanks could be moved forward with a minimum of fuss. Their watchword became "Tanks and Surprise".[610] Indeed, great care had been taken to make the attack a surprise. Telephones had been removed from the front line, so that German listening posts could be denied intelligence from tapping into British telephone lines. At night, gun positions were set up, carefully camouflaged. The troops and guns were to be brought up only at the last moment. The battalion transported special light cylinders of gas, designed to be fired electrically from mortars.

The situation did not look promising. "The enemy was occupying that wonderful trench system – the Hindenburg Line – a system which had been so well sited and protected by massive belts of

---

[610] *The History and Records of Queen Victoria's Rifles*, Major C.A.C. Keeson, 1923, p. 262.

wire that it was regarded as being more or less impregnable. Two important features – Tadpole Copse and Bourlon Wood – gave complete observation over our lines. Our own defences consisted of Platoon Posts, a number of which were unconnected. There was no support line, very little wire cut, and few communication trenches, whilst shelters were very few and inadequate."[611] The battalion took considerable pains to improve their trench system and even to expand the width of the Bapaume-Cambrai road to allow for the extra transport soon to be needed. Hours before the attack was due to start on 20th November, German artillery intensified. "Attack on Cambrai commenced. Evening. Patrols sent out and established contact with Division on Right. Posts established on Cambrai road. Battalion HQ moved to Sturgeon."[612] The battalion had laid down a smoke barrage (presumably with trench mortars) at 6.20a.m. and then attacked. But "During the early morning, 2nd lieutenant May, who had only recently joined the battalion and showed promise of being a good officer, was killed by shell-fire."[613] Whilst his commander, Lieutenant Colonel Follett, and the chaplain wrote sympathetically to his parents how he died "instantaneously by the explosion of a shell"[614] he was simply swept away in the advance. He was buried near where he died as one of the first to be laid to rest in a newly-opened cemetery at Hermies Hill, south of the road from Bapaume to Cambrai.

Arthur Mosley fought that day. Arthur had managed to gain a short leave after his recuperation from being wounded in the Battle of Arras and did not fight at Ypres. On the evening of 9th October, the 2/4th King's Own Yorkshire Light Infantry Battalion was called away from the Bullecourt front and for two weeks towards the end of October, Arthur and the others of his battalion and the 62nd Division were subjected to intense training designed to encourage open, not trench, warfare and to bring out the initiative of the junior officers. From 2nd November, they had several days training alongside a company of tanks. They went into the line near Havrincourt on 17th November. Their division was part of VI Corps whose objectives were to capture the German front line and support systems, then the villages of Havrincourt and Flesquieres in the first 'bound', followed by extending the line further. After this the cavalry was to pass through the gap created, followed by the triumphant infantry. The plan seemed to get hazy once success was planned. According to this plan, the assault troops would penetrate 3,000 yards before the cavalry rode through to victory. As a surprise attack, instead of an artillery bombardment designed to weaken the enemy, tanks were to roll forward to break down the enemy wire which was laid so thickly in front of the German line. The artillery was forbidden to send out ranging shots which might forewarn the enemy, even if that meant they were less confident about the ranges they needed.

Arthur's battalion was in the 187th Brigade, the left (northern) assault brigade for the division, with the 185th on their right. Thirty tanks would support the brigade – about fifteen each for the assault battalions. Zero hour was to be 6.20a.m., 20th November 1917. Facing them, the Hindenburg Line defences were particularly strong with three main systems of defences, including a maze of trenches just in the first line. There were up to four separate depths of barbed wire in front of these trenches and many well-sited machine-gun posts. All British preparatory movement was at night and surprise was maintained. Tapes were placed to guide men and tanks using the ruins of Havrincourt Wood for some further cover. Even the tanks had been modified. "On the back of each

---

[611] *The History and Records of Queen Victoria's Rifles*, Major C.A.C. Keeson, 1923, p. 263.
[612] War Diary, 9th London (Queen Victoria's Rifles), 20th November 1917.
[613] *The History and Records of Queen Victoria's Rifles*, Major C.A.C. Keeson, 1923, p. 264.
[614] *The Bournemouthian*, April 1918.

Tank was a huge fascine resting on a giant pair of arms. An ingenious contrivance provided means by which the fascine could be dropped into an unusually deep trench across which the Tank could pursue its way, without having to dip its nose into the trench with the possibility of getting stuck. The wire cutting Tanks were in the front line."[615]

The men waited anxiously on the jumping-off line – Arthur's battalion on the front right of the brigade front. Against them were ranged multiple battalions, including the German 107th Division which had only arrived from the Russian front on the 18th-19th November. At 6.20a.m., the British artillery opened up with a rolling barrage in front of the tanks. Field guns fired smoke shells and heavy and medium trench mortars attacked the German outposts and front line. British machine guns fired in front of the infantry. The infantry was ordered to keep 100 yards behind the tanks. The battalion was allotted three wire crushing and eight fighting tanks for the assault.

Unfortunately, the tanks which were supposed to precede the battalion were not in position. General Taylor had ordered in advance that whether or not the tanks were ready, the battalions must advance at Zero Hour. Arthur's company commander was fatally wounded just before the assault was due to start, and Arthur was ordered to lead the company instead. The whistles blew and Arthur led his company into the attack, relying on the artillery bombardment for protective cover. Soon some tanks caught up. The battalion over-ran the German outpost line, but encountered heavy machine-gun fire from their right, where there were several machine-gun posts. Some machine-gun posts were dealt with by tanks, but the infantry had to tackle others, especially an enemy strongpoint on the left in a crater, code-named Etna, and other German machine-gun posts based on a crater, code-named Vesuvius. As well as the machine guns, they had to deal with snipers.

By 9.00a.m., the battalion had reached their objective line and had taken two hundred prisoners, ten machine guns and three trench mortars. By nightfall, the division had advanced four and a half miles, captured two powerful German defence systems and over-run two villages in "a brilliant achievement" according to the official dispatches. This advance was not only the best of the war so far, but remained a record advance in battle over the whole war. Everyone had played their part – infantry using their initiative as well as the technical troops. Later, General Sir Walter Braithwaite wrote, "After the battle I asked a private of the 187th Brigade, what he thought of the barrage and he replied: 'It was perfect: just in the right place. I could have stroked it as it rolled along in front of me!'"[616]

Sadly, like John, Arthur would not have known much about this success. In the course of the attack he was wounded. He was probably taken back to the advanced dressing station near Havrincourt rather than the dressing station for the walking wounded by Mill Farm, and then back to Number 21 Casualty Clearing Station at Ytres. Three days later he died of his wounds, and was buried at Etricourt, which received casualties from the 21st and 48th Casualty Clearing Stations at Ytres. He was not alone. The battalion war diary recorded the names of two captains and three lieutenants (including Arthur) who had been killed, and of six more officers wounded. Of the men, two hundred and eleven had been killed, wounded or gone missing.

George Mossop was also in this assault. He had been at the school, alongside his step-brother Felix,

---

[615] *The History of the 62nd (W.R.) Division*, Edward Wyrall, Vol. I, pp. 76-77.
[616] ibid, p. 91.

from September 1909 to July 1912 when they went their separate ways – George to Lancing College in Sussex. (They were to have separate war experiences, George in the Army, and Felix as a highly decorated young Naval midshipman.) George had been born in 1898. When the war began, George was still too young to serve. He had built on his exam achievements at Bournemouth when at Lancing College and gained a place at Cambridge University, where he hoped to study to follow his father into the medical profession. Meanwhile, however, there was a war to be won, and instead of spending much time at Cambridge, as soon as he was old enough, in August 1916, George applied for a commission in the Army. His training was swift – he was commissioned 2nd lieutenant on 28th February 1917 and was posted to the 7th Sussex Battalion. After fighting earlier in 1917, George had been granted leave from 12th to 26th October but was back with the battalion in late October. He was probably in either 'A' or 'B' Company. The conditions of secrecy attached to the preparations were strict, including the warning to all ranks that they must on no account answer questions from unknown officers. Even Colonel Impey, their battalion commander, was rebuffed whilst the battalion was moving forward towards the start line. "The Commanding Officer, Lieut-Col. Impey rode up to one of the Companies on a very dark and moonless night and said 'Who are you?' The answer came back 'We're Kitchener's... Army'".[617] Whilst the men enjoyed hot tea and rum, the officers showed a preference for the "'vin jaune superior of Scotland"! One lieutenant, a platoon commander, slept on a ground sheet but, when the battle was due to start, the ground sheet was suddenly removed and he found himself in front of an 18-pounder gun of whose position he had no idea. Secrecy was almost complete. "Towards 6am the first streaks of dawn began to show themselves, disclosing for the first time the tanks which had been made to look all the more fearsome by having a huge fascine, for the purpose of negotiating the broad trenches of the Hindenburg Line, fixed on their tops. Zero hour was at 6.20 am and from now onwards the minutes seemed like hours. At length 6.10 came, then 6.15, still a dead silence – could it continue? Would the enemy forestall us at the last moment? The remaining minutes passed like months, the suspense was awful; 6.20 came at last and a most terrific barrage opened from guns of all calibre, to the accompaniment of a regular Brocks' Benefit Display of S.O.S. rockets of all colours from the German lines which had also become a mass of bursting shells. In addition to all this, the familiar sound of aeroplanes was also heard, dozens of our planes coming over which owing to the misty morning and bad visibility had to fly very low. The advanced guard tanks started at Zero, in order to make gaps in the broad and formidable belts of wire, and were followed ten minutes later by the main guard tanks accompanied by the Infantry in special 'tank' formation consisting of 'blobs' in file about 50 yards behind each tank, 16 of which were operating on our front. There was no doubt that from the first opening of the attack, surprise was complete."

Although a hidden machine-gun post opened up to inflict some casualties (including killing one subaltern), "the attack was the most successful ever undertaken by the battalion". They gained their objectives quickly with the loss of two officers and 106 men killed or wounded. One feature that stood out was the successful deployment of the tanks. "Mention must again be made of the completeness with which the Tanks carried out their task, all the gaps in the wire were crushed absolutely flat, no difficulty being experienced in crossing them and all M.G. nests were quickly subdued. In fact it is not too much to say that complete confidence in the tank prevailed throughout the brigade." However, there was a lost opportunity. 'A' Company – which might have included George Mossop – sent a patrol deep into former German territory, finding two deserted villages

---

[617] These and the excerpts following on the battle are abstracted from the War Diary, 7th Royal Sussex Battalion, Account of the Battle of Cambrai.

and the St. Quentin Canal unguarded, which they crossed without incident. They even found two abandoned German trench lines, code-named 'Pelican' and 'Bitch' Trenches, which overlooked and guarded the canal. When this was reported back via brigade, the senior commanders showed no interest and the battalion was not allowed to occupy these positions. When their significance was later realised, many men died in vain attempts to capture them from the Germans who had flooded back into them once the pressure had eased. Indeed, one day, later in November, the battalion lost another officer and over a hundred men in a vain attack on Pelican Trench.

The new Mark IV 'male' tanks used in the battle had many improvements on the old Mark I version: reinforced armour, a relocated fuel tank, an extra front machine gun and better trench crossing equipment; but even so the power-to-weight ratio was so feeble that big slopes and deep craters proved impassable. The tanks were initially armed with Lewis guns, but later were equipped with lighter Hotchkiss guns.

On 20th November 1917, Harold Head's tank section was engaged to assist 153rd Brigade of the 51st Division. The company had twelve tanks in action on that day, in three sections. Their orders were to assist the second wave attack, leading forward the 7th Black Watch and 7th Gordon Highlanders of 153rd Brigade, and to that end they fought in two groups rather than the normal three sections, with six tanks attached to each infantry battalion. They were supposed to assist in the capture of Flesquieres village and move forward beyond that afterwards. Of the four tanks of Harold's section, all managed to attack and to engage the enemy. However, two suffered direct hits – one was then burnt out. The other two turned back just before the second objective. One of them then broke down though the other did get back but with its guns out of action.

Reginald Winch's battalion, the 1/3rd London Battalion, had fought at Ypres in August 1917, but in September they had moved back near to Bapaume in the Cambrai Sector. They manned trenches across or near the road from Bapaume to Cambrai to confuse and deceive the Germans. "On night of 19th dummy tanks were placed out in 'No Man's Land' and dummy figures placed in position. Formation of Battn dumps completed. Generally quiet. 20th. 9.0am. Zero Day. Company of Special Brigade, REs discharged gas on the Left of the Battalion front, to which enemy made no reply. Zero was fixed for 6.20am at which time the Battn was 'standing to' ready to carry out a smoke feint attack, in conjunction with the dummy tanks and figures mentioned above. Smoke attack was most successful, wind being very favourable. Enemy reply very feeble and scattered. Casualties – 1 OR killed and 2 OR wounded."[618] They continued to hold the front line and to patrol. After several tours they were pulled back north of Arras for Christmas.

Another Old Boy there, fighting with the infantry, was Wilfred Bailey. He was one of the earliest members of the school, leaving aged 14 in July 1903. He was probably a boarder. He had returned to London, where he had been born, to work in the London Railway Clearing Office, an organisation which dealt primarily with the precise financial arrangements between the different private railway companies to ensure the different companies got the correct proportion of fares for passengers or freight when journeys involved travel on more than one company's tracks or using their rolling stock. By 1914, he was working as a clerk, but one with two years' military experience in the Hertfordshire Yeomanry. On 27th October 1914, he enlisted in London into the unglamorous, but extremely necessary, Army Pay Corps. He was promoted pay corps corporal on 29th April 1916,

---

[618] War Diary, 1/3rd London Battalion, 19th-20th November 1917.

and as acting sergeant on 21st June 1916. On 15th May 1917, he was compulsorily transferred from the Pay Corps as a private (though keeping his sergeant's pay) to the 87th Training Reserve Battalion, despite having poor eyesight. On 16th September he was transferred to the 1st Inniskilling Fusiliers Battalion. On 27th September he crossed the channel to Boulogne.

The battalion he joined had already fought its way through much of 1917 and needed replacement soldiers. Most recently, the battalion had fought in the Battle of Langemarck, 16th-18th August. When Wilfred arrived, the battalion was in trenches north of Langemarck, but was pulled back to the canal zone at Ypres to resupply and support other units. In the middle of October, the battalion was entrained south to Arras to prepare for the coming battle. Whilst they trained, their commander also agreed to divert men to help the local farmer with his harvest, and for battalion limbers to help him carry away the produce! In the first half of November, the training continued.

Wilfred and his battalion carried forward with their Lewis guns on the evening of 18th November. To preserve secrecy, there was a complete embargo on lights or even on smoking. As they moved forward into position in the line on the south-eastern side of Marcoing, south-west of Cambrai on 19th November, one company commander and eleven men were wounded. The first assault wave had already gone in when they arrived at 2.30p.m., and their commanding officer decided to join the assault immediately. The battalion spread out in company line on the east bank of the St. Quentin Canal. "On debouching from the cover of the bank, the battalion proceeded until it came under heavy machine gun fire and rifle fire. The battalion then halted and advanced by platoon rushes under its own covering fire, for a distance of 500 yards, when the Commanding Officer came forward and led the charge against the nearest gun pits. Before reaching the gun pits, it was necessary to get through 30 yards of barbed wire. While the wire cutters were going forward the remainder of the battalion covered them with rifle fire, standing. One officer placed a Lewis gun on the shoulder of a man and used it that way. When the battalion charged the first line of pits, the majority of the enemy retired to pits in rear, and those remaining were either killed or captured. On reaching this point the two centre companies kept up a heavy fire, while the right and left companies worked round their respective flanks. When this movement was completed the battalion again charged and converged on the pits from three sides. The majority of the enemy retired on to the Marcoing-Rumilly road. Two strong points… held out stubbornly – one was manned with guns, and the other with three machine guns. These were soon captured, and three dead German officers were found. The possession for each pit was stubbornly contested. No time was lost in pushing on beyond these pits. The battalion advanced right up to the wire in the Battalion area, and came under heavy flank fire from houses on the Masnières-Cambrai road, and were also fired upon by a machine gun… The Battalion was therefore withdrawn about 100 yards as it was impossible to get through the wire. On seeing that there were no troops on our right the Commanding Officer decided to form a defensive flank, and for that purpose withdrew the right company and placed them facing the Masnières-Cambrai road. The right centre was withdrawn into support. The Battalion then commenced to dig themselves in."[619]

This attack had been made without the support of the tanks, which had not been able to cross the canal, and it had been costly. On first count, it seemed that six officers had been wounded (one dying of his wounds), twenty soldiers killed, 116 wounded and five went missing; but when they rechecked they realised that actually forty-six men had been killed. They had, however, captured

---

[619] War Diary, 1st Royal Inniskilling Fusiliers, November 20th 1917.

fifty-four prisoners, including five German officers, and taken five German machine guns.

Special measures to try to maintain secrecy had also applied to Maurice Hellier and the 6th Shropshire Light Infantry Battalion. At the end of September 1917, they had been withdrawn from the Third Battle of Ypres and for some weeks had undergone special training with tanks. From 16th November, officers and men were confined to camp in daylight. But the night before the attack, the Germans raided one of the outposts to their trench and took one of their wounded men prisoner. The battalion still attacked at 6.20a.m. in conjunction with the other units on 20th November. Maurice, with 'B' Company was in the middle of it. "A Coy attacked on the Right, B Coy Centre, C Coy left with D Coy in Reserve. Numerous prisoners, Guns and other war material was captured."[620] Over the following days they remained under fire, holding a ridge for defensive purposes. Overall, three officers were killed, five wounded, whilst eleven had died, eighty been wounded and two gone missing.

After that they were pulled back into support. At one point, so intensive was the German shelling, the battalion had to evacuate the support camp for some hours. Then, on 30th November, the battalion was re-deployed and joined the defensive fighting, which had become very fierce. That day they took seventy casualties. Maurice fought on the St. Quentin Ridge with his 'B' Company behind 'A' Company on the right of the line. The battalion took its casualties from machine-gun fire to their front and flank. 'B' Company was sent forward to rescue the right flank. Heavy fighting continued on 1st December until an attack by the Guards Division, supported by tanks, drove the Germans back. Then, once again, Maurice and the battalion were taken out of the line and returned to training, parades, baths, work parties and similar duties until, on 6th March, they returned to the southern sector, to a position east of the Somme.

The British success of late November was incomplete. The furthest advance on 20th November was on the flanks. In the centre, the 51st Highland Division had made less progress. In places an advance of up to four or even five miles had been achieved but the cavalry could not get forward; when units did try to advance they were repulsed by German defenders at Noyelles. The Germans also managed to destroy 179 out of 350 assault tanks, and inflicted over four thousand British casualties, and retained some of their key defensive positions. Within twenty-four hours it was clear that the great encirclement of Cambrai by cavalry was not going to happen. To add to his difficulties, Haig was required by Lloyd George and the government to detach two divisions and to send them to the Italian Front instead. He tried, in vain, to change the government's mind.

In position near Marcoing, Wilfred Bailey and his fellow soldiers spent the days after the attack trying to consolidate their new trench line, harried by snipers who took a regular and heavy toll. On 23rd November, German shelling began. They continued shelling and sniping, and a lack of supplies meant "the physical endurance of the men in the Battalion was by this date sorely tried."[621] Their relief by 1st Essex on 25th November was most welcome.

Overall, the British attack continued until 27th November, when the British attempted to dig in to consolidate their gains, hampered by sleet and snow, which was rapidly making the ground unsuitable for surviving tank actions. The next day, Wilfred and the 1st Royal Inniskilling Fusiliers returned to the fight, relieving the 1st Essex and 1st Hampshires on their previous line. But the

---

[620] War Diary, 6th Shropshire Light Infantry Battalion, November 20th 1917.
[621] War Diary, 1st Royal Inniskilling Fusiliers, November 24th 1917.

Germans had brought up substantial reserves and struck back against what were essentially improvised British positions. That day, the Germans launched heavy gas attacks against the forward British position in Bourlon Wood, and on November 30th sent mass troops against the exposed British positions which rapidly began to collapse. Wilfred faced several hours of hard fighting to repulse the attacks which, from 6a.m., the Germans launched against the 1st Inniskillings. Even after their failed assault, the Germans were shelling Wilfred and the battalion with both shrapnel and high explosives. That day the battalion lost a further seven dead, twelve wounded, whilst five more were missing.

Men in other battalions were also feeling exhausted, and on December 1st the battalion carefully withdrew a short distance to shorten its own line whilst extending rightwards to cover the weakness of adjacent regiments, as far as possible destroying their advanced trenches and blocking them with wire. Some Monmouthshire soldiers were sent forward to reinforce them. On their right (but on the other side of the canal) were now the 2nd South West Borderers, and on their left was the Border Regiment. All the time the German guns were shelling them. Unfortunately, their new position meant that the trench on their extreme right was subject to enfilade machine-gun fire from across the canal. The Monmouth men were particularly badly hit, and their captain was killed. All day the men were subjected to German artillery fire, though it only occasionally hit the exact trench positions. That night, relieved by the 14th Durham Light Infantry, the battalion retired to dug-outs on the Hindenburg Line. At some point that day Wilfred was killed. His body was never recovered, and today his name is inscribed on the Cambrai Memorial at Louveral.

The Battle of Cambrai petered out in disappointment and frustration. British machine-gun barrages, especially those fired by the 47th, 2nd and 56th Divisions, had inflicted heavy losses on the Germans, but the salient the initial British advance had created was untenable and, on 3rd December, Haig ordered a pull back to shorten and straighten the line. Overall, both sides had lost some ground by the end of the battle, and the line took on the shape of waves so each side had a salient to defend. Both sides had lost approximately 45,000 men but for the British this was a massive disappointment – no breakthrough, significant losses, and the apparent squandering of resources. But at the same time, tactics combining tanks, infantry and artillery had shown promise for the future. Meanwhile, the war dragged on over another winter.

The final stages of the battle turned out to be defensive actions against German counter-attacks, not the hoped-for breakthrough. Another Christmas was still to come, with no victory for either side. William Mitford, who had returned from hospital, played his part in the final defensive fighting of the battle.

At the Battle of Arras in 1917, William had again been wounded. However, he recovered from a shell fragment remarkably quickly and on 14th August 1917 was held fit enough to be transferred to yet another battalion in France – the 17th Royal Fusiliers. Strictly, this battalion bore a longer title, 'the 17th (Service) Battalion, Royal Fusiliers (Empire)'. The 'Empire' in their title came from a group of English gentlemen who styled themselves 'the British Empire Committee' and who suggested raising the unit along with two brigades of Field Artillery, a Field Company of Royal Engineers and a Divisional Signal Company of Royal Engineers, all of which they then paid for in terms of clothing and equipment, as well as their original quarters in England. Corporal William Mitford's new battalion had already served with honour. Its men had fought in 1916 on the Somme at Longueval and Delville Wood, as well as on the Ancre and at Courcelette. They too had fought at Arras in 1917.

In the autumn of 1917, William was in the thick of battle once again. When General Byng was drawing up his plans, Haig had strenuously recommended that on the northern flank of the advance, and still east of Cambrai, Bourlon Wood should be attacked in strength, but Byng had planned differently. Consequently, by the time the 17th Royal Fusiliers were there, the position was vulnerable. The battalion was placed to defend a small section of the northern line of the salient created by the thrust on Cambrai, between Bourlon Wood and the village of Moeuvres. They were in the 5th Brigade of the 2nd Division, between the 56th and 47th Divisions. They were in the front line, with the 1st Royal Berkshires on their right and 1st King's Royal Rifle Corps on their left, occupying a long trench known as 'the rat's tail' which ran forward one thousand yards almost at right angles to the main British line. At the end of their trench, 'B' Company manned a post overlooking the German positions.

On 30th November 1917, two hours after the Germans launched their counter-attack on the southern flank of the salient, the men of the 17th Royal Fusiliers could see what appeared to be a solidly packed advance of the Germans. In fact, the Germans were hurling four of their divisions at them, with three more divisions in support. Ordering back most of his men, Captain Stone kept one platoon with him to hold off this enormous German advance to try to give his friends time to organise the defence from a less vulnerable position. These men were all killed as the Germans swept over them, but not before Captain Stone had stood upon the parapet, field telephone in hand, sending accurate messages back about the strength and direction of the enemy. He was last seen falling, shot through the head. He was awarded a posthumous Victoria Cross.

His actions had given the 17th Royal Fusiliers just enough time to organise a defence, but when they were relieved that evening they numbered only twenty officers and three hundred and fifty-one men.

On 4th December, they took up positions in front of Lock 7 on the Scarpe to help to cover the British retreat. Guns were pulled back through their position, and dug-outs were systematically destroyed. Two days later they prepared to cover the withdrawal of the rear guard, which was being closely followed by the Germans. They were ordered to establish three posts about five hundred yards in front of the line, to be held at all costs. These were established about dawn on 7th December, and on the 8th December the Germans reached their positions. All day both sides threw grenades at each other, and by the afternoon the German guns began to register hits on the 17th Royal Fusilier front line. Still they held on and the shelling continued all through the night. But they continued to hold, even though the next day they were repeatedly attacked, and by now were two thousand yards in front of the new British front line. They were finally relieved on the night of 9th December, but the line they had held remained the new front until the German Ludendorff Offensive of March 1918. William emerged unwounded.

William and the battalion remained in the Cambrai Sector that winter. At 10a.m. on 21st December, the Germans suddenly launched a thirty man raid on their trenches, but made the almost incredible mistake of forgetting to pull the strings to arm the fuses of their grenades, which consequently did not explode. As a result, not only was the raid beaten off by 'D' Company, but they took a German prisoner who was armed with the new German automatic pistol. This gun had a magazine of thirty-two rounds and proved of great interest to the British authorities. The next day, the 17th Royal Fusiliers tried to mount their own raid in retaliation, but this was quickly aborted when the covering fog lifted.

Geoffrey Gilbert, born in 1888, at school from 1905-1906, and older brother of Leslie, was involved in trying to halt the German counter-attack at the end of November. Geoffrey had emigrated to New Zealand after he had left school. In 1911 he lived at Kiore Station, and later at Paparatu Station, Gisburne Tolago Bay, where he worked as a shepherd. It is not clear if he had already returned to England before the outbreak of the war, or if he returned specially, but on 11th September 1914 at Winchester he enlisted in the Hampshire Carabiniers, a Yeomanry Cavalry regiment, part of the 1st South Western Mounted Brigade. It had four squadrons, and 'D' Squadron was based at Bournemouth. When mobilised, the regiment was moved to help to defend Portsmouth, but this was soon followed by further moves, ending up in the vicinity of Eastbourne. In March 1916, the regiment was split up, and three squadrons were sent to France attached to different divisions, whilst 'D' Squadron seems to have been disbanded. The three remaining squadrons landed on different dates at Le Havre, and Geoffrey had crossed from Folkestone to Boulogne on 6th April 1916. It is not clear what he did in France for the next few months, but on 1st August 1916 he was transferred to the Machine Gun Corps (Cavalry) and sent to join the 11th (Mhow) Squadron. This unit had been formed from three former cavalry units the previous February to serve in the 5th (Mhow) Brigade of the 1st Indian Cavalry Division.

Geoffrey's new unit was a cavalry squadron of eight officers and about two hundred men. They comprised six, two-gun machine-gun sections. As a unit it was never involved in battle, though sometimes they were called upon to help hold the line. It was broken up on 14th April 1918. The only battle in which his brigade fought was this action at Cambrai. On 1st December, the whole brigade massed in low ground north and north-west of Peizière. The idea had been that they would advance when an assault by the tanks had opened up a suitable opportunity, but in fact the expected tanks did not materialise for such an assault. This mass of cavalry provided an irresistible target for the German artillery which fired high explosive and shrapnel over them, causing considerable casualties, though they stood firm, until, after about an hour they were withdrawn again. A quarter of an hour later they were ordered to advance despite the absence of tanks. Four machine guns were supposed to seize control of strategic ravines, three thousand yards ahead of their starting line. Whilst the assault failed, their actions did at least help to stem the German counter-attacks.

On 2nd January 1918, Geoffrey was promoted lance corporal, but on 5th April 1918 he was wounded, receiving gas in his face. After passing through the casualty system he was invalided aboard the hospital ship *Stad Antwerpen* on 10th April to a series of hospitals in England. Gradually he recovered, though his eyesight was affected and he had to wear glasses. Having passed through a sequence of hospitals he was granted some home leave, though he was caught out by Military Police on Bournemouth Station for overstaying that leave, as a result of which he was admonished and fined a day's pay! He was demobilised on 20th February 1919, and after the war returned to New Zealand.

Meanwhile, the Battle of Cambrai provided something of a 'cover story' for Bernard Hame of the 5th Royal Engineers Field Company. The school magazine described one version of the events: "Lieut. B. W. Hame, M.C., R.E., was recently reported 'missing' under the following circumstances:—He was 'wiring' in Bourlon Wood during the counter-attack of last November 29th when a 5.9 German shell exploded in the middle of a party of eleven men, of whom Hame was one. He was 'knocked out' and remained unconscious from the shock for several hours, but he eventually reached a distant dressing station and afterwards made a splendid recovery. It was a very narrow escape for Hame, inasmuch as only one other (of the party of eleven) is known to have survived."[622] Dramatic though the event described was, it actually illustrates for us why we cannot take any account for granted. The truth was much more prosaic, though very unpleasant for him.

On 24th October, Bernard Hame had returned from leave. At the time, the 5th Royal Engineers Field Company was training and enjoying some sport, behind the lines at Chocques, a suburb north-west of Bethune. On 4th November, the company had moved to Poperinghe and on to Ypres. The next day, "Lt Hame and 1 NCO per section went forward to reconnoitre work on St. Julian-Winnipeg road. General repair to road to be carried out."[623] This work started the next day under "heavy hostile barrage fire" costing six casualties. They continued under fire, building a new tramway and took more casualties. Because the British focus now switched from Ypres to Cambrai, on 24th November they moved by train via Poperinghe to Rocqeny (near Bapaume) and moved up to Doignies the next day to work on the Demicourt-Graincourt road as far as the canal. They were repairing bridges across trenches and their approaches, clearing wire and generally making repairs to the road surface. On 27th November, the company switched to repair the Bapaume-Cambrai road, creating a new temporary road adjacent to it, one group assisted by the 252nd A.T. Company R.E.; and another group helped by 10th D.C.L.I. Pioneers, 226th Field Company R.E. and 483rd Field Company R.E. At the start of December there was to be work going on in Bourlon Wood, but Bernard was not there. The reality is revealed through the medical board reports in his Army file[624] and corroborated by the company war diary. He had suffered from dysentery in South Africa in 1904 and again in Bombay in 1914. This had returned whilst he was in the trenches near Doignes, to the west of Cambrai, and for six weeks he had suffered until, on 27th November 1917, he reported sick; he was weak and debilitated, and had to live off a restricted diet for the next ten months (for example, not managing to eat meat). He might have decided that he needed a 'cover story' as, although initially hospitalised and granted home leave in Plymouth for a while, he was later treated at Mont Dore Hospital in Bournemouth and his next posting was to the R.E. Training Centre at Christchurch on 23rd April 1918, where he might easily have been recognised and questions asked: it would be better to have a more heroic story ready to offer! So, on 5th-6th December 1917, he was sent home sick on the SS *Essquibo* to England and his employment on the front line had ended. On 1st July, *The London Gazette* noted his promotion to temporary captain with effect from May 1918. This was because he had by then been employed as assistant instructor at an officers' convalescent hospital. He temporarily relinquished that role on 23rd June 1918 when he returned to his substantive rank of temporary 2nd lieutenant. A medical board had decided he was fully fit on 3rd September 1918, but the Army did not seem to rush to bring him back into general service. For a short while he continued in the temporary captain's assistant instructor role at the convalescent hospital until 19th October 1918. On 30th October, his effectiveness was further limited by an injury whilst playing rugby in a match between the Depot and the Cadets, when he was accidentally kicked in the head. On 21st November he was sent to France, but was hardly there any time before he had to leave the R.E. Base Depot at Rouen on 6th December 1918, crossing to Southampton from Le Havre the next day, suffering from influenza. Even heroes get sick. After the war he was demobilised on 11th April 1919 and resumed work as an engineer for which he took employment in Singapore.

---

[622] *The Bournemouthian*, April 1918.
[623] War Diary, 5th Royal Engineers Field Company, 4th November 1917.
[624] Army File, Bernard Hame, WO 339/63884.

As the Battle of Cambrai drew to a disappointing end, Eric Paice and the artillery did good service covering the infantry and defending the established line. Eric had been born in 1890, and with his younger brother Francis joined the school in April 1906. When he attested on 9th December 1915, for military experience, Eric cited the two and a half years he had spent in the school O.T.C. After a posting in the 2nd Artists Rifles, he was commissioned on 13th January 1917.

Unfortunately, he spent much of March to May 1917 unwell – initially in an officers' convalescent hospital. It was not until 22nd November that he disembarked at Le Havre. Two days later he was posted to join the 34th Divisional Artillery, and was placed in 'B' Battery of 152nd Brigade, Royal Field Artillery. When Eric joined them they were firing on targets south-east of Arras, from positions near Vis-en-Artois. 26th November was a day of action, as – despite poor visibility – the batteries fired steadily all day and received counter-battery fire from German howitzers. After a three hour gap, they resumed with night firing, and repeated the same pattern the next day. The only visible target, however, was a horse and cart on the Hendicourt-Dury road, which was smashed by 18-pounder fire. For his first few days, Eric's guns fired in support of the 16th Division, but soon they had pulled a couple of miles westwards to Heninel, south of Wancourt and south-east of Arras to support their own 34th Division. There was drama on 29th November when they came under heavy German artillery fire which destroyed two gun pits and their cook house. One gun had to be sent away for repairs, but the other – though completely buried in the morning – was dug out and got back into action by the late afternoon. The next day it was their communication trenches which bore the brunt of the German attacks.

Throughout December and into January 1918, fire and counter-battery fire continued, in daytime and for many nights. The artillery brigade had three batteries, and Eric's was rested for a third of the time in sequence. January ended unpleasantly with a heavy German bombardment, with an estimated 60% shells containing poison gas on its penultimate day. The pattern was finally broken when they were relieved over two days, 7th and 8th February 1918, and spent the rest of the month 'at rest' and in training behind the lines.

Proportionately, the 28th London Battalions took heavy losses over the years 1917-1918, partly because they were in the thick of the action, and William Webber of the 1/28th London went through it. His battalion was not directly involved in the Battle of Cambrai, unsurprising considering the numbers killed or wounded at Passchendaele, but in the aftermath of that action, and at the turn of the year, William and the battalion fought in a vicious affair known as the Battle of Welsh Ridge. Attached to the battalion was the famous official war artist, John Nash, and he painted one of his most famous paintings, *Over the Top* depicting William and the others going over the top in this battle. The action took place near Marcoing, south-west of Cambrai. At the time, the 63rd Naval Division held its part of the front with all three brigades, the 188th (on the right), the 189th (in the centre) and the 190th (on the left), committed to the trenches. The battalion was therefore on the left, more northerly, part of the position.

On 30th December, at 6.30a.m., the Germans launched a heavy, fifteen minute, bombardment of the division's trenches followed by an infantry attack, including men with flamethrowers. The British defended vigorously against the German assault, and their rifle fire took its toll of the Germans. Even so, in various places the German infantry was able to get into the forward trenches, especially in places where the British had suffered heavily from the German bombardment. In particular, the other brigades lost ground: Corner Trench, Welsh Trench and Welch Support were lost by the

188th Brigade whilst the 189th Brigade found itself in peril as the Germans got into trenches on both its flanks – trenches known as Ostrich Lane on the right and Battery Lane on the left, and the 7th Royal Fusiliers of the 190th were pushed back and lost a trench known as Eagle Avenue.

At 8a.m., William's 190th Brigade came under particular pressure. The Germans moved forward along a sunken road to their north and pushed back the 1/4th King's Shropshire Light Infantry, which was their most northerly battalion. That battalion tried to form a defensive position. The 1/28th London Battalion had been the brigade reserve battalion, and two of its companies, supported by two companies of K.S.L.I., counter-attacked about noon and managed to clear the Germans from the sunken road and to establish on the sunken road a new defensive line. Although the other brigades also counter-attacked, only the 1/28th London had much success, and even so part of the former ground (which had been a small salient) remained in German hands.

For the next three weeks the division tried to hold the reduced line, and on 22nd to 23rd January 1918 it moved back into support trenches as the 2nd Division took over the front line. After this the division spent a few weeks to "rest and recover" – which meant working parties to strengthen the front line defences. Meanwhile, replacements were sent to the battalions to restore their fighting capacity.

Arthur Baker of the Tank Corps probably also worked on this battlefield in the aftermath of the battle. At the school from 1907 to 1909, Arthur was the youngest of five sons who joined the service. His next older brother, and fellow Old Bournemouthian, Percy (Walter) Baker had been killed at Gommecourt in July 1916. Arthur had volunteered at the start of the war and had first served as a private in India with the 7th Hampshires, and returned to England in September 1916. He had only enjoyed three days of a month's home leave in England from the 7th Hampshires when he was summoned to the Cadet Training School at Newmarket. "Shortly after my arrival a notice was posted that Cadets were wanted for Tank instruction, and those who had experience in machine gunnery would have the preference. As in India I had been for some time in the Armoured Car Unit, I put forward my name and shortly after was sent to Pirbright. I will not detain you with a description of our life there – suffice it to say it was grind and drill from early morning until late at night. In due time I found myself under instruction with the Tanks at their headquarters, but here I must not give you a detailed description of them. At last I was certified and soon afterwards left for France, where I have been for the last six months, and am now home on 14 days' leave."[625]

Arthur Baker

He was commissioned 2nd lieutenant in the Tank Corps, on 25th February 1917, and left for active service in France on 24th June, 1917, taking charge of a tank. For a time afterwards he had worked as an assistant instructor with the Tank Corps, so clearly was reckoned to have some expertise, but

---

[625] *The Bournemouthian*, December 1917.

he had relinquished that post on 1st October 1917. That was a period when the Tank Corps was preparing for Cambrai, and it was very important to train enough officers and men to take the corps forward. Arthur was clearly a capable and heroic soldier. It seems he specialised in support work with the tanks.

In 1916, the crew of a Mark I tank had been one officer and seven men, with each tank section having six officers and forty-three other ranks. For every two companies there was a quartermaster's establishment of one officer and four men, and a workshop of three officers and fifty men. By 1918 the organization had been improved and extended to create specialized technical field companies and we know that in 1918 Arthur was working in the 1st Field Company of the Tank Corps – a unit dedicated to the support, repair and salvage of tanks in the midst of battle. Even before the Mark I tanks were deployed, their designers had realised that they were going to need specialists and the Army had gradually created a set of such units, starting with a small initial group formed in December 1916, which was developed into a company in February 1917.

This was joined by a second company and a Special Salvage Detachment was created during the Third Battle of Ypres. These units soon proved their worth – in the Third Battle of Ypres it was calculated that they recovered tanks, parts and stores worth £1.3 million. By 1918 he was part of the team which not only recovered and safeguarded crucial war materials for the British but also prevented them falling into German hands during a counter-attack. This meant that Arthur and the unit had to work in the field in the midst of the battle – it was not the job of a field company to hang back and await the outcome of a battle before moving forward to the damaged tanks. "The work carried out by the Tank Field Companies was particularly dangerous, and many casualties amongst their personnel occurred. In the actual reclaiming of machines or parts they were constantly under shell fire, and the actual carrying to and fro of the material made use of required great physical strength, since the ground to be traversed was frequently a mass of shell-holes; incidentally a great deal of work had to be done at night since many of the machines to be salved were frequently situated in full view of the enemy."[626]

In a letter published in the school magazine of December 1917, Arthur gave a detailed description of what it was like to salvage a tank. "At present I am in charge of a section of the Tank Salvage Coy. Our duty is firstly to lend a helping hand when a 'stunt' is taking place and afterwards to recover if possible the derelict Tanks. On a recent occasion I was ordered to salve whole a Tank that Fritz had evidently made good target practice on. A Tank fully equipped weighs about 30 tons, i.e., equals the weight of say three of the Corporation steam rollers. Under skilful manipulation it can perform marvellous operations, from climbing over trenches and through shell craters to standing on its head or its tail or climbing over a sister tank, but the chief trouble of the commander is the awfully boggy ground. We found that the particular Tank referred to had been badly ditched, or in other words had sunk deep into the bog. The first thing to do was to get inside of it and find out if the engine were in likely working order. We found two of the cylinders and the radiator smashed by shell fire, and the gears damaged, but otherwise it appeared to be all right. Preparations were then made for clearing a passage way – this had to be done by the men with their hands. Once the spade was in the mud, one could not lift it up, but had to pull the whole spade-full off by hand – some game! The next job was to take away the damaged cylinders and renew the gears, also fix up an

---

[626] *Tanks in the Great War 1914-1918*, Col. J.F.C. Fuller, 1920, p. 128.

improvised radiator made from empty oil drums. After much labour we at last got away, but I found we could steer only a straight course. Owing to the condition of the ground we could not swing right or left, and in front of us was a belt of trees and more marshy ground. However there was no help for it but to go straight ahead and trust in Providence. A large tree was the first obstacle, and the Tank was elevated in front and put in motion, so that by sheer weight it brought down the tree, which, falling across part of the boggy ground, gave us a fairly good footing by which to crawl across. We had not proceeded very far on our way when we came across an artillery officer with about 100 men vainly attempting to drag a big gun out of a similar plight. Labour as they might they could not make it budge. I then asked the officer if I could be of any use, and looking at our battered old 'bus he says, 'No thank you, that thing is no good.' I then bet him a 'Gold Flake' that if he would let me try I would fetch it out. This he willingly agreed to and we soon had our hauling tackle fastened to his gun, much to the astonishment and gratification of the Tommies, who soon had the pleasure of seeing gun and tractor hauled out bodily by the derelict old 'bus. Shortly afterwards we came under gas shells, but we were well equipped against gas attack, and we wended our way homewards, and in due course arrived at our destination. There I had the satisfaction of drawing a sovereign from my C.O., who had made me a bet that we would not bring it back within a given time. This I divided among the crew, who well deserved it."[627]

On 3rd June 1918, he was awarded the country's third highest military honour, the Military Cross. This M.C. was awarded in the King's Birthday Honours, and in such cases no specific dedication survives to explain precisely what he had done to earn the award. Once again, the boys of the school were delighted at having yet another hero to follow, and getting another half-holiday in his honour, which was taken on 1st July 1918! The local paper, *The Bournemouth Visitors' Directory*, stated this award was in recognition of his gallantry and devotion to duty.

Arthur Sear had not been at Cambrai, but he was actively involved on the front line that winter. His work was as a wireless operator in a divisional signal depot, and his story reveals for us something of the frustrations – and successes – of trying to keep open the communications between division, brigades and battalions.

Arthur was born in 1897. He attended the school from September 1909 until July 1914, receiving a Bournemouth scholarship to pay his fees. On 8th December 1915, he attested under the Derby Scheme and was placed in the Army Reserve, as the authorities were aware he was a civil servant. On 23rd January 1917, the Civil Service was requested to release him for military service at Worcester, unless there was reason for him to be exempted. There wasn't and so, on 2nd February 1917, he was mobilised and posted as a pioneer to the Royal Engineers Training Centre, to train as a telegraphist. Arthur then spent the next months at Worcester training as a telegraphic wireless operator with 46th Divisional Signals Company. On 6th October, he was re-mustered as a sapper, having proved himself proficient as wireless operator at the Wireless Training Centre and embarked for France on 24th October 1917. On 4th November 1917 he reached the 46th Division Signal Company on the Western Front.

At that time, the company was based at Sailly-Labourse, on the south-eastern outskirts of Béthune, undergoing reorganisation. Communications were still largely being maintained by cable, by runners, and attempts were made to use visual communication via aeroplane, though these were

---

[627] *The Bournemouthian*, December 1917.

frequently unsuccessful due to air conditions. Most communications were made by telephone line, and cable trenches were being dug five and a half feet deep to try to maintain contacts for the general with his brigades. This could be a frustrating business, and sometimes wires were laid above ground in places nearer the front. For example, on 10th November one of the above ground cables on the forward slope of Hill 70 near Lens was heavily shelled in a retaliatory German bombardment, in response to a raid by the 11th Division just to the south of them, and when checked the next day was found to be broken. It took them until 12th November to be able to reconnect the cable. On 22nd November, it was again broken when the Germans raided Hill 70. This led to a request that all cables should be buried, even to battalion companies, which would require an immense amount of work and be hard to achieve in practice. Even so, with the help of infantry 'resting' this was managed by 26th November, and the cable was buried over six feet deep.

On 4th January 1918, Arthur helped to establish a "wireless intercept Station… at Cambrin to pick up enemy code calls and messages, which are forwarded to 'Intelligence', 1st Corps."[628] Soon after, on 23rd January, the company moved to Labeuvière, a short distance but this now placed them south-west of Béthune. Here, the company began a training programme for the signallers of the three brigades (137, 138 and 139) and of 230 Brigade R.F.A.

---

[628] War Diary, 46th Division Signals Company 4th January 1918.

8: 1918 – Difficulties and the Ludendorff Offensive

Although 1918 led to the Allied victory, the course of the year leading to that victory was anything but smooth for the Allies, and once again Old Boys (and not so old) played their part in the struggle, the costs, and the ultimate success. In fact, for members of Bournemouth School, this was the year of greatest participation on the Western (and other) Fronts.

The winter of 1917-1918 was grim for both sides. Although the Germans had beaten the Russians against all expectations, they faced the fact that in the west they were on the defensive, and things could only get worse once the Americans began to arrive in sufficient numbers to reinforce the French and the British. The Germans called this the 'Potato Winter' because at home shortages were grim. The British too were struggling. At home, 1917 had seen a desperate effort to maintain sufficient food supplies, involving heroic work by the Royal and Merchant Navies as well as sacrificial work to extend farming and food production within the country. On the Western Front, brigades, which had almost always consisted of four battalions (two in action; two in support) were now reorganised to be brigades of three battalions. Some service battalions were amalgamated, or even abolished, as manpower shortages took their effect. However, the wider use of Lewis guns helped to compensate for the reduction of manpower within the infantry.

The winter was a period of holding on for both sides. The school magazine for the spring term 1918 published a humorous account written by Maurice Hellier of life inside a 400 man dug-out when the battalion was 'in reserve'. Written in a 'tongue in cheek' style, it gives us a vivid idea of how confined and confusing such a place could be – and at the end it includes a recognition of the efforts of the Royal Engineers who made it, with whom his brother Stanley was serving.

Having described how frequently the lights failed, and how the Tommies could crack jokes even in the face of adversity and three days' worth of mud caking their fatigued bodies, and how they tried hard to shave and clean up, he explained that he was writing whilst lying in his bunk. Apparently, men tried to lie down as much as possible as this saved space and prevented men from knocking into each other. "When the mere fact of A moving his foot will certainly knock B's cup of tea over, or, if he is lucky enough to avoid that, will be bound to result in the treading on C's shaving brush, and when B stands up, C inevitably falls down as they are both sitting on a home-made bench with one central leg – it will be seen there are occasions when lying down has enormous advantages over any more upright position." He also described these dug-outs. "It is well when one takes a walk in this labyrinth not to attempt to get to any particular place, but to adopt the mental attitude of a sightseer who is prepared to go anywhere and see anyone or anything. Should you be so foolhardy as to attempt the strong-minded course of setting out with a purpose you will probably be still engaged on the job when peace is declared… Another playful little habit of the builders was to make all, or nearly all, the dimensions a size too small. In the passages there is seldom room for two to pass and one has always to go about in a stooping attitude to avoid severe collision between one's head and the roof."

In the first months of the year, German artillery continued to pound the British positions. Archibald Rogers reflected, in another letter published in the school magazine, after the German Offensive and before the British counter-attack of 1918 had begun, on the confusing change to places he knew after the British had driven the Germans back at the end of 1917. His description of the conditions before the extent of the disaster was clear: "I had hoped to be on leave by now, but the day after I applied for it all leave was stopped for reasons that you are well aware of. We are in a different sector of the line, though not far away from where we were before, and here our lines are much nearer the Boche, so that in addition to the inevitable 5.9's, etc., we also have to put up with 'Minnies' —very unpleasant they are, too. I say 'we' advisedly, for I am not in the line, but back with the Brigade, but I visit the forward areas daily and don't waste any time about it either. However, we are tolerably safe—safer in fact than if we were further back, for the Boche shells back areas regularly now and huts do not offer the best protection against H.V. shells and 9 inchers. The country round here is more devastated than any part of the line. I have seen huge woods absolutely blown to atoms. I often wonder how on earth we ever took these places; it speaks volumes for the efficiency of the gunners that they ever were taken—the Boche must have literally been blown out of them. He certainly chose his places well, for the observation that he must have got from them is truly remarkable."[629]

The number of German prisoners of war taken had grown over the war years, and that raised issues for the Army. Charles Peel's career gives us an insight into how the Army dealt with the situation, though before he became involved with prisoners of war he had already had an interesting service record. His story is also of interest as he was a Bournemouth School member whose parentage was German.

Dealing with German Prisoners of War

Charles was one of the original members of Bournemouth School – he attended for two terms in 1901. Born in Bournemouth about October 1885, his name then was Carl Francis Samuel Ratsch. His father, a florist and nurseryman called Hermann Ratsch was a German from Silesia. Herman had been naturalised and taken the oath of allegiance at Bournemouth in November 1897. Carl became Charles and was a British subject by right of his birth in Bournemouth. However, when he joined the school, he was still called Ratsch. Later he turned that into a middle name or sometimes called himself Ratsch-Peel. In the forces, however, his surname was always Peel.

Charles initially had been much more interested in the Navy than in the Army, and from 1908 to 1912 had served in the Naval Reserve. Charles volunteered for the Navy on 12th April 1915, and served as a naval rating between 23rd March 1915 and 14th July 1917 in the Royal Naval Volunteer Reserve (R.N.V.R.). Although a naval man, Charles had been on the Western Front, serving in the Royal Naval Division – the 63rd Division, and by 1916 was quarter master sergeant. In 1916 he had appendicitis. At the end of January 1917, a Royal Navy medical board classified him as only 'C3' – he would not be fit for general service for six months. He was then serving with Number 3 Reserve Battalion (R.N.V.R.) at Blandford. From this unit, on 8th March, he applied for an Army commission in the Labour Corps (an application which was agreed by the Officer Commanding the 63rd (Royal Naval) Division on 22nd March. This application was accepted and he was ordered to join an officer cadet battalion at Cambridge on 22nd May.

With all his experience, officer training was brief: he was given a commission as a 2nd lieutenant in the Labour Corps on 16th August 1917. By the end of the war the Labour Corps consisted of about 380,000 men, some of whom were medically unfit for active service, and some were fit enough but

---

[629] *The Bournemouthian*, July 1918.

used as a kind of reserve before being moved into active service battalions of the fighting regiments to make up for losses. He reported to the Labour Corps Depot in France, and soon afterwards was given a posting which matched his talents from his very particular background: on 17th March he joined Number 3 Prisoner of War Company, moving to Number 16 POW Company on 15th July.

These were specialist companies associated with the Labour Corps. (Technically they worked for the Labour Corps, but were not part of it, because the workers were foreign prisoners, although the officers and men guarding the prisoners would be from the Labour Corps or from units attached to the Labour Corps.) Until the middle of 1916, enemy prisoners had been sent back to England. For example, Dorchester in Dorset was 'home' to thousands in a special camp. Men whom it was felt could reasonably be trusted, and who had useful skills (especially in forestry and engineering) were placed in special POW companies, usually formed of about one hundred men, with sufficient guards to be used as POW forestry companies, or with the Army Service Corps or in Royal Engineer workshops. Others were placed with the Labour Corps, particularly for forestry work in one of forty-seven labour companies. Some were used in the dockyards.

German POWs at work

The International Red Cross took photographs of the working conditions as illustrated in this photograph:
http://grandeguerre.icrc.org/en/PostCards/fr

In creating such companies, the British were following the example of the Germans, who from 1915 had been sending British prisoners to live and work in small working units in agriculture, forestry or mining – industries badly short of manpower due to the war effort. Some of these companies were based in specialised POW camps, but in other cases the word of honour of a man not to try to escape was accepted, and they lived in the community. In either case, officers were not included as international conventions stated that they could not be asked to work. Charles spent the spring and summer with these companies, and earned UK leave from 17th August to 31st August 1918. When he returned to France he was posted on 4th September to Number 220 Prisoner of War Company. Whilst this was not as dramatic a role as that of the front-line infantry, it was an important one. After the Armistice, Charles was allowed briefly to serve an attachment to the Royal Army Ordnance Corps, and was promoted to full lieutenant. A Protection Certificate which he received in February 1920 rated him medically in category 'B1', not fully fit.

Another man whose war service was limited by fitness, and confined to the Labour Corps and a POW company, was William Seare, though his POW company was a different one from that of Charles. Born in 1899, William was a boarder at the school from January 1910 to March 1915. On 5th June 1917 he enrolled at Winchester, and he was posted to the 35th Training Reserve Battalion (formerly known as the 7th (Reserve) Dorset Battalion), but he was moved to the 33rd Training Battalion in August 1917. These training reserve battalions were products of the reorganisation of the infantry reserve which had followed the Battle of the Somme, after which the government was determined not to allow further 'Pals' units which – if smashed as on 1st July 1916 – could devastate communities. Some regiments like the Guards were not included, and the Territorial forces continued to have their reserve and depot units, as did the Regular battalions (normally the 3rd or 4th Battalions). From May 1917 these training reserve battalions became 'Young Soldier' or 'Graduated' battalions of specific regiments: William's battalion became the 51st (Graduated) Battalion of the Hampshire Regiment, and part of 201st Brigade, 67th Division. Whilst with them, William went down with measles, and he spent a fortnight in late March 1918 at the 316th Field Ambulance in Ipswich. After his discharge from hospital, William was posted and sent to Rouen to join the 2nd Wiltshire Battalion, on 2nd April 1918, but William was never with them. When he was medically checked before leaving for the front, on 8th April, he was classified as medically 'B1' – not fit for general service with a fighting battalion. This was confirmed by a second medical board, still at Rouen, and so he was posted instead to remain at the Base Depot for the Wiltshires. There was limited work for him, and on 22nd May, still a member of the 2nd Wiltshire Battalion, he was posted to the 31st Prisoner of War Company. He remained with this unit for several months, but gradually it became clear that he was never likely to attain 'A1' fitness, so on 15th July he was transferred to the Labour Corps, though remaining attached to the 31st Prisoner of War Company.

Thomas Stanton's role was also with a POW Company. Born in 1896, he also was still at school when the war began. His father, originally a tailor, had trained to become a clergyman. This might explain why, after school, Thomas lived at a mission in Harrow. He had been at the school from May 1911 until December 1914, and for most of that time was an active member of the O.T.C., rising to the rank of corporal. A single young man, he was called up in March 1916 and was commissioned 2nd lieutenant on 2nd May 1917 to the 5th Hampshire Battalion in India. Before service, however, a medical condition arose which required him to attend a number of medical boards.

Thomas Stanton

He had developed synovitis of the knee, which the Army said was not caused by military service. His knee locked frequently, causing him great pain, and stiffness. The condition is typically a secondary consequence of arthritis, despite his young age. The medical boards decided that, with such a condition, he was not fit for general service, but could serve abroad with a labour battalion or on garrison duty, although he could not cope with activities such as route marching. Only in September 1918 was he sent to France. So he embarked on 21st September 1918 as an officer seconded to the Labour Corps, and found himself posted to number 291 Prisoner of War Company. Soon after going to France he had been promoted to lieutenant. Thomas' company worked behind the lines, although sometimes they were relatively close to the action. They were, of course, subject to inspection by the International Red Cross. He was demobilised in May 1919.

Behind the Scenes 1917-1918: German 'Old Bournemouthians'

Charles Peel, despite his German parentage, seems to have had a successful career in both Navy and Army, but Adolf Bergmann's story throws an uncomfortable light on some of the attitudes and of the British Army and its government. His father, also called Adolf, was a hotel waiter in Bournemouth. He had become a naturalised Englishman (married to a girl from Pelham) but he had been born in Bavaria in about 1868, just before the unification of Germany. Adolf himself was born in Southampton in 1892, and had a younger brother John, born in Bournemouth five years later. It is not clear if John went to Bournemouth School, but Adolf certainly did. He was clearly intelligent and gifted – in April 1908 it was reported that he was one of a select group of boys who had been exempted from London University Matriculation because of his excellence in the Cambridge Senior Local exams (the equivalent of 'A' Levels).[630] By 1911 Adolf had left school but was still living in Bournemouth with his parents and working as an accountant clerk. At some point Adolf had enlisted in the Middlesex Regiment, and eventually found himself attached to the 7th Infantry Labour Battalion, whilst still a member of the Middlesex Regiment.

A near contemporary with a very similar story was Alexander Otho Kur, sometimes known as Alec. He was born in Dresden, Germany, in 1894, though he was British by parentage. He attended Bournemouth School initially as a day boy from 1908, though later he boarded in the house run by the headmaster, Dr. Fenwick. Whilst at school he was a member of the Officer Training Corps. He left in July 1911. On 6th August 1914, he volunteered. He was initially recruited into a Territorial Force unit, the Western Cable Signal Company, Royal Engineers.

At some point Alec was moved into the 4th Independent Labour Company of the Middlesex Regiment, and rose to the rank of sergeant. This company grew from an Army Council Instruction of 1916 to make use of fit and able men of German background. The Middlesex Regiment formed two labour battalions (the 30th and 31st (Works) Battalions) of naturalised British citizens, but born of enemy alien parentage, which remained in the United Kingdom. The regiment also raised eight Infantry Labour companies, which seem partly to have drawn on men from the two battalions, including men like Adolf and Alexander. Some of the men of these companies were transferred in from other units – and sometimes those units protested. This led the Army Council to allow exceptions to be made so that they could stay with their original units. This probably explains why Adolf's younger brother John was allowed to remain in the Motor Transport Section of the Army Service Corps, where he became a sergeant. However, Adolf was placed in the 7th Independent Labour Company.

These eight Infantry Labour companies, numbering in total about four thousand men, did not directly remain under Middlesex Regiment control, but came under the command of the GHQ Labour Directorate (itself only formed in February 1917) and in 1917 all eight were sent to work in France. Adolf's company was sent there in July 1917. Their work was not publicised and it is hard to ascertain precisely what Alec and Adolf did. Alec's company went to France on 26th March 1917. Like many of the battalions of the Labour Corps, the I.L.C.s did not keep war diaries. In theory, they worked away from the front, and were unarmed. Their duties included such things as road and railway maintenance and repairs, or unloading railway wagons. It is known that Alec's company were working in the Nieppe Forest, south of Hazebrouck and west of Armentières, in June 1917. These companies were not safe – they were sometimes subject to attack from the air or from long-distance shelling, and there were cases of men from these companies being gassed. Restrictions were placed on where the Independent Labour companies could be posted. They were not allowed closer than sixteen kilometres from the front line, nor near Prisoner of War companies, nor any base port. Additionally, they were not allowed to move either ammunition or hay.

---

[630] *The Bournemouthian*, April 1908 p. 3; p. 5 gives further details of his exam achievement. The following term the July magazine explained that his successes had been achieved in 1906 and 1907.

Before the formation of the Labour Corps and the Infantry Labour battalions, this work was done by men who were 'resting'. Whilst that euphemism continued, the burden was reduced on the men at the front by the work of men like Adolf and Alec. Both survived the war, but although entitled to his medals, Adolf never accepted them.

Lionel Sturmer's experience was a bit different. He was born in Bloomsbury in January 1896. He attended the school from September 1907 to December 1909, when illness forced him to leave. His brother Lancelot was both a pupil (September 1903-July 1912) and also a teacher (1915-1916) at the school before enlisting in the Royal Flying Corps and serving in France for a year. Their father Herbert was a journalist and a writer. Despite the name, and the fact that they were declared 'British by parentage', their parental antecedents were originally known as von Sturmer, though born in Britain for the previous three generations at least. Lionel clearly suffered with his health, but by 1911 had secured a job as an assistant librarian with Bournemouth Corporation. On 6th July 1915 he enlisted as a private in the 23rd London Regiment which had three 23rd battalions. It is not clear into which Lionel was placed. By the time of his enlistment the 1/23rd was already fighting on the Western Front, and Lionel would have required at least a year to train. The 2/23rd landed at Le Havre in June 1916 and later moved east to Salonika and Egypt until brought back to France on 26th May 1918 and was placed in the 30th Division, 21st Brigade. The 3/23rd London Battalion was the reserve battalion based in Winchester, moving to Chisledon in November 1917, and eventually to Norfolk for the last year of the war. Lionel's record card shows that at some point he served abroad, either within the 23rd London Battalion or else within the Labour Corps. We cannot be sure that he served on the Western Front, as all details are missing, but it is likely. When he received a comparatively early discharge, on 7th March 1919, it was done on the grounds of ill-health.

Behind the Front Line: Other 'Old Boys'

Charles Austin of 315 Company A.S.C. worked hard, driving and maintaining vehicles behind the lines. He had a couple of weeks leave from 21st February to 7th March 1918, and soon after his return was promoted to corporal. In 1918 he seems to have been driving for field ambulance units: mostly attached to 48th Ambulance Care Company, although for about a month in the summer of 1918 he drove for an auxiliary petrol company for the 3rd Australian Ambulance Care Company. Each field ambulance had a sergeant, ten drivers and four officers' batmen attached from the Army Service Corps as well as an A.S.C. driver attached for duties with the cook's wagon. The 48th Field Ambulance was part of the 37th Division. Although great use was made of horses for field ambulance transport (fourteen riding and fifty-two draught and pack horses, which worked the twenty-three wagons, three water carts, three forage carts, six general service wagons, ten ambulance wagons and the cook's wagon) they also had seven motor ambulance vehicles from the end of 1914. In June 1918, his unit supported the troops near Amiens from positions just south of the city, but in August they relocated to the northern edge of the Somme battleground, south of Arras, and then followed the advance across eastwards, north of Peronne. When the Armistice occurred they were at Bristre, just north of Le Cateau, and east of Cambrai: almost where the British Army had first encountered the Germans in 1914. This means that he was behind the scenes in the offensive which had begun with the Battle of Amiens and which was to end near Le Quesnoy. Charles survived the war and in 1919 returned to England where he was released from duty in March 1919, assessed as medical category 'B2', not fit enough for front line fighting duties. He had been judged to have been sober, reliable and intelligent as a motor vehicle driver.

William Avins had the briefest of service time on the Western Front, on the coast near Dunkirk, on the edge of the offensive. The account published in the school magazine, *The Bournemouthian*, seems to have been confused or embellished. William was born in 1898 and was at the school between 1910 and 1914, leaving a few days before war was declared. He was mobilised and posted on 15th December, joining the 2/28th London (Artists' Rifles) and on 27th June 1917 was posted 2nd lieutenant in the 9th Manchester Battalion. He joined his battalion with three other young officers from the reserve on 27th September 1917. At that point the battalion, which had seen a lot of fighting over the years, was stationed in the relatively quieter area near Dunkirk on coastal defence duties. The main hazard was from enemy aircraft. On 3rd October, William was invalided sick from the battalion to the field ambulance. The school magazine said, "Second-Lieut. W.W. Avins was in action at Ypres on August 26th when he was knocked over by the concussion of a 5.9 shell. The hospital behind the lines (to which he was sent) was bombed by the enemy on November 12th, and Avins was literally blown out of bed. He has now been invalided home and appears to be making a very good recovery."[631] But he was not with the battalion on 26th August, which in any case was on church parade behind the lines, and no shelling occurred. Unfortunately, his Army record does not mention what illness he had contracted, but it must have been serious for two reasons – firstly the length of his stay in hospital, and then his fitness level being such that he was not able to return to the front afterwards. Perhaps the incident of the air raid did occur, prolonging his time in hospital. After a prolonged stay in hospital in France, at the start of January 1918 he was allowed to resign his commission on the grounds of ill-health, but was re-instated in June 1918 when he was regarded as fit enough to resume work, but not fit enough to return abroad on active service. He joined the 86th Training Reserve Battalion, created from the 31st (Reserve) Battalion of the Northumberland Fusiliers to act as a unit to train or re-train soldiers. Some of these could be men who had recovered from wounds or sickness, but who still needed time to continue to recuperate and to be helped to regain their physical fitness, although by 1918 more of the men in the unit were conscript recruits. In 1918 it was classified as a reserve battalion for the Machine Gun Corps, and was later known as 'C' Battalion M.G.C., part of the 1st Training Brigade in September 1918, and about that time, William was formally attached to the Machine Gun Corps, though he ended up in 'A' Battalion. In December 1918 he was promoted lieutenant. When he was demobilised in April 1919, at that stage he was medically classified 'B1', which meant he was well, but not fit enough for active service abroad. He too never claimed his medals.

At the start of April 1917, Harold Brooks, having recovered from the wounds he had received on the Somme, had been moved briefly to the Manitoba Regiment. Deemed only to have a fitness level of grade 'B', in May 1917 he had returned to France with the 3rd Canadian Labour Battalion after a day's leave. He was again a private – known as a sapper in his new battalion which had only been organised in January 1917 in England. They worked as pioneers and their work was essential but not glamorous. Much of the time was spent on three main tasks – cable laying, railway line creation (both narrow and broad gauge), and plank road repairs, although from September their main task was unloading ships at Dunkirk. Trench and dug-out repairs were also important. On 29th November 1917, the battalion was re-designated the 11th Battalion Canadian Railway Troops and joined an organisation which was doing incredibly important transportation work for the British and Allied war effort. On 15th December 1917 he was re-promoted to lance corporal.

The C.R.T. (Canadian Railway Troops) were indeed very important. One of the earliest tasks of

---

[631] *The Bournemouthian*, April 1918.

these Canadian railway troops (before Harold joined them) had been to supply the Belgian Army holding the line at Dixmuide north of Ypres with a light railway system. However, for a time the British authorities were hesitant about exploiting the potential of narrow gauge, light railways, partly because that might be seen in some quarters as to be taking a defensive, static view of the front, rather than a dynamic, forward-thrusting and ideally mobile image which the British had tried to maintain despite the reality of trench warfare. That attitude had changed rapidly in 1916, and then from the middle of 1917 to the end of the war all the light railway construction was done by the Canadian Railway Troops. This new job officially detached Harold and the others from the Canadian Corps. Instead, their specific command headquarters was within the British General Headquarters in France. Before Harold joined them, other battalions of the C.R.T. had pushed forward narrow gauge railways to supply the British as they followed up the German retreat to the Hindenburg Line, and then in preparation for the Battle of Arras. (Credit must be paid to the C.R.T. for the creation of a narrow gauge railway almost to the Canadian front line on Vimy Ridge despite dreadful cold and wet weather conditions and ground that was incredibly glutinous and muddy. This railway system then brought supplies and ammunitions forward to feed the attack at Vimy Ridge, and carried back the wounded to the different stages of the treatment system. Amazingly, within a week of the Battle of Vimy Ridge, the C.R.T. had a light railway running on the top of the ridge itself, carrying further rations and supplies forward to the troops who had reached the plains to the east of the ridge.)

When Harold and his comrades joined these troops, they had been trying to deal with the quagmire of the Third Battle of Ypres. They had to contend not only with the thick and squelchy mud, but also with the reality that, on average, German artillery broke a gap in the railway lines a hundred times each day, or on average four times an hour in the sectors of the British 2nd and 5th Armies. Harold and the men of the 11th Battalion were moved from Dunkirk to Neuf Berquin, west of Armentières, in mid-December 1917. Changes were immediately obvious – musketry practice was introduced, for example, even before the move. Apart from a day's rest for Christmas Day, they were soon hard at work on a new narrow gauge railway line, which required bridging the River Lys. Despite the awful weather, some days they made great progress, laying up to 1,600 yards of new track. There was clearly great satisfaction on 2nd March 1918 when their new line opened for operations with two narrow gauge engines, though much work remained to be done, and more engines and trucks followed.

The German onslaught of the spring of 1918 directly affected them, as the German heavy artillery began to shell them and to cause the first casualties they had suffered for months, and soon wounded men came back along 'their' railway to a first aid dressing station established at Neuf Berquin. The battalion was moved forward to dig new trench lines and then, later in the month, pulled right back to build new bath houses and a hospital. But in the summer of 1918 they were back making railway lines – this time a full gauge track to support Haig's planned counter-attack further south. Harold and the battalion were kept working up to and beyond the end of the war. Unlike many of the fighting battalions, they did not stop work on 11th November, and it was only on 17th November that they were allowed a day's rest. It was at this point that Harold reported sick again. The hospital re-diagnosed him with the same heart disorder as before, which he admitted had pained him for some time, though he had kept working. After again passing though the casualty system in France he was sent back to England to convalesce and he spent some time in Epsom before being discharged from the Army in March 1919. He chose not to return to Canada, but instead went back to his mother in Boscombe.

Another who served throughout 1918 in a new capacity was Stanley Seymour. On 19th August 1917, Stanley transferred back from the 6th Northamptonshire Battalion into the Royal Engineers (and was re-appointed sapper on 1st March 1918). At that point he was listed as "Proficient as a Survey Post Observer" – in the 4th Field Survey, in which unit he served for the rest of the war. The role of these R.E. field battalions had developed with the changing nature of the war. Their task was to study the topography of the battlefield and to identify which positions were being held by the Germans. Four such companies had been formed in France in March 1916. Each had several sections – a headquarters, a topographical section, a map section, an observation section and a sound-ranging section. Later they also had a map printing section. Their work would allow the artillery and infantry to attack those positions and try to pin down or eliminate the enemy. When the war had turned to deadlock with lines of trenches, the longer-range artillery could no longer always directly see their enemy targets. It became crucial to have men who were skilled in surveying the lie of the land, creating maps, and plotting enemy positions onto them. Some of this work was much aided by aerial photography from the air force, but the field survey teams played a crucial role. In 1918 they were re-organised into battalions – the 4th Field Survey Battalion worked on behalf of the 2nd Army under General Sir Herbert Plumer, and included six sound-ranging sections and six observation groups (numbers 1, 3, 6, 7, 12 and 23). They came directly under the command of the general who commanded the artillery of each of the five British armies. Stanley's role and experiences are hard to discover, although General Plumer and the 2nd Army fought their way through from Amiens to the Armistice, pushing east across France and Stanley would have been there with them, often right at the front. He survived the war and was demobilised on 3rd February 1919. Back in civilian life he took up a career in trading, to Lagos, Nigeria, in 1920.

The Reverend William Williams is one whose story is very different from the norm. Though not himself a fighter, his story is important for various reasons, not least because he won the Military Cross. He was a master at Bournemouth School from 1907 to 1912. Indeed, in January 1907 he turned out for the masters' football team in testing conditions: "several degrees of frost together with a strong and biting east wind. Only Spartans could have turned out on such a day, but though we felt like Spartans we were clad more like the people of the Artic regions."[632] Needless to say, the masters were beaten by a Boscombe team 4 - 0. In the game William played alongside others who were to serve in the war, such as Leonard Taylor and Arthur Ridley (later in the Ceylon Planters Rifles). Perhaps such conditions helped to toughen William up.

William was first interviewed for an Army chaplaincy on 9th November 1915, and at that time he was living at Langland Bay, the Mumbles, in Pembrokeshire. The Anglican parish in which he worked had a large population of 6,000, served by a team of four clergy. Most such volunteer Anglican chaplains were interviewed at the War Office in London by the Chaplain-General, Bishop John Taylor Smith. The bishop noted that William liked to preach extempore, without notes. On 22nd February 1916 he was appointed to serve as a chaplain fourth class (equivalent to a captain), after being certified fit for active service the previous day. When he finally ended his military service on 10th June 1920, his address had become St. Thomas' Rectory, Haverfordwest.

Chaplains were drawn not only from the Church of England, but also from the Roman Catholic Church, and from the free churches (often Presbyterian). One chaplain from each denomination was posted to hospitals and casualty clearing stations, and groups of four to brigades (one of each

---

[632] *The Bournemouthian*, March 1907.

type, and a fourth of the denomination of the majority of the soldiers of that brigade). William was placed in 36th Brigade in the 12th (Eastern) Division. This meant one of 'his' battalions was George Mossop's 7th Royal Sussex Battalion. He renewed his commitment to serve as a chaplain on 9th December 1916 so might well have known George. The 7th Royal Sussex Battalion was specifically mentioned in his record. During William's time as its chaplain, the battalion took part in the Battle of the Somme – fighting in the sub-battles of Albert and Pozieres as well as the Battle of Le Transloy. During his first year of service, Rev. Harry Blackburne DSO, the Assistant Chaplain General of the 1st Army, recorded his views on William's work in a series of entries: "Can form no opinion yet. March 13th /16. 9th Fusiliers. Elliott Corpew speaks well of him. March 30th /16. Doing good work. May 1st /16. An excellent chaplain in every way."[633] As chaplain he had his work cut out – the brigade and battalion fought in several phases of the Battle of Arras and the Battle of Cambrai in 1917, and it was very active too in 1918 – in the Battles of Bapaume, Amiens, Albert, Epehy, the St. Quentin Canal, and was in the final advance into Artois, ending the war in Landas in north-eastern France. In the New Year's Honours, January 1918, he was awarded the Military Cross. Needless to say, only those chaplains who had performed some outstanding action or shown outstanding commitment to service were awarded the MC. Three chaplains won the VC in the war. William must have behaved with some degree of heroism, and in 1921, in recognition of his services, was appointed Honorary Chaplain to the Forces.

The Ludendorff Offensive: On the Somme and at Ypres

Using troops released after their armistice, and later their peace treaty, with Russia, the Germans decided to try to end the war before the Americans could arrive in numbers significant enough to ensure Allied victory which, at the start of 1918, was anticipated to be impossible before about 1920. It seemed a reasonable gamble.

After a planning conference in December 1917, Ludendorff decided on a four stage attack. First, Operation 'Michael' would strike the British on the Somme at the junction of British and French forces, trying to drive a wedge between them, cutting the British off from the main French forces further south. It was believed that this might force the British to retreat to the ports, or even to evacuate France and Belgium if the other stages of the attack went well. Stage One would also force the British to reinforce their defences on the Somme by reducing them further north. A month later the Germans planned to launch their main attack – Operation 'Georgette'. In the planning, this was meant to be the killer strike. This operation was to be an attack on the Ypres Salient. With weakened forces, the British were expected to break at Ypres, and so the Germans would be able to push westwards to the ports – or at least force the British troops from the south to flood north to get out before the Germans could stop them. Either way, the British would evacuate. Two further operations would complete the German victory: 'Gneisenau' and 'Blücher-Yorck'. The idea was that if Operation 'Georgette' were halted, a further attack, Operation 'Gneisenau', on the French north of the Marne would force the Allies to pull troops south to defend the threat to Paris – allowing the northern advance on the channel ports to resume. Finally Operation 'Blücher-Yorck' would punch back through between any remaining British and French forces in the middle ground near Compiègne, and destroy all Allied hopes of resistance.

---

[633] I am indebted to David Blake, Museum Curator, Museum of Army Chaplaincy, for finding this entry in Harry Blackburne's notebook and for providing the details of William's chaplaincy record card.

The Germans were aware that they had not been able to pull as many divisions as they wanted from the east because of their on-going operations in the region, not least because they had annexed vast territories of the former Russian Empire, and needed to keep troops there to control them, but Ludendorff was still confident that this plan would win the war before the Americans arrived.

The first blow, Operation 'Michael', was therefore hurled at the junction of British and French on the Somme. Like the British and French, the Germans had been learning and perfecting new techniques. Just as they had amended their defensive tactics two years before, now they were to use an amended attacking tactic. They knew that the British had begun to emulate the German revised system of lightly-held front line trenches with scattered machine-gun posts. This meant gaps would be left in the defence line. Instead of mass attacks on the British front line, they planned to use smaller, heavily-armed groups of 'stormtroopers' to infiltrate the forward British positions and turn on the British forward positions from the flanks or even the rear, preceded and supported by heavy artillery bombardments. With the British already in disarray, the main force would move forward to occupy the British positions. They had tried this tactic out on the Eastern Front in 1916-1917 with great success.

Twice the Germans were lucky. For both Operations 'Michael' and 'Georgette', the British had limited visibility due to fog. This helped them enormously, because it meant the British forward machine-gun posts could not catch silently infiltrating troops in a cross-fire if they could not see them!

From the end of the winter the British had been expecting a major German attack. In December, a High Command dispatch had given orders "having for their object immediate preparation to meet a strong and sustained hostile offensive." When, on 17th March, it was noticed that there was a lot of movement in the German lines, and as the British commanders needed to know which units were in those trenches and in what strength, a new raid by the 17th Royal Fusiliers (in which William Mitford was serving) was sent out which got into the German trench, killed eight or ten of them, and brought back three shoulder straps so that the unit could be identified. Only one casualty was sustained in this raid. The battalion was praised for this raid, but it did not provide enough information to prevent the onslaught which followed.

Archibald Rogers for one was optimistic that the Germans would be repulsed. On 26th September 1917, he had been posted as 2nd lieutenant with No.4 Special Gas Company, part of a special brigade of the Royal Engineers. There were four special companies designated to handle gas shells, which were fired from 4-inch Stokes mortars. Each company had 48 gas weapons. No. 4 Special Company was attached to the 3rd Army. After a spell as a platoon commander in late winter of 1917-1918 he became 49th Brigade Gas Officer, within 16th Division, south of Arras. This brigade was mostly composed of Irish battalions. Writing before the attack, Archibald explained his new job in a letter to the headmaster: "I expect you know that I have acted as Brigade Gas Officer for the last few weeks and find the work much more congenial than acting as a Platoon Commander in the line. We are out resting at present and my work consists largely in visiting the units in the Brigade and watching their box respirator drill, inspecting respirators and lecturing the N.C.O.'s. I have four Battalions, a T.M.B. and M.G.C. to visit, and as the area in which they are billeted covers about 20 square miles I have my work cut out and my mornings are pretty well filled in. Of course, I have the usual difficulties to contend with. Still I hope they may be remedied. I rather enjoy lecturing the

N.C.O.'s, it's a bit like being back at school again, and altogether the work is interesting, though a bit trying when in the line."[634] In December their division had moved further south to St. Emilie, a front line area north of St. Quentin and east of Peronne where the German artillery became more and more active, registering its shells not only on the front lines but also on the back areas. Archibald described the difficult conditions in which he was now working, as well as of the senior officers amongst whom he found himself: "You must please excuse my letter if it is somewhat incoherent; for Fritz is bumping the pillbox I'm in and has been bumping for an hour and a half monotonous regularity at the rate of one shell per minute. A motley crowd of runners, etc., are collected outside in the corridors, not daring to put their noses outside, while, to the rear of us, is an 18-pounder battery, which is, I think, Fritz's objective. It is all in the day's work. A machine gunner has just literally blown into our mess, chased down the duckboards by 5.9's for about a mile, and is perspiring freely. We are trying to revive him with the usual stimulants! A night journey on the duckboards is an experience that no one wishes for if he can avoid it. I have a pretty tough proposition on at present in trying to render our Brigade area gas proof and although my job is quite an interesting one, it is by no means a sinecure. I have a R.E. corporal and 4 sappers at work, but they carry on with the energy characteristic of the British workman at his best! Also I get an awful lot of clerical work to do; in fact, I run a small 'Q' branch on my own! There is no doubt Fritz is stirring himself these days. His shelling has increased enormously this last fortnight and we get the S.O.S. going up pretty frequently nowadays. Fortunately we are well supplied with artillery, and they respond to the S.O.S. with extraordinary promptitude. I shouldn't care to be in Fritz's part of the world when they start their barrage. I don't think he will ever break through here—we've done an awful lot of work during the winter strengthening our positions, and I could tell you quite a lot about it if I were allowed to. Since I've been on Brigade H.Q., I've changed my views about the staff considerably. I don't think anyone outside has any idea of the immense amount of work to be done and Brigade Majors and Staff Captains are literally worked to death. Our Brigadier is an awfully good chap—very energetic—he's round the line every day without fail, and he's always willing to help his staff in any way that he can. Through being on Brigade, I come across gunners, R.E.'s, Flying Corps people, and in fact all sorts of people, so that I've learnt a great deal that I should not have learnt if I'd simply stayed with my Battalion as a Platoon Commander. To use a vulgar expression, I'm 'sweating' on leave now, as I'm due next on Brigade, but I don't expect to get it for at least a month, as I can't very well go on leave till my house, so to speak, is in order. Well, I must end this, our artillery has just started on the Boche, thank goodness, and he's stopped shaking this old pillbox up."[635]

Operation Michael: March 1918

At 4.40a.m. on March 21st the Germans struck. They poured a million artillery shells onto the British 5th Army and then hit hard with their stormtroopers. The British were shocked by the turn of events. The British had decided at the end of 1917 to adopt the new German defence system but they were only part way through the process of training and preparing for this new system by March 1918. This caused some chaos. Even British commanders were confused as to whether they should hold or retire from the front zone in the face of a heavy German attack. At the same time, the British were in the process of taking over an extra twenty-five mile trench line from the French.

---

[634] *The Bournemouthian*, April 1918.
[635] ibid.

The British had also decided to 'improve' the German defence system. Accordingly, the British front zone was still heavily garrisoned (to "do all in their power to maintain the ground against every attack") but with outposts and strongpoints rather than holding every section of the trench line. Provided the weather and visibility were good, cross-fire from these outposts could cut up any German advance aiming to cross between the strongpoints. British defences in the designated battle zone – up to two miles behind the front zone – were incomplete: for example, by March 1918 dug-outs had not yet been prepared in the battle zone for most British forces (including no machine-gun dug-outs). The rearward zone from which the counter-attack was meant to be launched was almost completely unprepared in March 1918 – with only some shallow trenches in double lines at some points, or even just pieces of tape to mark where trenches were to be dug when time should permit. To match the new pattern for defences, brigades were expected to use their three battalions in a new, matching, standard pattern – the two front brigades of a division were expected to place one battalion at the front; one in support in the designated battle zone; and one at the rear in reserve.

When the Germans struck in the mists of 21st March and smashed their way through the British defences, a lot of Old Bournemouthians were involved in the attempt to thwart them. When the main German assault troops followed up the stormtroop forces, British forward defences were overwhelmed or forced to flee.

At the end of January 1918, the battalion of which Reginald Winch had been a member was amalgamated with other units to become, instead of the 1/3rd London Battalion, simply the 3rd London Battalion. The War Office had been forced by a growing manpower problem to reduce the number of battalions. Even then it was not a fully manned battalion. It went into a 'swampy area' of the line again on 8th February 1918, on the River Oise, south of St. Quentin, where it spent a fortnight and suffered over forty casualties from a gas attack. On 11th March, they were strafed by three low flying enemy planes and hit by gas shells both at 8.10p.m. and at 10p.m., forcing them to wear gas masks for five hours. Yet otherwise things seemed quiet – except for the sounds of German work parties which the British supposed to be building a bridge or improving a road.

Then the German offensive of 21st March hit them like a tidal wave. On the day of the onslaught, they were in a relief phase, but that didn't last: "Offensive commenced. Battalion ordered up from Viry Noreuil. Two companies reinforced 2/4 Battalion at Fargniers, leaving Viry Noreuil at 11am. Later C Company went up to Fargniers. A Coy went to Tergnier. Effective strength 47 officers 909 OR. Weather – very misty. March 23rd. Heavy fighting. Line of Canal bank Tergnier. Battalion fell back to Noreui in evening."[636] This fighting retreat continued and on 24th March their commanding officer was wounded. By then casualties had risen to eighteen officers and three hundred and forty-one men. Eventually they were relieved by the French on 27th March, and the next day a new composite fusilier battalion was formed of remnants – though even that unit only totalled twenty-nine officers and 583 men. The next day they were needed in the line to defend Manicamp – whilst Germans swept further west to the north of them.

Close by to Reginald in the middle of March was Harold Martyn of the 2nd Wiltshire Battalion. By then Harold was a captain, in command of 'D' Company. On 17th March 1918, the battalion was ordered to hold the front line near St. Quentin, from the canal on their right to the St. Quentin-Savy

---

[636] War Diary, 3rd London Battalion, 21st March 1918.

road on their left. This was part of the line which the British had taken over from the French during the past two months.[637] The battalion placed two companies, including Harold's, in trenches at the front on either side of the Roupy road, each with a platoon forward of the remainder of the companies. Behind these companies, in dug-outs off a sunken road, was a third company, designated the 'counter-attack company'. The fourth company formed a 'keep' on a small hill and guarded the battalion HQ with all-round defences. A little less than two miles to their north the 16th Manchesters had a similar 'keep'. "It was hoped that, should all defences in the front break down, these two keeps, with our artillery putting down a barrage between them, would hold up the enemy in this gap, while the troops in the battle zone would break up any attack in rear and then counter-attack to regain the forward zone."[638]

On 19th March, "Information was received from prisoners captured that the enemy was expected to attack on the night 20/21st inst., and preparations were made accordingly. At 10pm gas was emitted from our front line. No enemy retaliation was forthcoming."[639] Actually, this happened because an accident had occurred. About ninety yards in front of the forward line, and guarded constantly, the engineers had placed 3,000 gas projectors, and that night they were fired accidentally without first withdrawing the guards, who fortunately were unharmed as the projectors all worked and carried their gas shells into St. Quentin to explode. The next day the officers were told by the commander of the 2nd Yorkshires that the German attack was expected within the next twenty-four hours. "His information was that there would be ten hours' bombardment, including mustard gas, before the attack was launched. He... was not optimistic... After the news had spread round the ranks, officers and men alike, although they knew they were up against it, were very cheerful. Everyone was determined to make the Hun pay heavily for any of their trenches they attacked."[640] Despite the warnings, the battalion was hit hard when the assault occurred. At 4.30a.m., the German bombardment hit the battalion. For five hours it was intense and mixed with gas. Trench mortars also piled in. The explosions added smoke and fog to the heavy ground mist. At 10a.m. two German divisions attacked the battalion front. "Owing to the dense mist which prevailed [they] broke through on our flanks surrounding the Battalion in spite of the strong resistance which was offered."[641]

It was a desperate battle, and the adjutant writing the war diary from within the headquarters group in reserve did not know much of what was happening. He continued: "No definite information was forthcoming owing to the Battalion being cut off but a message was received by pigeon carrier at 1.30pm from Lt. Col. A.V.P. Martin to the effect that he was still holding out in the Redoubt with 50 men. The Battalion transport moved back from Fluquieres to Dury at 4.30[pm] and again moved at 11pm to Esmery Hallon. St. Quentin... 22nd March. No news received from the Battalion. Enemy were reported advancing on our right flank." The circumstances were exceptional, and it took time for the full horror of effectively the loss of most of the battalion to

---

[637] Many of the details following are based on the account in *The Second Battalion Wiltshire Regiment (99th): A Record of their Fighting in the Great War, 1914-1918*, p. 135 onwards.

[638] *The Second Battalion Wiltshire Regiment (99th): A Record of their Fighting in the Great War, 1914-1918*, p. 135.

[639] War Diary, 2nd Wiltshire Battalion, 19th March 1918.

[640] *The Second Battalion Wiltshire Regiment (99th): A Record of their Fighting in the Great War, 1914-1918*, p. 137.

[641] War Diary, 2nd Wiltshire Battalion, 21st March 1918.

filter through. The author of the history of the battalion continued his account of the day: "It was afterwards known that the actual force which attacked 'C' and 'D' Companies of the 2nd Wiltshires was two divisions. They did not make a frontal attack, but assaulted the Battalion's front on each flank, and were able practically to surround the two front companies and 'B' Company before they were seen. Actually, 'C' and 'D' Companies were attacked from the rear. They put up the strongest resistance possible, and undoubtedly did the Hun great harm. But, of course, before such masses the thing was impossible. They were quickly overwhelmed, and our men either killed or captured. A runner from 'C' Company succeeded in getting away and carrying this news."[642]

Harold Martyn was killed. 2nd Lieutenant C.D. Baker wrote to say, "All I know about him is that Mr. Hubert, the other officer in our company who was captured and is now in another lager – I don't know where – told me when I saw him 2 days after we were captured that Martyn was shot by a machine gun bullet in the head and must have died instantaneously. At the time I was captured I was in a small post in the front observation line and had not seen the Captain since 3am that morning when I left Headquarters to go around the trenches. The Company Head Quarters where he was killed was on top of Epine D'Allon near the Ham-St. Quentin road and about ¼ mile from St. Quentin. I was very sorry when Hubert told me, for Capt. Martyn was the best officer I have served under – a fine Company Commander and beloved by all the ranks."[643] The confusion can be understood when it is realised that the battalion was wiped out – even the keep taken (not having been helped by the British artillery shelling it when they assumed it must have fallen already!). Harold's Army file contains several eye witness statements about his death, which agree he was killed though not on when or how he died. "I saw him killed outright in the trench at St. Quentin about 8.30am on the 21st" stated Private Nelson Smith. "The Bosche was on the parapet and parados when I saw one of them throw an egg bomb on the Capt. from behind. I turned him over to see if alive but he had been killed outright." Another statement was sought out with the assistance of the Germans and the Red Cross from prisoner of war 2nd Lieutenant H.J. Hubert who could only confirm that Harold had been killed, and later two statements were made by a Private J. Windsor. In a statement given at Dunraven Castle Red Cross Hospital on 9th December 1918, Private Windsor said, "On March 21st about 2.30 pm at St. Quentin I was standing in a trench (we were No.14 Platoon C Coy) and looking over a parapet where No.15 Platoon were stationed. I saw a shell drop and kill an officer. Afterwards one of the men of No.15 Platoon came over to us and informed me that the officer just killed was Capt Martyn who would have soon been transferred to another Coy. As far as I know, no identification disc was taken off the officer. The body was roughly buried and immediately… No.15 Platoon had orders to move on."[644] This statement showed some confusion in Private Windsor's mind, however, as previously on 26th October, when questioned whilst wounded and on a hospital ship sailing from Le Havre, he was reported to have said, "He was O.C. of B Coy. on the 21st March during the retreat from St. Quentin, Captain Martyn during the morning was in a trench near me, when a shell got him full, blowing his body badly about. Death was instantaneous. His body had to be left as we were retreating." Harold's body was never recovered, so he is now commemorated on the Pozières Memorial to over 14,000 Britons and 300 South Africans, from the period 21st March to 7th August 1918, with no named grave. Unfortunately, Harold was not the only Old Bournemouthian whose body was lost in the attack.

---

[642] *The Second Battalion Wiltshire Regiment (99th): A Record of their Fighting in the Great War, 1914-1918*, p. 139.
[643] Army File of Harold Martyn, WO 339/54017.
[644] ibid.

Captain Arthur Hame was also swept away in this attack. By 1915 he was already a highly experienced soldier. Amazingly, given the seriousness of his wound that year, he returned to service in France on 8th July 1915 now as an artillery officer. He must have been highly regarded: he only officially applied for a commission on 6th July 1915, but was gazetted 2nd lieutenant on 9th July 1915. As he went through the war, so he gained in experience and was promoted full lieutenant on 14th September 1917 with seniority dated from 1st July 1917. On 10th May 1917 he was posted to 'B' Echelon of the 59th Division Artillery, but within days was switched to the 42nd Division Artillery. On 7th July 1917 he was posted to Y42 Trench Mortar Battery. At the time the division was on the Somme battlefield, but on 31st August they moved up to the Ypres Salient, having spent much of August training for their part in the Third Battle of Ypres. A few days later, on 7th September, he joined No.1 Section, 42 Divisional Artillery at the time when the division was moving its brigades into the front line. By the end of the month the division had been moved north to protect Nieuwpoort and the coast. They remained there until the end of November when they moved further south to the Béthune area. On 3rd December he was posted to 7th Corps, Royal Artillery and then on 8th December was posted to X21 but allowed leave in the United Kingdom first, from 17th December to the end of the year. He was promoted to captain whilst commanding X21 Trench Mortar Battery on 2nd January 1918 and returned from his last leave two days later on 4th January 1918. When he joined the 21st Division it was stationed east of the Somme battleground, north-east of Péronne.

He was a specialist in heavy trench mortars. The systematic development of trench mortars had only started in the British Army in the first half of 1915. Heavy trench mortars were attached to divisions rather than battalions. Although their operators were specialists, they remained members of their own regiments from which they had been drawn. So Arthur was 'attached' to X Battery of 21st Division Heavy Mortar Brigade, in a battery of six medium 6-inch mortars within 21st Divisional Artillery. On 20th March, the intelligence summary for the 62nd Brigade, part of 21st Division to which Arthur now belonged, ominously reported, "Visibility has been extremely bad and except at rare intervals when the rain ceased and the mist lifted for a short time, observation of the enemy's activity has been impossible. The movement on the Banteaux road reported in yesterday's summary continued and small parties were seen at intervals up to 6pm always in full marching order and mostly approaching Gonnelieu."[645] "At 4.45am on March 21st, a day of heavy mist, an intense bombardment was opened on the forward system along the whole front, together with heavy shelling of all artillery positions and back areas. The bombardment lasted over four hours, developing towards the end into a more intense barrage."[646] Arthur was killed that day, 21st March 1918, presumably in this bombardment. (Ironically the Commonwealth War Graves Commission has wrongly registered the death as 21st May 1918, but the various letters and notes in his Army file make the correct date clear.) His body was lost. Today he is one of those commemorated on the Soissons Memorial to those killed during the Battles of the Aisne and Marne 1918 and who have no known grave.

Captain Maurice Hellier was another company commander caught up in these attacks. On 19th March they had been relaxing behind the lines, at Cugny, south-west of St. Quentin, where various men were receiving medal ribbons for their contribution to the Battle of Cambrai, but by 21st March they were desperately trying to hang on despite the casualties. Maurice was in command of 'B' Company.

---

[645] Intelligence Summary in the War Diary, 62nd Infantry Brigade, 62nd Division, 20th March 1918.
[646] War Diary, 62nd Infantry Brigade, 62nd Division, 21st March 1918.

The first alarm was received on 20th March, but it was on the afternoon of 21st March that the battalion left Cugny in battle order and took up station a little south of the road which stretches between St. Quentin and Ham, at Bray St. Christophe. Here they were a little north of the River Somme and positioned to block the German advance. Their first night was quiet, but "The morning of March 22nd was very misty, and the situation quiet; but the troops holding the line in front stood to, expecting an attack. At about 1.30pm the mist cleared and the Hun attacked and drove in the Irish Regiments who were holding the line in front. The Corps was now very thickly held by men of the R.I.Rs and Inniskillings who had retired back. At about 4pm the Hun came on, and in places pushed us out of the front line, especially on the right where he had succeeded in working down the canal and getting well in on the right flank. He also succeeded in getting round the left by the 12 R.B. and getting behind D Company's keep platoon, and so cutting off a great number of the Company. At 7.15 the R.I.Rs and Inniskillings retired, and I think that the Hun got the idea that the whole line had retired, as he could see the Irish Regiments withdraw. He then pushed on in the valley on the right, and opened fire with his machine guns getting enfilade fire. At 7.30 pm, the situation had reached a very critical stage, and the order was sent up to the Companies to withdraw to the Bray St. Christophe Line."[647] They had spent 22nd March fighting in the rear zone defences at Bray St. Christophe and at dusk had received orders to withdraw as the battalion was concentrating a little further west along the road to Ham, where the Royal Engineers had managed to dig out some posts across the road for them to occupy. At this stage, Maurice's company was in the centre of the line, with 'C' Company to their right and 'D' Company to their left. Behind them, in support, lay 'A' Company.

For a time Maurice was able to maintain contact with the supporting companies, and he sent about a third of his company back to Battalion Headquarters to collect rations and water, and to report their position. However, that evening the mist descended again and they lost touch with the flanking companies, though he sent out a patrol to try to regain contact. At about 1a.m. Maurice heard shouting and bugle calls coming from the rear, where the Battalion HQ lay, and at that moment he realised that the Germans had not only outflanked his position but were about a mile behind him. He also realised that the division had not managed to hold the line which he and his company were occupying, because there had been no sound of fighting from his flanks. He had had orders to hold that line at all costs but decided on his own initiative to try to get his company back to re-join the battalion. Later he realised that 'C' Company must have retired about half an hour before he realised he was cut off. 'A' Company had already retreated, but he did regain touch with what was left of 'D' Company.

In fact, the fighting had already been lost. The report in the war diary continued: "At about midnight, A and D companies were surprised by enemy patrols who creeping up under cover of the mist opened fire with their machine guns... Col. Welch... decided to attack them with Battn HQrs. He led this attack himself and charged the enemy, but the position he held was strong, we were forced to retire. D Coy, by this time had also got disorganised while the enemy had got in behind B Coy and had taken practically the whole company with all officers prisoner."

How had this happened? In the middle of the night Maurice had begun to march his men back in the dark. "I marched the Company & a portion of D Coy through the German troops, keeping off roads and tracks, and reached a point about 1½ miles E. of Ham. The men were in a very exhausted

---

[647] From a report included within the War Diary, 6th Shropshire Light Infantry.

condition having been on duty since dawn 21st March & no water or rations for over 12 hours. At this point I was forced to cross the main Ham road to locate my position and encountered enemy troops and transport. Large reserves were also further down the road."[648] The thick mist which had cut him off in the night was lifting, and visibility was increasing rapidly. He had about one hundred men, and a German column stood in front of him, and another was marching up rapidly behind him. He was the senior officer, though he had with him two lieutenants from 'D' Company and two 2nd lieutenants from his own company. None of the officers had been wounded, but everyone was exhausted. "The position of our own troops at that time being as far as one could judge on the Canal at Ham, there was no chance of breaking through and no alternative but capture except wholesale massacre of exhausted men." So Maurice surrendered his unit and he and his men were taken as prisoners of war. He was sent to a prisoner of war camp in West Prussia. The conditions he experienced as a prisoner may not have been too severe as, when on 19th December 1918 he was returned to the United Kingdom, he was medically examined and found to be fully fit. He was required both to write an account of his actions that night, from which these sections have been extracted, and also to be interviewed by three senior officers in a commission of enquiry. He was demobilized on 11th March 1919 and on 15th May he received a letter officially exonerating him from any blame for the surrender. He had survived.

Arthur Elcock was born in Bournemouth in 1899 and began at the school in 1913. He was still at school when the war began. After initially leaving to become an apprentice at Boots the Chemist at the end of 1915, Arthur returned for an extra term from September 1916 until he left that Christmas, first to help his father, and then to join the Army Training Reserve. Later he served in the 2nd Devonshire Battalion, in the 23rd Brigade, 8th Division. In January 1918, the battalion served in the Ypres Salient. An NCO and five men joined the battalion on 18th February, whilst another fifty-eight men arrived on 7th March, and seven more men on 14th March. It is probable that Arthur joined them then, joining 'C' Company. If so, this a relatively quiet time for the battalion though eight men had fallen victim to gas shelling whilst they were in reserve trenches on 20th February, and there was some excitement when 'A' and 'C' Companies launched a 'dummy' raid on 3rd March to confuse the Germans whilst the 2nd Middlesex Battalion, on their flank, made a raid in earnest which was successful. The 2nd Devonshire Battalion came out of the line on 4th March and returned to Brandhoek, about half-way on the road between Poperinghe and Ypres. Here, on successive days, hundreds of men were deployed to help on building up the defences near Wieltje in anticipation of the anticipated German offensive. On 22nd March they suddenly received orders to make a route march to Wizernes, across the border in France and there to entrain for the south. Overnight the train trundled down to the southern Somme area and they detrained the next day at Chaulnes, south of the river and of Peronne, and due west of St. Quentin. On arrival they were "immediately rushed into the line in front of Villers Carbonnel"[649] astride the direct road between St. Quentin and Amiens, on the banks of the river just before it turned west near Peronne. They were in action almost immediately, beating off several German attacks on 24th March. The next day, however, they were forced to withdraw westwards along the road to Estrées. Then, on 26th March, the battalion was in brigade support as the brigade tried to mount a defence on a line north-south through Rosières, a couple of miles west of Chaulnes.

The climax for the battalion came on 27th March: "Battalion was called upon to counter-attack

---

[648] Maurice's own account, in his Army File, WO 339/19694.
[649] War Diary, 2nd Devonshire Battalion, 23rd March 1918.

through Harbonnières which they did with great success. Details which were left behind were also called out and successfully beat back an attack just n. of Rosières."[650] Though this counter-attack was called a success, the next day they were in line a mile further west at Caix. The battalion was withdrawn from the defensive battle on 29th March, and when the casualties were reckoned up it was found that (including men detached to the 23rd Trench Mortar Battery) sixteen officers had been killed, wounded or gone missing, whilst at least 304 men had likewise suffered. However, Arthur had survived.

William Mitford of the 17th Royal Fusiliers also fought against Operation 'Michael'. His unit was slightly further north and west of St. Quentin. The day before the attack they had observed a number of German staff officers in their front line trenches, and also hundreds of men moving in or out of those trenches in full pack as well as machine guns being brought up to the front and support lines. However, they had been relieved and sent back into reserve at Rocquigny, south-east of Bapaume and north of Peronne that night and so were not at the front when the storm broke.

On 22nd March they moved a little way forward, and the next day established what the British called 'the Green Line' near the village of Bus which they hoped to hold to destroy the German advance. By this time the brigade was not very strong: there were only 428 men and sixteen officers available in the 17th Royal Fusiliers and the other battalions were no better off: 1st King's (Liverpool) had 410 men and twenty officers, and the 2nd South Staffordshires had 529 and 21 officers. By 2a.m. the 17th Royal Fusiliers were 'standing to' anticipating an imminent attack. Their position was not good. The brigade diary recorded their fall-back line as "old German wire with a few lengths of trench dug west of the wire"[651] although later the trench was dug to a depth of about four feet – little more than a ditch. At 10a.m. and at 1p.m. in their forward line, they were heavily shelled; and at 4.30p.m. they realised the Germans were already at Bus as shells fell all round them. Threatened with being outflanked from the south, they withdrew a short distance west to the fall-back line and only fought off a German attack at 10p.m. with some difficulty.

Over the next days, the Germans maintained the pressure. The brigade war diary describes the Germans as advancing in large numbers under a heavy barrage and supported by light trench mortars and machine guns. It also reported that the British inflicted heavy German losses with rifle and Lewis gun fire – but not enough to stop the German advance. On 24th March, the 17th Royal Fusiliers were the last to withdraw in their sector, fighting hard and briefly taking a new stand at Ligny Thilloy, before continuing the westwards retreat until they were moving down the Bapaume to Albert road. The next morning the battalions of their brigade tried to hold a position between Pys and Le Sars and to hold off the on-coming Germans but soon they realised that the Germans were outflanking them to the south through Le Sars. After a brief counter-attack, near Miraumont which was followed by a heavy German attack, they again retreated, now joined by men from lots of different battalions caught up in the retreat. That night they paused near Hamel, just south of the River Ancre. The next day they fell back on Beaumont-Hamel and then on to Aveluy Wood and had two days of comparative respite, though their positions in the wood were shelled again on 30th March.

By that stage the entire brigade was being commanded and operating as if they were only a couple

---

[650] War Diary, 2nd Devonshire Battalion, 27th March 1918.
[651] War Diary, 6th Infantry Brigade, 22nd March 1918.

of companies in total. The casualty figures tell a stark story. The Brigadier – who had also taken command of 5th Brigade temporarily – reported that both 5th and 6th Brigades were reduced to about one hundred and fifty fighting men each by 25th March. Between 20th and 31st March the battalion had lost two officers and twenty-two men definitely killed; eight officers and one hundred and six men wounded; eight more men were known to have been wounded and then gone missing, and a further one hundred and seventy-seven men were missing. There was not much left of the battalion, but William had survived.

From this point the battalion was no longer placed in the main line of the German advance or battle, and it was a question of holding on, regrouping, re-supplying, training and making preparations. The attention had moved both further south and further north. When, in the summer, Haig launched his offensive to drive back the Germans, the 17th Royal Fusiliers were initially in support. William Mitford's comrades found themselves caught up in the Battle of Bapaume, but William had come out of the line on 7th August 1918, probably wounded. He was eventually discharged from the Army on 25th January 1919.

Even the Pioneers were caught up by this attack. Amongst them was Captain Edwin Hill, with the 8th Royal Sussex Battalion (Pioneers). In the new year of 1918 Edwin and the battalion had come south to the British lines opposite the Hindenburg Line east of Peronne. Their work, especially that of improving the defence line continued. They salvaged pickets from further back and screwed them in again in front of the new lines, and strung the wire, although suffering casualties. The battalion was reorganised into three companies rather than four. Edwin was a captain, probably in command of 'B' Company. They were reminded that as soldiers they needed to be prepared to fight but mostly they worked away, digging posts for the new system battle zone.

All that suddenly changed on 20th March. At 3p.m. that day they suddenly assumed 'battle positions' south of St. Quentin. The next day, March 21st, was a day unlike any other they had experienced, as their war diary made clear: "HQ Coy – Manned Battle Positions at 5.15 am and remained there all day. A Coy – Heavy Barrage on Remigny at 4.30 am. Coy moved off to Battle positions at 5.45 am. Company maintained Switch and held up enemy attack throughout day. B Coy – Manned Battle Positions at 5.15 am and remained there all day. C Coy – Left Remigny at 6 am and manned Battle Positions; work was carried on when possible. 2 platoons sent forward to reinforce A Coy about 6 pm."[652] The next day they retreated south-westwards, crossing the St. Quentin Canal. That day the different companies fought a defensive action, at one stage in conjunction with the 8th East Surreys. Each of the next days saw them continue a fighting retreat, now alongside the 7th Bedfords. The battalion was in danger of splitting up in the crisis – 'C' Company even found itself temporarily acting separately and attached to the 54th Brigade. They did manage to reunite on 26th March, and made their way back until eventually they were transported out of the action. At the end of these dreadful days, the officers had been hit but not as badly as the men: one officer had died of his wounds, three were wounded, and one missing (believed captured); but of the men, at least eleven were killed, ninety wounded, and eight missing. Edwin had come through unwounded. The survivors were immediately put to work at Boves, east of Amiens, digging new strongpoints and trenches, setting up new wire, and doing their best to prepare for the coming onslaught. Even here, there were casualties, wounded and men killed. Edwin was 'Mentioned in Dispatches' on 24th May for his part in the fighting retreat.

---

[652] War Diary, 8th Sussex Battalion (Pioneers), 21st March 1918.

Another man working with the Pioneers in 1918 during this German onslaught was Frank Hayes. From his Army Medals Roll, we know that, after recovering from the wound he received early in 1917, Frank had gone on to serve as a corporal in the 19th Middlesex Battalion, a Pioneer battalion, which originally had landed in France on 2nd May 1916. It had gone to Italy, but returned to France in March 1918. It made sense to send Frank to this battalion rather than return him to his old battalion, because he had not fully regained the use of his arm and his fitness. From 19th to 22nd March they were working on the system of defences in the Arras area, but when the storm of the Ludendorff Offensive broke they were called back once more into the line. They found themselves under attack near Bapaume on 25th March. Although they reckoned to have inflicted heavy casualties upon the attacking Germans, they too were forced to fall back at the end of the day. By 30th-31st March they had retreated as far as Ablainzevelle near Gommecourt. In early April they were switched to the Ypres Salient where they were put to work, initially creating defensive positions, and then on roads and tracks, or on digging new communication trenches. This was their work through the summer but in the autumn they followed the advance, working especially to assist the artillery advance. The Armistice found them working on bridging the River Scheldt. After the war they were moved by train into Germany where they put to work guarding bridges and important buildings, especially in Cologne. Corporal Frank Hayes survived.

A bit further north, William Webber of the 1st Artists' Rifles, joined by Joseph Lonsdale, and Edgar Ayling of Drake Battalion (both in the 63rd Royal Navy) Division also had a hard time fighting to try to stem the German advance.

Joseph had been a company quartermaster sergeant in the 2/5th London Battalion, which had suffered heavily casualties in 1917 and seen its numbers fall as a result. At the end of the year it seemed that the numbers were being replenished, but after a further month of training, they had received orders on 27th January that the battalion was to be disbanded. On 29th January 1918, Joseph was in a group of half the officers and 450 men of 'C' and 'D' Companies transferred to the 1/28th London (Artists' Rifles). When they joined the 1/28th London Battalion it was at Beaulencourt, just south of Bapaume on the Somme.

In the middle of February the 63rd (Royal Naval) Division, including the 1/28th London Battalion within 190th Brigade, was pulled further back into reserve at Fesquières – still in the Cambrai region but about eight miles behind the front line. On the right, to the south, was the 47th Division, which itself stood next to the most northerly units of General Gough's 5th Army. About this time, William was given what was to be his final UK leave, but he was back with the battalion in the middle of March. Able Seaman Edgar Ayling had never fully recovered from his illnesses, but he had continued to serve in France with Howe Battalion until the battalion too was 'dispersed' and the men sent to different units. On 22nd February 1918 he was placed in the 7th Entrenching Battalion of the Royal Naval Division, and then transferred from that to 'A' Company, Drake Battalion on 14th March 1918.

From March 12th, the Germans had been bombarding the British lines with gas shells, and the division suffered 2,000 casualties when the Germans unleashed their Operation Michael offensive in the early mists of 21st March. Drake Battalion was in the trenches in front of Ribecourt, a village about 10 kilometres south-west of Cambrai. According to Drake Battalion's war diary, the first they knew of the attack was a "heavy gas bombardment of Unseen Trench system for 5 hours with mustard gas and Ribecourt with Phosgene gas".[653] Then from 9a.m. there were three hours of a

---

[653] The account is described with excerpts taken from the War Diary, Drake Battalion, Royal Naval Division, 21st-25th March, 1918 and from the War Diary of the 190th Brigade, 63rd Division, 22nd-24th March 1918.

heavy barrage of all kinds of shells which particularly targeted the support system and Ribecourt. Drake battalion now began several nightmare days of fighting. "By 11:00 am the enemy was in possession of 20 sight posts of front line battalion." In the mad see-saw of war, the battalion was now relieved by Hawke Battalion in Neet Trench, a move which was completed by 9p.m.

William and Joseph's battalion had been in support when the attack started, but whilst they were there they had "been exposed to a protracted shelling, with gas, and then, without food or rest, had returned to the line".[654] They were ordered to advance to help, and ran "plump into the arms of the enemy! For several hours we had been marching at ease in apparent security, and were therefore taken completely by surprise on the first challenge in a foreign tongue. We scattered in open order on to the fields on either side of the road, and lay flat awaiting developments. A sergeant shouted out that he knew the place as the site of an Indian Labour Corps encampment. An officer and one or two men went forward, calling out that we were English! and were promptly shot. The fight that followed remains in my recollection as a confused medley of bursting bombs, rifle and machine-gun fire."[655] The support companies of Drake Battalion started to withdraw at 10p.m. Unusually, the brigade – although exhausted and suffering the effects of the gas shells – managed to hold its position to the end of the day with relatively few casualties, but because the brigades on either flank had been driven back they too were ordered to retreat that night. First, the 1st Artists' Rifles destroyed their gas projectiles by placing them in dug-outs which were then blown up. The division was still in a fighting condition, and planned a counter-attack but this was called off when it was realised how much damage had been inflicted on the neighbouring units.

By 3a.m., the next day, Drake Battalion had "successfully withdrawn to the Unseen Trench system until 10:00 am when German scouts were seen coming through the village and across the open. At 10:00 pm we commenced our withdrawal to Neuville. Rearguard left Unseen Trench system at 12:30 am 23rd March." William and Joseph's unit lay across the path of the German advance, protecting the retreat – "22/3/18. The 7/RF and 4/Bedfords are now located side by side in the Intermediate System, each two companies in the front and two in Support. 1/Artists in Second System. TMB in Intermediate System. Fairly Quiet in the early morning and very misty."[656] The next day, 23rd March, in the early hours, Drake Battalion again retreated – "At 02:30 am we evacuated the old British front line (Hermies-Trescault Line) and proceed via Trescault and Plank road through Havrincourt Wood & Neuville, where we arrived at 5 am. Battalion moved at 5 am in the direction of Ytres and at 1 pm commenced to dig in in front of Ytres." "23/3/18. Brigade ordered to withdraw to the second system and later to Metz Switch owing to the situation on our flank." At this point, a little south-west of Bapaume, Drake Battalion again attempted to make a stand to hold off the German advance – on their right was the 190th Brigade (including William) and Hood Battalion was to their left. There was a brief lull before the Germans caught up with them. "All quiet until 4 pm when light shells were fired into the village. By 9 pm 47th Div had withdrawn from the right of 190th Bde, leaving flanks open to the enemy. Offensive flank was formed by swinging back 190th Bde, and A & D Coys of Drake through RE Dump, Ytres and along the Bus-Ytres Rd. This was completed by 8 pm." The manoeuvre of swinging round to change front was not, however, sufficient to halt the Germans. So the retreat was resumed the next morning, 24th March. "We

---

[654] *Memories of Private R.G. Bultitude, 1st Battalion Artists' Rifles.* First published in *Everyman at War* (1930), edited by C.B. Purdom and displayed on www.firstworldwar.com website.

[655] ibid.

[656] War Diary, 190th Brigade, 63rd Division, 22nd-24th March 1918.

commenced to withdraw at 8 am, under MG barrage and HE shrapnel to Beaulencourt via Barastre. After 2 hours rest we withdrew from Beaulencourt about 3 pm and proceeded to a position in High Wood, via Flers. Our casualties up to this time were extremely light. Lt Com Turrell MC 'missing', presumed killed, T/Surgeon HAH McKerron missing, believed PoW. No rations received on this day. A large German patrol proceeded along valley on far side of High Wood." "24/3/18. Brigade continued to withdraw fighting line by line in conjunction with remainder of the army. During the night troops on our right were driven in leaving our right open. We threw out a defensive flank but enemy succeeded in getting round 3 sides and part of the 4th. We were able to withdraw next morning."[657]

The 1/28th London Battalion (1st Artists' Rifles), and the division was in retreat – and as they did so, in what the official histories describe as in good order, they performed a complex set of movements whereby the battalions took it to turn to hold a temporary line whilst the others retired back through the positions formed. At each point the British fought with determination to hold off the advancing Germans with machine-gun and artillery fire. From about 23rd March they were back on the old Somme battlefields and had lost touch with the 5th Army to the south – the Germans were driving a wedge between the British armies.

They were now back on the old Somme battlefield of July 1916, which must have added to the depression caused by a lack of sleep and being continuously driven back. Edgar and the others might have welcomed the fact that the night of 24th-25th March was "An exceptionally quiet night". But 25th March 1918 turned out to be another terrible day. "By 7 am our right flank was again exposed owing to withdrawal of 47th Div. From daybreak onwards rifle and MG fire was carried on. At 9 am Drake Bn advanced 250 yds and captured 3 MG's, 1 of which was turned on the retiring enemy. About 10 am orders were received to withdraw to ridge behind village of Martinpuich (Courcelette Rd). This was successfully carried out but with heavy losses."

Edgar Ayling was found to be missing on 25th March 1918 in the fighting near High Wood. In the early hours of the next morning the battalion was again retreating, and a relief came only at the end of the next day. There was no opportunity at the time to seek out the bodies of those who fell during that bitter period. In the end, his body was never found, so he was commemorated on the Arras Memorial.

The 189th Brigade had made a determined stand against the advancing Germans which, however, only delayed them for hours and that night they were retreating through Courcelette. On 26th March, William Webber and his comrades had the disquieting experience of once again standing on the west bank of the Ancre where the battalions had stood in 1916. The division finally held a line on the Mesnil Ridge, almost west across the valley from Thiepval. They fell back towards Aveluy Wood. The 63rd Division had been hit badly. From the start of the preliminary bombardment with gas to March 27th when they were attempting to consolidate in Aveluy Wood on the Mesnil Ridge, the division lost six thousand men and four battalion commanders. Most battalions – despite some hastily rushed forward replacements – were down to two hundred and fifty men (including men pulled off transport or headquarter duties, or drafted in from remnant groups of other battalions). William, Joseph, and the 1st Artists' Rifles survived and stayed in this precarious position, trying to consolidate the new line, until the division was relieved by a reorganised 17th Division on April 15th. They had then been in action continuously for about twenty-four days. Between 21st March

---

[657] War Diary, 190th Brigade, 63rd Division, 22nd-24th March 1918.

and 3rd April they had had lost six officers and eighteen men killed; eight officers and 135 men wounded; and four officers and 129 men went missing. The battalion remained on the defensive though it received a boost between 7th and 9th April when reinforcements were received as other battalions were closed down.

At Aveluy Wood, William and Joseph came to a position where George Mossop and the 7th Royal Sussex Battalion had been digging defence positions. (William Mitford with the 17th Royal Fusiliers also fell back to the wood at this stage.) Two days before the others reached the wood, George and his comrades had begun their hurried preparations. After the Battle of Cambrai, the 7th Royal Sussex Battalion had been pulled back to positions on the Somme near Albertand. On 26th December, George had temporarily left the battalion with thirty men for an attachment to 70th Coy R.E. for work in the forward area but he was with them again by the spring. On 25th March the battalion returned to Warloy, west of Albert, and was immediately rushed forward. By 6.30a.m. the next morning they were in position, attempting to guard the Ancre crossings north of Aveluy and Albert and preparing defensive lines: "26/3/1918. Positions established by about 6.30am. Bn frontage from S. end of Aveluy Wood to Black Horse Bridge. Dispositions – C & D Coys Front Line; A & B in support. 11.30pm Report received that enemy had broken thro on the left of the Bn sector. A defensive flank as formed by the left support Coy. Aveluy Wood. 27/3/1918. About 9am the enemy attacked on our right & the Bn on our right fell back. A Coy formed a defensive flank along the S. edge of Aveluy Wood & later B Coy were also put in on our right flank to bridge a gap between D & A Coy. The Bn was now formed on 2 sides of a square – C & D facing E, & A & B facing S. About 5pm enemy attacked on the whole front & succeeded in breaking into the wood on the SE Corner. A Coy retired slightly, killing a large number of the enemy. 2/Lt Rogers was taken prisoner but succeeded in escaping. D Coy retired on Bn HQ which were at Quarry Post. The attack was held up at Bn HQ which were temporarily surrounded. 28/3/1918. During the night 27/28 the line was readjusted. A & D on the Left in touch with R Wks, & B coy in Quarry Post. No news was heard of C coy. During the morning the enemy attacked & drove in the line slightly. A counter attack restored the position. B Coy at Quarry Post completely repulsed the enemy. During the afternoon, touch was joined with C Coy & B Coy. After dusk a continuous line was formed across Aveluy Wood, facing SE from Quarry Post exclusive, which was taken over by the 9th RF to the right of the OX & Bucks (2nd Div). B coy were in support."[658] They had held up the German advance.

The next day, the 7th Royal Sussex Battalion was pulled back from the line to recuperate. In the circumstances of such desperate fighting, their losses had been relatively light: one officer and eighteen men killed, and five officers and seventy-three men wounded. A further twenty-four men were missing, believed taken prisoner. On 2nd April they were sent back into the line north of Albert. In the afternoon of 4th April German artillery fire became intense, and the next morning the Germans again attacked them. George was not so lucky this time. "5/4/18. 7am. Enemy attacked all along the Front. Barrage heavy and considerable gas used. C Coy was sent to support 9th RF on the left. Enemy penetrated front held by 5th R Berks. A & B Coys counter-attacked (under 5th R Berks) at 8.45pm. Attack unsuccessful. Bn relieved 5th R Berks during the night. Lieut Collins missing. 2 Lt Mossop wounded. 6/4/18 Relief complete 4am. C Coy Left Front Line. D Coy Right Front Line. A & B Coys, amalgamated, in support. "[659]

George had been wounded. There is no detail, and his evacuation is not recorded. When the

---

[658] War Diary, 7th Royal Sussex Battalion, 26th-28th March 1918.

[659] War Diary, 7th Royal Sussex Battalion, 2nd-5th April 1918.

battalion was relieved later on 6th April their total casualties had been the two officers and 127 men. Once again we have uncertainty as to what happened to George next. The war diary does not mention him again until September 1918, so we do not know how seriously he was wounded, nor when he returned – if indeed he ever left the battalion. The summer of 1918 could have been when (and if) he was with the 12th Royal Sussex. His surviving Army file makes no mention of this wounding, nor of what happened to him. Given he was fighting with them again in September, the wounds could not have been too severe. His Army file also makes it clear that he served in France throughout the period.

William Webber and Joseph Lonsdale returned to the front line in the middle of May, manning positions on the northern flank of the German advance, including in Aveluy Wood, with reserve time spent partly at Forceville near Beaumont-Hamel.

Until the German attack, Robert Wakely's experience on the Western Front had been quite limited. Robert had been born in 1897 and attended the school from October 1907 until December 1913. The only son of a grocer, Robert was probably already intending to become a Congregationalist minister, something he achieved after the war. When he attested under the Derby Scheme on 10th December 1915, he was already managing to combine his job as a clerk with studying for the ministry. Under the scheme he was placed in the Army Reserve, but was mobilised on 28th March 1916 and posted to the 3/7th Hampshire Battalion. This battalion had been formed in Bournemouth in March 1915 as a reserve unit. The school magazine reported his progress in the summer edition: "R. A. Wakely joined the 3/7th Hants and passed through the Machine Gun School, being very highly commended for his work. He has been promoted Lance-Corporal and sent to the Southern Command N.C.O. School at Tidworth for a course of training."[660] This promotion to lance corporal was made in February 1916. Clearly he showed an aptitude for machine guns, as his Army record recorded that he had attended and qualified at the School of Musketry, Hayling Island, a year later, in March 1917, noting that he had "a fair knowledge of the Lewis Gun".[661]

In spring 1917, his application to become an officer had been accepted and as 2nd Lieutenant Wakely he was sent to join the 18th King's Royal Rifle Corps Battalion, known as the Arts & Craft Battalion, which had been in France since May 1916. When Robert joined it on 23rd October 1917, it was on coastal defence duties just inside Belgium at La Panne, immediately west of Nieuwpoort and east of Dunkirk. The battalion had suffered heavy casualties previously, and was short of numbers. Conditions were possibly not too onerous, perhaps because they had already suffered a great deal. Instructions issued included: "No bathing is permitted in front of the residence of the King of the Belgians… or in front of Hopital de l'Ocean. All bathers must wear drawers when bathing in front of La Panne Plage and within 500 yards of each end of La Panne Plage." By day security was in the hands of the police, and the battalion had the task at night. Robert was one of eight new 2nd lieutenants that day. A week later, on 30th October, 190 men also joined, though the war diary of the battalion disparagingly describes them as "'count-outs' from ASC & AOC." There was just time to prepare for a major change: the first real experience of war for Robert came, not in France or Belgium. The battalion moved to Italy in November 1917.

Between 3rd and 5th March 1918, the battalion returned from Italy to Pommera, a reserve position

---

[660] *The Bournemouthian*, July 1916.
[661] From his Army File, Public Records Office, WO 339/91771.

near Doullens and west of Arras. Their period of training had a precise purpose: "12. ABC Coys route march. D Coy baths. Officers & NCOs to <u>see</u> model of ground between Lagnicourt and Hermies Spur. Battn training throughout this period as counter-attack Bn in GHQ reserve in readiness for threatened Enemy offensive at and S of Arras."[662] In the event they neither used their new-found knowledge of the land between Bapaume and Cambrai nor earlier experience of the land immediately south of Arras. Instead, they were swept up into the defence against the German Spring Offensive further south, on the Somme itself. Their railway journey of 21st-22nd March was more eventful than might have been anticipated: it was only at 1a.m. on the 22nd that they reached Achiet-le-Grand station just north of Bapaume, and just as they left the station the Germans began to shell it. After a few hours' sleep, they were moved forward to create a reserve trench line immediately to the north of Bapaume. Late the next day, at 11p.m., they were ordered to move forward to relieve the South Staffordshire Battalion defending the area west of Beugny, which they managed to do by about dawn. Now they came under 123rd Brigade. The 19th Division was on their right and the 25th Division on their left. As they took up position, five men fell wounded.

The result of this move was a disaster for the battalion, following the pattern others experienced. After initial enemy bombardments, and the wounding of their colonel by a sniper, a bad morning turned into an awful afternoon:[663] "At 3pm troops on the right were seen to be withdrawing from their positions and 'C' Coy was therefore thrown out as a defensive flank to the Battn. Very heavy rifle and machine gun fire developed on the right, but the smoke from a burning dump to a large extent concealed the enemy's movements. About 3.30pm troops on the left were seen to be falling back gradually. An attempt was therefore made to extricate the Battn to prevent it being cut off, but owing to the facts that there was wire behind both front and support lines, that all Companies were by then heavily engaged & that the enemy was advancing very fast on both flanks, especially on the right, it was not possible for more than a small proportion of the garrison to be withdrawn. Casualties during the withdrawal were heavy as the enemy had managed to install machine guns of the railway line E of Fremicourt and was enfilading the embankment & neighbourhood. At the same time a moderately heavy artillery barrage was put down behind our front line, & behind it his infantry continued their advance. The remains of the Battn were collected and occupied a continuation to the S of the line dug on the 21st & 22nd, but were forced to leave this position as troops both on the left and right were withdrawn."

Robert was one of the officers who had managed to extricate himself, and he now joined the remains of the 123rd Brigade, which were collected together by the brigadier at Bihucourt, at a distance north-west of Bapaume. Quickly they were turned round and dug two lines of trenches due north of Bapaume at Biefvillers to try to protect the route to Achiet-le-Grand as by then the Germans had reached the outskirts of Bapaume. "This position was, however, rendered untenable the next morning by the enemy working up the valley between Biefvillers and Favreuil [a short distance to the north]. During the day the line gradually fell back to a final position on the line of the Albert-Achiet-le-Grand railway. At about 9pm the remains of the Division in this line were withdrawn on relief by the 62nd Division and the remains of the Bn endeavoured to find the 122 Inf. Brigade. As this could not be located, night was spent at Essarts. Weather fine, cold." The next morning reports indicated that their brigade had pulled back to Gommecourt. At midday the

---

[662] War Diary, 18th King's Royal Rifle Corps, 12th March 1918.
[663] As illustrated by the included, relevant extracts from the War Diary, 18th King's Royal Rifle Corps, 24th-25th March 1918.

remnant of the battalion re-joined their brigade at Gommecourt, and in doing so picked up another group, mostly of men from 'C' Company. There were not many of them left. The whole battalion – only about 60 strong now – was reorganised into a single company, and that night was withdrawn north-west to Bienvillers where they spent a very cold night in a field. As weak as they were, not a man could be spared, and on 28th-29th they were ordered forward into support first at Gommecourt, and then west of Bucquoy slightly further east, relieving a battalion of the 42nd Division. It was encouraging that that day more stragglers got through to re-join them and they were able to reorganise into two companies. This was partly made possible because the remains of the battalion was located – perhaps unknown to themselves – above the northern edge of the German advance, which was pushing past them towards Albert and Amiens. So, although he had survived, Robert Wakely and the remnant of his battalion had been swept aside by the German assault.

Frederick Furness was also back from Italy and in action against this offensive, and like so many of the others, his battalion was cut to shreds by it. When Frederick's battalion, the 11th West Surrey Regiment (or 'Queens') had shifted south to Italy, Frederick had been taken off to a French hospital, but he had re-joined the unit in Italy on 23rd January 1918. His experiences were remarkably similar to those Robert Wakely had encountered. On 21st March, they too were moved to Achiet, near Bapaume and the next day began to dig a new defence line across the old Bapaume to Cambrai railway line. This was hurriedly stopped on 23rd March when the battalion was moved forward to Beugny, astride the Bapaume to Cambrai road. Frederick and the battalion found themselves reinforcing the Royal Welsh Fusiliers, but when the Germans attacked they felt the pressure. "The enemy infantry attacked at about 4.30pm. As the battalion on the right had been forced to withdraw... A, B and C companies withdrew through Beugny at 5.30pm. They came under intense artillery and machine gun fire. It is reported by an NCO that a great many of A and B companies were unable to reach the village owing to a flanking movement by the enemy. The remainder of A, B and C companies were reorganised in Beugny and they took up a position with other units in a line south of the village which was partly dug. They remained in this position all night. When the enemy attacked at 4.30 pm, D Company retired from their support position on to the Bapaume-Beugny road where they reorganised and took up a position in the line started that morning across the railway. When the Battalion moved up to the position north of Beugny, Battalion Headquarters were made in the Vaulx-Beugny road and according to the report of a HQ runner, Battalion HQs were cut off at the same time as the portion of A and B companies in the retirement to the village."[664] Two junior officers had died; six officers were missing (including the lieutenant colonel in charge), five more were wounded. Frederick emerged unscathed. Amongst the men, five were dead, forty-three wounded and missing, and a colossal three hundred and seventeen missing.

The next day they retired to try to hold the line across the railway, in conjunction with men of the Cheshire Regiment, but were again broken on 25th March, after which they were temporarily pulled back to be reorganised a short distance west of Achiet at Bucquoy. In this dire situation, however, they could not long be out of the line, and by 28th March they were again at the front trying to protect the front directly north of Achiet, under the control of another battalion, the 10th Royal West Kents. On 1st April they were again detached, but so desperate was the situation that command of what was left of the battalion fell upon a lieutenant – Lieutenant Chetty. This officer

---

[664] War Diary, 11th West Surrey Regiment, 23rd March 1918.

then led them out of the front line, and the Army sent them north by train to Poperinghe, at the entry to the Ypres Salient on 4th April.

Alex Copp, born in 1889, had also returned from Italy. He had attended the school in the period from about 1903 to 1905 (probably as a boarder). He volunteered in 1914. He was placed in the Inns of Court Officers Training Corps from which he was gazetted 2nd lieutenant on 9th March 1915. By the time he married in October 1916 he had already been promoted to be a full lieutenant in the 2/5th East Surrey Regiment. This battalion was a Territorial, second line, home service unit in the 200th Brigade, 67th Division, tasked with defending Kent should there be a German invasion. In November the battalion was disbanded, and Alex landed in France on 15th October 1917 to join the 12th East Surrey Battalion, a New Army (Service) battalion which had gone there in May 1916 within 122nd Brigade, 41st Division. He had arrived at the front on 19th October 1917 in time to join the battalion at almost the most northerly part of the line for the British in the Ypres Salient. He joined the battalion under intermittent shelling and was placed as a full lieutenant in 'C' Company. By 11th November 1917, the battalion was up to numerical strength again, and it was sent off by train to Italy.

On 3rd March 1918, the 12th East Surrey Battalion returned to France, arriving at the railway junction of Amiens on 4th March for a spell of training and preparation. When the Germans attacked, leave was cancelled and the battalion moved forward to support the resistance; they too dug in on a line north of Bapaume on the old Somme battlefield on 22nd March though they had to withdraw two days later. The battalion war diary noted how much the German aircraft seemed to dominate the skies. With the Germans already outflanking them by occupying Mory directly to their north, they were perhaps uncertain upon which axis they should defend. On the 25th they realised that once again they were outflanked. Co-operating with the Hampshires they made a fighting withdrawal, as the war diary accounts: "The enemy commenced an attack on the line held by C. Company and a few Machine Gunners but were repulsed and held up until 10.30 am when the C.O. finding that the enemy were getting round both flanks as well as attacking frontally gave orders to retire, only the C.O. and 1 NCO escaped. This stand by C Company gave great assistance to the Hampshires who were digging a line in front of Bihucourt and also saved 60 guns at Achiet-Le-Grand which but for this stand would have been captured. The rest of the Battalion under Captain Walker helped to hold a line between Sapignieres and Bihucourt but withdrew to the Bihucourt line at 1 pm, where they dug in to support the Hampshires. Here a stand was made, the Battalion also supporting a counter-attack made by the Hants on Bihucourt Wood. Lieutenants Davencourt, Copp, Linford and Goulding were wounded, 2nd lieutenant Warland wounded and missing and 2nd lieutenant Johns and Lieutenant Dawson missing."[665]

For the next two days the battalion continued to withdraw. But by the end of the week, the retreat seemed to have come to a halt and the battalion began to rotate the defence of the new line. At the end of May the battalion war diary records that Alex learned that he had been awarded the Military Cross for his part in the fighting. When the citation was printed in *The London Gazette* on 16th September it read, "Lieutenant Alexander Foreman Copp, East Surrey Regiment: For conspicuous gallantry and devotion to duty. As a company commander he showed exceptional capabilities. In the most difficult positions against greatly superior enemy numbers, he handled his men skilfully and showed fine courage and initiative." When he learned this news, he was in Londonderry House

---

[665] War Diary, 12th East Surrey Battalion, 25th March 1918.

Hospital. (There were two called by this name, one in Park Lane, Westminster and the other in Londonderry, Northern Ireland.) He had spent over two months lying on his back in a hospital in France. Even there he had not been safe, having "eventually getting bombed out of the hospital I was in, and had a very lucky escape, as not only did the bombs drop around, but one actually fell on the ward I was in, doing a lot of damage. I am getting on nicely now and am glad to say sitting up in a chair, and, to relieve the monotony occasionally do a trip round the room on crutches. I hope to soon get out in the park."[666] Probably he did not return to his battalion, but he did survive the war, and lived to play a part again as an officer in the Second World War.

Since Cambrai, Harold Head and his tanks had seen a number of changes and a bewildering number of re-designations: From 20th November, Harold's 'D' Battalion was moved from 1st Brigade to 1st Tank Brigade, and then in January 1918 all the battalion letters were changed to numbers, so that 'D' Battalion became the 4th Battalion. His tank brigade was part of the 5th Army and from 24th March became the '4th Tank Brigade – Lewis Gun Brigade', though on 10th June it was amalgamated into the 2nd Tank Brigade. The reason why it temporarily became the Lewis Gun Brigade was the disaster of the German offensive which burst over the Army on 21st March 1918.

In this offensive, the battalion's sections were reduced to three tanks each. Between 21st and 25th March 1918, the 4th Battalion deployed nine of its tanks in four forward positions, whilst the other tanks of the battalion were held in reserve at the Buire Wood Tankodrome, south-west of Albert. These too were committed to the battle the next day. The battalion lost all but one of its tanks during the retreat; its sole survivor, number 8118, was handed over to 1st Battalion.

Harold's 10 Section now contained three of the tanks (4022, 4052, and 4690) which were held in reserve on 21st March. In company with six tanks of 9 Section, Harold's section deployed forward from Buire Wood at 1a.m. on 22nd March and reached Spur Quarry about 6.30a.m. Their intention was to support a counter-attack by the Royal Sussex Regiment, but because the Germans had already broken through on the right, the attack was abandoned. Harold's tanks nevertheless did their best to stem the German onslaught. They attacked from Spur Quarry at 7.45a.m. and even though they had no infantry support, they managed to inflict severe casualties on the Germans. Two tanks drove along the German front line doing great damage until eventually both had been hit and knocked out of the battle. His other tank got only six hundred yards out of the quarry before the commander, 2nd Lieutenant J.C. MacIntosh and four of his crew had been wounded.

Harold had lost his tanks, but this did not stop him fighting on. As the war diary for the 105th Brigade Headquarters (also in his division) explained on 23rd March: "The situation at present is not clear. Each unit will therefore be responsible for its own protection against surprise."[667] He formed a detachment of men from the survivors of the battalion, armed with Lewis guns. These were placed under the command of the 106th Brigade, and they placed themselves across the Bray to Albert road on 26th March. From 10a.m. to 4p.m. they remained there, just south of Albert, trying to hold back the German advance, with the support of two tanks. Eventually, however, their position was outflanked and Harold had to withdraw his men. (After this, the records of Harold's next movements are hard to uncover, but we know that on 23rd August 1918, Harold left his tank battalion for good. He returned to England where he transferred to the newly-formed Royal Air

---

[666] *The Bournemouthian*, December 1918.
[667] War Diary, 105th Brigade HQ, 23rd March 1918, Appendix 8.

Force. By September he was attending initial R.A.F. training, and he joined No.1 Flight School on 9th December 1918. This initial R.A.F. career did not last much longer than the completion of the war, and on 31st May 1919 he relinquished his commission though he was allowed to retain the title of captain. Twenty years later, however, he was back in action and in the Second World War he again served with the R.A.F., working with squadrons which supported covert action in occupied Europe. At that point he was a captain with the Special Operations Executive, and he helped in the operation which led to the assassination of Reinhard Heydrich in 1942, though Harold was shattered by the extent of the Nazi retaliation which followed when they killed or imprisoned 15,000 Czechs. He lived until the 1960s.)

Despite his earlier optimism, Archibald Rogers, 49th Brigade Gas Officer within 16th Division, also knew what it was to see whole units disappear around him when the offensive was launched. In early March the Germans seemed to step up their patrols but otherwise there is no hint in the brigade diary of the attack they were about to receive. Then, as elsewhere, all Hell seemed to be let loose on 21st March. "4.30am – Hostile bombardment opens. Apparently mainly gas shell. 4.35am – Practically all wires were cut. Communication by visual impossible owing to dense mist. 5am – Right Company of S.I.H. sent 'S.O.S.' by a message to Battalion Headquarters reporting gas. 7am – S.I.H. report 'All Coys. in Battle positions by 5am. Good deal of Gas about. All lines 'diss' to Coys at 7am but up to then Coys reported O.K. Fairly heavy hostile shelling.'"[668] By 1.30p.m., the 2nd Royal Irish Regiment reported its ammunition exhausted. It then became clear that they were being outflanked by a rapid German advance. Then the pattern became the familiar one seen elsewhere. By 9a.m. on 22nd March, the whole brigade had lost so many men that it was reorganised into a mere two companies. Later that day they were reinforced by a Pioneer battalion, despite the continued attacks from the air by German aircraft. Three battalions advanced to support the brigade that evening but these reinforcements turned out to be a drop in the ocean required, and the brigade continued to fall back across the Somme in stages, and presumably Archibald fell back with them. When they had a chance to review their numbers on 1st April, they read more like an 'April Fool' than a fighting force. (Because men had become mixed up, and stragglers were attached to non-brigade units in different places, some of these numbers did subsequently improve.) "Strengths. Brigade HQ – 3 Officers, 30 O.R.; 2nd Royal Irish Regt – 1 Officer, 19 O.R.; 7th (South Irish. Horse) Royal Munster Regt – 0 officer, 13 O.R.; Royal Inniskilling Fusiliers – 0 Officer, 8 O.R.; Strength in line with 48 Inf. Brigade: 2nd Royal Irish Regt – 6 Officers, 105 O.R.; 7th (S.I.H.) Royal Munster Regt – 3 officers, 60 O.R.; Royal Inniskilling Fusiliers – 2 Officers, 82 O.R.; Brig. HQ – 1 Officer, 15 O.R."[669]

Unsurprisingly, on 13th April, the decision was taken that the remnants of the battalions of the division (originally nine infantry battalions and supporting troops) were to be amalgamated into one composite battalion. To all intents and purposes, the division as a fighting force had ceased to exist, although soon replacements started to arrive, and over the coming weeks and months the battalions were rebuilt, though when the brigade was eventually reconstituted it was with an entirely different set of battalions from England.

Fellow schoolmaster Leonard Taylor was also caught up in the attempt to hold back the German advance. In the first week of February, Leonard and the 5th Durham Light Infantry Battalion were

---

[668] War Diary, 49th Brigade, Appendix – Record of Events 21st to 27th March 1918.
[669] War Diary, 49th Brigade, 1st April 1918.

back on Passchendaele Ridge, but by this time the conditions were much improved both because of the better communications up onto the ridge by the duckboards, and also because secure points had been created, including a shelter for one hundred and fifty men at a time under Crest Farm. As a result, in a week they lost only one man killed and another wounded. On 12th February, they had switched from the 150th Brigade to the 151st Brigade, but still in the 50th Division. The change occurred because the whole British Army was being reorganised and brigades slimmed from four to three battalions.

After a further spell on the Passchendaele Ridge, they were moved to the Somme in the middle of March and took their place in trenches at Nobescourt, east of Peronne on 22nd March, hours after the German assault began. The fighting quickly became so intense that first they withdrew a short way, and the next day they were ordered to pull back to west of the river Somme itself, covered by 'C' Company. They then prepared to counter-attack the bridgehead at Biaches (a south-western suburb of Peronne), but in fact the Germans crossed the Somme slightly further south at Eterpigny, and the battalion moved to thwart them: "A and C Companies were ordered to counter attack. The high ground NW of Eterpigny was occupied by them, and the Enemy held up for some time. Lt. Green was wounded in this fighting when about 4 pm 'A' and 'B' Companies were forced to withdraw and Lt. Slack was found to be missing. 'A' and 'B' Companies withdrew to a redoubt E of Barleux and here 'C' and 'D' Companies again joined them." [670] For a few hours they held up the German advance, but again and again were ordered to withdraw by stages, ever westwards. They were retreating south of the River Somme now, falling back towards Villers-Bretonneux and Amiens. On 26th March, the battalion attempted to hold a position near Rosières, but fell back the next day to try to hold the line of the railway between Rosières and Guillancourt. While two companies tried to establish that line, 'C' Company launched a counter-attack to try to delay the enemy advance. Three officers, including the major now commanding the battalion, were wounded in this attempt. The number of ordinary soldiers killed or wounded was not recorded. Then there was a brief respite. "During the afternoon the Enemy were driven back by a counter attack by another division, and at about 7 pm orders were received for the battalion to move up again into positions north of Rosières station. 28th During the early morning the Enemy broke through on the left of the battalion and about 9 am orders came to withdraw again down the railway line and positions were taken up NE of Caix with the French on the Left. Captain L W Taylor became wounded and missing, and 2nd Lieuts Smith and Joules wounded in this withdrawal. 'D' Company now held the bridgehead at Caix while a further withdrawal of the line took place."

After the war, Leonard described these events in more detail, and how he ended up in a prison camp on two islands at Stralsund on the Baltic: "It was on March 28, 1918, at Rosieres, while engaged in reconnoitring work, with his battalion of the Durhams, as he was going along a railway line, that he ran into four Germans. He succeeded in warning the battalion and then retreated before the enemy. But he had to take a line across an open field, and a rifle bullet in the knee brought him down, and another shot in the foot stopped all further progress. So he fell wounded into the hands of the Germans. He was taken to a casualty clearing station, but it was nothing like ours, where friend and foe alike had their wounds skilfully treated before being sent towards the base. There was no attempt whatever made to dress his wounds, or those of other wounded men, and for 24 hours he had no food. At the end of that time he was given some so-called 'soup'. After this Capt. Taylor was moved to another place, of which he never learned the name, and was kept

---

[670] War Diary, 5th Durham Light Infantry, 23rd March 1918.

there about four days with a lot of German privates, and during all this time his wounds were only given one dressing. The German wounded were treated in just the same fashion. For six weeks Capt. Taylor did not get a wash or a change of clothes. His next quarters were at St. Quentin, where he was kept ten or twelve days. As to the medical organisation at all these places there was none, and the sanitary conditions of Germany so far as he saw them were inconceivably bad. The latrines were in a most filthy state, and the orderlies seemed to be slipshod in their methods and thoroughly lazy... The doctors were just as lazy as the orderlies... and they were callous to trouble themselves about the sufferings of those under their care, whilst there were only paper dressings and bandages to be obtained."[671]

For a time it was believed in England that Leonard might have died from those wounds, and there was considerable anxiety for him and for the others similarly caught up in these events. On 20th April 1918, the local newspaper, *The Bournemouth Visitors' Directory*, reported him missing. Later it was realised that he had been taken prisoner and sent to a camp for officers in Germany. *The Bournemouthian* of December 1918 was able to quote from the Darlington Grammar School magazine that "All will be glad to hear that Captain Taylor is safe and not seriously incapacitated by his wounds. Captain Taylor was posted wounded and missing at the end of March. After many days of anxiety and gloom, we were all greatly relieved to hear that Mrs. Taylor had heard, via Copenhagen, that Captain Taylor was still alive. Since then two reassuring messages have come through from Captain Taylor himself, at the Internment Hospital Camp, Zerbst-in-Anhalt. A great load has been taken from our minds, and we hope soon to have the pleasure of welcoming Captain Taylor amongst us once more."[672] Indeed, he was repatriated to the United Kingdom on Christmas Day 1918, and was able to resume his career as a headmaster, for which he received the OBE in 1947.

As planned, the German attack had hit at the junction of the British and French Armies. General Pétain sent French reinforcements, but these were too few, too late. British troops, including Australian battalions, were rushed to the major railhead at Amiens to stiffen the desperate defence. Even so, from about March 24th the German advance began to falter as their communications extended and re-supply and reinforcement problems developed. Even after the initial onslaught slowed, things remained desperate for the British for some time. Three Old Bournemouthians were serving as infantry privates in the 15th Hampshire Battalion alongside Lieutenant Horace Tollemache.

Edward Preiss, born in 1897, was five years younger than his brother Russell (who attended the school from 1904-1910). Edward left in December 1915 but soon joined the Hampshire Regiment and was posted as a private into the 15th Hampshires and would therefore have served alongside other Old Boys, some of whom were his officers. Because he was a private, details of his career are sketchy, but he was slightly wounded in 1917 either on the Western Front (when the battalion fought in the opening actions of the Third Battle of Ypres, before moving up to the Belgium coast) or after it moved to Italy on 12th November 1917, arriving at Mantua to bolster the Italian forces who had suffered a significant reverse at the Battle of Caporetto.

Roy Rawle was born in 1894 and attended the school from May 1908 to March 1909. He was a member of the 1/1st Hampshire Yeomanry (sometimes known as the Hampshire Carabiniers). In

---

[671] Extracted from an account in *The Bournemouthian*, April 1919.
[672] *The Bournemouthian*, December 1918.

August 1914 this was part of the 1st South-West Mounted Brigade, and was used, initially, to strengthen the defences of Portsmouth and later of Eastbourne in Sussex, but by 1916 it was recognised that it had little useful role in southern England. Accordingly, it was sent, in separate troops, to France in the period 1916-January 1917. After separate deployments without battle, the regiment was reunited before the end of January 1917 and served then as the IX Corps Cavalry Regiment until 25th July 1917. By this stage it was clear that infantry were needed more than expensive Territorial cavalry, and a month later the regiment was 'dismounted' and its soldiers re-trained to become infantry. On 27th September 1917, they joined the 15th Hampshire Battalion. Roy was to survive the war, but died young in 1925.

Robert Meredith had also come out to join the battalion as a private soldier. Robert had been born in 1897. He was at the school from May 1911 to November 1913. He too either volunteered, or was conscripted, into the 15th Hampshire Battalion. He also survived the war, serving on the Western Front in the second half of the war, but died in 1929.

The official Hampshires' history describes their period in Italy as something of a respite. After a gruelling and forced march to the front, the battalion faced off the Austrians and Germans across a river in places one mile wide, and the Germans made no attempt to assault them. In consequence, only one man was killed, and barely ten were wounded – mostly in the first week of December. The Italians rallied, and in 1918 it was felt safe enough to redeploy the 15th Hampshires to France. So, in February these men, with Horace, were recalled from Italy, travelling from Campo San Piero by train and went into billets at Warlincourt, east of Doullens on 5th March 1918. After a fortnight training, they were just moving away when the German assault began. Quickly they were pulled back and on 21st March marched in fighting order to support the 12th East Surreys and the 18th King's Royal Rifles digging a defence line north of Bapaume. This whole movement was done so quickly that the battalion found itself without its Lewis guns – an important omission, and these did not catch up with the battalion for another week. However, the need was clear and urgent – the corps they reinforced had suffered badly from the attack of March 21st "and had been forced back to the rear line of its Battle Zone, after losing heavily."[673] Soon the line was adjusted and at 7a.m. two companies lined up on the left of the Surreys facing Mory, and the other two companies were positioned with the 13th Middlesex on their left and 10/11th Highland Light Infantry on their right. As the day drew on to evening, the battalion began to take heavy losses from hostile fire – fourteen killed and a further thirty wounded. Their line was situated on a reverse slope which exposed attacking Germans to view, and although the Germans pushed forward to within fifty yards of the Hampshires, the corpses of the Germans fell in piles on the British wire, and no Germans broke through.[674]

They took part in dramatic fighting from 24th-27th March 1918: "24th 11pm. Enemy attack in force and Battalion repulsed the enemy with heavy losses. Casualties very slight." This understated the drama of the events – at one point the Hampshires charged forwards in company with some men of the Argyll and Sutherland Highlanders to push the Germans back. Things were becoming increasingly desperate. As a sergeant described the day in a private diary mentioned in the official history, "Dug in and held enemy in large numbers." Five British divisions faced fifteen German

---

[673] *The Royal Hampshire Regiment 1914-1918*, C.T. Atkinson, p. 322, 1952.

[674] *The Royal Hampshire Regiment 1914-1918*, C.T. Atkinson, p. 323, 1952. Further details which elaborate on the battalion war diary are also drawn from this account.

divisions. German patrols pushed forwards and on the flank of the Hampshires ground was again given. Gradually the line was pushed back and "During the withdrawal 2 prisoners were taken, who informed us that enemy were advancing on both flanks. 26th 4 am. The Battalion took up a position E W of Bihucourt Wood and waited till dawn to dig in. 11 am. The troops in an immediate front retired on to a line and the enemy attacked. In the hollow in our rear were a Brigade of the Manchesters and as the enemy advancing carried our right flank, a message was sent addressed OC Manchesters informing him of the situation and asking what assistance he was going to render. The orderly who was dispatched with the message delivered it to the Brigadier who remarked 'Are they?' and dispatched one Battalion to our right flank and another to our support, one company being already mixed up in the centre of our line. 1pm. Situation very serious as the enemy was massing in Bihucourt Wood. 2pm. Three tanks advanced over our front and 8 on our right flank. All did extraordinary good work and after being in the enemies' lines for one hour, returned to our lines where two of them were knocked out. All endeavours were made to inform the OC of remaining tanks they were urgently required to go through Bihucourt Wood without success. 3pm. The enemy dug in on ridge opposite our front and the situation quietened down… Casualties on 26th… 18."

In the midst of this fighting, Edward distinguished himself in the very dangerous post of battalion 'runner', carrying messages. He was awarded the Military Medal – the equivalent of the Military Cross for 'other ranks', introduced in 1916. A proud headmaster recorded a letter from the major-general in the school magazine, which is very helpful as the citations for the Military Medal were not generally published in *The London Gazette*. "To Pte. E. C. Preiss, Hampshire Regt. I wish to place on record my appreciation of your gallantry and devotion to duty on the night of 25/26th March, 1918, when you carried urgent messages to Battalion H.Q. under heavy fire. You set a fine example of courage. (Signed) Major-Gen. Commanding 41st Division."[675] Edward was one of sixteen NCOs and men in the 15th Hampshire Battalion to receive the Military Medal for the fighting during this crisis. Several officers received the Military Cross whilst the colonel and two sergeants won the D.C.M.

By the end of March the battalion had got off lightly compared to many, but still it was calculated that four officers had been wounded; sixteen men killed, sixty-one wounded, and five were missing. In one of his letters, written in summer 1918, Archibald Rogers mentioned how Edward had failed to get entry to a commission because someone in the Army took too literal a view of the hierarchy, even at such a time: "I was interested to see that Preiss had the M.M., as I have discovered that his battalion have just come into the village where I am, and I am going to seek him out to-morrow and have a few words with him. One of his officers was telling me that he has been doing jolly good and that he had put in for a commission, but had been rejected because he was not a full corporal. Oh, the Army!"[676]

Between August and December 1917, Ernest Parsons had not been with the 1st Royal Fusiliers Battalion, and it is likely that he had been wounded. He had returned to the 1st Royal Fusiliers on 12th December 1917 when the battalion was in divisional reserve, at Vendelles, east of Peronne. The diary notes his arrival from the Infantry Base Depot I.B.D.,[677] the holding unit usually used for

---

[675] *The Bournemouthian*, July 1918.

[676] *The Bournemouthian*, December 1918.

[677] The Infantry Base Depot was a holding camp. Its purpose was to receive men from England, keep them in training, and then send them on when they were posted to join their battalion. Originally, each division had had its own such camp, and Étaples was the main Army base on the coast. Gradually, such was the need to replenish men, especially after the Battle of the Somme, and to deal with the numbers following

dispatching men who had been away wounded, or who were new reinforcements. He spent a bitterly cold and snowy Christmas in the front line near Hervilly, though the severe weather meant neither side was active and no casualties were sustained. Even so, the chance of baths on 29th December must have been very welcome! The first two months of 1918, though involving further front line tours and working parties, were largely uneventful, though the thaw did cause difficulties with sodden trenches. After a quiet tour in the trenches in the middle of March the battalion was lulled into a sense of relative security – their patrols showed little sign of the Germans, let alone any sign of an impending attack. However, they had not long been pulled back into support when the Germans opened up a "furious bombardment" at 4.30a.m. on 21st March 1918. Gas shells were used against them, meaning that for about an hour they wore their gas helmets continuously. In the furious fighting that followed, three officers and an unspecified number of men were killed or seriously wounded. This continued the next day when another five officers were killed, seriously wounded, or went missing. "Many casualties in the ranks"[678] was the best the war diary could manage – the action was too fierce for accuracy, and they were forced back.

Like the other units, the next week saw the battalion attempt to establish a line and then be forced to retreat every day. After a week, they tried in vain to counter-attack: "28/3/18. Battalion changed position slightly owing to left flank giving way. At 11.0am Battalion retired from line as left flank was in the air. Battalion made a local counter-attack with 3rd Rifle Bde but were driven back & retired. Battalion marched through Caix and again took up a position facing NE to protect the French who were about to counter-attack. The enemy, however, outflanked our line & the Battalion withdrew to Villers-aux-Erables, then marched to Castel where Battalion rested for night."[679] At the end of the month they estimated that over two hundred men and thirteen officers had fallen casualty of one sort or another. Mercifully, at the end of the month it rained heavily and this seems to have helped to slow the German advance. At this point their position became more stable. They were south of the River Somme, near Villers-Bretonneux and east of Amiens. Soon they moved to train near the coast and to receive substantial reinforcements to rebuild the battalion after its losses.

On 30th March, Oliver Cooper's experiences in the attack reached a climax. Oliver, born in 1898, had left school in July 1913. On 12th October 1916, he had joined the 1st Grenadier Guards Battalion. This battalion had been in action since the start of the war, and was very active in the two years during which Oliver served. In 1917 they had been hassling the Germans as they withdrew to the Hindenburg Line, and acting as support in the Battle of Pilckem Ridge, the first phase of the Third Battle of Ypres. They had continued to be involved in that battle – in the battles of Menin Road, Poelcappelle, and the First Battle of Passchendaele. Afterwards they had been at Cambrai in the Battle of Bourlon Wood, and facing the German counter-attacks. Now they faced the Ludendorff Offensive.

The official history of his regiment contains an interesting insight based on original battalion documents of the view the 1st Grenadier Guards had of the Germans making an initial attack, which

---

the introduction of conscription in 1916, that the I.B.D.s were subtly changed to supply new drafts for the battalions of a group of regiments rather than for a division. From the beginning of 1918, the number of I.B.D.s was reduced, though each now supplied even more regiments.

[678] War Diary, 1st Royal Fusiliers, 22nd March 1918.
[679] War Diary, 1st Royal Fusiliers, 28th March 1918.

the Guards were able to drive back: "The troops employed by the enemy seemed to have been well trained in the new method of attack, and men were dribbled forward to their assembly positions, where they deployed into waves for the attack, but when they came under our machine gun, Lewis-gun, and rifle fire, they soon began to bunch in groups. It seemed as if the enemy's troops had started with the intention of carrying out the operation at the double for the whole 3000 yards. In order even to attempt this, they must have undergone a considerable training to reach the standard of physical fitness necessary for such an attack. Round discs were used to maintain the correct direction, and the flanks of the attack were marked by flags. In other respects they appear to have evolved no new ideas in minor tactics, and the absence of any covering fire during the advance was most noticeable. Light machine guns followed up in the rear of the assault, and only came into action to cover the retirement of the defeated 'Sturm-Truppen'."[680]

Oliver's experiences would initially appear to have been less dreadful than some of the others. The battalion was on the northern edge of the assault, and initially their machine guns managed to slow up the German advance. However, from 26th March, they had to fall back, though in good order. Perhaps their worst day would have been 30th March, just as some of the others began to find the situation easing. The battalion had been out of the fighting since 27th March, but over the night of 29th-30th March they returned to the line. On returning to the front trenches, Oliver and his friends were confronted by very active enemy machine-gun fire, which was soon followed up with a heavy German artillery barrage, which was itself added to by precise use of minenwerfer aimed at targets of specific tactical value. Shells hit both the front trenches and the back areas. "The whole Battalion had a terrible time. But the Germans, with characteristic thoroughness, were not content with this: they thickened up their barrage with machine gun fire, and sent fourteen aeroplanes to drop bombs behind the trenches. They not unnaturally thought that, after three hours of a bombardment of this kind, no one could possibly remain to resist their infantry attack, but in this they were mistaken. The 1st battalion remained unmoved. Shattered, covered with earth, deafened by the constant explosions, dazed by the spectacle of maimed and mutilated men, the Grenadiers hung grimly on to their line, though in some places the trenches were completely obliterated."[681] A mass attack by two regiments of Germans followed. But they had misjudged. Considering that it was safe to do so, they attacked in a dense mass, assuming an absence of organised defence. They were met by withering defensive fire which stopped them in their tracks. Driven back, the best the Germans could do was to try to dislodge the Grenadiers with a heavy machine-gun and rifle fire for the rest of the day, but amazingly the Grenadiers had suffered only about eighty casualties despite all they had suffered. Oliver appears to have emerged unscathed.

Young Ralph Cheshire also survived despite the desperate fighting. Born in 1898 and a member of the school from 1910 to 1913, at the age of 14 he had started to take junior public exams, but left to take up junior work as a junior solicitor's clerk at a local practice. At the end of 1916 he moved to work as a post office clerk, but joined the Army in February 1917. He was posted to 93rd Training Battalion, formally the 15th Gloucesters, re-designated the 262nd Graduated Battalion in May 1917. In October 1917 he had been sent to France as a private of eighteen and a half (the new minimum age for overseas) to join as a replacement in the 2nd Royal Berkshire (Princess Charlotte of Wales's)

---

[680] *The Grenadier Guards In The Great War Of 1914-1918 Volume II*, Lieut.-Colonel Sir Frederick Ponsonby, Macmillan And Co., Limited, London 1920, pp. 354-355.

[681] *The Grenadier Guards In The Great War Of 1914-1918 Volume II*, Lieut.-Colonel Sir Frederick Ponsonby, Macmillan And Co., Limited, London 1920, pp. 357-358.

Regiment, 25th Brigade in the 8th Division. For the first twelve days of October 1917, the battalion had been 'resting' in camp, but from 13th October was back in the trenches. The war diary mentions the arrival of three 'other ranks' on 14th October, so that might be when Ralph joined the war. If so, it was no sinecure – one man was wounded that day. Casualties continued steadily at a few each day until 23rd October when one hundred men joined the battalion. After a period in reserve for work parties, rest and training they returned to hold the line north-east of Passchendaele from 17th to 19th November. More casualties followed including men lost when they attacked on 2nd December. They were still in this reserve when the Germans launched Operation Michael. On March 22nd, the battalion went by train towards the British front line near St. Quentin. They did not reach the old line as they encountered the German attackers at Bethencourt-sur-Somme where they tried to hold the line of the Somme Canal. They fought a retreating battle from 23rd March until the end of the month. At this time they had taken many losses, and the battalion was replaced by a French battalion. Ironically, the battalion war diary merely sums up these days – "Battalion took part in Rear Guard Actions during these dates. Casualties (Officers) T/Lieut Colonel C.R.H. Stirling DSO MC Wounded. 4 Officers killed, 16 wounded, 4 Missing, 1 Wounded & Missing. Casualties Other ranks. Killed 30, Wounded 170, Wounded & Missing 3, Missing 99."[682]

Eric Paice was with the Field Artillery trying to support these infantrymen. From November to the middle of February, Eric and 'B' Battery of the 152nd R.F.A. Brigade had been in almost continuous action. At the start of March, they had again moved forward and gone into action, this time at St. Léger. In the scramble caused by the offensives the drafts of the diary were lost: "4th to 20th. I regret that in the subsequent happenings the Brigade Diary got lost & so this summary will not be so complete as desired. From the 13th inclusive we put down Cover for Preparations A & B & during all nights put down very extensive harassing fire… 21st After heavy harassing fire from Midnight to 3am the Enemy attacked, his Barrage extending from the front line to the Battery positions & was continued with the same intensity until about 12 noon. By this time the Division on our Right had fallen back & hostile infantry were advancing without artillery support. The Enemy on our front were held for most of the day. 8pm Orders given for detached sections to withdraw and join main positions. 9pm 23rd battery 3rd Div attached to Left group. 10pm Orders given for A C D & 23rd Battery to retire to selected positions near Boyelles."[683] As the Germans advanced on St. Léger, Eric's 'B' Battery, supported by two of the others, briefly tried to push forward again, firing on the advancing Germans. However, very soon they were forced to pull back. The pressure eased just before the end of the month, however, as Arras was not the Germans' target.

Reverdy Dyason, born in 1897 was also with the R.F.A. trying to stem the offensive. He had left school in March 1914 to become an engineer in shipbuilding at Swan Hunters at Newcastle on Tyne, after first travelling with his father on a voyage to South and North America. As an apprentice he was refused permission to enlist in the Army because the authorities were in need of trained and trainee shipping engineers. Indeed, the school magazine reported him as being "employed in the Government Shipyard at Walker-on-Tyne, repairing ships damaged in naval warfare".[684] This was important work, but Reverdy was frustrated. Eventually, he quit the shipyard and went to Tynemouth where he persuaded the recruiting major to enlist him as a gunner in the Royal Field Artillery in February 1917. After six weeks training at Athlone he was promoted to

---

[682] War Diary, 2nd Berkshire Battalion, 24th-31st March 1918.
[683] War Diary, 152nd Brigade, Royal Field Artillery, 4th-21st March 1918.
[684] *The Bournemouthian*, July 1916.

lance bombardier, and soon after he refused the opportunity to train as an infantry officer. In October 1917, he went to France in the 116th Battery, 26th Brigade – then a mobile artillery brigade known as an army field brigade – to support the infantry in different places. His battery was brigaded with two other batteries of the R.F.A. (117th and 118th) and at the end of that October was fighting alongside the Canadians: initially with the 4th Canadian Division of the Canadian Corps, and then with the 2nd Canadian Division. From 22nd November 1917, his battery was with the 33rd and the 34th Divisions into the New Year, 1918. After serving next with the 3rd, 59th and 40th Divisions, it was transferred to support the 42nd Division when, on 25th March, it unsuccessfully attempted to counter-attack the German assault with the aid of seven tanks but was forced to retreat from Ervillers to Bucquoy. Finally, once that position seemed secure, Reverdy's artillery brigade was moved to support the 62nd Division for the middle two weeks of April, when it took over the line from the 42nd Division. This would be a comparatively quiet period, but an important one. The history of the division recounts, "Much work was necessary, both to the front line and on the communications, for which purpose every available man who could be spared joined the working parties which, by day and by night, were employed in strengthening the defences and in digging new defensive lines, of which between April and July, Sir Douglas Haig stated, '5,000 miles of trenches were constructed'. Truly a prodigious performance."[685]

As the German assault developed in March 1918, Richard Barfoot and the 24th Field Ambulance had moved westwards by stages, keeping south of the River Somme. It was not until the last day of the month that they were able to stop retreating, when they handed over their dressing stations, etc., to the French. The war diary gave testimony to the hard work of the unit: "Every patient that was brought to all A.D. Stations has been evacuated to C.C. Stations though some have been carried from the A.D. Stations on stretchers by the bearers for some miles, since the cars and wagons were loaded and the Germans were entering the villages. The most striking feature, from the Ambulance point of view was the enormous amount of good work done by the drivers of the Motor Ambulances who carried on driving for the first 7 days of the retreat without any rest at all, as there were no spare drivers available. Approximately 1200 wounded have been collected and brought to the A.D. Stations of the 24th Field Ambulance during the retreat. Many more than these were dressed & passed through the Dressing Stations. Unfortunately it was not possible to keep any accurate check on the numbers passing through. It is gratifying to note that no wounded man whatsoever who came under the care of the 24th Field Ambulance, or who was put under the charge of the Ambulance bearers at the various Battalion aid-posts, fell into the hands of the Germans. This was due to the perseverance and efforts of the M.O.s in charge of advanced posts and of the personnel generally, some bearers carrying wounded stretcher cases some miles from R.A. posts and if that had to be hurriedly abandoned."[686]

Former medic Gordon Collingwood had managed to move from the R.A.M.C. and been commissioned 2nd lieutenant on 23rd September 1915 in the Army Service Corps with duties concerning the supply of the fighting forces. After training at the Supply School of Instruction at Boulogne from 11th October, on 15th November 1915 he joined 386 Company in 1st Corps. For a year he served in the Army Service Corps on supply, but towards the end of 1916 was clearly frustrated and wanting to play a fighting role in the actions unfolding. By then he was a lieutenant. The infantry was not an option, given his need for glasses, but in the autumn he applied to switch

---

[685] From the *History of the 62nd (West Riding) Division 1914-1919 Volume 1*, p. 165.
[686] War Diary of the 24th Field Ambulance, 3rd April 1918.

to the Royal Artillery. On 1st February 1917, he was sent back to England, and on 9th February transferred to the Royal Field Artillery on probation, though at the cost of accepting demotion to 2nd lieutenant. He joined the Royal Garrison Artillery (R.G.A.) on 11th April 1917. Gordon was sent back to France with 405 Siege Battery, which left for the Western Front on 3rd May 1917. Ten days later it joined IX Corps Heavy Artillery, though it was switched between 51 and 41 Heavy Artillery groups that summer and autumn. For part of that summer at least it was operating near Ypres. On 3rd December 1917, it was moved to 99 Heavy Artillery Group, about the time when these units were re-designated brigades of the R.G.A. By the end of the war it was firing four 6" guns, and it is likely that this was its armament whilst Gordon served in the unit. It is hard to know Gordon's precise actions during the crisis, but at 2.15p.m. on 28th March 1918 Gordon died of wounds at No. 8 Casualty Clearing Station which was at Etrun, north-west of Arras. He died from the effects of wounds to his left foot and his right buttock. He was buried at the Duisans Cemetery extension at Etrun.

Douglas Tuck was also with the R.G.A. in this struggle. Douglas, originally called William Douglas – his Army record used those as his first names – was known by the school as Douglas William. When he tried to persuade the Army to call him Douglas, this was refused as they had a copy of his birth certificate showing the correct order of his names! He was born in 1897. When he attended Bournemouth School (from January 1910 until June 1917) he lived with his aunt, although it was his mother who counter-signed his application for the Royal Military Academy at Woolwich. At school he was keen on the Officer Training Corps and became a sergeant within it. In the summer of 1916 he passed the exam for entry to the academy and left school and moved on to attend the Royal Military Academy at Woolwich to train for a commission into the artillery. He began as a 'Gentleman Cadet' at Woolwich on 6th June 1917 and was commissioned as a 2nd lieutenant in the Regular Royal Garrison Artillery. After a period of further training (in which he bumped into fellow Old Bournemouthian William Ray at Lydd in Kent) he went to France, arriving on 26th November 1917. Initially he had reported to the R.G.A. base, but he was posted to the 95th Siege Battery, which had arrived in France the year before, armed since August 1917 with six 9.2-inch howitzers. The idea was that they would fire large high explosive shells high into the air to come down hard on fixed enemy positions, such as German artillery batteries, or key points such as ammunition dumps, communication lines like roads and railways, or enemy strongpoints. Fighting in the 90th Brigade, R.G.A., it was re-armed with six Mark II 9.2" howitzers on 12th January. His battery fought against the German Offensive in 1918 but their war diaries have not survived.

Finally, another R.G.A. man fighting against this assault was Edward Harlow. In about February 1917 Edward had left the 109th Siege Battery to begin his studies for a commission at the No.2 R.G.A. Cadet School in Uckfield, Sussex and was commissioned 2nd lieutenant on 18th August 1917. He sailed from Southampton to Le Havre over the night of 11th-12th December 1917. After a few days at a depot, he joined his new unit, 222nd Siege Battery R.G.A. (sometimes known as the Hampshire Royal Garrison Artillery), on 8th January 1918. This battery was armed with four 6-inch Mk. VII guns rather than the howitzers of his previous battery and was attached to the 4th Army. Its guns were to be used to try to suppress German artillery fire and destroy their artillery positions. On 6th March 1918, Edward was attached to the Cavalry Corps for a 'Physical Course' but as the emergency developed he re-joined the 222nd Battery on 23rd March 1918. At that time the 222nd battery was in action against the offensive near St. Quentin. He fought on through the year, with leave from 26th August 1918 to 11th September 1918. He was promoted to be lieutenant, although he was demobilised on 25th June 1919.

Operation Georgette: The Attack on Ypres, 9th April 1918

The second wave of German attacks, Operation 'Georgette', took place less than a month after Operation 'Michael' and had been planned to be the main German attempt to smash the British out of the war. The attack was launched on 9th April, and the Germans extended it south against Armentières the next day. The Germans attacked the Ypres Salient in force, trying to capture the city, drive past it to Poperinghe and then on past Dunkirk and the Channel ports. They won back all the land gained at the Third Battle of Ypres, but could not get the city. They were halted on its outskirts at Hellfire Corner. They regained the Messines Ridge to the south and swept on towards Mount Kemmel. This offensive is sometimes called the Battle of the Lys. Later, historians criticised the German High Command for being seduced by the successes of 'Michael' into reducing the number of soldiers involved in 'Georgette' and reinforcing 'Michael' in an attempt to capture Paris as well.

Wireless specialists like Arthur Sear monitored the situation: "Wireless messages received at Divl Directing stations from 55th Div Stns and other stations north of La Bassée during attack by enemy. Heavy gas shelling by enemy on roads and Hill 70 St Pierre sector. Despatch riders unable to reach left Brigade HQrs owing to gas shell barrage on Philosphe-Lens roads. Heavy traffic in Div HQrs Signal Office. A B & C messages total 959. Phone calls 780."[687]

These were desperate times for the British Army. On 11th April, the Commander-in-Chief, Sir Douglas Haig, issued his famous 'Backs to the Wall' Order to the troops. "Three weeks ago to-day the enemy began his terrific attacks against us on a fifty-mile front. His objects are to separate us from the French, to take the Channel Ports and destroy the British Army. In spite of throwing already 106 Divisions into the battle and enduring the most reckless sacrifice of human life, he has as yet made little progress towards his goals. We owe this to the determined fighting and self-sacrifice of our troops. Words fail me to express the admiration which I feel for the splendid resistance offered by all ranks of our Army under the most trying circumstances. Many amongst us now are tired. To those I would say that Victory will belong to the side which holds out the longest. The French Army is moving rapidly and in great force to our support. There is no other course open to us but to fight it out. Every position must be held to the last man: there must be no retirement. With our backs to the wall and believing in the justice of our cause each one of us must fight on to the end. The safety of our homes and the Freedom of mankind alike depend upon the conduct of each one of us at this critical moment."[688]

Brigadier John Charteris, Staff Officer with Haig, and a man sometimes criticised for his over optimism, was very anxious. He criticised the French for saying they were going to support the British, but seemingly doing nothing. "It looks as if we shall have to fight out this battle alone, and we have no reserves. It will decide the War. God grant the decision is not against us! Everything else fades into insignificance."[689] He doubted the wisdom of Haig's appeal in the order: "D.H. has issued a finely worded appeal to the army to fight to the last, saying that French troops are hurrying to our assistance. I wish they were. It is all so like 1914 when we were told the 1st Corps that French were coming, and they did not come. Yet then we won alone, and I believe we shall now. All the same, I wish D.H. had not issued his order. It will immensely hearten the Germans when they hear of it, as they must. I do not think our own men needed it to make them fight it out."

---

[687] War Diary, 46th Division Signals Company 9th April 1918.
[688] Sir Douglas Haig, from General Headquarters, Tuesday 11th April 1918.
[689] John Charteris, *At GHQ*, Cassell, 1931.

2nd Lieutenant Eric Paice of the Royal Field Artillery was on the receiving end of this German 'hammer blow'. At the start of April the R.F.A. batteries were re-deployed to try to counter the issues caused by the attack. Eric Paice and his men had to fire without fixed positions from which to operate, which their diary called "on the march". On 10th April, they fired off a lot of shells from positions south of Bailleul in response to reports of desperate fighting in Estaires and near Steenwerck. For Eric, the next day when Haig issued his order, was a turning point: "11th... Weather fine. 6am Heavy Machine Gun Barrage was heard on our Right after which our line fell back... 11am The 151 Inf Bde fell back & were holding the line L'Epinette to Zeldbese. 1.30pm Batteries retired... 3pm Bde HQ moved... 6pm Batteries retired... 8pm Bde HQ moved. Quiet night... Casualties 2/Lieut E.B. Paice wounded & 17 O.R."[690] Eric described the place where he was wounded as being at Robermetz. A piece of high explosive had gone through his right elbow, taking off part of the humerus. Later the doctors realised that as well as fracturing his bones, the German projectile had damaged at least one of his nerves – he subsequently lost the complete use of two fingers and had little or no sensitivity left in the little finger of his right hand. He was taken back, via field ambulance, to Calais, and thence aboard the *Princess Elizabeth* to Dover. From there he spent four months in Kitchener's Military Hospital at Brighton. After discharge he was not fit to resume active service in September 1918, so was redeployed to R.F.A. sites in Yorkshire and then to Shropshire. He was demobilised on 22nd March 1919 and then he married, but sadly died in December 1920.

After surviving the crisis of March 1918, the 15th Hampshire Battalion, including Horace Tollemache, Roy Rawle, Robert Meredith and Edward Preiss had been withdrawn and sent north to Poperinghe in Belgium, arriving on 4th April. Within days of their arrival in the Ypres Salient at the start of April 1918, the 15th Hampshires were on the Passchendaele Ridge, but the situation had seemed normal – with little sign of German activity and no further casualties. That had all changed on 11th April. The night before there was a marked increase in German artillery activity on their right, to the south. Then the Germans struck. "11th April. Situation critical owing to enemy advance on our right, a retirement thought probable and plans made to cope with same – however a counter attack in which our troops took [part] took back some of the lost ground rendered our position less anxious."[691]

Their relief was short-lived. Even though they had suffered no casualties they had been replaced on the front line by the 5th South Staffords, and pulled back to the northern outskirts of Ypres at Irish Farm. The next day they were sent back onto the ridge and held it for the next few days with only one casualty, as they helped to cover the British withdrawal to the outskirts of Ypres. Then, based about a mile north of Ypres, they were aware that the city was being shelled, including with gas, and that there was heavy fighting further south on the Messines Ridge and west towards Kemmel. They also noted a lot of German air activity, but for a time they were left in peace.

Eugene Holland was on the southern flank of the German attack from 10th April. Eugene's experiences the previous year, 1917, are hard to trace, but on 8th February 1918 he joined the 1st Border Battalion (87th Brigade, 29th Division) with the rank of lieutenant. The 1st Border Battalion was in the trenches on the Passchendaele Ridge. Eugene seems to have written a good deal of the battalion war diary in his capacity as adjutant (he was promoted to captain on 14th April). For a couple of months this was a comparatively quiet time though even when they were in reserve,

---

[690] War Diary, 152nd Brigade, Royal Field Artillery, 11th April 1918.
[691] War Diary, 15th Hampshires, 11th April 1918.

nearer to Ypres, they were shelled by a long-range German gun. They were sent south on 9th April and brought up into reserve west of Éstaires on 10th April 1918. This placed them just south of the Belgian front, a short way east of Armentières inside France, on the new front line facing the German assault. That evening they formed an eastward facing support line but, as the war diary put it, "The situation was very obscure."[692]

What had happened was that when their brigade had arrived in this new area, Eugene and the 1st Border Battalion had been sent out to cover the rest of the battalions. The German assault had been fierce and the British were indeed uncertain precisely how far the Germans had advanced. Because the threat was severe, a Pioneer battalion was sent out to replace them, and the 1st Border Battalion was re-deployed to act as brigade reserve, as their brigadier had been warned that there was a possible gap in the British line which needed to be filled by the 86th and 87th Brigades. The 86th Brigade was echeloned behind them. When reports came in of German infantry digging assault trenches in front of them, and of German artillery observed to be on the move, a general German attack was expected to follow on 11th April. The 1st Border Battalion worked in conjunction with the 2nd South Wales Borderers. "At 9.40am the O.C. S.W.B. reported that the troops in front of him, after bombardment, had retired. They had gone back very fast on the left, and the gap – how large he did not know – had been made. He had stopped a few, and with these and his reserve Company he had prolonged and reinforced his left flank. Assistance was urgently needed to restore the line, but the enemy had been temporarily stopped... Four Vickers Guns were placed at the disposal of the O.C. Border Regiment and four with the O.C. S.W.B."[693]

The fighting then became intense and at times desperate with 'D' Company suffering heavy casualties. Slowly they were pushed in, but there were moments when they made a considerable impact. "11th April, 5.30pm. Heavy attack on the new line repulsed with heavy loss generally. The enemy were caught in the open with Vickers and Lewis Gun fire. 7.0pm. Second attack was repulsed but many casualties were caused from accurate shelling."[694] That night they were forced to withdraw as the Germans got past their flanks, and the next day the Germans drove in their new position as well. As they were pushed further and further back, so the position became increasingly desperate – at one point they had to improvise a line with Guards and Pioneers on either side. By the end of 12th April things were completely desperate. A defence line was being improvised with whatever survivors were available. The remnants of 86th and 87th Brigades combined – but this composite unit only amounted to 352 men and eleven officers (including Eugene). They had the use of twelve Lewis guns and two Vickers machine guns between them. The 1st Border Battalion (with eight officers and one hundred and ninety-five men) formed the core of this defence line. Usually, to combine two brigades would have meant five to six thousand fighting troops, not three hundred and fifty! Things were desperate. Fortunately, the German attack eased off for some hours and the men were able to consolidate and dig in, helped by some Royal Engineers, and to regain contact with the brigades upon their flanks. Only at 9.30a.m. on 13th April did the Germans again push in an attack, which the composite unit was able to break up, causing heavy German casualties with well-judged Lewis gun fire. Further attacks that morning were also broken up by Vickers and Lewis gun fire. But in the afternoon the situation again became critical again: "4pm. Two Companies of enemy advanced... in small parties. There were heavily engaged by rifle and Lewis

---

[692] War Diary, 1st Border Battalion, 10th April 1918.
[693] War Diary, 87th Brigade, 29th Division, Diary of Operations 9th-13th April – entry for 11th October 1918.
[694] War Diary, 1st Border Battalion, 11th April 1918.

Gun fire and stopped but they dug in under very heavy rifle fire. Throughout the afternoon the trench was heavily trench mortared while snipers and MGs were very troublesome both from immediate front and from both flanks. Brigade HQ had withdrawn in the morning… Communication for most of the day was cut off. In the afternoon the 92nd Brigade on the Left withdrew, swinging their Right back… This was seen by one of the Brigade Staff who was on the spot who got them back into position but this withdrawal again took place in the evening which was followed up by the enemy. This left both flanks of the Battalion and the other small remnants of the two Brigades very much in the air. 10pm. The remnants of the two Brigades withdrew. Orders for this withdrawal had been issued by Division but had not been received at the time by the troops. Marched back unmolested through new line of defence being dug by 92nd Brigade… through a second line of defence being dug by 1st Australian Division… Brigade HQ then established… The march was then continued according to orders back to the St. Sylvestre area. Casualties. Officers: killed 1; missing 3; wounded 7. Other Ranks: killed 42; missing 185; wounded 160."[695] (The casualties listed would have been only for Eugene's 1st Border Battalion.)

Once back behind the new British line the battalion rested and reorganised temporarily into another 'composite' battalion, drawing in stragglers and combining with the remnants from the other units. The 1st Border Battalion made up two companies of the new composite battalion. It was soon moved forward back into the line, where it again suffered as it tried to support a French counter-attack. "17th April. No attack materialised. Stood by till 4am. Moved into close support to French Right and Australian Left, taking up position behind hedges etc. near Court Croix… by 5.30am in response to urgent request of French commander. Very quiet till 8am when considerable air activity took place. Low flying scouts carrying apparently British markings flew over in first appearance of enemy planes marked with circle and faint Iron Cross. (8 am). 9 am. Crash barrage on whole position and extending North and South indefinitely – all High explosive of all calibres, combing barrage in depth searching particularly farms, hedges and nullahs [sic]. Barrage continued till 12 noon inflicting casualties as follows: 10 officers, 60 men in 87th Composite Battalion. Border casualties: Officers 3, OR 31. Relieved at 8pm by 5th Brigade Australians and moved back to St Sylvestre Cappel area arriving 2am 18th."[696]

On 19th April, with more than a hundred additional Border stragglers coming in, the composite battalion was broken up and the 1st Border Battalion was re-formed. Over the next few days, assisted by some R.E. soldiers, they dug a new reserve line. By 26th April they were in line, with the battalion comprising two companies, and with two Tank Corps companies in support. They tried a raid to catch a German prisoner, but with hundreds of Germans facing them, all they managed to do was to attract hostile shell fire on their own positions. A third attempt at a raid, supported by British artillery, did succeed in taking one prisoner with his light machine gun, though at the cost of the loss of another officer (to 'friendly' artillery shell fire) and two men who fell to German machine guns. May and June saw them maintaining a static line as the German advance halted, but they were clearly outnumbered by the opposition, and it was with some satisfaction that they received a reinforcement of three hundred and five men from the Manchester Regiment on June 14th. For much of the rest of the month and into July they trained for a forthcoming attack, and in July they took over forward trench positions despite the inevitable casualties from German

---

[695] War Diary, 1st Border Battalion, 11th April 1918.

[696] War Diary, 1st Border Battalion, 17th April 1918. A 'nullah' is a ravine or gully, a word from southern-Asia which he might have picked up from Empire contacts.

shelling. On 25th July, Eugene was one of the first three officers to reconnoitre the area for the coming attack near Mont des Cats.

The 18th King's Royal Rifle Corps Battalion had also been rebuilt. Robert Wakely had survived the March Offensive and in the last days of March enough stragglers had made it back to Bucquoy that the battalion had been able to make up two companies again. They had been relieved on 2nd April and moved, by stages, to Poperinghe in Belgium. It was hoped that in this way they would be out of the German attack and could recuperate and re-build. On 5th April, they received sufficient reinforcements to reform into the customary four companies, and the next day they were theoretically back up to strength. Now they were moved forward to the support line, south-west of Passchendaele, relieving the 2nd Royal Fusiliers. After a few days were spent in salvage and repair work, and without casualties, the battalion was withdrawn on 16th April on the evacuation of the Passchendaele Salient. They now occupied a position east of Ypres. Here they spent the next week constructing new defence lines, and again suffered no casualties

For several days running at the end of April, they were given notice of an expected attack and ordered to be ready to move at short notice. Each time, after hurried moves, the orders were countermanded as false alarms and the battalion returned to its positions. Although one man was wounded on 29th April, it came as a shock when, on 30th April, their camp came under artillery attack: "30. Battn standing by to move at short notice. Enemy shelled Camp with Ground shrapnel, about 6 shellings falling in vicinity of huts, causing following casualties: 2nd Lt. R.A. Wakley wounded, 9 OR wounded."[697] Robert had been seriously hurt. A half-inch splinter of a high explosive shell had hit him on the left side of his neck and penetrated to within a half-inch of the connections between his 3rd and 4th cervical vertebrae. He risked paralysis if the shell splinter moved further, if not death from contamination. He was taken back through the casualty chain to the field ambulance, and on to a hospital in France. Remarkably, he wrote to tell his old headmaster that he was alright, making a joke of having German shell fragments in his neck: "Lieut. R. A. Wakely... says he is quite fit, although he belongs to a 'stiff necked and perverse generation', but hopes it will not be for long, as he is being operated on very shortly and hopes to be relieved of his duties as 'Boche Ammunition Carrier.'"[698]

He was operated on in France on 30th May, a month after he was wounded, and the operation was a success: "The operation wound is now healed. There is some stiffness of the neck & the head cannot be turned easily."[699] He was brought back to England on 6th May. Initially taken to Mont Dore Hospital in Bournemouth, as "very seriously wounded"; he was transferred for a time to the Prince of Wales Hospital for Officers, Marylebone, and then returned to Mont Dore to convalesce. Only on 23rd December 1918 was he finally passed as fit at the Command Depot, Eastbourne. He was released from duties on 3rd April 1919, and afterwards achieved his ambition to complete his theological studies and to be ordained as a congregational minister. His middle name was 'Angel', which seems very appropriate.

On 3rd April 1918, Alexander Corbet had been sent back to France. Having re-joined O.C. Depot Special Brigade on 9th April, he was quickly re-deployed: on 13th April he re-joined No.2 Special

---

[697] War Diary, 18th King's Royal Rifle Corps, 30th April 1918.
[698] *The Bournemouthian*, July 1918.
[699] Robert Wakely, Army File, WO 339/91771.

Company. "At the end of March I was sent overseas at about 24 hours' notice and without any 'draft' leave, shortly after the German offensive started. When I joined my company again they were holding the front line just out of Neuve Eglise. I was in this part of the line last year, and I could hardly credit the change in things. Ammunition dumps were being cleared, guns brought back, and everything made ready for a retirement."[700] The Bavarian 22nd Regiment, assisted by elements of the 363rd Regiment, attacked and captured Neuve Eglise on 14th April 1918 after a protracted fight with the 2nd Worcesters, who were also supported by the 33rd Battalion of the Machine Gun Corps. Other battalions in the front line close by included the Glosters, Shropshire Light Infantry, 1 /4th K.O.Y.L.I., 1 /4th York and Lancaster, and remnants of the 6th K.R.R.C.

The German attack on Neuve Eglise (now known in Belgium as Nieuwkerke) was their major effort to break through and capture Mount Kemmel on the western side of the Ypres Salient, and was an integral part of 'Georgette'. The attack had started with a massive bombardment on 11th April, followed by a mass infantry attack the next day which pushed the defence back inside the village, and then soon afterwards the village was captured. Trying to consolidate, the British were forced to abandon the Passchendaele Ridge and pull back towards Ypres. Alexander wrote about his resumption of working with gas: "When the advance stopped we were moved further south and started our usual 'gas stunts.' There were new improvements in this department, but none of them could be described as labour saving. Things are much easier, however, when we have good roads to work on, but the absence of communication trenches means continual night work." Alexander was again gassed. Army records suggest that he may have been hit once, or twice – either on one or both of 10th and 12th May 1918. Alexander stated that this new gassing "made my eyes bad again and I was returned to England." The medical notes stated that he had been gassed by 'shell gas' after which he was observed to have vomited and suffered nausea, headache, and then the gas irritated his eyes, setting off blurring and irritation to the cornea. He also suffered minor physical damage to his right ankle and shoulder. Initially, he was taken back through the system to the 2nd Australian General Hospital. This hospital was at Wimereux, just north of Boulogne, near to where he had been the year before. On 18th May he was transferred from the 2nd Australian General Hospital to England, and on 7th June 1918 was sent to Royal Victoria Hospital, Netley. This was based on the pre-war military hospital, the Royal Victoria Hospital. Sending him to Netley suggests that he was in some mental anguish, as it was really a specialist facility for military mental illness, with a separate unit for men who had lost limbs.

He partially recovered and from 13th June 1918 to 17th July 1918 was back with the Royal Engineers at Devonport. At Devonport, on 26th June, he was rated 'B2' medically, which restricted his future deployment. On 17th July he transferred to Tyne Electrical Engineers and was re-mustered as a skilled electrician on 30th August 1918 at Portsmouth, after completing a course of instruction with ant-aircraft searchlights. He was officially rated as having a "very good knowledge of all duties – keen". He explained, "The work here consists of courses in engine driving, electric lighting, and sound location, and this promises to be very interesting. It is all for coast defence and anti-aircraft stations." Having got started in his new role he was appointed acting lance-corporal (unpaid) on 30th November and so finished the war in England. He was demobilised quite quickly on 22nd February 1919. Given the opportunity to try to claim a pension for injury to his eyes, he declined and stated that he finished the war with his eyes in much the same condition as they had been when he was examined back in January 1916.

---

[700] *The Bournemouthian*, December 1918.

Former boy-soldier Eric Rey was sent back to the Western Front and into the fighting around Ypres. In late March he was attached to the 10th Royal West Kent Battalion (118th Brigade, 39th Division), although on the medal rolls he is listed as a member of the 1/4th Battalion. That battalion was in India and remained there throughout the war, but the 10th Royal West Kent Battalion had been in France since May 1916, except for a spell in Italy between November 1917 and March 1918. On its return from Italy it was rushed into the line in the attempt to stop the westward lunge of the Germans on the Somme. By Easter 1918, its colonel had been captured, and even with reinforcements rushed into line, its fighting strength was only eighteen officers and two hundred and four men on 25th March. The reconstructed battalion was taken out of the line for further reinforcement and training, and was then transferred to the Ypres Salient. They were for a time lucky – finding themselves north of the area initially attacked in the second phase of the German assault on 9th April, though they did have to take part in the withdrawal of the British line from their advanced positions round Broodseinde and Passchendaele to lines much closer to Ypres itself. Their withdrawal was not contested by the Germans so that even the covering rear guard made it safely. But there was a minor disaster when the ammunition dump at their base camp blew up under German shelling, killing an officer and seventeen men, and injuring about thirty others. In May 1918, the battalion lost two hundred men wounded or killed by gas shelling. To make matters worse for them, they also suffered badly from the 'flu epidemic. Three weeks and some training later, Eric and the battalion were moved to near La Clytte north of Kemmel where their division relieved a French one. Here, there was some additional interest raised by the attachment of some American officers, and then of two companies of the 106th American Regiment, for instruction and training. So here they were close to the 15th Hampshires, including Horace Tollemache and Edward Preiss.

In the 1918 emergency, Thomas Chaffey and the XV Corps Cyclist Battalion had briefly returned to cycling patrols. Two patrols were sent out on 9th April to try to locate the German advance troops. Both patrols (and the main unit) were on the receiving end of heavy shell fire, and their cycles were damaged. From 10th to 13th April, the battalion was heavily involved in fighting near Estaires as they tried to help to stem the German advance. The battalion took quite heavy casualties: one officer and two men killed, four officers and thirty-eight men wounded, and twelve more men missing (two believed prisoners).

Until 21st March the sector further south around Arras seemed reasonably secure. Douglas Collingwood had probably fallen sick after a leave between 2nd and 19th December, but on 1st March had returned to the 2nd Canadian Pioneer Battalion. On 22nd March they were placed on one hour's 'stand by' notice to move forward. The next day, they were transported to Roclincourt outside Arras on the evening of 23rd March and in the morning Douglas and his company began work on a new strongpoint to defend Arras. Several days later they were rushed along the Doullens road south-west of Arras to spend some uncomfortable nights under canvas, waiting to be called upon, before starting work on a new defence line known as the 'Purple Line' to cover the southern approaches to Arras. Each day they were taken to the new defence system by light railway. For a while the work was continuous but apparently not bothered by hostile action. However, on 20th April they began taking casualties from gas shells. The next day, men from the 18th and 20th Canadian Infantry Battalions were sent to assist the work of 'C' Company on the new trench system. As the war diary commented, when they arrived the area had virtually no defensive trenches but by a month of hard work a significant defence system had been created.

On 6th May, they were visited by five American infantry officers on a tour of instruction – a moment of reassurance and hope that future reinforcements would arrive to help. The work on the defence lines continued without respite, including new artillery dug-outs and building a tunnel under a main road. Sometimes they were assisted by men from the 27th and 29th Canadian Infantry Battalions. On 1st June, Douglas would have learned that he had been 'Mentioned in Dispatches' on 28th May for his hard work before and since the crisis. In a reorganisation of the Pioneers (partially a reflection on the manpower shortage and partly to distinguish Pioneers from the men of the Labour battalions) the Pioneer battalions were now absorbed into the Royal Engineers. Accordingly, the 2nd Canadian Pioneer Battalion was disbanded and divided between three Engineer battalions. Douglas went with his commanding officer to take over 'C' Company, the 5th Canadian Engineer Battalion, which was formed from a similarly disbanded 5th Canadian Field Engineers Company. He was promoted to major.

Although the second offensive had been intended to concentrate on the Ypres Salient and the north, in the end much of the fighting was further south, west of Albert, essentially in a continuation of Operation Michael. A major battle raged south-east of Amiens, around Villers-Bretonneux.

The Battles of Villers-Bretonneux

West of Arras, at Le Quesnoy-en-Arras, Ralph Cheshire and the 2nd Berkshire Battalion had reorganised and trained. After their losses against Operation Michael, three hundred and eighty-three replacement soldiers joined the battalion on 5th April. The war was going badly for the British. On the night of 20th to 21st April Ralph and the battalion moved forward to relieve the 54th Australian Battalion north of Villers-Brettoneux. This village was the last village of significance east of Amiens. The British battalions trying to hold back the onslaught had been relieved by Australians who were tasked with holding the villages of Dernancourt and Villers-Bretonneux. (Villers-Bretonneux was south of the River Somme, and Dernacourt was on the north bank, south-west of Albert. Albert itself had fallen.) The British 4th Division and the Australian 9th Brigade tried to hold the southern flank at Villers-Bretonneux whilst other Australians held the north bank.

On 4th April, the Germans had captured part of Hill 104, east of Villers-Bretonneux. In the First Battle of Villers-Bretonneux, the Australians and British had stopped the Germans capturing the village but the position was far from secure. On 18th April, the Germans resumed their drive to capture Amiens. On 20th-21st, the 25th Brigade, including Ralph's battalion, relieved the 14th Australian Infantry Brigade in the line to the north of the village and for four days the battalion held its place in the line.

The Second Battle of Villers-Bretonneux began on 24th April when German forces, spearheaded by tanks, captured from the British earlier, broke the British defences south of the village. The first ever tank-on-tank battle was fought, both sides fighting with British tanks and the British won! But the Germans captured the village and pushed west of it, forming a salient in their advance. That night, The Australian 13th and 15th Brigades counter-attacked that salient from north and south, cutting the German lines east of the village. Some Germans surrendered, others retired eastwards, and the village was saved for the British. North of the village, Ralph Cheshire and the 2nd Berks attacked at 6.30a.m. on 25th April in support of the night operation. The battalion war diary sums up the attack laconically: "Counter attack by battalion at 6.30 am on Villers-Bretonneux. Village cleared and mopped up. 35 machine guns and 300 prisoners captured."[701] For two more days the battalion stood in line in the trenches to defend the village until it was withdrawn on 27th April. Nine officers had been killed or wounded. Of the ordinary soldiers, fifty-five had been killed; one hundred and sixty-six wounded; a further nineteen suffering from wounding by gas; and ten were missing completely. Whilst often the battle is hailed as a great Australian victory, which it was, it was also a joint British-Australian effort.

This time, Ralph did not come through. In *The Bournemouthian*, the account of his death says he was fatally wounded on Kemmel Hill on April 24th. This must be an error, for the battalion was far from Kemmel that day (indeed the French were at that time guarding the hill, not the British, and no Berkshire battalion was even in the vicinity). Ralph would have been one of the one hundred and sixty-six wounded at Villers-Bretonneux. He suffered multiple wounds, but there were hopes that he might survive. He was taken back through the casualty clearing system to the hospital at Le Trépot on the Somme coastline, south of St. Valery-sur-Somme. By 1918, there were a number of different hospitals there: three general hospitals (the 3rd, 16th and 2nd Canadian), the No.3 Convalescent Depot and Lady Murray's B.R.C.S. Hospital. In one of these the doctors tried to save him but the operation failed, and he died on May 14th 1918. He was buried in the new cemetery at Mont Huon because the main Le Trépot Cemetery was already full. And there were many more casualties still to come.

The second battle which had led to Ralph's death finally brought Cecil Tollemache the opportunity to be in the midst of battle. After recovering from his first wounds, he had returned to France in May 1916 and re-joined his Pioneer battalion. During 1916 his battalion, the 11th Hampshires, had been involved as Pioneers in the Battles of Guillemont and of Ginchy, within the Battle of the Somme. Those were bloody affairs. On 8th March 1917, Cecil had been promoted to full lieutenant and was transferred to the 18th Middlesex Regiment (another Pioneer battalion) in the 33rd Division. Eventually, in March 1918, he was attached to the 2nd Northamptonshire Battalion, 8th Division. Finally, he was where he always wanted to be: in a fighting, infantry battalion.

Cecil joined the 2nd Northamptonshire Battalion on 15th March 1918 and was posted to 'B' Company. When, in March 1918, they had fought against the German onslaught in the battle of St. Quentin, for reasons not clear from the battalion war diary, Cecil is not among the officers listed as taking part in the fighting. We are told that he and another officer 're-joined' the battalion on 7th April and he was now switched to 'A' Company, and the battalion war diary twice makes explicit mention that he took part in the later and equally dramatic events of 23rd to 28th April. At that time the battalion had just been pulled back into Blangy Wood after a period in the line near Villers-Brettoneux. On 22nd April, "A prisoner captured by the Sherwood Foresters said that the enemy were attacking on the morning of 23rd. All precautions were taken & a fighting patrol with a Lewis gun was sent out by each Coy. In the line at 2am (23.4.18), returning at dawn but no enemy were met with & the attack did not take place. The order in the line was D Coy on the R, B next, A on the Left & C Coy in reserve… 24.4/18. During the early hours of the 24th the wood [Bois de Blangy] was heavily shelled both with Gas & H.E. 2/Lt Howard was killed & several men killed & wounded. With some difficulty Coys were got out of the wood & reorganised on the open ground S of the wood. A message was received between 4 & 5am ordering the Bn to take up its battle position in the reserve line… We were in touch with the 8th Londons on the R & the 1st Worcesters on the L, &

---

[701] War Diary, 2nd Berkshire Battalion, 25th April 1918.

were supported by 1 section of Vickers guns. As the frontage was of considerable length it was decided to have 4 Coys in the Front trench with the Demonstration Platoon & Bn HQrs acting as a reserve, dug in about 400x in rear. Wounded men coming in reported that Villers Brettoneux had been taken by the enemy. At this time we were being heavily shelled & Cachy also was being bombarded."[702]

After sending out more patrols during the day to check on the situation, that night the battalion was ordered to attack Villers-Brettoneux from the south in conjunction with the 22nd Durham Light Infantry, after the 51st and 52nd Australian Battalions had first attacked to clear a route to allow the English battalions to attack the village itself. This attack was made in the teeth of a heavy German bombardment in which the battalion commander, Colonel Latham, was killed. Ironically, casualties mounted when they reached what had been their own thick band of barbed wire, and until they could locate a suitable gap they were subject to heavy German machine-gun fire. Once they got through the former British wire, they reformed in an extended line. "The signal was given to advance & attack the village. The high ground… was covered without any difficulty but on moving down the slope the enemy fired numerous Very lights from the direction of the village & also from a point towards the Bois d'Aquenne – lights from this last position were fired parallel to us, lighting up the whole valley & m/e guns opened very heavy fire on our troops going down into the village. Our casualties were very heavy. As it seemed useless to proceed in this direction we withdrew slightly & side slipped to the R & tried to get through again, but the enemy had evidently massed m/e guns all along the S side of Villers-Brettoneux."[703] To their right, the Australians were also being held up by the German machine guns, so the battalion commanders decided to co-operate by using their entrenching tools to dig a defensive line, with the Northants facing north towards the village and the 51st Australians facing east.

In the morning they were cheered to see a British tank working its way along the edge of Aquenne Wood, smashing the Germans who were there in strength. Many Germans broke and tried to flee back to the village, and Cecil and the Northants men used a captured German machine gun to fire on the retreating Germans as they broke cover. This was part of a bigger British effort to clear the village of its German defenders, so the decision was taken jointly by the commanders of the 2nd Northants and 51st Australians that they would rush the one hundred and fifty yards of open ground (despite being already subject to enfilade German fire from an uncaptured defence point at Monument Farm). "At a suitable moment the advance was signalled & the men rose & dashed forward. It was about ¼ minute before the enemy grasped what was happening & opened very heavy fire & only the men who were slow suffered, about 12 casualties in all." Patrols were again sent out, which discovered from hostile machine-gun fire that the Germans were still occupying the eastern end of the village. By this time, 'A' Company had been reduced to only ten fighting men, though the other companies had more. The rest of the day saw some tricky fighting against German snipers in the village, and also a terrible German counter-barrage, but fortunately this did not last long. "25.4.18. Hot soup & tea came up & were much appreciated as the men had gone into action the day before without water or rations. Two platoons of A Coy under Lt. Tollemache who had been cut off joined the battalion making it up to a strength of 8 officers & 190 O.R.s."

---

[702] War Diary, 2nd Northamptonshire Battalion, 22nd-24th April, 1918.
[703] War Diary 2nd Northamptonshire Battalion 24th April 1918; the following extracts were also taken from the diary with entries taken from 24th and 25th April.

At dawn the next day, a French unit unsuccessfully attempted to dislodge the Germans from Monument Farm. When the Northants men realised that a weak Australian company had also survived, they linked up and decided to push forward when the French should attack again. However, the new attack did not materialise, and Cecil and the men of the 2nd Northants were relieved and sent back to regroup. Between 23rd and 28th April, the battalion had suffered fifteen killed, nineteen missing – not too bad really considering what they had experienced – but also two hundred and fifty-one wounded. They had managed to capture eighteen Germans and two machine guns, though they could only manage to bring one of those back into the British lines.

Earlier, in March, as the situation deteriorated, Haig had asked French General Pétain for reinforcements. Pétain refused, but Haig had pushed again for a joint Allied conference which had been held at Doullens on March 26th. This was a dangerous move for political reasons by Haig as he knew Prime Minister Lloyd George disliked him but rated the French more highly. At the conference it was agreed that General Ferdinand Foch would take supreme command of the Allied forces, but Foch tacitly agreed to support Haig and not to interfere in British actions. Soon the advantage of an overall command strategy began to bear fruit. Operation Michael had begun to slow down, and troops were moved around. For example, in April, soon after Ralph Cheshire's death, the 2nd Berks were sent south to help the French further south in the battle to save Paris.

Reginald Winch also fought to thwart the attempt by the Germans to push forward to Amiens. His unit was pulled out of line on 2nd April – and two days later reformed and renamed again, as the 3rd London Battalion. They had fallen back towards Paris where briefly they went back into line near Ambleny before being switched north to take position to the south of Amiens. They were attacked on 24th April when "Enemy attacked. Heavy barrage and gas bombardment at 3am. Attack developed at 6am. Battalion held Front Line all day in spite of Flanks falling back. Heavy fighting throughout the day. British and French counter-attacked at 10pm and restored line in parts in the left flank. Situation on the left flank obscure in Bois de Hangard. 25th. Battalion held line. Enemy endeavoured to attack during the afternoon, but attack broken up by artillery fire. Casualties:- 6 Officers and 219 Other Ranks. Battalion relieved by 7th and 8th Battalions, London Regiment."[704]

There had also been little rest for Richard Barfoot and the men of the 24th Field Ambulance. The ambulance had been moved forward to Villars-Brettoneux to relieve an Australian medical unit, and to treat the numerous gas cases coming through from there. So it was that they were caught up in the battle on 24th April 1918 when the Germans attacked at 7a.m. The forward regimental aid post, and some advanced dressing stations had to be abandoned when they became subject to direct German machine-gun fire. Richard Barfoot might well have helped Ralph Cheshire of the 2nd Berkshires, as this ambulance found itself responsible, with some limited help, for the medical support of the whole 8th Division. Nine of their men were wounded – three had to be evacuated through the casualty system, but the other six remained on duty. As far as we know, Richard survived unscathed, but two of their cars were hit by shells and a further ten cars were disabled in the fighting. Withdrawn afterwards into Amiens, they were still not safe. On the night of 2nd-3rd May, they were bombed by German aeroplanes, and whilst none of their personnel were injured (though some engineers were killed) more of the equipment suffered. The next day they were moved south-east by train in support of their division to assist the French west of Reims. In that fighting they were again forced into a hurried retreat as the Germans pressed on towards Paris. A

---

[704] War Diary, 3rd London Battalion, 24th-25th April 1918.

captain, a lieutenant and forty-three men went missing, before they stopped the retreat; another man had been killed, and four wounded. But once again, Richard had come through.

Meanwhile, further north, a youthful John Nutman had arrived to play his part in stemming this German advance. John was the second of four brothers who attended the school. John, born in 1899, was more commonly known as 'Jack' by his friends and contemporaries. When he left school in March 1915 he was too young to be allowed to volunteer, and for a time assisted his father in his duties as Borough Accountant for Christchurch, but in July 1917, after his eighteenth birthday, he enlisted. After training, he was sent to France in March 1918 to fill the gaps caused by the heavy casualties, joining the 2/4th Oxford and Buckinghamshire Light Infantry Battalion. Only about fifty men of the battalion had survived the onslaught of March by combining with an intact battalion of the Gloucesters and only one front line officer, Major Jones, had survived. John joined them in April in a fresh draft of three hundred men and officers who acted as "an infusion of new blood and vigour... Many of these were boys."[705] Other remnant Buckinghamshire soldiers joined them (without orders!).

John Nutman

The battalion was part of 184th Brigade, 61st Division. The general's intention had been to give the newly recreated battalion time to train and to gel together, but the German attack of April 1918 thwarted this idea; instead the battalion was sent straight into the new battle zone. The Germans had broken through the Portuguese defence line and had reached Merville. "My orders were to take up a line, which was at present covered by the 51st Division, between Robecq and Calonne and for that object to detrain and move forward immediately... Still the situation at 9 a.m. [April 12th] was both obscure and difficult. Until their ammunition seemed to be expended, our artillery, which had withdrawn behind the La Bassée Canal, kept up a fire upon the open ground between Les Amusoires, where the Battalion was concentrating, and the Calonne road, which it was necessary for us to cross. Doubtless this untoward shelling was due to the reports spread by stragglers, of whom there was a considerable number from different units. Shortly after this occurrence I had the good fortune to meet a gunner subaltern, and for the next few days, pending a reinforcement of the artillery, what guns there were gave us excellent support"[706].

By the next day, with some heavy fighting, the battalion established its base at a farm called Les Amusoires, and for several days the battalion helped to prevent further German advances. After this the battalion made 'tours' of duty, holding the line in rotation with others from the brigade, suffering heavy German shelling and with episodes of intense patrolling activity. From the middle of June, the battalion began suffering from the 'flu epidemic which began to take a major effect on both sides. Nevertheless, the battalion had to remain in the line until it was moved back on 10th July and was switched to General Plumer's army.

Meanwhile, further north again, the remnants of the 11th West Surrey Battalion (or 'Queens'

---

[705] *The Story of the 2/4th Oxfordshire and Buckinghamshire Light Infantry*, by G.K. Rose, 1920, p. 175.
[706] ibid, pp. 177-178.

Regiment) of which Frederick Furness was an officer had been moved north to Ypres by 8th April, and the Army had begun to pull in some more senior officers to help reorganise the battalion. With the German offensive developing in the north as well, they were needed, and soon were digging in new defence lines supporting those troops further forward. From 14th April, they were again in the front line. The attack broke on them on 27th April as the Germans attacked heavily with artillery as units probed forward and laid down harassing fire on the Surreys. Frederick was promoted to captain in charge of a company. There was little respite from the continued attempts by the Germans to move round or through them – the British had to keep a careful and continuous watch on their lines to prevent infiltration or even a major probing assault, while keeping their heads down under heavy German artillery fire.

It almost seems incredible that on 13th May – despite constant German artillery attacks – that, even allowing for their being rotated back into reserve, some of the men still managed to attend a concert (although the war diary does not make it clear if this was put on by the men or by visiting players). After another spell in the front line, they were tasked on 24th May to clean up and repair the defences of Ypres itself.

Meanwhile, further south, on 24th April, Arthur Elcock of the Pioneer Section of 'C' Company of the 2nd Devonshire Battalion had moved into the Villers-Bretonneux defence line to face and hold off a German attack four days later.

On 21st May 1918, at Béthune, south of Ypres, another Old Boy, Frank Game, was fatally wounded. Born in 1897, and at school from 1906 to 1914, Frank was more generally known as Freddy. In his first year he won the Thomson Scholarship and from then excelled in his exams, becoming particularly distinguished in pure and applied maths. As early as 1912, he gained First Class Honours in the senior exams and was photographed soon after. A mainstay of the O.T.C., he was also a school prefect. He won many awards, and in 1914 left school having won both a £50 higher education scholarship and also the Clothworkers' Scholarship of £60 a year (then a very significant sum) to attend the City and Guilds (Engineering) College in London. Here too he excelled by winning the John Samuel's Scholarship for £38, but he suspended his studies in order to work for Thorneycroft Engineering, making motor transport for the Army.

Frank Game, 1912

A local newspaper remarked later that he "was a young man of high Christian character, and during his school life not only carried off the large awards referred to above, but won various prizes for Christian knowledge. He became Registrar to the East Cliff Congregational Sunday School, and also filled the office of Sidesman at that church."[707] He was enrolled under the Derby Scheme at the end of 1916 and called up for service on June 11th 1917. When the Army assessed him it was no surprise that he was rated "excellent" and sent to the A.S.C. (Army Service Corps) to work in the Mechanical Transport Section. In the baffling way military administration sometimes managed to confuse and bungle, some unknown idiot deployed him as a clerk instead.

---

[707] *The Bournemouth Visitors' Directory*, 15th June 1918.

But later in the year he was sent with a large group of men to be assessed for the Tank Corps. Once again military bureaucracy got it wrong. Instead, he was deployed to the South Staffordshire Regiment as an infantry private, although the Tank Corps tried hard unsuccessfully to get him back. His battalion commander, however, recognised his potential and recommended him for officer training. A new War Office memo, however, had come out saying that to be so recommended a man must have had overseas experience, and so, on April 3rd 1918, he was sent, still as a private, to France to join the 1/6th South Staffordshire Battalion, 137th Brigade, 46th (North Midland) Division. On May 18th, his battalion relieved the 5th Leicesters in trenches near Verquin, in the Loisne Sector on the southern outskirts of Béthune. Almost immediately they came under a series of gas attacks. On 19th May, at 2a.m., the battalion headquarters was bombarded with gas shells. No one was hurt but on the night of May 20th-21st Frank was hit by poison gas. He was sent back to a casualty clearing station. "21 May 1918 – The enemy put over a terrific bombardment of gas shells between 11pm 20th to about 4am 21st. The number of shell estimated exceeded 10,000 including 500 8". Owing to the great concentration we suffered heavy casualties i.e. 6 officers and 134 other ranks of 'D' and 'A' Companies."[708] The gas blinded him for four days. Then, as sometimes happened in such cases, he seemed to start to recover. But his condition deteriorated and Frank died after seventeen days on 7th June 1918. He was buried in the cemetery at Pernes which had only been started that April when 1st and 4th Canadian Casualty Clearing Stations had set up in Pernes, west of Béthune as the British fell back before the German advance.

Frank Game

Operation Blücher-Yorck: May 27th 1918

At the end of April 1918, five divisions of Commonwealth forces (making up IX Corps) were sent south to join the French 6th Army to rest and refit following the German offensives on the Somme and Lys. When Operation Georgette ran out of punch, the third assault, Operation Blücher-Yorck was launched on May 27th. With a mass of artillery in support, the Germans attacked in what is sometimes known as the Third Battle of the Aisne. They smashed their way over the Chemin des Dames battlefield and on to fight at Chateau-Thierry and Belleau Wood. The British divisions found themselves facing this massive German attack. Although the British and French fought ferociously, they found themselves pushed back across the Aisne to the Marne. Jack Derrett was one of those who felt the impact of this third big German attack.

Jack had been born in 1897. On 15th September 1914, he and his younger brother Charles joined Bournemouth School. He immediately decided to join the O.T.C. (alongside William Alder and others) and when he left in September 1916 he enlisted in the Army. The headmaster believed he had gone to Liverpool to join the Liverpool Scottish, but he actually joined the 2/5th South Lancashire Battalion as a private. This battalion had been formed at St. Helens in September 1914, but – despite the Headmaster's belief! – was no longer in the north. In 1916, it was training near Aldershot in Surrey. Jack wrote a letter for the school magazine, which unfortunately was never published. On 16th February 1917, the battalion landed at Boulogne. It is not clear if he served on

---

[708] War Diary of the 1/6th Battalion, South Staffordshire Regiment, May 21st 1918.

the Western Front with them at this time, but he was accepted for officer training in the latter part of 1917.

Jack was commissioned 2nd lieutenant in the 4th Yorkshire Battalion on 29th January 1918. This battalion was better known as the 'Green Howards', a name dating back to its origins in the Seventeenth Century. It had been in France since April 1915, part of the 150th Brigade, 50th (Northumbrian) Division. He was one of a very large number of reinforcements who virtually twice recreated the battalion in April 1918 after dramatic fighting between 2nd April and 17th April had twice brought about heavy casualties. It is not clear in which batch of reinforcements Jack arrived. The battalion had been sent to help defend the crossings over the River Lys. Their job was based on a position on the northern (west) bank of the river opposite a bridge at Sailly-sur-la-Lys. On 9th April they managed to blow up a footbridge over the river whilst Royal Engineers prepared to blow the main bridge at Sailly. British and Portuguese troops were withdrawn across the river, but the charges to blow the bridge then failed. This battalion then had to hold off the Germans from crossing it, which they managed to do, inflicting heavy casualties on them. However, the Germans managed to cross the river further north, and soon they found themselves facing German attacks both from the front and from the left – their northern flank. Four officers were killed or wounded in the next day's fighting. The battalion then was split up as a general westward retirement was made, with the inevitable additional casualties. Even as they retreated, further casualties were received before the battalion again reorganised at La Lacque, just inside the French border with Belgium. Five officers had been killed or wounded, and 353 men, over the course of the month, whilst an additional twenty-two officers and 802 men had joined them – including Jack. In May, the battalion, as part of its division and brigade, were deployed to try to defend the route to Paris. By the middle of May they were in trenches at Craonne between Reims and Laon. Things were far from secure: "19th May. After a heavy bombardment the enemy raided our forward posts at Carponiere Vincent. Enemy took two prisoners. Flanking fire from our Lewis Guns caused the enemy casualties."[709]

A few days later they were in the trenches at Craonne when the Germans attacked in force. This was the start of the third big German offensive, Operation Blücher-Yorck. This time the Germans made use of tanks – probably captured and refitted British ones, since the Germans did not really have tanks of their own to make readily available. "Craonne. 26th-27th May. Battn took up a support position round Craon[n]elle and La Hutte. Enemy bombardment started about 1am 27th May. Heavy gas shelling as far back as Maizy. The enemy broke through on our left & pushed on towards Beaurieux arriving there about 10am. The enemy also came through on our right using tanks over the flat country to the east of Craonne. This party also pushed on towards Beaurieux and surrounded the Brigade in the line. The enemy then pushed on towards Maizy. All troops in Maizy and the few who had got out of Beaurieux then made a stand on the hills to the south of the village. At about 11.15am these troops were withdrawn from this position. The next position was held at Glennes, and later a line on the hill north of Fismes."[710] The battalion continued to be pushed back, but Jack had been captured on 27th May. When the situation was reviewed at the end of the month, it was recognised that twenty-four officers had been lost – most, like Jack, listed as 'missing', though in a couple of cases it was known they had been wounded or killed. Of the men, three were known to have been killed and fifty-two wounded, but five hundred and sixty-six were missing.

---

[709] War Diary, 4th Battalion Yorkshire Regiment, 19th May 1918.
[710] War Diary, 4th Battalion Yorkshire Regiment, 26th-27th May 1918.

Effectively, the battalion had been wiped out. Later, after the war, an enquiry was made into the circumstances in which Jack had been taken prisoner, and he was exonerated from any blame.

Meanwhile, he disappeared into the German system for prisoners of war, ending up in the POW Camp at Stalsund. There he recognised fellow Old Bournemouthians. Harold Le Roy, at school between 1910-1916, in the R.F.C./R.A.F., and whose birthday was almost the same as Jack's, was a fellow prisoner. The school magazine described Harold's experiences there, "…finally to Stralsund. Apart from the delay in receiving parcels of food and clothing, and the hardship which that involved, Le Roy's letters indicate that he has not been badly treated and that he has kept in good health and spirits. Strangely enough he met, in the prison camp, two of our old boys, J.H. Derrett and H.W. Burry, and attended a lecture by Mr. Taylor, who was formerly second master here."[711] (Harold Burry was a R.F.C. pilot who had only learned to fly in 1917-18.) Jack was repatriated on Christmas Day 1918. Before he could be demobilised, he had to face the aforementioned enquiry, but at the start of 1920 he was free to marry, and he went on to settle running the 'Half Moon' pub in Sherborne, where he died in 1954.

Cecil Tollemache also fell prisoner to the Germans in this offensive. On 15th May, whilst the 2nd Northamptonshire Battalion was in brigade reserve, Cecil was among a group of officers and men sent off for a course of instruction on the Lewis gun, but when he returned to it at Mont Notre Dame, near Reims, on 27th May, a "very heavy bombardment commenced at 1.00 am and continued for 4 hours, Gas shells falling in Back areas… The Enemy made a surprise attack on the Right of the Bn. Front and completely surrounded the Bn. The Adjutant, Capt. Blave M.C. and Regt. Sergt.-Major were the only two to escape. Lieut. J.C. Lobb, Lieut. C.H. Tollemache, Lieut. G.M. Edmonds, 2/Lieut. V.S. Copping, and 76 other ranks returned from Lewis gun course at 9th Corps School Lhery and were Brigaded under Lieut. Col. Davidge, 1/Worcester Regt and proceeded up the line as reinforcements, details and transport moved to Montigny via Ventelay at 1.00pm. A Guard under 2/Lieut S. Mason was left behind to take charge of Baggage, etc., which eventually had to be destroyed by fire…"[712]

That day "As a Lewis Gun Officer I went into action with a detachment of the 2nd Northamptonshire Regiment on the 27th May 1918 near Rouchy. About 1 p.m. that day I was shot through the chest, the bullet passed through my left lung. I was carried to an Aid Post where my wounds were dressed. Shortly afterwards I was put into an English ambulance car and driven to a C.C.S. at Mont Notre Dame, some distance behind our Front Line. I was unconscious when I arrived there and two days afterwards (29.5.18) on recovering consciousness I was informed that the Germans had advanced and captured the entire hospital and staff. I being a patient in the Hospital became a prisoner of war."[713] The military record also described his wound: "Wounded on 27.5.18 by bullet which entered just to left of Sternum 2nd intercostal space, and gained exit behind just below scapular spine (left). There was Haemoptysis for a week after the wound." The Germans required the British medical teams to continue to care for the wounded, although Cecil later said that as the Germans looted the stores, this became increasingly difficult. He remained in the hospital for about six weeks, during which time, on 17th June, the Kaiser himself visited on a tour of inspection, had

---

[711] *The Bournemouthian*, December 1918.

[712] War Diary 2nd Northamptonshire Battalion, 27th May 1918.

[713] Army Record papers, Cecil Herbert Tollemache, National Archives, WO – statement given on 27th January 1919.

his photograph taken, and talked to some of the prisoners, including Cecil. According to Cecil's account, "He asked me where I was wounded and how I was getting on; what battalion I belonged to, and he told me the battalion fought very well at Cambrai. He seemed to know all about it. He saw Captain French, a cousin of Lord French. He told him he knew Lord French very well, that he [Lord French] did very well in South Africa, but he had not spoken to him since the outbreak of the war. I think he said that more in a joke."[714]

(Later, in April 1919, the school magazine published quite a long account of his experiences, derived from an interview he gave to a journalist of *The Bournemouth Visitors' Directory*. Some details as reported do not exactly fit with his Army record file details. However, his account made clear the very poor conditions which he endured as a prisoner of war. He described in some detail the lack of food and the insanitary conditions, though pointing out that the ordinary soldiers fared worse than the officers. He had spent time at an overcrowded officers' camp at Rastatt and later was sent to Kamp Stigall at Bei Pillau near Danzig. He described privations such as being made to travel in cattle trucks, to eat and drink substitute food and drink, to cope with the outbreak of 'flu, not having soap (so that some officers were willing to barter up to two hundred cigarettes for a piece), and not being allowed boots. Perhaps one of his most critical comments was the way that their parcels were intercepted – he reckoned to have received only two of twenty sent to him. This fits closely with similar complaints recorded in Foreign Office files, despite Red Cross and neutral inspections of the camps. He also gave an interesting account of the way the German guards' attitudes changed as the war came towards its end: "they became more considerate to their charges and had taken to muttering about their conditions. They had passed from boasting about their Army and Kaiser to abusing both and saying what they would like to do with the latter.")

Meanwhile, after further reorganisation and training on 12th May, Arthur Elcock of the Pioneer Section of 'C' Company of the 2nd Devonshire Battalion took over the front line from the 317th French Infantry Regiment in the Juvincourt Sector, north of Reims, in the south where the British were helping to bolster the French defences north-east of Paris. Two days later they were reorganised so that three companies manned the front with one in support. They were heavily shelled, and that continued for the next day. After a few quieter days, the Germans tried to rush the front line posts on 18th May, but although grenades were thrown, the battalion suffered no losses and the German effort was thwarted. Two days later they tried a raid of their own, but this failed to bring back any prisoners or means of identification. Then the 2nd West Yorkshire Battalion relieved them.

On 26th May, the battalion moved into support at the Bois des Buttes in the expectation of a German attack. Sure enough, the next day they suffered a heavy bombardment followed by a German assault. Under heavy shelling and machine-gun fire they were forced to retreat. They fought many rearguard actions, and men went missing as they retreated. According to the records of the International Red Cross, this was when Arthur was captured by the Germans. He too remained a prisoner of the Germans for the rest of the war, and survived to be demobilised in April 1919. In December, the school magazine reported that he had been "taken prisoner by the Germans in March, 1918, and in lodged in a prison camp at Anhalt"[715] but this was an error of detail – he had survived until April.

---

[714] Interview with *The Bournemouth Visitors' Directory*, quoted in *The Bournemouthian*, April 1919.
[715] *The Bournemouthian*, December 1918.

So, brushing aside the French and British opposition, the Germans swept on towards Paris and there were tensions within the Allied Command as a result of the German attacks. In the first two days of June, there was a difficult meeting of the Supreme War Council. In a preliminary meeting to the full council, the key British leaders (Prime Minister Lloyd George, Lord Milner of the War Cabinet, Wilson Chief of the Imperial General Staff, and Haig) argued about whether Haig should be required to release the American troops then training with the B.E.F. to help relieve the French divisions, and Haig spoke vehemently against it because he believed the French lacked sufficient fighting resolve: "From what I heard from Foch and Weygand, I inferred that French reserves once in the battle did not last but 'melted away': this was due to coddling them last summer, and to want of discipline and to the lack of reliable officers and N.C.O.s."[716] Eventually, Haig reluctantly agreed to release eight American divisions to the French on 3rd-4th June, although he continued to resist further French requests for him to weaken the B.E.F. position by transferring three further British divisions south to protect Paris. (Instead, the British divisions already committed for that task were transferred back to Haig by the end of June.)

Operation Gneisenau: 9th June 1918

On 9th June, Ludendorff launched Operation 'Gneisenau' – an attempt using eighteen divisions to strengthen the salient his previous southern attacks had created by capturing land on its northern flank, pushing north-west from the Aisne Salient to link up with German positions to the north. The apparent success of 'Michael' compared to 'Georgette' (which had been held up on the outskirts of Ypres) had distorted the whole German plan. As local German commanders pulled in ever greater resources to try to push for Paris, Ludendorff reduced his efforts immediately south of Ypres.

A massive French artillery bombardment caught the Germans as they gathered in the jumping-off trenches on 7th June. The Germans countered with their own bombardment – huge quantities of poison gas mixed with high explosives. This was a pivotal moment. The Germans were unaware that French intelligence had succeeded in breaking the German codes on 3rd June, and had gained further intelligence from aerial reconnaissance and from interrogating German deserters, and so the French had been generally aware of the German plan. Although conceding more ground on 9th and 10th June, Foch had gathered forces for a counter-attack by five divisions and nearly one hundred and fifty French tanks. His orders included this accurate summary: "Tomorrow's operations should be the end of the defensive battle which we have been fighting for more than two months. It should mark the definite check of the Germans and the renewal of the offensive on our part. It must succeed. Let everyone understand this."[717] On 11th June, the Allied counter-attack began – tentatively at first, and then with greater confidence, culminating in the great Battle of Amiens in August. On 11th June, four French and two American divisions supported by tanks and airplanes drove into the German spearhead, bringing the German attack to a halt. This was a defensive success: the Germans were checked but not significantly thrown back. The advance of Operation 'Gneisenau' had been halted within about two days, and Ludendorff called off the attempt within a week, but the fighting went on. Almost immediately the Allies began preparing their own set of offensives.

---

[716] *The Private Papers of Douglas Haig, 1914-1919*, Eyre and Spottiswoode (London) 1952; quoted in J.H. Johnson, *1918 The Unexpected Victory, Arms and Armour*, 1997, p. 75.

[717] Quoted in J.H. Johnson, *1918 The Unexpected Victory, Arms and Armour*, 1997, p. 77.

In Between the Offensives

Arthur Sear and the signallers of the 46th Division Signals Company began training for open warfare and a wireless communication scheme was created. As April had drawn to a close, so did the intensity of the fighting, and its impact on signals communications south of Béthune. In consequence, much of May was spent digging and renewing underground telephone cables to the forward positions. Members of the Signals Company were reminded of the different methods of communication which they should use – in what looks like an order of priority: Telephone and Telegraph; Visual; Wireless (including Power buzzer & Amplifier); Runners; Despatch riders (horse or cycle); pigeons; contact aeroplane. For a day, a practice was held in which only urgent medical calls might be made by telephone – all other use of the telephone was forbidden. This allowed them to practice for conditions when all wires might be cut; the results were found to indicate that the company could successfully maintain communications for the division without using the telephone. On 2nd June, a similar practice day was held across the entire corps, and two days later some members viewed a demonstration on the potential of communication to 137 Brigade by message-carrying rocket.

On 2nd May, though still unfit, Frederick White had returned to France and re-joined the 6th Dorset Battalion. He probably re-joined the battalion a few days later when they came out of the line, having been holding trenches near Aveluy Wood. This was a time of training for the counter-attack, and the battalion trained at Forceville, a few miles west of Beaumont-Hamel. The enlightened battalion colonel tried to give his men a sense of competition and accomplishment: "Note. The period of Rest and Training – May 10-25th 1918 – was highly successful from the point of view of training, individual, collective and tactical. All ranks were enabled to fire rifles on ranges, and almost all ranks fired from a Lewis Rifle. Competitions were held in rifle shooting, drill, cooking, Lewis Rifles and rifle grenadiers, for which money prizes were given, the Battalion receiving a grant of 600 Francs thro' Brigade for this purpose. The Sports held on the 25th were a great success and highly popular with the men. As a result the battalion were much benefited in physique, general efficiency, and morale."[718] However, the good days were not to last. On 26th May, they relieved the Cambridgeshire Regiment in support trenches amidst a heavy gas bombardment, and the Germans maintained heavy artillery activity over the next few days. At this time one of Frederick's officers was fellow Old Bournemouthian, Bernard Allbon.

From the start of June they were practising for a large scale raid in conjunction with the 7th East Yorkshire Regiment. On the night of 7th June, they took up their positions on the assembly trenches west of Beaumont-Hamel. This was the same battleground where the 2nd Hampshire Battalion had attacked in 1916, and in the area now preserved as 'Newfoundland Park'. They were to make a raid on the evening of 8th June. "During the day the raiding party of the battalion lay quiet in their assembly trenches. At 10.5 pm the barrage opened and the Battalion Raiding Party with a strength of 16 officers and 500 men on the Right in conjunction with a raiding party of a similar number of the 7th East Yorkshire Regiment assaulted the German lines near Beaumont-Hamel to a depth of 500 yards. The Raid was a great success – the Battalion killing many Germans in hand to hand fighting, capturing about 40 prisoners and 4 machine guns. Nearly 20 prisoners however, did not reach Battalion HQ and owing to the carriers of Enemy MGs depositing guns to fetch in wounded,

---

[718] War Diary, 6th Dorset Battalion, 25th May 1918.

only 2 machine guns actually reached Battalion HQ."[719] The objectives of the raid had been "to kill Germans, secure identifications, destroy defences and demolish dug-outs."

As a member of 'A' Company, in the 1st Platoon, Frederick would have started by assembling in the front line. His company was to be the first wave into the raid. Their specific task was to capture the German front line trench, secure it, and then hold it throughout the raid whilst two Lewis guns were to fire down along 'Y Ravine'. Then the rest of the battalion raiding party – three waves – would pass through 'A' Company and spend fifty minutes in the German trenches before the withdrawal started. Then 'A' Company would cover the withdrawal and be the last men back.

They advanced with wire cutters attached to their rifles and carrying spare ammunition and full water bottles slung round the back of their belts. In the event, casualties were high for a successful raid: seven officers were wounded, with two more missing. Twenty-nine of the men were also missing at the end of the raid, one hundred and ten had been wounded, and nine were dead. One of those killed was Frederick. The school magazine said he was killed in a raid at Mailly, Thiepval Ridge – but that was a mistake. The survivors from the raid were gathered at Mailly afterwards, before being taken back for rest and report writing. Frederick's body was never found and identified. Today he is commemorated on the memorial to the missing at Pozières. It is a bitter irony that the cousins and firm friends, Edgar Ayling and Frederick White, both died within months of each other within a few miles of each other, and that the bodies of neither of them could be recovered.

For the 6th Dorsetshire Battalion and for Bernard Allbon the war went on. Bernard was born in 1896 and was at school from 1909-1914, becoming a prefect. On 21st July 1915, at the minimum age, he applied for a commission and went to Balliol College, Oxford for six weeks training after which he was gazetted on 26th August 1915 as 2nd lieutenant in the 3rd Dorsets. After a camp at Wyke Regis he was sent to France, joining the 1st Battalion of the Dorsets in July 1916. However, he had been detached on other service a good deal that autumn, and in November had developed trench fever whilst serving near Albert. On 18th January 1917, he was admitted to Mont Dore Hospital, suffering from trench fever, influenza and acute tonsillitis. The doctors also decided he was debilitated. He was discharged from hospital on 26th February 1917and was placed on light duties with the 3rd Dorsets: the doctors said he was "somewhat weak and incapable of much exertion".[720]

When eventually Bernard had returned to France, instead of returning to the 1st Dorsets, he had changed battalions and had joined the 6th Dorsets on 3rd July 1917. *The London Gazette* reported his promotion to lieutenant from 1st July 1917, in the same batch of promotions as his fellow Dorsetshire Regiment and fellow Old Bournemouthians, Hubert Dinwoodie and Ralph Drayton. (By this time, Ralph Drayton was in England on Salisbury Plain, where he was seen by Alfred Burt during his training. Ralph was still on light duties, recovering from his gunshot wound and nervous shock. In November 1916, he had unsuccessfully applied to join the Machine Gun Corps to work with the tanks. After a frustrating year in England in 1917 he successfully applied to join the R.F.C. in 1918 as a wireless equipment officer, a position he started on 20th February 1918. Ralph was demobilised on 12th January 1919.) On 28th August 1917, Bernard had been sent to the 3rd Army

---

[719] War Diary, 6th Dorset Battalion, 8th June 1918.
[720] Army File, Bernard Allbon, WO 339/39204.

Musketry Camp as an instructor on secondment from the 6th Dorsets Battalion. The Army had established specific instruction schools for a range of different skills but the Army Musketry School essentially ran training courses for junior officers and senior NCOs to enable them in their turn to train their men in the use of the rifle and machine gun. (Although muskets had long since been phased out, the Army kept the term 'musketry' to cover all sorts of 'small-arms' firing. It was a requirement that only a qualified instructor was allowed to instruct in, and pass on, the skills of rifle firing to others. Any other soldier, however experienced, was not allowed to do this, so the Army expanded its original instruction school to establish additional schools known as Infantry Schools and Musketry Camps in France by 1917, and Bernard was attached to the one which serviced the 3rd Army, which was based near Albert, at Warloy-Baillon, though it was moved in a hurry after the German offensive of 1918.)

What was it like to be with Bernard at such a training school? There is an interesting account of a month spent at an army school by Siegfried Sassoon in his *Memoirs of an Infantry Officer*, though this dated from the spring of 1916. Sassoon had been sent "on a month's refresher course" at the 4th Army School at Flixecourt (rather than 3rd Army's school where Bernard instructed) with two other officers from each of the battalions in the brigade. In his reminiscences, he tells of training in the art of sniping, explosions and smoke bombs, the employment of the Mills bomb, use of barbed wire and screw pickets, and bayonetting on a battle course. Sassoon's overall view was that the school was run as a holiday for officers and NCOs who needed a rest. Whilst this could be true, it was written when Sassoon was very cynical about the Army and his experiences.

By May, Bernard had returned to the 6th Dorset Battalion where he was posted as battalion musketry officer. Needs change, however, and in June 1918 he had a new role, as signalling officer and was second in command of 'A' Company. So, when they made their raid in strength on the German positions near Beaumont-Hamel on the Somme, which had cost Frederick White his life, Bernard had worked within the Battalion HQ, coordinating signals and passing information back to Brigade HQ. Later, General Byng wrote in praise of the raid: "I consider this raid to have been very well prepared and carried out and reflects great credit on the two battalions."[721] In July, Bernard's job had changed again to that of battalion intelligence officer. The battalion had a lot of hard fighting in August and again in September. By September he was a captain, commanding 'D' Company.

In May 1918, the Canadians instituted an impressive development to harness the abilities and intelligence of their men in a way alien to standard British thinking of the time: "Platoon Commanders inaugurated a system of interchange of ideas, gathering their Platoon around them 'at ease', and debating on subjects appertaining to the war, and the system or systems in use for the prosecuting of the war to a successful issue (from a soldier's point of view). The benefits derived from this form of exercise is twofold. Not only does it bring out the trait of originality in a man, whereby the Officer (in addition to the men) received the benefit of ideas probably expressed by a thinking and intelligent member of the platoon, but the man who thinks out problems for himself, but is probably backward owing to natural shyness in giving expression to them, suddenly finds his interest aroused, and by tactful handling by his Officer finds (much to his surprise) that he is expressing his ideas to an attentive and interested audience including the Officer himself, who will give advice, or criticise as the case demands, but all from a 'we are willing to learn' standpoint. This

---

[721] Included in the 6th Dorsets War Diary, June 1918.

system has many and manifold advantages to commend it."[722]

Amongst these Canadians, as the war went on, Reginald Wrenn of the Canadian Corps had gained quite a reputation for his courage. His obituary in the local newspaper recalled details such as how, after the Second Battle of Ypres, he had gone on to fight at Festubert and Givenchy as well. According to his obituary, he was mentioned three times by his Sergeant-Major for his brave deeds.[723] He had even volunteered for a mission after which he was the only survivor – six others were killed, and one wounded. Eventually, he was transferred to the same unit as his brother. Frank later wrote of his brother Reginald's courage in a poignant letter to his parents: "Every man of the unit speaks of Reg as the bravest man they have ever met. On many occasions in the past he demonstrated acts of bravery. We buried him at 2pm on Sunday afternoon, June 30th. It was a beautiful service. I made arrangements with a Church of England chaplain, and the whole unit attended the funeral. A coffin was made for him, and the Union Jack was placed on top. I am having a cross made for him, so I think everything has been done as you would wish it… I hope the shells from Vick's gun will avenge for Reg. and I will continue with a good heart to beat the inhuman pest of the world, if it takes another four years. Our American friends are in tooth and nail. France and Italy are fighting with great vigour, and our own dear Empire more solid than ever. This combination will make Germany pay for every life lost for humanity."

Reginald Wrenn

At the time of his death on 29th June, Reginald was at St. Omer, away from the fighting. The town was a considerable hospital centre with the 4th, 10th, 7th Canadian, 9th Canadian and New Zealand Stationary Hospitals, the 7th, 58th (Scottish) and 59th (Northern) General Hospitals, and the 17th, 18th and 1st and 2nd Australian Casualty Clearing Stations all stationed there at some time during the war. He and Frank had come out of the fighting forces, and were now in the Canadian 1st Division's Butchery unit – applying for the benefit of their comrades the pre-war skills that Frank had developed. (Frank had been transferred to the unit before Reginald.) But St. Omer suffered air raids in November 1917 and in May and June 1918, and a bomb had dropped from a German plane and crashed through the roof of the hut and killed Reginald as he slept. He was 23. He was buried in the Longuenesse (St. Omer) Souvenir Cemetery.

But June 1918 had turned out to be a much quieter month for Frederick Furness and the men of the 11th West Surrey Battalion. They had pulled back from Belgium into France, for training and recuperation. On 1st July, the battalion relieved the 104th French Infantry Regiment taking up support positions just north-west of Mount Kemmel, the highest point on the western extension to the Messines Ridge, which the Germans had managed to capture in their offensive. In front of them was the 23rd Middlesex Battalion, and both units suffered from active German machine-gun fire. The next day, the Germans heavily shelled their positions, destroying several shelters and dug-outs. The West Surreys soon began to dig a new trench line, known as the 'Redoubt Line', and

---

[722] War Diary, 1st Canadian Infantry Battalion, 29th May 1918.
[723] *The Bournemouth Visitors' Directory*, 20th July 1918.

casualties became relatively lighter though still significant. Each day that month at least one man seems to have died, and normally two or three were wounded.

On 18th July, Frederick assembled a large scale raiding party. Because it was a light night, the Germans were able to observe the men assembling, and fired on them with machine guns. Even so, by midnight they were ready to move forward. Their object was to capture prisoners and to do as much damage as possible to German personnel and material. At 1.27a.m. on 19th July, a few British field guns opened a barrage on the Germans, followed two minutes later by covering machine-gun fire. Because the barrage did not begin with a simultaneous burst of explosives, the raid got off to a bad start – the line did not jump forward simultaneously as had been intended. Nevertheless, one lieutenant called Trotter managed to lead his men forward at Zero Hour in a dash to the forward shell holes. After desperate fighting they took three prisoners. Trotter was badly wounded in the shoulder. Other Germans tried to take cover under corrugated iron covered shell holes, and had to be prised out. When those who did surrender were asked why the defenders had fought with such desperation, they replied "English take no prisoners".[724] Trotter briefly fainted from the pain, but recovered and was carried back to the British lines on a stretcher. Apart from Trotter, fifteen men of the platoon had also been wounded and one killed. Later, it was realised that two more were missing, presumed killed. Another lieutenant, called Moon, had also led his platoon forward into desperate fighting and reached the enemy's line, established in the shell holes. Moon personally bayonetted two Germans and captured a third. He also captured a light machine gun, though this and the prisoner were later lost when the men taking them back fell under German shell fire. Moon was shot three times but even so, with so many casualties amongst his platoon, carried by a private, managed to lead his men back to the British line, ably supported by the sergeant in charge of the 'moppers up'. Moon and twenty-three others had been wounded, whilst two were missing, believed killed.

What of the part played in this by Frederick Furness? His part was summarised in the citation with which he later received the Military Cross for his actions: "For conspicuous gallantry and skill in command of a raid. He superintended the placing of the assembly tapes the night before the raid under circumstances of great difficulty, exposed to the fire of the enemy posts, which were only 30 yards away. During the attack he was wounded in the leg, but declined to retire, and, propped up by two men, he fired the prearranged signals. He directed the evacuation of the wounded and the return of the various parties, and was carried away only when he had successfully achieved his object. His leadership and fine example of endurance were worthy of high praise." He had been wounded at about 1.55a.m., after which he was greatly assisted by a Lieutenant Jackson, who directly supervised the evacuation, himself passing through the enemy barrage three times. Frederick's lieutenant colonel wrote in his report, "Capt. Furness was magnificent throughout. He inspired his officers and men to great efforts." He was a hero. His gallantry was announced more widely in *The London Gazette* on 15th October 1918.

In the following December, the school magazine published a letter which Frederick wrote from hospital describing his wound as "a nice 'cushy' wound. I have stopped a piece of shell this time in my right calf… In a few days' time I hope to be on my way to England. Am I not lucky?" In the letter he also briefly described "the whole show" and quoted his colonel's reaction, in which the colonel had written to him, "I cannot tell you how much has been said about your raid; most charming letters have come from the Corps Division and Brigade. The whole affair is looked upon as a

---

[724] Details of this raid are included in an appendix to the War Diary, 11th West Surreys, July 1918.

tremendous success, and you are responsible for it. I wish you to appreciate this fact. I compliment you on your very excellent work and wish to thank you for the whole-heartedness with which you tackled your job."[725] Frederick was taken back through the casualty system and on 30th July was sent back from Boulogne to Dover. On arrival in England he was sent to the Fort Pitt Military Hospital near Chatham, an old military hospital constructed out of a Napoleonic defence work and extended in 1915, and then on to the Military Families Hospital, also in Chatham, where the wound quickly healed. (He had been operated upon whilst in France.) His main problem then was muscle wastage and some lack of mobility for which he would need massage and rest. It was estimated that he would not be fit to return to service for about six weeks, although in the end it was not until 14th November, three days after the Armistice, that a medical board at Tonbridge Wells deemed him fully recovered and again fit for active service. Some months later, Frederick was able to leave the Army, and after the war he returned to live in London, and later to work at the National Provincial and Union Bank in Wimborne.

Ernest Parsons was also on the front during the period between the German and Allied offensives. Ernest and the 1st Royal Fusiliers Battalion had returned to the war zone in May 1918 to the Lens Sector. When the battalion was next in the front line, for an eight day spell, there were unpleasant spells of heavy shelling, including the use of poison gas. For example, "17/5/18… Our forward positions were bombarded with Gas shells for about 1 hour. Respirators were worn. The effect of the sun on the gas during the morning caused about 16 casualties in spite of the necessary precautions having been taken."[726] The gas in question was mustard gas, though known to these troops as 'Yellow Cross' after the symbol colouring the shell case. For the rest of the month, gas attacks of varying ferocity became the norm. In June, the effectiveness of the battalion reduced as ever larger numbers of men were admitted to hospital with fever: a crisis which peeked on 23rd June. However, we cannot know if Ernest was himself sick as the diary revels only the names of the officers. Despite this, the battalion spent much of June, July and August in the front line, with occasional spells in divisional reserve. Because they were stationed in the Loos area, they were not involved in the start of the counter-attack and the Battle of Amiens.

After the emergency, Thomas Chaffey and his fellow cyclists returned to fatigue duties, particularly a lot of digging. On 7th July 1918, it was agreed that the XV Corps Cyclist Battalion should gain experience of trench warfare, with a tour of duty in the front line, so two officers and forty-six men were sent into the trenches, though we do not know if Thomas was one of them. On 11th-12th July, a group attached to the 10th East Yorkshire Battalion took part in an attack from Le Grand Hazard (on the outskirts of Hazebrouck) in which Tern Farm was captured. With pride their war diary reported that "The Cyclists took 1 Off and 20 O.R. prisoners and 1 M.G. The position was consolidated and held until the party were relieved by 10th E. Yorks R. at 3 am 12 July when cyclists went into Support Line… Casualties during these operations were 3 O.R. wounded."[727] After this there was some further participation in patrols, and in the advances from August, interspersed with training and fatigues. Once the war became more mobile in the autumn the number of patrols increased. The final two days of the conflict saw them helping to push forward into land ceded by the Germans as they retreated. At the end, one platoon had reached east of Lille and north-east of Tournai. Thomas survived and was demobilised on 12th March 1919.

---

[725] *The Bournemouthian*, December 1918.
[726] War Diary, 1st Royal Fusiliers, 17th May 1918.
[727] War Diary, XV Corps Cyclist Battalion, 13th July 1918.

The Battle of Hamel, 4th July

After the defensive actions of the early part of the year, Haig now turned to offensive actions. On 28th June 1918, a relatively minor assault by the 5th and 31st Divisions in the Lys Salient, against German positions east of Nieppe Forest, had succeeded. The divisions had advanced behind a creeping barrage, taken the Germans by surprise, captured their objectives, and taken over four hundred prisoners with their trench mortars and machine guns. Haig then tasked General Rawlinson and the 4th Army to make a bigger probing attack. Rawlinson deployed the Australian Corps with the objective of capturing Vaire and Hamel Woods, and the village of Hamel, strongly fortified German positions on the ridge between Villers-Bretonneux and the River Somme. The village of Hamel lies near Villers-Bretonneux, south of the mid-way point between Amiens and Albert. In the summer of 1918, the British still held Corbie, west of Hamel, south of the River Ancre, and north of Villers-Bretonneux. The Somme flowed to the north of Hamel but meandered south of Corbie. The capture of Hamel would strengthen British defences near Villers-Bretonneux and help to safeguard Amiens. If the British were to counter-attack eastwards from Amiens, Hamel would block their advance.

This time, ten infantry battalions were to attack, supported by sixty tanks, mostly drawn from the 8th Tank Battalion, but with some from the 13th Battalion. Command was given to Lt. General John Monash. This was his first operation as a corps commander and he was anxious to prove himself and to promote the Australians as well as to deliver a British success. He explained his thinking, "It was high time that the anxiety and nervousness of the public, at the sinister encroachments of the enemy upon regions which he had never previously trodden, should be allayed by a demonstration that there was still some kick left in the British Army. I was ambitious that any such kick should be administered, first, at any rate, by the Australians." To overcome Australian objections to the tanks – which they partially blamed for their losses at Bullecourt in May 1917 – Rawlinson organised practice sessions with the tanks before the battle, which convinced the Australians that they would be useful.

General Monash was allocated sixty Mark V tanks and four supply tanks, and he deliberately ordered the tank and infantry men to mix and form friendships before the battle. Indeed, infantry badges were painted onto the tanks designated to support their attack. Arthur Baker and, probably, Stanley Hughes, were based near Corbie to the west of Hamel. The tanks were drawn from the 5th Tank Brigade. They prepared alongside the Australians at Vaux en Amienois. Although the 2nd, 3rd and 4th Australian Divisions were the main assault troops, Rawlinson decided to use four companies of the 131st and 132nd American Infantry Regiments of the 33rd American Division, and to encourage them he chose to fight on 4th July 1918 in honour of American Independence Day. This decision nearly back-fired as he explained to Colonel Wigram, the King's Private Secretary: "I selected the date of Independence Day, as it was the first occasion on which American troops had taken part in an actual attack alongside our own fellows; and I was not a little put out when, at the last moment, I got a direct order from Pershing that no American troops were to be employed. It was then too late to withdraw them, so I am afraid I had to disobey the order."[728]

The tanks to be used were the new Mark V tanks, and this was to be their first outing. The Mark V tank was the first 'one man drive' tank, the first to have an engine specially designed for tank work.

---

[728] From Major-General Sir F. Maurice, *The Life of General Rawlinson*, Cassell London, 1928, quoted in *1918 The Unexpected Victory*, J. H Johnson, Arms and Armour Press London, 1997 p. 85.

With its one man control it enjoyed better manoeuvrability as well as better observation and ventilation though it still required four men and the driver to get it started. All the early tanks were designed to cross trenches up to ten feet wide but both Mark IV and Mark V tanks could be fitted with an extra set of tracks (known as the 'tadpole tail') which gave each an extra nine feet in length, though reducing their rigidity and stability. General Monash used his artillery to good effect, concentrating its fire on the German batteries and ammunition dumps. He was able to order the use of a good mixture of high explosive, shrapnel and smoke shells. In addition, he had forty-six heavy machine guns to support his infantry, who were now well armed with plenty of Lewis guns.

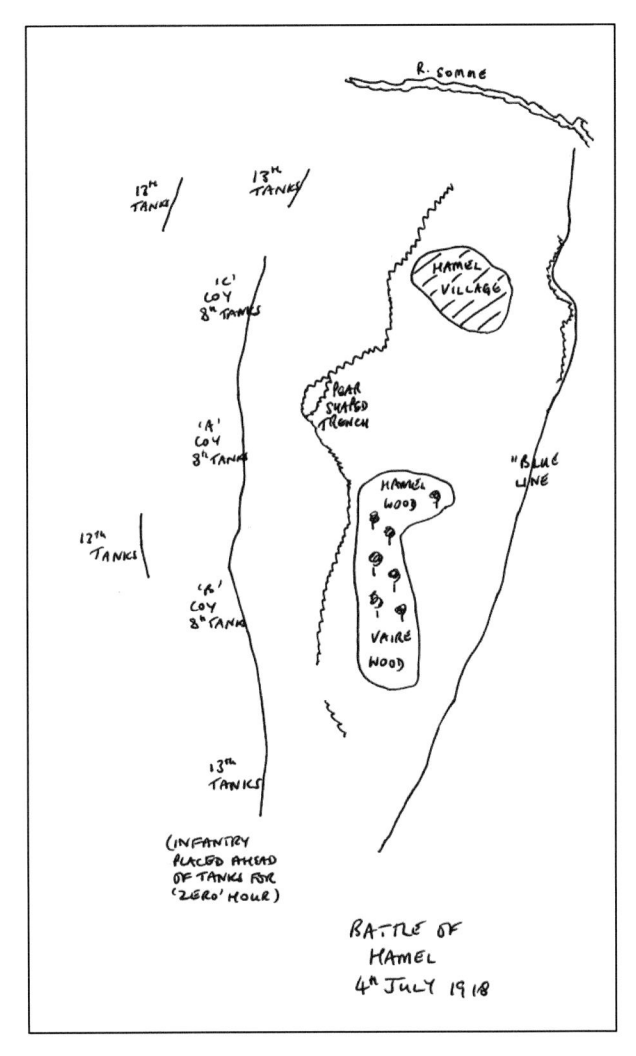

The plan called for a surprise attack to be launched at 3.10a.m. on 4th July 1918. The tanks were lined up further back and – partly because of Australian suspicions – the tanks were to follow the infantry assault, carrying forward additional ammunition and water for the infantry. The tanks were only meant to pass in front of the infantry if resistance was encountered. In the event, the battle did not work exactly according to that plan. Although the Australian accounts have a natural and justifiably triumphant tone about them, it was not at all a 'walk-over', but in two hours the objectives were attained. The Tank Corps played a big part to achieve this British success.

In the Tank Corps, Stanley Hughes (at the school from June 1910 until the end of July 1911) had been born in 1899. When war broke out he was far too young to serve, but under the Military Service Act he was called upon to attest in January 1917 at the age of 17 years 11 months, and was placed for a month in the Army Reserve. At that time he was working as a motor driver, though later this was described variously as a motor cyclist or motor engineer. On 12th February 1917, he was mobilised and sent to the Motor Transport Section of the Army Service Corps, at Grove Park. Here he was tested and found to be a fair motor cyclist. For the next few months he trained within the A.S.C. However, on 20th June 1917, he was transferred into the Machine Gun Company (Heavy Section) at Wool – which of course meant the new Tank Corps base at Bovington. The next day he was posted gunner within the M.G.C. (H.S.). This was a time when the Tank Corps had been recognised as a separate unit of the Army, and was in the process of a dramatic expansion. The original four companies were supplemented by an extra four companies (and in 1918 this expansion increased even more dramatically). "The First Tank Brigade, under Colonel C.D. Baker-Carr, had consisted of 'C' and 'D' battalions. These two battalions had taken part in the recent battle. The Second Brigade, under Colonel Courage, was formed provisionally of 'A' and 'B' Battalions. The arrival of new battalions, who had been raised and trained at home, made a Third Brigade necessary. 'C' battalion was taken from the First brigade and two new battalions from home. 'E' and 'G', added to it. The Third Brigade, under Colonel J. Hardress Lloyd, DSO, was made up of 'C', 'F', and 'I' battalions. 'H' battalion was to join the Second Brigade in due course. That was the second stage of the growth of the Tank Corps – from twelve companies to twenty-seven."[729]

Stanley's training was successful, and on 24th March 1918 he was appointed 'Tank Mechanic Class II' though retaining the rank of private soldier. On 8th April 1918, he embarked for France from Folkestone to Boulogne, where he joined the Tank Corps reinforcing depot. Four days later, he was posted to 'H' Battalion (soon to be renamed the 8th Battalion). He served as a tank driver in 'A' Company, 8th Tank Battalion.[730] The four sections of the tanks of 'A' Company, 8th Battalion, were involved in the Battle of Hamel on 4th July 1918, as was the 13th Tank Battalion.

All the tanks of the 8th Battalion assembled in the Fouilly Chateau grounds and moved up to the battle line at night. Aeroplanes supported them: by making aerial attacks on Hamel, and by using older planes to mask the sound of the tanks getting into position. Air power was also to be used in novel and important ways – dropping marked-up maps from reconnaissance planes to dispatch riders below who then drove them to the appropriate units, and even by dropping ammunition and supplies by parachute to the troops on the battlefield. The tank commanders were instructed to cooperate with the 15th Australians in the capture of Pear Shape Redoubt, after which they were to continue forwards to the second objective, the 'Blue Line'. To confuse the Germans, as the tanks advanced, smoke shells were fired by the artillery and trench mortars, and the attack began at 3.10a.m. The 6th Brigade attacked on the right, overcoming resistance in the woods with the help of the tanks. The 11th Brigade captured Hamel itself, taking many Germans by surprise in their dug-outs. To the north of the river, 15th Brigade too captured their objectives by 5a.m.

The tanks themselves had started to move forward eight minutes before Zero Hour, covered by an artillery bombardment – to the Germans a repetition of similar bombardments made for several days previously. After a one minute pause, the barrage had lifted to fire for four minutes onto the German front line. This had allowed the tanks to advance for twelve minutes, reaching the infantry line four minutes after Zero Hour. Generally, they advanced in front of the Australian infantry and good use was made of the capabilities of the Mark V tanks, especially their much improved manoeuvrability, which allowed them to swing towards danger points such as German machine-gun posts.

An official Australian account of the action recognised the contributions of the artillery and of the tanks: "At ten minutes past three our barrage came down with ferocious suddenness upon the enemy's front line area, and pounded, battered, and chopped it to pieces with shells of every calibre – light, medium, heavy, gas, shrapnel, high explosive, and phosphorous shells. The Boche here suffered four minutes' hell before the barrage began to lift in hundred yards' stages every minute, allowing our first wave to advance to the attack with the cooperation of the 'tanks' which smelt out the vicious machine guns in the enemy strong-points, and summarily dealt with them in their own quaint manner. Not many minutes passed before the first waves had taken the first objective, and the on-coming tide of the 44th Battalion swept over it and on up the coveted ridge, 'A' and 'B' companies working round the left and 'C' and 'D' companies round the right of the village of

---

[729] From W.H.L. Watson, *With the Tanks 1916-1918*, William Blackwood & Sons, Edinburgh & London, 1920.

[730] An Army Certificate dated 22nd October 1918 stated that he had been excellent in this capacity.

Hamel, leaving the village to the mercies of Hotchkiss and the Pounder aboard six 'tanks'. Three 'tanks' accompanied each half of the battalion around the village. Whilst our advance was in progress the enemy followed his usual procedure by filling the air with Verey lights and rockets – white, red, green, golden and showers – but whatever their significance, this barrage remained particularly feeble, and our boys advanced with practically no resistance from artillery, the machine guns giving the most trouble. A kind spurt from the uncanny 'tank', however, soon disposed of the defending 'gallants'. A feature of the offensive was the effectiveness of the smoke barrages which were used on either flank to cover our advance. These consisted of thick white clouds of smoke which were worked across the front by the action of the wind… As darkness gave place to day, our men could be seen working their way steadily but surely to the crest of the ridge, whilst eight tanks wobbled here and there over the slopes and summit of the ridge clearing the Boche out of his strong defences commanding our old forward area."[731]

Fifteen hundred Germans were taken prisoner in this battle, together with field guns, machine guns and trench mortars. The Australians lost nearly nine hundred casualties and the Americans lost one hundred and thirty-four. Haig was delighted. He wrote in his diary: "The attack by 10 battalions of the Australian Corps preceded by some sixty tanks was entirely successful this morning. Reports up to midday state that over 1100 prisoners taken and [our] casualties under 500. Our line has been advanced on a front of 4 miles to a depth of 1½ miles, and the village of Hamel and the ridge to the east of it captured. This greatly strengthens our positions on the Villers-Bretonneux Ridge."[732] This success encouraged the French use of massed tanks later in the month, and formed a prelude and preparation for the mass attack of the Battle of Amiens in August.

Stanley's records are not clear. Probably he had driven one of the tanks, but afterwards, he might have been sick or have been wounded. Certainly he was admitted to the 5th Australian Field Ambulance soon after the battle. The reason was sufficiently serious for him to be referred back, albeit in a slightly unorthodox order – to the 5th Casualty Clearing Station and then on to the 16th (USA) General Hospital at Le Trépot. On 31st July 1918, he was sent back to England aboard the *Laconia* and put in hospital in England from 1st-15th August 1918. At some point – possibly whilst he was with the 5th Casualty Clearing Station, he was given an anti-tetanus injection, which sounds as if he was being treated to guard against a wound infection, but on the other hand he gave a blood transfusion to help a badly wounded man. After this spell in hospital, Stanley was awarded a fortnight's leave before he was posted back to Bovington Camp for the rest of the war. Just after the Armistice he was reposted to the 22nd Battalion, and then later to the 20th Battalion from which he was demobilised in October 1919 and returned to Birmingham.

Arthur Baker of the Tank Corps was also in action in this battle, and his part in it was very noteworthy. His job in the attack was to direct tank salvage operations during the action on the north-eastern sector at Hamel, near Corbie. He was with the assault troops going 'over the top' into the attack. Ahead of the assault, a rolling barrage covered the advance of tanks and infantry. Although the position of the tanks relative to the infantry changed from time to time, overall the tanks led the way and opened the path for the infantry. It was said that sometimes they were immediately

---

[731] From *Narrative of Hamel Offensive, July 4th-6th 1918*, War Diary, 44th Australian Infantry Battalion, 23/61/22 Part 1, July Appendices, AWM4. Quoted on the website, www.ww1westernfront.gov.au/le-hamel/on-this-spot-australian-corps-memorial-lehamel.php.

[732] From *Douglas Haig, War Diaries and Letters 1914-1918*, edited by Gary Sheffield and John Bourne, p. 426.

behind the busting shells. In places, the German machine gunners fought back ferociously and threatened to hold up the infantry, or even to smash them, but the tanks concentrated fire on the German machine gunners and prevented a British disaster. They destroyed the German machine-gun posts so effectively that there was no question of the Germans being able to emerge from concealment to re-start the use of the machine guns against the Australians or the British, from in front or from behind. The Australians were duly impressed. It was later realised that the bulk of Australian casualties had occurred where their infantry had advanced in front of, rather than with or behind, the tanks. Lessons were learned accordingly.

Arthur was with these troops as they reached Hamel itself. When he reached the village he found a tank with one track completely ripped off. He had to assess whether or not it could be put back into action. If a tank were deemed to require salvage rather than mending, horses and wagons might be sent for so that all parts that were not needed for the actual salvage operation could be removed and sent back behind British lines to prevent their further loss from German shell fire (which tended to concentrate on stationary tanks) or to protect the parts from potential capture by a German counter-attack. In this case he believed he could fix the tank. So he organised a work party and in about four hours managed to have lifted the track back into position so that the tank could again be available to fight. However, even then his work was not done. "There was another tank in Hamel village which had received a direct hit, and 2nd Lieut. Baker at once started work on this with a party of the Tank Field Company. He worked continuously between the morning of Thursday, July 4, zero being 3.10 a.m., until nearly midnight on Saturday, July 6, 1918, with only six hours sleep. During practically the whole time Hamel village was exposed to heavy shelling and saturated with gas intermittently. Work had to be carried out in gas masks, and there were six casualties admitted to hospital." His commanding officer was both impressed and concerned: "I visited Hamel to inspect the work, and in order to avoid casualties which would have interfered with further salvage operations I ordered the temporary withdrawal of 2nd Lieut. Baker and his party during the afternoon of Friday, July 5, 1918, as the shelling and gassing were so intense. He showed an utter disregard for personal danger and set a splendid example throughout." In this way Arthur achieved the rare distinction of a 'Bar' to his Military Cross – that is, he was awarded it for a second time. This 'Bar' was gazetted on 7th November 1918, but was awarded for the work he had done that July. In the end, although five tanks (from the two tank battalions) had been knocked out in the battle, all had been salvaged by the night of 6th-7th July.

Afterwards, Major Keith, on behalf of General Monash, sent the following congratulations from Sir Douglas Haig to all those involved in this attack: "Headquarters July 5, 1918... Will you please convey to Lieut.-General Sir John Monash, and all ranks under his command, including the Tanks and the detachment of 33rd American Division, my warm congratulations on the success which attended the operation carried out this morning, and on the skill and gallantry with which it was conducted. In forwarding this message the Army Commander desires most heartily to congratulate the Australian Corps, and especially on the way in which the scheme was drawn up and the gallantry with which the operation was carried out. The part played by the tanks and the artillery was a prominent factor in bringing about success, and reflects great credit upon them."

Also labouring to keep the tanks working and fighting was Douglas Besley, although his precise experiences are harder to ascertain. He was born in 1893. Douglas was at the school from 1906 to 1908. On 12th December 1916 he joined the 2/28th London ('Artists' Rifles'), and from 1st May 1917 trained for a commission in the Machine Gun Corps at the No. 2 M.G.C. Cadet Battalion (or No. 35

Depot Company Officers' School). He was gazetted 2nd lieutenant in the Tank Corps. On 27th April 1918, he was posted to the 4th Advanced Workshops and was sent out into the field to work on tanks, from 19th June until the 18th October 1918, though, unfortunately, details of where he worked are not clear. He was released from France, and from the Army, in October 1919.

The Second Battle of the Marne, 15th July

That summer, the 15th Hampshire Battalion were in a defensive action in the north. By 1st May 1918, only eighty of the 15th Hampshire Battalion who had originally landed in France were left. That month they had worked to strengthen the defences of Ypres. On 4th June, Lieutenant Horace Tollemache and Privates Edward Preiss, Roy Rawle and Robert Meredith and the others were pulled back from Ypres and on the last day of the month moved into the line at La Clytte, a little north of Mount Kemmel, relieving the 1st Battalion of the French 103rd Regiment. Here, like Eric Rey and the 10th Royal West Kents, they had American officers and NCOs attached for training on 15th July. Two days later there was a burst of heavy German shelling on the British front line trench. In this shelling on 17th July 1918, Horace Tollemache was killed. His burial was at Lijssenthoek Military Cemetery, several miles west of Ypres, on the road to Poperinghe. Edward, Roy and Robert continued with the battalion through the battles of 1918. They fought on through the counter-attack of July and in August as well as in the advance into Flanders, the final Battle of Ypres and the last advances. All three survived these horrors.

Meanwhile, Ludendorff decided that the only option left that summer 1918 was to capture Paris. He hoped that if he attacked Paris the British would weaken their northern flank, as the French demanded, and even hoped that the Channel ports might become vulnerable. So, on July 15th, he attacked the French in the Second Battle of the Marne, from both sides of the city of Reims. At first, Ludendorff was encouraged by the excellent progress his forces seemed to be making. It was not long, however, before his troops began to slow down and then to stall in their advance. These were not the disciplined troops of 1914; many were relatively young and ill-trained. Apparent success led in some cases to over-confidence. Once Paris was again threatened, the French too put up greater resistance than expected of them.

To add to Ludendorff's woes, American troops – albeit some scarcely trained – had begun to arrive in significant numbers in France. The Germans were on the defensive now despite their initial spectacular gains. Although they were in sight of Paris, this was really just a diversion from the original vision of splitting the British and French and making the British run back to the Channel ports and Britain. Instead, Ludendorff's offensives had led to greater Anglo-French co-operation, and had pulled his remaining men and resources off-target. Unless Paris should fall and France surrender, he had no way to gain the victory.

On July 18th, the day after Horace died, French troops, supported by some newly-arrived American battalions, counter-attacked, trying to catch the German assault battalions within the salient their advance had created. Although on a relatively small scale, this attack by the French was – in hindsight – the beginning of the end for the Germans. This was the first, and virtually the only time, that the French attacked with tanks on a large scale – three hundred and fifty, mostly light Renault tanks, were thrown into the attack and, despite encountering significant losses from German artillery, helped to push the Germans back onto the defensive. An Old Bournemouthian, Sidney Seeviour, arrived on the Western Front and was with the French when they began the counter-attack.

Sidney had arrived at Marseilles from Egypt with his battalion, the 2/4th Hampshires, on 1st June 1918. This battalion was attached to 186th Brigade, 62nd (West Riding) Division, otherwise mostly full of Yorkshiremen. They were clearly needed! "During the night A and C Companies of the 2/4th Hants Regiment relieved D and B Companies 5th Duke of Wellington's Regiment. On relief D and B Companies went into Brigade Reserve... The 2/7th Duke of Wellington's Regiment ceased to be a unit in the Brigade today on being disbanded and posted as drafts to other units. The 2/4th Hants Regiment took their place as third battalion in the Brigade."[733] In July, the battalion, as part of 62nd Division, XXII Corps, had been placed at the disposal of Marshal Foch who had requested support from Haig. Foch knew that French intelligence had been forecasting a new German offensive in the Marne Sector and felt that the French required support. The corps was moved to Vitry-le-Francois and placed in reserve for the French 5th Army under General Berhtolet. So this Hampshire battalion played a supporting role in a mostly French battle, joining in the Battle of the Tardenois, which developed the counter-attack that had started on July 18th.

Sidney's brigade held the line from the Bois de Reims to the Ardre until they advanced on the evening of 27th July-28th July against a retreating German force, which nevertheless defended itself fiercely. Sidney and the men of the 2/4th Hampshires spent a difficult night under heavy rain. When they lined up in the early morning of 28th July, they shivered through a cold mist. At 4a.m. they deployed in line with the 2/4th Duke of Wellington's to spearhead the attack, but immediately faced twin hazards from both machine-gun fire against their positions and by a German artillery barrage which swept the open ground they had to cover. Rather than advance in line, they attacked by sending forward small parties of men in rushes, with others providing covering fire. They finally achieved their battle objective for the day at 4p.m. – long after the planned success deadline. Alongside other members of the division and corps, they had pushed forward about a mile. Despite their exhaustion and the impact of the continuous rain and fighting, the French general ordered that the British battalions must not stop. Even though they received this order, the battalion was able to make no further significant progress, though other battalions and brigades did, and at the start of August they were pulled from the battle to rest. The division had advanced about four miles in the eleven days to July 31st but it had lost one hundred and eighteen officers and two thousand nine hundred and fifty soldiers. Victory did not come cheap, but the British reported huge numbers of German dead, and they had taken many prisoners and captured one hundred and thirty-five machine guns and recaptured thirty-two French and Italian artillery guns. General Bertholet praised them for their success in the heavy fighting in extremely difficult country.

Sidney had survived. If you believe the official view of the Hampshire men from the history of the 62nd Division, after this fighting they were viewed almost as honorary Yorkshiremen – quite an accolade from a fiercely proud part of the country. "For the first time since the 62nd Division landed in France in January, 1917, troops belonging to other County Regiments had fought side by side with the Yorkshiremen; they had been welded into the Brotherhood of the men from the West Riding. With pardonable pride in their own achievements and a greater regard for the splendid reputation the Division had won for itself it is possible that the Yorkshiremen looked, at first, on these new divisional units with something akin to fear lest they should fail to keep bright the glorious record of the past. For the feeling of *esprit de corps* ran very high indeed in the Division. But the Hants and the Devons responded nobly to all calls made upon them, just as the Londoners of the 2/20th Battalion London Regt were, in the future, to help add further lustre to the brilliant

---

[733] War Diary of the 5th West Yorkshires (Duke of Wellington's), June 17th 1918.

record of what was probably the finest Territorial Division which ever trod the soil of France. What is there a Yorkshireman cannot do? And what is there he cannot do again and again when aided by the Londoners and the men of Devonshire and Hampshire?"[734]

Elsewhere, other units were also probing the German lines and testing their defences. Alfred Bishop was possibly mixed up in one such raid, on 25th July. Born in 1899, Alfred joined the school in 1910. When he left in December 1913 he had become a boy clerk in the Civil Service, making good use of his considerable success in a wide range of public exams, and took up a significant position in the Indian Store Office in London. He was a keen scout and in London he became Junior Scoutmaster to the 67th South London Scout Troop. He enlisted in February 1917. Ironically, for one who ended up as a rifleman, Alfred needed glasses, and his foreign service was delayed because of the difficulties he had with fitting his gas mask. Eventually, he was placed in the Rifle Brigade and attached to the 8th London Battalion (known as the 'Post Office Rifles'). His eyesight delayed him going to France until July 1918, by which time his division had been in almost continuous action from the launch of Operation Michael in March to the Battle of Villers-Bretonneux in April. When he joined his battalion, part of the 174th Brigade in the 58th Division, it was recouping and reorganising ahead of the counter-attack at Amiens. Alfred probably arrived in a group of forty-six 'other ranks' on 21st July. The battalion made a raid in strength on the evening of 25th July. Three companies attacked under a barrage, whilst the fourth remained as a reserve and afterwards worked as stretcher-bearers to bring back the wounded – the men of the flanking companies having suffered from machine-gun fire. Two officers and ten men had been killed, four officers and fifty men wounded, six men wounded but who were able to carry on, and fifty-five men were missing: "[The] Reserve Company... did less conspicuous but excellent work in providing relays of Stretcher Bearers, Control Posts, Escorts, etc. essential to the success of the operation... After the barrage on both sides had died down, parties went out under the Red Cross Flag into 'No Man's Land' and brought in all wounded they could discover. The enemy did not molest these parties and was himself engaged on similar work. 7th London Regiment, 2/10th London Regiment and 1/132rd American infantry Regiment rendered valuable assistance in bringing in and carrying back wounded."[735] The short history of the battalion describes how Alfred and his fellow recruits played their part: "Actually, with the exception of a few days at Neuf Moulin,[736] no opportunity had been given to train the Battalion, a large number of whom consisted of youngsters hurriedly sent out as reinforcements to make good the gaps caused by the enemy offensive. These lads were soon to show their mettle, even without the advantage of training."[737]

Ludendorff was forced to pull his vulnerable spearhead back from the salient his assault had created. Paris had been saved, and the Germans had run out of options. The Kaiser's heir, the Crown Prince, who commanded part of the German Western Front forces, now privately gave his opinion that the war could no longer be won. A high level German command meeting was less conclusive. Ludendorff conceded that victory in 1918 seemed to have eluded the Germans, but argued that there was no need for peace negotiations. He maintained that at the worst the Germans could resume a defensive war to wear down Allied resolve, despite the arrival of the Americans.

---

[734] *The History of the 62nd (West Riding) Division 1914-1919 Vol. I*, p. 219.

[735] Within the War Diary, 8th London Battalion (Post Office Rifles). Report on Special Operation by 8th Battalion London Regiment on 25th July 18.

[736] An area next to Abbeville, north-west of Amiens on the Somme but close to the estuary at St. Valéry.

[737] *History Of The Post Office Rifles 8th Battalion City of London Regiment*, Aldershot, 1919.

The Americans might not accept the political cost of a long-term commitment in Europe, which was so contrary to their previous policy. The French might again lose heart. The British had borne the main impact of the casualties inflicted since March, and were running out of reserves. Ludendorff believed he could hold any counter-attack on the Somme and, if necessary, at the end of the campaign season perhaps he might withdraw to his line in front of Peronne or to the Hindenburg Line. Yet the Germans made no serious attempt even to consolidate their new front line or to create strong lines east of the Hindenburg Line, though some half-hearted attempts were made to delineate such lines: for the time being, the men's capacity was used up in holding onto their gains. When the Kaiser's confidential aide-de-camp Niemann asked Ludendorff, in the light of the Crown Prince's memo to his father, "Can I assure His Majesty that your Excellency will shorten the line? It appears to me that the positions in which our attacks have left us are awkward for defence and require too many troops," he was vigorously rebuffed. Ludendorff is said to have responded, "Defence! I hope we shall soon have our attack on Amiens in full swing, when the men have pulled themselves together." [738]

---

[738] C.R.M.F. Cruttenwell, *A History of the Great War*, p. 547, 1934 – second edition 1936.

9: The Counter-Attack: The Battle of Amiens and the 100 Days

But it was Haig, not Ludendorff who was to make the decisive attack near Amiens.

Although the fight-back had started with the Australians and the tanks at Le Hamel at the start of July, that had been a relatively small-scale action. On 18th July, the French attack further south had been much bigger, but still effectively an action to prevent a further German advance. The major battle, which opened up the 'Hundred Days' of Victory was Haig's attack known as the Battle of Amiens, which was fought from 8th to 11th August 1918. Marshall Foch was later to describe the actions of Haig and the British as the "hammer blows" which smashed the German defences, and he described the sequence of British attacks which began at Amiens by saying, "they were classic examples of the military art, perfectly conceived and perfectly executed."[739]

At the end of July and beginning of August, however, neither Haig nor Foch – or indeed anyone holding a significant Allied political or military position – expected victory in 1918. Ironically, the Allied Command agreed with Ludendorff that this would take over a year. The counter-attack was expected to thrust to force the Germans back to the Hindenburg Line at best. Allied preparations began to prepare for the victory assault to be made in 1919 or 1920 when it was hoped ten thousand tanks would break the German lines, and ten thousand caterpillar tracked vehicles would carry forward the infantry and their equipment. American soldiers would provide the reinforcements the British and French lacked and give the Allies an overwhelming numerical advantage. Overhead, new airplanes would maintain the newly-won Allied air domination. These plans remained a dream for the future: for 1918 the British must restore the situation lost that spring.

The Counter-Attack in the North

Having been pushed all the way back across the Somme and past Albert, the British had held the important railway junction of Amiens, and it was from here that the decisive blow was struck. However, the Germans were also on the defensive further north where British probing actions kept them occupied.

After a spell in Salonika, Egypt and Palestine in 1917, Arnold Whitting had returned to the Western Front. Now he was attached to the 2/15th London Regiment, the 'Civil Service Rifles'. He had not enjoyed the desert war, but had taken part in significant actions whilst in the east. Conditions had not helped him: the school magazine had reported that "Lieut. A. Whitting Royal Fusiliers, has been in hospital with irritated eyelids, caused by sand."[740] Arnold had joined the unit in which Francis Holbrook had been serving since February 1916, in Salonika and the Middle East. Like Arnold, he had experienced the attention of the Army medics – in his case because he had been wounded in action. We do not know if these two men, of contrasting rank and position, realised that they had shared a common schooling, though their time at the school had overlapped. Arnold and Francis embarked with the 2/15th London Battalion from Alexandria on 17th June 1918, landed at Taranto in Italy six days later, and travelled with the battalion to the Western Front. This must have been

---

[739] C.R.M.F. Cruttenwell, *A History of the Great War*, p. 553, 1934 – second edition 1936.
[740] *The Bournemouthian*, April 1918.

an exhausting railway journey, for the train kept stopping and it took the battalion the rest of the month to reach northern France near to Calais. On its arrival, the battalion was sent to corps reserve, east of Hazebrouk and south of Poperinghe, and on 7th July 1918, Arnold – now a full lieutenant – was one of four officers sent forward to liaise with French officers and to reconnoitre the front line in case they were called forward into action. On 26th July, they relieved the 18th Highland Light Infantry in the front line. Otherwise, for Francis and the rest, the first few weeks of July were spent in training and in being brought up to scratch with the current situation. On 17th July, Francis had become a 90th Infantry brigade runner – always a hazardous duty, but one which he survived, and which seems to have earned him temporary promotion to corporal and two weeks leave back to the UK.

The battalion moved eastwards into Belgian Flanders, south of Poperinghe. On 28th July, 'A' Company suffered four wounded when the Germans attacked them with an estimated 150 to 200 artillery shells. For August they were in and out of the defensive line. Arnold went on leave from 6th to 24th August, but Francis would have been kept busy running with messages, especially between his company and the Battalion Headquarters. On 16th August, "Orders received that batt would relieve the 2/14 London Regt in the line. Enemy aeroplane brought down in flames. Second one believed to have been brought down by Lewis Gun fire from our A.A. Section. One Coy on duty with R.E.s."[741] When the British went on to the attack on 21st August, the battalion looked on as their sister battalion, 2/14th London Battalion, took a German position on the Dranouter Spur, but despite this success, conditions were difficult. "23/8/18. Batt. in line. Intermittent shelling by enemy during day. Wakefield wood shelled with gas shells. Work – improving parts of wiring. Impossible to work during daylight. Position overlooked by Kemmel. 24/8/18. 1am. Enemy artillery very active & heavily shelled front and support trenches. Enemy attempted to launch a counter attack but was driven off by our artillery. One prisoner taken by right coy (A Coy). 2nd Lt E. Jones & six O/Rs killed, 29 ORs wounded, and 2 O/Rs wounded & remained on duty."[742]

Sidney Street's unit, a little further south, began to advance before that of Arnold and Francis. Sidney, born in 1893, was at the school from 1905 to December 1909 as a Hampshire Scholar. He left to become an industrial chemist. By 1911 he was boarding and working in London as an assistant chemist at a chemical manufacturing works. Although it would therefore seem logical that he would be placed in the Royal Engineers special units for gas, that was not the case, perhaps because when he enlisted on 7th January 1915, poison gas had not yet been deployed on the battlefield. Sidney had volunteered in London, was passed 'A1' fit, and posted to the Oxford and Buckinghamshire Light Infantry. He had not been a member of the Cadet Corps, so needed to be trained from scratch, a process which would take a couple of years. During that time he was rapidly promoted through the ranks, so by 1st July 1916 had been an acting quarter master sergeant in the 9th Oxford and Buckinghamshire Light Infantry, a reserve battalion formed in Portsmouth in October 1914 as a Service battalion, but on 10th April 1915 formally converted into a reserve, training battalion. On 1st September 1916, Sidney was re-appointed acting company quarter master sergeant. On 16th April 1918, he was transferred as sergeant in the 3rd Oxford and Buckinghamshire Light Infantry Battalion. Finally, he was off to France, embarking from Folkestone on 24th April and reported to his new battalion, the 1st Oxford and Buckinghamshire Light Infantry, probably joining 'B' Company. This battalion was in the 10th Brigade, 4th Division,

---

[741] War Diary, 2/15th London Battalion, 16th August 1918.
[742] War Diary, 2/15th London Battalion, 23rd-24th August 1918.

and had been in France since August 1914. In May, the battalion was in and out of the trenches on the banks of the Canal d'Aire near Béthune, since the line had been pushed back by the German Spring Offensive. The Germans had an unusually high number of observation balloons out, overlooking the battalion, and their aircraft were active, particularly at night. On 24th May, Sidney's battalion, and the divisional artillery, aimed to show the Germans that they could not take the British retreat for granted: "At 2.57am & 3.0am we discharge 160 Gas projectors into Enemy's Support Line & Pacaut Wood. Very wet and cold day. Hostile artillery very quiet indeed. Our heavies shoot most of the day & 18 pounders carry out harassing fire at night."[743] This pattern had continued for the next couple of months – regular tours of the trenches, with varying degrees of artillery action, interspersed by the occasional special attack organised by one side or the other – more typically a raid in strength than an artillery barrage alone.

On 5th August, Sidney and his comrades began to see a difference in the Germans opposite. "5th. Dull morning, fine misty rain. Quiet. Word was received during morning that the enemy was reported to be evacuating his front line. Patrols confirmed that he had withdrawn from his shell holes line, but on a patrol going out at 6pm to occupy them, they were heavily fired on from these posts & had to withdraw, having two men wounded. Artillery quiet. Quiet night… Aug 6th. Fine morning, fresh breeze. About noon the Enemy was discovered to have evacuated his position in front of us. 'A' Coy pushed forward to a depth varying from 100 to 500 yards with very slight opposition. Battalion on right & left also advance & touch is maintained. 'B' Coy move to old front line trench & 'C' Coy come into old Support Line. 'D' Coy take up whole of reserve line."[744] The next day, the battalion pushed forward across the canal and occupied the village of Riez du Vinage, though not without casualties from machine-gun fire. At this stage they were moving north, but the battalion was held up trying to cross the Quentin road towards Calonne.

Just south of Belgium, John Nutman was serving in a different battalion of the same regiment, pushing the Germans back towards Bailleul. John Nutman and the 2/4th Oxford and Buckinghamshire Light Infantry Battalion were south-east of St. Omer and south-west of Hazebrouck with their backs to the village of Steenbecque in an area sometimes known as the Lys Salient. Between them and their next objective, Merville, lay the Nieppe Forest. August 7th started well with a successful attack organised at short notice on the German front line between the Hazebrouck-Merville road and Bonar Farm, with 'only' eighteen casualties. But poison gas was a particular hazard: "It was now a nightly programme of the enemy to drench the wood, which was low-lying and infested with pools and undergrowth, with his noxious 'Yellow Cross'—shells whose poisonous fumes bore the flavour of mustard. Throughout the night of August 7/8, when things generally were very active, a heavy gas-bombardment was kept up. The Colonel was away from his headquarters at the time. He returned after the shelling to find that gas helmets had been taken off. No harm was expected, but the next day, after the sun's heat had awakened dormant fumes, the Colonel, Symonds (the adjutant), Kirk, who had brought up the rations, and Cubbage, as well as the Regimental Sergeant-Major and many signallers and runners, all found that they were gassed. Their loss was serious."[745] The men named in this account were all officers, but thirty-eight other men were also gassed, whilst six were killed over those two days and seventeen others wounded. Of course, what made their loss doubly serious was the relative lack of experience in the battalion

---

[743] War Diary, 1st Oxford and Buckinghamshire Light Infantry, 24th May 1918.
[744] War Diary, 1st Oxford and Buckinghamshire Light Infantry, 5th-6th August 1918.
[745] *The Story of the 2/4th Oxfordshire and Buckinghamshire Light Infantry*, by G.K. Rose, 1920, p. 203.

after the devastation of the previous April.

For Sidney's battalion, August 9th showed that there remained plenty of fight left in the Germans: "Early morning, Patrols were pushed forward & one large patrol under 2nd Lieut P H Horsley having got well forward were surrounded by greatly superior numbers of the enemy. Three men escaped & the remaining eight & the officer were missing. This occurred about 7am, and about 7.30am, the enemy, about 30 strong, were seen advancing on to one of our outposts. Lewis gun fire was effectively opened & the enemy dispersed with casualties. Later in the morning, Trench Mortar (Stokes') fire was brought to bear on the house south end of Quentin & this was later taken by 'B' Coy & an outpost line was established well in front of Quentin, in touch with battalion on left, & thence falling back to West of Bobeme in touch with battalion on right. Enemy Machine Guns & snipers were active the whole day & there was also a certain amount of shelling of our supports & Coy HQ. The early part of the night was quiet and 'B' & 'D' Coys were relieved about 11.30pm by 2 Coys of the 1st Rifle Brigade who were taking over the whole of the 10th Brigade Outpost Line. On relief 'B' & 'D' Coys embussed near canal bank & were taken to Busnettes. 'A' & 'C' Coys were relieved earlier in the afternoon by 1st Hampshire Regt & marched to billets at Busnettes."[746] Further training, and some rest, followed. As a senior NCO, Sidney might have been one of the thirty-five NCOs chosen to attend a R.A.F. lecture on co-operation between ground troops and the aeroplanes, and to go, the next day, to a nearby aerodrome to be taken round the hangers, and – in some cases – to be taken on flights. On 15th August, they were back in the trenches, relieving the 2nd Essex Battalion. Several men were poisoned by 'Blue Cross' (mustard) gas the next day. On 18th-19th the pattern of a few days before was repeated with a further minor German retreat followed by stubborn resistance.

Further north, Bernard Richardson, formerly of the 5th London Battalion, was also in action. After being wounded in the battle at Gommecourt at the start of July 1916, Bernard recovered and was transferred to the 18th King's Royal Rifle Corps in their hour of need. The 18th K.R.R.C. had been in Italy but had returned to France at the start of March 1918 as part of the 122nd Brigade in 41st Division. This battalion was in the same brigade as the 15th Hampshire Battalion. After sharing in the heavy fighting – and losses – of March 1918 they had been moved alongside the rest of the brigade to Poperinghe on 3rd April where they received hundreds of reinforcements that allowed them to re-instate the four company system. Bernard had been in the UK until he returned to France on 30th March 1918.

The rebuilt battalion had trained and prepared. On 1st July, the 18th K.R.R.C. had moved into trenches at La Clytte, north of Mount Kemmel, where they were immediately shelled by the German artillery. After a few days they had been relieved by the 15th Hampshires, and on the night of 10th-11th July they in turn had relieved the 12th East Surreys. This pattern then continued as the brigade battalions rotated. On 7th August, the 18th King's Royal Rifle Corps again relieved the 12th East Surreys in the front line at La Clytte. They prepared to support the attack which the 15th Hampshires made the next day, pushing back the German front line and consolidating the gained line. On 10th August, the battalion relieved the 15th Hampshires on the new front line. This was accomplished without loss. But then all hell seemed to be let loose. "Early in the morning at about 3.30 the enemy dropped a very heavy barrage of all calibres on our forward system reaching as far back as the La Clytte – Dickebusche Road. This lasted about one hour. The mist was very thick and

---

[746] War Diary, 1st Oxford and Buckinghamshire Light Infantry, 9th August 1918.

no enemy were seen although when the Barrage had stopped a good deal of shouting could be heard. At about 5 am the Enemy attacked and succeeded in driving in our left coy front. The Post occupied by H Binns and his platoon was completely isolated and none came out but one man who took a message to OC Coy reporting their danger. The left front Company immediately reorganised in the Old Front Line and delivered a counter attack which succeeded in driving the enemy from all the posts he had occupied with the exception of H Binns' Post which was some hundred yards in front of our wire and strongly held by the Enemy. The attack on the Rt Coy front was equally determined but not so well organised with the result that it was beaten off although for some time the left post on the Coy front was for some time engaged with the enemy in front of them as well as behind. The situation for this post was relieved by the initiative and quickness of action of Sgt. Humphrey who was in command of the left support platoon on the Right Coy front. This NCO led part of his post in an immediate charge upon the Enemy in the Hollow between his own post and the front line post. They inflicted heavy casualties upon the Enemy with the sword and rifle and drove them out in front of the front line. The Enemy were in much greater numbers than he had at his disposal. This NCO was severely wounded in the spine. At about 8am the situation was reported normal by patrols sent forward by the Support Companies. All telephone communication was cut and inter communication had to be carried on by Runners. Casualties: 3 officers wounded, 1 officer missing; 4 OR killed, 20 OR wounded, 19 OR missing."[747]

Bernard Richardson must have been the runner from the outlying post, as according to *The Bournemouthian*, on 11th August 1918 Bernard found himself completely surrounded by enemy troops, yet fought his way out to re-join his company.[748] For this he was recommended for a gallantry award, though this does not seem to have been awarded. The battalion then held the line in rotation within the brigade, and on 20th August the Germans attempted another determined attack, which was also driven back at a cost and with the loss of one outlying post. After this the battalion was pulled back out of the front line for a time and went with the brigade to the St. Omer training area for a week.

The Germans had regrouped on 20th August. Four days later, John Nutman and his comrades of the 2/4th Oxfordshire and Buckinghamshire Light Infantry moved into the front line – here known as the 'Outpost Line' in front of Neuf Berquin. John and the others could see the palls of smoke rising from the explosions as each day the Germans blew up structures which could be of help to the Allies, whether economically – like mills and factories – or strategically – like bridges or church towers which could be used as look-out posts. The Germans were expecting to have to retreat. "Often, when idly scanning the horizon or watching aeroplanes, eyes were arrested by huge jets which sprang into the air to become clouds as large as any in the sky. Combining with this present orgy of destruction numerous booby-traps were left behind, whose action was delayed till our advance should provide victims for their murderous art. Cross-roads and level-crossings especially 'went up,' or were expected to, and so many houses were mined that it became impossible to rest secure in any."[749]

The battalion remained opposite Neuf Berquin, under shell fire (including gas) until they launched an attack on 28th August. That day, the battalion attacked the Germans, trying to disrupt their

---

[747] War Diary, 18th King's Royal Rifle Corps, 11th August 1918.
[748] *The Bournemouthian*, April 1920.
[749] *The Story of the 2/4th Oxfordshire and Buckinghamshire Light Infantry*, by G.K. Rose, 1920, pp. 212-213.

preparations to retreat. The Germans had taken a position astride the Neuf Berquin to Estaires road. "'B' and 'C' Coys., who commenced to advance at 11.30am under cover of a creeping barrage, pushed forward a distance of 500 yards, but were unable to cross the Laudick Brook owing to M.G. fire from Bowery Cottages, which the 40th Division operating on the Battalion's left, failed to capture. The enemy afterwards held the houses about Rue Montigny strongly, and further progress having become impossible, the original outpost line was resumed at dusk. South of the Neuf Berquin – Estaires Road 'A' Coy, by means of patrols, occupied the German wired position east of the Skelter Cross – Obos Cottage Road in two places and held on all day. At dusk the enemy, with half a Company moved up from the enclosures at Skelter Cross and commenced to take these patrols in the rear, whereupon they withdrew after treating the Germans with Lewis Guns. During the night 'A' Coy held its previous outpost positions East of Hemerie Chapel. During the attack hostile artillery did not retaliate with much vigour, but during afternoon and evening the Neuf Berquin – Estaires and Neuf Berquin – Robermetz Roads as well as all tracks and approaches to the village were severely harassed. 'C' Coy, who held the ground E. of Cochin Corner received much attention from hostile T.M. Casualties: Killed 4 O.R.; Wounded 2/Lt W.A.H. Goodman and 22 O.R. Wounded & Missing 1 O.R."[750]

After a brief relief, the battalion moved back into the line at Neuf Berquin on 31st August. That night, German 4.2 guns shelled their position and one man was killed – John Nutman. He was initially buried near where he died in a cemetery hurriedly dug in the hamlet of Caudescure, but after the war was transferred to Aval Wood Military Cemetery at nearby Vieux-Berquin.

Sidney Street's 1st Oxford and Buckinghamshire Light Infantry had moved with their division from 5th Army to 1st Army, and in consequence was sent by train back to Pernes and then south to Buneville. From there they had to make a tiring, long march to Mont St. Eloi, north of Arras, to take part in a day's brigade training for a forthcoming assault. On 28th August, they moved east to Arras by bus, and then moved forward between Monchy-le-Preux to their north and the Arras-Cambrai to their south for the relief of 5th Canadian Mounted Rifles Battalion in the front line positions in front of Vis-en-Artois. The next day, despite active German artillery, 'A' Company was able to occupy Remy village, north of Vis-en-Artois, and the battalion prepared for the onslaught scheduled for the next day.

This was to be a day of heavy casualties for the battalion. "30th. No orders are received from Brigade until about 10am which say that the Battalion is to move forward into assembly position SE of Remy Wood & village. Coys dribble forward, but the movement is observed & a heavy Machine gun & Artillery barrage is put down. 'B' & 'C' Coys are much disorganised & suffer severe casualties. Lieut A J Adams is killed, Capt P H W Hicks MC, & Lieut J B Coventry wounded, & 2nd Lieut T F Hyde Gassed. Our Artillery is asked to shell opposite ridge & hostile fire is considerably reduced. 'D' Coy, ably led by Capt E J A Maunsell MC get into position with only a few casualties. At noon the CO is called to another conference at Brigade HQ & receives instructions to attack at 4pm in conjunction with 2nd Duke of Wellington's on the right & 11th Brigade on the Left. Orders are issued, but owing to the difficulty of getting hold of officers (assembly area still being shelled) it is impossible to promulgate these effectively. Capt E J A Maunsell MC takes his Coy & elements of A, B & C forwards at the arranged time. They have to cross a stream and swamp, some of the men wading through waist deep in mud & water. Line of 2nd Objective is reached without much

---

[750] War Diary, 2/4th Oxford & Bucks Light Infantry Battalion, 28th August 1918.

opposition on the part of the enemy, a number of whom were shot down as they attempted to run away. Lieut L J C Seaman is killed, Lieut C W Rowntree & 2nd Lieut F G Kitching are wounded. 2nd Lieut J E Hosking Gassed. Owing to delay in crossing river & swamp, the Artillery barrage gets too far ahead. This, in conjunction with shortage of men, prevents 3 Objectives being taken. Capt W G B Edmonds MC collects about 60 stragglers & takes them up to reinforce Capt E J A Maunsell MC who has established a line 100 yards west of the 2nd Objective & has obtained touch on his right flank with the 2nd Duke of Wellington's. At about 6pm a Coy of 2nd Seaforth Hrs is sent up in support to the Battalion in O.24b. At midnight orders are received that the battalion is to be relieved by the 2nd Seaforth Highl'rs before dawn. The CO visits the line, is slightly wounded, but remains at duty. Relief is completed about 4.30am. The battalion comes back into support in Gory trench."[751]

That day six officers and 166 men fell casualty. Sidney Street was wounded with a gunshot wound in his left forearm. Taken back to a casualty clearing station and then to a field ambulance, it was decided to send him back to England where he arrived on 7th September. He was moved to the Wharncliffe War Hospital, Sheffield and there he made a good recovery, being discharged to leave on 8th October 1918. He did not return to the front but to a depot at Knowsley Park. He was demobilised on 25th February 1919, once again rated 'A1' for fitness.

So, when the great blow against the Germans was struck at Amiens at the start of August, British troops further north had played their part in ensuring that the Germans were unable to reinforce their defences there without letting the British push forward their lines elsewhere.

The Battle of Amiens: 8th to 11th August

Haig and his men had prepared in great secrecy for the attack in front of Amiens. Haig's plan was to combine an army assault featuring good use of two thousand artillery guns, substantial infantry, and four hundred and fifty tanks with air support provided by the newly-formed R.A.F. In the event, so great was the success that later Ludendorff called 8thAugust "the black day of the German army". When Haig attacked at Amiens, the French attacked in support further south in the Battle of Montdidier.

The British 4th Army under General Rawlinson attacked – ten divisions including Australian and Canadian troops. Rawlinson's tactics were very different from those he used in 1916. In preparation, 38,000 air photographs were taken of the German defences so that the British could be fully briefed on their objectives. The Canadian Corps, which had not been involved in the defensive campaigns of the spring and so was fresh, after undertaking some deceptions to trick the Germans, was secretly brought into the jumping-off zone. To preserve the surprise the gunners were required to plan their initial barrage by plotting the first shots using maths and their maps: there were to be no 'ranging' shots! The maths worked. The infantry (British, Australian and Canadian) advanced at 4.20a.m. behind a creeping barrage fired by seven hundred field guns, whilst tanks attacked German strongpoints. Light tanks, known as 'whippets' pushed forward into gaps in the German lines. Above them, the R.A.F. dropped bombs on the German defences. Every ten minutes, the field guns were moved forward to maintain contact with the infantry. For once, the weather favoured the British – early morning fog concealed the advance.

South of the River Somme, the Canadians and Australians, in flatter ground where the tanks could

---

[751] War Diary, 1st Oxford and Buckinghamshire Light Infantry, 9th August 1918.

operate most effectively, made greater progress than the British divisions to the north of the Somme whose attack had to move forward in hillier ground. They broke through the German line, and by 13th August the British and French forces had pushed forward in places up to eleven miles. Rawlinson felt confident enough to throw forward twenty thousand cavalry to support the light whippet tanks and these certainly helped push forward the assault, despite taking heavy losses.

What made this an even more remarkable victory was that the attack was made across a front of forty-seven miles. The Germans lost 48,000 (killed, wounded or taken prisoner) in just three days. Towards the end the heavy British losses of aircraft and tanks took off some of the shine, but within the German High Command more secretly recognised that the war could no longer be won. A large number of Old Boys were involved in this battle and its aftermath.

Ernest Snelgar was involved in the deception to make the Germans think that a blow was planned in the Ypres Salient. After the Second Battle of Passchendaele, Ernest and the 4th Canadian Mounted Rifles had remained for a time in support, whilst others finished the assault and the capture of Passchendaele. On 13th November, they had pulled back to a camp just south of Poperinghe. From here they were moved to Loos – to Hill 70 – where they spent Christmas and the New Year, and then down to Vimy Ridge again. They were still there when the Germans launched their 1918 offensives south and north of them. In April 1918 Ernest and the Rifles had moved back to the Loos Sector to reinforce that area. They were not caught up in the immediate fighting to hold the line nor required to repel the onslaught. In June they began to suffer badly from the Spanish 'flu, but in July 1918 they returned to the sector just south of Arras and then back to Vimy.

For the deception the battalion was moved first north to Mount Kemmel to try to make the Germans think that the Canadian Corps had all moved north to the Ypres front. The battalion moved by a specially named 'Strategic Train', so that spies could report its movement. Near Kemmel they temporarily took over a trench from the 15th Hampshires on 1st August, but on 6th August, having been transferred to General Rawlinson's 4th Army, they were secretly brought near to Amiens by train via Boulogne. It was let known that the Canadian commander, General Currie, had been drawing up plans for an attack in front of Arras and that the tanks had been concentrated near St. Pol. Fake radio messages in code the Germans could decipher were sent out and the troops and materials for the battle were only rushed to Amiens at the last minute. As they arrived, the final preparations for the great battle were underway.

The war diary of the Basil Keogh's 1st Canadian Field Artillery Brigade explained that from 3rd August 1918 no movement of any description was allowed on the roads. Batteries arriving by railway had to spend the night in woods. "4th... Batteries all placed in woods and horses and vehicles are all under cover. No movement is allowed in the daytime and everything possible is to be done to prevent the enemy knowing there is a concentration of troops taking place."[752] The next night they moved guns forward to support the attack. (From then onwards they moved forward with the Canadian Corps as it fought its way eastwards.) Airplanes were flown so that their noise could drown out the whippet tanks being moved into position as the camouflage over the big guns was removed only at the last moment. At nearby Mericourt on 6th August, "The streets were very much congested with tanks, artillery, ammunition columns, motor lorries and troops. So dense was the traffic at some points that the men had to pick their way in single file. The whole mass of

---

[752] War Diary, 1st Canadian Field Artillery Brigade, 4th August 1918.

fighting material was moving south east wards."753 By the evening of 7th August the formidable preparations were coming together. "Soon after twilight, from hidden crannies came creeping tractors, lumbering tanks, huge guns, thousands of waggons and innumerable limbers, all preparing to move towards the front. Out of the houses poured troops who formed up wherever they could find a space. Drivers, who had been cleaning and oiling their harness during the day in their billets, were limbering up their teams. Lorry drivers were tinkering at their engines. No one would recognise the innocent little place of the day time."754

At the end of July, Douglas Collingwood of the 5th Canadian Engineer Battalion had worked to make an infantry and tank manoeuvring ground just west of Amiens. (In June they had still been south of Arras working on defensive artillery positions and gas-proofing the Artillery Brigade HQ. Much of July had been taken up with training and sports: the men of the two units forming the new battalion being bonded together.) Amidst the preparations for the coming battle, they had moved forward around the south of Amiens. No difficulties were experienced on the march until the battalion reached Fluy. At this point, the Fluy-St. Fuschien road was blocked with heavy traffic and the battalion had been unable to move for over an hour. From here on, their march was very difficult because of the intense traffic on the road, which included tanks, motor and horsed transport, and infantry. The next day, "Orders from 2nd Brigade C.E. are received to repair Cachy-Marcelcave Road from Cachy to Front Line. Reconnaissance of this work is made in the afternoon by Major Morphy, Captain Collingwood and Captain McGhie MC, and arrangements made that 'C' Company commence work at night." 755 (Douglas' old second in command had been promoted and given command of 'B' Company.)

Douglas and his men worked on this road on the day of the assault, though they were under shell fire and took four casualties. This was the main road south of the Somme linking Amiens with St. Quentin. Soon they would be exploring the old German trenches and filling in old British ones (which had crossed the road) to make possible forward movement of British transport and supplies.

George Rees was with the tanks as these final preparations were made for the battle. George was born in 1918. He attended the school from January 1910 to June 1912. He was called up for service from 15th February 1917, and the next day was posted to the Royal Flying Corps, then part of the Army. Initially, he had begun work as an air mechanic, though he had an unpleasant – and unusual, given his age – bout of shingles which required him to stay in the Connaught Hospital at Aldershot in July 1917, and then to remain in Farnborough. He recovered only slowly – medical boards continued until 27th March 1918. On 31st March 1918, he was compulsorily transferred into the Tank Corps, in which he became a corporal. He was posted to join the Carrier Units Tank Corps at Wareham on 21st April 1918. His unit worked on transporting the tanks behind the lines. He was placed in the 4th Tank Carrier Company, otherwise known as the 4th Tank Supply Company, part of the 4th Tank Brigade. This company was only formed at Bovington in February 1918 and its men came from a variety of sources: eighteen officers who had served overseas (three with the Tank Corps) including thirteen who had served in the ranks; 64% of the men were drawn from infantry

---

753 War Diary, 8th Canadian Infantry Battalion, 6th August 1918, Alexander Sandbrook's unit.
754 *The 4th Canadian Mounted Rifles*, Captain S.G. Bennett, Murray Printing Company Ltd, Toronto, 1926 p. 114
755 War Diary, 5th Canadian Engineer Battalion, 4th-5th August 1918.

in France; of the remaining 36%, 20% were Royal Engineers from the UK, 7% were from Motor Transport sections of the Army Service Corps, and 9% came from the Machine Gun Corps. He might well have been the only man sent from the R.F.C.

By this stage of the war, it had been decided that each tank brigade should have its own tank carrier company, divided into four sections, each with six Mark IV tanks. The first two companies were sent out to France in February (though not deployed in active service) and George went out with his company and the remaining two when they were deployed to France. Initially, the plan had been that these older tanks, armed only with a single machine gun, would carry the infantry forward into the attack. There were visions of the fighting tanks blasting through the German lines, closely followed by carrier tanks, which would empty out the infantry into the German positions. This impressive vision of mechanised infantry was not to be fulfilled in the Great War however; reality kicked in, and the tanks were used instead to re-supply the fighting tanks.

On 12th June 1918, the company had paraded at Bovington for the last time, and George was given a more senior mechanics post, and sailed with his unit aboard the SS *Archimedes* ("a large and comfortable steamer, which had been employed continuously on the transport service since August 16th 1914"[756]) from Southampton, landing in Le Havre the next day. Almost immediately the company was hit hard by 'flu, a serious attack which made them suffer for several weeks. They were initially based at the central workshops at Blingel (west of Cambrai). By 26th June, men were fit enough to draw twelve Mark IV tanks and take them to the Tankodrome at Blangy (south-west of Abbeville and west of Amiens) to be used for training purposes, since no tank carrier company had yet been deployed in action, and the men still had much to learn. Whilst the company remained at Blingel until 20th July, they were busy: amongst other activities they trained with tanks and Hotchkiss guns. (There was also a scare that they might be re-formed into a Lewis gun section.) Then, on 20th-21st July, they moved forward to Caucourt, north-west of Arras and west of Lens. There was much to do, and as a mechanic, George would have been busy: "The tanks which had been taken over from the 1st Tank Supply Company were in a most deplorable condition. Not only had they been left without the necessary daily attention, but they had reached the state at which practically every working part required renewal. Strenuous efforts were made to repair and tune the tanks."[757] On 2nd August, they were sent south by train to the northern outskirts of Amiens, and then forward to Querrieu Wood, astride the Amiens-Albert road. By 4th August their tanks were in forward positions, camouflaged, ready for final adjustments to be completed so that they could support the 5th Tank Brigade and be ready for action by the night of 7th-8th August.

The British attacked, opening the Battle of Amiens on 8th August. The company was very busy. "At the hour of Zero, on the 8th August, a dense grey mist prevailed. Not until 9 o'clock had the sun's rays split up, and mastered it. Even at that hour, filmy shreds still hovered in the hollows, between the series of low, brown ridges that ran roughly parallel to the front of the attack. This mist was all in our favour. Not dense enough seriously to hamper Tank Commanders and drivers, it yet hid the approach of Tanks from the Hun. Hardly had the threat of a lusty barrage told him he was about to be smitten, when the fighting tanks were upon him. His resistance was weak. Only on the relatively high ridge above Chipilly, protected, except from the north, by a loop-like bend of the Somme River and Canal did he hold out. Generally speaking our advance was rapid. The Supply Tanks followed

---

[756] Narrative, p. 6, War Diary, 4th Tank Carrier Company.
[757] Narrative, p. 13, War Diary, 4th Tank Carrier Company.

as rapidly as their heavy loads permitted… The result of their use was good. Dumps were made at Battalion Rallying Points, amply in time on the first day of the operations. This, and the subsequent making of dumps in forward positions, involving treks up to 8 miles long, over ground none too good for heavily loaded Mark IVs, cannot be considered a mean achievement, having regard to their condition at the start."[758]

On 10th August, George was detached temporarily from the 4th Supply Company, possibly to work with the 4th Tank Brigade in the field. The narrative account with their war diary mentions a tank which was temporarily left behind with mechanical problems which, once repaired, came back into action. Whatever the reason and circumstances, his work was clearly satisfactory. On 24th August he was back with his company and was made 2nd class tank mechanic. (On 13th October he was promoted to lance corporal.) Although his company was not officially with the fighting tanks, their role still could bring them into close proximity, and even contact, with the Germans. There were accounts of men in the supply tanks driving them up and over No Man's Land, once the lines had become more fluid as a result of the British success. In the narrative account there is even an amusing anecdote of a supply tank intercepting a German on a horse, forcing him to hand it over. It was then used by the section commander for the rest of the day as he enjoyed riding around directing the tanks of his section!

The supply tanks might carry forward all sorts of necessary stores – or even senior officers on occasion. In battle, whilst initially these supplies tended to be fuel and ammunition for the fighting tanks, they might also come to include items such as wire, water, rations, picks, shovels and sandbags. Although at first there had been arguments because it seemed they might become glorified R.A.S.C. transport machines, in battle they turned into an essential armoured and versatile elements of the Tank Corps, even though they always had to make do with older equipment. It was typical that their crews were men of experience of the front but until 1918 with little knowledge of the machinery of a tank – they had had a lot to learn, quickly. In fact, with his R.F.C. mechanic experience, George was probably better qualified than many of his comrades. As they operated each tank section with a skeleton crew, all had to be prepared to lend a hand at any task placed before them.

Major W.H.L. Watson, in command of Number 5 Tank Carrier Company – doing the same sort of work as Number 4 Company in which George served – wrote of the work in August 1918: "It had become increasingly difficult for us to convince ourselves that we were not 'fighting troops'. We had followed the infantry 'over the top'; we had dumped supplies in full view of the enemy; one of my tanks had received a direct hit, and had been set on fire; another tank had been abandoned practically in No-Man's-Land because every man in the crew except the tank commander had become a casualty; a third tank, with a Highland colonel on board, had started to mop up a machine-gun nest. We began to wonder whether, after all, we were a fit receptacle for 'crocks'. And we did not forget that Carrier Tanks were manned only by skeleton crews, and that, in consequence, every member of the crew was driven to work day and night."[759] One section of the 4th Tank Supply Company suffered such heavy losses in the Battle of Amiens fighting alongside the Canadians that for a time the 5th Company had to help out with its the carrier duties. Carrier tanks

---

[758] Narrative pp. 20 and 22, War Diary, 4th Tank Carrier Company.

[759] *A Company of Tanks* by Major W.H.L. Watson, D.S.O., D.C.M., author of *Adventures of a Despatch-Rider*, William Blackwood and Sons, Edinburgh and London, 1920.

did not have the reinforced steel sponsons (gun posts) of the fighting tanks – theirs were made of non-armoured material, so they were more vulnerable as well as lacking much weaponry.

This was also a busy and valuable time for the tank salvage units. It has been reckoned that in the four weeks between 8th August and 8th September, the salvage companies of the Tank Corps worked on 544 tanks which were handed over for salvage; saved 269 tanks; sent off 96 tanks by train for the central workshops; and prepared a further 42 tanks at the railway depots ready to be sent off by train. On 25th August, Arthur Baker was promoted full lieutenant. He survived the war and lived in Bournemouth until his death in 1948. He even volunteered to serve again as an unpaid 2nd lieutenant in the Second World War, and when he finally retired on 1st January 1946 was given the rank of captain.[760]

Crucial though the role of these tanks and tank carriers was, it was the infantry that provided the main element of the assault, and men like Reginald Winch and Alfred Bishop were heavily involved in the battle.

Reginald and the 3rd London Battalion had moved into the front line south of Ville-sur-Ancre, a village south-west of Albert and just east of Heilly on the 27th July. Although they were relieved by the 1/132nd American Infantry Battalion on 1st August and pulled back north of Amiens for a few days rest in safety, on the evening of 7th August Reginald and the battalion moved into position, poised to attack the Germans holding Malard and Celestine Woods, on a bend of the river south of Albert. The battle was not easily won.

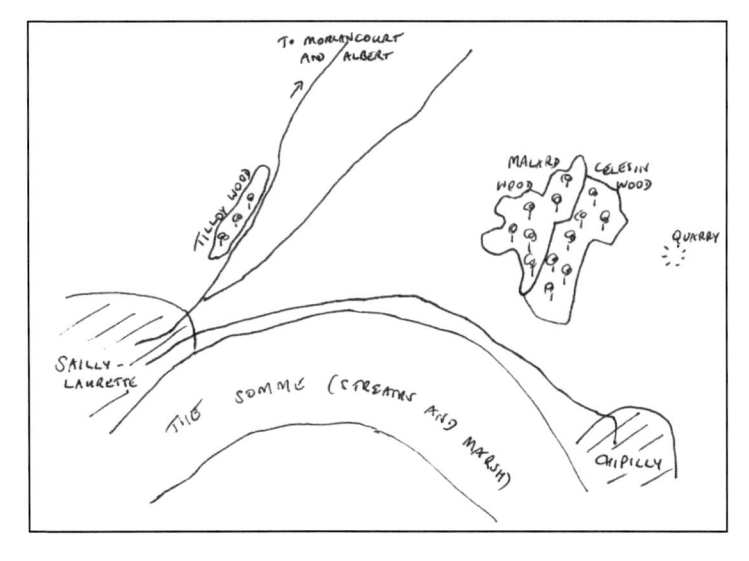

"The Battalion formed up in the Assembly position for the attack behind the 174th Inf. Bde, with the 2/4th Bn. London Regt on the left. The attack started at 4.20am: owing to the thick fog, companies somewhat lost direction and became involved in the fighting before the 174th Inf Bde gained their objectives. Battn HQ pressed on and attacked the Quarry beyond Malard Wood, capturing 4 MG and over 70 prisoners. During this operation the Acting Adjutant was severely wounded and the Intelligence Officer killed. A large number of HQ personnel also became wounded. By the time the objective of the 174th Inf Bde was reached, owing to the number of casualties and disorganisation caused by the fog and heavy fighting, the Battalion was unable to press on. A further attack was launched in the evening by the remnants of the 3rd and 2/4th Battns and also the 2/2 Bttn who had not been involved in the previous fighting, while the 2/10th Battn attacked Chipilly. This attack was unsuccessful. Posts were dug and an outpost line taken up for the night. Casualties: 7 officers. August 9th. The battalion in conjunction with the 2/2nd Battn, the 2/4th Battn and an American Battalion attacked at 5.40pm., Celestine Wood the final objective. After heavy fighting the objective

---

[760] Further information was supplied by members of the Great War Forum, www.greatwarforum.org.

was gained and the Battalion consolidated on the new line. Casualties: 7 officers."[761] Relieved from the line the next day, there was a chance to count up the cost of this attack – their casualties from 8th to 11th August were 226 men. Three days later, reinforcements restored the strength of the battalion. There was a brief period for rest and training.

Alfred Bishop and the 8th London Battalion had also moved up for the battle to a position near the Bray-Corbie road. On the night of 4th August, the battalion had moved up through an uncomfortable drizzle until they reached the badly damaged front trenches – only immediately to be attacked by German 18th Division assault troops (which they managed to thwart with some difficulty) and to suffer from continuous bombardment from the German 5.9 shells, gas shells, and minenwerfers. As their battalion history put it, "By the morning of the 8th, the date fixed for the great counter-offensive, the men of this Battalion were caked in mud from head to foot, had had practically no rest (this was only possible by leaning against the parados), and had repelled a determined attack by the enemy."[762]

The 8th London Battalion was meant to be in reserve for the attack, but within minutes of the start of the battle in mist so thick that visibility was less than ten metres, they found themselves in the action. Indeed, so well did they fight that they managed to capture two German battalion commanders, five hundred German soldiers, and many trench mortars and machine guns. As the fighting continued, many officers and men were killed or wounded. By the start of 9th August, the battalion had been reduced to eleven officers and two hundred and thirty-four men still available to fight, though nearly half of these were scattered amongst the 6th and 7th London Battalions and with Brigade HQ. That evening, after hurriedly collecting the men with the 7th Battalion, they made an evening attack. So rapidly were events unfolding that the colonel noted, "The few minutes available were utterly inadequate to explain all details to my officers & I had to give rough guides as to route & objectives & send them off."[763] Later he reported how the defending German artillery exploded a shell which killed the entire group of runners at his Battalion Headquarters.

Eighteen-year-old Horace Croft was also in the assault, even though his battalion had been designated to be in support not in the attack. Horace was aged 14 when the war broke out and still at the school, so he spent most of the war at school. By the end of 1917 he was old enough to train as an officer. From the start of 1918 he was training with the 2/28th London Battalion ('Artist's Rifles'), in France. In July 1918, he was sent as a private soldier to the 7th Royal Sussex Battalion, 36th Brigade and 12th Division. As the battalion moved forward to its assembly position on 7th August it too came under heavy shell fire and two officers were killed and two more were wounded. According to the official accounts, the division was brought into the battle when 35th Brigade recognised that the Germans were starting to withdraw. Its three battalions – 7th Norfolk, 9th Essex and 1st Cambridgeshires – advanced to consolidate a new line. As these attacked on 8th August, the 7th Royal Sussex Battalion moved forward in support. "Front Line. 8/8/18. Zero hour was 4.20am. Attack took place in thick mist that did not lift until 10am. All coys were disorganised owing to mist and on lifting it was found that the battn was behind its objective, patrols pushed forward and coys moved up to near their final objective."[764] Horace was unlucky. Somehow in the

---

[761] War Diary, 3rd London Battalion, 8th-9th August 1918.
[762] *The History of the 62nd (West Riding) Division 1914-1919 Vol. I.*
[763] War Diary, 8th London Battalion, Operation Report 9th August 1918.
[764] War Diary, 7th Royal Sussex Battalion, 8th August 1918.

midst of this he was shot through the heart. It was only his first day in action. He was buried in the Beacon Cemetery, Sailly-Laurette.

Also in support, the 8th Canadian Infantry Battalion of Alexander Sandbrook had also advanced that day, in their case at 6.20a.m. following the 10th Canadian Infantry Battalion. For the first time in their history, their commander and his second-in-command were so confident that they rode out on horseback leading the battalion. After passing the first objective they became directly involved in the advance but reached their new position with only three casualties. The next day they led the brigade assault (after a delay) at 1p.m. The tanks didn't get through the German barrage to support them so their only support was a battery of field guns. They suffered heavy casualties but managed to take 300 prisoners and a "great number of machine guns" though "now the battalion had suffered between 300 and 400 casualties, and 14 officers gone. Sgt Donaldson and Sgt Garrett jointly took command of 'A' Coy and carried on. Lieut Barlow and Lieut Pope remained with 'D' Coy, and these two Coys now constituted the first line of our advance on right and left respectively." Those two were followed by the other two companies. They just about gained contact with the 14th and 5th Canadian Battalions with the help of some of the 14th Canadian Battalion. That evening, 9th August, they consolidated by gaining touch with the 25th Battalion with the help of a squadron of the 9th Lancers covering the gap, and the arrival of four whippet tanks. But in the battle their casualties had mounted: three officers had been killed and seven wounded; of the men, fifty-nine had been killed, 309 wounded, forty-five were known to have been wounded but gone missing, and seven others were also missing. They were down to about four hundred men, but according to the war diary still "ready for action".

Ernest Snelgar and the 4th Canadian Mounted Rifles Battalion were in reserve for the first day, north of the River Luce, and only went into action on the second day of the battle. The hurricane bombardment and surprise attack had been a great success – for the brigade all objectives for Day One had been taken by 9a.m. When the battalion moved into action on the afternoon of 9th August, the Germans were trying to consolidate and put up greater resistance. The battalion took casualties, including a company commander, even before they moved up to their final attack line. There, assisted by three tanks (two of which were knocked out quite quickly) they attacked the town of Folies. The tanks and some field artillery helped them to advance through heavy German machine-gun fire. By the evening they had achieved their objectives and advanced four kilometres. They had captured three officers and one hundred and twenty-three men, machine guns, and even a complete three-hundred pigeon unit. Sadly, they had also lost two officers killed and three wounded, twelve men killed and sixty-two wounded. One of the officers lost was their hugely brave and popular chaplain, whom Ernest must have known well since he was one of the original members of the battalion. Although other Canadian units fought on for about a week, this battalion was rested, and later moved with the rest of the Canadian Corps north to Arras.

For Douglas Collingwood of the 5th Canadian Engineer Battalion eastward progress was fast after the first day of battle, and the company was for a time detached from the rest of the battalion to work directly with the 6th Canadian Infantry Brigade as it pushed eastwards. On 9th August, Douglas reconnoitred cross-country tracks and established a Royal Engineers dump at Rosières Railway Station and a German search light plant, over which he set guards. By the middle of the month the reunited battalion had reached Chilly, near the line of the modern motorway. Later, Douglas was to learn that he had been awarded the Military Cross for his actions during the Battle of Amiens. Then, pulled back, they were sent by stages by train to Arras on 21st August to enjoy a few days' rest before resuming the task of filling shell holes and clearing debris, and improving roads in their old ground near Neuville St. Vaast. He missed the work of the battalion supporting the Canadian advance at the start of September because, from 2nd to 21st September, he was given leave to return to England. After that he worked with his company to support the advance, improving roads and preparing sites for necessary constructions, such as new field ambulance posts. He survived to the end and was demobilised at the end of March 1919. Afterwards, he became prominent in the oil industry in the USA.

Donald Spickernell was probably also back in action in August, fighting south of the Somme. Born in 1891, he had attended the school from 1904-1908. He had enlisted on 18th January 1915, beginning his war service as a private in the Royal Army Medical Corps. (Although eventually he was commissioned into the Hampshire Regiment (and attached to the Dorsetshire Regiment), most of his service had been on Salonika. He had been briefly on the Western Front before when he was in the 66th Field Ambulance, Royal Army Medical Corps serving with the 22nd Division, part of the New Army. On 6th September 1915 they had sailed from Southampton aboard the SS *Tintoretto* to Le Havre. The division had concentrated near Flesselles in the vicinity of Amiens in early September 1915, which Donald and his comrades reached on 9th September. They then advanced south of the River Somme and established a hospital; at Harbonnières. He described this as a time when "we saw plenty of active work".[765] The unit war diary shows this to have been a mixture of caring for the healthy (baths and vaccinations); caring for the sick; and caring for the wounded. They moved to Marseilles by train and embarked for Salonika on 27th October. From Salonika, Donald wrote informative letters which were published in the school magazine.) Whilst serving as a private with the R.A.M.C. on Salonika, Donald had applied for a commission. On 28th June 1917, he was sent back to England, officially arriving on 14th July, when he was granted leave (and married, in Warwick) the next day. On 7th September 1917, he was sent to the 18th Officer Cadet Battalion at Bath. He was commissioned on 29th January 1918, 2nd lieutenant in the 2nd Hampshire Battalion. This posting was finalised on 23rd April 1918 and he crossed overnight from Southampton to Le Havre on 29th-30th April. At Rouen he formally joined his battalion on 2nd May but was actually attached to the 1st Dorset Battalion. On 7th August 1918, the 1st Dorset Battalion marched into Fourdrinoy, slightly west of Amiens, and then moved forward until opposite the German lines at Damery, south-east from Amiens and south of the River Somme. Here the battalion split – the fighting portion prepared to attack whilst the reserve section retired. We do not know which was his portion of the battalion, though later he was placed in 'A' Company, and that part of the battalion was certainly in the attack.

The battalion was on almost the extreme south of the British line, almost adjacent to the French Army. They went into the attack several days after the start of the battle. The battalion attacked on 11th August at 9.20a.m. when the barrage opened, and immediately encountered heavy German machine-gun fire. Although two tanks assisted in the capture of the village of Damery, losses were heavy: all but one officers of 'C' Company were killed or wounded, as well as 80% of the men, and the remnant joined up with 'A' and 'B' Companies as they were no longer capable of independent action. They had made considerable progress but in view of the heavy losses incurred by all three companies engaged, the battalion was not able to hold all the captured trenches, and consolidation was made with the help of other battalions, notably the 2nd Manchesters and 15th Highland Light Infantry. By the end of the day's battle the battalion had lost seven officers killed; seven more

---

[765] *The Bournemouthian*, July 1916.

officers wounded; twenty-six men were dead, forty-two missing, two hundred and forty-one wounded. Their overall commander, Brigadier-General L.P. Evans, wrote of this engagement that "the loss of many valuable lives is deeply to be regretted but they have not been lost without result. The 5/6th Royal Scots, the 1st Dorset Regt, and 'A' Coy 32nd Bn M.G.C. have good cause for pride in the action fought on 11th August, and the admiration of those of us in the Brigade who took no active share in the fighting is both deep and sincere."

The Battle of Albert: 21st-23rd August

Next, Haig attacked further north, using General Byng's 3rd Army. Foch removed the French 1st Army from Haig's command, though French forces went onto the attack further south. Haig switched the Canadian Corps north to join General Horne's 1st Army. William Webber and Joseph Lonsdale of the 1/28th London (Artists' Rifles) who had moved to the Amiens Sector were not in the initial battle but their moment came on 21st August.

William Webber

The 1/28th London Battalion had regrouped after the March Offensive. It remained in 190th Brigade, 63rd (Royal Naval) Division, and this division was brought in to support the offensive in the Battle of Albert to be launched on 21st August. On 20th August, William Webber was sent to bring water and rations to his battalion. This involved a two-day's movement in the thick of the battle across ground which was under heavy shell fire from the Germans. According to the obituary in the school magazine, he "had almost succeeded in taking his party to their objective, when, in Longeast Wood, near Achiet, an enemy shell struck and felled a tree immediately above him."[766] As was customary in these obituaries, we are told that the twenty-seven-year old died instantly. He died on 22nd August, and his body was never recovered. Today he is commemorated on the memorial in Vis-en-Artois.

Joseph Lonsdale was in the front line of the battle itself. "Zero hour 4.55am. Objectives 188 & 189 Brigade Railway Embankment... 190th Brigade Achet le Grand to Behucourt... Barrage at 4.55am when Infantry arrived with tanks. – Misty morning necessary to move by compass. Difficult to keep in touch. No retaliation from enemy. Then moved... M.G. fire from huts... Touch lost with other units. Enemy shell heavily. Batt man trenches... Not in touch with Batt HQ. 2 Lt V.L. Eve wounded. Drake Battn & elements of Hood Batt found in trench... 22.8.18. 4.30 am Enemy barrage... Enemy Counter Attack 7th RF's twice... repulsed both times. At 11.0am 37th Division advances under barrage & go through. Enemy retaliation. Battalion ordered back to Essarts."[767] After this confused advance, there was a time of holding on and the repulse of counter-attacks whilst other brigades advanced. On 27th August, Joseph and his comrades went back into action with the attack on Thilloy, just south of Bapaume. After bitter fighting, they were withdrawn to recuperate the next day and for a couple of days, but were soon back in the line – which had now reached the Hindenburg Line – on 1st September. But when 'D' Company made a forward thrust on 5th September, they were driven back by German machine-gun fire.

---

[766] *The Bournemouthian*, December 1918.
[767] War Diary, 1/28th London Battalion, 21st-22nd August 1918.

In the Battle of Albert, 21st to 23rd August, the 3rd Army, supported by US II Corps, had recaptured Albert on 22nd August. This attack by General Byng's 3rd Army was on a narrower, thirty-three mile front than for the first stage at Amiens. A German counter-attack on 22nd August was speedily defeated. By 23rd August the way across the old Somme battleground of 1916 was open. An additional 34,000 German prisoners had been taken, along with two hundred and seventy guns. Now Haig could order a general advance by the 3rd Army and part of the 4th across a front of over thirty miles. On 22nd August, Haig sent to his commanders a letter which was almost unbelievably optimistic. He urged them, "Risks which a month ago would have been criminal to incur ought now to be incurred as a duty... The situation is most favourable. Let each one of us act energetically and, without hesitation, push forward to our objective".[768]

Donald Spickernell was fighting at the extreme southern end of the British assault. On 18th August, the 1st Dorset Battalion had moved by bus to Harbonnières to take up a reserve position whilst their division relieved the 2nd Australian Division. Here they were in the Amiens Defence Line, south of the River Somme but astride the road to St. Quentin and due south of Albert. Although in a reserve position, the battalion suffered each day from German shell fire. On 24th August, the battalion moved forward to trenches near Herleville, and Donald, as a member of 'A' Company, was in the front line. The next day, "on right front A Coy pushed forward by bombing up trenches and occupied the trench system... 2 Lt Spickernell and 4 O.R. were wounded. Herleville and vicinity of B Coy Headquarters were heavily shelled at intervals during the day."[769] Indeed, on 25th August, Donald was "Very seriously wounded".[770] He had gone out on a daylight reconnaissance patrol but had failed to locate the Germans and "so had orders to advance his line. He then went on himself to reconnoitre in front, and suddenly came on a bombing block. Spickernell got a Mill's bomb amongst the Boches, but a stick bomb from them burst close to him, wounding him in ten places, one a bad one in the hip."[771] He had suffered multiple wounds – one fractured his left wrist; a second smashed through his upper left arm; a third made severe wounds to the front and back of his right hip; and a fourth hit him in the right chest breaking a rib; and finally he suffered three further wounds to his back. He was sent back to England from Le Havre to Southampton on 2nd-3rd September and taken to hospital in Birmingham for further treatment and recuperation. With such wounds this treatment lasted many months and well beyond the end of the war, but he survived and after prolonged treatment lived in Birmingham after the war. However, before the end of the autumn term he was able to visit his old school.

On the day Donald was wounded, from a new position due south of Albert, Reginald Winch and the 3rd London Battalion attacked "hostile positions behind Happy Valley in conjunction with the 140 Bde, 47th Div. Zero Hour was 2.30am. The attack was carried out under a creeping barrage of field guns and Hows. and was entirely successful. All objectives on the Divisional front being gained... The Battalion followed closely behind the 140 Bde & consolidated on a line running N & S of the Fricourt-Bray Road... The enemy retired well beyond the final objective & for a time contact was lost." Hours later they advanced again. Other battalions attacked ahead of them and then "Enemy offered vigorous resistance supported by heavy counter barrage. In spite of this all objectives were gained on a line running N of Peronne road through W edge of Billon Wood. Weather – Hot during

---

[768] C.R.M.F. Cruttenwell, *A History of the Great War*, p. 553, 1934 – second edition 1936.
[769] War Diary, 1st Dorset Battalion, 25th August 1918.
[770] Army File of Donald Spickernell, WO 339/11415.
[771] *The Bournemouthian*, December 1918.

the day, heavy downpour during the early part of night. Battn HQ moved from Bonfray Farm road to Battle HQ of the 2/2nd." This was followed by three more days of pressuring attacks, capturing "Numerous prisoners, MGs & enemy stores" on the 26th August, and the next day attacking "the village of Maricourt, supported by a rolling barrage of field guns & a concentration of heavies on the village... The attack was entirely successful & all objectives were gained by an early hour in the morning. The village of Maricourt was cleared and a line was taken up in the old German front line W of Maricourt."[772] On the third day, 28th August, they again took all their objectives and moved their Battalion HQ into the former German reserve line.

Nearby, Oliver Cooper of the 1st Grenadier Guards also fought their way through the fierce and tough battle of Albert from 21st August. On 25th August: "the King's and No. 4 Companies moved up Mory Switch supported by one tank, while another worked on the southern flank. The fog was still thick, and as the first tank advanced it was suddenly engaged at very close range by a stray machine-gun post. Armour-piercing bullets were used, and the engine and water jacket were penetrated. It was therefore necessary to find the other tank, which could be heard working in the fog, and after an unsuccessful attempt to get it going in the right direction, it eventually succeeded in moving forward at 8.30 a.m., supported by the King's Company and a platoon of No. 4 Company. But soon afterwards the fog lifted, and the tank was immediately put out of action".[773]

Alfred Bishop and the 8th London Battalion were also involved in this phase of the assault. Their brigade had been re-assigned to the 18th Division for the battle. On 25th August, the 8th London Battalion moved up to the front line on an intensely hot day which left Alfred and his friends exhausted by the heat and by their frequent moves, and the lack of sleep and water. As they advanced to Billon Wood that evening, Major Priestley, who was in temporary command of the battalion, was wounded by a shell, and this later caused the company commanders some confusion. "The night was exceedingly dark, the movement a very complicated one, the Valley up which the advance was to take place was being heavily bombarded with Blue Cross and H.E., and a violent thunderstorm did not lessen the difficulty of keeping touch, direction and control."[774] Even so, at 4a.m. the next morning they went into the attack, coming immediately under heavy artillery fire as well as very strong hostile machine-gun fire from their flanks. They found themselves isolated – no unit was in 'touch' on either flank, so they had to use their own men to form defensive flank positions until, eventually, the 7th London Battalion came up onto their right. For a day they were in an exposed forward position driving off German counter-attacks, even though – because of the hurried nature of their advance after last-minute orders – Alfred and the men had neither rations nor water. (Although some men were supplied with some rations and water on the night of 26th-27th August, this was only with great difficulty, and many of the men had to wait until the following night and the early hours of 28th August before receiving any. So they had fought since the night of 24th-25th August without food or drink.) On the night of 26th-27th August, despite exhaustion and terrain that was broken up by trenches, wire and shell holes, they managed to make yet another successful attack in support of the 6th and 7th London Battalions. Despite the loss of various officers over these days, and in the attack, and despite continuous German machine-gun fire even as they assembled, they managed to reach their objectives with surprisingly light casualties. However, they

---

[772] War Diary, 3rd London Battalion, 25th-28th August 1918.
[773] *The Grenadier Guards in The Great War of 1914-1918, Volume III*, Lieut.-Colonel Sir Frederick Ponsonby, Macmillan And Co., Limited, London 1920, p. 76.
[774] War Diary, 8th London Battalion, Operation Report, 25th August 1918.

had to make an emergency re-organisation of the companies to re-balance the officers and men between them. For a time they managed to capture some German machine-gun posts which had been holding them up, but afterwards they were bombed out by a German counter-attack. Overall, they managed to consolidate a new forward position, although the shelling – and the casualties as a result – continued all day, until they were relieved by the 10th Londons by 4a.m. on 29th August.

This relief was only temporary. That day they rapidly reorganised and re-equipped themselves. Two of the officers and fifteen men had been killed; five officers and one hundred and sixty men wounded; and eleven men were missing. On the other hand, they had taken one hundred and fifty prisoners, many machine guns, and even three German field guns. They had also captured forty German pigeons. There was to be no rest. On the evening of the next day, 30th August, they were moved by bus from near Maricourt and driven for two hours until they were dropped off on the Peronne road about five hundred yards west of Hen and Howitzer Woods. They bivouacked for a short while that night under heavy shell fire. In the middle of the night, the company commanders were briefed for an early hours attack. Alfred and the others moved forward at 2.15a.m. and brought up to a position from which to attack at 5.10a.m. Final preparations were not helped by British 18-pound artillery exploding a shell which killed one of the company commanders. The suggestion was later made that they had been instructed to assemble too close to the barrage. "What happened was that some of our guns, probably two guns, were firing short during the whole of the barrage. While the barrage remained stationary shells from these guns were bursting on my Battn HQ, which had to be hastily evacuated and was re-established… When the barrage lifted these guns overtook our own troops and caused the casualties inflicted by our own barrage."[775] This attack was again a success, though they lost a further two officers and nine men killed, five officers and seventy-one men wounded, and lost a further twenty-one men missing. Alfred though had survived unhurt. They had captured another three hundred and twenty prisoners and many more machine guns. Finally, they were relieved and allowed a brief rest.

Once the infantry were on the move, the role of tanks in general temporarily diminished and George Rees and the 4th Supply Company went into reserve. Tanks simply could not keep up! This changed once the German retreat reached the higher ridge which ran north to south through Bray and down to the River Somme. "On the 20th the O.C. received orders calling for the co-operation of his Company in actions to be fought to the north of Somme, on the 22nd by the 47th Division, and on the 23rd by the 1st Australian Division, and the 32nd Division to the south. This time we were to do infantry supply work."[776] Each day the company moved ammunition and materials forward to the front. This was extremely hazardous. For example, on 22nd August, 'E' Section was sent forward – three tanks delivering loads but "1 Tank knocked out by direct hit. 1 Officer killed. 1 Officer wounded at duty. 1 O.R. killed and three wounded. 1 Tank had to be abandoned. 2 of crew missing believed killed. 1 wounded and missing. 1 O.R. to hospital sick."[777] Unfortunately, this was not an isolated occurrence. Some days were better. One tank commanded by 2nd Lieutenant H.H. Baker was on his way to deliver one load of supplies forward when: "on the outward journey found five Huns skulking in a dug-out. They had been missed in the mopping up. He brandished his revolver and ordered them to the rear. What an opportunity he missed. What if he had taken them forward

---

[775] War Diary, 8th London Battalion, Operation Report, 31st August 1918.
[776] Narrative p. 28, War Diary, 4th Tank Carrier Company.
[777] War Diary, 4th Tank Carrier Company, 22nd August 1918.

as unloading party and brought them back as tank prisoners – Supply Tank prisoners?"[778] The narrative account paid tribute to men like George: "The efforts of Lieut. N. Read, the Tank Engineer, and his staff contributed especially to the excellent result gained."[779]

On the northern flank of the advance, north of the River Somme, after the recapture of Albert, the fighting mostly centred on the struggle to secure Bapaume, at the eastern end of the old Somme battleground. Sidney Seeviour and the 2/4th Hampshire Battalion had returned to the main British forces after helping in the French Battle of the Marne in 1918. The battalion marched for four days continuously to reach a position just north of Bapaume and north-east of Achiet-le-Grand in the early part of 26th August. The 2/4th Hampshires were in support of the 5th Duke of Wellington's. Behind them was the small village of Gomiécourt. They were to be the assault battalions for the brigade, targeted to drive eastwards to cut the road from Bapaume to Arras and to capture Béhagnies and then on to occupy the land south of the village of Mory. The idea was that by attacking the retreating Germans they would prevent them creating any defence west of the Hindenburg Line, but it was not going to be easy. The ground to be covered would present many obstacles: "Thick belts of old wire, rusty and torn in places, still protected (inversely) the battered and tumbled trenches, many of which, however, were capable of being turned to good account."[780] At Zero Hour, 9a.m. on 25th August, the 5th Duke of Wellington's attacked with a rolling barrage. They encountered heavy machine-gun fire from Mory to the north-east and Favreuil to the south-east and suffered heavy casualties. Sidney and his comrades held the line while the 5th Duke of Wellington's advanced, and the next day, August 26th, made their own attack. "The attack starting at 6am was successfully carried out. 1st objective was gained without difficulty, except for enemy barrage which was fairly heavy. Considerable difficulty was experienced in getting the final objective owing to heavy M.G. fire from the road and high ground immediately beyond the final objective. This was especially so on the left, but Captain Cave handled his Coy with considerable skill and by 9am all objectives were gained and the Bn reorganised."[781] A captain was then killed just as orders were received to move forward to gain a further line of trenches, which they achieved by dusk. By the end of the day, one officer and nine men had been killed, and another officer and thirty-nine men wounded. Another seven men were missing. For his actions that day, August 26th, Sidney was awarded the Military Medal for bringing in five wounded Australians whilst under fire.

The next day, August 27th, as the 5th King's Own Yorkshire Light Infantry attacked eastwards south of Mory, the 2/4th Hampshire Battalion pushed out patrols to try to secure the line of the road from Beugnatre to Ecoust – which meant crossing the line of the modern A1 motorway. The official divisional history described the machine-gun fire from in front of them as "murderous". "Hostile machine gun fire now became more intense and it was evident that the enemy had reinforced his line with additional guns." Not surprisingly, "The patrols sent out… were unable to make headway."[782] That evening, Sidney was brought back to a casualty clearing station, very seriously wounded in both legs and arms. He had been hit by this heavy machine-gun fire whilst on a patrol

---

[778] Narrative p. 34, War Diary, 4th Tank Carrier Company.

[779] Narrative p. 36, War Diary, 4th Tank Carrier Company.

[780] *The History of the 62nd (West Riding) Division 1914-1919, Vol. I*, p. 231, E. Wyrall Publisher: John Lane, The Bodley Head Limited.

[781] War Diary, 2/4th Hampshire Battalion, 26th August 1918.

[782] *The History of the 62nd (West Riding) Division 1914-1919, Vol. II*, p. 4.

sent out by 'C' Company. They did their best for him, and at first had some hope, and he was taken a long way behind the lines – past Arras to Ligny-sur-Canche where there were three casualty clearing stations: 3rd Canadian, 19th and 43rd Casualty Clearing Stations. Despite all their efforts, Sidney died on 28th August and was buried in the small cemetery established by the casualty stations. The school magazine adds a note of additional sorrow: "The sad event gains additional pathos from the fact that he was engaged to be married, and that, before he received his wounds, a message was on the way to him granting him the leave of absence during which he was to have celebrated his wedding."[783]

Slightly further north again, James Miller also did not emerge unscathed. Born in 1898, and at the school between 1911 and July 1914, he had left to become a clerk. On 21st September 1916, he enlisted as a private in the Machine Gun Corps. From 1916, the infantry battalions were gradually and increasingly equipped with the lighter two-man Lewis guns, but to work the heavy machine guns the Machine Gun Corps soldiers were attached to brigades and deployed at the need of the brigade. The Army seems to have had mixed views on the Corps, which was disbanded in 1922, and its records are notoriously difficult to trace. James was posted near Arras. He had been picked out for officer training and on 21st August his general had approved his transfer to an officer cadet battalion. Meanwhile, though still a private, he have been given charge of a multiple-man team operating a heavy machine gun: to work and fire a heavy machine gun like the Vickers required, at least in theory, an eight-man gun team. The gun itself weighed about 42.5lbs. It took a man each to carry the gun and its tripod, and six others to carry the ammunition boxes and cooling water, as well as a spare barrel (since the gun could only be fired for a maximum of a minute and a half continuously before the barrel had to be replaced to avoid overheating destroying the gun). Each belt box of ammunition (a belt carrying 250 rounds) weighed 22lbs.

Machine gunners on the move would be a prime target. Both sides made every effort to destroy enemy machine guns and kill their crews because these machine guns were so damaging to the opposition. The Vickers machine gun (by 1918 the main British heavy machine gun) could fire to a range of 2,800 yards and shoot off a complete belt of ammunition in less than a minute. It had not been normal to attack with the heavy machine guns since they were seen as essentially defensive weapons – their low trajectory was more likely to shoot down their own men than the enemy if the assault troops were in front of the gun. According to a German manual, they had learned that for the purposes of a British attack the Vickers were "deployed as far as possible on the flanks. They work best when they are sited in such a way that they can keep up their fire for the greatest length of time, i.e. exploiting for as long as possible their capacity for sustained fire. In the attacks reaching to a greater depth the machine guns are to be brought forward by stages. Covered positions will have been prepared for them in advance by designated detachments of the attacking infantry." But by 1918 tactics had developed. They tended to be used from behind an infantry assault as 'light artillery' giving arcing overhead fire to barrage specific enemy defensive points.

James was badly wounded on 23rd August 1918. "We were just going 'over the top' when a 'Jerry' shell burst within a few yards of my gun team. Five of my men were killed and also my officer who was just behind me. The No.2 and myself were wounded, but I hear the No.2 has since died." He crawled to the aid post where his wounds were dressed, after which he was helped back to the advanced dressing station. His wounds were extensive, though he tried to make light of them. He

---

[783] *The Bournemouthian*, December 1918.

had shrapnel from the shell in his right thigh and also in the left frontal area of his head. He had also been hit by shrapnel in his left shoulder and his back, and his jaw was damaged and a number of his teeth blown out. At each stage he received treatment of some kind, varying from X-ray to shrapnel removal or other operation. After arriving at the advanced dressing station, "I was put on a stretcher and taken to the C.C.S. in a motor ambulance. I was kept there until late in the evening, when I was put on an ambulance train and taken to the 53rd General Hospital [at Wimereux, north of Boulogne]… I stayed at this hospital for a week, and then I was transferred to 'The Dublin' 83rd General Hospital for special treatment to the jaw [in Boulogne itself]. After three days at this hospital they operated on the jaw… A fortnight later I was brought back to England and taken to the Queen's Hospital at Sidcup. My stay here was not long, for on the fourth day I was transferred to Stanford Road Hospital, Croydon."[784]

The Queen's hospital – actually Queen Mary's Hospital, Sidcup – performed plastic surgery on men's faces between 1917 and 1925, and they kept a record of the work done on James' face, which was sufficient to earn him discharge from the Army and the award of the Silver War Badge on 25th February 1919. Although James made light of his injuries in his letter, his story is a salutary reminder that the impact of the war lingered on for years for some of the Old Boys and their widows.

On Saturday 24th August, the headline in *The Times* proclaimed "Gains along the Line" and the article explained that "The whole British front is now ablaze about four miles south of Arras to five or six miles below the Somme, attacks almost to Lihons. Roughly a distance of 28 miles is now all battlefront, and everywhere, except for local counter-attacks, it is we who are on the offensive, and the Germans everywhere are being beaten back."[785] Whilst German reports mentioned heavy British losses (exaggerated), not surprisingly British newspapers played those down. But there was a general delay after the success of the Battle of Albert, despite the urgings of Marshall Foch who wanted 4th Army to push on through the Germans. Haig resisted, because he was anxious to regroup, and especially to bring forward his artillery. In any case, Haig recognised that the Germans had retreated to stronger defences than those held on August 8th 1918.

The Second Battle of Arras

On 26th August, near Arras, General Horne committed the right wing of the 1st Army to join in the offensive, and this extended the front to forty miles. This part of the battle is sometimes known as the Second Battle of Arras. Haig used the Canadians in a battle designed to disrupt the north flank of the Germans resisting his attacks further south.

Ernest Snelgar and the 4th Canadian Mounted Rifles went back into action. They attacked at 3a.m. on 26th August after a brief, but powerful, bombardment, and following a creeping barrage. They achieved their objectives despite strong German defensive machine-gun fire and consolidated under artillery fire whilst other units moved the line forward. Two days later they attacked again, successfully. As a result of these two attacks, the battalion had once again lost a substantial number – three officers killed and twelve wounded (one died later); and twenty-two men killed and two hundred and fourteen wounded. But they had captured ten German officers and four hundred and

---

[784] *The Bournemouthian*, December 1918.
[785] *The Times*, 24th August 1918.

fifty-nine men; six field guns; and very many trench mortars, light and heavy machine guns. The machine guns could only be counted in tens, rather than the odd ones which previously had seemed such a trophy. The battalion was again pulled from the battle, which continued for a further week. Once again Ernest had survived. In an address, the out-going divisional general congratulated them on their successes over the last two years: "At Vimy you distinguished yourselves; at Passchendaele you made the hole through which the 9th Brigade was able to pass through and capture Bellevue Spur. These actions came to a climax in the three recent actions, at Amiens and in front of Arras."[786]

In the same battle, Alexander Sandbrook and the 8th Canadian Infantry Battalion pushed along a line from Arras towards Cambrai, in action from 29th to 31st August, near Arras and Vis-en-Artois, across the Sensee River. Now that the British Army was advancing, it was not always possible to maintain a continuous line, so their exposed flanks had to be defended by outposts, shelled both by high explosives and Blue Cross (mustard) gas. They also found themselves being machine gunned from German aeroplanes. With the Allied line temporarily held up, they attacked at 5a.m. on 31st August, supported by the 2nd Canadian Machine Gun Company. They captured the German line within 20 minutes but were then held up further by intense machine-gun fire. The attack was costly: their casualties were five officers and ninety-three men.

On 2nd September, after a million shell bombardment, the Canadians, with the 52nd and Royal Naval Divisions, broke through the German defences known as the Drocourt-Quéant Switch, south-east of Arras. The 8th Canadian Infantry Battalion was in support for this attack, crossing the river behind the 10th Battalion and taking part in the fighting. One German group they encountered indicated the way the tide of war had turned: "The German officer here did not want to surrender, but his men thinking otherwise, killed their Officer and threw up their hands."[787] Next, they helped to capture Villers les Cagnicourt after which they advanced in conjunction with 7th and 10th Canadian Infantry Battalions west of the Canal du Nord. "As our first troops crossed the high ground west of the canal du Nord the enemy directed fire over open sights with his artillery from the far side of the Canal. This caused great annoyance and many casualties. One shell knocked out a whole Company HQ though the Captain thrice wounded, still briefed his men, as did two lieutenants, both wounded in the leg (one shattered). Finally relieved morning of 4th September."

Douglas Tuck and the howitzers of the 95th Siege Battery were supporting the infantry. He had returned from leave to the UK on 17th August 1918, in time to fight with it as it supported the advance of late August. On 10th September 1918, he was slightly wounded in the right cheek by flying shell splinters. For a few weeks from 14th September 1918 he was attached to IV Corps Heavy Artillery Headquarters and was judged only well enough to re-join his unit on 1st October. On 28th October, he reported to the Commandant of the School of Instruction at Berkhamstead for the 1st Instructors Course. Whilst on this course, on 6th December, he was promoted to lieutenant. After completion of the course, he reported again to his battery in France on 28th December 1918. After the war he continued his military career as a full lieutenant in the Indian artillery. He served on the North-West Frontier with Afghanistan in 1919 with the 6th Mountain Artillery, and then with the 28th Mountain Artillery, 7th Meerut Division of the Royal Garrison Artillery, from which he

---

[786] Quoted in *The 4th Canadian Mounted Rifles*, Captain S.G. Bennett, Murray Printing Company Ltd, Toronto, 1926, p. 133.

[787] War Diary, 8th Canadian Infantry Battalion, 4th September 1918 (for this and the subsequent entry).

resigned in 1921 in order to go to university to study chemistry and electricity. His battery was returned to India and for several years he went with it. One curious end to his military career was that, when he was sent home from India he was a member of the Regular Army reserve and was temporarily attached to the 4th Wiltshire Regiment to conduct home some of its soldiers and to "serve during the present emergency from 16/4/21 to 6/6/21"[788] and this delayed his final demobilisation by three months. He died on war service in 1940.

Meanwhile, the ANZACs too were distinguishing themselves. The New Zealanders captured Bapaume on 29th August and the 2nd Australian Division captured Mont St. Quentin overnight between 30th and 31st August, allowing them to capture Péronne on 1st September despite heavy casualties. The German attempt to hold the old Le Transloy-Loupart trench defences east of the Somme had failed, and the British held a line which ran roughly north to south from Arras, through Bapaume to Peronne.

After a month of offensive fighting, despite the losses, British confidence was high. The newspapers began regular speculations on what should happen "after the war" and how Germany should be made to pay. In a Special Order issued to the troops in France, Haig wrote, "The capture of 73,000 prisoners and 750 guns in the course of four weeks' fighting speaks for the magnitude of your effort and the magnificence of your achievement… The enemy has now spent his efforts, and I rely confidently upon each one of you to turn to full advantage the opportunity which your skill, courage, and resolution have created." Yet almost at the moment of this triumph, on 29th August Haig received a telegram from Sir Henry Wilson, Chief of the Imperial General Staff, which warned him of the dangers of incurring heavy casualties should he continue the advance and attack the German Hindenburg Line. Haig was understandably furious. He recognised the political motive behind this telegram in his diary, "The Cabinet are ready to meddle and interfere with my plans in an underhand way, but do not dare to say openly that they mean me to take the responsibility for any failure though ready to take credit for every success! The object of this telegram is, no doubt, to save the Prime Minister (Lloyd George) in case of any failure… What a lot of wretched weaklings we have in high places at the present time."[789]

The Belgian Old Bournemouthians

There were several members of the school from European citizenships, and at least two of these were Belgians. One at least was directly involved in these events of 1918. G. Maistriau is one of the most obscure Old Bournemouthians – we do not even know his forename, when and where he was born, nor even when he attended the school, though it was in its earliest years. The only positive detail is an entry in the April edition of the 1917 magazine which read, "G Maistriau is on the Belgian front in a .75 battery".[790]

The Belgian Army had adopted a defensive role from the autumn of 1914, holding an expanding line of 'trenches' which often had to be built up from the level rather than down into the ground because of the low land and the high water table. These trenches were hazardous to hold, and the issues caused by the Germans were compounded by the illnesses which their frequently water-

---

[788] From his Army File, WO 339/127093 William Douglas Tuck.
[789] From *Douglas Haig, War Diaries and Letters 1914-1918*, edited by Gary Sheffield and John Bourne, p. 453.
[790] *The Bournemouthian*, April 1917.

logged conditions brought to the men. From the end of 1916, the Belgian Army had begun to be re-equipped to furnish the men – many of whom were trained in the safety of England – with more modern and more appropriate weapons, though their equipment never included tanks. In early March 1918, the Belgians had flooded further sections of their country when it was clear that their trenches there were close to collapse. When the Germans had begun their April Offensive they attacked the three Belgian infantry divisions in the line in an attempt to pass north of Ypres and so to try to encircle the British positions there. On 17th April, they tried to punch their way through the Belgians using three German divisions, with a further four in reserve. Although they fairly rapidly broke through the Belgian front line and reached their support line by lunchtime, they encountered surprising resistance from the Belgian artillery in which G. Maistriau may have participated. Belgian artillery thundered its shells both on the German assault forces and also on the reserves, and then the Belgians shocked the Germans by attacking out of their support trenches. The Belgians then broke the German troops (who were not their prime soldiers, since a relatively easy victory had been anticipated) and that afternoon regained the ground lost in the morning. Therefore, the Germans had to be content with the fruits of their more successful southern attacks (they were to capture Mount Kemmel from the French on 25th April) but not the pincer movement they had hoped for. The British, though driven back to the edge of Ypres, held on there, and the Belgians to their north supported them by denying the Germans their advance.

Later in the year, on 28th September, under the nominal leadership of King Albert I (but 'supported' by the French general Jean-Marie Degoutte), ten of the twelve Belgian infantry divisions, with British and French divisions alongside, began to advance and managed to liberate about forty miles of Belgian territory before the Armistice. We do not know the extent of Maistriau's involvement or even whether or not he survived.

Benoni van Hecke was born in Belgium in December 1884. We know that he was educated in Bruges from 1898 to 1900, and after that that he moved to the Bournemouth area. He married a Mathilde Deschutter at the start of 1916, and joined the school as a part-time French teacher whilst also working as a private French tutor in the area, from 3rd May 1917 to 1st June 1918. The school magazine of July 1918 recorded that he joined the Belgian Army "early in June". Unfortunately, it is not possible to trace his actions with that army, or even if he managed to join them in time to take part in the offensive which helped to liberate his homeland. Unfortunately, we know no more, except that the British had a couple of van Hecke agents near Mons during the war, who might have been related to him.

10: The Autumn Advance to Victory

Despite the political doubts and arguments which so exasperated Haig, the Army pushed on against the retreating Germans. George Mossop was involved: in August 1918 the 7th Royal Sussex Battalion had taken heavy casualties in the attack on the Germans – twenty officers were killed or wounded, and 416 men. It is not entirely surprising that the diary was written in less detail than usual. However, on 31st August 1918, the diary stated, "Draft of 253 joined Bn. 13 officers joined – re-joined Bn."[791] George Mossop must have one of them, if he was not already with them because we know for certain that he was with them that September.

On 1st September, the battalion rested and re-organised, but at 4a.m. they moved forward via Maricourt and Maurepas to trenches about 2,000 yards east of Le Foret, close to a six howitzer battery. They were moving across the south of the old Somme battlefield to a trench line close to the site of the modern A1 motorway. That day, George was formally promoted lieutenant. The next day they suffered some slight shelling, but no casualties. Then they moved east again to take over positions near Rancourt, south-east of St. Pierre Vaast Wood, replacing the 7th Queen's Battalion. All that night they suffered from heavy gas attacks.

On 5th September, when the battalion went onto the attack driving eastwards, George was badly wounded. "5/9/18... 6.45am. Battalion attacked with Nurlu as objective. Held up along Nurlu Ridge by Machine Guns. 2/Lts Branson, Mossop, & Bennett wounded."[792] A bullet had hit him in the face, and it had penetrated from the left side of his nose and moved upwards into his brain. It was lodged in the left frontal lobe. But he was still alive. George was carried back through the casualty clearing system and the doctors clearly believed he had a good chance of survival, because he was regularly moved back up the medical chain. On 13th September, he was sent from Le Havre to Southampton on an overnight crossing, and from there to the 5th London General Hospital (St. Thomas' Hospital), a Territorial Force hospital in Lambeth. Here, X-rays were used to locate the bullet, and he was operated upon to remove the bullet on 7th November. The operation was a success. However, he remained in hospital to until the middle of February 1919, after which he was discharged into his father's care, now at home in Maldon, Suffolk. On 21st August, though still invalid, he was demobilised and allowed to retain the rank of lieutenant. However, by February 1920, it was clear to George's father that George would never recover fully. He made a major effort, in vain, to secure a larger pension benefit than that which had been granted – the Army took the view that he had not lost a limb so that whilst his injury was "very severe and permanent" it did not merit the higher level of pension. George's father maintained that George could not work or study, and was "very weak minded" in contrast to his former self. The doctors examining him admitted he suffered "some loss of memory for recent events... his memory is impaired for recent happenings and he lacks initiative. He is able to do a day's work in the office but feels that he is unable to study or work for examinations."[793]

Two days after George Mossop was wounded, Machine Gunner Harry Finch had come into action.

---

[791] War Diary, 7th Royal Sussex Battalion, 31st August 1918.

[792] War Diary, 7th Royal Sussex Battalion, 5th September 1918.

[793] Medical Board Review, 25th February 1920 in the Army File of George Mossop, The National Archives, WO339/72677.

Harry was the older brother of Harold Finch who had been killed on the Somme in November 1916. He had been born in 1889. Harry, who was at the school from 1902 to 1907, had had something of a golden school career. He won senior honours and a prize in 1905, after which he was a prefect and then Head of School – the equivalent of the later designated 'School Captain'. He was a member of the school O.T.C. from January 1904, rising to the rank of colour sergeant by the time he left in December 1907. With his exam results (including a distinction in geography) he gained exemption from the exams to matriculate for London University. After leaving school and following further education, he became a teacher. On 29th November 1915, he enlisted at Newhaven and was placed in the Army Reserve while he continued to teach at Harrow View Prep School in West Ealing, and then at Lexden House School, Seaford. He attested at Chichester on 16th August 1916 and was posted to the 3rd Royal Sussex Battalion, though soon he was moved to the 7th Oxford and Buckinghamshire Light Infantry on 19th October 1916.

For part of the next year he had served with his battalion in the campaign in Salonika, but he had come back to England in July 1917 to prepare for a commission. "Schoolmaster before joining Army & consequently has the knack of imparting his military knowledge to others."[794] He was attached to No.3 Officer Cadet Battalion on 6th October 1917, in Bristol. In his application to become an officer, he asked to be commissioned into the Oxford and Buckinghamshire Light Infantry, or into the Railway Section of the Royal Engineers. However, later, on 28th February 1918, when he had come to the end of his training his stated preference had changed, to the order: the Hampshires; the Worcesters; and then the Dorsets. So in that way of thinking which is so special to the Army, he was commissioned into the Dorsetshire Regiment and then almost immediately switched to a 2nd lieutenant attached to the Machine Gun Corps. He was placed in the 58th Battalion of the Machine Gun Corps. This battalion had been formed in the early months of 1918 when the corps was reorganised and the different companies melded into a new, single command structure. As each battalion then took its number according to its division, his was part of the 58th Division. Before he went to France with the M.G.C. he studied at Grantham, and later the school magazine reported his success with pride – he passed out top of his list; in maths he scored 88% and had an overall exam average of 81.5%. Harry went to France on 16th August, arrived at the M.G.C. Depot in France on 24th August, and joined the 58th Battalion on 31st August.

Fighting on the Somme, the battalion was supporting the various infantry units of the 58th Division trying to push the Germans back. They were still operating on the Somme in early September 1918 in the southern area of the battleground near Carnoy and Montauban. On 1st September, 'A' and 'D' Companies were fighting in support of the 173rd Brigade, after which the battalion moved swiftly eastwards along the southern flank of the Somme battleground and beyond. On 6th September, the battalion split to place its companies with the different brigades of the division. 'D' Company went into divisional reserve, 'B' Company joined with the 174th Brigade; 'C' with the 175th; and 'A' with the 173rd Brigade. On 7th September, 'C' Company went into action alongside the 175th Brigade and in the evening 'D' Company carried out harassing fire in support of the 174th Brigade. The other two companies were not directly involved in the fighting that day.

The 175th Brigade – 2/9th London and 2/10th London – attacked the railway line south of Ephey at about 8a.m. Ephey lies about half-way between Cambrai to the north and St. Quentin to the south. Their assault was soon held up by German machine-gun fire and a shrapnel barrage was used to

---

[794] Army File of Harry Finch, The National Archives, WO339/106270.

try to force their way forward. There were many casualties, and Harry was one of them. He was shot by a machine-gun bullet through the left shoulder. Fortunately, the bullet passed cleanly from the point where the left shoulder meets the arm and out behind his left scapula, without causing additional complications or infection. He was evacuated from the battlefield and brought back to 55 Casualty Clearing Station, which then was at 'Edgehill'. It was also known as No.2 London Casualty Clearing Station, and when Harry arrived it was at Dernancourt, a village immediately south of Albert. The site had only been recaptured on 9th August, but by early September was being used by three casualty clearing stations: the 47th, 48th and 55th, and was code-named 'Edgehill' because of the rising ground to its north-west. Later in the month it was again moved forward, to Doingt, east of Peronne. It was really a mobile hospital with operating theatres, resuscitation and pre-operation wards, huts, marquees, and sisters' quarters.

After checking his wounds, the authorities moved him further down the line to Le Havre where he embarked for Southampton, crossing on the night of 10th-11th September. He was admitted to Lady Cooper's Hospital, Hursley Park, Winchester on 11th September 1918. Although his wound was no longer life-threatening, it was too bad to send him quickly back into action, and the war was over before he was healed. Consequently, he was released from the Army on 11th January 1919, although as early as 30th September 1918 he was fit enough to visit the school. Afterwards he was awarded a wound pension because, although his wound had healed, and his power of movement returned, as late as his final medical board at the Kitchener Hospital, on 2nd June 1919, he lacked all power to lift with his left arm. The board decided he had 20% disability as a result of his war service.

Alfred Bishop was in action again the day after Harry was wounded. At the start of September, Alfred and the 8th London Battalion had been allowed a short rest. But after little under a week to recuperate, on 8th September at 6.15a.m., when it was already light, they received orders to attack. "Companies were ordered to creep forward as far as possible and then to catch up with the barrage as soon as they could."[795] They attacked over one thousand yards but came under heavy machine-gun fire. All four companies reached the enemy trench, and thirty prisoners were taken and they were able to destroy a number of German machine guns. At that point they received a message telling them to make a further attack. "This message was received at 12.30pm on the 8th. However, it was impossible owing to heavy M.G. fire to reach those objectives – my left flank were unable to get in touch with the 21st Division, who did not advance – consequently I put all my machine guns there to protect this flank." They had made progress but had lost another two killed and four wounded officers and another one hundred and forty-one men killed or wounded. Alfred was fast becoming one of the veteran soldiers surviving in the battalion. To compound their misery, they had then spent over twenty-four hours in the captured trench, which had been shallow, affording them little protection from the heavy storms and high wind which set in over them. It must have been a considerable relief, at the end of September, to be sent into 'peace trenches' at Loos, having been replaced by the American 105th Regiment.

In the same area, after a short respite, the 3rd London Battalion, including Reginald Winch, attacked yet again, assaulting the village of Épehy on 10th September, "in a heavy storm of driving rain". This time the casualties were seven officers and eighty-seven men. Afterwards, on 17th September, the

---

[795] The description of the fighting from 8th to 10th September is taken from the Narrative, Appendix I to the September entries, War Diary, 8th London Battalion.

depleted battalion had to be reorganised into only two companies. Even so, the next day they attacked Pezieres-Épehy. The fighting took all day because of the persistence of German machine gunners and snipers. Afterwards, the battalion struggled to regain sufficient strength to fight on and they were moved north, to near Lens. The respite was short. On 4th October, they were back in the trenches and began attacking eastwards, pushing the front east beyond the suburbs. Then they made a rapid advance which swept them south of Lille to Nomain by 20th October. On 25th October 1918 Reginald was transferred to the Royal Army Service Corps for what were to be the last days of the war. He was discharged – sick and no longer able to serve – on 26th March 1919. Perhaps his health was fatally affected by all he had been through – he died in London in 1923.

Meanwhile, at the end of August, Oliver Cooper and the 1st Grenadier Guards moved, after five days rest, to Noeuil, close to Merville where John Nutman had just been killed. At 5.20a.m. on 3rd September, the battalion had attempted to attack the retreating Germans, but although they took prisoners and captured guns, the Germans were too intent on reaching the Hindenburg Line to stand and fight. Oliver and the others must have been exhausted since they had moved forward on foot twenty miles, over the hills, in full fighting kit. When they tried to advance further the next day they found the Germans entrenched in strength on the old Hindenburg Line, so they occupied the earlier British front line trenches. For the next three weeks, the Grenadiers fought their way forward. Each night the Germans had shelled the British assembly positions with heavy gas attacks. On 12th September, the battalion was in the outer zone of the Hindenburg Line and at dawn attacked up 'Brown' Trench and secured the line of 'Alban Avenue'. British artillery then put up a barrage to support an attack on Havrincourt but this led to heavy German artillery in retaliation which killed an officer and several other soldiers. German enfilade machine-gun fire cut across the Grenadier position, making 'Alban Avenue' very dangerous for them. That afternoon the German 225th Infantry Regiment carried out bombing attacks on Grenadier posts, code-named 'Beatty' and 'Babs', but the German attackers were repulsed with heavy casualties. The Germans, nevertheless kept up a heavy fire all day against the Grenadiers and tried again to attacked 'Beatty' and 'Babs' posts in the evening but were again driven off. Somewhere in the midst of the fighting Oliver was fatally wounded. He was buried in Vaulx-Vraucourt, north-east of Bapaume, close to a field ambulance station to which he had probably been evacuated.

Four days later, near Lens further north, Harold Deans organised a raid on a German trench. In the autumn of 1915, Harold had been invalided to UK and had taken a 'gas course' in Scotland whilst he recuperated. After doing well on this course, he was sent to America on 13th November 1917 as a staff officer with the British Mission, as gas instructor to the American Army. Once the American troops he was training were ready, he returned to Europe with the American 79th Division and landed in France on 16th July 1918 and was then offered an additional six months instructing in gas warfare. According to *The Bournemouthian*,[796] he refused this offer of a "soft job" when "fit men are wanted so badly at the Front" and we know from his Army file that he quit his staff appointment and was attached to the 7th/8th Scottish Borderers on 2nd September. This battalion was near Maroc in a position on the western edge of Lens. They could approach their position partly by means of a long tunnel. They manned the trench system to the north-west of Lens until relieved and pulled back to Marzingarbe, between Béthune and Lens. The battalion took advantage of Harold's specialised knowledge, and on 5th September he gave a lecture to the NCOs on protection against gas.

---

[796] *The Bournemouthian*, December 1918.

On the 8th September, they moved back into the trenches in the 'Puits 14 Bis' Sector (in what is now a northern suburb of Lens). On the whole, this part of the front line was temporarily quiet, apart from one heavy spell of mustard gas and high explosive shelling and patrolling. Once the Germans attempted a raid but were driven off easily. On 14th September, preparations began for a major raid on the German lines of which Harold Deans was to take charge, whilst 'C' and 'D' Companies were left to man the front line. The Battalion HQ and 'A' and 'B' Companies were withdrawn to Mazingarbe to prepare. Ground was taped out to the known shape of the enemy lines, and the practices began the next day. After practising, they re-joined the front line companies in the trenches, although Harold and the designated raiding companies remained in the rear trenches. The main aims behind the raid were to capture prisoners for interrogation, and to assess the quality of the German trenches and their defences.

Zero Hour was set for 4p.m. on 16th September. The raiding parties moved up to the assembly zone to be ready fifteen minutes before. The war diary of the battalion describes the raid in some detail. "The... artillery... came down promptly and the men jumped over the parapet and moved forward at a steady pace. At this point a few shells of the 18 pounders on front... fell short. Sweeping through the enemy front line and through the support practically uncontested, they were then met by a murderous machine gun fire. The company between 'Hobs' and 'Honey' were particularly affected at this point. 2nd lieutenant Hopkins in the front... sustained two wounds about this time, one bullet passing through his right hand and a second bullet striking his arm, about 20 yards further on. Finally he fell dead – shot through the head as he reached the junction of 'Hall' and 'Honey'. Some 30 yards behind, Captain Deans who was encouraging the men under the heavy fire was shot through the chest. He died shortly afterwards. 2nd lieutenant Pritchard fell hit in two places. He was afterwards able to reach our line. A party of 'A' company finding the open ground not comfortable struck the Honey Alley and ran along the trench toward Hulloch trench. Immediately west of the trench a German officer got to his feet, fired a few shots at the advancing men, then dropped his automatic and scurried back, although fired on and pursued by Private Raife who had picked up the pistol."[797] The raid continued until the men were able to get back to the British front line, abandoning their dead, including Harold, and those wounded who could not make it back.

The diary explains that "patrols were pushed out in the evening to recover any wounded or material left by the raiders, but could only recover material." Attempts the following day were also unsuccessful. *The Bournemouthian* described Harold's death: "He had reached the German support line, where he was to establish his Headquarters, but seeing his men on the right flank to be held up by heavy machine-gun fire, he ran forward, rallied the men, and himself led them in a charge towards the next trench. Near this he fell, shot by a bullet from a machine-gun."[798] When his body was found later, Harold was buried at the Philosophe British Cemetery, Mazingarbe.

William MacAdam was also there, in the role of a Pioneer rather than as a front-line infantryman. He was born in 1892 and attended the school from 1903 to 1906. On 11th November 1914, William volunteered and became a private with the 2/4th City of London Royal Fusiliers. On 31st December, William and the battalion were sent to Malta to relieve the 1/4th City of London Battalion, then to Egypt, and finally to land at Cape Helles on Gallipoli on 15th October until they were evacuated in

---

[797] War Diary, 7/8th King's Scottish Borderers, appendix to 17th September 1918.
[798] *The Bournemouthian*, December 1918.

January 1916. After training at No.8 Officer Cadet Battalion in Lichfield, he was posted to the 7th Nottinghamshire and Derby Battalion, but immediately seconded for duty with the 29th Provisional Battalion (which was then at Walton on Naze) on 28th November 1916. Perhaps his health was deteriorating, since on 5th April 1917 he appeared before a medical board at Walton on Naze, suffering from dysentery. The board declared him fit only for service at Home, not for General Service abroad. Successive medical boards repeated this assessment, saying that he needed access to hospital treatment. The medical boards continued, though at widening time frames. On 6th December 1917 he was officially restored to duty with the 7th Nottinghamshire and Derby Battalion, but then remained in England. A number of reminders about medical boards were sent by the War Office to Eastern Command, only to be told (eventually) that on 4th May 1918 he had already gone abroad with the 2/6th Durham Light Infantry.

This battalion had been stationed in Frinton since September 1917. It landed at Calais on 1st May 1918 as a garrison guard battalion, under the orders of 177th Brigade, 59th Division, though its title of 'Garrison Guard' was dropped on 16th July. On 11th August 1918, he was transferred from the 7th Nottinghamshire and Derby Battalion (attached 2/6th Durham Light Infantry) for duty with the Labour Corps. At the end of August he was working in France with the 788 Area Employment Company, and then, after a short UK leave in October, he was posted to take command of the 787 Area Employment Company. Though they had also been used as emergency infantry earlier in the year when the Germans launched their Spring Offensives, these were units of the Labour Corps manned by officers and men whose medical rating was below the 'A1' rating needed to serve in the front line battalions. These particular units, the Labour Corps Area Employment Companies, had first been formed in 1917 for salvage work. Most of the company would be 'other ranks' with very few officers. Some of the men might well be quite skilled and specialist as they had to carry out technical tasks in salvage as well as manual labouring tasks. Another Durham officer, Captain G.S. Fillingham of the 2nd Durham Light Infantry, said after the war, "A typical pioneer job was this – be present under shell fire all day in support of the main attack. Then move forward and grab ground and dig trenches in so called no man's land under enemy fire at night. Go back before day break, sleep and start all over again. Casualties no object."[799] The comment used the phrase "pioneer job" in describing the work of the Labour Corps, though as we have seen the real Pioneers were skilled specialists rather than men of a lower physical fitness providing support to their comrades. However, by 1918, there was such a confusion of terms that the true and original Pioneer troops were re-designated Engineers. This was William's life, but one which he survived.

The Germans were now under intense pressure. The Germans were retiring to the old Hindenburg Line and Haig wanted to break it. He had hesitated to attack this line before, but was encouraged by the plan that Pershing's American troops would attack further south in the St. Mihiel Salient (12th-16th September) which would limit Ludendorff's ability to reinforce his line.

The 2nd Canadian Division moved forward from reserve and into the line for 6th September, tasked with establishing bridgeheads over the Canal du Nord wherever they could find intact bridges, and "to take up dispositions to deny the passage of the Canal to the enemy... Particular attention should be given to anti-gas precautions in the area near the Canal, near Baralle and near Buissy."[800] "At this time the enemy was retiring along the whole front of the Canadian Corps with the apparent

---

[799] Quotation derived from www.longlongtrail.co.uk.
[800] War Diary, 2nd Canadian Division, 3rd September 1918.

intention of taking up a position on the Eastern bank of the Canal du Nord, the 1st and 4th Canadian Divisions being in pursuit. In view of the possibility of a future advance the policy laid down for my Division was to establish bridgeheads on the Eastern bank of the Canal wherever possible and to deny any crossings of the Canal to the enemy. Since it appeared that the enemy was not in any immediate force, being somewhat disorganised, and at the same time there was a possibility of my Division being utilized in future operations, I decided to take over this frontage with one Brigade, the extent of the total front being 5,200 yards."[801] The Canal du Nord formed a north-south barrier to the advance against Cambrai. In the event their orders to take intact bridges were thwarted as the Germans had mostly destroyed them as they retreated, but the anti-gas warnings turned out to be prescient. This was illustrated in the early hours of 7th September when the Canadians reported: "2nd Canadian Divisional Artillery report considerable hostile artillery mainly in forward areas. Fire is usually sent over in rapid bursts – some gas shells sent over between 7pm and 10pm last night… Considerable enemy aerial activity around dusk. British plane brought down and attempted rescuing party fired on by 77mm battery. Bombing machines up from 8pm till midnight. Remainder of night quiet… The 6th Canadian Infantry Brigade report in their Morning Situation Report a heavy bombardment of gas."[802] The British and Canadians retaliated with gas shells of their own, but on 9th September there were again reports of very heavy gas shelling, including in the support area. Dull, cloudy and wet weather quietened things down the next day, and then in the early hours of 11th September there were fresh reports of "intermittent shelling of Support and rear area. At 3.25am there was a fairly heavy concentration of gas – Yellow and Blue Cross."[803] Even so, that evening, against determined machine-gun fire in defence, the Canadians were able to push up to parts of the west bank of the canal.

Reverdy Dyason was supporting the 2nd Canadian Corps when it went into action, still serving in the British Field Artillery. The 116th Battery had remained in support of various divisions for the defence of Bucquoy through the summer, apart from about three weeks rest, from 24th June to 18th July 1918. In July 1918, Reverdy had served in the Soissons Sector in the Battle of the Marne when the Germans began to be pushed back, supporting the 42nd, 37th and 5th Divisions. Then he was with the New Zealand Division, fighting in support in the Battle of Amiens and its aftermath up to 30th August. Finally, after a week in the Canadian Corps reserve, he and his battery once again fought alongside the Canadian Corps, supporting the 2nd Canadian Division (6th to 26th September). He wrote home, "I am as happy as it is possible to be in France, and I would not be anywhere else in the world in these times. We are winning."[804] But in the middle of September Reverdy was acting as brigade orderly for his battery at Brigade Headquarters when it was hit by a German gas shell. We do not know the exact date, but 14th September saw a bad attack: "Hostile artillery was very active throughout the night, especially from 11.50pm and continued till 12.40am (14th instant). There was a heavy concentration of gas… Our heavies retaliated. At 12.40am the enemy fire slackened/from 12.50am to 2.55am enemy again carried out a gas concentration on the same area."[805] A German gas shell gained a direct hit and Reverdy was gassed along with his colonel, adjutant and others of the headquarters staff. He was sent back through the casualty system and on

---

[801] War Diary notes, 2nd Canadian Division, 30th August to 2nd September.
[802] War Diary, 2nd Canadian Division, 7th September 1918.
[803] War Diary, 2nd Canadian Division, 11th September 1918.
[804] Quoted in his obituary, *The Bournemouthian*, December 1918.
[805] War Diary, 2nd Canadian Division, 14th September 1918.

16th September was admitted to the 54th General Hospital at Boulogne. However, he died on 19th September, aged 20, and was buried on the northern outskirts of the town.

The Battle of Épehy: 13th September

On 13th September, Haig authorised Rawlinson to attack with all three corps of the 4th Army and with the support of Byng's 3rd Army in what is sometimes called the Battle of Épehy. The aim was to drive in a wedge between Cambrai and St. Quentin. One and a half thousand guns and three hundred heavy machine guns supported a forward thrust spearheaded by two Australian divisions advancing behind a creeping barrage which gained about three miles – and helped further to weaken Ludendorff's morale.

Bernard Barnes was in this battle. On 14th October 1918 Bernard's widowed mother, Emily, wrote a poignant letter to the Secretary of the Territorial Forces. She must have become frantic, but her letter is a marvel of restraint as she wrote, "I have not heard from my son since the 15th September and as he was in the habit of writing every few days… [manuscript torn and lost]… if you can give me any information about him. Today I have had one of my letters returned with the words 'Address unknown. Present location uncertain. Wounded 18/9/18' and an officer's signature which I cannot read. Any information you can give me regarding him I shall be grateful for."[806] You always hear of the sadness of the telegram being delivered, not of the mother having to beg to learn the sad news of her only son's death. It seems particularly poignant that, as the war drew towards its close, young men still had to die, and especially when they were young men of as much promise as Bernard was and when they were their parents' only son. Born in 1897, he had been a successful student at school (1908-1913), gaining first class honours in his senior exams in 1912, when a school photograph was taken of him. His mother had already endured so much. Her son had already been in three separate campaigns: in the trenches near Arras on the Western Front during from 26th June until December 1916; in Salonika; and in Palestine against the Turks. Indeed, his battalion of the Queen Victoria Rifles was the only battalion to march in state into Jerusalem when it was captured. On 3rd July 1918 he had left Alexandria for a two week voyage along the Mediterranean, putting in briefly at Taranto, and landing in France on 15th July. Here the 24th London Battalion (the Queen Victoria Rifles) was put into the 173rd Brigade, 58th Division. He was given a two week UK leave in the middle of August though he had to return to his battalion on 23rd August.

Bernard Barnes

In September, the 2/24th London Battalion was in the area near Gouzeaucourt. They had occupied the trenches from 12th-14th September, temporarily operating under 175th Brigade. Then, after rehearsing for an attack on Peizieres, they had returned to the front line on 16th September. Over the next two days they suffered from some German shelling, including gas shells, and one junior officer had to be evacuated with shell shock. On 18th September, the battalion was in close support for an attack on Peizieres next to Épehy, between Cambrai and St. Quentin. The day was a confusing one: two 2nd lieutenants were killed, and two captains and another 2nd lieutenant were burned by splashes from gas shells. As company signaller, Bernard was vulnerable because he could not stay under cover. Afterwards, his body was found near the company headquarters, and it

---

[806] Army File of Bernard Frampton Barnes.

looked as if he might have been killed instantly. Aged just twenty-two, he was commemorated on the memorial which forms the backdrop to the Vis-en-Artois British Cemetery, because later his body could not be recognised for burial.

The 6th Dorset Battalion including Bernard Allbon and Aubrey Godfrey also took part in this offensive. Aubrey was the son of the Bournemouth Corporation Musical Director, Sir Dan Godfrey. Born in 1899, he was only fifteen when the war began. He attended the school between 1913 and 1916. He must have heard lots of stories of what his predecessors had done in this war (and of his older brother who was a lieutenant in the Dorsetshire Regiment), and as soon as he was old enough he joined the 3rd Dorset Battalion, being commissioned as a 2nd lieutenant from 1st May 1918. He went to France on 8th Sept 1918 and joined the 6th Dorset Battalion, from its base, on 16th September 1918. When he arrived, Bernard Allbon was the Officer Commanding 'D' Company, and it would be interesting to know if Aubrey was attached to his fellow Bournemouthian's company, or to one of the others. When he joined the battalion it had been heavily involved in the fighting – fourteen new 2nd lieutenants joined that day to make good the losses. The battalion was at Rocquiny, south-east of Bapaume – but before assault they were reminded of the reasons for the assault – the enemy still held Beaulencourt, Le Transloy and Morval, just north and west of them, and this would mean that should they press forward they would be leaving the Germans behind them on the flank. Their task was to be to advance and to cover the flanks of another brigade which would make the actual attack.

The evening after Aubrey arrived, the battalion moved away from Rocquiny to take up their assault assembly positions. On the evening of 17th September, the tapes were laid out with other markers so that they could get into place, though this process was hampered by heavy rain storms. Between 1.30a.m. and 4a.m. on 18th September they got into position, with 'A' Company on the front right and 'B' on the left; 'C' supported 'A' and 'D' supported 'B'. At 5.20a.m. the barrage opened up and at once the battalion moved forward, close behind the men of the 52nd Brigade, pushing forward in the dark despite the driving rain, trying to keep up with the rolling barrage which helped them to keep their sense of direction. The German counter-barrage seemed rather weak, and by 6a.m. they had passed their first objective. As dawn broke, visibility hardly improved because there was so much smoke. By 8a.m. all companies had reached their objectives and were consolidating their new positions.

Casualties so far had been relatively light, and the consolidation continued despite long-range German shelling and machine-gun fire. That afternoon, new orders were received to press home a second attack in the evening. They began moving forward at 7p.m. and made the attack northwards with 'B' to attack on the right, 'C' in the centre, and 'D' on the left, with 'A' in support. This time the attack was less straightforward, and progress was hampered by a counter-attack about 9p.m. further south, and because the battalion covering their left had been unable to move forward and therefore was not protecting their flank. Nevertheless, the right and centre companies of the 6th Dorset Battalion established themselves in the German St. Quentin Redoubt, capturing more than fifty prisoners and taking six machine guns – all without loss. The left company, Bernard's, had switched across the front, but had been driven back by a counter-attack and had to be reinforced by the support company. Progress was hampered by a shortage of grenades and rifle grenades, until a fresh supply was brought up to the front.

On the afternoon of the next day, 19th September, the Germans made frequent counter-attacks, using flammenwerfers and trench mortars, as well as grenades. German machine guns racked the new British lines and the British advance was halted. Even so, much had been attained – they had taken one hundred and twenty-four prisoners from the German 402nd Infantry and 6th Cavalry regiments; they had also captured twelve machine guns, three trench mortars and three anti-tank rifles. They had earned their relief that night. Aubrey had won his spurs! The next day, their brigade commander, Brigadier-General Sanders, was killed as the relief battalions were heavily shelled and strafed. Aubrey, Bernard, and the 6th Dorsets had a little over a day to recuperate before returning to the line. Fortunately, their next spell in the trenches was uneventful and was followed by more rest and renewed training.

Arthur Sear of the 46th Division Signals Company was in support for this attack. In front of them, on 24th August, the Germans had begun to fall back, followed by the British, and a wireless section was pushed forward to maintain communication links until additional cables could be laid. His company remained near Béthune until 12th September. Within days they were pushing eastwards beyond Peronne. Soon they reached Vendelle, north-west of St. Quentin. As their division prepared to attack the St. Quentin Canal, orders were issued that "this route will be reinforced between Division and Brigade by Visual D.R., Mounted Orderly and Spark Wireless Routes and between Brigade and Battalion and forward of Battalion by Visual, Loop Set, Power Buzzer-Amplifier, and Runner Routes and Rockets… Wireless. One Wilson set and three Trench sets are available for the main Divisional Route and normally these will be disposed as follows: (a) Wilson set. At Advanced Divisional HQ. Keeping constant watch: controlling forward communications; and acting as a transmitting and receiving station allotted to the Divisional Observation Officer. It will also endeavour to get into communication with the Corps Directing Station and so act as a supplementary means of communication back to rear Divisional HQ via Corps HQ. (b) One trench set at or near the Brigade communication centre or in supplementary position with regard to brigade Headquarters and will form communication both with Wilson set at ADHQ and with the trench set assigned to the DOO. (c) One trench set with means of transport will be assigned to the DOO. This set will be erected in a naturally concealed position as near his HQ as possible and will be available to dispose of the hourly pieces of information referred to in Divisional letter M. D. If possible this set will communicate direct with the Wilson set at ADHQ, but if the range is too great will relay through the Brigade trench set. (d) The third trench set will be kept in reserve at ADHQ."[807]

As a wireless operator, Arthur was clearly going to be busy. On 29th September, the 46th Division advanced across the St. Quentin Canal and broke through the Hindenburg Line. "Communication was carried out as per attached instruction. Visual proved useless until late in the day because of intense mist. Wireless functioned to the D.O.O. throughout the day and to 139 & 137 Bdes towards the close of the day. Lines found impossible to maintain between CC & HP & the Old Hindenburg Line until the evening when comm' was successfully established. 29 & 30/9/18… Action continued by 138 & 139 Bdes until final objectives were reached when 32 Division passed through. Commn with 138 & 139 Advd HQ established by lines laid by Cable Section, by Wireless but visual not functioning forward of our original front line, the HQ being in the hollow and out of sight. Sufficient personnel for manning necessary transmitting stations not available."[808]

---

[807] Orders included in the War Diary, 46th Division Signals Company, September 1918.
[808] War Diary, 46th Division Signals Company 29-30th September 1918.

The Counter-Attack Continued in the North

Whilst the main thrust was on the line in France, pressure was also brought to bear in the Ypres Salient. On 18th August, Eugene Holland and the 1st Border Battalion had gone into the attack east of Hazebrouck, capturing a hamlet called Outtersteerne just west of Bailleul, despite determined German defensive action. By the end of August it was clear to them that the Germans were in retreat in this sector: "29/30th. Numerous dumps being blown up behind enemy lines and huge fires. Lt. J Pattinson, 2nd Lts. E W Chicken and W E King took out their platoons and established posts... No enemy encountered. 2nd Lt. W E King pushed on to cross roads... and found no signs of occupation. At 2am Intelligence reported that enemy was withdrawing from our front and that patrols were to push forward at 5am with Coys following in support... There was no opposition, but owing to the bad nature of the ground, it became very difficult to maintain touch with the flanks. Communication to Btn HQ front line was very poor, and the situation in front was obscure during the whole of the morning."[809]

Periodically, they came up against rearguard German machine-gun posts, and suffered some occasional German shelling, but otherwise at last there was significant progress. Bailleul had fallen back into British hands, and the concern now was to ensure that the advance was co-ordinated and secure. After greater opposition on 1st September was encountered, they took heavier casualties, but still continued the advance until relieved.

In September, Bernard Richardson also went back to the front with the 18th King's Royal Rifle Battalion. They relieved the 27th American Division on the Dickebusch Front (closer to Ypres), but on 3rd September an entire company had fallen casualty to determined and persistent German gas shelling. Even so, two days later they had taken part with the brigade as it made its advance southwards, though this was very costly, especially amongst the 15th Hampshires.

Arnold Whitting and Francis Holbrook also advanced. Arnold had missed the previous defensive fighting near Ypres in which Francis and the rest of the 2/15th London Regiment had participated as he had been on leave from 6th to 24th August, but when he had returned to the battalion it was still in a tricky trench position overlooked by the Germans of Mount Kemmel (the highest vantage point in the area) and they were being shelled heavily by the Germans. The encouraging rumours which had started as early as 3rd August that the Germans were imminently expected to withdraw finally came true at the start of September when they fell back on to the main Messines Ridge. On 4th September the battalion pushed forward. "Disposition of companies: 'B' Coy on the right... 'D' Coy on the left... 'C' Coy in support to 'B' Coy at Wulverghem and 3 platoons 'A' Coy... and 1platoon in reserve at Battalion Headquarters. Casualties – 2nd Lieut E J Martin killed; Capt RBWG Andrew, MC, wounded in action and remained at duty; 4 OR's killed; 3 O/R's missing, believed killed; 13 O/R's wounded in action. During the afternoon 'C' Coy's position heavily shelled and 'C' Coy moved forward at T6c. Platoon in reserve rejoined 'A' Coy at dusk. Capt KA Wills, MC, to hospital. During the night patrols were pushed forward and posts established."[810]

For his part in this advance, Arnold was honoured by the award of the Military Cross : "Lt. Arnold Whitting, 2nd Bn., attd. 2/15th. Bn., Lond. R. For conspicuous gallantry and devotion to duty. When his supporting company was severely shelled and headquarters received three direct hits, killing

---

[809] War Diary, 1st Border Battalion, 29th-30th August 1918.
[810] War Diary, 2/15th London Battalion, 4th September 1918.

or wounding several, this officer, though severely shaken, remained helping the wounded and encouraging the men. Later, while the bombardment continued he reconnoitred for a better position, and eventually moved his men without further loss."[811] From 7th September Arnold took charge of 'C' Company as its acting captain.

On 28th September, he led his company forward onto the Messines Ridge: "Information received pointing to the probability of the enemy withdrawing. Battalion received orders to advance in conjunction with battalions on right and left, and capture and secure Messines. At 5.30am A & C Coys pushed forward fighting patrols – object being to capture Big Bull Cottage and secure the line… At 6.45am objectives gained. Captured 3 MGs, 15 prisoners. D Coy moved forward from Neuve Eglise and remained in reserve at Battalion HQrs. At 3 pm barrage opened for attack by right battalion and our line was pushed forward to the Steenbeck. General advance was ordered at 6 pm. Advanced guards were sent forward and A Coy reached Messines but had to withdraw owing to battalion flanks not being up. A Coy established HQrs at Hospice Mill. C Coy's line was echeloned back so as to keep touch with A Coy and right battalion. At 9.30pm our line was approx Hospice Mill, Sniper's House and W2c95.5Q. B Coy were ordered to keep close touch with forward Coys. D Coy moved up to old front line. Verbal instructions were received from Brigade that advance would be continued on the following day to Comines Canal, Houthem being this battalion's objective. The advance was to commence at 5.30am and the dispositions of the battalion were then organised as follows: D Coy in front line, B Coy in support, followed by A Coy. C Coy in reserve. Captured up to 12 midnight 9 MGs, 17 prisoners. 29/9/1918. Messines was captured with small opposition and the battalion made good progress towards Houthem, object being to secure the Canal Crossing. 1 MG and 1 Field Gun captured at Messines. Few casualties were sustained from enemy shells in E Slopes of Messines Ridge. Information was received at midday that 41st Div had crossed the Comines Canal and were moving southwards, crossing our front. Battalion reached within 1 mile of Houthem and then struck SE to form flank guard to Div. A line facing SE – South of Houthem was held during the night. The 2/14th London Regiment came up on right flank to fill gap between battalion and 31st Div who were held up at Warneton. Casualties during operations 12 O/R's killed, 40 O/R's wounded. Capt FH Du Heaune and 3 O/R's wounded and remained at duty."[812]

The next day the war diary recorded the capture of eleven 77cm guns and three 10cm guns, ten machine guns and one light trench mortar. In a memorandum at the end of the month their philosophy was laid clear: "It is the intention of the Commanding Officer to press close on the heels of the retreating enemy but avoiding casualties as far as possible."[813]

Eric Rey of the 10th Royal West Kent Battalion was one of those attempting to press close on the German heels. For August and much of September, former boy-soldier Eric and the battalion had been out of the main action, varying trench duties with reserve training, taking only low casualties as the Germans facing them were content to hold their ground. About this time, Eric was promoted to lance corporal. From 10th to 18th September they had gone into the line near Dickebusch just to the east of La Clytte, awaiting their opportunity to help to push back the Germans. On 18th September they completed what in the end proved to be their last bout of orthodox trench duty.

---

[811] *The Edinburgh Gazette*, 4th December 1918.
[812] War Diary, 2/15th London Battalion, 28th-29th September 1918.
[813] Order no LXVI by Major A.C.H. Benke MC, 27/9/1918, included in War Diary, 2/15th London Battalion, September 1918.

The British counter-offensive in the Ypres Salient formally started on 21st September 1918. Eric and the 10th Royal West Kent Battalion were not involved on that first day as their division was in reserve. However, they were brought up to share in the actions a week later, on the 28th September, halting in Ravine Wood and Kortewilde, south-east of Ypres and east of Wijtschate on the Messines Ridge, ready to attack the next day. "September 29th opened fine, but with a ground fog, which made direction keeping difficult but helped to conceal the advance and so contributed to the surprise of the Germans. So complete was this that the crews of a 4.2-inch howitzer battery were at breakfast when the 10th came rushing in on top of them, and in addition three 77-mm field guns, five machine guns and many prisoners were taken with surprisingly low casualties. By 9.15 the battalion was on the railway NE of Comines, but the 23rd Middlesex on its right had been kept back by meeting some very stubborn opposition on the canal bank and both that unit and the 10th had outrun the troops on their flanks and found themselves in a pronounced salient under a heavy converging fire from artillery and machine guns. It was necessary to fall back; and under cover of B Company, which was well handled by 2nd Lieut. Weston, a successful withdrawal to a position a little in advance of the Houthem line was made, though casualties were heavier in the withdrawal than they had been in the advance... If losses had been severe – three officers and 35 men killed, 20 men missing and five officers and 90 men wounded – important gains had been made."[814]

Unfortunately, Eric was wounded that day. He was sent back to a casualty clearing station and there they did their best for him. He was taken back as far as Lijssenthoek to the west of Ypres. He lived on for nearly two weeks, but died on 11th October 1918. He was buried in the enormous cemetery there, which, with 9,901 Commonwealth and 883 other graves (mostly French and German) is the second largest in Belgium. "It is a coincidence that his last resting place is where he first fought with the Hampshires in 1916."[815]

On 29th and 30th September, Eugene Holland and the 1st Border Battalion fought a significant action, pushing back up along the Menin road. Though they took heavier casualties than in the previous month, especially from the machine guns – three wounded officers; twenty-four men killed, ninety-seven wounded and five missing – they managed to capture a German battalion HQ complete with its colonel and staff, and to move eastwards a considerable distance. The early hours of the next morning were more sombre – not only did intense German machine-gun fire prevent a further advance, but their brigadier was shot by a sniper. When, later in the afternoon, they were able to advance, after flank attacks in their support by the East Surreys, their war diary informs us it was "in face of intense MG barrage fire." October saw a further mix of experiences for Eugene. Sometimes they were fighting and sometimes they were pulled back behind the line. Overall, the brigade continued to push forward. At this stage Eugene was based at headquarters as adjutant, though that did not mean he was much further back than the attack troops in the companies, and the HQ was also periodically liable to enemy shelling in particular.

By the end of September, the British Army was not only pushing the Germans back across a wide front in France, but was also ready to support the King of the Belgians in the campaign to throw the Germans out of Belgium. Haig agreed that General Plumer should supply the men to push south-

---

[814] *The Queens Own Royal West Kent Regiment 1914 to 1919* by C.T. Atkinson, Compiled from materials supplied by Colonel G.W. Maunsell (CMG) & Lieut-Col. J.P. Dalison, London: Simpkin, Marshall, Hamilton, Kent & Co. Ltd., 1924, pp. 432-433.
[815] *The Bournemouthian*, April 1919.

west against Zandvoorde and Ghevevult, and then beyond.

On 2nd October there was a spirited fight outside Menin in which Bernard Richardson and the 18th King's Royal Rifle Battalion found themselves between the 15th Hampshire Battalion and the 2nd Hampshire Battalion. Afterwards they were pulled back into reserve at Zandvoorde, a little further south and west. Over the past month they had lost another two hundred or more casualties and needed to regroup and to re-train.

In December 1918, Archibald Rogers had three letters published in the school magazine. In the first he described his position as a specialist gas officer with the Royal Engineers, in the Ypres Salient, as the Allies had begun the liberation of Belgium. "Since returning from leave I have visited several parts of the front, being sent, first of all, to work for an American Division on our extreme right. As we found when we got there that we were not wanted we had a very pleasant fortnight building a camp for ourselves and collecting souvenirs. No sooner had we completed our camp and really made it first class (being R. E.'s we ought to be able to!), than we were ordered north, and here we are in the same desolate region that I was in last winter in the infantry. But what a difference! Nurses now visit the places of interest that we used to hurry past with tin hats and S.B.R.'s on, and Chinese are working on the roads that last year we never ventured on unless necessity compelled us. I visited a town—one of our most recent captures—the day before yesterday. I had often viewed it in the distance from an O. P. where it lay before us like the Land of Promise, and it was with feelings of elation that I sallied forth one day to explore it."[816]

He commented on the progress made in liberating Belgium. "One has to be pretty careful of booby-traps now-a-days, though the Boche does not seem to use them as much as he did; indeed, I do not think he has time to bother much about them. If only we get decent weather I do not see why Belgium should not be cleared by Christmas; but I am inclined to think that the Boche will put up a pretty stiff fight sooner or later. Refugees are pouring back, and our people have liberated no end of civilians during the past ten days. One of the most remarkable things to my mind has been the work of the Belgian Army. If ever one man deserves credit for his work during the war I think the King of the Belgians does. We did a gas shoot a week ago, but with the rapid advance there is little chance of our doing anything owing to the difficulty of getting anything like a decent target. Still, most of us in this unit have had our fair share and we shall not grumble over much if we do not get another chance. I hope that this time next year will see me once more settled down to civilian life, though I am afraid it will be a difficult matter settling down to the routine of an indoor life again."

In another letter he discussed the evolution of British Army organisation and the role of the gas officer. "I expect you know that I have transferred into the Special Brigade R.E., who do all our gas stunts. I have been at the depot and have been through a course of instruction for the past fortnight. The work is very interesting, particularly the projector work, which is done by electricity, but I am afraid I am not at liberty to go into details about it. The whole thing is kept very secret, and we do not know ourselves the composition of some of the gases we use; but we are quite content to know they cause the Boche a horrible death. I was very loth to leave the 49th Division 1st Line Yorkshire Territorials—a finer crowd you will not find anywhere—as I had made many friends there. I unearthed one day a doctor in one of our Field Ambulances who was in the same form with me at school in 1892, and we had never met since then. It was a great wrench to leave,

---

[816] *The Bournemouthian*, December 1918.

but I hope that eventually I may get back to them as Divisional Gas Officer. When G.H.Q., in the wisdom of their hearts decided that Brigade Gas Officers were unnecessary (they still keep a Canteens Officer at Division) the only alternative for me was to go back as a Platoon Commander under people over whom I had had more or less authority, and so I decided to transfer, more especially as an order came out that all Divisional Gas Officers had to serve in the Special Brigade first. Still, I shall always treasure very pleasant recollections of my stay with the 49th. I have finished my course here now and expect to go to a company any day. The first thing I shall do is to apply for my very overdue leave, so I do not think I shall be very popular when I get there. I do not think the Special Brigade has a very rosy time in the line, for as soon as the Boche gets wind of gas his guns begin strafing like mad; but the great point is that one does not stay in the line for days and days but gets back to a decent billet. I am afraid that my long stay at Brigade H.Q. has made me rather chary of the discomfort of the trenches." [817]

At the end of the war he felt pleased that he had used his expertise one last time: "I'm pleased to say that we got one gas shoot in before the armistice. We were on one side of the Schelt [Scheldt] and he was the other, and as he cleared out a night or so after, we were able to cross over and see what damage had been done. There is little doubt that we gave him a hot time, and I found direct evidence that my guns had made one or more Boche very sick (literally, I mean). The day before he went back we had one of the worst bombardments that I have ever known both with H. E. and gas, and one mustard gas shell burst in our garden, fortunately without doing any damage. Consequently I am devoutly thankful that I have a whole skin at the present moment."[818] After the war, Archibald returned to teach at Bournemouth School, where he remained until his retirement in 1946.

Meanwhile, Reginald Dare, after rather a mixed military career, had been in action on the Menin road, which was still blocked at Hooge. Reginald had been born in 1896 and attended the school from 1908 to 1912. His father was a National Provincial Bank Manager in Ringwood, but had also been a soldier since 1885, and had become a captain in the 2/9th Hampshire (Cyclist) Battalion. Reginald was in the school O.T.C. After school, he too entered the bank, as a bank clerk. In 1915 he was living in Tamworth, in Staffordshire, when he attested under the Derby Scheme. He was initially placed in the Army Reserve, but on 20th January 1916 he was mobilised and posted to the 2/6th North Staffordshire Battalion. He probably saw unexpected action when, in April 1916, the brigade was sent to Ireland to help to deal with the Easter Rising and the associated Republican troubles. On 25th July 1916, he had been allowed to transfer into 'C' Company, 2/9th Hampshire Battalion – his father's battalion, a Territorial Army battalion stationed in Sussex. Almost immediately, on 31st August 1916, Reginald applied for a commission, though he had not served a year on the front, the normal rule by this stage of the war. On 5th October, the colonel of the 2/9th Hampshires wrote in especial support of the application: "This cyclist is recommended for attachment to an Officers Cadet Training Unit with a view to obtaining a Commission in my battalion."[819] Reginald received his commission as 2nd lieutenant on 6th February 1917. However, immediately, there was a short time complication when he was posted to the 5th Hampshires – who served in India for the duration of the war. Once again, the colonel wrote to request that the Army

---

[817] *The Bournemouthian*, December 1918.
[818] ibid.
[819] Reginald's Army File (WO 374/17855) seems to have become mixed up with that of his father, Frank (WO 339/139467). This supporting recommendation is included in Frank's file.

changed the posting, and that Reginald should return to serve (alongside his father – though that was not mentioned) in the 2/9th Hampshires at Bognor. The colonel succeeded, and this was done.

It is possible that this posting was not really in line with Reginald's personal ambitions – in 1917 the July edition of *The Bournemouthian* magazine reported that he was in the Royal Flying Corps, but attached to the 1/5th South Staffordshire Battalion. In the end, on 20th March 1918, Reginald was seconded as 2nd lieutenant attached to the Machine Gun Corps. A few months later, on 25th July 1918, he was promoted to lieutenant but switched as a 2nd lieutenant to the 15th Hampshire Battalion, to which Reginald reported near Ypres. The battalion had suffered terrible casualties in September 1918 – suffering sixteen officer casualties on 4th September alone (with the fighting force reduced to the command of a 2nd lieutenant) as well as over three hundred men because they had been smashed by German machine-gun and sniper fire when British artillery supporting the advance had misdirected and missed its targets. He was certainly with them by 13th October. That afternoon the battalion moved up through Ypres and took up positions on the Menin road near Hooge. They assembled for the attack in the early hours of 14th October, and "The enemy put down a harassing barrage between the hours of 04 & 05 which caused casualties to A & B Coys. At 5.35 our barrage opened and the Battn went forward in a very thick mist. Considerable opposition was encountered from Pillboxes at the commencement of the advance which were soon overcome by the dash and determination of the Battn who took every advantage of the very heavy mist, which was the cause of some of the men of other units mixing themselves up with us."[820] The battalion went on to secure their objectives, suffering casualties in the assault, but Reginald was not with them. "When ready to attack he was wounded by shell fragments in left buttock & right side of neck. He was treated at No. 10 CCS and in 14th Genl. Hospital and reached 2nd W G H on October 17th, & subsequently a small foreign body was removed from left buttock… [he received a shell wound on the] right side of neck 1½" below right ear – superficial now healed."[821]

He had been with his battalion for only a few days before he had to be invalided home wounded. He embarked from Boulogne to Dover on 17th October and was taken to the 2nd Western General Hospital the same day. Fortunately, his wounds were relatively superficial and after treatment he had a Christmas holiday and re-joined the 3rd (Reserve) Battalion of the Hampshire Regiment at Gosport on 28th December. His last posting was to serve as an officer attached to the 5th Northern Company, Non-Combatant Corps, although not for very long as he was demobilised on 5th February 1919.

That day, the 14th October, Bernard Richardson and the 18th King's Royal Rifle Company also attacked along the Menin road in a thick mist which made it difficult to maintain accurate bearings. They managed to secure their objectives despite casualties and despite the disorganisation of troops caused by the hampering effects of the mist.

Arnold Whitting has left us a personal view of the attack in which Bernard had taken part and before which Reginald was wounded. After returning on 8th October from a gas course he had resumed command of 'C' Company, 2/15th London Battalion. "We are certainly having pretty exciting times now, but as long as we are winning the war it doesn't much matter… We had a pretty good bag the other day. Our fellows 'went over' at 5.30 one morning under a splendid creeping

---

[820] War Diary, 15th Hampshire Battalion, 14th October 1918.

[821] Medical Reports of 7th and 9th December included in the Army Files of Reginald and his father Frank, WO 374/17855 and WO 339/139467.

barrage which completely demoralised the Hun. We secured 9 officers and 304 other prisoners. Our casualties were almost negligible."[822] Before the assault began, the "Enemy heavily gas shelled front line and area near Battalion HQrs. At 0535 Barrage opened and at 0538 B & D Coys moved to attack. Enemy artillery replied fairly vigorously. At 0700 hours Right Coy (D Coy) reported by pigeon objective gained and pushing on to railway… B Coy on the left reported objective gained and in touch with both flanks. At 0740 hours A Coy moved up to old front line. C Coy was in close support to two forward Coys. D Coy had to move back from railway owing to MG fire from right rear. B Coy reported at 1000 hrs whole line held up and battalions on right and left digging in. Battalion consolidated line gained and pushed patrols forward. Total prisoners 9 officers, 304 O/R's. casualties 7 O/R's killed, 35 O/R's wounded."[823]

The next day Arnold and his company took the lead and pushed on to reach the River Lys, which it then crossed in conjunction with 'A' Company. They were now entering France, to the south and west of Menin, though moving fast south-eastwards driving back the Germans. After a few more days they stopped to recuperate whilst other battalions took over the lead. In this last month of the war the advance had slowed with the deterioration of the weather. "Unfortunately the weather has now broken up for a while which makes the going very difficult. But, still, that effects [sic] both sides." Despite the weather, he was optimistic. He described their new position favourably and, as the battalion broke through into territory previously behind the German side of the battle lines, was pleased that the liberated locals had welcomed the British, and that the advance was also helped because "We have now got into good country and amongst civilisation, which is a great relief after nothing but shell-holes and ruins."

Afterwards, Francis Holbrook rejoined Arnold, returning from brigade runner to normal duties with the battalion in the field on 18th October. By this time huge progress had been made by the battalion, which had now reached to the south of Menem, and was positioned just south-east of Menin at Hallouim. The day he returned, their Lewis guns once again brought down a German plane.

Now the 122nd Brigade too was making rapid advances – two days later Bernard Richardson and the 18th King's Royal Rifle Company were at Gullegem, north-east of Menin (still in Belgium) and heading eastwards, before turning south-eastwards around the outskirts of Courtrai. On 19th October, they crossed the River Lys on the north-east outskirts of Courtrai and then advanced to a line on the road between Courtrai and its eastern suburb of Swevegem. The 35th Division was at that time consolidating in Swevegem itself, but the next day, 21st October, Bernard and his comrades were marched eastwards to the edge of Swevegem to make the next attack. They were heading in the general direction of Brussels and were involved in a struggle for the higher ground to the east of the Courtrai-Bossuyt canal on 21st – 22nd October. Eugene Holland (with the 1st Border Battalion and 29th Division) also fought in this attack. "At 0715 attack commenced. The Courtrai-Bossuyt canal was reached without opposition and Coys crossed by Pont Levis No 2 which had been blown up but was still passable by infantry. On reaching the Eastern bank, all Coys came under heavy M.G. fire, but pushed boldly on and seized ridge… Later it transpired that 29th (British) Division on left had made but little progress. To enable effective artillery support to be afforded for

---

[822] This and the other extracts from his letter following were published in *The Bournemouthian*, December 1918.
[823] War Diary, 2/15th London Battalion, 14th October 1918.

them to continue the advance our line was withdrawn from the ridge… arrangements had been made for 41st and 29th (British) Divisions to continue the advance at 1215 but orders to this effect were not received until 1258, by which time our artillery supporting fire had ceased. Brigadier-General S.V.P. Weston, DSO, MC, GOC 122nd Inf. Bde saw our CO at Battn HQ about 1320 and issued preliminary instructions for an advance…. At 1530 29th (British) Division attacked. It was ascertained from a Coy Commander of a Battn of R. Fusiliers that their objective was identical with ours, although this was trespassing within our Divisional boundary. Orders were issued for Coys to stand fast on their present line. Later, orders were received for a resumption of attack at 0900 Oct.22. Throughout the morning much inconvenience was caused by a 6" Howitzer Battery which shelled the neighbourhood of Battn HQ in Swevegem. Artillery fire in support of the attack of the 29th (British) Division attack at 1530 also fell short and caused casualties to our men. Two Vickers Guns, one section R.E., one section RFA, and 1 Stokes Mortar were attached to the Battalion during these operations. The light Trench Mortar was not used. The section RFA fired on machine gun nests during the day. The section RE worked on Pont Levis No.2, preparing the damaged structure for wheels. This bridge was fit for 18 pdrs by 1900 hours. About 1300, the 2 Vickers Guns took up a position on the East Bank of the canal to cover Banhout Bosch, as the situation on the left was obscure."[824]

After this confused fighting, the Germans still held their ridge. The next day, 22nd October, from their position by Pont Levis Bridge and the canal, Bernard and the 18th King's Royal Rifle Battalion were ordered back into the attack. "When orders for resumption of the attack were received, the forming-up line fixed was found to be still in the hands of the enemy… The advance on the left was found to be unnecessary, the area having been cleared by 29th (British) Division. On the right, direction was lost and the advance carried too far. Heavy MG fire was encountered and Lieut. S. Pye and 2nd Lieut E.J. Hacking and 20 OR were subsequently reported missing. At 1210 the advance was stopped all along the line, and 18 KRRC remained as Battn in Reserve."[825]

These machine guns had been causing problems for several days. The 10th Royal West Kent Battalion (in the 123rd Brigade, also of the 41st Division) were also thwarted by them the next day, October 23rd, when they came under heavy fire from a chapel, the roof of a farm, and from the mill. It was only swept aside by a heavy artillery barrage and a mass attack by 123rd Brigade on 25th October. The heavy machine-gun fire mentioned probably cost Bernard his life. *The Bournemouthian*, which is by no means always reliable, reported that he was killed in the attack on the ridge by Hoogmolen Mill on 22nd October. However, according to *The Bournemouthian* of March 1920, the news of Bernard's death had only just reached the school.[826] Probably he was hit on 22nd and died of wounds on the 26th October, the date the Army records show for his death. (Although those Army records state he was 'Killed in Action' rather than 'Died of Wounds', the war diary of the 18th K.R.R.C. reveals that on that day the battalion was marching back to billets behind the line, with no casualties.) Bernard was buried at the Heerstadt Military Cemetery, south-east of Courtrai (now called Kortrijk) which was created in 1919 when Belgian farmers were allowed to clear the area of the battlefield graves. It must have been heart-breaking for his parents to receive the news of his death at what turned out to be almost the same time as the news of the Armistice.

---

[824] War Diary, 18th King's Royal Rifle Corps, 21st October 1918.
[825] War Diary, 18th King's Royal Rifle Corps, 22nd October 1918.
[826] *The Bournemouthian*, April 1920.

The advance of Arnold Whitting and Francis Holbrook in the 2/15th London Battalion continued, bringing them from Flanders into the Belgian Walloon region. They halted and drew breath for a few days before returning to the front line at the start of November. But as their advance stalled for several days, Arnold went down with the 'flu and on 31st October was sent to hospital in a serious condition. He was sent back to Calais where a medical board ruled on 12th November that he was debilitated and anaemic, and needed two weeks home sick leave in Parkstone. In this condition, Arnold survived the war, but was in hospital when the wonderful news of the Armistice was broken to his men. However, he had come through the whole length of the war, and was well enough to be able to return to command his company until he was demobilised in 1919, leaving the Army on 23rd March 1919. Later Francis too contracted the 'flu. Two weeks after his return to the battalion, on 2nd November, he was admitted to the 98th Field Ambulance. His case was not as serious as that of Arnold. He was in hospital for about a week before re-joining his battalion for the final week of the war. On 8th November, about the same time as he returned to the battalion from hospital, news reached them that German delegates had crossed the lines at Guise. Victory was on the way! Francis was with his comrades to celebrate those epic last moments of the war: "9/11/18. Warning order received that the enemy is retiring. Batt to be ready to move at short notice. 10/11/18. Batt moved at 10.00 to Heeteert. Night rumours of Armistice. 11/11/18. Information received that hostilities would cease at 11.00 hrs. Thanksgiving Service held at 15.00 hrs."[827]

Actually, Heeteert does not exist and the writer of the war diary meant Heestert, a short way north of the River Lys, and some miles east of Menem. This was where Francis and the battalion reached the end of their particular war journey. It would be fascinating to know for sure if his brother Harold was with him in the battalion rather than away with the 1/15th London elsewhere. We do know that early in 1919 Francis was allowed to return to England for early demobilisation on 7th February 1919. Harold had to wait a few more months until 14th June 1919 for his demobilisation. But both survived.

As the war in the north drew to its conclusion, Joseph Lonsdale and the 1/28th London Battalion found themselves under fire as they entered the outskirts of Blaugies in Belgium, south-west of Mons, though they achieved all their objectives despite the heavy fire from German machine guns. The next day their advance continued as the Germans retreated before them, and they reached the southern outskirts of Mons. However, that evening, the battalion had to withstand machine-gun, light artillery and trench mortar attack. Sadly, on 10th November as they advanced north-east across the outskirts of Mons, three more officers and two men were killed, and one officer and twenty-five men were wounded. Joseph himself survived, finishing at Mons where the British fighting had begun, and after the war he returned to Montreal.

Forcing the Hindenburg Line (up to 26th September)

Further south, in France, Ludendorff's defences relied on the Canal du Nord and the old Hindenburg Line. Ludendorff himself recognised that this was an increasingly forlorn situation. Unless the Allies could be split politically, the war could not be won by Germany. Nevertheless, although they had lost men and resources which they could ill afford, as the Germans were pushed back, their defence line shortened and consolidated. By the end of August it has been estimated that the Germans had fifty fewer miles of front to defend, which would have required twenty-five

---

[827] War Diary, 2/15th London Battalion, 9th-11th November 1918.

divisions. So the more successful the British attacks were, the harder their target became. The Hindenburg Line was formidable both in its own right, and also because of the memories it provoked of the end of 1917. In places, defence canals had been dug to thwart the tanks, and the barbed wire was incredibly dense and deep. Facing the forty British divisions and two supporting American divisions, the Germans had fifty-seven divisions.

Echoing the telegram from Sir Henry Wilson of 29th August, Lloyd George now felt it necessary to write to Haig that heavy casualties from an attack on the Hindenburg Line would have a grave impact on British public opinion. But Haig had powerful friends. Not only the King supported him, but some key ministers, and when Haig came to London to argue against Lloyd George's caution, the majority of the Cabinet backed Haig. On 21st September, Haig confided in his diary, that he had told Lord Milner that "In my opinion it is possible to get a decision *this* year: but if we do not, every blow that we deliver now will make the task next year [much easier]."[828] (Lord Alfred Milner was an important member of the Cabinet. He had been a member since 1916 and Secretary of State for War since 19th April 1918 when Lloyd George had replaced the Earl of Derby (a genuine supporter of Haig). Milner had been a champion of the appointment of Foch as Supreme Commander, but Haig had to deal with him as Milner also chaired the Army Council until the end of the war.)

Despite its strengths, the Hindenburg Line failed to stop the advancing British. In a series of four major Allied offensives, the German line was broken entirely by the end of September. Originally, Foch had reckoned on two significant attacks to capture key railway junctions behind the German lines. This, he hoped, should force the Germans to retreat further. He wanted an assault from Arras to capture Lille in the north and a Franco-American attack south of Reims. The main British forces would attack in the centre against the Hindenburg Line whilst the flanks were turned in north and south of them. Foch's pincer attacks were planned to start on 26th September.

In the south, French troops would be supported by Pershing's American Army. Although a few American divisions were still with the British, as far as possible, Pershing had insisted on consolidating them into a distinctive U.S. Army which he would lead. They had been bloodied in a costly assault on the St. Mihiel Salient, south of Verdun – pointless really because the Germans had already started to withdraw from it when the Americans attacked, and the American assault meant the Germans were forced to turn and fight. The Americans soldiers did well, and took a lot of prisoners, but the land they gained had already effectively been conceded by the Germans. In his campaign, the American transport system had completely broken down, but the Germans had withdrawn before the impact of that debacle could be felt.

Now Foch wanted to have Pershing's forces available to aid the French in the Argonne Sector. This would give the Franco-Americans four times the number of troops that were available to the Germans. After one brilliant day of advance, once the Franco-Americans reached the German battle zone they found themselves faced by a magnificent defence. The Americans took heavy casualties, both from the German machine guns but also caused by their own weaknesses. For example, transport again went wrong – it is estimated that seven hundred Americans starved to death on the front line, whilst other American units left the front line to search for the rations that had not

---

[828] From *Douglas Haig, War Diaries and Letters 1914-1918*, edited by Gary Sheffield and John Bourne, p. 463. The authors point out in a footnote on the same page, "In his diary for 23rd September, Henry Wilson noted that Milner thought Haig was 'ridiculously optimistic and is afraid that he may embark on another Passchendaele'."

reached them for four days.[829] British and French officers were sent to sort out the American transport system.

Two days before the main British attack started, Ernest Marshall was killed. Born about 1894, Ernest was a member of the school from 1906-1909, being particularly skilful in drawing and maths. He volunteered in October 1914 and joined the Royal Garrison Artillery in Hampshire. Most of his experience of the war came fighting in Palestine and there he was eventually promoted to the rank of sergeant. His unit was moved from the Eastern Expeditionary Force on 21st May 1918 and he was sent to the Western Front to fight in the 379th Siege Battery. This was a battery with four six-inch howitzers, and was part of the 13th (Mobile Brigade) of the 3rd Army under General Byng. He arrived back in France from a short leave only two days before he was killed on 24th September 1918. Because of a confusion in the records and artillery designations, it is difficult to ascertain his precise role at the time, but he was buried at the Hermies British Cemetery, half-way between Bapaume and Cambrai, and a short distance to the west of Havrincourt. He and his battery would have been supporting the British advance in that area. The area of the cemetery had only just been recaptured by the British in September 1918.

The main British attack in the centre was also launched on 26th September. The northern flank began with an eight-hour barrage; further south near St. Quentin the bombardment lasted two and a half days. Another million shells crashed down on the German defenders, targeting enemy batteries, headquarters, and dug-out entrances with British-made mustard gas.

The Canadians were given the task of attacking north of Cambrai to try to capture bridgeheads over the canal, whilst the 3rd Army attacked to the south in a parallel assault. The idea was to break through and open the way to the undamaged countryside behind where an advance could be made unhindered by wire or prepared trenches. On 27th September, the Second Battle of Cambrai began.

The Second Battle of Cambrai: 27th September

Norman Wragg fought in this battle. Whilst the 5th Dorset Battalion regrouped and retrained after its losses at Ypres in 1917, Norman had been seconded to do a six week signalling course behind the lines at a chateau which served as Army Headquarters. He was away from them when his battalion had taken part in the Battle of Poelcapelle – part of the Passchendaele debacle. After his course, Norman had returned as signalling officer at Battalion Headquarters. The winter had been spent in a mixture of holding the line, raiding and repulsing enemy raids, and resting and training. On 25th April 1918 Norman had been promoted full lieutenant. The battalion was not directly involved in countering the Ludendorff Offensive as it was in the line nearer to La Bassée and Arras, near Noyelles (where the unit war diary reports they regularly bathed – once or twice a month!) but on 27th August, some days after moving to Frevillers, the battalion had moved on to Givenchy-le-Noble where the brigade was formed into a mobile unit in conjunction with the 1st Cavalry Corps. They had lorries attached to them for transport. After further training in conjunction with the cavalry, the battalion moved towards the end of September into the action.

On 26th September they were at Vis-en-Artois, and the next day advanced from Villers-les-Cagnicourt, north-west of Cambrai. They advanced at 9a.m. behind the Northumberland Fusiliers. At midday they crossed the canal, but then came under heavy German artillery fire at a place called

---

[829] C.R.M.F. Cruttenwell, *A History of the Great War*, p. 567, 1934 – second edition 1936.

'Keith Wood'. They reached Sauchy Cauchy Farm and established their headquarters in a trench slightly north of the farm, deploying the companies into new positions. This advance was costly – that day (September 27th) three had died, five went missing, and a further thirty-five were wounded, together with one of the subalterns. Norman Wragg advanced with the headquarters group. This position allowed them the following day to relieve the Northumberland Fusiliers in the front line at Oisy-le-Verger, though at a further cost in dead and wounded. Here they attempted to strengthen their position with an unsuccessful further attack whilst the battalion suffered especially both from machine-gun fire and from German gas shells before the end of the month. They then were switched south-east to Épinoy to make a full-scale attack on 1st October. This advance was made at great cost to the 5th Dorsets. At the end of the attack, having secured the new position, they had lost a further one officer killed and five wounded, with sixteen men killed and two hundred and nine wounded, whilst thirty-four had gone missing. Additionally, another man had been caught by the German gas.

The Germans were far from giving up. Over the next two days, German defensive fire was very heavy: "Shelling was heavy at frequent intervals and machine gun fire swept rolling [across them]… Hostile trench mortars also active… Heavy shelling during morning. Aid post destroyed. Medical officer badly wounded and four stretcher bearers and chaplain killed. M.O. died later in day. C.O. was wounded about 400 yards from railway line. Battalion was relieved by Northumberland Fusiliers who side-slipped into our position."[830] After re-organisation, the battalion continued in action in conjunction with the 8th Northumberland Fusiliers, the 7th South Staffordshires and the 11th Manchesters. There were emergencies and further casualties. On 8th October they broke up a concentration of about two hundred Germans who were grouping for a counter-attack by firing their rifles and Lewis guns at them – having waited thirty three minutes in vain for the artillery to respond to S.O.S rockets which they had sent up when their telephone communications had been broken by a heavy German barrage. As signalling officer, Norman must have been in the thick of this emergency.

In the middle of the month they had a brief respite as they were pulled back and a new commander took over to replace their colonel, who had been fatally wounded in the attack on 3rd October and who had died of his wounds on 4th October. After this, the battalion trained hard under the watchful eyes of their new commander for the rest of the month.

A few miles further south, Canadian Edward Newman was in action east of Inchy-en-Artois. He had been born in 1887 and had been one of the earliest members of the school – leaving in 1903 after specialising in chemistry and physics. After school he took an apprenticeship with the Bournemouth and Poole Electricity Supply Company and continued to work with the company as an electrician until 1909. Then he took a job with the London County Council, but by 1916 he was in Vancouver, British Columbia. On 19th July 1916, he attested for the 11th Regiment, the Irish Fusiliers of Canada, a training and depot unit which supplied over four thousand men for service overseas in other battalions rather than acting as a fighting unit in its own right. Edward ended up in the 3rd Canadian Division, Trench Mortar Group. In this mortar group there was a battery for each of the 7th, 8th and 9th Canadian Brigades in the division, as well as a divisional heavy mortar battery. On 25th September, orders had been received to bring forward their six-inch mortars to a position in front of Inchy-en-Artois (west of Cambrai) to cut the wire in front of the Canal du Nord

---

[830] War Diary, 5th Dorset Battalion, 2nd-3rd October 1918.

so that the 1st and 4th Canadian Divisions would be able to open their attack. "All available men in camp with exception of 2 mobile mortar gun crews, which were kept in reserve to follow infantry of 3rd Cdn Division, proceeded to forward area in the evening to commence work on new positions and transport ammunition to the magazines. Sept 26 1918. Mortar emplacements completed and ammunition transported to guns. Guns all ready to fire in preliminary bombardment on the 27th… Attack by 1st and 4th Canadian Divisions. 160 rds expended cutting wire in front of Canal du Nord… 2 mobile mortars moved forward in support of infantry of 3rd Canadian Division. 28. Attack continued. Mobile mortars moved forward with infantry."[831] His division was heavily involved in the fighting round Cambrai. Commenting on the fighting of 30th September, the commander of the 3rd Canadian Division stated in the war diary in a report on the fighting, "It was a day of very bitter fighting and the enemy fought well, and very noticeable was the lavish use of his M.G.s of which he had an abnormal quantity."[832]

Alexander Sandbrook and the 8th Canadian Infantry Battalion were in action again, from 27th to 29th September, forcing a crossing of the Canal du Nord, east of Inchy, and attacking through Bourlon Wood. Once again the battalion took heavy casualties – five officers were killed and nine wounded. Of the other ranks, fifty-nine were killed, 272 wounded, thirty-two were found to be missing and a further three had been gassed. One of those, missing and captured, was Philip Tollemache who had returned to the battalion sometime after recovery from shell shock in 1916. He was sent to a German prison camp, where his treatment was monitored by the Red Cross.

Ernest Snelgar and the 4th Canadian Mounted Rifles had been held back in reserve for the battle, but the battalion moved forward behind victorious Canadian forces to await its turn to attack. As they moved forward on 29th September they came under a German barrage. By 7a.m. on 30th September they were in the trenches, ready in case they were called upon to attack. There was a heavy ground mist. The Germans were only three hundred yards away. The battalion remained in these support trenches until the night of 2nd-3rd October. Twice they stood by, expecting to attack. "During this period, support and reserve companies were living in what had formerly been an enemy ammunition dump. Some men had ferreted into shell shelters and others had cover adjacent to a cordite dump. During the evening of October 5th there was intermittent shelling but about 2.00 a.m. on the 6th the enemy threw salvo after salvo into the support area and set on fire a large dump in front of 'B' Company's Headquarters. Then the cordite dump in front of 'A' Company Headquarters caught fire. Everyone fled without waiting for personal treasures; it was the part of wisdom for in a few minutes there was an enormous explosion. The dump 'went up' blowing a crater seventy feet wide and thirty feet deep where the hurriedly vacated billets had been. It was estimated that the enemy threw over 500 shells into these two companies; despite this and the explosion there was not a single casualty."[833]

The fighting was quite desperate against the Canadians as the Germans fought hard to prevent a collapse, and the British and Imperial forces fought to bring that collapse about. "In this battle the Canadian Corps touched its pinnacle of fame. Beyond question the battle, and especially the fighting of September 30 and October 1, was the most savage and sustained in which the Canadian

---

[831] War Diary, 3rd Canadian Division Trench Mortar Group, 25th to 28th September 1918.

[832] Special report included in the War Diary, 3rd Canadian Division, September 1918.

[833] *The 4th Canadian Mounted Rifles 1914-1919*, Captain S.G. Bennett, M.C., Murray Printing Company Limited Toronto, 1926, p. 137.

Corps ever engaged. Only the utmost heroism and tenacity of our infantry, ably supported by our gunners, enabled us to cling on to the salient we had driven into the heart of the enemy's defence in face of withering fire and there withstand wave after wave of counter-attacks by almost overwhelming numbers... But that we had gained the decision was by no means clear on the evening of Oct.1. Our losses had been so severe, our reserves had been so freely drawn upon, that there was anxiety on all hands that night as to whether the morning might not see a last final thrust such as we might be in no condition to fight off."[834]

In such fighting, the work of Ernest Snelgar and his fellow signallers was of especial importance: "During the progress of the battle a tremendous strain is thrown on Signals, which must keep all units in close touch with their headquarters; the brigades with their divisions; these latter with Corps headquarters. Nor is this all. They must maintain uninterrupted the all-important liaison between the infantry and artillery. A loss of communication at a critical moment of the advance must mean the useless sacrifice of many lives, for our counter-battery work is of vital value to the attacking troops."[835] Therefore, on 1st October, it was essential that the senior staff should know accurately what was going on. So a forward observation post was established near the outpost line. At this point the battalion was still in support, but the Germans were resisting and counter-attacking. It was vital that the colonel should know accurately what was going on, and that this information could be sent back to inform the brigadier. Ernest was running the work of communication with Brigade Headquarters, and according to his later citation, "the success obtained was due only to his untiring energy and disregard for personal safety. During the morning, under very heavy shell fire, he repaired upwards of thirty breaks in the line, and brigade headquarters were never out of touch with brigade outposts."[836]

For his actions that day, Ernest was later awarded the Distinguished Conduct Medal (D.C.M.). This was the non-commissioned soldiers' equivalent to the D.S.O. It was awarded to warrant officers, non-commissioned officers, and men, serving in any of the sovereign's military forces, for distinguished conduct in the field. It was the second highest award for gallantry in action (after the Victoria Cross) for all army ranks below commissioned officers and was awarded for distinguished conduct in the field. Ernest was the highest decorated 'Old Bournemouthian' of the war.

In hindsight, the Germans at Arras were beaten by 2nd October, and although this was not entirely obvious to the Canadians the almost complete cessation of their counter-attacks gave a new optimism to the men. Then, on the night of 8th-9th October, the attacks of the British 3rd Army were so successful that the Germans defending Cambrai broke. At 1.30a.m., in the novelty of an attack in the middle of the night, the battalion attacked and crossed the formidable obstacle of the Scheldt Canal. There was some resistance at the canal, and to deal with it two men swam the canal, landed on the far bank, and bombed the German machine-gun post. Yet by 8a.m. the battalion was in the outskirts of Cambrai itself, and had suffered no casualties. And so the 4th Canadian Mounted Rifles was the first battalion to enter the city.

Further north, near Lens, Alfred Bishop and the 8th London Battalion had enjoyed a brief respite. Then, on 2nd October, the battalion had again moved forward and went onto the attack on 4th

---

[834] *Canada's One Hundred Days*, J.F.B. Livesay, Thomas Allen, 1919, pp. 271-272.
[835] *Canada's One Hundred Days*, J.F.B. Livesay, Thomas Allen, 1919, p. 345.
[836] Citation to his D.C.M., as published in the *Supplement to The London Gazette*, 2nd December, 1919, p. 14903.

October against the German position at Cité St. Auguste, a suburb of Lens. Two days of fighting followed with considerable casualties, particularly from German gas shell attacks, but also from heavy trench mortars and machine guns. Alfred Bishop, despite his eyesight, had held out.

On 10th October, Ernest Snelgar and the 4th Canadian Mounted Rifles received a surprise visit from the Prince of Wales. This was a reflection of advice given on 20th September when Haig had suggested he should be allowed to visit the Australian and Canadian Corps, and if possible to join one of their staffs. The prince had managed to persuade the government to allow him to be a staff officer, though instructions were given to preserve his person, if necessary despite himself. He had been attached to the Canadian Corps, and seems to have overcome the doubts of many by the way he lived amongst them (at least at corps level) and visited various units whilst managing to put men at their ease as he showed genuine interest and curiosity.

From the start of the month until 16th October, the men like Edward Newman who would normally have worked the heavier trench mortars, served within the 3rd Canadian Division Field Artillery batteries instead. By the start of October they were in the northern suburbs of Cambrai, and then moved northwards to a position east of Lens and south of Lille. By the middle of October, when Cambrai had fallen, the 3rd Canadian Division had been fighting for twelve days continuously. Whilst we cannot be sure from the records if he was with the mobile mortars or with the field artillery, we can know that Edward would have been hard at work almost continuously over that fortnight. On 18th October, the group war diary recorded, "2 O.R.s evacuated sick to Field Ambulance. All available personnel still attached to Batteries." So, Edward's war experiences came to an end. On 16th December 1918 he wrote to the headmaster, Dr. Fenwick, explaining, "I came down the line from Cambrai on October 18 with sores on my hands and legs, and made the usual round of casualty clearing stations, hospital, and convalescent camps... This is the first time I have been 'down the line' since I have been out here, and as I am in good health I can count myself pretty fortunate."[837] After the war he returned to Vancouver.

Between 11th to 19th October, Alexander Sandbrook and the 8th Canadian Infantry Battalion were fighting in the line near Norman Wragg, east of Le Cluse, advancing north-east towards Estrées where they were held up at the bank of the Canal de la Sensée. Once again they were working closely with the 10th Battalion. On 17th October they crossed that canal without opposition, and as their advance continued the next day they were joined by an attachment of the corps cyclists and another of light cavalry to help with patrolling the flanks of the advance. Only as they pushed on fast did they come under machine-gun and artillery fire.

After another short period of rest, Alfred Bishop and the 8th London Battalion had moved into the attack yet again, this time to try to gain a bridgehead across the canal near Courrières, a small town twelve kilometres north-east of Lens and further north of Cambrai – and Alfred's luck ran out. On 14th October, as they tried to gain the far bank, they encountered determined German defenders and many were captured, whilst two officers and eighty-nine men were killed or wounded – amongst whom was Alfred. Ironically, the next day, when the attack was renewed, the Germans made only token resistance as most of them retreated, and the battalion gained the bridgehead with no further casualties. Alfred was one of just ten men to be buried in the Courrières Communal Cemetery. Sadly, however, he was not the last Old Bournemouthian to make the supreme sacrifice in the war.

---

[837] *The Bournemouthian*, April 1919.

On the other hand, for some, this advance was marked by previously unknown scenes of euphoria. On 19th October, near Wandignies Hamage, east of where Alfred had died, the 1st Canadian Field Artillery Brigade of Basil Keogh had such an experience: "It was in this town the Brigade got its first glimpse of the civilians liberated from the enemy. The joy of these poor people on seeing for the first time Allied troops in their village was beyond bound and could not be described. Old men and women and young girls came forward to meet our soldiers as they approached the village and amid shouts of 'Vive La Canada' 'Vive L'Anglaise' and 'Vive la France', our troops realised for the first time probably the reward for their labors for the past three and a half years. The civilians could not do enough for us. Houses were thrown open for our use and everyone settled down for the night in comfort."[838]

Forcing the St. Quentin Canal and Eastwards

Montague Pickard was in action in the main thrust further south, with the 16th Tank Corps Battalion. Martin Luther Montague Pickard, known as Montague, had been at school from September 1913 to December 1914. He was born in 1898, probably in Cape Town. After he left school he had soon become a member of the Gloucestershire Regiment and had landed in France on 10th October 1915 as a boy soldier aged seventeen with a group of men reinforcing the active battalions. From his records it is not clear which battalion he initially joined since ten Gloucestershire battalions were in France at the time. At that stage he had been promoted to lance corporal. However, he later transferred as a private into the 16th Battalion of the Tank Corps which was formed in the winter of 1917-1918. Montague's battalion left Bovington Camp for Southampton early in September 1918, sailed on the SS *Nirvana* and the SS *Archangel*. Soon they were working up their skills with the tanks, ready to move forward in the week of 21st to 27th September to Tincourt-Boucly, and then up to the front where they were attached to the 3rd Australian Division, east of Peronne and north of St. Quentin.

At this stage of the technology there were many difficulties faced by those wishing to communicate between the infantry and the tanks in an attack. Radios were not yet sufficiently mobile so if a tank commander wanted to give messages to the infantry it had to be done by a system of flags. Showing a green and white flag would tell the infantry to 'come on', a red and yellow flag would mean 'out of action', whilst a tricolour flag shown told them that the tank was 'coming back'. It was even harder for the infantryman – a helmet raised on his rifle was supposed to mean 'tank assistance required'.[839] All these signs, however, would have required clear visibility rather than fog, and one wonders how infantry in difficulties would be able to raise rifles and helmets in the teeth of German machine-gun fire! Still, the tanks were there to assist the attacks, and they seem to have done a good job overall.

Montague's precise role is unclear, but the tanks of 'A' and 'C' Companies of the 16th Battalion were in action on 29th September at Bellicourt, north of St. Quentin, in dense fog. This made it tricky – especially as they came under heavy machine-gun and artillery fire even before they reached the start line. The 27th American Division attack ahead of them had failed, and it was up to the tanks and the Australians to try to sort out the situation. In a vain attempt to manage this, all the tanks involved were put out of action and it was left to the survivors from the crews to establish

---

[838] War Diary, 1st Canadian Field Artillery Brigade, 19th October 1918.
[839] War Diary, 14th Infantry Brigade instructions, Autumn 1918.

machine-gun posts alongside the Australian infantry. In that action the battalion losses have been calculated at about two-thirds, so the battalion's scope for further action was limited.

The Americans involved were fighting under Rawlinson's command with II Corps. Rawlinson put their failure down to their keenness but also their inexperience: "My heaviest losses in this battle have been the American Corps. They were too keen to get on, as gallant new troops always are, and did not pay enough attention to mopping up, with the result that the Germans came out of the dug-outs, after they had passed, and cut them off."[840]

George Rees also continued to serve with the tanks through these latter months, assisting some of these Americans for a time, and then helping in the push beyond Cambrai. Whilst the men of the tank carrier units were not meant to fight (despite attempts by some senior officers to 'steal' experienced men to reinforce other units when they arrived that spring) their role still could bring them into close proximity, and even contact, with the Germans. Some tanks were destroyed when driving over land mines the Germans had left as they withdrew, or which had been laid as a minefield in March 1918, and for the location of which the British lacked accurate maps, particularly in the vicinity of the Hindenburg Line.

At the end of August, George's unit had been sent by train to Boisleux-au-Mont near Arras to support operations in that sector, and enjoyed a quieter time (though with multiple illnesses), transferring from the 5th Tank Brigade to the 4th Tank Brigade. From there it was sent by train down to Manancourt, east of Bapaume and north of Peronne in late September. Here, their tanks once again went into the forward sector and they suffered battle casualties. One of their tasks was to detach a section to assist the American 27th Division, operating alongside the 301st American Tank Battalion. October saw a lot of action with the 4th Brigade Tank Carrier Company supporting both Americans and their own 4th Brigade tanks. This was a month of "strenuous activity" until the company was again rested. "During this period it took part in several of that magnificent series of fights which led up to the smashing of the 'impregnable' Hindenburg Line, protecting Cambrai and St. Quentin, and finally drove the Hun helter skelter towards his own frontier."[841]

At first they had supplied the 106th American Infantry Battalion. One tank struck a German mine and was then hit by a shell but – with wounded men aboard – managed to dump its supplies for the Americans whilst under heavy fire, but sadly struck a second mine, received a direct hit and was burned out. Other tanks suffered similarly. Tragically, these were British, not German mines, which had been inaccurately recorded on the available maps, and were 500 yards out of position. (Later they were engaged in re-supplying 104th Army Brigade R.F.A. As they did so, the company moved forward and by the end of the month were at Roisel, near St. Quentin, before being pulled back once more to the area around Arras. In contrast, for the final month of the war they were engaged in training whilst some officers and men were granted leave.)

On 2nd October, 'B' Company of the 16th Tank Battalion fought slightly further east at Nauroy; two days after that 'A' Company was in action at Beaurevoir; and after yet another two days a composite company drawn from each section of the battalion fought slightly to their south at

---

[840] Rawlinson is quoted in *Borrowed Soldiers: Americans under British Command, 1918*, p. 184, Mitchell A. Yockelson, University of Oklahoma Press, 2008; the author blames Rawlinson and the Tank Corps for the American failure.

[841] Narrative p. 45, War Diary, 4th Tank Carrier Company.

Joncourt, attached to the 6th Australian Brigade in the Battle of Montbrehain; and finally 'B' Company was attached to 9th Corps for the action of 17th October at La Selle River. In between, from 6th to 16th October they were working on salvage, refitting and training for that final battle. After the war, the battalion formed part of the Army of Occupation, and it was not until 19th August 1919 that Montague was demobilised.

In between, on 3rd October, the men of the 46th Division also had been back in action, also to the north of St. Quentin and across on the east side of the canal where George Rees was working. The night before the attack, Arthur Sear and the signallers were very busy sorting out new cable lines and checking wireless communications to keep the general in touch with his brigades. As this action succeeded the division continued to press forwards, eastwards and within days its HQ was at Fresnoy-le-Grand, east of Joncourt and south-west of Le Cateau. The war diary tells us how the leading brigade now had a permanent cable-laying section attached to it, whilst the wireless communications continued to work well.

From September, Joseph Lonsdale and the 1/28th London Battalion fought in the costly attacks on the St. Quentin Canal, and the advance south of Cambrai. On 8th October, they attacked in darkness and immediately 'A' Company found themselves under fire from a machine-gun post of which the British had been unaware. This was taken out and eight machine guns and one hundred prisoners taken as a result. Meanwhile, 'C' Company took an additional sixty prisoners. When the Germans counter-attacked at about 10a.m., unusually, the German attack was supported by tanks which were put out of action using a captured anti-tank gun and the counter-attack was repelled.

It was at the time of the Second Battle of Cambrai and the push north of St. Quentin that the German Government began to make clear their desire for an armistice, based on President Wilson's Fourteen Points, though that move was not enough to satisfy those 'in the know' who wanted an unconditional surrender – a sentiment shared by those troops in the battle line amongst whom the rumours began to circulate. Some comments from the time have been preserved in Livesay's book: "'He knows he's beaten; we'll have our own peace this winter,' says a private from the Ottawa Valley. A Tommy from the West Riding: 'When Gerry comes knocking at the door with his pride in his pocket, he must be in a pretty bad way.' ...A sergeant who was reputed to have charged a machine-gun nest in Blecourt with his bare fists: 'The Hun is bankrupt. We must make him liquidate to the last cent of his assets. Our widows and orphans demand it. That can be done only by the sword.' ...The Captain of an Imperial heavy battery, working his guns from the slope of Bourlon Wood, is of the same opinion, 'I don't like it,' he says, 'The enemy is short of men and material. He is crippled for lack of field-guns and his ammunition seems running low. He'll drag on peace negotiations for three months, and then go at us again.'"[842] So for a time the fighting went on.

The Second Battle of Le Cateau: 8th-12th October and the Final Advance

Various Old Bournemouthians were caught up in the Second Battle of Le Cateau as the British continued to put pressure on the retreating Germans, including Bernard Allbon and Aubrey Godfrey of the 6th Dorsets. They had had a spell of training and recuperation after the fighting of 18th and 19th September until they moved back into the lines to prepare for their next assault. By October the battalion was pushing the Germans back onto the Hindenburg Support Line. The

---

[842] *Canada's One Hundred Days*, J.F.B. Livesay, Thomas Allen, 1919, p. 321.

battalion arrived in the lines at Selvigny, south-east of Cambrai at 11.30a.m. on 9th October. That evening they moved up to the outpost positions (the standard trench system had been breaking down all autumn, and had largely been abandoned now the war had returned to being one of movement). Bernard attended a company commanders' briefing about the attack planned for the next day. He received his final orders at 12.30a.m. The 50th Brigade was to pass through the 51st Brigade with the Dorsets on the left of the advance.

On 10th October, the attack began. As the brigade attacked, the Dorsets were on the left with the 10th West Yorks on then right, and 7th East Yorks in support. They captured Audencourt, Beaumont and Inchy without any significant opposition. (Bernard Allbon's company took Inchy.) They were now close to the western fringe of Le Cateau. However, on their left the 37th Division held been held up. This led to troublesome machine-gun and shell fire from Béthencourt, which was now behind the Dorsets, to the north. 'B' Company formed a defensive flank, and the other battalions of the brigade pushed on past to reach the outskirts of Neuvilly, north of Le Cateau. This progress had been made by 8a.m.

At 1p.m. on 10th October, the other two battalions were ordered to attack Neuvilly immediately north of Le Cateau, with the 6th Dorsets in support. 'D' Company was one of the two companies which acted as the support. 'B' and 'C' remained in the position holding the flank. But when the attack was made at 5p.m. it was repulsed. Though the East Yorks had succeeded in crossing the River Selle, flowing through Neuvilly, they had to cross back again. Bernard then led his company forward into the village to support them but the company was met with heavy machine-gun fire from some houses and had to withdraw. In this attack, four officers fell wounded, two men were killed and three more wounded. Casualties were officially "slight",[843] but amidst the wounded officers that day were both Bernard and Aubrey.

"Whilst giving his last orders preparatory to leading his men into battle, he [Bernard] received a severe wound in the leg."[844] Afterwards, the two companies dug in within nearby trenches until the following afternoon when the other two companies attacked the village supported by the East Yorks and the remaining two companies, though their attack was also repulsed with heavy machine-gun fire, and they too were forced to withdraw. (On 11th October the casualties were much worse amongst the men – twenty-five killed, one hundred and two wounded and fifteen missing, and five officers wounded and one killed.) Both had to be invalided out. Aubrey had been wounded by a shell explosion, but fortunately not too seriously. When the shell burst near him, shrapnel bruised his ankle and some of it wounded him in the leg. He was hospitalised in Sunderland for a time. His was thus a 'short war'.

Bernard Allbon was less fortunate. He had been struck by a fragment of the same shell that had hit Aubrey, but in his case it had hit him in his right thigh, and this had partially fractured his femur, and had left six fragments inside his thigh. He was passed down the casualty chain to a base hospital and on 13th October back to England. He was taken to the Red Cross Hospital in Brighton. Three times he was operated upon, and things seemed to be going well. There was some optimism in November 1918 that in five months he might have recovered fully. But though he lived to know of the Armistice, he spent his last months in the hospital system. Then, still in hospital, he caught

---

[843] War Diary, 6th Dorsets, 10th October 1918.
[844] *The Bournemouthian*, April 1919.

the 'flu and died on 3rd February 1919, officially of heart failure, leaving his estate to his parents who grieved the loss of their only son. The Army file attributed his death to "Died of wounds". He was buried with full military honours at the Wimborne Road Cemetery, Bournemouth. The headmaster, Dr. Fenwick, and the O.T.C. officers of Bournemouth School attended. In his school obituary, a fellow soldier said, "He was a fine soldier, and his men would have followed him anywhere. He was one of the best, cool and determined under fire, and always thoughtful for his men."[845]

Ernest Parsons of the 1st Royal Fusiliers Battalion was involved – almost to the last – in the battle and the advance to victory. At the end of September the battalion had been pulled back west of Arras for training, and then sent in October to advance through Cambrai and into a position to attack eastwards at Rieux-en-Cambrésis on 11th October. The action shows both that the Germans still had much fight left in them. "Battalion went through a heavy barrage at Rieux when assembling for attack at 4am. The intention was to pass through the 73rd Brigade. The Battalion was held up by enemy Machine Guns before reaching the first objective. Casualties were very heavy. It was impossible to advance against such fire owing to the nature of the country. Had there been artillery co-operation or a single tank the 3rd objective could easily have been gained. During the morning and whilst the 73rd Brigade were actually being relieved the enemy sent 1 tank forward which fired a few bursts of Machine Gun fire and a few shrapnel and immediately returned. During the night, patrols were pushed out and the enemy having retired, posts were established on high ground west of Villers en Cauchies and St. Aubert. Casualties: Killed in Action [three named officers] 40 O.R.; Wounded – [6 named officers] 181 O.R.; Missing – 4 O.R."[846] However, despite these losses, the next day the battalion advanced without loss: "At dawn reconnoitring patrols were pushed further forward. These advanced very rapidly, the Battalion following up closely. The enemy was reported by Royal Air Force to be East of La Selle River. Enemy Machine Guns were reported in vicinity of Salzoir which prevented a further advance and posts were established at dusk on high ground west of La Selle River. The artillery rendered excellent support this day."[847]

After these advances the battalion was pulled back into reserve to recuperate and to retrain. For the rest of the month they were out of the direct action, but on 3rd November began to march forward again towards the front line. On 4th November they entered Jenlain under shell fire; they were east of Valenciennes, just beyond the Belgian border and the town of Mons. The next day they were back in the thick of the action, pushing forward until again held up by German machine guns. This was to be a miserable day, despite the advance. It rained continuously. The next day the effort was made to push forward again, as the diary reveals: "River Hogneau and St Waast La Vallée. 6/11/18. At dawn an attempt was made under a barrage to reach high ground on East side of River Hogneau. It was however unsuccessful and 2 platoons of D Coy supported by A and HQ Lewis Gun team were compelled to dig in along East side of River Bank. The enemy was holding in strength line of Railway about 300 yards distant with machine guns. An attempt with 6" Newtons was made to dislodge the enemy but without success. Our troops were under observation by the enemy and the close proximity, about 300 yards, prevented the artillery from opening. At 2000 hours the 2 forward platoons were withdrawn to billets in Western outskirts of St Waast La Vallée which was

---

[845] *The Bournemouthian*, April 1919.
[846] War Diary, 1st Royal Fusiliers, 11th October 1918.
[847] ibid.

being shelled when they entered and casualties caused, C Company held the high ground further West. It rained almost without ceasing throughout the day which had been a hard one for the battalion. Casualties: Killed 3 O.R.; Wounded 20 O.R. (2 remain); Gassed 2 O.R."[848] Ernest was one of those wounded.

This was Ernest's last action in the war, and ironically it was also the last action made by the battalion – the next day a different battalion advanced without opposition, and the 1st Royal Fusiliers Battalion was withdrawn to billets. By then Ernest was in the casualty clearing system. He had been wounded on the back by shrapnel, and scarred both above his left eye and above his left knee. But he had survived.

Richard Barfoot was one of those helping to tend the wounded like Ernest. In late June and July, the 24th Field Ambulance had been given a period of respite in the west, near Abbeville, and Richard Barfoot might have attended the concerts arranged or the Divisional Horse Show in which the ambulance representatives won three prizes. From the summer until the end of the war, they were dealing with (and suffering from) cases of the Spanish influenza in addition to wounded and the normal sick of a military campaign. The 24th Field Ambulance was not called upon to support the counter-attack of August-September 1918, but in October moved east near to Lens in support of the attack in that area. Once again, they regularly shifted their headquarters, but this time they were advancing, and casualties were pleasingly light. When the Armistice came they were at Pommeroeul, by Le Cateau and close to where the B.E.F. had started its campaign back in August 1914. Richard too had survived.

On 17th October, the 46th Division attacked again, in conjunction with a French division to their south. Once again the cables laid by signallers like Arthur Sear held – despite German artillery fire – and the wireless system was even more successful, this time even including one battalion of the leading brigade. It is interesting to note in the preparatory orders that much greater prominence was being given to wireless communication as warfare had become mobile and systems and sets more reliable. After this successful attack, the division was withdrawn from the line for a fortnight to recuperate and prepare. When they returned for the push in November, progress was resolute and dramatic; their HQ moved forward each day, and by 11th November they were at Sains-du-Nord, south of Mauberge and Mons, near the Belgium border. As they advanced they laid pairs of cables, but "Wireless stepped up as required by means of Wilson & Trench set at Divl HQ. Bde sets up but not used much. DOO's wireless set used throughout the advance. All Bde & forward sets in touch without intermission. No visual used. Special DR service as required. Communications satisfactory throughout."[849] Two days after the Armistice, Arthur was allowed fourteen days leave to England before returning briefly to France. He finally left France on 11th January 1919 and was demobilised on 9th February 1919.

On 17th October, the Canadian Corps, including Ernest Snelgar and the 4th Canadian Mounted Rifles had crossed the Canal du Nord, and three days later, on 20th October, they joined in the final advance against the demoralised enemy. Suddenly they found themselves liberating territory and welcomed by civilians who decked out towns with bunting and flags, and called out 'Vivre Canada!'

The battalion still had one part of the campaign to fight – the final forcing of the German retreat to

---

[848] War Diary, 1st Royal Fusiliers, 6th November 1918.
[849] War Diary, 46th Division Signals Company, November 1918.

Mons. The warfare was now across open country, but the Germans still resisted as best they could, and some Canadian attacks were repulsed. They also had the problem that the speed of their advance was leaving their supply depots far behind. At the start of November they managed to cross the Canal du Nord and capture Valenciennes. On 6th November, the brigade attacked across causeways through swamps and marshes and, in heavy fighting, captured Crespin and crossed the Honneau River. For the next few days heavy fighting continued over increasingly water-logged terrain, made worse as the weather deteriorated. As they extended north towards the Conde Canal they increasingly received thoroughly demoralised German prisoners. A counter-attack was repulsed, and on 9th November they secured positions north of the Conde-Mons Canal whilst helping to capture an increasing number of southern Belgian villages. The advance of their division on 10th November brought Canadian troops to the south-western outskirts of Mons itself, which was also reached by another Canadian division, the 2nd Division. The town was occupied by the 7th Canadian Infantry Brigade, in the battalion's division, in the early hours of 11th November. Finally, the news of the coming Armistice was received, and that morning divisional headquarters was moved to Mons market place. Ernest Snelgar was able to come home safely.

Behind the scenes, Alexander Miller had had time to train and be reclassified as an army coppersmith on 3rd September, though he remained with the Motor Transport Company of the 63rd Divisional Supply Column. He had been working as an A.S.C. driver with the 63rd Division when the Germans struck on the Somme in March 1918, and with his unit was forced back before the onslaught. In the middle of that, on 4th June 1918, he had been awarded a 'Good Conduct' badge. He suffered another bout of 'flu for which he was hospitalised ('sick leave') from 6th to 25th October. When his illness struck, the 63rd Division too was pushing deep into former enemy territory, having crossed the Canal du Nord. This time his 'flu was regarded as more serious, and he was sent back to England and to hospital at Christchurch, but fortunately recovered well. On 25th October he was well enough to be sent back to his work in France, re-joining his unit on 7th November, four days before the Armistice. So Alexander survived three years of warfare in France. After several postings within the R.A.S.C. in France, in 1919 he was eventually sent back to England at the end of May 1919, though he was not demobilised until 21st September 1919.

Although William Hoare's part in these events was much less dramatic and much more limited, he too was with the troops pushing on towards and beyond Le Cateau. Born in 1895, he attended the school from January 1905 until March 1909. His younger brother Reginald (who was a draughtsman before serving in the R.A.F. in 1918) attended the school for these same years. William attested on 25th February 1916. There was some hesitation about calling him into service, as he worked in charge of the drawing rooms of a chemical explosives company, and was designated a Group 36 (Munitions Worker). Finally, he was posted to the Royal Horse Artillery on 21st August 1916. On 1st September he joined 'P' Battery, R.H.A., part of X Reserve Brigade, based at Woolwich. On 13th November 1916 William had landed in France and was initially posted to the base in France as a gunner. Although he remained in France for the rest of the war, he did not immediately serve with the guns, as two days after his posting he was admitted to the 39th General Hospital at Le Havre, probably with an illness contracted before he left England. He was to remain in the hospital and at a specialised casualty clearing station until he was pronounced fit by a medical board on 14th May 1918, after which he was posted back to the R.H.A. base at Le Havre. He remained at the base until posted to 'F' Battery, R.H.A., on 12th October 1918. A battery was the main active unit of the artillery, and three batteries were brigaded under a lieutenant colonel, together with an HQ unit and an ammunition column. This meant that William was in an overall unit of about eight hundred men – which closely matched the size of the infantry battalions. By this stage of the war, 'F' Battery was part of 14th Army Brigade. The guns it fired were eighteen-pounders. It was brigaded with 'T' Battery and the 400th and 401st Batteries of the Royal Field Artillery, and so was an unusual formation designated as a force in support of 3rd Army.

At this time, the 3rd Army was pushing forward in the final advance through Picardy, crossing the La Sambre River on 4th November, after pushing eastwards beyond Cambrai in the direction of Le Cateau. By the end of October, William and his battery were south-east of Le Cateau, on the west bank of the Sambre-Oise Canal assisting the 1st Dorset and 5/6th Royal Scots Battalions, with the 15th Highland Light Infantry in support. On 4th November at 0545, the artillery laid down what the 14th Brigade War Diary described as a "very effective" barrage supporting the 1st Dorset Battalion as it crossed the canal. This assault turned out to be the last fighting experienced by the brigade. They managed to take 342 prisoners, 28 guns, 51 machine guns, 1 trench mortar and 1 anti-tank rifle in the action. When they advanced again a week later they were unable to engage the retreating Germans. William remained with 'F' Battery (apart from some Christmas leave to the UK) until he was returned to the UK on 4th January 1919 for discharge through the R.H.A. Centre.

By the end of the war – once the Army had broken through into open warfare again – the carrier tanks with which George Rees served had established themselves as vital elements of a successful advance. Watson wrote of his own company: "We had, to my mind, given conclusive proof of the utility of Carrier tanks, properly employed, even in semi-open warfare. Before the battle we had helped to build a bridge. During the battle we had kept the Divisional Commander in communication by laying cable forward as the advance progressed; we had carried stores for three brigades, supplying them on the spot with the necessaries of warfare; we had transported an enormous quantity of shells from the roadside over country impassable to horse transport. And this we had accomplished with obsolete tanks, entirely unsuitable for carrying bulky loads. On no single occasion did we fail 'to deliver the goods'."[850]

He also described one action in which a company – possibly George's – made a real difference east of Cambrai, a month before the Armistice: "Coxhead's Company continued the good work, until the 4th Army had passed beyond the Mormal Forest. Near Landrecies a section of his tanks captured an important bridge-head in curious circumstances. 'The tanks were laden with bridge-building material, heavy girders, timbers, hawsers, and so on. According to programme the bridge-head should have fallen to the infantry, the tanks arriving with material for the reconstruction of the bridge, which it was anticipated that the enemy would have destroyed. There was unfortunately a little hitch. When the tanks came on the scene, the enemy were still defending the bridge-head with the utmost vigour. The section commander did not hesitate. His tanks continued to move forward as though they had been fighting tanks. The infantry, who had trained with tanks, advanced in the proper formation. The enemy broke and fled. It was a bloodless victory gained, curiously enough, by officers and men who were not rated as 'fighting troops'."[851]

Reginald Lapthorne was with a Pioneer battalion in the closing months of the war. In the summer of 1918 he had been sent to the 11th Hampshire Battalion, a Pioneer battalion which had been in

---

[850] *A Company of Tanks* by Major W.H.L. Watson, D.S.O., D.C.M., William Blackwood and Sons, Edinburgh and London, 1920, pp. 288-289.

[851] *A Company of Tanks* by Major W.H.L. Watson, D.S.O., D.C.M., William Blackwood and Sons, Edinburgh and London, 1920, p. 289.

France since December 1915, but in the emergency of the German offensive it had been almost wiped out. The remnant, 'cadre strength', had been brought back to England on 18th June and over the next month, combining with the 13th Border Battalion, was rebuilt. They re-landed at Boulogne on 1st August 1918, and resumed their role as the Pioneer battalion for the 16th Division. The battalion then took part in the final advance as the Germans were pushed back. At the end of the war the battalion ended at Antoing, a village just south-east of Tournai in Belgium. Reginald was granted leave from the 11th Hampshire Battalion from 6th to 20th January 1919 in order to make a start at sorting out his dental practice. He wrote asking for an early demobilisation, citing the needs of his firm, but also explaining that he still suffered from shell shock. This request was granted and he was released from the Army on 9th March 1919.

Hindsight is a wonderful thing, and today we might imagine that, since the Germans had begun negotiations for an armistice, the fighting might have died down as October drew on. This did not happen. Edwin Hill was kept very busy. He had been on the Western Front since the middle of 1915 and, since 10th April 1918, had been second-in-command of the 8th Sussex (Pioneers) Battalion. Once Haig launched his counter-attack, and trench warfare was superseded by mobile warfare, the work of the battalion tended to be based on improving communications and transport links, with some groups on guard duty on bridges and key places. On 10th August, Edwin Hill had been promoted to major, a rank more appropriate to his responsibilities.

As the British assault developed, the battalion moved forward behind the attack troops, working hard each day to restore and improve the communication roads across the battlefield. Tasks included marking out dry weather tracks for the use of horse transport, putting up sign posts to give directions to roads, names to trenches, woods, and other localities. The roads needed to be improved to allow military resources and ambulances their free use. Sometimes they had the grimmer duty of digging graves, burying dead horses or dead Germans in the aftermath of battles. By early October they were north of St. Quentin and west of Peronne, and moving fairly fast north-eastwards following the line of British advance.

Harold Pike, who had been sent home in 1916 with Jaundice and synovitis, had returned to France in 1918 with the 2nd Battalion Life Guards Machine Gun Regiment. (On 3rd March 1917 Haig had written to say, "The situation with regard to man-power has made it necessary to convert to other uses certain units now in the field, and, in consequence, the Army Council, with the consent of the King, have issued orders that the three Household Cavalry Regiments are to be dismounted and converted into Army Machine Gun Battalions. I feel confident… that this reorganisation… will be accepted with the loyalty and devotion with which every turn of fortune has been met by British officers and men throughout the war, and that the Household Cavalry Regiments will in their new role as Machine Gun Battalions maintain their old esprit de corps and add further honours to their very distinguished record."[852]) He ended the war at St. Souplet, near Le Cateau. Harold was allowed to return again to England where he was demobilised on 15th March 1919.

In late October, 8th Sussex (Pioneers) Battalion also reached Le Cateau. As their colonel had 'flu, Edwin Hill temporarily took command of the battalion. On 23rd October 1918. three companies were all working on road repairs, and Edwin went forward to inspect the work. It was a day of casualties. Six men were wounded and one was killed. Two subalterns were wounded. As he

---

[852] Included in the War Diary, 2nd Life Guards, March 1918.

returned from making his inspection a shell burst beneath the car. Clearly seriously injured, he was taken down the line to the casualty clearing station, and then all the way back to No.41 Stationary Hospital of the Royal Army Medical Corps at Pont Remy, near Abbeville. The shell had smashed him, and he had multiple wounds to his left foot. A telegram was sent to advise his mother that he was "dangerously ill" and his left foot was amputated. This unfortunately did not prevent gangrene setting in. A blood transfusion was tried, but it failed to stem the infection. On the same day that his wife received a letter from the chaplain saying he was dangerously ill, a telephone call to the hospital led to a relative being told he was already dead. He actually died on 26th October 1918 and was buried in the Hospital Cemetery, Drury, south of Amiens, but after the war he and those around him were exhumed and reburied at a new concentration cemetery established at Villers-Bretonneux on the road between Amiens and St. Quentin.

For his mother and sister the anguish continued, and on her behalf his brother-in-law tried to get the Military Cross for him, writing a letter which is included in his Army file: "Just prior to his death he was mentioned in dispatches and was recommended for the Military Cross, and I understand, this decoration was never issued to him or his next-of-kin."[853] There might have been some confusion because there was a Captain Hall who did gain the M.C. in the battalion that autumn, but Edwin did not receive the award. His mother was sent into a downward spiral of ill-health by the news of her son's death, and followed him to the grave a couple of years later. She had written to the ministry begging for an allowance to let her travel to see her son's grave, but there is no indication that the request had been satisfied. Edwin was probably the last Old Bournemouthian to die on the Western Front.

---

[853] Army File of Edwin Hill, WO 339/389.

11: The Armistice

In the days leading up to the Armistice the Allies maintained the pressure, as reflected by the diary of the 1st Canadian Field Artillery Brigade (in which Sergeant Basil Keogh served) for 9th November: "The Mons Road is a living stream with guns, lorries, vehicles, battalions and cavalry going East, and civilians dragging or pushing vehicles of all descriptions travelling towards Valenciennes."[854] Afterwards they moved for a short time into Germany but were demobilized at Ottawa on 24th April 1919. Basil had survived.

In early November, Norman Wragg and the 5th Dorset Battalion repeatedly moved forward in anticipation of action against the Germans. In a letter of December 1918, Norman described the exhilaration – and frustrations – of this last phase of the war: "I can't tell you how glad I am to have been in at the death. I think it will always be one of the 'prides' of my life. We were busy chasing after the Boche (for one could hardly call it pushing him back; we had been unable to find him!) on the Monday morning of the 11th, when at 8 a.m. the news came through 'Advance cancelled; hostilities cease at 11 a.m.' on which I think we went wild for an hour or so. We were just four miles south of Mons, quite close to the battlefield of Malplaquet, in a small cluster of farms, which is greatly flattered if called a village… The Germans have conducted their retreat in a marvellous manner. They have left no war material behind, and every cross-road is mined and blown up."[855]

Norman, now as battalion adjutant, described the joy with which the Armistice was greeted: "Les Trieux. At 8am news arrived that hostilities were to cease at 11am. The band at once fell in and paraded up and down the main road, the whole battalion falling in behind as it passed by – Popular airs were played, and then the officers took over the band instruments, and headed by the Quartermaster, the column then marched back down the road. At 11am the battalion paraded and were addressed by the Commanding Officer… In the afternoon impromptu sports were arranged, free beer being issued to the men."[856] In the days that followed, the battalion war diary kept by Norman showed most of the men's time being spent playing football – or 'footer' as he called it. On 11th December 1918 it must have given Norman some quiet satisfaction to list the awards for gallantry conferred by Field Marshall Haig with the authority of the King – which included his own Military Cross. When later his citation was published it hearkened back to the events of late September: "As battalion signalling officer in the operations on Oisy le Verger and Epinoy from 27th September-2nd October, 1918, he did gallant work. He found an advanced report centre under very heavy fire and remained there sending back valuable information. He went forward on several occasions with his linesmen, and set a fine example to his men. Later, he took on the duties of adjutant, and was untiring in his energies in reorganising the battalion, which had received heavy casualties."[857]

Of course, other Old Bournemouthians also experienced the Armistice in the field. After being behind the lines in reserve for the first week in November, Eugene Holland and the 1st Border Battalion were advancing. The diary noted with some satisfaction, and surprisingly knowingly

---

[854] War Diary, 1st Canadian Field Artillery Brigade, 9th November 1918.
[855] *The Bournemouthian*, December 1918.
[856] War Diary, 5th Dorsets, 11th November 1918.
[857] *The Supplement to The London Gazette*, 10th December 1919, p. 15378.

(perhaps because it was written later?), that on 8th November: "German delegates arrived at French GHQ and given until 11.00 on the 11th to accept armistice terms."[858] As the battalion moved forward the next day, they received the news that the Kaiser had abdicated and that the Crown Prince had renounced his right to the German throne. On 10th November, they were unable to "get in touch" with the enemy, and then of course the next day they heard the news of the Armistice. Many battalions like Norman's then celebrated with games of football in the afternoon, but for the 1st Border Battalion, 'A' Company was set to work on road repairs, filling in craters. We are not told how the other companies spent the day, except that the officers had a conference at 5p.m. Then it was a question of preparing for a ceremonial parade the next day! Eugene stayed with the battalion for a few months after the Armistice. On 16th January 1919, the battalion diary reported that he had been awarded the Belgian Croix de Guerre. On 3rd March he finished his military service: "Captain E. L. Holland having proceeded to England on duty struck off strength from 1-3-19."[859] However, he did not quit the regular army – he was still an adjutant in the Border Regiment in September 1919; and later was confirmed in his rank of captain and also served in the Second World War.

The start of November had found Alexander Sandbrook, by now a sergeant in the 8th Canadian Infantry Battalion, resting north of Cambrai and east of Douai, at Auberchicourt. "At 08.45 hours the wonderful news was received over the wire that hostilities with Germany would cease at 11.00 hours. The information was immediately communicated to the Battalion on parade, and three thunderous cheers went up."[860] Alexander and the battalion ended up in Germany.

Tank man George Rees and his company were at rest when news of the Armistice arrived. They certainly celebrated. That night a huge bonfire was lit, songs were sung and speeches made. "Everyone sang who could or thought he could. The rest shouted. It didn't matter. Noise was the thing."[861] But after the Armistice George fell ill. On 2nd December he was sent from the 4th Supply Company to hospital in St. Pol, and was transferred to the 56th General Hospital in Étaples. He remained in hospital through into the New Year but was released on 1st February 1919 and joined the Central Base Depot the next day until he could re-join his unit, the 4th Tank Carrier Company, on 4th February. Leaves followed, including one sad one as his father died, and he got a new posting in May 1919 to the field battalion being again re-rated, to 1st class mechanic. His final promotion, to corporal in August 1919 was accompanied by new work as a clerk. On 23rd October he was sent back to England. Finally, on 21st November 1919, he was demobilised.

On 26th September 1918, Leslie Gilbert's 1st Honourable Artillery Company Battalion (which since 26th June 1917 had been designated General Head Quarter troops) had transferred to the 4th Guards Brigade, which at that time was in the Cavalry Corps. This was a period of being ready to move forward when the breakthrough should occur, but not actually doing so. Much of the time was spent near the sea at Criel Plage, and it was there that the news of the Armistice reached them: "A great day! From an early hour various unofficial indications of the Armistice having been concluded arrived in Criel Plage, including an ambulance decked with flowers, 'chaufferattes' and cabbages. The official news arrived about noon, and was received with acclamation. The Massed Drums played Retreat on the Front. A very good and well attended concert was held in the large

---

[858] War Diary, 1st Border Battalion, 8th November 1918.
[859] War Diary, 1st Border Battalion, 3rd March 1919.
[860] War Diary, 8th Canadian Infantry Battalion, 11th November 1918.
[861] Narrative p. 65, War Diary, 4th Tank Carrier Company.

Marquee at 6.0pm. The 'Lilywhites' and selected performers from the rest of the Brigade provided a most enjoyable programme."[862] On 27th November 1918 he was granted leave to return temporarily to the UK and was sent back to the UK via Dunkirk on 29th January 1919 for demobilisation, and was discharged on 6th March 1919.

Archibald Rogers described the great excitement of the news of the Armistice. "At last! I hope and trust now that there will be no objection to my being with you once more for next term. I feel very thankful that the war has come to an end while I am out here, for I cannot conceive that hostilities will be renewed. I don't expect anyone in England can conceive the feelings of the people out here when the news came through. Verey lights and rockets were sent up all over the place and I should think every flashlight in our lines was turned on. I don't think any one of us quite realises the situation; it has literally taken our breath away. I have visited many of the big cities which have been under Boche rule, and everywhere I hear terrible tales of Boche cruelty. The people give us a very warm welcome and can't do too much for us."[863]

The Aftermath, 1919

That Christmas was very special for the surviving Old Bournemouthians and their families. What *The Bournemouth Visitors' Directory* called a "note of gladness and rejoicing" was felt across Bournemouth. "In every land and in every home there will be thankfulness that the long nightmare of war is over, and although the grief and sorrow it has caused in countless families cannot be effaced, there is everywhere an uplifting feeling of relief that its horrors and desolation are at an end."[864] There were three reasons for the grief and sorrow. First, for some mothers and wives there was the news or memory of a son or husband's death. Then, for very many, the parting continued whilst the soldiers remained in khaki and with their units, in case the Germans re-started the fighting. Some indeed were wounded and were still to die in the military hospitals and a large number were to die from the Spanish 'flu epidemic which had started and was to continue for many more months. Finally, of course, many loved ones were still far away – returning prisoners of war, or still with the Army in far-flung outposts of the Empire or on campaign fields far away. For example, it soon became clear that many of those in the Hampshire Regiment in the East or in India would not quickly be returning home.

Representative of those still with an Army job to do despite the Armistice was John Sinclair. As John was a 2nd lieutenant in the Royal Garrison Artillery (R.G.A.) who had only qualified as an artillery officer in spring 1918, his disembodiment was not a priority for the Army compared to older men who had served much longer. When the war ended, his battery was in Belgium, and later it was moved into Germany, part of the Army of Occupation whilst talks turned the Armistice of November 1918 into the Treaty of Versailles of June 1919. In a letter written in December 1918, he described having been moved from 145 Battery to 174 Battery (still in the same brigade) and the very different pre-occupations of the Army in these months. "We are very busy just now cleaning and polishing the guns, for we are going to Brussels en route for the Rhine on the 7th of this month. Although this 'spit and polish' business is rather boring, it is better than hearing that nasty whistling sound and 'crump' which shows that there is a war on. Every man is being educated now,

---

[862] From the War Diary, 4th Guards Brigade, 11th November 1918.
[863] *The Bournemouthian*, December 1918.
[864] *The Bournemouth Visitors' Directory*, 21st December 1918.

for we hold classes on practically every subject a man wants to know. I myself am taking a class in English composition."[865] In his last war letter, he explained that, as billeting officer, he had had to ensure appropriate billets for both men and horses, but that after leaving Belgium his battery became part of the British Army of the Rhine, occupying western Germany. With a fellow officer he was living for a time in a German billet, which at first had seemed a bit dangerous, but which he had come to realise was rather good. To his surprise he was welcomed by his hosts. He enjoyed the cheaper prices of Germany. "It was quite an experience. Two unarmed British Officers in a village full of Huns. Yet we were the top dogs, and we tried to impress this upon ourselves, as we sat at night, smoking and yarning to each other, for it would have been nasty if the Hun had got his back up. The Burgomaster of one of these villages had been wounded in France, Roumania and Italy, and could not say a good word for the Kaiser… A mark is worth an English shilling to the Hun, but we get three marks for our shilling, so things are cheap over here… I bought an iron cross, 2nd class, the other day for 11 marks. It was the genuine article and there were dozens of them in the shop! I am going to make my fortune by laying in a store of them and selling them for two or three guineas when I come home. We are all ready to start the war again: Guns in position, observation posts chosen, and alarms arranged. At night time we have to carry revolvers, but I think the Boche would rather have us, than not have us. We are feeding him and safe-guarding him from Spartacists and Bolshevists."[866]

Gaston Caudron, having fought earlier in the war itself, continued to serve in the Army of the Rhine in occupied Germany after the war. Gaston had been born in August 1895 in Fulham, but his father was French – a chef de cuisine in various hotels. So in childhood he moved around. He was at the school from 1908 to 1910. He joined up on 2nd May 1916 and was placed in the 6th Gloucestershire Battalion. At some point Gaston switched to serve in the Tank Corps, in which by the end of the war he had risen to the rank of sergeant. Then he served in the Army of the Rhine. Whilst his records have largely been lost, we know that he was in 'B' Company of the 5th Tank Battalion when it was at Bickendorf, Germany, in February 1921. This battalion was in the 4th Tank Brigade in 1918, and in the second half of the year was equipped to fight with forty-two Mark V tanks. He remained in the Army until April 1938. However, he was recalled to the Tank Corps in July 1939. An interesting post-script to his story is that in 1941 he was made a lieutenant as an Assistant Commissar in the Indian Army Department. By then he had been awarded the Military Medal. Later he became a major in the Indian Army Commissariat.

Others were away because they were still to be repatriated as prisoners of war, or because they were sick or wounded. One such was Cecil Tollemache who, as we have seen, had fallen wounded through the chest in May 1918, and was taken prisoner whilst lying unconscious on a hospital bed. Afterwards, Cecil had been taken back into Germany where he was treated. A later Army report, included in his Army records, described his treatment and conditions: "He was a prisoner of war in Germany for 7 months. He was treated by the Germans for his last wound, and he states that he suffered very considerably from privation." When eventually he was rescued after the defeat of Germany he was brought back from Danzig aboard the hospital ship *Russ* to Leith, and was medically checked at Scarborough, where he began to cough blood. At first this did not seem too significant, and the Army concentrated on checking out his reasons for being captured (he was officially informed that after the official enquiry he was exonerated in June 1919 for being made

---

[865] *The Bournemouthian*, April 1919.
[866] *The Bournemouthian*, July 1919.

P.O.W.) Remarkably, he still seemed keen and was well enough to be one of those sent to Russia in April 1919 as part of the North Russia Force opposing the Bolsheviks. In that campaign he was promoted captain, and afterwards was awarded the M.B.E. for his role as 'Movement Officer' for the North Russia Force. However, after his return to England, the coughing up blood became worse and he became debilitated by tuberculosis, and later by the long-term effects of the chest wound he had suffered. Although he lived until 1976 he never fully recovered, and the Army accepted that he had been permanently 80% disabled by his war service. For him, as for so many other Old Bournemouthians, their families and friends, as well as so many across the country, in many ways the war never ended.

Roland Hobern was also in France with the Army in 1919 and 1920. It is not clear if he joined his battalion on the Western Front before the war ended. He was an officer in the Labour Corps. He was born at Clapham in August 1898, the son of a greengrocer; he gained a scholarship to the school from Sept 1911 to July 1914, and was a member of the O.T.C. from 1st May 1913. After leaving school he became a clerk, and was called up on 16th February 1917. His potential was quickly recognised and after only a few weeks, on 2nd March, he was promoted to lance corporal. On the completion of his basic training he was posted to the 3rd Gloucestershire Battalion, and then to 'B' Company of the 262nd Infantry Battalion at Foxhall Heath Camp, Ipswich, for further training, though still designated as a 3rd Gloucestershire soldier. He was accepted for training for a commission, asking to be allowed to join the Hampshire Regiment – or any other battalion! In the event, after training with 20 Officer Cadet Battalion at Cookham, on 25th June 1918 he was commissioned to the 3rd Devonshire Battalion at Plymouth on 9th July 1918.

Roland Hobern

About that time he had his photograph taken in Boscombe, wearing this new uniform. He was a single man with a temporary regular commission, which probably explains why he remained in service so long after the war. It is not clear when he landed in France, nor when he was promoted lieutenant, as the next record shows him reporting to the 86th Labour Group at Caudry near Cambrai on 26th November 1919. He was officer in charge of No. 71 Labour Company in February 1920 before returning to England for his discharge in May 1920.

12: Conclusions

It is difficult to be sure precisely how many Old Bournemouthians served in this war. Very many served on fronts other than the Western Front, and therefore have fallen beyond the scope of this account. In December 1918, long before an accurate list could be regarded as in any way definitive, *The Bournemouth Visitors' Directory* published its preliminary assessment of the contribution of Bournemouth School. The newspaper reckoned that five hundred and ninety-four former members of the school were known to have served in the war. They reminded their readers that many others had volunteered but were not allowed into the forces because they were needed in munitions or other work regarded by the government as necessary to carry on the war. (Research indicates that the total was actually about six hundred and seventy-five.) In making this study, it has not been possible to track down all the stories of all those who went to the Western Front, and therefore it has to be admitted that this can be only a partial account. *The Bournemouth Visitors' Directory* calculated that two hundred and twenty-four had received commissions. They stated eighty-five had been killed in action or died from causes directly traceable to the war, though we now know that was an under-estimate. Of the survivors, about one hundred and eighty were reckoned to have been wounded. At the time of publication they believed sixteen had received the Military Cross, two the Military Medal, and seventeen had been Mentioned in Dispatches. An indication that in this too they had only an imperfect knowledge and under-estimate was the omission of any reference to the soldier who received the Distinguished Service Medal, the second highest in the hierarchy of military awards. Other awards were to follow, but so too were further incidents of loss, death or disability. When does a man's death count as a war death? Some lingered for several years, and are missed from any official statistics. Few school families were untouched; the commitment had been huge.

Old Bournemouthians had served on the Western Front for the entire duration of the war, from the Battle of Mons in August 1914 to the defeat and occupation of Germany. Most served as private soldiers or sailors, but a large minority contributed as commissioned officers in the relatively junior ranks: the most badly affected section of the Army. A newly established borough school had risen magnificently to the challenges posed by the war, and its commitment had made a really significant contribution to the war on the Western Front.

At the beginning of this study the question was posed: What sort of commitment was shown by members of this local grammar school? Even drawing on the evidence of those who fought on the Western Front, the answer has to be that the commitment was huge. And many, many others fought in the air, or at sea, or in the other campaigns, bleeding and dying in places like Gallipoli or in Mesopotamia. For a very new school, the 'Old Boys' had done it proud. But it was a sad kind of pride. In one of his letters, written in January 1919, John Sinclair, whose story we have recounted above, summed up the sadness with words focussed on his friends but which might stand for all those Old Bournemouthians who had lost their lives or survived with physical or mental scars: "Mother sent me the School Magazine last week and it made me rather sick to read it. L. Bell, O.I. Cooper and others who were personal friends of mine at School gone. It seems too awful for words."[867]

---

[867] John Sinclair's letter of 3rd January 1919, printed in *The Bournemouthian*, April 1919, p. 327.

Appendices: Others Who Served but whose Service Details are Currently Limited

Appendix 1: British Soldiers on the Western Front

It is to be regretted but the details of some of those who served on the Western Front are currently unknown to the author. Those who served in that way on the Western Front (there are unfortunately many others who served but it is not clear upon which war front) included:

George Butler (b. 1897; school 1910-1912) served in the Army Service Corps.

Harry Caines (b. 1897; school boarder 1907-1910) was a sapper in the Royal Engineers and rose to become a lance corporal. In December 1918 the school magazine reported that, whilst he was working as a motor dispatch rider in the Royal Engineers, he fell from his motor bicycle. "A motor lorry ran into him, with the result that he has been for four weeks in hospital in France, but is now going on satisfactorily."[868]

Reginald Curties (b. 1898; school 1912-1916) 2nd lieutenant in the Royal Garrison Artillery went to France on 14th December 1917.

William Dunford (b. 1896; school 1910-1913) volunteered for the 2/9th Hampshire Cyclist Battalion and afterwards transferred to a battalion of the Dorsetshire Regiment (possibly attached from the Hampshire Regiment) and was wounded in France in the latter part of 1916.

William Dunford

Lauriston Fitz (b. 1898, school 1910-1912) enlisted on 18th January 1916 and served first with the 26th London Battalion and then as a lance corporal with the 'Black Watch'. Twice he served on the Western Front: initially from 13th January 1917 to 11th March 1917 and then again in France from 25th April 1918 until his discharge after 24th April 1919. In this latter period he was in the R.A.F., having joined the R.F.C. on 1st March 1918. At this time he worked as a wireless operator and a rigger until he was transferred to the reserve on 15th February 1919.

Duncan Foster (b. 1898 in New South Wales, Australia; school 1912-1914) volunteered to join the Australian Army, and from 11th October 1918 was a private in the 12th Australian Battalion, which was on the Western Front. He was discharged from the battalion in October 1919.

Eric Frampton (b. 1895; school 1904-1907) volunteered on 18th January 1915, stating, "I am desirous of joining the Army Service Corps as a clerk, to do a little for my King & Country. I passed out of school in class VA at the age of 13 & am able to do Fractions & Decimals. (Signed) Eric Chas Wm Frampton." He was promoted lance corporal on 19th May 1915 and corporal shortly after, on 19th July 1915 and on 29th July 1915 he sailed from Folkestone to Boulogne where he was attached to the 18th Railhead Supply Detachment. On 22nd November 1916, he was promoted sergeant and on 23rd February 1918 transferred to Number 32 Railhead Supply Detachment. After this he moved between similar units quite frequently but on 7th August 1918 a medical board rated him in category 'B2'. In *The Peace Gazette* he was gazetted as winning the Meritorious Service Medal –

---

[868] *The Bournemouthian*, December 1918.

something of an unsung hero. (The Meritorious Service Medal (M.S.M.) was a silver medal for distinguished service, or for gallantry, principally by non-commissioned officers of all of the British armed forces and of Queen Alexandra's Royal Naval Nursing Service.)

Stanley Frampton. (b. 1895; school 1909-1910) joined the Royal Army Medical Corps, and went as a private to France on 16th November 1915. He was reported amongst the wounded in June 1917.[869]

Alfred Gascoigne (b. 1901; school 1914-1915) was a boy soldier whose older brother Arthur had managed to enlist in the 6th Hampshire Royal Field Artillery, and had gone off to India with them. Despite his age, Alfred managed to enrol as a bugler in the 3/7th Hampshire Battalion, according to the list published in the school magazine in June 1915, although the school records also show him as still a member of the school at that time. This battalion was only formed in Bournemouth in March 1915 and had a limited life before becoming part of the reserve battalion structure for the Army. In the meantime, Alfred had been allocated to the 2/4th Battalion of the Hampshire Regiment. Perhaps Alfred was recognised as too young to be sent abroad to India with them as he was moved into the 16th Royal Warwickshire Battalion. This battalion fought on the Western Front, apart from a time in Italy between November 1917 and April 1918.

William Hall-Simmons (b. 1894; school 1907-1910) joined the Royal Engineers as a sapper, working in the Railways Section. In this capacity he went to France on 7th April 1915.

Philip Hankinson (b. 1889; school 1901-1908) served in the 1st Hampshire Royal Garrison Artillery and in France. He was a bombardier and corporal in 351st Battery in 1917, a siege battery which was armed with four six-inch howitzers. Philip was commissioned 2nd lieutenant, still in the R.G.A., on 21st October 1918, just before the end of the war.

John Harrison (b. 1896; school 1904-1910) became a private in the 17th London Battalion, known as the 'Poplar and Stepney Rifles'. It is uncertain when he went to France. The 1/17th London landed in France on 10th March 1915, and on 11th May became part of the 141st Brigade, 47th (2nd London) Division. Later he was a rifleman in the 9th Royal Irish Rifles. This battalion had landed in Boulogne in October 1915. He applied to change to the Royal Naval Air Service, in which he trained as an observer. Eventually, he was commissioned sub-lieutenant, and so joined the R.A.F. when it was formed in 1918. He went on to pass his observer course, coming out top of his class, and was promoted to lieutenant in the R.A.F. (Naval Wing).[870]

Gordon Hillier (b. 1891; school 1904-1908) was commissioned 2nd lieutenant respectively in the West Buckland School O.T.C. and later in St. Peter's School O.T.C. On 29th November 1916, he was appointed 2nd lieutenant in the West Lancashire Divisional Engineers, part of the Royal Engineers. He landed in France on 26th July 1917 and was promoted to be lieutenant on 30th May 1918.

Douglas Howson (b. 1895; school 1905-c.1910) began his Army career in 1913 as a Territorial volunteer in the Hampshire Yeomanry. This unit split up into troops and dispersed – some as cavalry in France, some as cyclists in Ireland, and some as infantry (in 15th Hampshire Battalion) in France over 1916-1917. In some way he distinguished himself, earning the Military Medal.

---

[869] *The Bournemouth Visitors' Directory*, 2nd June 1917.
[870] *The Bournemouthian*, July 1918.

Therefore when, on 6th August 1918, *The London Gazette* published its list beginning "His Majesty the King has been graciously pleased to approve of the award of the Military Medal for bravery in the Field to the undermentioned Non-commissioned Officers and Men" his name appeared, although the entry was slightly obscure: "100151 Pte. D.G. Howson, Yeo., attd. H.L.I. (Boscombe)."[871] The puzzle is that H.L.I. to which he was listed as attached was the Highland Light Infantry. Perhaps this attachment, and his award for bravery, preceded his deployment with the Royal Field Artillery in which his Army career concluded.

Henry King (b. 1895; school 1909-1910) enlisted in April 1915 and went to France with the Army Service Corps at the end of September.

George Kingsnorth (b. 1892; school 1902-1904) volunteered for the Territorial Force before the war, on 23rd January 1913. He served in the 14th Hampshires, and was later transferred at some point to the 2nd Worcestershire Regiment. The 14th Hampshire Battalion landed at Le Havre on 6th March 1916 and fought on the Somme in various parts of the battle. In 1917, they went on to fight throughout the Third Battle of Ypres, but by then he must have moved on to the 2nd Worcestershire Battalion, which had landed at Boulogne on 14th August 1914 and remained on the Western Front for the duration of the war. However, there must be other details in his story because his later, R.F.C./R.A.F., record shows he served in Mesopotamia from 5th December 1917 when he had been transferred as a 3rd level air mechanic to the Royal Flying Corps, and then into the R.A.F. on 1st April 1918. His 'trade' within the R.A.F. was that of a wireless operator. After four years in service, and aged 21, on 21st January 1918 George's service would have been concluded, but with the exigencies of war, the Army retained him for an extended period, for which he was awarded a bounty payment of £15 (payable after the war).

Henry King

Henry Lane (b. 1889; school 1903) joined the Army Ordnance Corps. He landed in France on 23rd July 1915.

Ernest Laxton (b. 1890; school 1904-1905) served in the Army Service Corps, initially as a private, but rose to the rank of staff sergeant, indicating that he was talented and used those skills wisely. He was on the Western Front from when he landed on 25th July 1915 until he was sent back to be demobilised on 5th July 1919.

Frederick Lewin (b. 1895; school 1905-1907) emigrated to South Africa and for a time was a private in the Cape Town Highlanders – from 1913 this unit was known as the 6th Infantry, Active Citizen Force of South Africa, and it served through the First World War – in South-West Africa, in North Africa (the Senussi Campaign) and later in France – especially at Delville Wood in the Battle of the Somme as part of the 4th South African Infantry Battalion. By then, however, Frederick had moved on. Probably, he returned to England to apply for a commission, which he attained on 12th July 1915. He disembarked in France with the Army Service Corps on 7th September 1915 and was promoted lieutenant on 13th May 1916, and became temporary captain whilst serving as his unit's adjutant from 12th August 1917. He held that role until 7th August 1918. On 5th February 1919 he was allowed to resign his commission on the grounds of ill-health, and he was awarded the 'Silver War Badge' as one who had been wounded or made infirm by the exigencies of the war.

---

[871] *The London Gazette Supplement*, 6th August 1918.

Alexander Maddox (b. 1895; school 1911) was commissioned 2nd lieutenant in the Royal Engineers on 21st July 1915. He was sent to France on 26th December 1915. On 16th March 1917 he was forced to relinquish his rank on the grounds of ill-health. Circumstances and health changed, however, and on 21st August the same year he resumed his service and rank. At some point he was raised to lieutenant, and after the war became acting captain for three months from the end of January to April 1919.

Philip Mendoza (b. 1898; school 1911) served as a private in the 2nd and 10th Yorkshire Light Infantry Battalions, although the details of that service are unknown. We know that both battalions fought in the Battle of the Somme and for the rest of the war (though the 10th Battalion was disbanded in France on 13th February 1918, after which at least some of the men were sent to the 20th Entrenching Battalion).

Hannam Miles (b. 1891; school 1903-1908) was initially a member of the 6th Suffolk Regiment, which was one of the cyclist regiments. He moved to the Royal Engineers as a sapper and became an acting sergeant within the corps. On 18th January 1919 he was, like Eric Frampton, awarded the Meritorious Service Medal "in recognition of valuable service rendered with the Armies in France and Flanders".[872]

Percy Montgomery (b. 1888; school c.1904-c.1905) was a doctor and was gazetted as a temporary lieutenant in the Royal Army Medical Corps on 8th March 1917. On 3rd March 1917, he landed on Salonika, but according to the register of the Middlesex Hospital, as well as serving on Salonika from 1917 to 1918, at some point in 1918 and through into 1919 he served in France.

Arthur Pepworth (b. November 1898; school 1913-1914) was an apprentice to a chemist. It is not clear when Arthur joined up: from his Army service number it was probably in one of the middle or later years of the war. He joined the 6th Somerset Light Infantry. It is clear that Arthur saw some active service in France, possibly from 1st August 1918 when a reconstructed 6th Somerset Light Infantry Battalion re-landed at Boulogne, within 49th Brigade of 16th Division.

Leonard Pretty (b. 1895; school 1908-1913) served in the Royal Engineers. He went to the Western Front in the summer of 1916, as a member of the 1st Battalion Special Brigade Royal Engineers, the branch of the Royal Engineers responsible for the chemical war effort. On 24th August 1916 he survived a dramatic incident, which was reported in some detail a year later in the school magazine: "L. A. Pretty, 2nd Corpl., R.E., had a narrow escape in August, 1916, when a shell burst in the middle of a party of about 16, of whom he was one. Six were killed outright and several severely injured. Pretty himself escaped with a wound in the hand, being saved by the buckle of his belt from more dangerous injury. His wound was not considered sufficiently serious for him to be sent back to 'Blighty', and he went back to his unit after two months in a French hospital." He finished the war with the rank of sergeant.

Leonard Pretty

Walter Randall (b. 1895; school 1910-1911) enlisted into the 2/9th Hampshire Battalion – the Cyclist Battalion on 22nd November 1915. He then was moved into the 1st Somerset Light Infantry with whom he served on the Western Front and was promoted to become lance corporal. In April

---

[872] Citation in *The London Gazette*, 18th January 1919.

1917 his battalion played a full part in the Battle of Arras. He was discharged from the Army because of serious sickness on 3rd July 1917. Sadly he died young, on 1st June 1920, and on his probate record he was described as "ex-private Somerset Light Infantry" which suggests that in his last years he was too ill to take up any work, and that his experience with the battalion was the defining feature of his life.

Edwin Reasey (b. 1894; school 1909-1910) enlisted on 20th December 1916 as a private in the Coldstream Guards. Unfortunately, although we know he served on the Western Front in the war, since all the battalions of the Coldstream Guards fought only there, the details of his service, and the battalion to which he belonged are currently unknown. He was discharged on 20th May 1919 suffering from exophthalmic goitre, which meant his thyroid gland was infected, producing a protrusion of the eyeballs.

Edwin Reasey

Haydon Richmond (b. 1890; school 1906-?) was a gunner in the Royal Horse Artillery (and then with the Royal Field Artillery) and gained the '1915 Star' as one who arrived on the Western Front on or before 19th March 1915. At some point he transferred to the Royal Engineers.

Charles Robertson (b. 1886; school 1903-1904) was the older brother of Percy. He was a gunner in the 74th Siege Battery Royal Garrison Artillery in the summer of 1917. This battery was part of the 43rd Heavy Artillery group and went to France on 30th April 1916. It was a battery of the South African Heavy Artillery, but part, too, of the Royal Garrison Artillery. We don't know whether Charles went out with them or if he landed later. The battery was certainly involved in the Battle of the Somme, initially in the attack on Gommecourt on 1st July. It took heavy casualties 1916-1918. By the spring of 1917, the battery was in action near Arras, and later in the year it fought in the Third Battle of Ypres. By the end of the war, one hundred and sixty-seven men had lost their lives fighting with this battery. However, Charles was not with them by the end, at some point, he served instead as a corporal with 111th Siege Battery. This battery had been on the Western Front since May 1916.

Raymond Tanner (b. 1893; school c.1905+) was in the Mechanical Transport Section of the Army Service Corps. He clearly made a good start, and on 7th August was promoted to acting (but paid) corporal. He embarked at Portsmouth on 18th August 1917 aboard the SS *Huntscape*, but perhaps because of the submarine danger, the trip took over a day and he only landed at Boulogne on 20th August. He was sent to join Number 275 Section, H.A.M.T. However, he was rapidly then placed in 406 Mechanical Transport Company, but attached to 375 Siege Battery. The 406 Mechanical Transport Company had been formed in July 1915, initially as an ammunition column for the 27th Brigade of the Royal Garrison Artillery, though later it became the X Corps Siege Park, and after that transport for II and IV Corps Heavy Artillery. Raymond's attachment to 375 Siege Battery brought him into a unit formed the previous February and which was deployed to France that August 1917. On 20th September, he was moved back via 406 M.T. Company and placed in Number 886 Mechanical Transport Company where his promotion was confirmed. These companies seem to have inter-changed a number of men, perhaps to maintain a balance of experience and expertise. This company was also attached to the Heavy Artillery – in this case to XVIII Corps.

Wilfred Tizard (b. 1894; school 1906-1910) enlisted on 27th November 1915 as a private in the Royal Army Medical Corps. He was wounded in 1918, almost certainly on the Western Front as the newspaper article explaining how he had been moved from Southampton to Christchurch Hospital was in the context of men who had been wounded on the Western Front.[873]

Adolfo Zanetti (b. 1887; school c.1901-1902) left the Merchant Navy to volunteer and became a private in the Army Service Corps, in which role he went to France on 21st June 1915. On 1st June 1918 he was transferred into the R.A.F.

Wilfred Tizard

Appendix 2: Canadian Soldiers on the Western Front

Wilfred Gosnell (b. 1894 in Adelaide, Australia; school 1909) in 1911 worked as a 'manufacturer day plates and paper, photographer'. On 3rd May 1911 he sailed on the *Royal Edward* from Bristol to Montreal where he married and became a farmer. He enlisted in Victoria, British Columbia, on 28th November 1916 and was sent to the A.M.C. Training Depot No.11 of the Canadian Expeditionary Force. From that time, his record is currently hard to find though we know he survived to serve as company quarter master sergeant with the Royal Canadian Engineers in World War Two. He died at Vancouver in 1959.

Wilfred Hawkes (b. 1889; c.1901+). Both he and his younger brother Lionel were members of the school. He called himself 'Will'. In April 1910 he sailed from Liverpool to Quebec aboard the *East Britain*. He moved west to British Columbia to work in real estate. Later, he worked as a chauffeur, and was doing this when, on 30th August 1915, he enlisted in the Canadian 62nd Infantry Battalion at Vernon in British Columbia. He gave as his next of kin, not his wife Grace, but rather his father who was still living in Bournemouth. The battalion which he joined had been established earlier that year and they set sail for Britain on 20th March 1916. Whilst it mobilised in Vancouver, it recruited along the British Columbia coast, from Victoria and Vancouver to Prince Rupert in the north. However, the 62nd Infantry Battalion had no fighting life of its own. After it arrived in Britain it was used to provide reinforcements for the Canadian infantry battalions already in the field. Unfortunately, we do not know to which battalion Wilfred was sent. (The remnant of the 62nd Battalion was absorbed into the 30th Reserve Battalion on 6th July 1916. It was formally disbanded entirely on 8th December 1917.) We know that he served on the Western Front. He sent a series of four postcards home and wrote two letters to his nephew Jack in Victoria. Curiously, one of the postcards he sent shows the emblem of the 158th Battalion – the Duke of Connaught's Own – which had recruited in Vancouver State in 1915 and sailed after Wilfred's battalion, in November 1916. Like his original battalion it was absorbed into the 1st Reserve Battalion on 6th

Wilfred Gosnell

Wilfred Hawkes

---

[873] A short reference was made in *The Bournemouth Visitors' Directory* on 21st September 1918.

January 1917. The first letter, dated 10th August 1916, was headed "somewhere in France". He promised that "some day when we have killed all the Germans I am going back to Victoria to see you, and I will tell you all about it… I am quite well too, but am very busy getting my machine gun ready to kill some Germans for you." Four months later, on 26th December, he wrote again. He had been wounded or was ill: "I am a long way away, over the sea which is as blue as the water mamma uses when she washes the clothes. I am in hospital, and I wear blue trousers and coat, with a red tie, but when I am well, and I have my gun… I am going up to the hills where the big guns are roaring, and perhaps I shall be able to tell you some more about it one day." From the description in this second letter it is possible he had been placed in a British regiment sent to Italy or further afield after a time in France, but that is speculation.

Harold James (b. 1894; school 1908-1909) became a tailor on leaving school. Before the war, he had left home and gone to Canada, and there became a rancher. His spirit of adventure was complemented with a sense of loyalty and duty, and he volunteered on 1st February 1915 at Pincher Creek, Alberta. Interestingly, like several others he 'stretched' his school experience when he enlisted by making the most of his time in the school O.T.C., declaring that he had spent two years in an officers training corps in England. He joined the 13th Canadian Mounted Rifles as a trooper. This unit was recruited from volunteers from the south-western part of Alberta. Although Harold was clearly quick to volunteer (the authority to recruit was only given in December 1914) others who chose to volunteer for that unit were much slower to respond. In June and August 1915, two groups of fifty men were sent across to England, but even by January 1916 the unit had not recruited enough men to form a cavalry regiment of mounted rifles – six hundred were needed. By that stage, the Canadian Mounted Rifles in service had all been changed to infantry battalions, and the unit was eventually reconstituted as an infantry battalion. Even so, it was disbanded as soon as it reached England, and the men were dispersed to reinforce other Alberta infantry units. We know that Harold was sent to England in the second reinforcing draft in August 1915. By then the British Government realised that they had sufficient cavalry, so men like Harold were placed in another unit from Alberta, but at the moment it is unclear which battalion he joined, although it was probably the 10th Canadian Infantry Battalion. (On 4th September 1915, the 10th Canadian Infantry Battalion received reinforcements of two lieutenants and one hundred and seventy-nine men from the reserve battalion in England.) This battalion was in the thick of the actions in which the Canadians were involved, including the fighting around Ypres in 1916, the actions on the Somme, the Battles of Arras and Passchendaele, and the fight for Hill 70. So it is possible that he fought alongside men like Alexander Sandbrook and the 8th Canadian Infantry Battalion. We know he survived, and after the war, in December 1919, he was married in Putney before returning to Canada where he died back in Alberta.

Wilfred White (b. 1894; school 1910-1911) left to become a bank clerk. Soon he emigrated to Canada and became a farmer in Toronto. On 25th February 1916 he attested in Toronto and joined the 170th Battalion of the Canadian Expeditionary Force – Mississauga Horse. Despite its name, this was an infantry battalion. Based in Toronto, the battalion began recruiting that winter, and then trained in Canada. The battalion sailed to England in October 1916, but when it had arrived it was absorbed into the 169th Battalion of the Canadian Expeditionary Force on 8th December 1916. This too was a battalion founded and recruiting in Toronto in the winter of 1915-1916 and sailing to England in October as well. However, the 169th Battalion was itself absorbed just over a month later when its men were taken in to the 5th Reserve Battalion. This was only a holding unit, from which men were sent to reinforce the 1st and 2nd Canadian Divisions on the Western Front, or to become a base for the 3rd and 4th Divisions as they were formed in England. Unfortunately, it is not currently possible to trace further where and how Wilfred served or in which battalion but it is extremely likely that he was in France in 1917.

Victor Williams (b. 1897; school 1908-1913) spent three years in the O.T.C. When he left school, he too went off to British Columbia to farm. He attested at Sidney Camp in British Columbia on 24th August 1916 and joined as one of the original members of the 231st Overseas Battalion of the Canadian Expeditionary Force. This battalion, based at Vancouver, had started to recruit there early in 1916. They sailed to England in April 1917, where, on 22nd April, they were absorbed into the 24th Reserve Battalion. After that it is currently not possible to trace his actions, but as many of the members of this unit seem to have been placed into the 4th Canadian Division, and especially into the 72nd Battalion (the 'Seaforth Highlanders') which fought at Passchendaele at the end of the Third Battle of Ypres. It is likely that Victor was there with them in that gruesome and bloody phase of the battle.

Index of Old Bournemouthians on the Western Front

Aitken, John, 32
Alder, William, 298, 415
Allbon, Bernard, 420, 421, 468, 487, 488
Allen, Victor, 94, 95
Atkin, Jesse, 23, 25, 39, 57, 163, 164
Atlee, Charles, 285
Austin, Charles, 301, 368
Austin, Harold, 18, 262, 267
Austin, William, 17, 18
Avins, William, 369
Ayling, Edgar, 290, 383, 421
Bagshaw, Eric, 11, 13, 25, 26
Bailey, Walter, 107, 188
Bailey, Wilfred, 351
Baker, Arthur, 359, 426, 427, 429
Baker, Percy, 162, 201
Baker, Walter. *See* Baker, Percy
Ball, Bertram, 63
Barfoot, Richard, 39, 74, 144, 145, 300, 400, 412, 490
Barnes, Bernard, 467
Bartlett, Bernard, 280, 324
Bennett, John, 101, 104, 186, 205, 277
Bergmann, Adolf, 366
Besley, Douglas, 430
Birdseye, Stanley, 124, 167, 168, 172, 198, 213, 263, 268, 269
Bishop, Alfred, 433, 446, 447, 452, 462, 483, 484
Bolton, Arthur, 72, 78, 148
Bott, Eric, 150
Bott, Harold, 146, 150
Brooks, Harold, 369
Brudenell, Cyril, 285
Budden, Henry, 60, 61, 72
Budden, Ronald, 238, 306, 309, 319
Butler, George, 501
Caines, Harry, 501
Caudron, Gaston, 498
Chaffey, Thomas, 119, 152, 290, 408, 425
Challis, William, 107, 108
Cheshire, Ralph, 398, 409, 412
Chudleigh, Eustace, 169, 211, 217, 265, 272, 309, 319
Clark, Richard, 54, 55, 56, 83, 145, 174, 207
Clough, Bernard, 92
Colborne, Reginald, 285, 334, 339

Collingwood, Douglas, 105, 259, 288, 343, 443, 448
Collingwood, Gordon, 40, 400
Cooper, Cyril, 103
Cooper, Oliver, 397, 452, 463
Copp, Alex, 190, 390
Corbet, Alexander, 235, 406
Cornwall, Joseph, 98
Couch, Claud, 192, 217
Couch, Wilfrid, 192
Cox, Edward, 66
Cox, Frank, 103, 106, 183, 257
Croft, Horace, 447
Curties, Reginald, 501
Curtis, Oswald, 218
Dare, Reginald, 474
Day, John, 96, 158, 168, 208, 270
Deans, Harold, 14, 55, 56, 72, 90, 463, 464
Derrett, Jack, 415
Dinwoodie, Hubert, 102, 103, 210, 421
Drayton, Ralph, 57, 58, 90, 118, 421
Dunford, William, 501
Dyason, Reverdy, 466
Elcock, Arthur, 380, 414, 418
Fairley, Reginald, 72, 80, 226, 229
Farwell, Howard, 110, 132
Feather, Stanley, 152
Finch, Harold, 216, 461
Finch, Harry, 460
Fitz, Lauriston, 501
Footner, Henry, 302
Forman, Francis, 162, 164, 298
Foster, Duncan, 501
Frampton, Eric, 501
Frampton, Stanley, 502
Friendship, Henry, 202, 203
Froud, Harold, 181, 269, 297
Fuller, Wilfrid, 57, 90
Furness, Frederick, 119, 179, 305, 321, 389, 414, 423, 424
Game, Frank, 414
Garrad, Arthur, 214
Garrad, Harold, 214
Gascoigne, Alfred, 502
Gilbert, Geoffrey, 356
Gilbert, Leslie, 27, 57, 205, 212, 223, 496
Gladney, Reginald, 259

Goddard, Edward, 262, 293, 326
Godfrey, Aubrey, 468, 487, 488
Gosnell, Wilfred, 506
Gosschalk, John, 115
Gould, Alfred, 87
Grantham-Hill, Clermont, 18, 50, 96
Gunning, Edwin, 220
Hall, Edward, 65
Hall-Simmons, William, 502
Hame, Arthur, 26, 57, 60, 246, 378
Hame, Bernard, 278, 356, 357
Hands, Leslie, 198, 237, 240, 243, 244, 245
Hankinson, Philip, 502
Harbord, Cecil, 200, 202, 203
Harlow, Edward, 401
Harlow, John, 283
Harrison, John, 502
Harrison, William, 45, 46
Hawkes, Wilfred, 506
Hayes, Frank, 211, 243, 248, 383
Hazard, Douglas, 58
Head, Eric, 53, 55, 127, 181, 225
Head, Harold, 191, 193, 194, 195, 208, 217, 257, 278, 323, 351
Hellier, Maurice, 72, 74, 88, 181, 195, 316, 324, 353, 378
Henry, Joseph, 72, 76
Hickling, Edward, 19, 23
Hill, Edwin, 93, 143, 299, 382, 493, 494
Hillier, Gordon, 502
Hoare, William, 491
Hobern, Roland, 499
Hodges, William, 28, 127, 128
Holbrook, Francis, 219, 220, 435, 470, 476, 478
Holbrook, Harold, 219
Holland, Eugene, 116, 139, 142, 166, 403, 470, 472, 476, 495
Hollies, Henry, 72, 78, 79, 114, 184
Horsey, Cyril, 145, 215
Howard, Cyril, 109, 307, 326
Howson, Douglas, 502
Hughes, Cecil, 58, 84, 190
Hughes, Stanley, 426, 427
Ing, Albert, 168
Ingram, John, 28, 30, 33, 34, 36
James, Harold, 507
Jones, Joseph G C, 72, 85
Kent, Frank, 282, 321
Keogh, Basil, 43, 50, 62, 63, 69, 254, 346, 442, 485

Kerr, Harold, 94
King, Henry, 503
Kingsnorth, George, 503
Kur, Alexander Otho, 367
Lambert, Harold, 170
Lane, Henry, 503
Lapthorne, Reginald, 109, 145, 209, 492
Lawrance, Francis, 21
Laxton, Ernest, 503
Lever, David, 72
Lewin, Frederick, 503
Little, Edward, 331
Lobley, Arthur, 256, 342
Lobley, Owen, 46
Lonnen, Frederick, 217
Lonsdale, Joseph, 105, 280, 383, 450, 478, 487
Lonsdale, Thomas, 87, 105, 314
MacAdam, William, 464
Maddox, Alexander, 504
Maistriau, G, 458, 459
Markham, Charles, 146, 147, 148, 149
Markwick, Alan, 99, 169, 249, 250
Marshall, Ernest, 480
Martin, Charles, 288, 329
Martin, Victor, 109, 131
Martyn, Harold, 142, 169, 170, 211, 217, 265, 310, 320, 375, 377
May, John, 126, 128, 347
Mendoza, Philip, 504
Meredith, Robert, 395, 403, 431
Miles, Hannam, 504
Miller, James, 455
Miller. Alexander, 284, 491
Mitford, William, 124, 159, 160, 167, 168, 198, 249, 272, 274, 354, 373, 381, 382, 386
Montgomery, Percy, 504
Moorey, Frank, 33
Moorey, William, 160, 161, 334
Mosley, Arthur, 247, 278, 347, 348
Mossop, George, 349, 350, 372, 386, 460
Nethercoate, John, 57, 58, 90, 91, 133, 135
New, Brian, 313
New, Jack, 163, 210
Newman, Edward, 481, 484
Novarra, Cecil, 138, 158, 291
Nutman, John, 413, 437, 440, 463
Okey, Leslie, 281, 282
Omer-Cooper, Joseph, 196
Omer-Cooper, Wilfred, 196
Paice, Eric, 358, 399, 403
Parsons, Ernest, 214, 304, 425, 489

aumier, Ronald, 318
Peake, Bruce, 136, 264
Pean, Percy, 123, 164, 222
Peden, Andrew, 109
Peel, Charles (Carl Ratsch-Peel), 364, 366
Pepworth, Arthur, 504
Phillips, Jack, 332
Pickard, Montague, 485
Pike, Harold, 135, 159, 176
Pitfield, Percy, 149
Preiss, Edward, 394, 403, 408, 431
Pretty, Leonard, 504
Prichard, Russell, 317
Quaife, Eric, 57, 297
Randall, Walter, 504
Rawle, Roy, 394, 403, 431
Ray, William, 221, 237, 238, 343, 401
Reasey, Edwin, 505
Rees, George, 443, 453, 486, 492, 496
Rey, Eric, 109, 408, 431, 471
Richardson, Bernard, 125, 126, 438, 439, 470, 473, 476
Richmond, Haydon, 505
Ridout, Harold, 337
Robertson, Charles, 505
Robertson, Percy, 32, 111, 171, 237
Rogers, Archibald, 94, 363, 373, 396, 473, 497
Sandbrook, Alexander, 44, 62, 67, 106, 203, 256, 261, 288, 343, 448, 457, 482, 484, 496, 507
Sear, Arthur, 361, 402, 420, 469, 487
Seare, William, 365
Searls, Thomas, 42, 97, 113, 114, 182, 203, 276
Seeviour, Sidney, 431, 454
Seymour, Stanley, 186, 206, 310, 371
Shears, Haswell, 205, 223, 245, 331
Sherwood, Dudley, 41, 45, 52
Short, Herbert, 88, 152, 176, 273
Simpson, Alexander, 205, 212, 213, 223, 245, 274
Sinclair, John, 345, 497, 500
Sinton, James, 118, 133, 135
Snelgar, Ernest, 101, 106, 108, 182, 204, 253, 334, 442, 448, 456, 482, 483, 484, 490, 491
Snelgar, John, 65, 112, 113, 114, 153, 154, 155
Spicer, Harold, 237
Spickernell, Donald, 449, 451
Stagg, Arthur, 42, 129, 130
Stanton, Thomas, 366
Stay, Howard, 265
Street, Sidney, 436, 440, 441
Strudwicke, Ernest, 151
Strudwicke, Montague, 44
Sturmer, Lionel, 368
Tanner, Raymond, 505
Taylor, Leonard, 269, 270, 297, 339, 346, 371, 392
Tizard, Wilfred, 506
Tollemache, Cecil, 111, 410, 417, 498
Tollemache, Horace, 44, 108, 188, 294, 303, 322, 394, 403, 408, 431
Tollemache, Philip, 44, 62, 67, 203, 482
Trask, Eric, 222
Tuck, Douglas, 401, 457, 458
Tucker, Stanley, 284, 328, 336, 338
Turner, George, 57, 90, 92
Turner, John, 11, 14, 34, 57, 99
Tyson, Robert, 70
Van Hecke, Benoni, 459
Wakely, Robert, 389, 406
Webber, William, 285, 334, 339, 340, 341, 358, 383, 385, 450
Wellum, Frank, 107, 108
White, Frederick, 421, 422
White, Herbert, 89
White, Wilfred, 507
Whitting, Arnold, 68, 155, 435, 470
Wilkes, Joseph, 342
Williams, John, 231
Williams, Victor, 508
Williams, William, 371
Wilson, John, 146, 149
Winch, Reginald, 126, 310, 311, 351, 375, 412, 446, 451, 462
Winton, John, 86, 155
Wolfe, Arthur, 36
Wragg, Norman, 308, 311, 329, 331, 480, 481, 495
Wrenn, Reginald, 43, 49, 423
Wright, Howard, 41
Wroth, Edward, 119
Zanetti, Adolfo, 506

PRINTED AND BOUND BY:
Copytech (UK) Limited trading as Printondemand-worldwide,
9 Culley Court, Bakewell Road, Orton Southgate.
Peterborough, PE2 6XD, United Kingdom.